The Logic of International Relations

EIGHTH EDITION

Walter S. Jones

University of Cincinnati

 LONGMAN

An imprint of Addison Wesley Longman, Inc.

New York • Reading, Massachusetts • Menlo Park, California • Harlow, England
Don Mills, Ontario • Sydney • Mexico City • Madrid • Amsterdam

Acquisitions Editor: Margaret Loftus
Project Coordination: Electronic Publishing Services Inc.
Text Design: Electronic Publishing Services Inc.
Cover Design: Paul Lacy
Cover Photograph: Keith Tishken
Art Studio: Electronic Publishing Services Inc.
Photo Researcher: Julie Tesser
Electronic Production Manager: Christine Pearson
Manufacturing Manager: Helene G. Landers
Electronic Page Makeup: Americomp

Library of Congress Cataloging-in-Publication Data
Jones, Walter S.
    The logic of international relations / Walter S. Jones. — 8th ed.
      p. cm.
   ISBN 0-673-52478-7 (pb)
    1. International relations. I. Title.
JX1395.J66   1996
327—DC20
                                                96-18900
                                                 CIP

ISBN 0-673-52478-7

To Sally and Steven, Cristine and Doug, and Sarah,
That the New World Order might bring peace to their century.

And to William deNeergaard and Emil Gerard,
Two uncommon gentlemen.

Brief Contents

Detailed Contents

Part Three   The Logic of the International Political Economy

Part Four   The Logic of World Order

Preface

When the seventh edition of *The Logic of International Relations* was published in 1991, the world was celebrating the end of the Cold War. But it was also agonizing over its sad realization that the post–Cold War era produced neither global tranquility nor the anticipated economic "peace dividend" that would divert a long habit of luxurious defense funding into domestic revitalization and international development. The disintegration of both the Soviet Union and its Eastern European empire sparked several civil wars; a UN-sponsored and U.S.-led coalition of forces crushed the Iraqi invasion of Kuwait; Yugoslavia broke apart in genocidal hatred, provoking the first-ever combat by NATO after its old nemesis and *raison d'être*, the Soviet Union, had ceased to exist. Bloody civil wars in Somalia, Rwanda, Mozambique, Liberia, Algeria, and elsewhere underscored the seething temperament of the Developing Nations. Terrorism reached new heights. The former constituents of the Soviet Union, Russia foremost among them, struggled—often violently—to find their way both politically and economically as the transformation of their socialist economies sparked inflation, unemployment, and the kind of incipient class conflict that the Bolshevik Revolution presumably had eradicated. By the end of 1995 communism had become fashionable once again, this time in open elections, in Russia and Poland. Except for the absence of the global nuclear confrontation, it was tempting to think that the world was retrogressing, encouraged by Russia's brutal war with the breakaway republic of Chechnya.

But there were countervailing trends as well. Peace came to Cambodia and independence to Namibia. The Palestine Liberation Organization and Israel adopted accords that turned the governance of former occupied territories over to Palestinians, even as Lebanon stabilized after decades of war, Jordan and Israel found peace, and Syria consented to peace negotiations. Apartheid was abandoned through free elections in South Africa, and Nelson Mandela, imprisoned for much of his adult life as an enemy of the state, was elevated to the presidency. A peace accord between warring religious factions in Northern Ireland staggered between tranquility and renewed violence. An unpopular NATO peacekeeping mission, with Russian cooperation, began the process of enforcing a shaky peace agreement among Serbians, Croatians, and Muslims in Bosnia and Herzegovina.

As all this unfolded, the world attempted, however interruptedly, to address its intended post–Cold War agenda: the global economy. And if less visible to a media- and communications-rich world than the atrocities of war, economic events struck an equally brisk pace. Globalization of securities and currency markets; completion of the European Common Market and initiation of final steps to European Union; the regionalization of agricultural and industrial trade; the effort to promote free market economies where socialist planned economies had prevailed in Eastern and Central Europe; a refocusing on economic development in full awareness that the world's rich-poor gap is widening; efforts to accommodate to the heralded successes of the

Dynamic Asian Economies and to cope with the contradiction of China's growing economic might and its regressive policies on human rights and civil liberties; creation of a new World Trade Organization to promote the evolution of an equitable global trade regime and to resolve steadily increasing trade conflict—these and many more issues struggled for the attention of governments unexpectedly preoccupied with the geopolitical detritus of the Cold War.

Buoyed by Moscow's cooperation with the Western reaction to Iraq's invasion of Kuwait and confident from arms reduction agreements that the Cold War had run its course, President George Bush proclaimed his vision of a New World Order. He inarguably was correct that the Cold War's demise would reorder world politics and change both the international objectives and strategies of governments. But the images of an idyllic world order with which his hopes were received were smashed both immediately and frequently in the ensuing years. To be sure, the world was different; but it was not peaceful, so how could there be a New World Order?

Because the preceding edition of *The Logic of International Relations* was prepared at the outset of the transition, I wrote the following words in its Preface: ". . . [W]hile I have attempted in this edition to demonstrate the causes and consequences of the Cold War's demise, I have not attempted to paint a sweepingly new view of the global order." Although in this new edition the view is something less than "sweeping," I have attempted, nonetheless, to capitalize on five years of events, facts, and trends to elucidate what the New World Order is and what it is not, and how various perspectives on it have altered foreign-policy behavior among governments in their many bilateral and multilateral settings. In doing so, I have made some format changes, some of which I previously had resisted despite critical comment, and I have increased the economic content and brought the military content into line with the current circumstances. I also have increased references to the domestic-international interface to illustrate causal factors in foreign policy.

Tabular material has been increased in the hope of easing the student's burden.

I wish to thank the following reviewers who were selected by HarperCollins to critique the seventh edition and the manuscript of the eighth: Robert M. Brown, Troy State University; Beau Grosscup, California State University—Chico; Michael Kelley, University of Central Arkansas; Alan C. Lamborn, Colorado State University; Gary Prevost, St. John's University; Craig Warkentin, University of Kentucky; Professor Michael C. Williams, York University. It seems that with each edition of this book, the reviewers become more incisive and critically thoughtful in the most helpful of ways. I have tried to utilize their suggestions and to restructure my own thinking as much as possible without distorting my principal goals.

With the greatest pleasure do I also acknowledge the role of the readers and the professors who have used previous editions of *The Logic of International Relations*. The message of this book—that an effective understanding of contemporary international relations requires a method both interdisciplinary and multinational—has reached many thousands of young people throughout the English-speaking world. These students have been alerted to the need to view world politics through more than a single set of national lenses. Despite the transition to the post–Cold War world, that message is no less important today. That the international relations professoriate and its students should turn to this book for this message is the author's everlasting reward.

For the instructor, we offer an instructor's manual/test bank prepared by Joe D. Hagan of West Virginia University. The manual includes chapter summaries, multiple choice questions, discussion topics and essay questions, and suggestions for further reading.

Perhaps the most courageous contributors to this book are the people at Longman who carried this work to completion after having learned that their company had been offered for sale. Thus I have benefited not only from the skill but from the calm perseverance and steadfast dedication of Leo Wiegman, Margaret Loftus and Reka Simonsen, and from the artistic care of Julie Tesser. Rob Anglin and his colleagues at Electronic Publishing Services Inc., to whom responsibility for production was given, did their work expertly and were gentle in their efforts to keep me on schedule as I moved first to Florida and then to Ohio in a space of less than four months. In his work as copy editor, Andrew Schwartz perfected the details of the manuscript.

Aside from those who contributed to this work by way of their knowledge and expertise, there are many who did so through the more subtle, yet invaluable gifts of helping me to find the requisite strength and discipline as I attempted to balance writing with the daily vicissitudes of an academic vice presidency, and as I prepared to leave Long Island University for the University of Cincinnati. Their special contributions are their friendship and good humor, and their concern for my exhaustion. Gale Stevens-Haynes, Lee Kelly, and George Sutton share a genius for knowing where work stops and life begins and, together, they found a way to impart their message to me. Nancy, Ron, and Nicole Naskashian welcomed me into their home as I went through the domestic phase of a complicated move west. Had Owen Smith not invited me into his office and Marilyn Bernstein not set with him the perfect tone and environment for sustained writing, it simply would have been impossible for me to complete this work. Melodee Gandia's unwavering friendship was a constant source of strength. Ellen McHugh, who for nine years organized my life, was more than an assistant; she is a friend whose irreverent humor and devil-may-care reassurances made for great joy where it would not otherwise have been. The thoughtful care and help of Shirley Johnson and Susan Ruby in my hopscotch-like move eased my complicated transition as I raced the publisher's clock. Mere thanks can only begin to express how much these people have given me, but the importance of their security and happiness leads me to hope that *The Logic of International Relations* might make some small contribution to international understanding and global stability.

For any shortcomings and imperfections that might have survived all this assistance, the author alone is responsible.

W.S.J.
Cincinnati, Ohio
August 1996

Introduction

There are several questions of style and organization in this book that may at first seem odd and will be misleading without explanation. The book begins with an analytical description of the New World Order emphasizing its conceptual content and its practical limitations, followed by a theoretical introduction to *perceptual analysis*, the book's chief mode of presentation. The succeeding five chapters explore the world outlooks of five principal "actors" (or group of actors) in the contemporary international system: the Russian Federation, the United States, the principal partners of the United States (Canada, Western Europe, and Japan), China, and a composite of the Developing World. This is done by examining the way in which each viewpoint is influenced by concepts, values, national interests, and ideologies, rather than a statement of universal laws and regularities describing all actors, as is done in most texts. This emphasis on perceptual analysis is based on the thesis that differences in national goals and perceptions are the origin of most international conflicts.

For the fullest appreciation of the differences among perceptions of the international system, this book uses an experimental method of presentation. Instead of taking a detached, objective, "scientific" perspective and looking at each actor's view critically, it tries to step into each nation's shoes to look at the world from its own point of view. This is an exercise in role-playing, or more nearly exactly, in role-writing, imagining first the outlook of a Russian citizen, then seeing the world from an American point of view, then from that of a partner of the United States, then as a Chinese communist, and finally from a synthesized Developing World perspective. This differs greatly from the usual approach of newspapers, histories, and most of our sources of information, which stand above their subjects as "neutral and objective" observers. The task of understanding viewpoints that differ profoundly from our own is so difficult that it is necessary temporarily to suspend judgment the better to appreciate the perspective of the other. To achieve this, the reader will try temporarily to be the figure he or she wishes to understand.

A few reservations and caveats about the experiment at this point. First, the various perspectives are presented in a mixture of original texts and the words of the author acting as an intermediary organizing the original texts for a predominately American audience. This provides some flavor of the original, while permitting a quicker pace than would be possible with full texts.

Second, the book concentrates on idealized pictures of each actor, emphasizing values and professed beliefs without succumbing to propaganda. There is a danger here in mistaking mere rhetoric for the actual motives; we know that speechwriters often use idealistic disguises for less lofty goals, such as the pursuit of power. The differences among nations are undoubtedly exaggerated when only ideals are presented, but they would be understated if, like most introductory texts, this one concentrated instead on universal modes of behavior that ignore critical differences among actors. In a sense, then, this book errs on the side of principles, drawing caricatures that highlight the unique and defining features rather than completely proportioned portraits.

Third, the author concedes that it is partly artificial to speak of the perceptual system of the United States or of any other party, particularly that of the greatly varied Developing World. Within each national actor there are elites with differences of opinion regarding the national interest, the optimal course of strategy, and other issues. This book tries in each case to develop a characterization that subsumes these differences, at least as far as the dominant elites are concerned. Yet the analysis gives less importance to dissenting opinions within each national actor that have not in the post-war period influenced policy directly or substantially. For example, in the American case the analysis centers mainly on the anticommunist perspective that in fact guided policy from 1948 through 1988, and only in passing does it review various revisionist challenges to the dominant outlook. In other words, the analysis focuses on various orthodoxies, not on minority views or factions that have been consistently out of power.

Fourth, one feature of the presentation may be especially controversial. Considerable attention is given to internal political features and to problems of the various actors that shape their external outlooks. Conventional analysis draws a fairly sharp distinction between domestic politics and foreign policy, but many international relations specialists find this rigid boundary a hinderance to understanding the roots of international behavior. To a considerable degree, the foreign actions of nations are continuations of essentially domestic processes and demands, and certainly international perceptions cannot be separated entirely from the broader value base that generates them. This explains the emphasis on domestic matters at key points.

Fifth, the analysis presented here takes the nation-state to be the principal actor in international affairs. To some extent this is no longer accurate, as international organizations, integration movements, and some less formal transnational phenomena rise in importance. These newer actors are treated at length in the latter half of this volume. Their importance notwithstanding, the key actors are still nation-states and their official bureaucracies, accounting for perhaps 80 percent of real power in international relations. The first two parts of the book, comprising ten of the book's seventeen chapters, stress these national actors over others.

Sixth, since the publication of the first edition of *The Logic of International Relations* in 1974, the role and character of the Cold War changed entirely. For about half the life of this book, détente between the Soviet Union and the United States and the relaxation of Sino-American tensions reduced the probability of serious confrontation, except between China and the Soviet Union. From 1980 to 1988, however, détente failed as a regulator of Soviet-American relations, and the decade was marked by mutual suspicion, accelerated arms production, and angry rhetoric. The new wave of American conservatism coincided with the revival of Soviet adventurism (as in Afghanistan) and tightening of the Soviet grip on Eastern Europe (as in Poland), so that the celebrated period of détente seemed only to have been a brief interlude in the Cold War. Then, unexpectedly, the pace of global events accelerated, and by the autumn of 1990 the Cold War was history, followed by the Soviet empire in Eastern Europe and finally by the Soviet Union itself. A great transformation of the international system began fitfully, with war in the Arabian Peninsula, some of the former Soviet republics, and in scattered spots within the Developing World; but also with peace in Central America, Cambodia, and in much of the Middle East. Namibia became independent; apartheid was eliminated from South Africa; but China became more oppressive. As a consequence, whereas previous editions of this book were dictated by Cold War conditions, this new edition takes its lead from the perceptions and policy changes of the New World Order.

And finally, a word about the political implications of perceptual analysis. It has been said that this method tends to be forgiving of sins, and that it views each actor in the sympathetic light of its own values and experiences. Ultimately, it is charged, each actor is free of responsibility, each the victim of respective misperceptions. The author concedes that an agnostic analysis of positions, giving the internal logic of each case and avoiding absolute external judgments, may introduce greater moral ambiguities than fixing a single position from which to assess all the alternative views. These dilemmas of relativism and ambiguity are inherent in international relations, and it is necessary to leave the comforts of one's own belief system in order to understand other, equally compelling contributions to global coexistence. Relations among nations are in their very nature a meeting place of divergent perceptions.

CHAPTER 1

The New World Order and National Perceptions

With the surrender of German forces in May 1945 and the fall of Japan barely three months later, the forty-five-year process of dividing the world into two giant armed camps began. War-weary and war-wary allies arranged occupation zones in the eastern and western sectors of Germany, the German capital city of Berlin, Eastern Europe, China, Korea, Japan, Southeast Asia, and many Pacific islands that would portend the most fundamental element of the post-war world order. When the Soviet Union broke the American atomic monopoly in 1947, both the political and territorial lines hardened. President Harry S Truman, who had ordered the atomic bombings of Hiroshima and Nagasaki, faced down a leftist guerilla movement in Greece with the pledge that the United States would use any measures, including force, to prevent the spread of Soviet influence (the Truman Doctrine, 1947). Despite American aid and diplomatic pressure, it became apparent that Chiang Kai-shek's Western-oriented Chinese government would fall to the communist revolution of Mao Zedong. The course of events had already inspired Winston Churchill to declare in 1946 that "an Iron Curtain has descended across the [European] continent,"[1] a barrier that for nearly a half-century would divide the world between democracy and capitalism on one side, and communism and socialism on the other, and across which hundreds of billions of dollars in conventional

and nuclear arms would be aimed. A year later, the influencial journalist Walter Lippmann characterized the world order as "The Cold War."[2]

Unlike a shooting war that begins with the first assault and ends with the last, the Cold War had no precise dates. In general, however, its origin is set at the end of the Second World War in 1945 and its termination in 1990. It did not, in fact, terminate. Its end was not celebrated in treaties or joint declarations. And while there are many conflicting theories as to why it ended, the evidences of its passing were several. Among the most important were (1) conclusion of a treaty on Intermediate-Range Nuclear Forces in Europe (1987), a giant step in pacifying the East-West division; (2) Mikhail Gorbachev's revised diplomacy with the West and loosening of domestic political controls, and Washington's enthusiastic endorsement; (3) Soviet tolerance of democracy in Poland and Gorbachev's open advocacy of free elections (1989); (4) the agenda for peace resulting from the Bush-Gorbachev conference at Malta in 1989 (Figure 1–1); (5) unprecedented Soviet-American

---

[1] Quoted in *The New York Times*, March 6, 1946, p. 4.

[2] Walter Lippmann, *The Cold War* (Boston: Little, Brown, 1947), collected essays published in the same year. While Lippmann is generally credited with having originated the expression, some attribute it to American financier Bernard Baruch. Lippmann himself disclaimed originality, saying that he had taken it from a French expression used to describe Hitler's psychological tactics, often called *la guerre froide*, translated "the cold war." See for brief discussion Ronald Steel, *Walter Lippmann and the American Century* (Boston: Atlantic-Little, Brown, 1980), p. 445.

The President and Chairman Gorbachev exchanged views on a variety of issues during their meetings in Malta, including the remarkable events leading to peaceful and democratic change in Eastern and Central Europe.

The President noted his strong support for *perestroika* and suggested that the two leaders work to give major new impetus to the U.S.-Soviet relationship. The President conveyed his strong personal commitment to this goal.

In this spirit, the President put forward the following ideas:

Next Steps

1. Holding the summit in the United States during the last 2 weeks in June.

2. Having the next meeting of Foreign Ministers next month in the Soviet Union to prepare for the summit.

Economics and Commercial Relations

1. Targeting the 1990 summit for completion of a trade agreement granting most-favored-nation status to the Soviet Union so that the President can grant a Jackson-Vanik waiver at that time. To reach that goal, the President proposed beginning negotiations on a trade agreement now and urged the Supreme Soviet to complete action on its emigration legislation early next year.

2. Supporting observer status for the Soviet Union in GATT after the Uruguay round is completed next year. The President urged the Soviet Union to use the intervening time to move toward market prices at the wholesale level so its economy will become more compatible with the GATT system.

3. Expanding U.S.-Soviet technical economic cooperation. The President presented a paper proposing specific economic projects covering topics such as finance, agriculture, statistics, small business development, budgetary and tax policy, a stock exchange, and antimonopoly policy.

4. Exploring with Congress the lifting of statutory restrictions on export credits and guarantees after a Jackson-Vanik waiver.

5. Beginning discussions of a bilateral investment treaty that would provide protections for American business people who want to invest in the Soviet Union.

6. Improving ties between the Soviets and the OECD, and East-West economic cooperation through the economic basket of the CSCE process.

Human Rights

Resolving all divided family issues by the time of the 1990 summit. In this regard, the President handed over a list of people wishing to emigrate.

Regional Issues

Expressed disappointment with Soviet policy on Central America, noting it was out of step with the new Soviet direction domestically in Eastern Europe and in arms control. Nicaragua/Cuba remains the single most disruptive factor in the relationship.

Arms Control

1. Speeding achievement of a chemical weapons ban by offering to end U.S. production of binary weapons when the multilateral convention on chemical weapons enters into force in return for Soviet acceptance of the terms of our U.N. proposal to ban chemical weapons.

2. Proposing to sign an agreement at the 1990 summit to destroy U.S. and Soviet chemical weapons down to 20 percent of the current U.S. level.

3. Suggesting joint U.S.-Soviet support for a CFE summit to sign a CFE treaty in 1990.

4. Accelerating the START process in order to resolve all substantive issues and to conclude a treaty, if possible, by the 1990 summit. To this end, the President suggested that Secretary Baker and Foreign Minister Shevardnadze concentrate on resolving at their January meeting three of the outstanding START issues: ALCM's [air-launched cruise missiles], nondeployed missiles, and telemetry encryption.

5. Completing work on the Threshold Test Ban Treaty (TTBT) and the Peaceful Nuclear Explosions Treaty (PNET) for signature at the 1990 Summit.

6. Proposing that the Soviet Union join efforts to constrain missile proliferation more effectively by observing the limits developed by the U.S. and its allies in the Missile Technology Control Regime.

Military Openness

Making public more information on military programs. The President suggested that the Soviet Union make public the details of its military budget, force posture, and weapons production figures, just as the United States now does.

Olympics

Suggesting joint U.S.-Soviet support for Berlin as the site of the 2004 Olympic Games.

Environment

1. Hosting a conference next fall to negotiate a framework treaty on global climate change, after the working groups of the U.N.-sponsored Intergovernmental Panel on Climate Change submit their final report.

2. Convening an international meeting at the White House next spring for top-level scientific, environmental, and economic officials to discuss global climate change issues. The President expressed hope that the Soviets will join us by sending their top officials in the field.

Student Exchanges

Increasing significantly university exchanges so that an additional 1,000 American and 1,000 Soviet college students are studying in each other's country by the beginning of the 1991 school year.

FIGURE 1–1   White House fact sheet on the meeting with Soviet Chairman Mikhail Gorbachev in Malta, December 4, 1989.

Source: The Public Papers of the Presidents: George Bush, 1989, Volume II, pp. 1642–1643.

diplomatic collaboration on the Desert Storm War against Iraq and on peace initiatives in the Middle East (1990–91); (6) the peaceful reunification of the two Germanys (1990); (7) conclusion of the Strategic Arms Reduction Treaty (START) (1991); and (8) collapse of the Soviet Union itself (1991). The Malta peace agenda of December 1989 was trumpeted by *The New York Times* as a declaration of the Cold War's end.[3] Ten months later, in an address to the General Assembly of the United Nations, President Bush referred to "the Revolution of '89," and he declared that the "long twilight struggle that for 45 years has divided Europe, [the United States and the Soviet Union], and much of the world has come to an end."[4]

Only three weeks earlier, in an address to Congress on the Persian Gulf crisis (Iraq had attacked Kuwait, but the U.S.-led coalition had not yet launched its counteroffensive) and buoyed by Moscow's collaborative policy, the President had laid out his objectives, and at one point said:

> We stand today at a unique and extraordinary moment. The crisis in the Persian Gulf . . . offers a rare opportunity to move toward an historic period of cooperation. Out of these troubled times, our fifth objective—a new world order—can emerge: a new era—freer from the threat of terror, stronger in pursuit of justice, and more secure in the quest for peace. An era in which the nations of the world . . . can prosper and live in harmony. A hundred generations have searched for this elusive path to peace, while a thousand wars raged across the span of human endeavor. Today that new world is struggling to be born, a world quite different from the one we've known. A world where the rule of law supplants the rule of the jungle. A world in which nations recognize the shared responsibility for freedom and justice. A world where the strong respect the rights of the weak. This is the vision that I shared with President Gorbachev. . . . He and other

leaders from Europe, the Gulf, and around the world understand that how we manage this crisis today could shape the future for generations to come.[5]

He repeated this theme at the United Nations, saying, "It is in our hands . . . to press forward to cap a historic movement toward a new world order and a long era of peace."[6]

There is, of course, no assurance that the New World Order or any world order will be so uniformly progressive and pacific as these passages promise. But the essence of President Bush's observation was accurate: that the passing of the Cold War with all its oppressive and restrictive markings, coupled with other major contemporary themes of international politics, did so fundamentally alter the environment that the world order could no longer be defined as it had been for nearly a half-century. What, then, is the New World Order?

The New World Order

We start by dispatching three erroneous assumptions. First, the New World Order and the end of the Cold War are *not* synonymous. True, giving an end to the Cold War was an essential precondition. But the important point is that when the Cold War was swept from the scene, what world order characteristics replaced it? What did the change mean for Russian-American relations? What suppressed political forces were unleashed as others were being contained? What have the United Nations and other organizations been able to achieve that they could not earlier? With the Cold War's emphasis on arms gone, what became the focal point of world order? With the collapse of the Soviet empire and the disintegration of the Soviet state itself, what

---

[3] *The New York Times*, December 4, 1989, p. A1.
[4] *The Public Papers of the Presidents: George Bush, 1990*, Volume II, "Address Before the 45th Session of the United Nations General Assembly in New York, New York, October 1, 1990," pp. 1330–1334 at p. 1331.

[5] *The Public Papers of the Presidents: George Bush, 1989*, Volume II, "Address Before a Joint Session of Congress on the Persian Gulf Crisis and the Federal Budget Deficit, September 11, 1990," pp. 1218–1222 at p. 1219.
[6] George Bush, "Address Before the 45th Session of the United Nations General Assembly in New York, New York, October 1, 1990," p. 1332.

new dynamics place demands on the global political system and the international political economy? What new avenues of conflict have replaced the old, and what mechanisms for conflict resolution?

Second, the New World Order does *not* claim that everything is perfectly orderly, or that harmony prevails, or that the end of the Cold War has ushered in a world without conflict. The New World Order is likely, in contrast, to have as many foibles as the old, but they will differ as to who is involved, how conflict arises, how it is conducted, and how it is resolved. One need only look at Bosnia, Somalia, or Chechnya to see all this vividly. The contradiction is not that aggression and genocide can occur in the New World Order, but that it would be assumed from the title that force is nothing but a historical memory. Based on international events and the debate over the future of U.S. foreign policy, one observer writes of "the new world disorder."[7] Another more accurately characterizes the conditions as "new instabilities, new priorities," and says of the New World Order:

> One thing seems assured: Given the present confidence about the international scene, there will be disappointments aplenty for Americans in the years ahead. Although the world after the Cold War is likely to be [a] far less dangerous place because of reduced risks of a cataclysmic clash, it is likely to be more unstable rather than less. The Bush administration has coined the phrase "new world order." If the phrase means that the world order has been sharply *altered* from the strict divisions of the Cold War, then clearly it is correct. If it means that the world order will be *novel*, marked by a new stability, then it is unduly utopian.[8]

And third, just as the Cold War did not end instantaneously, the New World Order did *not* just appear fully formed on the global scene. Indeed, many of the New World Order's components long coexisted with the Cold War itself. Take among

them the integration of Western Europe, which has been in progress with varying degrees of earnest since 1954. The Developing Nations have been searching for their piece of the economic pie since the first United Nations Development Decade was launched in 1960. Throughout the Cold War, however, these were secondary issues. From the American perspective, for example, European integration was always secondary to trans-Atlantic security through the North Atlantic Treaty Organization (NATO), and each renewal of Soviet-American dispute revealed the underlying tensions between economic growth and collective self-defense. In fact, therefore, just as the Cold War evolved out of existence, the New World Order evolved into existence. The end of the Cold War so altered the environment as to enable what were previously secondary issues to converge into the primary components of world order.

We know now what the New World Order is not. Let us explore what it is by comparing some of its building blocks with those of its predecessor. Table 1–1 summarizes these comparisons.

1. Military Characteristics

The characteristics of the Cold War period were primarily military. It was an era marked by a continuous Soviet–American nuclear arms race, with Britain, France, and China developing smaller nuclear arsenals. Accompanying this was an alliance structure that girded the globe, with American troops on every continent except Antarctica, and including the Soviet Union's failed attempt to deploy missiles to Cuba in 1962. Furthermore, although the tight bipolarity of the early Cold War years evolved almost into multipolarity, the global military standoff was always bipolar. Even the many regional power confrontations, such as the two Koreas and the Middle East, could not have been so richly armed had it not been essential to the hegemonic policies of the two superpowers not only to sponsor the opposing sides, but also to keep them tightly controlled and balanced. On all this the United States, the Soviet Union, and their respective allies lavished hundreds of billions of dollars annually.

---

[7] Ted Galen Carpenter, "The New World Disorder," *Foreign Policy,* fall 1991, pp. 24–39.
[8] James Schlesinger, "New Instabilities, New Priorities," *Foreign Policy,* winter 1991–92, pp. 3–24 at p. 4. The emphasis is from the original.

TABLE 1–1

COMPARING TWO WORLD ORDERS

	Cold War World Order	New World Order	
Primary	Military		Secondary
	Spiraling nuclear arms race	Staged reduction of nuclear arms	
	Alliance—with troop deployments	Troop withdrawals; base closings	
	Annually increasing defense budgets	Defense budget reductions	
	Global military bipolarity	Survival of only one superpower	
	Tight controls on regional arms	Uncontrolled proliferation of regional arms	
Secondary	Economic		Primary
	Capitalism vs. state-controlled economy	Decline of state-controlled economies	
	East-West trade barriers	Most-favored-nation trade status	
	Economic nationalism and regionalism	Growth of regionalism	
	Faltering trade regimes	Expansion of trade regimes	
	Development	Development	
Tertiary	Political/Ideological		Tertiary
	Militaristic hegemony	Peaceful competition	
	Inflammatory rhetoric	Cooperative rhetoric with candor	
	Bloc-oriented foreign policy	Revitalization of multilateralism	
	Intervention for tactical advantage	Intervention for stabilization	
	Paralysis of Security Council	Unprecedented use of Security Council	

Throughout the 1980s, for example, the U.S. defense budget absorbed an annual average of over 6 percent of the gross domestic product (GDP, the value of all goods and services produced). By 1990, the Pentagon's budget crossed $300 billion, an amount only slightly smaller than the combined GDP of all African countries. Despite the enormous costs, and notwithstanding the raging of three large wars during this period (Korea, Vietnam, and Afghanistan), successful mutual deterrence prevented both global nuclear war and conventional war in Europe.

The New World Order has strikingly different characteristics. The collapse of the Soviet empire through Gorbachev's willingness to allow self-determination in Eastern Europe (1989) changed the face of the trans-European conflict. The Warsaw Treaty Organization, the Soviet counterpart of NATO, went quietly out of business, and some of its former members petitioned for membership in NATO. Disintegration of the Soviet state followed two years later when Yeltsin and the leaders of Byelorussia (now Belarusse) and Ukraine jointly declared that "the U.S.S.R., as a subject of international law and geopolitical entity, is ceasing its existence."[9] Among the former constituent republics that broke away were six of the largest and most industrially advanced: Georgia, Ukraine, Belarus, Lithuania, Latvia, and Estonia. Even the Soviet nuclear deployment was no longer intact. There remained only one nuclear superpower: the United States. Gone in only two years were the nuclear confrontation, global military bipolarity, a European continent separated by the threat of war, the Soviet empire, and the integrated Soviet state.

These new features of world politics negated the need for massive armaments that were so central to the Cold War. Soviet and American intermediate-range nuclear forces (INF) in Europe were all but dismantled, and strategic arms reduction greatly accelerated. (Presidents Bush and Gorbachev actually signed the START treaty with pens

---

[9] Quoted in *The New York Times*, December 9, 1991, p. A1. The text of the agreement establishing the Commonwealth of Independent States is reproduced in full on page 22.

consisting of metal recovered from dismantled missiles.) Both Washington and Moscow announced intentions to retarget their dwindling nuclear forces as a way of defusing the nuclear trigger. Chemical weapons were set for gradual reduction and destruction. Russian troops left Germany, the emancipated republics, and most of Central Europe; and American troop deployments in Western Europe were sharply curtailed. In a rush to rebuild its economy and convert it from state controlled to market driven, Russia reallocated its defense budget to economic development and social stability. In the United States, defense funding was leveled in dollars, and actually reduced both as a percentage of gross domestic product and of total federal spending.

Consistent with the warning that the New World Order could be less stable rather than more, post–Cold War international relations are not, despite all the foregoing, without troubles in the military sphere. For one thing, Soviet military dissolution has meant that relatively modern military hardware has fallen into new hands outside of Russia itself. (This explains in large measure why the breakup of Yugoslavia, especially as seen in the war among Bosnian Serbs, Bosnian Muslims, and Croats, has been so ferocious.) It has also flooded both the public and underground international arms markets with virtually every kind of conventional weapon. Moreover, the absence of the old hegemonic controls over arms races has invited more nations to participate in international arms trade in increasingly sophisticated items. There is less assurance today than there was at any time during the Cold War that surface-to-air missiles, high-grade plastic explosives, weapons-grade radioactive materials, and even tactical nuclear weapons will not fall into the hands of irresponsible governments or international terrorists.

2. Economic Characteristics

The dominant economic theme of the Cold War was the challenge between Western capitalism and the socialist, state-controlled economies of the Soviet empire. To some extent, the entire period was understood from the Eastern side as a struggle for socialist survival against capitalist encirclement. Marxism-Leninism posits that capitalism is an instrument of class warfare, and international capitalism for suppression of true democratic progress throughout the world. Encirclement by global capitalism was thus a threat to the Soviet way of life, especially when it was armed and poised for either conventional or nuclear war. From the Western perspective, Nikita Khrushchev's dictum "we will bury you," at first taken as a nuclear threat, was really a challenge to capitalism and to American domination of the global economy. Any Marxist foothold in the Third World was, therefore, a threat to America's supply of natural resources and markets for its goods. Under these circumstances, neither side was eager to strengthen the other economically; in fact, part of the Cold War was to weaken one another as much as possible through economic means. For Canada, Western Europe, and much of noncommunist Asia, this was an unwelcome barrier to trade and growth, and gradually the standoff became unique to the Soviet Union and the United States. For much of the final decade of the Cold War, Washington imposed trade sanctions on the Soviet Union under the Jackson-Vanik amendment, a Congressional act restricting Soviet-American trade because of Moscow's prohibition on Jewish emigration except after payment of an exorbitant education tax.

Outside of the Soviet-American ideological confrontation, the global economy of the Cold War era was marked by a gradual but halting growth of regionalism over economic nationalism. We have seen, for example, that the path to Western European integration opened in 1954. Britain and France included many of their former imperial holdings in trade protections through special multilateral treaties. Nations in South America, the Caribbean, the Pacific Rim, Africa, and the Middle East all experimented with regional arrangements at one time or another. In some cases, these were traditional common markets—elimination of trade barriers among the members and common trade policies with respect to outside states. In others, they were instruments of multilateral assertion. The Organization of Petroleum Exporting Countries (OPEC) is the outstanding example, as it used controls on the volume and price of oil exports to raise development capital and to influence the policies of the capitalist industrialized countries on Middle Eastern military politics. Other cartels organized around exports of primary products from coffee to tin were far less successful, but also far less disruptive.

On the global level there was an era-long effort to improve the international trade regime, that is, the rules and regulations under which nations trade or restrain trade. This occurred principally under the General Agreement on Tariffs and Trade (GATT), part of the post–Second World War international economic structure. But it was not until the close of the Cold War that the Uruguay Round of negotiations was concluded, making major advances in trading equity. The new regime also put the GATT out of business, establishing in its place the World Trade Organization (WTO) (something the United States had resisted after World War Two), and giving it authority as an arbiter in trade disputes.

Development of the poor states was also a major part of the agenda in the former world order, through both national and multinational means. Individually, governments offered foreign aid, but in many cases primarily as part of the Soviet-American ideological challenge. Multilateral aid was made available by the International Bank for Reconstruction and Development (IBRD or World Bank) and the International Monetary Fund (IMF) as well as a number of regional organizations. United Nations programs such as those concerning development and population and others also provided aid.

The bipolar military imperative of the Cold War has yielded to economic competition and prosperity as the defining characteristic of the New World Order. The march toward democracy has been joined by a new enthusiasm for market economics among the former Soviet allies and in

Russia itself. State-controlled economies are waning except in China, North Korea, and Cuba. Russia and China both enjoy growing trade with the West and have most-favored-nation trade status (i.e., except for Mexico and Canada under the North American Free Trade Area [NAFTA], they trade with the United States on terms equal to the best available to anyone). Despite recurrent political differences with China, Western capital moves there as well as to the former Soviet world, and formalization of diplomatic relations between the United States and Vietnam in 1995 was much the result of corporate pressure to facilitate competition with Japan in Southeast Asia.

Economic nationalism is now rapidly giving way to regionalism. The European Union (EU) and NAFTA are continent-wide attempts to expand markets and facilitate the free flow of labor, capital, and goods. While to some extent they are new and larger instruments of competition, and to some observers new sovereign entities, they are also instruments of regional multilateralism. Thus they reduce nationalism within regions, but contain the danger of making regionalism a new form of economic hegemony from a global perspective. The intrinsic defense against this threat is that they are themselves the products of international lawmaking, and they are regulated by an international economic regime that, thanks to the Uruguay Round of GATT negotiations, is subjected more and more to peaceful regulation.

In the New World Order, development is elevated as a global goal because it is no longer tied to hegemonic ideological challenge. In addition, the more modern development programs fully recognize the relatedness of development, population control, environmental preservation, and nutrition as a basis for increased multilateral assistance. The economic rights of women and education are also part of the formula. On the other side, however, the end of the Cold War has made bilateral aid politically unpopular, particularly in the United States, where there is growing demand to discontinue it. And given Russia's economic problems and the removal of its ideological motivation, its aid program has already suffered. The current depressed economic climate in Cuba, for example, is a direct result of Russia's foreign policy in the New World Order.

3. Political/Ideological Characteristics

The disappearance of military hegemony has changed the face and the sound of international politics. Gone with the alliances and the nuclear confrontation is the inflammatory rhetoric that added so much to the temperature of the Cold War: mutual assured destruction, nuclear utilization theory, first strike, massive retaliation, multiple independently-targeted reentry vehicles, civilian targeting, and so on. American homes are no longer built with atomic bomb shelters, equipped with enough food and water to support families until the winds carry away the worst radiation danger. City buildings are no longer visibly designated as fallout shelters. An entire generation will remember Richard M. Nixon as vice president berating Soviet officials at a consumer-goods fair in Moscow, and Nikita Khrushchev pounding his shoe on a table at the United Nations. And gone from television are ads depicting an egg rolling toward the edge of a table, covered by a map of Europe, that shakes more and more as the sound of artillery mounts, only to have the egg fall softly into hands marked "NATO." In place of all these is a tone of peaceful competition marked by calm candor. No one would argue, for example, that the Japanese-American trading relationship is happy, but only the most irreconcilable economic nationalists resort to verbal bashing and threats of force.

Twice in this century—after World War One (League of Nations) and after World War Two (United Nations)—the world has turned to multilateralism to preserve peace in favor of power politics. There is evidence that this is in progress once again, and much advocacy for it. After having been paralyzed for fully nine-tenths of its lifetime by Cold War politics, the Security Council now shows signs of achieving what the great powers meant for it in 1945, namely, to mandate common action to preserve international peace against threats to the peace, breaches of the peace, or acts of aggression. In what some consider to have been the acid test of mutual trust in ending the Cold War,[10] the Soviet Union joined the other permanent members of the Security Council in calling for joint action against Iraq in the Gulf War (1990–91). Other successful multilateral acts have followed, including common action to restore peace and humanitarian treatment in civil wars in Cambodia, Haiti, Rwanda, and Somalia. Even in Bosnia, troops serving under UN command have played many roles including combat, and NATO warplanes have fought from above. Only after the bombings turned the advantage on the ground to Bosnian Muslims and Croats did the Russian government object, fearing not only a Serb defeat, but a forceful redistribution of territory that might diminish Serbian interest in a peace arrangement under discussion. Even in the area of intervention, then, the renewed preference for multilateralism and a revised motive for intervention—stabilization rather than tactical advantage—have been much in evidence in the early years of the New World Order.

These, then, are the elements of the New World Order. Once again, the expression "New World Order" is not a statement of peaceful perfection, but of a new historical phase and the revised characteristics of the post–Cold War world. Before turning to the perceptions of the global system held by the principal contemporary actors, we explore how opinion about and, therefore, action in the international arena, is formed.

Perceptions in World Politics

In political debate as well as any other, we all like to assume that the sides begin with facts. But in

---

[10] Paul Sharp, "The Great Test: Soviet Diplomacy and the Gulf War," *Diplomacy and Statecraft*, July 1992, pp. 272–302; and Michael R. Beschloss and Strobe Talbott, *At the Highest Levels: The Inside Story of the End of the Cold War* (Boston: Little, Brown and Company, 1993), particularly chapter 13.

politics, are facts actually facts? Is political subject matter what it is, or what it seems to be? How is it that hundreds of millions of people on each side of the Cold War could have experienced the same events and had such hugely different understandings of them?

In each of the remaining chapters of this section we will examine the world view of a different actor (or group of actors) in the international system. We will explore the manner in which each one's world view evolved from historical, ideological, and economic origins. In one chapter we will view the world from the perspective of a Russian student, then from the American, then from the Chinese, and so on. The objective is to elucidate the many ways in which national perceptions are formed and the ways in which their respective imprints on the system make international politics and economics so vastly complex. Because most people in the Western world are at least fairly satisfied with the system's operation, they struggle with the idea that more than half the world yearns for fundamental changes. And with the birth of a New World Order and the close of the Cold War, they would like to think that all would be peace and prosperity if only "they would be just like us." But a multicultural world replete with different cultures and national histories, different problems and goals, and vast discrepancies in both economic and social capital forbids the molding of its diversity into uniformity. The dynamics of the international system are of a piece with the diversity of peoples, and a reflection of how those diverse peoples want the world to conform to their visions and their needs.

National perceptions spring from an array of facts, ideas, beliefs, values, and cognitions, all of which are manipulated and shaped, either consciously or unconsciously, by leaders, commentators, news analysts, critics of government, scholars, teachers, clergy, jingoists, and even novelists. Shaping also comes from outside, particularly in an era of universal mass communications, as anything said by the president of the United States about global economics is likely to have a different meaning to a Japanese businessperson. And when

NATO planes bomb Serb military targets to hasten diplomacy in the Bosnian civil war, fears are ignited in Russia about the redivision of Europe along military lines, especially when states formerly in the Soviet orbit are seeking membership in NATO. So while a fact may still be a fact, it is subject to multiple meanings, each shaped by the different and conflicting perceptions brought to bear on it.

Each perceptual outlook supports itself with an array of data and historical analyses. Each may seem to its proponents so well supported by facts that it needs no further substantiation. Each perceptual system regards the others as inaccurate and dishonest. Proponents of the other points of view are victims of misperception or are dissimulators who know the truth but for ulterior motives pretend to have a different perception. In short, laypersons and national policymakers believe their own perceptual systems to be true, accurate, proven, justifiable, and worthy of accepting; and they consider those of their adversaries to be at least partly false, inaccurate, and distorted for dishonest policy purposes.

How is it possible for each perceptual system to resist change when confronted with contradictory information? Why don't the leaders of the world sit down and iron out their differences, correct one another's misperceptions, and resolve at least the portion of their conflicts that is rooted in misunderstanding? Why don't they get down to the facts and replace all this confusion with an understanding of reality?

To answer these questions, it will help to understand some of the propositions in the theory of international perceptions—propositions adapted from social psychology and applied to the study of international relations.

Facts

In everyday life, we generally assume that our understanding of reality flows directly from that reality itself. It is common sense that certain things are facts whereas the opposite assertions are not, and that if we can ascertain the facts, certain conclusions will follow. The purpose of information gathering, for both the scientist and the decision maker, is to determine the facts from which knowledge of reality can be drawn.

Perceptual theorists do not accept this simple conception of knowledge. To them, knowledge has a subjective as well as an objective component: The facts do not speak for themselves but are given meaning by each interpreter from his or her own analytical point of view. The conclusion that follows from facts depends on the interpretation that is given to the facts.

Furthermore, facts do not spring from reality but are, rather, particular pieces of information from reality that are selected by an observer as having importance, while other pieces of information are rejected as lacking importance. "Reality" consists of an infinite amount of potential information, from which only a tiny part is taken as a set of facts. For example, in writing the history of a particular war, the historian must select only a small portion of the available data to report. Millions of individuals are involved in billions and trillions of acts; billions of decisions are made by participants; the patterns of interaction are beyond imagination. The historian must select from all this a few pieces of information that seem, summarily, to describe the interactions and succinctly explain their causes. Students of history and historiography know only too well that the facts do not speak for themselves.

Social science summarizes this view of facts in a terse definition: A fact is but a peculiar ordering of reality according to a theoretic interest.[11] That is, the facts themselves are imposed on reality by the observer, rather than the other way around; and the very nature of the facts themselves depends on the questions the observer chooses to ask. Because each perceptual system asks its own questions, observers of divergent viewpoints naturally arrive at different answers or facts.

To illustrate from the Cold War: From the Soviet point of view, data on the profit structure of American corporations were the body of facts that one needed to understand the international system; from the American point of view, it is off the point entirely. Someone given twenty minutes to explain the Cold War who spent fifteen on the nature of American investments would have been regarded by a Soviet listener as having given "the facts," but by an American as having evaded them. To the American listener, the real facts had to do with Soviet aggression and American response, and examples of this kind of Soviet behavior would be pertinent. (This kind of dispute is called bias attribution.) "Facts" are thus subjectively defined and are themselves a phenomenon of perceptions. Perceptions cannot be corrected when confronted with facts if the facts themselves are perceptions.[12]

Values, Beliefs, and Cognitions

Perceptual theorists distinguish among three components of perception: values, beliefs, and cognitions. A value is a preference for one state of reality over another. For example, health is better than illness; green is prettier than blue. Values do not specify what is but, rather, what ought to be. Values assign a relative worth to objects and conditions.

A belief is a conviction that a description of reality is true, proven, or known. Often it is based on prior reception of information from the environment ("I have learned that . . . "), but it is not the same as the data themselves. It is an analytical proposition that relates individual pieces of data into a "proven" pattern. For example, democratic governments are less warlike than totalitarian governments; imperialism is the mature phase of monopoly capitalism. A belief is not the same as a value. One might believe that communism brings a higher rate of economic growth and that capitalism has a better record of protecting individual freedoms. Given these beliefs, one must decide whether capitalism or communism is better

---

[11] See David Easton, *The Political System* (New York: Knopf, 1953).

[12] For a series of quantitative studies using Cold War American perceptions to demonstrate many of the phenomena that follow, see Matthew S. Hirshberg, *Perpetuating Patriotic Perceptions: The Cognitive Function of the Cold War* (Westport, Conn.: Praeger, 1993).

according to one's own values. Which is worth more, economic growth or personal liberties?

There are actually three types of beliefs. The first, principled beliefs, form judgments of the most basic kinds, such as right and wrong, just and unjust, helpful and damaging. These are closely tied to the morality content of a political culture. The second are the causal beliefs, the ones that enable us to find cause-and-effect relationships in events around us. Their degree of uniformity in a political culture influences the consistency with which the public supports governmental policy because of consensus conversion with policymaking elites. And the third, world view beliefs, form the macroscopic notions by which a body politic understands the international environment and the nation's place in it: sovereign independence, self-determination, human rights, national identity, group loyalty, and patriotism.[13]

A cognition is data or information received from the environment; for example, China is selling missiles to Iraq. Cognitions are key elements in establishing perceptual systems and in changing them. The concept of changing national perceptions refers to introducing cognitions that will revise beliefs and values. If we had held a conference between the major Cold War actors to iron out their differences and misperceptions, our purpose would have been to influence perceptions by introducing new information. We would have tried to change stubborn beliefs and values that cause conflict by confronting each side with new cognitive data.

Unfortunately, it is well established that at all levels of human behavior, deeply held values and beliefs are highly resistant to change through new cognition, and that broad foreign policy postures such as militarism, nuclear deterrence, economic nationalism, and the like are more resistant than smaller and more transient issues.[14] Additionally, the political consciousness clings

more comfortably to stereotype-consistent information than to stereotype-inconsistent,[15] such as the Soviet Union as the Red Menace, China the Yellow Peril, or Germany the precipitator of two world wars in barely a quarter-century. Social psychological research also supports a theory of cognitive dissonance. Briefly stated, this theory holds that when a deeply held value or belief is contradicted by a new message from the environment (a dissonant cognition), the message (fact, cognition) will be rejected and the value or belief retained. Or there might not be outright rejection of the discrepant message; it may take the alternative form of reinterpretation of the datum to make it consistent with existing belief. But the effect is the same: the individual's value and belief system protects itself from external alteration.[16]

The essence of this is that incoming information is not intrinsic fact. It must be processed. Weighing information against existing beliefs or value systems, or heuristic processing, is especially important in the formation of foreign policy attitudes because the volume of information is so great and its content often mystifying. Furthermore, the guideposts our minds use to process domestic political information, such as liberalism and conservatism, big government or small, expansive social policy as against tax reductions, do not apply usefully to foreign policy.[17]

We might relate these phenomena to the idea of an economy of thought. It is very "expensive" to carry about in one's head all the information supporting one view and its opposite. Mental economy requires that we have a filtering system to fit a single reality to our preconceptions so that we are not constantly revising our basic perceptual systems, with all the readaptation and adjustment that this would require. Political organizations choose as their leaders individuals with known points of view

[13] Judith Goldstein and Robert O. Keohane, eds., *Ideas and Foreign Policy: Beliefs, Institutions, and Political Change* (Ithaca, N.Y.: Cornell, 1993).

[14] Marx Peffley and Jon Hurwitz, "Models of Attitude Constraint in Foreign Affairs," *Political Behavior*, March 1993, pp. 61–90.

[15] Matthew S. Hirshberg, "The Self-Perpetuating National Self-Image: Cognitive Biases in Perceptions of International Interventions," *Political Psychology*, March 1993, pp. 77–98.

[16] Leon Festinger, *The Theory of Cognitive Dissonance* (Stanford, Calif.: Stanford University Press, 1962).

[17] Peffley and Hurwitz, "Models of Attitude Constraint in International Affairs."

"The other side?" (*Source:* From Herblock's State of the Union (Simon & Schuster, 1972))

that concur reliably with those of the membership. If national leaders were relatively free to revise their perceptual frameworks, they would not be reliable. Hence the rigidity and predictability of the leadership's perceptual system is an asset to the group. The leader should not be quicker to change than are his or her constituents.

The constituents, on the other side, must not be overly vulnerable to perceptual change from external influences. If foreign leaders could appeal over the head of a national leader to his or her own constituents, they might manipulate these persons to their own advantage. For this and other reasons, it is functional for each nation to have its own system of authorities, public officials who determine the overall national interest with regard to other nations. These same public officials play a major role in channeling the cognitions that reach their publics. Many studies have shown that individuals will accept or reject the same information depending on whether it comes from a positive or negative prestige source. Thus constituents choose their

leaders partly for the relative inflexibility of their perceptual systems, and the leaders process incoming information in such a way as to maintain the existing perceptual system of the constituents. The national belief system is thus stable and resistant to change.[18]

For all these reasons, national perceptual frameworks will usually survive challenges from other nations and new experiences. They may make superficial or cosmetic improvements to adjust to new realities at times, but fundamental change is a long-term process. The vehicle of national policy is steered by looking in the rearview mirror; nations are influenced more by where they have been than by where they are going. For over a quarter of a century the United States continued to respond to the failure of isolationism and the ill wisdom of Munich. Soviet policy never abandoned the threadbare theory of capitalism that was more than a century old when the Cold War ended. China's policy has, until very recently, been shaped by recollections of the Century of Humiliation. The Developing Nations' concept of colonialism has scarcely evolved. Hardened perceptions, because of the conviction with which they are held and the information shaping for which they are used, are major obstacles to political progress.

Selective Perception in Big-Power Intervention

International events are selectively perceived by pertinent actors, and every reality has multiple meanings depending on the nationality and political

---

[18] Compare Herbert Kelman, ed., *International Behavior: A Social Psychological Analysis* (New York: Holt, Rinehart and Winston, 1965), especially "The Effects of Events on National and International Images" by Karl Deutsch and Richard Merritt; Ole Holsti, "The Belief System and National Images," *Journal of Conflict Resolution,* vol. 6, 1962, pp. 244–252; Kenneth Boulding, *The Image* (New York: Harper and Row, 1960); Robert Jervis, *The Logic of Images in International Relations* (Princeton, N.J.: Princeton University Press, 1971); and also by Jervis, *Perception and Misperception in International Politics* (Princeton, N.J.: Princeton University Press, 1976).

orientation of the perceiver. This principle can be seen sharply in a comparison of two big-power interventions in the middle 1960s: American military intervention in the Dominican Republic, and Soviet military intervention in Czechoslovakia.

The United States sent 25,000 marines into the Dominican Republic in the spring of 1965 to prevent that country from shifting leftward. Three years later, the Soviet Union initiated a military invasion of Czechoslovakia to choke that country's drift toward political liberalism. The Dominican Republic is in the traditional American sphere of influence in the Caribbean, and Czechoslovakia was a key element of the traditional Soviet sphere in Eastern Europe. To many outside observers, the two events were a clear demonstration of the dual-imperialism philosophy of the superpowers, dividing the world between them and intervening freely in the affairs of lesser states in their respective hegemonies. But to the superpowers themselves, these events had fundamentally different meanings; each justified its own behavior as different in kind from the lawless intervention of the other. Perceptual analysis provides a key to understanding these two cases.

The Dominican Republic, 1965

The Dominican crisis arose from a conflict between a right-wing military government and a rebellion by supporters of ousted civilian president Juan Bosch, the first freely elected president in thirty-eight years. Crisis erupted when a constitutionalist movement attempted to restore him to office. Some American officials viewed the rebellion as a communist conspiracy using the good name of Bosch as a mere convenience, and President Lyndon B. Johnson dispatched the marines to Santo Domingo to prevent another Cuba from arising in the Caribbean.

By what right did the United States intervene in what were manifestly the internal affairs of the Dominican Republic? American officials responded that although all the rebels were indeed Dominican, the rebellion was nonetheless part of the

international communist conspiracy and was, in the words of the legal adviser to the State Department, "an attempt by a conspiratorial group inspired from the outside to seize control by force" and was thus "an assault upon the independence and integrity" of the Dominican Republic.[19] American intervention was justified to protect the Dominican people from domination by a hostile, external political force.

The Soviet reaction was swift and indignant. Ambassador N. T. Fedorenko said at the United Nations, "There can be no justification for the invasion of the territory of a sovereign state by the United States armed forces, . . . a cynical violation of the elementary norms of international law." Fedorenko specifically rejected the assertion that intervention was justified by the principles of the Inter-American System as enunciated by the Organization of American States (OAS). This United States–dominated organization had passed several resolutions that affirmed and validated the American contention that communism was inherently a foreign threat to Western hemispheric nations, and on several occasions the OAS had endorsed American military interventions in Latin American countries to oppose developments believed to be communist inspired. This, he objected, amounted to a belief that

> the right to decide the fate of the Dominican Republic rests only partly with the people of that country and partly with their neighbors. . . . Such statements are incompatible with the obligations of the United States under the United Nations Charter, which prohibits any interference in the internal affairs of other countries. . . . The question of internal organization and regime is purely an internal affair of the Dominican people themselves and they alone . . . have the right to decide it without any pressure or interference from outside.

---

[19] Statement of Leonard C. Meeker, "Legal Basis for United States Action in the Dominican Republic," reprinted in Abram Chayes, Thomas Ehrlich, and Andreas F. Lowenfeld, *International Legal Process*, vol. 2 (Boston: Little, Brown, 1969), p. 1182.

The United States, Fedorenko insisted, cannot act in Latin America "as if it was [sic] in its own private domain, . . . as if it were a question of Alabama or Mississippi."[20] Thus the United States had invoked certain regional principles that allegedly superseded the usual rule of noninterference, while the Soviet Union rejected these claims and stood firmly on traditional international law and standards of decent behavior.

Three years later, these positions were exactly reversed, and the diplomats of the two countries demonstrated extraordinary rhetorical dexterity in reversing roles and taking opposite parts in the case of the Soviet invasion of Czechoslovakia. This time it was the Soviet Union that asserted a special regional right to intervene in the internal affairs of a sovereign country, and the United States that was outraged at the naked display of international gangsterism.

Czechoslovakia, 1968

The crisis in Czechoslovakia materialized when the government headed by Alexander Dubcek began to move its domestic and foreign policies in directions unacceptable to the Kremlin. Just as the United States had feared another Fidel Castro in the Dominican Republic, the USSR came to fear another Tito in Czechoslovakia. (This is a reference to Marshall Josip Tito, the long-time maverick leader of communist Yugoslavia, who had advanced the notion of "separate roads to socialism," a theoretical threat to Soviet monopoly over the political philosophy of the Eastern bloc.) To prevent this, several hundred thousand troops of the Soviet Union and other Warsaw Pact nations entered Prague to dismantle and replace the Dubcek government.

American officials, reflecting opinion in most of the world, labeled the Soviet action an outrage. Secretary of State Dean Rusk insisted that a small country is entitled to live its own life without having the will of a dominant neighbor forced

upon it. American spokespersons portrayed the Czech events as a plain act of foreign interference, comparable to the 1938 Nazi invasion of Czechoslovakia.

Defense of the Soviet action began with the proposition that the Dubcek government had become an agent of capitalist imperialism. Antisocialist forces were seeking to sever Czechoslovakia from the socialist commonwealth. Although these were Czechoslovak nationals, giving the conflict the appearance of an internal affair, Russia claimed to possess "irrefutable data concerning ties between the internal reaction in Czechoslovakia and the outside world," according to Soviet UN representative Jacob Malik.[21]

Furthermore, *Pravda* argued that the Czech government was responsible "not just to its own people, but also to all the socialist countries." Czechoslovakia occupies a crucial geopolitical position in the European balance of power, and "weakening of any of the links in the world system of socialism directly affects all the socialist countries, which cannot look indifferently upon this."[22] The Soviet argument invoked the very same regional right to intervene that it had rejected in the Dominican case.

American spokespersons were equally inconsistent. Officials rejected most strenuously the assertion that there are special rules within the socialist commonwealth that supersede the universal principle of noninterference, even though the United States had asserted precisely such a special relationship for the OAS in the Dominican case. "No matter what the intimacy of one country with another," a United States delegate at the United Nations argued, "neither may claim a right to invade the territory of its friend."[23] And yet the American nations could, in this view, determine

---

[20] Fedorenko's remarks as reprinted in Thomas M. Franck and Edward Wiesband, *Word Politics* (New York: Oxford University Press, 1972), pp. 97–102.

[21] UN Security Council, Doc. S/PV 1441, August 21, 1968, p. 32.
[22] *Pravda* statement reprinted in *The New York Times*, September 27, 1968, p. 3.
[23] Statement of the U.S. representative to the UN Special Committee on the Principles of International Law on Legal Aspects of the Invasion and Occupation of Czechoslovakia, September 12, 1968, in *U.S. Department of State Bulletin*, vol. 59, October 14, 1968, p. 394.

that no more communist governments would be tolerated in the Western Hemisphere, even if established by purely internal processes.

Thus the two superpowers sharply reversed their positions to accord with policy considerations. The Soviet Union rejected the idea that "the right to decide the fate of the Dominican Republic rests only partly with the people of that country and partly with their neighbors" but at the same time asserted that the Czech government "is responsible not just to its own people but to all the socialist countries." The United States asserted that the OAS, as the institutional expression of the Inter-American system, could make determinations regarding the internal movement of members toward a communist government, but the Warsaw Pact bloc could not exercise the same rights in the name of the socialist commonwealth.

Conflicting Perceptions

Underlying these disagreements of principle are critical differences in political perception. American officials see the Inter-American system as a free association of self-determined nations, whereas the Cold War socialist commonwealth was a mere collection of satellites and puppets of the USSR. Soviet officials, on the other hand, saw the OAS as a formal historical expression of American imperialism in Latin America, whereas the socialist commonwealth was an alliance of progressive states under the leadership of the USSR. Thus even if detailed cognitions of the two crises had been identical, interpretation would involve conflicting sets of prior contextual beliefs and values. To Americans, a shift toward communism would be a loss of freedom; Soviets would see a progressive and even inevitable development. However, Americans regarded the liberal movement of the Prague regime away from Soviet-style orthodoxy as progressive and hopeful, but Soviet observers saw it as regression toward capitalism. Officials of the two countries would have rejected the suggestion that their positions in the two cases were contradictory.

Each side could also defend its actions by pointing to certain factual differences favoring a given perception. The Soviet intervention interrupted the otherwise peaceful evolution of Czechoslovakia, whereas the smaller U.S. force helped end a fratricidal civil war that was already under way. The U.S. intervention was followed by reasonably free elections, but the Soviet intervention was followed by continued repression. On the other side, there was a pattern of U.S. economic domination in the Dominican Republic, whereas economic relations in Eastern Europe actually favored Czechoslovakia over the USSR. Also, Czechoslovakia was vital to the Soviet defense network, but the Dominican Republic was strategically minor for the United States—raising the argument that the Soviet intervention might have been the more justifiable in the name of necessity.

Facts of this sort can be raised to justify the rationalization of either side that its case is different. Unflattering parallels can be rejected by either side, and the perceptual framework can remain invulnerable to empirical or logical refutation. This comparison of two cases shows that an intelligent perceptual structure is highly resistant to change, even in the face of direct contradiction.[24] These two examples, although thirty years old and impertinent to contemporary world politics, are particularly illustrative of the problem of conflicting perceptions. Not only did the United States and the Soviet Union fail to understand each other in these instances, but each failed to recognize the contradictions in its own logic.

Although not all perceptual contradictions are so strikingly clear, recent history is filled with evidences of perceptual confusion. In 1980, for example, while the Iranian government was holding American hostages in retaliation for American support of the ousted shah, it invoked international law against Iraq for behavior that contributed

---

[24] For an extended comparison of the Dominican and Czechoslovak interventions, including thorough documentary citations, see Franck and Wiesband, *Word Politics.* For other comments, together with a comprehensive treatment of the roles of doctrines and perceptions in the management of international crisis, see Friedrich V. Kratochwil, *International Order and Foreign Policy: A Theoretical Sketch of Post-War International Politics* (Boulder, Colo.: Westview Press, 1978).

eventually to war between the two. Remarkable reversals in logic are also seen in the respective Soviet and American attitudes toward the Americanization of the Vietnam War and the Soviet Union's long and equally costly war in Afghanistan.

Special Problems of Major Power Perceptions

We will see later that power is used in international relations to influence the system in order to control the outcomes of events. During the Cold War, the balance of power (ranging from tight bipolarity in the early years to incipient multipolarity in the later years) enabled the Soviet Union and the United States to exert unprecedented influence. With very few exceptions, such as Japan's policy of economic expansion unassociated with strategic military matters and Western Europe's march toward economic integration, Cold War strategic imperatives dominated global politics. As these were fraught with mistrust, conflicting perceptions, and uncompromising ideological conviction on each side, the stances were hardened through the years against penetration by demystified facts.

With the end of the Cold War and the opening of the New World Order, these circumstances do not exist. And while most observers no longer speak about polarity in international politics, all acknowledge that there still exists a marked asymmetry. Western Europe, the United States, and Japan, in that order, are the global economic powers able without threats of force to use economic might to dominate world politics. It is important, then, in any world order that is asymmetrical to explore the special issue of perceptions and misperceptions among the major powers.

Mikhail Gorbachev at Westminster College in Fulton, Missouri, speaking about the end of the Cold War, beneath a likeness of Winston Churchill. It was on the same site that Churchill had earlier declared the falling of an "Iron Curtain" across Europe. (*Source:* © Reuters/ Dennis Garrels/Archive Photos)

Examples from the Cold War era are still useful. During that time, many Americans espoused the idea that the leaders of other countries tended to see the world through ideological lenses that created perceptual distortion, and that this was less true in the United States. Was it not true, they asked, that the United States has a free press in which diverse opinions and outlooks are represented? Virtually every point of view, no matter how silly or outrageous, has its own publication in the fantastic array of printed materials available. Even the mainstream press has a huge spectrum of editorial opinion trumpeted routinely, and the subtle differences of opinion that seep into the reporting of radio and television news influence the sources to which we turn. This contrasted sharply with the situation in the communist countries, and in most of the Third World, where political information was monopolized by the party in power and points of view were limited strictly. If the American press tended toward chaotic freedom of expression, those of the communist world tended toward state censorship. It seemed that the free market of ideas in the United States made Americans less vulnerable to self-deception and rigid ideological distortion.

It is undeniable, though, that certain crucial American misperceptions managed to persist over very long periods of time, despite the repeated efforts at correction by intelligent and responsible dissenters. For example, the American image of China as a satellite of the Soviet Union dominated foreign policy decision makers until at least 1960, long after this misperception ought to have been adjusted by available information. Dissenters who questioned the orthodox point of view in the early years after the Chinese revolution had their patriotism and loyalty to the American anticommunist cause vigorously challenged; only the bravest were willing to continue their dissent from the official mythology. That other pictures of China were freely obtainable is interesting but not particularly meaningful. The dominant misperception was reinforced by all the major publications and the broadcast media—information that

supported the official view. The free market of ideas was not then and is not now a guarantee against false orthodoxies and misperceptions, although it does help keep alive varying points of view.

A hazard of the American self-perception is the easy assumption that what Americans think is typical of world opinion. Like people elsewhere, Americans are prone to the delusion that when an opinion prevails among those they know, it is equally popular elsewhere. (It seems to matter little that a political value held zealously in New York City may have little or no popularity in New Mexico, let alone in Moscow, La Paz, or Manila!) During the Cold War, Americans were particularly subject to this error, because of their view of themselves as the leaders of the Free World. Samplings of public opinion in different countries showed, however, that the outlook of the United States was not universally popular and that there were many issues on which American public opinion was inconsistent with opinion abroad, even in countries that shared the basic American Cold War values and goals. For example, the Gallup organization conducted an eleven-nation public-opinion poll in 1967 on U.S. policy in Vietnam (see Figure 1–2). It found that outside the United States the military escalation policy was almost universally unpopular; within the United States, however, the majority of opinion favored even greater escalation. In nine of the eleven Free World countries polled, American withdrawal was overwhelmingly the favored opinion, but in the United States, 53 percent favored even greater escalation and only 31 percent favored withdrawal. On this issue, apparently, the American people isolated themselves from world opinion and deluded themselves that they were the shield of the Free World. Americans, despite a remarkably free press and apparent good intentions, are no less prone to errors and misperceptions than are other peoples, and they as much as others need to listen carefully to the opinions of both acknowledged friends and apparent enemies.

Moreover, although Americans regard other political cultures as ideological, they generally deny that their own foreign policy is ideologically

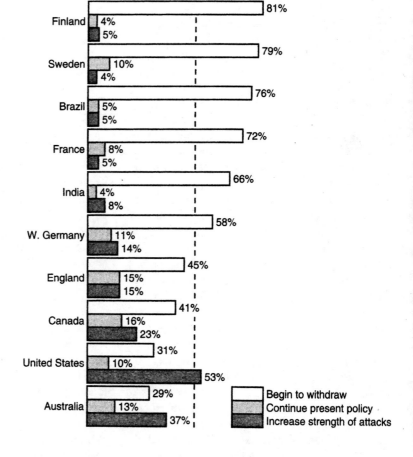

FIGURE 1–2   Eleven-nation Gallup poll on Vietnam.

Source: Gallup Opinion Index, no. 29; November 1967. Reprinted by permission.

motivated, too. They consider their ideology simply as democratic, and they dismiss skepticism concerning it. American foreign policy is virtuous, and dissent is un-American. Indeed, despite the health of the American two-party political system, the pages of the nation's diplomatic history are dotted with theories of foreign policy that proclaim either bipartisanship or nonpartisanship, that declare that politics stops at the water's edge, or that the best politics of foreign policy is no politics. In the effort to depoliticize foreign policy, particularly during periods of war or other national crises, episodes of messianism are not uncommon. In his first detailed report to the American public on the two atomic

bombings of Japan in 1945, for example, President Harry S Truman invoked heavenly authority:

> We must constitute ourselves trustees of this new force—to prevent its misuse, and to turn it into channels of service to mankind.
>
> It is an awful responsibility which has come to us.
>
> We thank God that it has come to us, instead of to our enemies; and we pray that He may guide us to use it in His ways and for His purposes.[25]

---

[25] "Radio Report to the American People on the Potsdam Conference," August 9, 1945. See *Public Papers of the Presidents of the United States: Harry S Truman, 1945*, pp. 203–214 at p. 213.

More than forty years later, President Ronald Reagan declared, "I have always believed that this anointed land was set apart in an uncommon way, that a divine plan placed this great continent between the oceans to be found by people from every corner of the earth who had a special love of faith and freedom." And ". . . we are enjoined by scripture and the Lord Jesus to oppose [the evil empire of the Soviet Union] with all our might."[26] Any American foreign policy, however ill conceived or inhumane and however offensive to international law, is justified by heavenly decree.

An analysis of this phenomenon less spiritual in tone deals with the ethos of the American vision of its world role. Because in foreign relations all states seek to express their cultural uniqueness and reinforce identity, foreign policy in general and security policy in particular tend to be derived partly from whatever myths and historical perceptions thrive in the body politic. In the case of the United States, those myths spring from a moral sense of historical separation from the banal politics of Europe, from a unique vision of a bountiful New World, and from a sense of moral exceptionalism. Hence Americans see foreign policy in terms of the good and the evil (as in democracy and naziism or democracy and communism) and in goals of reformism (leading to internationalist foreign policy) or self-conscious isolation.[27] The consequences of foreign policy based on this assumption are themselves threats to a stable world order, because it exempts American policy from the rule of self-restraint. Constitutional guarantees of freedom of expression and free press are thus crucially important balances to official orthodoxy.

The problems of Soviet Cold War perceptions and misperceptions were equally complex. In a world in which the superpowers daily flung invective

back and forth, it was not enough to label the Kremlin anti-West or anticapitalist. It did not suffice to conclude that the Soviet Union was, in former President Reagan's words, "an evil empire" or to determine in one's mind whether capitalist encirclement was a Western aggression against the East or a defensive reaction to the Kremlin's avowed intent to overtake the West. At issue was nothing less than a set of presumptions about world politics that evolved from Marxism-Leninism that differed totally from those that came to the West from the Renaissance and the Enlightenment. Although Soviet leaders may not have appealed to God, they did invoke a secular faith in Marxist-Leninist precepts regarding socialism, the world revolution, the dictatorship of the proletariat, the inevitable decline and destruction of capitalism, and notions of democracy that centered on economic equality rather than political liberty. On the occasion of General Secretary Konstantin Chernenko's death in 1985, the Communist party and the Soviet government released a joint letter to the Soviet people in which they proclaimed that

> The CPSU is equipped with the immortal revolutionary doctrine of Marxism-Leninism. It is unswervingly following the path charted by Lenin and will never deviate from that path.
>
> The party will continue to pursue its course toward the all-around perfection of developed socialism. . . . The party has always regarded dedication to Marxism-Leninism . . . and proletarian socialist internationalism as the supreme spiritual values of the Soviet people.[28]

It is against this background that Soviet images were formed for virtually the entire life of the Soviet state. Long before 1917, Marx observed that materialism is a vital expression of capitalism. Given two Western invasions in less than a half-century and post–World War Two capitalist encirclement, the nuclear arms race and the European

---

[26] For a review of the contemporary consequences of this kind of foreign policy thinking, see Arthur Schlesinger Jr., "Foreign Policy and the American Character," *Foreign Affairs*, fall 1983, pp. 1–16.

[27] Michael Vlahos, "The End of America's Postwar Ethos," *Foreign Affairs*, summer 1988, pp. 1091–1107.

[28] Letter reproduced in *International Affairs* (Moscow), April 1985, pp. 12–14 at p. 13.

military balance evolved not from transient political differences but from the necessity of capitalism to express and defend itself against historical inevitability through the economics of military arms. Moreover, as arms policy demonstrated its inability alone to adjust the course of history, in the early view of General Secretary Mikhail Gorbachev (1985), "the practical actions of imperialism, especially United States imperialism, ever more clearly elucidate [a policy] of social revenge on the basis of achieving military superiority over socialism."[29] The American target, then, was seen not as the Soviet territory or leadership, but as the future itself.

Soviet ideology was not a mere instrument of foreign policy. It was, rather, a scientific instrument that shaped and guided the world revolution. Indeed, the supremacy of socialism in world affairs was its objective ability through scientific substantiation and theoretical elaboration to understand the forces of history and the world revolution against imperialism. It was by these techniques that the inevitability of history was to be revealed, and it was these revelations that guided policymaking so as to advance the world revolution rather than permit the imperialist forces to retard it.[30]

Because Soviet ideology was viewed as a scientific instrument for interpreting and adjusting social forces, the perceptions of Soviet leaders were formed not by what the West said it was, but by what Marxism-Leninism determined it to be. Consequently, Western diplomacy, strategic policy, arms negotiation tactics, activities in the Third World, and so forth were seen not as isolated political events but as parts of a fabric of antisocialist aggression and antirevolutionary reaction. Doctrine anointed Soviet actions as the advancement of the irreversible forces of history, but Western policies were shaped by political orientation into an aggressive though fruitless effort to postpone the inevitable victory of peoples free from state oppression and imperialism.

Despite their tenacity, it is not true, of course, that perceptions never change, even in principal powers. Americans did eventually sacrifice the notion that all socialism is militaristic communism of Soviet origin, just as they abandoned the idea that China in communist control could never be dealt with.[31] Eventually the Vietnam War was abandoned because of a sharp turn in domestic public opinion. But the most remarkable revision of national perceptions arose after Gorbachev rejected the strict Marxist-Leninist interpretation of foreign affairs and the severe domestic controls of the Soviet state. With his policies of *glasnost* (openness at home and cooperation with the West in foreign policy) and *perestroika* (internal restructuring, free access to information, and free elections), an opportunity arose for U.S. foreign policy makers to review and revise their own perceptual framework. For President Reagan, the commander of the evil empire became "my friend Gorby." And at the end of the subsummit conference aboard ship off Malta, Gorbachev and President George Bush jointly announced a diplomatic agenda that amounted to an ending of the Cold War. The face of world politics changed rapidly and drastically into the New World Order, which could not have occurred without mutual perceptual reconstruction of revolutionary proportions. Without such occasional changes, the global political system cannot progress peacefully; without them, it can only leave to force the role of reallocating international values.

---

[29] General Secretary Mikhail Gorbachev in an address to the Plenum of the Communist party of the Soviet Union preparing for the Twenty-seventh Congress, quoted in *The New York Times*, October 16, 1985, p. D17. For the full text in English translation, see Mikhail S. Gorbachev, *The Coming Century of Peace* (New York: Richardson and Steirman, 1986), pp. 280–293.

[30] See, as an example, N. Kapchenko, "The Peace Potential of Soviet Foreign Policy," *International Affairs* (Moscow), July 1985, p. 86.

[31] Mathew S. Hirshberg, "Consistency and Change in American Perceptions of China," *Political Behavior*, September 1993, pp. 247–263.

CHAPTER 2

The Russian Perspective

I n the closing days of 1991, Boris N. Yeltsin joined the leaders of two other constituent parts of the Union of Soviet Socialist Republics and declared: "We, the Republic of Byelorussia, the Russian Federation and Ukraine ... state that the U.S.S.R., as a subject of international law and geopolitical reality, is ceasing its existence."[1] After three breathtaking years of events that had shaken global politics, the Soviet Union could cope no longer with demands for political liberties, economic collapse, ethnic violence, secession, and divergence of political wills so great that failure had met all efforts to forge new union out of old. Three-quarters of a century, much of it consumed in war or cold war, came to an abrupt close. Born of revolution against tsarist oppression at the end of World War One, forged in civil war, and a major victor over fascism in World War Two, this enormous state disintegrated only two years after the collapse of its international empire. A calm declaration did what forty-five years of capitalist encirclement could not: It ended a massive experiment in Marxism-Leninism and the evolution of a global nuclear superpower. Contrary to Leninist dictum, however, the state had not withered away in favor of a dictatorship of the proletariat (the working class) or fallen at the hand of capitalist aggression; it had collapsed of ignominious failure and disenchantment. Mikhail Gorbachev, former chairman of the Communist party of the Soviet Union, first

Soviet president, architect of *glasnost* (access to information) and *perestroika* (restructuring), and the man who ended the Cold War, had become a president without a state. In place of the Soviet Union would rapidly evolve a Commonwealth of Independent States (Figure 2–1).

The Soviet government and the Communist party had refused until the end to admit what many citizens had known, namely, that cohesion in the Soviet Union was less a result of legitimacy and voluntary compliance than of involuntary dependence on the state and fear of repression. In some quarters this was anything but news, but its political ramifications were unleashed by *glasnost*. The government news media had carried Gorbachev's request that the Polish government let the Solidarity labor movement become a political party, that it permit free elections, and then encourage the victorious Solidarity to construct a noncommunist government. The public was aware that Gorbachev had encouraged self-determination in Eastern Europe after decades of rigorous control and military intervention. Ethnic strife in the republics was common knowledge, as was the unfamiliar governmental forbearance. The Kremlin had acquiesced in the reunification of the two Germanys, signed a nonaggression pact, and blessed the new Germany's membership in both the United Nations and NATO. The government was in open diplomatic partnership with Washington on the Persian Gulf, the Middle East, and forging a New World Order. It was time for the republics, one by one, to proclaim their independence, and time for the Russian

---

[1] As quoted in *The New York Times*, December 9, 1991, p. A1.

Text of Declarations by 3 Republic Leaders

MOSCOW, Dec. 8 (AP) — *Following are the texts of two declarations issued today by the leaders of Russia, Ukraine and Byelorussia, as transmitted by the Soviet press agency Tass and translated from the Russian by The Associated Press:*

We, the heads of state of Byelorussia, Russia and Ukraine:

NOTING that talks on the preparation of a new union treaty have reached a dead end and the process of the secession of republics from the U.S.S.R. and forming the independent states has come to reality;

STATING that the shortsighted policy of the center has led to a deep political and economic crisis, to disintegration of the economy and catastrophic decline of the living conditions of practically all the sectors of the population;

TAKING into account growing social tension in many regions of the former U.S.S.R., which have led to ethnic conflicts and resulted in numerous victims;

ACKNOWLEDGING the responsibility before our people and the world community and the growing necessity of practical implementation of political and economic reforms;

HEREBY declare the formation of a Commonwealth of Independent States, about which the parties signed an agreement on Dec. 8, 1991.

The Commonwealth of Independent States, consisting of the Republic of Byelorussia, the Russian Federation and Ukraine, is open to all member states of the former U.S.S.R., as well as to other states who share the aims and principles of this agreement.

The member states of the Commonwealth intend to conduct a policy aimed at reinforcing international peace and security. They guarantee fulfillment of international obligations from treaties and agreements of the former U.S.S.R. and insure unified control over nuclear weapons and their nonproliferation.

> STANISLAV SHUSHKEVICH,
> *Chairman, Supreme Soviet of*
> *the Republic of Byelorussia*
> BORIS YELTSIN,
> *President, Russian Federation*
> LEONID KRAVCHUK,
> *President, Ukraine*
> Dec. 8, 1991, Minsk

ECONOMIC PACT

Preservation and development of the existing close economic ties between our states is vitally necessary for stabilizing the situation in the national economy and creating the foundations for economic revival.

The parties have agreed to the following:

¶To carry out coordinated radical economic reforms aimed at creating feasible market mechanisms, transformation of property and ensuring the freedom of entrepreneurship;

¶To abstain from any actions economically harmful to each other;

¶To develop economic relations and mutual accounts on the basis of the existing currency unit — the ruble. To introduce national currencies on the basis of special agreements which will guarantee the preservation of the economic interests of the parties;

¶To sign an interbank agreement aimed at curbing monetary emission, providing for the effective control over money supply and forming a system of mutual accounts;

¶To conduct coordinated policy of reducing the republics' budget deficits;

¶To conduct coordinated policy of price liberalization and social protection;

¶To undertake joint efforts aimed at providing for a single economic space;

¶To coordinate external economic activities, customs policies and to provide for free transit (of goods);

¶To regulate by special agreement the question of debt of the former U.S.S.R. enterprises;

¶To coordinate in a period of 10 days the amounts and procedure for financing of defense spending for 1992 and the expenditures for cleaning up the results of the Chernobyl nuclear disaster;

¶To ask the Supreme Soviets of the republics to take into account the necessity to coordinate the levels of sales taxes while forming tax policy;

¶To help create joint-stock companies;

¶To work out in December the mechanism for implementation of the inter-republican economic agreements.

For the Byelorussian republic,

> VYACHESLAV KEBICH,
> *Prime Minister*

For the Russian Federation,

> GENNADI BURBULIS,
> *Secretary of State*

For Ukraine,

> VITOLD FOKIN,
> *Prime Minister*

FIGURE 2–1 The Soviet Union is dissolved and the Commonwealth of Independent States launched.

Source: The New York Times, December 9, 1991, p. A4.

people, too, to claim the self-determination accorded others formerly under the omnipresent Soviet gaze. Gorbachev's "Second Russian Revolution" had taken an unforeseen turn.

How could all of this have occurred so rapidly in a state historically unfriendly to change, especially change that challenges orthodoxy? To understand the Soviet world view and the collapse of the Soviet state, it is necessary to explore the basic tenets of communist ideology as intertwined with the interests of the Russian nation. Communist ideology introduces a unique analysis of the basic behavioral laws underlying human relations and explains in an orderly way the otherwise unintelligible complexities of society. Karl Marx and Friedrich Engels provided the basic analysis of capitalism and the state, and Vladimir Lenin, using Marx's "objective truth," contributed the main analysis of the international system.

Fundamentals of Communism

1. Economic Determinism

Marxist–Leninist philosophy holds that the foundation of society is the economic system and the social relationships it produces. Josef Stalin said, "The basis is the economic system. . . . The superstructure consists of the political, legal, religious, artistic, philosophical views of society, and the political, legal, and other institutions corresponding to them." Communism is thus a branch of the materialist school of philosophy.

What distinguishes Marxism-Leninism as a materialist philosophy is its conception of class relations as the root of social interaction. In *The Communist Manifesto* Marx declared:

> The history of all human society, past and present, has been the history of class struggles.
>
> Freeman and slave, patrician and plebeian, baron and serf, guild-burgess and journeyman—in a word, oppressor and oppressed—stood in sharp opposition each to the other.

This theory holds that in every organized society, one class controls the ownership of the means of production, and it uses political authority and all-powerful institutions to maintain this control. The ownership class extracts surpluses produced by the laboring masses. Society is a pyramid in which the broad working class at the bottom produces wealth for the privileged elite at the top.

2. Feudalism and Capitalism

This principle is seen in the feudal pattern of agriculture in which ownership of land was concentrated in the hands of a small nobility, the lords, for whose benefit it was worked by impoverished peasants. The laborers lived in shanties on a minimum subsistence, sustaining themselves from disaster to disaster. The lord lived in a baronial mansion at leisure, enjoying his daily diet of sport and cultivation of the arts. The landlords were not, of course, chosen by God; they achieved their position initially by conquests, foreclosure on usurious loans, and royal grants, and they passed on their control through inheritance. Government was intertwined with feudal landownership: The lords gave a portion of their wealth and power to support the state, and the state used its physical force to guarantee the rights of property—that is, the position of the lords. The whole system was sanctified by the church, the "opiate of the masses."

Industry, the second and more modern form of production, displaced feudalism. A new class of owners was created, the capitalists, whose interests were tied not to land but to factories. In the capitalist mode, the bourgeoisie monopolizes control of machinery, assembly lines, and other modern means of production plus a financial infrastructure. Now the labor power of the workers itself has become a commodity, to be sold in the market to the highest bidder. By maintaining a surplus labor force—the pool of the unemployed—the price of labor (wages) is depressed. The industrial workers become proletarians where before they were serfs. The emergence of the capitalist mode of production shifts the center of power from landlords to industry. After a period of struggle, the bourgeoisie seizes the reins of state from the landed gentry. Now the power of the state is used to build infrastructure and supports for capitalist manufacture, trade, and finance. The controlling interests of the free market industrial state are those of the capitalists.

3. Origins of the State

Economic exploitation creates political relations in society. "The state," Engels wrote, "has not existed from all eternity. There have been societies that did without it, that had no conception of the state and state power. At a certain stage of economic development, which was necessarily bound up with the cleavage of society into classes, the state became a necessity owing to this cleavage."[2] Lenin added, "History shows that the state as a special apparatus for coercing people arose only wherever and whenever there appeared a division of society into classes, that is, a division into groups of people some of whom are permanently in a position to appropriate the labor of others."[3] The state, he concluded, "is an organ of class rule."[4]

4. Social Controls

This is not to suggest that the physical might of the state is the only (or even main) means whereby the elite protects its position. No social system, however oppressive, habitually uses force when there are less expensive and more efficient means of control available. Coercion is the most visible form of control, but it is the least reliable. It requires vigilance and an elaborate network of enforcing agents who themselves are loyal to the system, and it raises a constant danger of rebellion. A social system that

is forced to fall back on extensive coercion is on the point of collapse.

More efficient than coercion are market controls, meaning a structure of material rewards keyed to positive behavior—carrot in place of stick. Capitalism, for example, is superior as a form of exploitation to slavery, because now the workers have the illusion of free choice. Their victimization is masked by what appear to be impersonal market forces, rather than naked threats by identifiable enemies.

But the most effective form of behavioral control is neither coercion nor the market, because both depend on external regulation of the individual. Normative controls work through education and social training to produce a set of norms and to identify expectations that act as internal regulators of behavior. Individual consciousness is patterned to fit the desired social model. False consciousness exists when deceptive morals, ideologies, and religions are used to mask injustice behind a facade of legitimacy and legality. Individuals are betrayed by their own education, and they come to revere the very institutions that exploit them.

In general, normative social controls, supported by a structure of market rewards for cooperative behavior, are capitalism's first line of defense. Only in the last resort is brute force on the part of the state necessary. Control by the state ensures the smooth operation of all three forms of control. Public law and administration are thus extensions of the relations of production.

5. Revolution

Marxism prescribes a revolutionary solution to the problem of class rule. The aroused proletariat rips the instruments of control from the bourgeoisie and uses the state apparatus to seize the means of production, thus changing the entire basis of social relations. "Expropriation of the expropriators" gives land to the peasants and factories to the workers. A certain amount of violence may be necessary, because the ruling class will not give over its position voluntarily, but this is nothing next to the much

---

[2] Friedrich Engels, "Origin of the Family, Private Property, and the State," in *Selected Works of Marx and Engels* (Moscow: Foreign Languages Publishing House, 1951), vol. 2, p. 239.
[3] Lenin "The State" (1919), in *Selected Works* (London: Lawrence and Wishart, 1939), vol. 2, p. 644.
[4] Lenin, "State and Revolution," in *Selected Works* (New York: International Publishers, 1943), vol. 7, p. 9.

greater violence of the everyday capitalist system. As Nikita Khrushchev said, "The use or nonuse of violence in the transition of socialism depends on the resistance of the exploiters, on whether the exploiting class itself resorts to violence, rather than on the proletariat." Communism does not romanticize violence, but it regards pacifism as bourgeois sentimentality. The capitalist system will always rest on foundations of injustice and suffering, and it must be overthrown.[5]

Revolution is both desirable and inevitable. History is progressive, each epoch representing an inevitable advance. Capitalism itself outdates all previous forms of social order, as Marx's celebration of its accomplishments attests. But capitalism rests on class exploitation. Although it is progressive and necessary in the march of history, it is also unjust, and so eventually it produces the seeds of its own destruction. Mature capitalism increasingly is monopolistic and insatiable in its profit hunger. A point is reached at which the economy is saturated with enterprises, and the relentless search for investment opportunities drives the weaker capitalists back into the proletariat. Job shortage drives wages down, and the misery of the proletariat grows. The army of the unemployed mounts, production cannot be consumed, rates of profit fall, and general desperation prevails. Capitalism has created the machinery to satisfy human needs, but it cannot use this machinery rationally. It is driven by its inner dynamic to amplify its contradictions until only revolution can rationalize society again.

As recently as 1982, less than a decade before the Soviet Union's disintegration, in a speech commemorating the sixtieth anniversary of the founding of the Soviet Union (dated not from the 1917 revolution but from the close of the unifying civil war in 1922), Yuri Andropov noted that

> The imperialists have not given up the schemes of economic war against the socialist countries, of interfering in their internal affairs in the hope of

eroding their social system, and are trying to win military superiority over the USSR, over all the countries of the socialist community. Of course, these plans are sure to fail. It is not given to anyone to turn back the course of historical development. Attempts to "strangle" socialism failed even when the Soviet state was still getting on its feet and was the only socialist country in the world. So surely nothing will come out of it now.[6]

Despite the presumed inevitability of history, Marx's prediction that capitalism would collapse of its own weight has never been fulfilled. Although he apparently expected the collapse of advanced capitalist states by 1900, they have become progressively more secure. Meanwhile, revolution occurred in the Soviet Union, China, Cuba, North Korea, and Vietnam, none of which conformed to the Marxist premise that mature capitalism must precede communism. (The Soviet Union itself constructed a partial market economy, and no Marxist theorist argued that the purpose was to realign history by reintroducing capitalism and awaiting its presumably inevitable collapse.) How have these paradoxes occurred? In the Soviet view, the answer lay in the subtle ways in which capitalism manipulates the international system.

6. The International System and Imperialism

Lenin extended Marx's analysis of society to a conception of international relations. Capitalism saved itself, he argued, by reaching the stage of imperialism in which international dynamics temporarily ameliorate the domestic conflicts. Borrowing from the English economist John A. Hobson, Lenin showed that capitalism depends not only on oppression at home, but also on exploiting entire

---

[5] Robert C. Tucker, *The Marxian Revolutionary Idea* (New York: Norton, 1969).

[6] Yuri Andropov, "Sixty Years of the USSR," December 12, 1982. English translation from *Moscow News*, no. 52, 1982, and reprinted in Martin Ebon, *The Andropov File: The Life and Ideas of Yuri Andropov, General Secretary of the Communist Party of the USSR* (New York: McGraw-Hill, 1983), pp. 249–264, at pp. 259–260.

peoples elsewhere. Lenin called this the "internationalization of the class system." This is conducted through three principal imperialistic means. The first is foreign investment, by which capitalists seek high rates of return in capital-starved foreign countries to compensate for the stagnant investment climate at home. Second, they seek foreign markets for their excess production, the products that their underpaid workers cannot purchase, but the profit from which is essential to sustaining capitalism. The third device is controlling raw materials abroad, a motive that requires not only economic exploitation but often control of local governments and external regulation of social, political, and economic development.

During the earlier period of imperialism, capitalists were very crude in competing for the most profitable prizes. In the days of colonialism, the capitalist states actually fought wars over the benefits from subjugation. In the resulting colonies, bourgeois functionaries developed a political system and an infrastructure (rails, ports, and so on) conducive to profitable investment.

Subsequently this system became (with exceptions) more subtle and durable. Direct control offended the national spirit of the subject peoples, and so international capital relinquished formal colonialism. Titular control passed to the national bourgeoisie, a native class of capitalists comprising a subsystem of the international system, who were co-opted by rewards of minor profit-sharing from national exploitation (such as the royalties from a mining investment). There is a pleasant illusion of self-determination. In case of trouble, the imperialists can use their overwhelming position in the international economic system to deny markets to any subject state that refuses to comply (the boycott of Cuban sugar by the United States, for instance), and the national bourgeoisie can be relied on to put the recalcitrant former colony back on course. Occasionally, direct force is used to stop a revolution by those who see through this delusional system. In these and other ways, neocolonialism preserves and even extends the imperial system

while giving the Developing Nations a false sense of independence.

The development of the imperial system gives capitalism a temporary reprieve, postponing its inevitable collapse and forestalling revolution. In the poor countries, however, the class basis of the international system is only too visible. Hence the paradox that revolution seems to be ripest where capitalism is least mature. Stalin explained this phenomenon in *The Foundations of Leninism*:

> Formerly, it was the accepted thing to speak of the existence or absence of objective conditions for the proletarian revolution in individual countries, or, to be more precise, in one or another developed country. Now this point of view is no longer adequate. Now we must speak of the existence of objective conditions for the revolution in the entire system of world imperialist economy as an integral unit. . . .
>
> Where will the revolution begin?. . .
>
> Where industry is more developed, where the proletariat constitutes the majority, where there is more culture, where there is more democracy—that was the reply given formerly.
>
> No, objects the Leninist theory of revolution (imperialism); *not necessarily where industry is more developed*, and so forth. The front of capital will be pierced where the chain of imperialism is weakest. . . .[7]

Revolution may come first in the most progressive states of the underdeveloped world, and the centers of capital may be the last to fall. But eventually communism will be universal.

7. The Withering Away of the State

The relentless march of history requires that in the presence of mature socialism, the state will wither away in favor of a dictatorship of the proletariat. Marx and Engels were ambiguous on both how this

---

[7] Josef Stalin, *The Foundations of Leninism* (New York: International Publishers, 1931).

would happen and what the political characteristics of the proletarian dictatorship would be, other than that it would be a society without coercion. But to Marxist theory during the Cold War, the ambiguity became unimportant. Stalin was acutely aware that the old Russia was repeatedly beaten by foreign enemies—the French and English in the Crimean War (1856), the Japanese (1905), the Germans (1917)—because of its political and industrial backwardness. In the period of capitalist encirclement, a different threat of extinction, the new Russia would have to use the most modern and practical means to ensure the survival of the first communist advances in a still-capitalist world and to protect the Russian nation.[8] Until the worldwide socialist victory reaches the powerful capitalist states and removes the threat, the Soviet state had a special mission of ideological defense that postponed indefinitely the withering away of the state.

8. Democracy

Western critics always accused the Soviet Union of suppressing democratic principles by not adopting the Euro-American concept of electoral democracy and civil liberties. But in the classical Soviet view, bourgeois elections were part of the state apparatus of capitalism. Even if balloting were conducted without deceit, the outcome could not correspond to the objective interests of the masses. False consciousness, perpetuated by class control of the mass media and the educational system, blinds the voters. Pious electoral candidates, most of them leading capitalists, further obscure the issue, often by using a false demonology of the communist threat to stir up fears. Marxist-Leninists always rejected this as a meaningless version of democracy. To them, real people's or workers' democracy emphasized the objective nature of the social system rather than electoral mechanics. They insisted that work was universally available in the Soviet Union, and that the social decadence of the

so-called democracies of the West did not exist under mature socialism. The critical question of Marxism-Leninism was whether a social system, especially in its ownership of the means of production, can serve the interests of the masses. The meaning of social justice, in this view, is not a spurious procedural question, but one of real outcomes—of substance rather than process.

9. Diplomacy

Leninism also has its own view of making foreign policy, one that prevailed throughout the Soviet period. Unlike the pre-Soviet Russians, who formulated foreign policy secretly and without consulting the masses, Lenin's international policy required a "new socialist diplomacy "

> . . . destined to break down the wall which the exploiters had always carefully raised between foreign policy and the mass of working people, and thus to turn the masses from a mere object of foreign policy into a force actively influencing international affairs in their own interests. The birth itself of socialist foreign policy made it immediately possible to move crucial international problems out of the secrecy of closed tsarist offices into the street, which the bourgeoisie so completely scorned, and bring them within reach of the workers and all working people. This was a thoroughly class, thoroughly Party-type kind of change. For the first time, it enabled the masses effectively to influence politics. . . .

In contrast, however, nonsocialist diplomacy continued to be conducted beyond the reach of working people.

> What is Washington busy with now? One hysterical propaganda campaign after another. First the public is told of a "Soviet military threat." Then it is sold a bill of goods on the subject of the USA "lagging behind" the USSR strategically. People are also either being intimidated with tales of "international terrorism" or told cock-and-bull stories regarding

---

[8] Josef Stalin, "Reply to Comrades," *Pravda*, August 2, 1950.

the events in Poland, Central America and South and Southeast Asia. All this has its own logic, of course: the imperialists are able to indulge in creating new weapons of mass destruction only as a result of deceiving the masses.[9]

Russian National Interests

The foregoing is the political theory brought by Marxism-Leninism to Russia, where it was put to work in conjunction with the unique attributes of Russian history and culture. Stalin intertwined national and ideological imperatives in 1927 when he defined a revolutionary as "he who without arguments, unconditionally, openly and honestly . . . is ready to defend and strengthen the USSR, since the USSR is the first proletarian, revolutionary state in the world." Moreover, "to advance the revolutionary movement is impossible without defending the USSR."[10] Thus a historic accident married communism to the international position and national interests of a particular country.

Marx and Engels had been skeptical of nationalism, always considering class rather than nationality the dominant feature of society. The First World War convinced Lenin, however, that communist ideology would have to adjust to the continued potency of the national idea. The workers of every country dropped all pretense of proletarian internationalism when war broke out, and they marched blindly behind their national flags. The Second International in 1907 had called on all European socialist parties and trade unions to resist an international conflict, as it would serve none but competing capitalist interests. But grand expectations of worker solidarity shattered in 1914 when not a single major European socialist party opposed war, and the powerful German Social Democratic (Marxist) Party voted unanimously for government war credits. The lesson for Lenin was that communism must join with nationalism rather than oppose it.[11]

The Russian revolutionaries of 1917 found themselves at the head not just of an ideological movement but of a national state. They were an opposition party whose entire organization and philosophy had been geared to destructive action, suddenly in a position of responsibility rather than insurgency. Not just grand principles but physical Russian realities had to be dealt with, the first of which being amalgamation and federation of many separate pieces into a Union of Soviet Socialist Republics. By the time the process was completed, the USSR consisted of fifteen such republics, with the Russian Soviet Federal Socialist Republic (RSFSR) comprising almost 90 percent of the land mass. The other fourteen formed an almost continuous rim of incorporated territories beginning in the northwest at the Finnish border to the deep south of the Soviet Union, interrupted only by the Black and Caspian seas. (See Figure 2–2.)

Another condition imposed on the Soviet government was the necessity to insulate the state from excessive economic, cultural, and military penetration by the expansionist powers of Western Europe. From 1917 to 1940, the communists used an economic policy of autarky, a political policy of limited intercourse, and a strategic policy designed to equilibrate a European balance of power. Some Western observers dismissed these defensive

---

[9] Yuri Andropov, "Leninism: A Source of Inexhaustible Revolutionary Energy and Creativity of the Masses," April 22, 1982, in English translation by the Soviet press service, *Novosti,* and printed in the Soviet press on May 15, 1982. Reprinted in Martin Ebon, *The Andropov File,* pp. 224–238, at p. 235. A different translation of the same address appears in Y. V. Andropov, *Speeches and Writings* (New York: Pergamon Press, 1983), pp. 216–234, particularly pp. 228–229. The final sentence appears as follows: "There is a logic, albeit perverted, in this propaganda: indeed, to advertise weapons of mass destruction and to prod the world to war the imperialists have to deceive the masses."

[10] Josef Stalin, "The International Situation and the Defense of the USSR" (August 1, 1927), *Sochineniya* (Moscow: Gospolitizdat, 1949), vol. 10, p. 61.

[11] Adam B. Ulam, *Expansion and Coexistence: The History of Soviet Foreign Policy 1917–67* (New York: Praeger, 1968), pp. 13, 18–19, and 24–25.

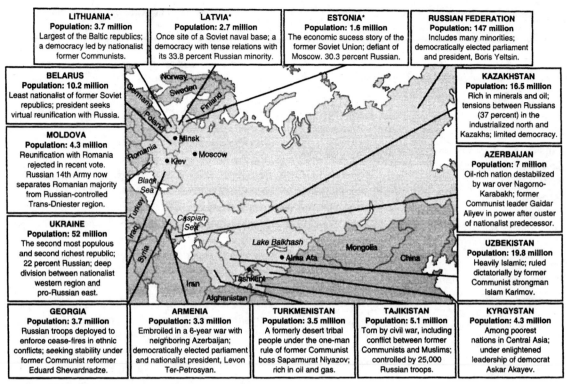

LITHUANIA*	LATVIA*	ESTONIA*	RUSSIAN FEDERATION
Population: 3.7 million	Population: 2.7 million	Population: 1.6 million	Population: 147 million
Largest of the Baltic republics; a democracy led by nationalist former Communists.	Once site of a Soviet naval base; a democracy with tense relations with its 33.8 percent Russian minority.	The economic sucess story of the former Soviet Union; defiant of Moscow. 30.3 percent Russian.	Includes many minorities; democratically elected parliament and president, Boris Yeltsin.

BELARUS
Population: 10.2 million
Least nationalist of former Soviet republics; president seeks virtual reunification with Russia.

MOLDOVA
Population: 4.3 million
Reunification with Romania rejected in recent vote. Russian 14th Army now separates Romanian majority from Russian-controlled Trans-Dniester region.

UKRAINE
Population: 52 million
The second most populous and second richest republic; 22 percent Russian; deep division between nationalist western region and pro-Russian east.

KAZAKHSTAN
Population: 16.5 million
Rich in minerals and oil; tensions between Russians (37 percent) in the industrialized north and Kazakhs; limited democracy.

AZERBAIJAN
Population: 7 million
Oil-rich nation destabilized by war over Nagorno-Karabakh; former Communist leader Gaidar Aliyev in power after ouster of nationalist predecessor.

UZBEKISTAN
Population: 19.8 million
Heavily Islamic; ruled dictatorially by former Communist strongman Islam Karimov.

GEORGIA	ARMENIA	TURKMENISTAN	TAJIKISTAN	KYRGYSTAN
Population: 3.7 million	Population: 3.3 million	Population: 3.5 million	Population: 5.1 million	Population: 4.3 million
Russian troops deployed to enforce cease-fires in ethnic conflicts; seeking stability under former Communist reformer Eduard Shevardnadze.	Embroiled in a 6-year war with neighboring Azerbaijan; democratically elected parliament and nationalist president, Levon Ter-Petrosyan.	A formerly desert tribal people under the one-man rule of former Communist boss Saparmurat Niyazov; rich in oil and gas.	Torn by civil war, including conflict between former Communists and Muslims; controlled by 25,000 Russian troops.	Among poorest nations in Central Asia; under enlightened leadership of democrat Askar Akayev.

* not part of the Confederation of Independent States

FIGURE 2–2 The 15 republics of the former Soviet Union

Source: National Times, Dec./Jan. 1995. Reprinted with permission of the Los Angeles Times Syndicate.

maneuvers as Stalinist paranoia overlaid onto a traditional Russian xenophobia,[12] but the same actions can also be seen as a realistic response to a distinct external threat.

Another part of the historic Russian policy that the communists inherited was the pursuit of influence in critical border areas: Poland, the Balkans, the Bosporus and Dardanelles straits, Manchuria, Finland, and elsewhere. The value of these policies is economic, strategic, and even cultural (pan-Slavism), in addition to the impetus given by communist ideology. Indeed, it is argued

by some that the all Soviet policy was nothing more than a continuation of the imperialism of the tsars, even in North Korea, Afghanistan, and Mongolia.[13] The Balkan wars, the Crimean War, and the Russo-Japanese War all anticipated the broad pattern of Soviet policy in later years, except that Soviet leadership succeeded, where the tsars failed, in achieving influence in Eastern Europe. Winston Churchill said that Soviet policy is "a riddle wrapped in a mystery inside an enigma. . . . But . . . the key is Russian national interest." This

---

[12] Basil Dmytryshyn, *USSR: A Concise History* (New York: Scribner's, 1965), pp. 143–153, 200–207, and 247–259.

[13] Tsarist and communist imperialism are compared in Michael Karpovitch, "Russian Imperialism or Communist Aggression," *The New Leader*, June 4, 1951, p. 18.

conclusion was almost certainly true from the beginning to the end of the Soviet state.[14]

The Soviet Union and the International System

The interplay of national and ideological themes in Russian policy can be seen in the Soviet interpretation of major international events after 1917. Until then, capitalist countries controlled the entire international system. All regions not part of advanced capitalism were dominated by it and exploited as subject markets and sources of raw materials. Russians call the First World War the Imperialist War because they see it as having been a struggle among rival imperialists for the most desirable spoils.

The capitalist countries understood from the outset that the Bolshevik Revolution of 1917 posed a threat to their international system. Britain, France, the United States, and other imperialist powers sent an international army to join domestic counterrevolutionaries in a struggle that lasted from 1917 to 1921. (The United States played a relatively minor role, sending 14,000 troops and suffering 1000 casualties. The intervention is relatively unknown to Americans today, although it is well remembered by Russians.) Though the Red army prevailed and the revolution was secured, the hostility of the capitalist world to socialism was manifest from the beginning. Though they failed in Russia, the capitalists did succeed in preventing other revolutions for many years by a combination of clever anti-Soviet propaganda and the repression of revolutionary movements. The Soviet Union was an island in a hostile sea and, as such, needed to spend huge portions of its resources on its defenses. Nonetheless, great progress was made from

1917 to 1940 in developing a revolutionary society, and in rebuilding the Soviet economy from the ravages of the First World War.

The second great European war erupted when a particularly virulent form of imperialism took hold in Germany. Its leadership was determined to extend its hegemony at the expense of the other capitalist states, making war inevitable. But Adolf Hitler also proposed to lead a holy war against communism—that is, against the Soviet Union. The German-Italian-Japanese Anti-Comintern Pact tempted the West with the idea of neutrality, to turn Hitler east and let the Nazis and communists bleed each other dry. Harry S Truman, then a U.S. senator, said on the occasion of the Nazi invasion of Russia, "If we see that Germany is winning we ought to help Russia and if Russia is winning we ought to help Germany and in that way let them kill as many as possible."[15] But Hitler's expansionism forced the capitalist states into a wartime alliance with the Soviet Union. The United States and Britain, still deeply anticommunist and dedicated to the overthrow of the Soviet government, opportunistically suspended this goal to deal with the immediate danger of fascist Germany.

The Western powers succeeded, however, in shifting most of the burden of alliance to the Soviet Union. The great victory over fascism was paid for by Russian blood and by the heroic efforts of the Soviet people, while the capitalist allies delayed opening the second front on the West until 1944. Of the 22 million Allied lives lost in the war, an estimated 20 million were Soviet. The United States, by comparison, although it made an important financial and military contribution, lost only 300,000 (1.5 percent of the Soviet loss). Eleven hundred Soviet towns and villages were plundered, while the Western Allies suffered only minor damage. Many historians hold that the Soviet Union came very close to defeating the Germans

---

[14] Winston Churchill, *The Gathering Storm* (Boston: Houghton Mifflin, 1948), p. 449.

[15] *The New York Times*, June 24, 1941.

America's participation in the 1918–1919 War of Intervention that attempted to overthrow the Bolshevik regime is now virtually forgotten in the U.S.—although it is well remembered in Russia. Here, the bodies of 111 American soldiers killed in Russia lie on the army piers at Hoboken, New Jersey. About 1,000 Americans died in the war, early martyrs in the struggle against communism. (*Source:* © AP/Wide World)

single-handedly. Churchill said that Russia's fighting men "did the main work of tearing the guts out of the German army."

These great sacrifices brought gains to Soviet revolutionary and national interests after the war. The Red armies liberated a number of countries from fascist occupation in 1945–46, particularly in Eastern Europe. Following the war, socialist governments were established with Soviet aid in Poland, Hungary, Bulgaria, Czechoslovakia, Romania, Albania, and the Soviet-occupied sector of (East) Germany. Other communist movements, with lesser amounts of Soviet aid, succeeded in Yugoslavia and China. Three years after the war, the Soviet Union had moved from isolation in a capitalist world to leadership of a communist bloc comprising half the world's population!

The American atomic monopoly after World War Two backed the demand that capitalist financiers and landlords be restored to their former positions in the Eastern European states, where the West accused the Soviets of imperialism. The Soviet Union, it seemed, was expected to reproduce exactly the conditions that led to the two world wars and then languish politely and await the next invasion. Instead, the Soviet Union committed itself to the establishment of a new order in Eastern Europe in cooperation with its new allies even as capitalist encirclement and the Truman Doctrine (an American declaration of willingness to use any means, including force if necessary, to prevent the spread of Soviet influence) precipitated the Cold War. By 1950, the new imperialist North Atlantic Treaty Organization (NATO) alliance was created and more than 50 American military bases constructed at the Soviet periphery, many of them to be equipped with atomic weapons. Once again, defense of socialism and of the Soviet state became one.

Konstantin Chernenko, who served as General Secretary of the Soviet Communist Party in 1984 and 1985, explained the origins of the Cold War in this way:

In pursuit of world supremacy, the U.S. ruling circles openly declared that their aims could be achieved only from a position of strength, and waged the so-called cold war. At their initiative the aggressive bloc of imperialist countries was formed in 1949 under the name of . . . (NATO). On a scale hitherto unknown, the United States expanded the arms race and began to step up the production of atomic, thermonuclear, bacteriological weapons and other types of mass destruction weapons. American military bases, targeted on the USSR and other socialist countries, were being quickly set up; new military blocs were formed. . . .

The Communist Party of the Soviet Union (CPSU) and the Soviet government could not ignore the dangerous course of American imperialism, which had the atomic weapons at its disposal, and openly proclaimed its intention to achieve the "rolling back" of socialism. We had constantly to build up the USSR's defense capability. The fact that the Soviet Union came into possession of atomic, and later thermonuclear, weapons, and mastered the production of intercontinental missiles, which put an end to U.S. atomic blackmail, is of immense principled significance.[16]

It is ironic that the imperialists convinced some people of Soviet aggressive intentions, when it was the Americans who kept their bases far from home on the borders of the Soviet heartland, and not the other way around! Leonid Brezhnev, General Secretary of the Communist Party of the Soviet Union, protested in 1971:

> The peoples will not be deceived by the attempts to ascribe to the Soviet Union intentions which are alien to it. We declare with a full sense of responsibility: we have no territorial claims on anyone whatsoever, we threaten no one, and have no intention of attacking anyone, we stand for the free and independent development of all nations. But let no

one, for his part, try to talk to us in terms of ultimatums and strength.[17]

Meanwhile the imperialists intensified their exploitation of Africa, Asia, and Latin America which, despite formal political independence, remained under neoimperialist control through reactionary puppet governments, military interventions, and the manipulation of international markets. Though the world socialist revolution was strong, its final victory was postponed by the might of the imperialists, with the Soviet Union assuming responsibility for defense of the revolution against imperial reaction. The international political system thus consisted of an imperialist bloc led by the United States, a socialist bloc led by the USSR, and the Third World nations at various stages of development toward socialism but in many cases still dominated by the imperialists.

To meet the Western threat in Europe, intensified by West Germany's membership in NATO, the Kremlin established the counterbalancing Warsaw Pact. Moscow used its strength as the dominant partner to support its allies by developing the centrally planned production and distribution system through the Council for Mutual Economic Assistance (COMECON), and it used forceful intervention where necessary to suppress Western-inspired antirevolutionary activities. In 1968, on the occasion of a Warsaw Pact invasion of Czechoslovakia to smother a West-leaning liberalization movement, Leonid Brezhnev pronounced a full rationale for such actions. Known as the Brezhnev Doctrine and often likened to the Monroe Doctrine under which the United States frequently intervened in Latin America and the Caribbean, it reasoned that the security and welfare of proletarian internationalism supersedes the policy directions of a single member. Although the 1968 invasion was the last of its kind (martial law was sufficient to restore order to Poland during Solidarity's liberalization

---

[16] Excerpt from a book reprinted in Victor Pribytkov, *Soviet-U.S. Relations: The Selected Writings and Speeches of Konstantin U. Chernenko* (New York: Praeger, 1984), pp. 127–162, at p. 140.

[17] M. Gribanov, *Security for Europe* (Moscow: Novosti Press Agency, 1972), p. 19. Originally stated at Twenty-fourth Congress of the Communist Party of the Soviet Union.

movement in 1980), the Brezhnev Doctrine remained a cornerstone of intra-alliance policy for more than two decades. It was the single most essential element in preserving a cohesive defense perimeter of the Soviet Union itself.

Disintegration of the Soviet State

When the Soviet Union ceased to be in 1991, it was fashionable in the West to declare that the Cold War had been won by the West; that the Soviet Union had fallen because of the innate inferiority of socialism to capitalism or of communism to democracy; that the Soviet Union was socially and philosophically bankrupt; or that the American defense investment of the 1980s had so escalated the price of the arms race that it destroyed the Soviet economy. None of these figures in the Russian explanation. The end of the Cold War and the flight from orthodox Marxism-Leninism occurred alongside an unprecedented recognition of political and ethnic pluralism within the Soviet Union and, with these, a reevaluation of the orthodoxy around which the Union had coalesced for seventy-five years. Andrei Kozyrev, Russian Foreign Minister, went so far as to characterize the "state ideology of communism" as "the main breeding ground for the Cold War."[18]

1. Democracy and the Communist Party

Until 1988, Mikhail Gorbachev's leadership of the Soviet Union departed little from that of his predecessors. He was dedicated to proletarian internationalism, concerned about signs of intensified Western imperialism in the Developing World, and

a devotee of single-party rule. But as a visionary, he knew that harmony could not be commanded from Moscow and that the Communist party had been made fragile by insurgent domestic factions. And so in twin acts of democratization, he introduced the policies of *glasnost* (access to information) and *perestroika* (restructuring). Under these he persuaded the party's Central Committee to abandon the party's seventy-two-year monopoly on political power, legitimizing for the first time a pluralism of ideas and even the possibility of a multiparty system. To some these were overdue reforms; to others they were practical necessities provoked by lightning-fast events in both the Soviet Union and Eastern Europe. These included a prolonged coal miners' strike, ethnic restiveness in several of the republics, civil war between Armenians and Azerbaijanis that required armed Soviet intervention, and threats of secession from Lithuania, Latvia, and Estonia. His allies in party liberalization rested their case on environmental degradation, explosives under unreliable supervisory control, and economic stagnation. Some had even urged him privately to split the Communist party to create a multiparty system as a way of isolating the hardline conservatives. Still others interpreted events at the periphery as requiring internal liberalization to avoid multiple uprisings amounting to civil war throughout the Soviet Union itself.[19]

In 1989, in a debate on the party's goals and future, Gorbachev had said:

> The [communist] party cannot gain authority by decree. No mighty decree or decision can do this now. Our authority was acquired at the first stage of *perestroika* by having offered society the policy of *perestroika*. And society trusted the party, supported it

---

[18] Andrei Kozyrev, "Russia: A Chance for Survival," *Foreign Affairs*, spring 1992, pp. 1–16 at p. 13.

[19] For comprehehsive treatments of this period see David Remnick, *Lenin's Tomb: The Last Days of the Soviet Empire* (New York: Random House, 1993); Michael R. Beschloss and Strobe Talbott, *At the Highest Levels: The Inside Story of the End of the Cold War* (Boston: Little, Brown and Company, 1993); and Steven Kull, *Burying Lenin: The Revolution in Soviet Ideology and Foreign Policy* (Boulder: Westview, 1992).

and followed it. Today authority can be won only by the decisive and consistent carrying out of the policy of *perestroika*. There is not nor will there by any other way for the party to win authority. If anyone thinks otherwise this is unrealistic, comrades.

. . .

If *perestroika* is a revolution—and we agree that it is—and if it means profound changes in attitudes toward property, the status of the individual, the basics of the political system and the spiritual realm, and if it is to transform the people into a force of change in society, then how can all this take place quietly and smoothly?

And do we really need to be overcome with panic when the revolutionary processes have become a reality? We have caused them by our policy.

. . .

The restructuring processes that have unfurled today are enveloping all realms of our life. They are revealing much unusual and much that is sometimes hard to accept. This is generating additional tension. But that is what these revolutionary years are all about! We must understand all of this and act like a revolutionary party. Otherwise forces will appear which, seeing that the party is lagging behind, will try to seize the initiative. This is already happening.[20]

Just six months later Gorbachev asked the Central Committee of the party to accept the fact that political pluralism already existed, and to permit the free exercise of multiparty politics unimpeded by the party's constitutional monopoly. The party that Lenin had labeled the Vanguard of the Proletariat in its march toward the worker dictatorship had given way to officially sanctioned political pluralism. If the state were to wither away, it would not wither into a proletarian utopia. Consistent with the new fashion of criticizing the past, Andrei Kozyrev subsequently wrote: "Soviet communism

was doomed from the start. . . . Most surprising is not the fact that the system collapsed, but that it lasted for over 70 years."[21]

2. The Defense Perimeter

Events in Eastern Europe lay prominantly behind the party's decisions. Hungary had broken the seal by opening its Austrian border to give political refugees a clear path to the West. Estonia, Latvia, and Lithuania all seceded from the Soviet Union with only brief military resistance. The Brandenberg Gate through the Berlin Wall was opened, ending a forty-five-year standoff between the vestiges of Soviet and Western occupation. The two Germanys were reunified, and the Kremlin offered no objection to the new Germany's membership in NATO. The Polish Solidarity union was elevated to a political party and permitted with Gorbachev's public support to participate in free elections. Everywhere it offered a candidate, it defeated a communist incumbent. At first only hinting that he would not attempt to intervene, Gorbachev eventually repudiated the Brezhnev Doctrine by declaring that he would let the Eastern European states determine their own futures since the Soviet Union has "no right, moral or political," to command their internal affairs.[22] One by one those governments fell, only one (Romania) with serious armed resistance. (Here Gorbachev hinted that Soviet troops might intervene on the side of the noncommunist interests.) Suddenly there was no defense perimeter and, more remarkably, no Soviet empire. As a final statement of independence, some allies petitioned NATO for membership, implicitly seeking Western protection from any retaliatory or future Soviet military adventure. For his part, Gorbachev declared his intention for the 1990s to be a "common European home" free of menacing military alliances and marked by self-determination in

---

[20] As quoted in *The New York Times*, July 23, 1989, p. 16. For an analysis of how the Gorbachev adaptations fit into Marxist-Leninist doctrine, see John Ehrenberg, *The Dictatorship of the Proletariat: Marxism's Theory of Socialist Democracy* (New York: Routledge, 1992), pp. 185–188.

---

[21] Andrei Kozyrev, "Russia: A Chance for Survival," pp. 4–5.
[22] As quoted in Michael R. Beschloss and Strobe Talbott, *At the Highest Levels*, p. 134.

Eastern Europe. And this concept, in the world of one Soviet analyist, "means decomposition of the empire, in our own interest."[23]

3. Diplomacy

Gorbachev extended the revolution of *perestroika* well beyond the boundaries of the Soviet Union and its sphere of influence. He broke the diplomatic shield with China by visiting Beijing in 1989. Some argue that his visit and the admiration among young Chinese of *perestroika* provoked the demonstrations that led to state violence in Tiananmen Square. He exploited the popularity that Washington's endorsement of *perestroika* had given him in the West, and he vigorously emulated the public relations style of Western leaders. By the time of his 1988 state visit to the United States, he was already one of the world's most popular figures among Americans, and he was *Time* magazine's man of the year.

But the substance of his diplomacy was more important than style. Consistent with the work of his predecessors, he pursued arms reduction as a practical matter of bloc defense. In 1986 he agreed to remove virtually all intermediate-range nuclear weapons from the Warsaw Pact arsenal and to accelerate strategic arms reductions talks to reduce intercontinental missiles and their multiple warheads. He also declared his willingness to discuss scaling back chemical weapons. On other fronts he ended the long and costly Soviet intervention in Afghanistan, declared his willingness to make payments long withheld from the United Nations for peacekeeping matters, and discontinued the costly and vexing economic support of Cuba. For six of his eight years as president, Ronald Reagan had maintained his "evil empire" rhetoric about Soviet diplomacy; but in the final two years it was apparent Reagan and Gorbachev had forged a relationship of growing trust.

---

[23] As quoted in *The New York Times*, November 30, 1989, p. A20.

Moscow and Washington capitalized on that trust in the years 1989 through 1991 especially. In that time the world was profoundly changed. The removal of intermediate-range nuclear forces was completed; START was signed; chemical-weapons reduction was under discussion; the Berlin Wall was dismantled; Germany was reunified; and Moscow withdrew its support of insurgency in Central America. In addition, the Soviet Union and the United States stood together at the United Nations Security Council denouncing Saddam Hussein's invasion of Kuwait and endorsing the first-ever use of Chapter VII (collective security in the face of an act of aggression), something previously impossible because of intractable Cold War stances. As part of a diplomatic practice, Gorbachev had insisted on Soviet inclusion in the broader issue of Middle East peace, an area from which US-Israeli agreement had always excluded Moscow. In the new spirit of the Malta Conference peace agenda, Washington yielded to Moscow. Presidents Gorbachev and Bush announced that the two nations would jointly sponsor a conference at Madrid to begin peace talks in earnest between Israel and the Palestine Liberation Organization. The Cold War was over, and a New World Order beginning.

4. Rebirth of the Russian Federation

Boris Yeltsin, a former Gorbachev ally, had abandoned the Communist party and his future in the Soviet government by being elected president of the Russian SSR when all signs pointed to the disintegration of the Soviet state. Except to hard-line communists who saw *perestroika*-related events as uniformly seditious, collapse of the defense perimeter and liberation of the Eastern European allies were welcome. The fizzling Cold War raised profound questions about the justification of central Soviet authority in domestic affairs. The rise of multiparty politics gave vent to a pluralism of ideas that had remained suppressed by communist orthodoxy for decades. Throughout the Soviet Union, the Lenin statuary was being toppled by mobs heady with elixir of political freedom. The Central Committee of the CPSU had either abandoned or so modified the role of state and party that orthodoxy was no longer a guide. Although Gorbachev was rescued from a brief *coup d'etat*, few thought that his restoration to office would signal the recovery of the Soviet state.

Shaky indeed was the Soviet state. Six months before the Russian election Eduard Shevardnadze, Gorbachev confidant and Soviet Foreign Minister, had resigned in fear of dictatorship. As the world speculated about Soviet reactions to secessionist moves within the USSR and decommunization in Eastern Europe, Shevardnadze had feared internal military attacks on strikers and anti-Soviet demonstrators. Because Gorbachev was less decisive on domestic than on international matters, Shevardnadze worried that pervasive disorder would provoke hard-liners to throw Gorbachev aside and establish a right-wing, Stalinist-style dictatorship backed by the military, the classic Soviet combination.[24] Many of the right-wingers were still smarting from a 1987 Gorbachev speech in which he, like Nikita Khrushchev before him (1956), had attempted to "de-Stalinize" Soviet politics by unapologetically telling the story of Stalin's lawlessness, cult of personality, mass repression, and other abuses of power.[25] Now, in these live-or-die moments for the CPSU and the Soviet state, Shevardnadze feared that the past would be summoned back by the power-starved right wing. For Gorbachev, all was progresing well externally; but what would be the outcome of *perestroika* at home? Yeltsin had his own plans.

The choices seemed clear. Either the hard-liners would seize power and roll back history to dictatorship, because of or in anticipation of revolution, or Gorbachev's self-proclaimed revolution would carry through to an unpredictable end. Efforts to persuade and then to force the Balkan states to remain within the union failed, as did efforts to reconstruct the terms of union. Now Yeltsin played his final card. Once again the Russian Federation would be the leader, this time of the Council of Independent States. Gone now were the four fundamental bases of Soviet strength: the Cold War, the political monoploy of the Soviet Communist party, the unified proletariat, and the Soviet empire. Now, with neither purpose nor popularity, gone too was the Soviet state. In its place were fifteen independent republics, preeminent among them the Russian Federation.

This, then, is how the Russian perspective on the international political system evolved. With that as background, we turn to Russia's contemporary view of the system and its other principal actors.

The Russian View of the United States

Literally from the birth of the Soviet Union in 1917 the United States and its capitalist friends were Moscow's aggressive enemies. Western intervention in the Soviet civil war underscored just how menacing the capitalists thought socialism to their imperialistic world order. Four successive presidents of the United States, representing both major parties, refused to recognize the Soviet Union, and by the time Franklin D. Roosevelt did, World War Two had already begun in Asia and loomed in Europe. Although Lend-Lease aid flowed to the Soviet Union from Washington after Hitler's invasion, the suffering and losses of war were felt disproportionately by the Soviet people. Through this time, however, Stalin's government worked

---

[24] Melor Sturua, "The Real Coup," *Foreign Policy*, winter 1991–92, pp. 63–72 at p. 66, argues that Gorbachev was "chronically indecisive on pushing *perestroika* toward its logical conclusion." Sturua was formerly foreign editor of the Soviet daily paper and mouthpiece *Izvestia*. See also Artyom Borovik, "Waiting for Democracy," *Foreign Policy*, fall 1991, pp. 51–60 at p. 60, where the author quotes Gorbachev as having said, "Ethnic conflict in the USSR is the last thing that worries me."

[25] David Remnick, *Lenin's Tomb*, pp. 50–51.

with the West both in wartime alliance and in planning the post-war world order. They were equal partners in establishing the United Nations. Behind the facade of trust, however, lurked the truth, namely, that with its atomic monopoly and unequaled economic power, the American resolve to bring down Soviet power would resume after the war. The Soviet Union and proletarian internationalism were the real targets of *pax Americana*.

American Economic Imperialism

Above all others, the United States embodied economic imperialism. American investors had penetrated the economies of more than seventy nations at a time when there were only about one hundred. So much of its wealth was produced overseas that the foreign economy of the United States equaled that of the fourth largest gross national product (GNP) on earth as long ago as 1966.[26] The fifteen largest American exporters had combined international sales equal to a quarter of the American GNP and more than 20 percent of the total GNP of the developing countries, then called the Third World. Here American imperialism was the most exploitative. Through its economic power, coupled with government aid, American investment capital determined the pace of nation-building. Industrial goods were exchanged for raw materials at terms of trade that ensured long-term Third World indebtedness and guaranteed the indefinite subjugation of peoples. Precious capital was drained from the Third World, where return on cash and portfolio investment was greater than in the investment-choked domestic market. From the Soviet perspective, "the siphoning off of financial resources from the developing countries in connection with their external debt [was] the most cynical and parasitic form of neocolonialist plunder and [was] an important element of the system of neocolonialist

exploitation."[27] The transnational corporations were cited in this connection as the special vehicle of imperialism.[28] That the United States had troops stationed in sixty-four countries and rapid-response forces ready to go elsewhere on short notice only solidified the capability of American capital to turn the world economy to Washington's primary Cold War objective—the destruction of proletarian internationalism.

The Soviet case regarding American imperialism was made in numbers. In the area of raw materials, for example, there are sixty-two industrial raw materials listed by the Defense Department as vital to American defense industries, more than half of the annual consumption of which has to be imported. In many cases, 80 percent or more is imported annually. Political-military control of the supplier countries is capitalist imperialism's natural solution to this problem.

Penetration of export markets is equally revealing. Just compare two years. In 1982 the top fifty U.S. exporters produced $629 billion in goods and exported $59 billion, barely 10 percent. But in 1988, only fifteen top exporters produced a total of $524 billion and exported $65 billion, or 12.5 percent. Now look at specific industries. In 1988, when the American automobile industry was widely believed to be crumbling under the weight of Japanese and European competition, the big three American automakers all ranked in the top six as exporters measured by value of exports. In the computer industry, where Japanese competition was also widely feared, IBM, Digital, Hewlett-Packard, and UNISYS all ranked in the top fifteen as exporters. The two largest manufacturers of commercial aircraft, Boeing and McDonnell Douglas, make the list annually. Looking at these figures from

---

[26] Leo Model, "The Politics of Private Foreign Investment," *Foreign Affairs*, July 1967, pp. 640–641.

[27] A. Shitnikov and G. Markov, "The West's 'Debt Trap' for the Developing Countries," *International Affairs* (Moscow), August 1985, pp. 35–43 at p. 39.
[28] Y. Stepanov, "The TNCs in the Strategy for Imperialist Expansion," *International Affairs* (Moscow), December 1985, pp. 68–76.

another angle, nine of America's largest industrial producers sold more than 20 percent of their total product abroad in 1988, with Boeing leading the list at 46.3 percent.[29] In Soviet analysis, these figures show unmistakably the American imperialistic reliance on foreign markets.

A third important body of evidence of America's capitalist imperialism is the concentration of investment abroad. Only about fifty firms control more than half of all U.S. foreign investments; fewer than two hundred control more than 80 percent. Thus the foreign operations of American capital are far more monopolistic than are the domestic operations: The largest and most powerful corporations tend to have a disproportionate interest in the foreign market. From the socialist perspective, this is significant because concentrated economic interests are better organized and more influential politically than are dispersed economic interests. A large industry that is concentrated, such as the General Electric Company, has more influence than does a large industry that is dispersed, such as retail drugstores, even though the total sales of all retail drugstores may be larger than those of General Electric. The huge concentration of power in the foreign investment and export sectors gives added weight to these interests.

In the Soviet Cold War view, the crux of American capitalist imperialism was the military-industrial complex, the nexus of government, the military, manufacturing, investment, and research that depends on militaristic foreign policy and defense spending. Military spending comprised another 10 percent of capitalist profits, more for large firms than small. In addition, a large percentage of the U.S. labor force was involved in defense production. If we add defense to exports and foreign investments and count only the largest firms, we may estimate that the world structure accounts for 35 to 40 percent of the Cold War profits of the top capitalist interests. The clear link was demonstrated

between capitalism as a socioeconomic system and the tendency to imperialism in American foreign policy.

How does this connection between the economic sectors of capitalism and government policy operate? There are both direct and indirect linkages. It has been shown, for example, that a relatively small number of individuals circulated among the top policy bureaus between 1944 and 1960. Moreover, about 60 percent of these came originally from big business, investment, or major law firms. There was an equally impressive circulation of personnel between the armed services and the top defense firms. For example, more than 2000 retired officers above the rank of colonel or naval captain went to executive positions with the largest defense corporations. One linkage between imperialism and capitalism is the shared interests of the top capitalists and key government officials in the United States.[30]

From the old Soviet perspective, the goals of this complex were three. The first was wealth through collaboration, exploitation, and the mythic fear of war. The second was to perpetuate the myth that socialism was a menace to capitalism through the might of the Soviet Union.[31] The third was pursuit of an international arms race so costly that the Soviet Union would be able to equal the imperialists' arms expenditures only at the expense of other economic priorities. In this way the military-industrial complex was an instrument of international economic warfare designed to strangle socialism. Writing as late as 1985, one Soviet analysis concluded that "modern militarism and its specific creation—the arms race—is the product of the entire socio-economic system of imperialism, primarily its most developed and most reactionary

[29] "America's Fifty Biggest Exporters," *Fortune*, July 17, 1989, pp. 50–51.

[30] Gabriel Kolko, *The Roots of American Foreign Policy* (Boston: Beacon Press, 1969), pp. 16–26.
[31] Georgi Arbatov and Willem Oltmans, *The Soviet Viewpoint* (New York: Dodd Mead, 1983), p. 107, and Georgi Arbatov, "A Soviet Commentary," in Arthur Macy Cox, *Russian Roulette: The Superpower Game* (New York: Times Books, 1982), pp. 182–183.

component—American imperialism."[32] Occasionally even the American press contributed to the Soviet analysis, as in this statement from an article reporting the resignation of a defense manufacturer's president:

> Retired Adm. Bobby R. Inman, whose military career included a stint at the helm of the National Security Agency, resigned as head of Tracor Holdings, Inc., conceding that even his years as a master spy didn't alert him to the impending end of the Cold War and its devastating effect on the highly leveraged defense contractor.
>
> "I never foresaw in the most optimistic forecasts the pace at which change has taken place in Eastern Europe," Mr. Inman said in an interview. "I'm elated to see it all unravel on that side [of the Iron Curtain] from the personal point of view, but from the investor's point of view, it isn't good news."[33]

Mikhail Gorbachev rose to power within weeks of Ronald Reagan's second presidential inauguration. It was a time of tension between the two capitals because of the American deployment of INF weapons in Europe and of cruise missiles, and because of accelerated American efforts to deploy a defense system in space (Strategic Defense Initiative, or Star Wars). His two predecessors, each of whom served for but a short time, had locked in a rhetorical contest with Reagan.[34] Concerned that American policy had taken an aggressive turn, Gorbachev told a *Time* magazine reporter that

Reagan's position was "truly a case of driving in nails, snipping off the heads and then expecting everyone to pull them out with their teeth!"[35] In his first year in office, then, there was little sign that Gorbachev foresaw better relations with the West. The issue of arms control in particular was complicated because under Reagan, the United States suffered from "social senility" that "augments its recklessness" in world affairs.[36] In these inauspicious beginnings, it remained the official position that the Kremlin would not be stared down by Washington. Already the Soviet Union had achieved three major landmarks in the march of history to mature socialism: revolution, the defeat of fascism, and military parity with the imperialists. Thus history could proceed without fear of American militarism.[37]

The era of *glasnost* and *perestroika* brought considerable change to these long-standing views. Mikhail Gorbachev's vision of world peace, Soviet political and economic modernization, and improved Soviet-American relations began to materialize before the end of the Reagan presidency. The most dramatic steps were the withdrawal of Soviet troops from Afghanistan, a Soviet admission that Soviet military participation there had been "immoral," and a Soviet-American agreement to dismantle all intermediate-range nuclear forces in Europe. They also agreed to mutual visits for on-site inspection of the removal and destruction of the weapons. As President Reagan left office, he dropped the rhetoric of the Soviet Union as "the evil empire" and began to refer instead to "my friend Gorby."

In 1989, even before the dramatic independence movement in Eastern Europe, the Soviet Union declared publicly that it no longer feared aggression from NATO. In an unprecedented

[32] Y. Katasonov, "Socio-Economic Factors of the Arms Race," *International Affairs* (Moscow), January 1985, pp. 39–47 at p. 47. On the subject see also E. Kuzmin, "Traditional Bourgeois Institutions of Power in Deepening Crisis," *International Affairs* (Moscow), August 1985, pp. 61–69.

[33] Michael Allen, *The Wall Street Journal*, December 27, 1989, p. B4.

[34] Yuri Andropov, "Text of Soviet Statement on Relations with U.S.," *The New York Times*, September 29, 1983, p. A14. The text was released by *Tass* on the preceding day. Also see Alexander Yakovlev, "The Harsh Soviet Line on Reagan," *The Washington Post*, October 16, 1983, p. B5. The author was director of the Soviet Institute of World Economics and International Relations; and a Chernenko speech in Victor Pribytkov, *Soviet-U.S. Relations*, pp. 120–124 at p. 123.

[35] Taken from the Soviet translation in *International Affairs* (Moscow), October 1985, pp. 3–16 at p. 11.

[36] Quoted in *Christian Science Monitor*, February 26, 1986, p. 28.

[37] V. Zagladin, "World Balance of Forces and the Development of International Relations," *International Affairs* (Moscow), March 1985, pp. 65–74.

appearance before the House Armed Services Committee of the U.S. Congress, Marshal Sergei Akhromeyev, Gorbachev's foremost military adviser, commented in part as follows:

> I am personally convinced that neither the United States nor its allies intend today to unleash a warfare against the U.S.S.R. and its allies. I openly make this kind of statement in my country. We are telling our people that the tensions in the world, and war danger, have diminished. And this has been the result of positive changes in the relations between the U.S.S.R. and the U.S.
>
> We are convinced that political means to achieve national security will predominate in the 1990's, while the role of military means must decrease. The U.S.S.R. intends to work to this end in the 1990's. This course was approved by the body of our supreme power, the Congress of the People's Deputies of the U.S.S.R.[38]

Under these circumstances, it became the new Soviet view that NATO and the Warsaw Pact could be disbanded or be disarmed and become merely political alliances. The Warsaw Pact was to be stripped of the power to intervene in the domestic political affairs of its members, as happened within the year.

We have already seen the foreign policy benefits of the unprecedented collaboration between Moscow and Washington in the last two Reagan years and the first three Bush years, 1987–1991, with emphasis on arms reduction and Middle East diplomacy. But there were other important areas of progress as well. Having acknowledged the diminished military content in foreign affairs, the Soviet Union took its place in the New World Order seeking economic partnership with the West. Even before the dissolution of the Soviet state, Gorbachev was securing pledges of economic assistance from the United States and its Western friends, now partners in peace rather than the running dogs of imperialism, and was seeking membership in the International Monetary Fund and privileges from the International Bank for Reconstruction and Development (World Bank). The Soviet government encouraged joint ventures with Western corporations to stimulate the economy, and central controls were dropped. Although orthodoxy did not evolve fast enough to admit the existence of capitalism, references to "market economy" became common. A small securities exchange opened. And in proportions and with a speed that would have horrified the original keepers of the Marxist-Leninist faith, a globe-trotting capitalist class arose. Processes were set in motion to privatize the means of production, a full reversal of one of the cornerstone policies of the old Soviet political culture.

In post-Soviet Russia the foremost priorities are stabilizing an emerging market economy and building a noncommunist managerial class, though the election of a communist majority in the lower legislative house in 1995 upset the pace of change. The continued softening of the world view is partly a product of abandoning anticapitalist hysteria and acceptance among the "new democrats" that democratization and conversion to capitalism—the word is now frankly used—must evolve together. They stress, however, that such a sentiment is not universal. Resistance to this ideological conversion is most common in the middle echelons of government still staffed by old-style socialist thinkers. The analogous problem in foreign policy is that it is being made under radically altered circumstances. Russia lacks "a usable foreign policy tradition after its break with communism."[39]

As maturation progresses, long-term foreign policy calls for a democratic Russia to be a full partner with the West in politics and economics. To this end, the contemporary debate centers on the underlying premise of Russian foreign policy. Meanwhile, however, Russia finds itself in a "new encirclement" consisting of possible conflict at virtually any point around its borders. The greatest dangers are closest to home. In the words of the Russian ambassador to the United States,

---

[38] *The New York Times*, July 31, 1989, p. A15.

[39] Vladimir P. Lukin, "Our Security Predicament," *Foreign Policy*, fall 1992, pp. 57–75 at p. 70.

To sum up, the intensification of all negative trends in Russia's relations with its neighbors would create a dangerous geostrategic environment for Russia. One can easily imagine, for instance, a concurrent unfolding of several crises along Russia's new borders: Muslim fundamentalists gaining power in key states of Central Asia, a new escalation of the Armenian-Azerbaijani conflict and of the conflict in Moldova, and a confrontation with Ukraine over Crimea. All that could occur in a context of mounting tensions with Japan over the Kuril[e] Islands and of deepening political crises in China and on the Korean peninsula. Even for a strong Russia, such a combination of threats would pose a formidable challenge, to say nothing of a weak Russia, which some might see as inviting such situations. Hence the central challenge of Russia's new foreign policy is to eliminate or at least radically reduce the chances for a worst-case scenario of that kind.[40]

With this in mind, Russia's first external priority is to solidify political and economic relations with the other republics through the Council of Independent States. This is necessary for several reasons. First, because the borders of Russia are smaller than those of the Soviet Union, Russia is now more isolated geographically from Europe, a major player in which it intends to become. Second, during the Cold War period Soviet economic planners had a preference for huge factories and centralized industries, many of which were not in Russia. Today, therefore, many vital industrial products are manufactured in other CIS states and not available to Russia except through harmonious trade. Third, an estimated 25 million ethnic Russians live in the other fourteen republics. Ethnic diversity and the current surge of national self-consciousness have placed many of these in danger, and in its new diplomacy Moscow wants to resist intervention on their behalf. Finally, many of the CIS states have no national defenses. Since many of them are not governed by "new democrats" or even "new thinkers" who recognize that the Cold War is over,

many feel a need for a defense structure for which they turn to Moscow. The Russian government rejects criticism from the West that in signing the Tashkent Treaty with five other CIS governments in 1992, Russia was attempting to structure a post–Cold War alliance. This is a system of collective regional self-defense that includes a pledge of nonaggression and mutual assistance in the event of an external attack.[41] Unknown at present is the long-term significance of a call for restoring the Soviet Union in a 1996 resolution of the communist dominated lower legislative house.

The second priority is to the east, of which it is said, "Once again, history is throwing an enormous challenge to Russia. But perhaps that is Russia's new mission: to become a guarantor of stability throughout the Eurasian heartland through its own democratic revival."[42] And beyond the eastern border region, long-range goals include normalization of relations with China, a peace treaty with Japan that includes disposition of the territorial issues in the North Pacific, and stabilization of the Korean peninsula.

The third foreign policy priority, though by no means less important, is European and trans-Atlantic relations.

The Russian View of Europe

Throughout the Cold War, Europe was the great divide. It was here that the NATO alliance members maintained in excess of 5 million troops organized in twenty-four divisions, armed with 7200 nuclear warheads and an abundance of conventional air, sea, and land materiel. Three NATO states—the United States, Britain, and France—were nuclear powers. All the world's largest economies except Japan were engaged in this massive confrontation. Quite naturally, the issue of security in Europe occupied the forefront of Soviet attention and dominated the Soviet world view.

---

[40] Ibid., pp. 64–65.

[41] Ibid., p. 68.
[42] Ibid., pp. 66–67.

To accomplish the key goal of preventing an attack from the West in the absence of a comprehensive European security system, three critical imperatives dominated Soviet strategic thinking until 1989:

1. Governments sympathetic to the USSR and socialist in orientation had to be maintained in the belt of Eastern European countries that lies between the Soviet heartland and the powerful countries of Western Europe, especially Germany. In the West, these Eastern European states were considered a buffer zone of satellite states. (See Figure 2–3.)
2. Germany, the most powerful and historically the most aggressive country of Europe, had to be neutralized as a threat. Preserving the division of Germany into East and West was a necessary and expedient means of reducing the German threat. A government sympathetic to the USSR had to be maintained in the East.
3. The military powers of the West European countries had to be counterbalanced by the military power of the USSR and the Eastern European countries. This was the mission of the Warsaw Pact.

This security formula remained relatively constant through the Cold War, even though there were great variations in the intensity of relations across the European divide. The least threatening time was the period of *détente* (approximately 1974–1981), which, in Moscow's view, rested on several bases. From a strategic point of view, increased fear of Chinese strength on the Asian borders was an incentive to more peaceful relations in Europe (although, paradoxically, improved relations between Beijing and Washington resulted in renewed suspicions in the Kremlin of American motives). Second, the phenomenon of Eurocommunism further loosened the economic dependence of Eastern Europe on the Soviet Union. It opened both intergovernmental (official) and transnational (popular and unofficial) avenues to improved relations between Eastern Europe and the countries of the European Common Market, thus greatly strengthening the potential for international trade

balances among the Eastern European countries. Third, and a matter of utmost importance to Soviet planners in all areas pertaining to economic modernization, agricultural production, and military preparedness, Moscow increasingly recognized its need for access to the superior technological capabilities of the United States, Japan, and Western Europe. Although American critics of technological trade with the Soviet Union argued that it merely strengthened the military potential of their country's principal adversary, the Soviets, in acknowledging that the gap between the two countries could be closed through such trade, recognized that its continuation depended on moderation in their foreign policy.

During this time, many on each side of the line spoke optimistically about the end of the Cold War. But the improvement did not survive long into the 1980s. Increasing Western hostility to the Soviet Union and its internal and external policies made it clear that the West understood détente to apply restraint to Soviet pursuit of great power interests. Examples abound: American destruction of the socialist regime of Chile; constant American attacks on the human rights policies of the Soviet Union; NATO charges of aggressive Warsaw Pact intentions in Europe; reconstruction of Sino-American relations as a form of tacit aggression against the Soviet Union by both Washington and Beijing; continued American intrusion in the affairs of the Eastern bloc by condemnation of Soviet actions in Poland, together with American economic retaliation; American plans to deploy an MX missile system, a major variant of the nuclear arms race threatening its stability; failure of the United States to ratify the SALT II treaty; emphasis in American nuclear targeting on countervalue strategy (aimed at population and industrial centers); deployment of highly accurate Cruise and Pershing II missiles in Western Europe; inflammatory rhetoric of the Reagan administration accusing the Soviet Union of planning military superiority designed to enslave the world; and so on. The militarism and anti-Soviet hysteria of the United States, together with the expanded threat of nuclear war following the deployment of new American

* the shaded area indicates the former East Germany, which was a member of the Warsaw Treaty Organization prior to German reunification

FIGURE 2–3   Eastern Europe in Soviet and Russian defense.

weapons, struck the Soviet Union as signs of hostility, not of an enlightened Western attitude called détente, which provided assurances of great power, peace, and freedom of action in areas not directly under the control of one another. Détente had been merely a ruse under which the West perpetuated the Cold War. In such an environment, it was necessary for the Kremlin to discontinue the Intermediate-range Nuclear Forces (INF) talks regarding Europe and the Strategic Arms Reduction Talks (START) on intercontinental nuclear weapons.

The era of *glasnost* and *perestroika* brought sharp changes to the Soviet perception of Western Europe as well. The Kremlin's willingness to permit its Eastern European empire to dissolve in the Kremlin's own economic interest, its willingness to permit NATO and the Warsaw Pact to evolve into political alliances, its apparent eagerness to denounce the Brezhnev Doctrine, all in favor of a "common European home," indicate a revolutionary revision of the official attitude toward Western Europe. Caught between a foundering economy and a restive public eager to enjoy the benefits of modern Western European living, and willing to come to terms with the capitalist powers even at the expense of the sacred anti-imperialist dogma, the CPSU set a course toward the West.

Attempts to build a partnership with the West have been frustrated by several factors, one of which reveals the close connection between domestic reform and foreign policy. Despite early changes toward democracy, the progress has slowed considerably. As early as the parliamentary elections of 1993, the public's frustration with economic reform showed in the success of candidates sponsored by the right-leaning party. This is attributed to a number of things, all of them related to the decline in living standards, unemployment, and the emergence of an ultrawealthy capitalist class at a time of general economic decline. Many Russians blame this on a failed reform policy designed by Westerners and even suspect the United States of having created a new economic instrument for permanently weakening Russia.

Simultaneously, Russians are concerned about "the near abroad," (the former Soviet republics) and the old Eastern European allies. Collapse of the empire has contributed to the Russian economic decline, and it has raised new security issues. The defense perimeter is gone and is seeking membership in NATO. The West fails to understand Russia's need to resume as close a relationship with these areas as possible, apparently fearing a renewal of empire. "What is wrong," the former foreign minister asked, "with Russia announcing as its goal the gradual reintegration—primarily economic

reintegration—of the post-Soviet space on a voluntary and equal basis?"[43] And the same principle applies to the security realm. The 1991 Tashkent Treaty that bound Russia, Ukraine, and Belarus into a regional organization pledging nonaggression and collective security was joined by all other former members of the USSR with the exceptions of Lithuania, Estonia, and Latvia by 1994. The agreement entails modest Russia military deployments (Table 2–1). Such a regional commitment pales against the military might of NATO, or even against the American portion of it.

In the face of concerns of (1) post-socialist economic decline, perhaps planned by the West, (2) a slowing pace of democratization, and (3) the future of the near abroad, fear has arisen of a popular reaction welcoming a new dictatorship. The possible results include a return to a state-centralized economy, neoimperialism in the near abroad, and a division of Europe that would have some of the characteristics of a new cold war.[44] These outcomes are made more likely by the West's failure to acknowledge Russia as a major power and to deal with her as an equal partner. In place of reciprocity, the West fails to speak out about discrimination against ethnic Russians in the near abroad, encourages NATO membership for former partners in empire, excludes Russia from the principal institutions of the world economy, and undertakes policies in Europe, such as bombing Bosnian Serb positions, without consultation with Moscow. "It would be hard to accept an interpretation of partnership in which one side demands that the other coordinate its every step with it while the former retains complete freedom for itself."[45]

The most important in all this remains the nagging problem of NATO, which stays in existence despite the end of the Cold War and the disappearance of the Warsaw Pact. Several of the former Warsaw Pact states have sought membership

---

[43] Andrei Kozyrev, "The Lagging Partnership," *Foreign Affairs*, May–June 1994, pp. 59–71 at p. 69.
[44] Georgi Arbatov, "A New Cold War?" *Foreign Policy*, summer 1994, pp. 90–103.

TABLE 2–1

RUSSIAN TROOP STRENGTH IN THE NEAR ABROAD, 1993 AND 1994

Location	Troops[1]	Tanks	Helicopters[2]	Aircraft	Missiles[3]
Armenia					
1993	5,000	90			
1994	5,000	80			
Belarus					
1993				272	
1994				130	
Georgia					
1993	20,000	21,335	35		
1994	20,000	230	35		
Kazakhstan					
1993				80	85
1994				0	0
Kyrgystan					
1993					25
1994					0
Moldova					
1993	8,000	120	10		37
1994	9,200	120	0		25
Tajikistan					
1993	8,500	200			10
1994	12,500	180			10
Turkmenistan					
1993	34,000	900	155		87
1994	28,000	900	179		75
Uzbekistan					
1993			30		45
1994			0		0

[1] In the case of Turkmenistan, troop count includes both Russian and Turkmenistani troops.
[2] Helicopter count for Georgia includes some fixed-wing aircraft.
[3] With the exceptions of 12 SCUDs in Moldova and 12 SSMs in Turkmenistan in 1993, all missiles are surface-to-air missiles for air defense.

Source: William H. Lewis, "Russia as Peacekeeper," *Problems of Post-Communism,* January–February, 1995, pp. 19–24 at p. 21. Reprinted with permission.

in NATO, and Russia has objected to their admittance. Former Foreign Minister Andrei Kozyrev wrote the following in 1995:

> In the West, many wonder why Russia is so opposed to Central European countries joining NATO since this does not constitute a threat to Russian security. Our East European counterparts have argued that for them, membership in NATO would be a psychological symbol of rejoining the Western civilization that Central and East Europe have allegedly been part of from time immemorial. But what we are dealing with is joining a military and political alliance. This fact inevitably makes the advocates of Central and East European membership in NATO seek arguments of a military and strategic nature, which in one way or another always boil down to the thesis of a threat from Russia—if not today's democratic Russia, then possibly from the imperial Russia of tomorrow. Those who champion this thesis eventually begin to believe that such a threat really does exist, although they disguise it by vague remarks concerning a "security vacuum."[46]

He concluded that "NATO's advance toward Russia's borders cannot but be seen as a continuation, though by inertia, of a policy aimed at containment of Russia."[47]

The 1995 NATO decision to bomb Serbian military depots in Bosnia accentuated this issue. Irked that NATO had ignored his pleas for moderation and then excluded him from consultation, Yeltsin renewed the call for NATO's transformation to a political institution with more reliable consultation provisions. "NATO has already shown what it is capable of. Only bombing, and then counting the trophies, of how many are killed among the civilian population." In an enlarged NATO, "When NATO approaches the borders of the Russian Federation, you can say that there will be two military blocs, and this will be a restoration of what we have already had." Such circumstances

would mean "a conflagration of war throughout Europe, for sure."[48] Despite these dire warnings, only a few days later NATO approved criteria for admitting new members. These include commitment to democracy, human rights, market economics, and civilian control of the military, mutual security in event of attack, and willingness to participate in peacekeeping outside of the NATO territories.[49]

As to the future, Russia calls for a transformation of NATO from a sixteen-member regional alliance into "a pan-European security organization and a joint instrument for the efficient response to new common challenges, such as ethnic conflicts, terrorism, proliferation of weapons of mass destruction, and drug trafficking." Only in this way, in the Russian view, can there develop across Europe a true Partnership for Peace.[50]

The Russian View of China

From time to time during the Cold War, China was high on the list of Soviet foreign policy problems. Defense of their long common border (6000 miles) was arduous and expensive. Mao's notion of peasant communism (as against proletarian socialism) and his commitment to the multiple-paths-to-socialism concept were fractious and dangerous, and these threatened to invade the Soviet Union's leadership of world communism. China's nuclear development was a potential military threat, and the principal testing site was near the Soviet border, which was considered provocative. Fitful though demonstrable growth in the Sino-Japanese trading relationship raised the specter of modern China asserting itself not only in Asia but in Eurasia, and possibly out of Manchuria into the warm-water ports on the Soviet Union's Pacific end. Each improvement between Beijing and Washington,

---

[45] Andrei Kozyrev, "The Lagging Partnership," p. 66.
[46] Andrei Kozyrev, "Partnership or Cold Peace?," *Foreign Policy*, summer 1995, pp. 3–14 at p. 12.
[47] Ibid., p. 13.

[48] As quoted in *The New York Times*, September 9, 1995, p. A5.
[49] As summarized in *The New York Times*, September 21, 1995, p. A6. See also *The New York Times*, September 29, 1995, p. A7.
[50] Andrei Kozyrev, "Partnership or Cold Peace?" pp. 13–14.

including diplomatic recognition, was seen as aggressive, because it threatened to give China access to American technology, military equipment and military intelligence. As long as China remained a regional power it was no threat to the Soviet Union, but in concert with Japan and the United States it could become rapacious.

For these reasons and more, the Soviet Union was wary of China's policies continuously from 1956 until the mid-1980s. At that time China's adoption the policy of equidistance—maintaining a safe distance from both the Soviet Union and the United States but dealing with each—diminished the Westward drift feared by the Kremlin and formed the stage onto which Gorbachev stepped when he rose to power in 1985. As part of his global diplomatic strategy, he intended to improve relations not only with the West, but with China as well. Exploratory trade talks opened in 1988, and they culminated with Gorbachev's historic 1989 visit to Beijing. This was the first visit ever made by the top-ranking Soviet official to China in the history of the Chinese revolution, and it might have had historic consequences had other events not intervened. Using the presence of the world press in Beijing to cover the Gorbachev visit, dissident Chinese students demonstrated in Tiananmen Square for freedom of the press and protested government corruption. The situation remained tense throughout Gorbachev's visit and turned violent after his departure, with the press still present to record the bloody events. Because the Chinese reaction was to turn inward and forsake at least temporarily Beijing's international goals, and because Gorbachev's policy was to align with progressive tolerance rather than repressive reactionism, the talks were temporarily and informally discontinued. In May 1991, however, before it was clear that the Soviet Union would collapse, the first-ever Sino-Soviet summit meeting was held in Moscow. The tangible result, the first in many years for the two parties, was settlement of territorial disputes and agreement on borders.

The basic progress represented in the Gorbachev visit survived the collapse of the Soviet Union, however, and pursuit of cooperation with China remained part of the new Russian foreign policy. In late 1992 Boris Yeltsin visited Beijing, and in a meeting in Moscow in 1994 the Russo-Chinese nonaggression pact was signed. Underlying Russian goals in Asia is the rapidly diminishing American military presence in the area, leaving a void that may prove dangerously tempting to China. As summarized by one observer,

> . . . detente with China is designed to maximize Russian policy leverage vis-a-vis the United States, turn Chinese policy in a desired direction, forestall the evolution of a Sino-Japanese entente, and attempt to shift Japan toward better relations with Moscow. At the very least, detente with China is designed to prevent Russia from becoming odd man out in the emerging regional structure.[51]

The resurgence of communism's popularity, growing economic discontent, and distrust of the West's motives regarding the expansion of NATO drove Russia closer to China in 1996. The most symbolic event was Moscow's agreement to provide 72 advance fighter bombers to Beijing just as tensions were rising over the question of Taiwan's future, tensions that sent two American aircraft carriers into the China straits for the first time since the Vietnam War.

Conclusion

Throughout the Cold War, the Soviet Union was forced into a variety of defensive strategies by capitalist encirclement and by Western imperialism and militarism. It was clear that international capitalism was so determined to obliterate proletarian internationalism and its leader, the Soviet Union, that all other objectives were subordinated to survival. In the Soviet Union's final years, the Communist party liberalized its ideology through *glasnost*

---

[51] Richard C. Thornton, "Chinese-Russian Relations and the Struggle for Hegemony in Northeast Asia," *Problems of Post-Communism*, January–February 1995, pp. 29–34 at p. 32.

and *perestroika* and oversaw first the collapse of the regional empire and then the disintegration of the Soviet state itself. With the Cold War receding into history, the rationale for both the empire and the communist political monopoly evaporated. The awakening of aggressive national self-conscience among the republics destroyed the class base of communist power. The squalid condition of the economy generated a widespread demand for economic reform. As the circumstances sounded the death knell of the Soviet state, fifteen republics, foremost among them the Russian Federation, reasserted their sovereign independence. Two of the foundations of the New World Order thus occurred almost simultaneously: the post–Cold War era and the post–Soviet era.

The contemporary dilemma of the Russian world view is that while Moscow seeks full partnership in the New World Order, it lacks many of the requisites. How far and how fast the new democracy and market economy will evolve is unknown, and until the signs are clearer, Soviet diplomacy is greeted with skepticism. How independent the other members of the CIS will be from Moscow is another critical issue, because any progress toward resurrecting the Soviet Union, as the parliament's communists wish, could doom Russian diplomacy. The Bosnian War revealed the military vitality of NATO, which never until then engaged in combat. How NATO and Russia would accommodate one another thus became a larger question right after the Cold War rather than a smaller one. Russia covets the prestige of a great power, but it is not one in either military or economic terms. In many ways Russia is still a backward country economically, and it is unable to play a strong role in a world order that turns on economic competition and prosperity. Finding its way in the New World Order will confront Russia with a difficult struggle, internally and externally.

CHAPTER 3

The American Perspective

Throughout most of the twentieth century, the American world view has been dominated by war or the threat of war. From the time at which neutrality and isolation were abandoned in favor of intervention on the side of Britain and France in 1917, only the decade of the 1920s provided a respite from military planning. During the 1930s there was a second flirtation with isolationism, but a string of events forced Washington to assert world leadership continuously thereafter: the rise of Adolf Hitler to power, Japan's invasion of Manchuria (China), formation of the Axis alliance (Germany, Italy, and Japan), war in Europe, and the Japanese attack on Pearl Harbor in 1941. The Allied coalition of World War Two, consisting principally of the United States, Britain, France, Russia, and (precommunist) China, won both the European and Asian wars in 1945 following the biggest industrial expansions in history. Though peace seemed to be at hand, the Cold War intervened to compel the United States to maintain its war-ready posture.

The Soviet threat in Europe was matched by the menace of China in Asia, as Mao Zedong's communist revolution succeeded in the final days of 1949 in forcing the Western-oriented nationalist government to flee to Taiwan. Only six months later Korea, divided at the thirty-eighth parallel between Russian occupation to the north and American to the south, was plunged into war by North Korean invasion. Following Western intervention on behalf of South Korea, which succeeded in pushing North Korean forces almost to China,

Mao's troops also intervened to force the allies back to approximately the original demarcation line, where an armed truce exists yet today. Although Japan was to have been disarmed after its 1945 surrender, Washington now reevaluated its geomilitary value and rearmed it as a full Cold War ally. Meanwhile, French forces were battling insurgent communists in Southeast Asia in events portending the Vietnam War.

The anticommunist zeal of the early Cold War years produced in the United States a remarkably consistent world view. This changed dramatically after the force commitments to South Vietnam in 1964. Gradually but measurably, first with the student generation and then with the public at large, opinion divided on the value of the commitment there. In this atmosphere, it became easier for many Americans to entertain a friendly picture of the Soviet or the Chinese world view than to appreciate the roles of officials in their own country. Americans divided between those who found withdrawal antihistorical and humiliating and those who condemned policies that cost so many American lives. The Watergate scandal that forced Richard M. Nixon from the presidency accentuated loss of confidence in government. A radical left emerged as a powerful force in reckoning American foreign policy. With the help of revisionist historians, many centrists became skeptical of the orthodox interpretation of the Cold War and its origins.

Ironically, it was the endgame of the Cold War, from 1985 to 1990, that reversed this trend. Using an image of Soviet strength that is now known to have been inaccurate, Ronald Reagan persuaded Americans of the need to multiply defense systems and to exploit new technologies as much as possible to offset Soviet gains. Part of the persuasion was a combination of income tax reductions and special tax increases that improved the standard of living and reduced unemployment, but which could not cover the cost of the arms program. The national debt tripled. Nevertheless, the Cold War ended in what most Americans considered their victory. The conservative wave hastened on, aimed now at retaining unequaled military strength with both tax and deficit reductions. The long-promised "peace dividend" vanished into realization that the policy of the 1980s had left the immensely powerful United States a debtor nation, faced with a national debt that costs more than 20 cents on every federal tax dollar to service annually.

As we have seen, the passing of the Cold War and the disintegration of the Soviet Union occurred simultaneously. Although it is a gross oversimplification, one reason for the latter was that in the absence of intractible Cold War confrontation, there was no longer a rationale for Soviet military dominance of Eastern Europe or of rigid domestic political controls. For analogous reasons, the American world view now struggles with the question, "Whither United States foreign policy?" in the unfamiliar circumstance of being the sole superpower in a world with no enemy.

Roots of the American World View

Whereas Marxism begins with a theory of class conflict and revolution, the American traditional world view evolves from questions of political freedom and tyranny. Freedom—understood as self-determination, majority rule, and the right of dissent—is the highest goal in the hierarchy of core values. "Give me liberty or give me death," demanded Patrick Henry. When Americans evaluate other social systems, their concern turns first to the degree of freedom of speech, press, and religion, the

right to vote, and tolerance of dissent, and only secondarily to economic well-being and questions of economic justice.

The relative unconcern of Americans for class injustices has been credited to the lack of a feudal experience. Absentee landlordism and other abuses of feudalism left in many other countries a bitter heritage of class conflict, which was much less pronounced here.[1] The promise of open land beyond the frontier before 1900 made America a land of opportunity where wealth was the direct reward for hard work and poverty the punishment for laziness.[2] Early settlers in the New World sought not class revolution but religious tolerance (for example, Puritans and Mennonites) and economic opportunity. Capitalism itself demanded a free market, entrepreneurial liberty, and political self-determination, at least for the commercial classes.

These origins were consistent with the evolution of a philosophy of the social contract. In this theory, the state is constituted by freely consenting individuals to protect the security and advance the common interests of society. Government "derives its just powers from the consent of the governed," in Thomas Jefferson's words. Revolution is justified not in terms of class upheaval but as a legitimate response to political tyranny.

The principal danger to liberty is the inherent tendency of government to expand without limitation and to extinguish the rights of citizens. "Power corrupts, and absolute power corrupts absolutely." Tyranny is averted and governmental power limited in the United States by constitutional restraints, majority rule, guaranteed minority rights, checks and balances among 80,000 separately elected governmental units, and the separation of executive, legislative, and judicial powers. Power is at every point balanced against power: civilian control of the military, judicial oversight of the constitutionality

---

[1] The importance of a nonfeudal past is explored in Louis Hartz, *The Liberal Tradition in America* (New York: Harcourt Brace and World, 1955).

[2] The significance of the frontier is explored in Frederick Jackson Turner, *The Frontier in American History* (New York: Henry A. Holt, 1920). See also David Potter, *People of Plenty* (Chicago: University of Chicago Press, 1954).

of legislative and executive actions, state versus federal authority, direct election of high officials, and other checks. The obsession of the entire design is eternal vigilance against despotism.

The American Image of International Relations

The problem of defending freedom against tyranny exists in international relations as well. The parallel to individual freedom in international society is the principle of national independence and self-determination, and the parallel to infringement of individual rights is the violation of territorial sovereignty and foreign interference in the internal affairs of a free nation. International freedom is threatened when one nation or coalition undertakes to extend its power to dominate others. Both domestically and internationally, injustice begins when one power center upsets the natural balance of forces and seeks an unwarranted expansion.

Historically, internal and external tyranny have been linked in the American view. Democratic governments and free peoples are thought to be naturally peace loving, whereas tyrannies and dictatorships have an innate tendency to expand beyond their own borders to make demands on their neighbors. An unchecked tyranny in one country is soon a danger to the entire world.

The Image of the Aggressor

The image of the International Aggressor is an important component of the American belief system. The Aggressor is a bully who employs military threats and actions to subdue weaker states and to seize from them any assets he wishes. He is immune to normal considerations of justice and regards international law and morality as mere sentimentality. His appetite for expansion is insatiable, especially when motivated by a messianic ideology, and success in one conquest does not appease him but whets his appetite for more. He is cunning in the use of propaganda to conceal his intentions, and he regards agreements and treaties as mere expedients rather than obligations.

The only restraint that the Aggressor respects is physical opposition. If the world is to be ruled by reason and not by force, and if weak members of the international community are not to be left at the mercy of the strong, it is the special responsibility of the larger democratic states to oppose international lawlessness. The United States in particular is obligated by its vast resources and its historic ideals to play a role of leadership in guaranteeing minimum standards of international behavior. Thus the dominant theme of twentieth-century American diplomatic history has been the search for an appropriate role, one in which to pursue a law-based and humane world order while staying within the democratic limits of power.

Aggression and World War One

Before the First World War, the United States was relatively uninvolved on the world stage. Although potentially powerful, it was insulated from foreign conflicts by vast oceans on both shores, and the dominant position of the United States in the Western Hemisphere ensured safety within this zone. Moreover, the global system from 1815 until 1914 was relatively stable and rarely called for American military participation. The major European states that dominated the world system pursued essentially conservative policies of maintaining the status quo (although redistributive goals were pursued in relation to colonial issues), and the security of American interests was hardly affected by the tides of world politics.

American foreign policy during this period had three cornerstones:

1. **Isolationism:** nonentanglement in the complex web of European military alliances and intrigues, perceived as having little consequence for Americans.

2. **The Monroe Doctrine:** an insistence on European nonintervention in the Western Hemisphere, in effect declaring Latin America as the United States' sphere of influence.

3. **Commercial expansion:** full participation in free international trade and access to world markets while avoiding foreign conflicts.

In general, these principles asserted for the United States a major role as a world economic actor but a minor role in world political and military affairs.

This relatively harmonious world was thoroughly upset in 1914 by the outbreak of the First World War. For the first time since 1815, a major power seemed bent on fundamental redistribution and alteration of the European balance, with vast consequences for the rest of the world. The United States, protected by geographic position from the main issues and confused by the morass of charges and countercharges, claims and counterclaims, stayed out of the war for three years.

But as the war progressed, America's early neutrality yielded to growing hostility toward Germany and an increasing sympathy to the Allies, especially Britain. Ties of language and custom with England, as well as strong commercial links, made true neutrality impossible. Moreover, the struggle was increasingly viewed as a deeply moral issue of democracy and decency (England) versus dictatorship and barbarism (Germany). This image of the German Aggressor was promoted by British propaganda and adopted by President Woodrow Wilson to build public support for entry into the war. When German submarines began sinking American commercial vessels with civilian passengers aboard, American opinion was enraged, and the image of the Aggressor was driven deep into the public consciousness. President Wilson's memorable war message on April 2, 1917, spoke directly to the key themes in the image. The war was caused by an attempt at territorial expansion by tyrants.

> We have no quarrel with the German people. . . . It was not upon their impulse that their government acted. . . . It was a war determined as wars used to be determined upon in the old, unhappy days when peoples were nowhere consulted by their rulers and wars were provoked and waged in the interest of dynasties or of little groups of ambitious men who were accustomed to use their fellow men as pawns or tools.

The United States had tried to stand apart, Wilson declared, but had discovered to its sorrow that it could not escape the responsibility to oppose massive aggression.

> A steadfast concern for peace can never be maintained except by a partnership of democratic nations. We are glad . . . to fight thus for the ultimate peace of the world and for the liberation of its peoples, the German peoples included; for the rights of nations great and small and the privilege of men everywhere to choose their own way of life and of obedience. . . . America is privileged to spend her blood and her might for the principles that gave her birth and happiness and the peace which she has treasured. . . . The world must be made safe for democracy.[3]

The United States would fight not for narrow national interests, but for the restoration of an international system based on principles of justice and nonaggression. This break with historic isolationism signified for the United States the beginning of an active role in the defense of Western democracy.

For the United States, post-war stability could not be maintained without redesigning the German political order. The Weimar Constitution, which was drafted largely by Americans and which borrowed heavily from Anglo-American constitutional experience, projected for Germany a model democratic system eliminating all traces of autocratic rule. Combined with a compulsory program of disarmament and industrial limitation, it seemed to guarantee that Germany would never again attempt aggressive expansion.

On the international level, the Wilsonian goal was systematic guarantees against future threats to stability. The idea of collective security was founded in the institutional form of the League of

---

[3] Woodrow Wilson, War Message, 65th Cong., 1st sess., Senate document no. 5 (Washington, D.C.: U.S. Government Printing Office, 1971), pp. 3–8.

CIVILIZATION

BOLSHEVISM

"On the Threshold!" (*Source:* © Los Angeles Times. Reprinted by permission. "On the Threshold" by Paul Conrad)

Nations (precursor to the United Nations). In effect, this modeled future international relations on the principle of an alliance of major powers permanently committed to oppose aggression. Unfortunately, the League had little success in fulfilling these goals when new threats to international peace developed. Domestic political opposition and a resurgence of isolationism prevented the United States from actively supporting the League in the way that Wilson had envisioned. Moreover, the major powers were not, in most cases, able to agree on joint policy toward expansionary movements, and it became clear that opposition to aggression on grounds of principle was less important to most leaders than was the pursuit of more narrowly

conceived national interests. The dream of collective security evaporated, and international relations reverted to the more familiar pattern of power politics from which, in fact, it had never varied.

Aggression and the Second World War

Within seventeen years of victory in the Great War, three new Aggressors moved to subdue new victims. First, militant Japan seized control of China's crucial Manchurian industrial region in 1931, and in 1937 extended its movement with an eye to the total conquest of China. Second, in 1933, Adolf Hitler used the ill-conceived emergency powers clause of the Weimar Constitution to over-throw the German Republic and establish the fa-natical and aggressive Third Reich dictatorship, and in 1935 he militarized the Rhineland in prepa-ration for war. Third, in 1935, Benito Mussolini led Fascist Italy into a war of conquest in Ethiopia. The stage was set for war on three continents—Europe, Africa, and Asia—as well as throughout the Pacific Ocean.

President Franklin D. Roosevelt warned the American people in 1937 that "the epidemic of world lawlessness is spreading," but Americans re-mained firmly isolationist. Reluctance to get in-volved was based on retrospective doubts about the First World War, including scandalous revelations about the activities of munitions profiteers and British propagandists in promoting the earlier war policy. A January 1937 poll showed that 64 percent of Americans questioned thought that it had been a mistake to enter the previous war. Many Ameri-cans resolved not to be trumpeted into foreign troubles a second time. The Neutrality Act of 1937 formalized this attitude in law.

Critical events in the deepening European cri-sis began in 1938. The German Anschluss absorbed Austria into Germany, and Hitler demanded that Czechoslovakia surrender the Sudetenland on the ground that its population was German speaking. Hitler and Mussolini agreed to a big-power crisis conference in the fall with representatives of Britain and France (but not of the Soviet Union). At Munich the democratic leaders took Hitler at his word that he would make no further demands if given the Sudetenland, and the Allies abandoned Czechoslovakia to its fate. Prime Minister Neville Chamberlain returned to London with the wishful declaration that he had achieved "peace in our time," on the grounds of Hitler's promise that this was "the last territorial claim which I have to make in Europe." These are now remembered as some of the most tragic statements in diplomatic history. The Munich sellout is universally cited as a classic case of appeasing an aggressor. Hitler quickly ab-sorbed the remains of Czechoslovakia and went on to Poland, finally triggering British and French

resistance. The last chance to stop Hitler had been lost, and Soviet fears were stoked that the Allies had conspired to turn Hitler east at Soviet ex-pense, a perception that led to the infamous Hitler-Stalin nonaggression pact that temporarily took Russia out of the antifascist alliance. Ameri-cans took from this bitter experience a deep skep-ticism about appeasers who would compromise with aggressors (a practice subsequently known as "Munich-mindedness").

Roosevelt warned Americans that "enduring peace cannot be bought at the cost of other peo-ple's freedom." What was truly at issue was the abil-ity of a tyrannical movement to commit aggression against other people at will. In an attempt to bring the war home and awaken Americans to future dangers to their security and their way of life, he warned that

> During sixteen long months this assault has blotted out the whole pattern of democratic life in an appalling number of independent nations, great and small. The assailants are still on the march, threat-ening other nations, great and small.[4]

Only after Japan's surprise attack on the Amer-ican naval and air base at Pearl Harbor, Hawaii, on December 7, 1941, did Americans abandon isola-tionism. Japan's purpose was to immobilize Ameri-can defenses against Japanese seizures of American, British, and Dutch possessions in the Far East, but many Americans perceived it as a threat to Hawaii and even California. An enraged public gave over-whelming support to a declaration of war against Germany as well as Japan. Once in the war, broad principles of an allied defense against aggression took precedence over purely national concerns. For example, a frequent poll question during the war was, "If Hitler offered peace now to all countries on the basis of not going further but of leaving matters as they now are, would you favor or oppose such a peace?" Support for peace on these terms was generally below 20 percent. In many concrete ways, American war conduct manifested a broad

---

[4] *Congressional Record*, vol. 87, January 6, 1941, p. 46.

commitment to principles of nonaggression and universal self-determination, rather than a pure concern with American self-interest.

Following the war, the United States and its allies once again set about to secure the future international system. The German and Japanese political systems were redesigned by occupation authorities along modern democratic principles, and the United Nations was founded to reestablish the machinery of collective security that had failed in the League of Nations. The extreme American view called for establishing world government with central control of armed forces, including those of the United States. The United States joined the United Nations immediately as a permanent member of the Security Council and was from the beginning one of its most ardent supporters.

The fundamental shift in American policy, then, was a strategic reorientation from isolationism to a permanent commitment to world responsibilities. This was taken as an inescapable duty of the world's strongest democracy. Moreover, it was now accepted that the interests of world stability and American security would be served best by involvement rather than by isolation. The problem has always been the extent of the involvement. How does a democratic foreign policy fulfill its leadership in a world threatened with tyranny without becoming tyrannical itself? How much involvement is enough? When is intervention appropriate and when is it not? When is it in the national interest and when is it not? Where does one draw the line between global leadership and arbitrary, self-serving policy? Where does leadership become aggression? Should a leader be a "world policeman"? The urgency of all these questions was redoubled when millions of Americans disassociated themselves from their government's foreign policy in the Vietnam War.

The unique innocence Americans brought to international politics has been a liability as well as an advantage. An optimistic people tends to reduce burdensome complexities to simplistic explanations and easy formulas, and Americans have often compressed their understanding of difficult issues into purified political and moral principles. Not every conflict can be understood as a struggle between good and evil. In particular, the tendency to interpret the motivations of all adversaries through the lens of the Aggressor theory may distort reality and lead to false solutions. This is especially dangerous when America's response is founded on the antiappeasement principle of countering perceived aggression by a strong willingness to use force. The twin problems of accurately defining threats to the peace and formulating appropriate American responses reached an acute stage as the post-war world order degenerated into the Cold War. The debate over the proper content of pax Americana became the driving force of United States foreign policy and of the American world view for forty-five years.

Origins of the Cold War

Almost immediately upon cessation of hostilities in 1945 the United States and the Soviet Union ceased to be allies and became locked in a struggle for political mastery of Europe, Asia, and the world. There are profound differences of opinion among informed Americans about the origins of the Cold War, and alternative interpretations greatly affect the understanding of many other issues.[5]

Although the wartime alliance with Moscow had been a matter of necessity against a background

---

[5] Studies of the origins of the Cold War abound. Among the most thorough full-length studies that represent a spectrum of viewpoints ranging from strongly pro-American to equally strongly critical of the United States are these: Herbert Feis, *From Trust to Terror* (New York: Norton, 1970); Denna F. Fleming, *The Cold War and Its Origins* (Garden City, N.Y.: Doubleday, 1961), two vols.; John Lewis Gaddis, *The United States and the Origins of the Cold War* (New York: Columbia University Press, 1972); David Horowitz, *Free World Colossus* (New York: Hill and Wang, 1965); Vojtech Mastny, *Russia's Road to the Cold War* (New York: Columbia University Press, 1979); Hugh Seton-Watson, *Neither Peace nor War* (New York: Praeger, 1960); Martin J. Sherwin, *A World Destroyed* (New York: Random House, 1973); Ronald Steele, *Pax Americana* (New York: Viking, 1967); and Daniel Yergin, *Shattered Peace* (Boston: Houghton Mifflin, 1977).

of intense hatred of Stalinism, Americans entered the post-war era with a deep ambivalence. On the one hand, they had gained respect for the Soviet people in their extremely costly struggle against fascism. Out of this developed the notion of a "grand alliance" in which wartime cooperation would spill over into the post-war world and Washington and Moscow together would ensure peace. On the other hand, however, Americans had a deep-seated suspicion of the Soviet government. Stalin's purges of the 1930s, his reputation for bloodthirsty oppression, and the hated Hitler-Stalin nonaggression pact all made for a wary American public on the subject of post-war collaboration.

Planning for the United Nations began as early as 1943, and the agreements for post-war occupations were made at the Teheran, Yalta, and Potsdam Conferences in 1945. (The Soviet Union joined the war against Japan only in the final few days, yet subsequently made large territorial demands.) For Europe, three Big Powers—the United States, the USSR, and Britain—agreed on several essentials. The Nazi war machine would be destroyed by Soviet armies moving from the east and American and British forces moving from the west. Temporarily, each of the Allies would be responsible for establishing civil order in the territories liberated by its forces, pending the assumed restoration of self-determination and free elections. Eventually, the occupation forces would withdraw, and the liberated nations would resume independent lives.

It was understood realistically that after two world wars, the Soviets could not agree to have potentially hostile alliances along their borders again and that the new East European governments would have to respect this principle in their foreign affairs. An informal understanding provided this formula to guide political development during the transitional period:

Romania	90 percent Soviet
Bulgaria	80 percent Soviet
Hungary	50/50 Soviet/West
Yugoslavia	50/50 Soviet/West
Greece	90 percent British

In addition, the Soviet Union wold not participate in the liberated Western European countries including France and Italy, but security imperatives would give the Soviets considerable influence in Poland and Czechoslovakia. Germany, the most serious problem, would be divided into four zones—under American, Soviet, British and French control—disarmed, and eventually reunified after pacification and political reconstruction. Additional understandings applied to Korea, Japan, and other countries and to the United Nations.

Unexpectedly, the Soviets left the Red armies permanently in control of the Eastern European states, creating a satellite chain linked by virtual puppet governments. Americans were outraged by the naked use of Soviet power to create colonies. In Poland, for example, the Soviets shocked world opinion by abetting in the extermination of antifascist but noncommunist freedom fighters and putting in their place an all-communist government reporting directly to Moscow. In Czechoslovakia, a democratic coalition of communists and noncommunist leftist parties was destroyed by a Moscow-ordered communist coup. In Germany, the Soviet zone of occupation was converted into a permanent puppet state, and the agreed goal of reunification was scuttled. The idea of free elections was forgotten. "Across Europe," Winston Churchill declared to the American people at Fulton, Missouri, in 1946,

> from Stettin in the Baltic to Trieste in the Adriatic, an Iron Curtain has descended across the continent. Behind that line lie all the capitals of the ancient states of central and eastern Europe. Warsaw, Berlin, Prague, Vienna, Budapest, Belgrade, Bucharest, and Sofia, all these famous cities and populations around them. . . . The Communist parties, which were very small in all these eastern states of Europe, have been raised to prominence and power far beyond their

numbers and are seeking everywhere to obtain totalitarian control. Police governments are prevailing in nearly every case.[6]

Even more alarming was the perceived Soviet effort to push this Iron Curtain forward. Subversive activities were encouraged in France and Italy; claims were advanced against Iran; the communist-controlled Viet Minh moved against French control in Indochina; threats were made against Turkey; and an insurgent movement was mounted in Malaya. In China, the communists reopened their struggle against the Western-oriented Kuomintang government. Throughout the world, insurgent parties fomented disorder and revolution in the name of communism. Many in the West concluded that the USSR sought not just security on its frontiers but expansion everywhere, and possibly even mastery of the earth.[7]

The Truman Doctrine

The case that finally produced a crisis atmosphere in Washington was that of Greece. There, the retreating Germans had destroyed railways, ports, bridges, communications facilities, and the network of orderly civil administration. More than a thousand villages had been burned. By 1947 a majority of children tested were tubercular. In this atmosphere, rival communist and monarchist factions of the former antifascist resistance were locked in civil war. It was widely believed in Washington that Stalin had unleashed the insurgents and that Soviet arms were flowing freely to them in violation of the understanding that Greece was to be under Western influence.

This crisis had special significance for the assessment of Soviet intentions. If indeed this were a Soviet move against Greece, Russian expansionary goals evidently included political issues quite remote from critical zones of national defense. Stalin

seemed to have in mind ambitious plans for the destruction of capitalism, in disregard of his agreements. On the other hand, some continued to see the Soviet Union as pursuing essentially defensive goals or, at worst, regional expansion along the familiar lines of tsarist imperialism, rather than a truly global power grab in the name of communism. A great debate about Soviet motives and a search for the wisest response began in the United States.

The dominant school of thought, given its classic expression in the "containment" philosophy of diplomat and scholar George Kennan, was that Soviet policy served ideological imperatives demanding global struggle and opposition to capitalism. He explained:

> Of the original ideology, nothing has been officially junked.... The first ... concept is the innate antagonism between capitalism and socialism.... It means that there can never be on Moscow's side any sincere assumption of a community of aims between the Soviet Union and powers which are regarded as capitalist.

The responsibility to oppose this policy of limitless conflict fell to the United States, which, Kennan said, must base its actions on the principle of containing Soviet power within its existing boundaries until internal changes within the Soviet leadership produced an abandonment of aggressive intentions.

> The Soviet pressure against the free institutions of the Western World is something that can be contained by the adroit and vigilant application of counterforce at a series of constantly shifting geographical and political points, corresponding to the shifts and maneuvres of Soviet policy.[8]

This point of view was shared by President Harry S Truman, who incorporated it in his enunciation of the Truman Doctrine in March 1947. His speech likened communist aggression to the Nazi aggression that preceded it: The "fundamental

---

[6] *The New York Times*, March 6, 1946, p. 4.

[7] See, for example, Elliot Goodman, *The Soviet Design for a World State* (New York: Columbia University Press, 1960).

[8] George Kennan (writing under the pseudonym "Mr. X"), "The Sources of Soviet Conduct," *Foreign Affairs*, July 1947.

issue" in the war with Germany and Japan had been "the creation of conditions in which . . . nations . . . will be able to work out a way of life free from coercion." Now, once again, we had to be "willing to help free people to maintain their free institutions and their national integrity against aggressive movements that seek to impose upon them totalitarian regimes." Note the themes of aggressive dictatorship versus peaceful democracy in the following passage from Truman's address:

> The peoples of a number of countries of the world have recently had totalitarian regimes forced upon them against their will. . . . At the present moment in world history nearly every nation must choose between alternative ways of life. The choice is too often not a free one.
>
> One way of life is based upon the will of the majority, and is distinguished by free institutions, representative government, free elections, guarantees of individual liberty, freedom of speech and religion and freedom from political oppression.
>
> The second way of life is based upon the will of a minority forcibly imposed upon the majority. It relies upon terror and oppression, a controlled press and radio, fixed elections and the suppression of personal freedom.
>
> I believe that it must be the policy of the United States to support peoples who are resisting attempted subjugation by armed minorities or by outside pressures.
>
> I believe that we must assist free peoples to work out their own destinies in their own way.[9]

Note also that the United States will "support peoples who are resisting attempted subjugation by armed minorities." This suggests intervention against aggression even when the rebels are nationals of the same country, blurring the distinction between international aggression and civil war.

The Truman-Kennan perspective was not universally accepted. The "realist" school, headed by

Hans Morgenthau, accused it of sentimentalism and moralism. The containment strategy was justified not by national interest, but by confusing national interests with universally applicable moral principles.

> As a guide to political action, it is the victim, as all moral principles must be, of two congenital political weaknesses: the inability to distinguish between what is desirable and what is possible, and the inability to distinguish between what is desirable and what is essential.[10]

Journalist Walter Lippmann, another realist, called the Truman Doctrine "a strategic monstrosity" that could not succeed in changing the situation in Eastern Europe. "No state in Eastern Europe can be independent of the Kremlin as long as the Red Army is within it and around it," he wrote. And the Red army would remain as long as Russia was threatened with hostile encirclement across the military line of division in Western Europe. "The presence of these non-European armies in the continent of Europe perpetuates the division," he continued. The wise course of American response would be to offer the Soviets a mutual withdrawal, U.S. forces to leave the Western sector and Soviet forces to return to the USSR. "If the Red Army is in Russia, and not on the Elbe . . . the power of the Russian imperialists to realize their ambitions will have been reduced decisively." The containment policy was seen as having exactly the opposite effect and therefore was an incorrect response to Soviet expansion.[11]

The "liberation" school of dissenters, headed by John Foster Dulles, who later became secretary of state to Republican President Dwight D. Eisenhower, took a position opposite to the realists.

---

[9] *Congressional Record*, vol. 93, March 12, 1947, pp. 1999–2000.

[10] Hans J. Morgenthau, *In Defense of the National Interest* (New York: Knopf, 1950), pp. 120–121.

[11] Walter Lippmann, *The Cold War* (New York: Harper and Row, 1947), p. 61. See also Ronald Steel, *Walter Lippmann and the American Century* (Boston: Atlantic-Little, Brown, 1980), chapter 34.

Dulles objected that containment was a passive policy that always left open the question, "Which of us will be the next victim?" It projected for the United States a static political role, allowing the Kremlin to determine the place and terms of conflict. It is a law of history that "the dynamic prevails over the static," and the correct response to Soviet imperialism was not mere defense but an active offense. We could not just contain communism at its present boundaries but had to carry the struggle across the Iron Curtain to pursue the liberation of captive nations that had already fallen to Soviet imperialism.[12]

A third school of dissent was the "dove school." Climaxing in the unsuccessful 1948 presidential drive of former Secretary of Agriculture Henry A. Wallace, the doves argued that the containment policy itself endangered peace and provoked the very Soviet posture that it deplored. He advocated cooperation in the United Nations rather than a worldwide anticommunist military crusade. He predicted that containment would force the United States to support dictators everywhere in the name of defense: "Every fascist dictator will know that he has money in our bank. . . . Freedom, in whose name Americans have died, will become a catchword for reaction."[13]

A similar view was argued by Robert A. Taft, the leading conservative of the time, who objected to the North Atlantic Alliance as "a treaty by which one nation undertakes to arm half the world against the other half," and predicted that "this treaty . . . means inevitably an arms race." Taft, like the doves, feared that "if Russia sees itself ringed gradually by so-called defensive arms, from Norway and Denmark to Turkey and Greece

. . . it may decide that the arming of Europe, regardless of its present purpose, looks like an attack upon Russia."[14]

Despite this dissent from all ideological quarters, the majority of Americans adopted President Truman's hard line. A Gallup poll asked, "As you hear and read about Russia these days, do you believe Russia is trying to build herself up to be the ruling power of the world, or do you think Russia is just building up protection against being attacked in another way?" In June 1946, just after Churchill's Iron Curtain speech, 58 percent favored the "ruling power" interpretation, as opposed to 29 percent for the "protection" interpretation. By November 1950, after the adoption of the Truman Doctrine and the onset of the Korean War, 81 percent favored the "ruling power" theory, as opposed to only 9 percent for the "protection" theory. In January 1948, 83 percent of Americans favored stopping all trade with Russia. The ratification of the NATO pact "to stop Soviet expansionism" was endorsed by 67 percent. Late in 1954, *Time* magazine defined the communist idea of coexistence as "a period of deceptive docility while gathering strength for a new assault." Clearly, the great debate had been won by the containment theorists.[15]

Hostility deepened after the promulgation of the Truman Doctrine and the establishment of the North Atlantic Treaty Organization. A constant stream of negative headlines concerning events in the communist world reinforced and strengthened the convictions of the containment model. The Soviets suppressed liberalization movements in East Germany in 1953, in Hungary in 1956, and in Czechoslovakia in 1968, to mention only the large-scale coercive actions. Oppression against captive peoples was also perceived in China's forcible annexation of Tibet and Soviet

---

[12] John Foster Dulles, "A Policy of Liberation," *Life*, May 19, 1952, pp. 147–148. See also Townsend Hoopes, *The Devil and John Foster Dulles* (Boston: Atlantic-Little, Brown, 1973), chapter 13.

[13] Speech by Henry A. Wallace at Madison Square Garden, New York City, on March 31, 1947, printed in *Congressional Record*, 80th Cong., 1st sess., appendix, pp. A1572—A1573.

[14] Speech by Robert A. Taft, *Congressional Record*, 81st Cong., 1st sess., pp. 9208–9210.

[15] *Time*, November 8, 1954.

policy toward non-Russian minorities within the USSR. These negative impressions were confirmed by millions of refugees who voted with their feet by fleeing communism to the Free World. Three million left East Germany for the West (prompting the construction of the Berlin Wall by the Communists); 180,000 left Hungary in 1956; and 500,000 came to the United States from Cuba. Even relatives of the ruling elite, including Josef Stalin's own daughter and Fidel Castro's sister, defected to the democratic world. To the majority of Americans these signs were the tip of an iceberg of repression. Communists retained power, it was thought, only by the massive use of police coercion.

Imperialism in the Cold War

In addition to political repression, Americans saw the Soviet Union impose a system of economic imperialism on its captive nations. While the United States poured billions of dollars in Marshall Plan aid into the devastated economies of former allies and enemies, restoring Europe and Japan to economic health, the Soviet Union milked approximately $20 billion out of its zone of occupation, through four devices:

1. Billions of dollars in war reparations were assessed against East Germany, Hungary, and Romania.
2. A special price system was imposed for trade within the communist bloc, characterized by high prices for Soviet goods and low prices for exports by satellite nations. One result was losses to Poland of about $500 million in discounted coal exports to the USSR between 1946 and 1956.
3. Joint stock companies were established as a highly exploitive form of Soviet foreign investment in East European economies. Former German firms were expropriated by Russia under the Administration for Soviet Property Abroad, and their value was counted as Moscow's investment against which fair

returns to Russia were calculated. Joint stock companies of this and other types transferred additional billions of dollars in value to the USSR.
4. Interdependence of production was forced on the satellite economies, restricting their trade with the West and giving priority to Soviet deliveries. Raw-material dependency is illustrated by the case of Poland, which, in 1957, imported from the USSR 100 percent of its oil, 70 percent of its iron ore, 78 percent of its nickel, and 67 percent of its cotton. From 1945 through 1956, exploitation of Eastern Europe was ruthless; economic relations were more nearly equal after 1956.[16]

For their part, Americans stoutly defended their economic system against Soviet charges of worldwide imperialism. Marxism-Leninism argues that imperialism is necesarily part of mature capitalism, because capitalism can only survive through exploitation of foreign markets, excess profits from overseas investments, and controlled access to foreign supplies of raw materials. Exploitation, it argues, is at its worst in the developing economies where profits are greatest and controls easiest to impose. From Moscow's perspective, all of America's Cold War foreign policy was imperialism disguised as fear of communist expansion. Orthodox capitalism responded to these charges in the following ways:

1. **Profits from foreign investments are not higher than for domestic investments.** Throughout most of the Cold War, return on domestic manufacturing investments were actually higher, making the Soviet claim statistically false.
2. **American capitalism does not depend on foreign markets.** In most industries, exports rarely

---

16 Zbigniew Brzezinski, *The Soviet Bloc* (Cambridge, Mass.: Harvard University Press, 1967), pp. 124–128, 282—287, and 376. See also Paul Marer, "The Political Economy of Soviet Relations with Comecon," in Steven Rosen and James Kurth, eds., *Testing the Theory of Economic Imperialism* (Lexington, Mass.: D. C. Heath, 1974).

exceed 10 percent of total sales. Computers, aero-space, and farm machinery are notable exceptions.

3. **American capitalism does not depend on exploitation of the Developing World.** Except for arms sales, developing economies are declining markets for American goods. Furthermore, because of both economic vitality and political stability, the industrial economies are more profitable places for American investments.

4. **There is no clearly defined capitalist ruling class in America.** Small businesses command much of the national means of production. Moreover, ownership of even the largest corporations is widely dispersed among more than 140 million stockholders, many of them through pension plans or insurance companies rather than individual holdings. In this sense the United States has achieved a unique "people's capitalism" that lacks the concentration claimed by Marxism-Leninism.

5. **Economic interests do not determine United States foreign policy.** Security interests and ideological principles, rather than economic profit, form the cornerstone of foreign policy. This was particularly the case during the Cold War, when the fear of Soviet military expansionism dominated most foreign policy debate.[17]

6. **The count of American bank branches abroad, even in the Developing Nations, is a valueless exercise.** First, international banking is not dominated by the United States. Of the world's top fifty commercial banks, only four are American and only one of them ranked higher in total assets than thirty-seventh in 1989 (Citicorp of New York ranked twelfth). Even the Beijing-based Bank of China ranked twenty-sixth, higher than all American banks other than Citicorp.[18] Second, while some American banks have much money abroad, they have suffered great losses through the inability of the Developing Nations to service their debt. By

1990, for example, under the Brady Plan for debt discounting in the most progressive developing economies, many American banks transferred current reserves into special accounts to offset imminent losses. These transfers totaled in the billions of dollars.

7. **American direct and portfolio investment abroad is no measure of imperialism unless it is matched to foreign investment in the United States.** By this more revealing measure, the United States is less imperialist than imperialized. In 1990, for example, the net foreign investment position of the United States—that is, value of American investments abroad as against value of foreign investments in the United States—was in deficit by almost $600 billion.

8. **The Vietnam War cannot be explained as economic imperialism.** Natural resources and market value cannot possibly repay the costs of the Vietnam War to the United States. The rice, tungsten, teak, and small offshore oil reserves of Southeast Asia are of relatively minor value. And the stock market averages that Marxism-Leninism would have predicted to rise during the war actually fell. The Vietnam War was not good for business.

From the American perspective, then, Marxist-Leninist charges of global imperialism were nothing but antiquated ideological rhetoric, while there was hard evidence of the Soviet imperial exploitation of its allies.

The Continuity of Policy: Korea and Vietnam

For forty-five years, American policy remained firm and unvarying in its opposition to communist aggression, both real and threatened. Isolationist impulses were suppressed, and the most extensive commitments ever undertaken by a single power were honored. The essential continuity of the policy can be seen in a comparison of statements in

---

[17] Robert W. Tucker, *The Radical Left and American Foreign Policy* (Baltimore: The Johns Hopkins University Press, 1971), especially pp. 124–138.

[18] *Fortune*, July 31, 1989, p. 286.

the Korean and Vietnam wars, separated by a span of 20 years.

In 1951, President Truman explained the problem in Korea in bleak terms. "The Communists in the Kremlin are engaged in a monstrous conspiracy to stamp out freedom all over the world," he said. "The whole Communist imperialism is back of the attack on peace in the Far East." He explained the American response to the North Korean invasion of South Korea as a product of lessons from Japan's invasion of Manchuria more than twenty years earlier.

> In the simplest terms, what we are trying to do in Korea is this: we are trying to prevent a third world war. . . . If [the Free World] had followed the right policies in the 1930's—if the free countries had acted together to crush the aggression of the dictators, and if they had acted in the beginning, when the aggression was small—there probably would have been no World War II. If history taught us anything, it is that aggression anywhere in the world is a threat to peace everywhere in the world.[19]

Strikingly parallel themes were later used to explain the necessity for American military intervention in Vietnam. A 1965 State Department White Paper portrayed that struggle as a typical attempt at communist aggression:

> South Vietnam is fighting for its life against a brutal campaign of terror and armed attack inspired, directed, supplied, and controlled by the Communist regime in Hanoi. . . . Aggression has been loosed against an independent people who want to make their way in peace and freedom.[20]

President Richard M. Nixon said in 1969:

> If Hanoi were to succeed in taking over South Vietnam by force—even after the power of the

United States had been engaged—it would greatly strengthen those leaders who scorn negotiation, who advocate aggression, who minimize the risks of confrontation. It would bring peace now, but it would enormously increase the danger of a bigger war later.[21]

In both wars American policy was based on four basic propositions: (1) that conflict is due to communist aggression against the Free World; (2) that communist expansion cannot be appeased and must be stopped by force, if necessary; (3) that as leader of the Free World, the United States is obligated to serve as a counterweight to communist aggression; and (4) that fighting a small war now will prevent a larger one later. This was the stern formulation of American foreign policy ideals from 1947 to approximately 1970.

America's Post-Vietnam World View

The withdrawal of American troops from Vietnam in 1973 signaled the end of an age of U.S. foreign policy. Abandonment by the Nixon administration of the costly anticommunist crusade in Asia gave larger meaning to the event: The United States was engaged in a major reassessment of its foreign commitments, its place in the international system, and the means that it would invoke henceforth to influence significant international events. It seems irrational that the immense investment of lives, resources, and political fortunes (the war destroyed President Lyndon B. Johnson's public life) in Vietnam in the name of freedom should suddenly have been overturned in favor of a unilateral withdrawal that would inevitably lead to reunification of the two Vietnams under a communist flag. Such a decision could have been made only in the context of other changes in the American world view. In fact,

---

[19] *The New York Times*, April 17, 1951.
[20] U.S. Department of State, *Aggression from the North: The Record of North Vietnam's Campaign to Conquer South Vietnam* (Washington, D.C.: U.S. Government Printing Office, 1965).

[21] "Address to the Nation on Vietnam," May 14, 1969. See *The Public Papers of the Presidents of the United States: Richard M. Nixon, 1969*, pp. 369–375 at pp. 370–371.

many converging perceptions and policy shifts rendered the American departure logical.

First, the communist bloc had come to be seen as having several competing centers of power rather than a unified command center in Moscow. Sino-Soviet disjuncture after 1960 had highlighted China's independence, and the competition between Moscow and Beijing over the wartime policy of North Vietnam had strengthened Washington's expectation of a deeper rift after the war. So the prevailing image of communism shifted from the fearful monolith to a differentiated theory of polycentrism, offering the possibility of exploiting more fluid international conditions by dealing with different factions in the splintered communist world. This same view led President Nixon to begin the process of normalization of relations with China, a policy consummated in formal diplomatic recognition (1979) by President Jimmy Carter.

Second was the hope of inducing more moderate Soviet policies. After fifty years of revolution and economic modernization, and twenty years after the death of Stalin, the Soviet Union had grown fairly satisfied with its own position in the world. The dominant elites in Moscow clearly favored coexistence with the West and minimizing the risks of war. Like the American government, Moscow was under continuing domestic pressure to hold down defense spending. The hawk group in the Politburo was on the decline, and new possibilities for cooperation with the West were open.

Third, the Cold War itself had come to be waged in less strident ideological terms. Positive economic achievement in the USSR, China, and Eastern Europe showed signs of gradual convergence of Eastern and Western economic systems. The Soviets were introducing economic reforms ("Liebermanism") and tolerating tendencies toward free enterprise, while the capitalist states accepted increased government planning and participation in their economies. Also, increased awareness of continuing injustices in the West itself, such as the suppression of African-American

rights, weakened the moral righteousness of anti-communism.

Amid these conceptual changes, many Americans had come to see the Soviet problem as a practical balance-of-power issue instead of a battle between the forces of light and the forces of darkness. A less moralistic foreign policy permitted a more pragmatic exploration of options. As perceptions of the USSR shifted from the image of Aggressor to one of more complex, less dangerous patterns of motivation, cooperative proposals were less vulnerable to charges of appeasement by domestic opponents. The popular growth of moderate Eurocommunism alongside democratic socialism in Europe helped to loosen the political environment as well.

In this atmosphere, the United States was able to open a new phase in its dealings with the communist world after withdrawing from Vietnam (1973). In both the military and economic realms, great progress was made with Moscow. This included a major increase in Soviet-American trade, completion of the strategic arms limitations talks (SALT I and SALT II, the latter of which was never ratified by the U.S. Senate), agreement on Germany's borders, and other business left over from World War Two. Washington even sanctioned a number of trade contracts involving technological products that might have immediate beneficial consequences for Soviet security. Similarly, relations with China changed dramatically. Following diplomatic recognition, the first cargo of goods from China since 1949 arrived in a Chinese vessel in 1979. Coca-Cola was invited to construct a bottling plant in China.

This progress tempted many Americans to claim an end to the Cold War. This, of course, could not be taken literally, since over $400 billion in defense expenditure continued annually by the Soviet Union and the United States alone as they glared, even if more tolerantly, at each other across military lines the world over. It seemed clear, nevertheless, that by the time of the American withdrawal from Vietnam, a new era of de-escalation was in progress, however gradual and interrupted. The revised international climate, and particularly the consequences for Soviet-American relations, ushered in the era of détente.

The period of détente was as brief as it was productive, lasting only until about 1979. Some observers interpreted it as a period of elevation in mutual Soviet and American tolerances simply because in the wake of the Vietnam War, superpower diplomacy seemed to work. Another group saw it very differently, interpreting it as a loss of consensus on the basic anticommunist goals of American foreign policy.[22] Still another group summarized détente as a self-imposed public mood in the United States resulting from exhaustion over Vietnam, loss of confidence in the morality and judgment of American leadership, discontent over global responsibilities, and skepticism over activities undertaken in the name of national defense. Under these circumstances a charitable view of the Soviet Union was preferred to the tough-minded decisions and policies that the United States needed to take to maintain its vigilance against the Soviet challenge.[23] Détente, therefore, came and went with attitude, not with events and landmark years.

With the retrospective advantage of twenty years, it seems that détente was largely a post-Vietnam illusion. While significant diplomatic progress was made, the communist world continued several of its Cold War habits. First, in 1975, Soviet and Cuban troops intervened in an Angolan civil war, raising fresh questions about Soviet expansionist aims, this time in Africa. Second, Moscow vastly increased its military capabilities by every measure: annual cost, deployment of new weapons systems, increase in size of armed forces, and so on. Third, contrary to a common Western perception, most of the buildup of the most modern arms was not along the Chinese front but in Central Europe.

Fourth, despite its agreement at Vladivostok, Moscow continued its physically brutal response to political dissent. And fifth, the pattern of arms sales exposed Moscow's goals of disrupting the global balance of forces and the regional balances in the Middle East, Africa, and Europe; extending its naval forces to areas of Western interest; and sponsoring armed communist revolution in Central America and the Caribbean. These prompted American concern about the long-range intentions of Soviet foreign policy and about the trustworthiness of Soviet commitment to détente.

In particular, the strategic buildup was considered evidence of a plan to maintain tension in Europe sufficient to prevent East-West economic ties from eroding Moscow's economic, military, and ideological stranglehold on its Warsaw Pact allies. The maintenance of continental tension was a way for the Soviet Union to prevent any reduction in regional socialist cohesion. An American study of official Soviet statements regarding the ideological foundations of foreign policy was summarized as follows:

> The growing "organic" relationships with the socialist commonwealth are represented as a "law-governed" process; this process is "organically" linked with "proletarian internationalism"; "proletarian internationalism" is "organically" combined with "peaceful coexistence"; and "peaceful coexistence," defined as a product of the changed balance of forces, is "organically" tied to the ideological struggle between social systems. Thus, the processes that are effecting the triumph of socialism over capitalism are functionally interconnected; a change in one structural relationship produces change in the others.[24]

Détente, then, had become a camouflage for a subtle resumption of classic communist methods of manipulating the international system to promote the triumph of socialism over capitalism, conclude the

---

[22] George Quester, "Consensus Lost," *Foreign Policy*, no. 40, fall 1980, pp. 18–32.

[23] Dimitri K. Simes, "The Anti-Soviet Brigade," *Foreign Policy*, no. 37, winter 1979–80, pp. 28–42, especially pp. 28–29.

[24] R. Judson Mitchell, "A New Brezhnev Doctrine: The Restructuring of International Relations," *World Politics*, April 1978, pp. 366–390 at p. 389.

American era, and reinforce Moscow as the center of worldwide socialism. Another American concluded from similar evidence that while the strategic policy of the Kremlin was to instill fear of its power everywhere, its diplomatic practice was an act of seduction designed to persuade others that Moscow had accepted its role in the contemporary world order and had abandoned aspirations of a Soviet world state.[25]

The turn of the decade demolished détente and the optimistic claims of the Cold War's demise. The first indicative event occurred in the waning days of 1979, when the Soviet Union invaded Afghanistan in support of a communist government, expelled the foreign press, and put down dissent and unrest with brutal force. This long, costly, and fruitless crusade became known in the West as as the Soviet Union's Vietnam. Meanwhile, as Iran and Iraq headed for war, Soviet troops moved ever closer to the Iranian border, arousing fears of expanding Soviet activity, intervention in a revolutionary Iran, and direct great-power confrontation in the Persian Gulf area. When the Solidarity labor union struck in Poland in 1980–81, the Warsaw Pact moved menacingly toward forceful intervention, but never went beyond martial law. Nevertheless, coupled with redoubled Soviet arms development and an increasingly bellicose tone regarding the American role in Western Europe, these events reinvigorated the Cold War. In both interbloc and intrabloc relations, the Soviets seemed to have resumed classic Cold War habits.

With hawks now seemingly in control of Soviet policy, fear was rampant in the West that a struggle for power within the Kremlin might touch off an irresponsible, politically inspired military adventure somewhere other than in Afghanistan or Poland. Secretary of State Edmund Muskie reported after a meeting of the NATO foreign ministers that the allies were united as they had not been for decades, even after the OPEC petroleum embargo of 1973–74. Policies of rearmament dominated

the American presidential and congressional campaigns of 1980. On the matter of military preparedness, the election spoke with historic voice: détente was dead, the Cold War had returned, and once again the United States had to multiply its arms development effort in face of the Soviet challenge. A congressional study estimated that overtaking the Soviets in both conventional and strategic arms might take as much as eight years and $80 billion. Despite the magnitude, American taxpayers were quietly resigned to the need. And SALT II, withdrawn from the Senate by President Jimmy Carter ostensibly as a protest of Soviet behavior, but probably out of fear that the Soviet-wary Senate would reject it, was declared by the Reagan administration to be defeatist and void.[26]

Leonid Brezhnev's death (1982) brought to power Yuri Andropov, former director of the dreaded KGB (the Soviet secret police) and Soviet ambassador to Hungary during the forceful suppression of revolt there in 1956.[27] The Reagan administration greeted his rise with unabashed verbal attacks on Soviet intentions around the world. Within a year, the USSR had walked out of all arms negotiations; both the Soviet Union and the United States had deployed new-generation missiles in Europe; and Soviet-American relations were at their lowest point since the height of the Cold War in the 1950s. American condemnation of continued Soviet policies in Poland and Afghanistan, together with proof that the Kremlin was providing arms to the leftist government of Nicaragua and the rebels in El Salvador, fueled the revived image of the Soviets as the Aggressor. The shooting down of a civilian Korean airliner in 1983 was seen as a statement of the inhumane Soviet

---

[25] Kenneth L. Adelman, "Fear, Seduction and Growing Soviet Strength," *ORBIS*, winter 1978, pp. 743–765.

[26] For a representative spectrum of American positions on the SALT II agreement concerning both international strategic and domestic political questions, see the five-article section entitled "SALT and Beyond," in *Foreign Policy*, summer 1979, pp. 49–123.

[27] Martin Ebon, *The Andropov File* (New York: McGraw-Hill, 1983), chapter 6, "The Hungarian Connection," chronicles Andropov's "duplicity" during this episode but holds open the possibility that Andropov attempted to prevent military intervention.

character; and a brief American invasion of Grenada to depose a leftist government and extinguish communist influence was an announcement of Washington's intention no longer to take a passive position on Soviet interference in the Americas. It was, in fact, in this context that the Reagan Doctrine was enunciated, under which the United States would use economic and military aid to attempt to win back countries and peoples previously fallen to communism. The United States and the Soviet Union were on a seesaw of moderation on one end, and militarism on the other. The challenge for the latter half of the 1980s was to balance their asynchronous mood swings.[28]

It was amid these circumstances that Mikhail Gorbachev succeeded to power in 1985. At fifty-four years, he was the youngest Soviet leader ever. Unlike his predecessors and most of his challengers, he was born after the October Revolution and was not rooted politically in the tsarist wars, the Russian revolution, or Stalin's purges of the 1930s. From the beginning, Americans viewed him as a different type of Soviet leader, not bombastic and boastful as Khrushchev or dour and sinister as Brezhnev. Instead, he seemed to be friendly, open, frank, relatively stylish—almost a Western-style politician. His manner earned credibility, and while there was ample speculation about his leadership ability, from the start the tone in the United States was optimistic. Among the large number of Americans who found him fascinating were Ronald Reagan and George Bush.

President Reagan, who throughout his first term had maintained an unbroken record of rhetorical hostility toward the Soviet Union, treated Gorbachev differently. By the time of his second inauguration (1985) and his State of the Union Address in 1986, it was well known in the West that the Soviet economy was in far worse condition than had been believed previously. The combination of this knowledge and a gamble that Gorbachev would conduct Soviet affairs differently prompted the president to alter his tone. Continuing to

acknowledge the differences in the two societies and political systems, he nonetheless opened the door to new attitudes.

... [T]he tensions between us reflect differences that cannot be washed away. But the future is not predetermined. Knowing this, and truly desiring to make the differences between us smaller and more manageable, the United States continues to pursue progress in all aspects of our relationship with the Soviet Union.

Our Administration seeks to ensure that this relationship remains peaceful. We want restraint to be the Soviet leadership's most realistic option and will see to it that our freedoms and those of our Allies are protected.

We seek a secure future at all levels of arms, particularly nuclear forces, through agreements that are equitable and verifiable. The soundness of our proposals, our renewed military strength, and our bipartisan determination to assure a strong deterrent create incentives for the Soviet Union to negotiate seriously.

We can move toward a better, more cooperative working relationship with the Soviet Union if the Soviet leadership is willing. This will require full Soviet compliance with the letter and spirit of both past and future agreements.

... I ... hope to see greater communication and broader contact between our peoples. I am optimistic that if the Soviet leadership is willing to meet us halfway, we will be able to put our relations on a more cooperative footing in 1986.[29]

This tone was rewarded by a rapid series of events that persuaded most Americans that this time the Cold War really was over. These included among others:

- Gorbachev's distancing himself from the military by downgrading the political staff of the defense minister
- Gorbachev's speech before the United Nations General Assembly in which he promised improved cooperation, announcing his

[28] James Schlesinger, "The Eagle and the Bear," *Foreign Affairs*, summer 1985, pp. 937–961, at pp. 939-940.

[29] State of the Union Address, February 4, 1986, in the *U.S. Department of State Bulletin*, April 1986, pp. 25–29 at p. 27.

intention to make up most unpaid Soviet contributions (excluding notably those for the Korean War and peacekeeping operations prior to 1967)

- The Soviet-American arms agreement in which all intermediate-range nuclear forces (INF) were not only removed from the European theater, but destroyed under witness of officers from one another's armed services
- Real reductions in Soviet defense spending
- The complete withdrawal of Soviet troops from Afghanistan after nine years of war
- Gorbachev's reversal of a five-year Soviet insistence that strategic arms reduction talks could proceed only if the United States would abandon the Strategic Defense Initiative (SDI, or "Star Wars")
- Gorbachev's announcement of unilateral troop withdrawals from Eastern Europe without requiring concessions of the United States or NATO, followed later by an agreement on much deeper bilateral cuts

With the effect of all this activity working on the peace-loving imaginations of Americans, President George Bush entered the White House faced with one of the most extraordinary contradictions in American foreign policy in the century: on the one hand, the promise of greatly improved Soviet-American relations, and even a close to the Cold War; but, on the other hand, despite its vast power, insolvency of the United States. The combination of huge annual budget and trade deficits and a net investment position of more than $350 billion deficit, including a national debt increasingly funded by the foreign purchase of U.S. Treasury securities, created an unprecedented contradiction between the power of the United States and its insolvency.[30]

Paradoxically, this contradiction was matched by the surge of Gorbachev's popularity throughout the West. He became the first Soviet leader to make the Gallup poll list of most popular figures, ranking eighth in 1988 and second in 1989. *Time* magazine named him Man of the Decade. In West Germany his popularity exceeded that of the respected Helmut Kohl. After he pledged to Pope John Paul II the restoration of religious freedom in the Soviet Union, the American Council of Chruches elected him its man of the year. As for his policies, in 1988 65 percent of Americans thought the Soviet Union was "undergoing major changes," and 76 percent thought peaceful coexistence with the Soviet Union more likely than ever before.[31] Six months later, 65 percent thought that *perestroika* would ultimately succeed; 61 percent agreed that social and economic changes in the USSR would "come about peacefully;" and 66 percent thought that *glasnost* would continue. In this same poll, 60 percent feared that if efforts to change the economy did not succeed within "the next few years," Gorbachev would be replaced.[32] The most compelling American concern was that Gorbachev's reforms would set off a conservative reaction that would end *perestroika* and *glasnost*, force Gorbachev from government, and plunge the world once again into Cold War.

A landmark test of the new Soviet diplomacy occurred in 1990, when the United States, the Soviet Union, the NATO nations, and the Warsaw Pact nations all met in Ottawa, Canada, with representatives of the two Germanys. From that meeting emerged a formal agreement to reduce Soviet and American forces in Europe to 195,000 each except that the United States might, at its option, retain 30,000 more provided that they be in Britain and southern Europe, far from the NATO–Warsaw Pact boundary. In addition, the meeting produced an agreement on a two-step process for the reunification of the two Germanys. There followed a series of "four plus two meetings" (a reference to the four occupying powers—United States, Soviet

---

[30] Several writers have addressed this so-called Lippmann Gap, referring to the dictum of the late columnist Walter Lippmann that "[f]oreign policy consists in bringing into balance . . . the nation's commitments and the nation's power." See as examples Samuel P. Huntington, "Coping with the Lippmann Gap," *Foreign Affairs, America and the World* 1987–88 edition, pp. 453–477, and James Chace, "A New Grand Strategy," *Foreign Policy*, spring 1989, pp. 3–25.

[31] *Gallup Report*, January 1989.
[32] *Gallup Report*, June 1989.

Presidents Bush and Gorbachev enjoy the concluding press conference of their Malta Summit in 1989 at which they laid out the principles of post-Cold War cooperation.
(*Source:* Patrick Robert/Sygma)

Union, Britain, and France—and the two Germanys). Here the parties settled three main issues: (1) the speed and process for the economic and political reunification; (2) settlement and guarantee of the Polish borders with Germany; and (3) the thorny question of the unified Germany's status in NATO. Eventually Gorbachev conceded to Germany's inclusion in NATO. By mid-1990 all parties were urging rapid political integration in an effort to meet the 1992 goal of economic union of the European Community. Reunification was set for October 1990.

Quite apart from their affection for Gorbachev, Americans watched with awe the dizzying events of 1990 and 1991: wholesale secession from the Soviet empire without resistance from Moscow; Gorbachev's denunciation of the Brezhnev Doctrine; formal efforts at constitutional democracy within the Soviet Union; the demilitarization of the East-West front; and the reunification of Germany. And they watched with breathless fright Moscow's armed intervention in an Armenian-Azerbaijani war and in Lithuania upon the announcement of its secession from the USSR. Gradually it became apparent to a skeptical American body politic that what was unfolding was the decomposition of the Soviet empire and the

disintegration of the Soviet state itself. The Cold War was, finally this time, over.

America and the End of the Cold War

After forty-five years of continuous commitment to containment, two costly wars, and trillions of dollars in tax-sponsored defense expenditures, perhaps it was natural for Americans to celebrate the end of the Cold War as their victory. The enormous respect for Mikhail Gorbachev and sadness over his disappearance from public life never went so far as to credit him with a share of the victory. To most Americans, he was the right man in the right place at the right time to see realistically that the Soviet Union could not survive economically, particularly in light of the American arms buildup in the 1980s. In this view, the cost of arms competition had been elevated to the point that the Soviet economy could not both compete with the United States and make sufficient domestic progress to preserve the state against the political forces unleashed by *perestroika*. Nor could it safeguard its interests abroad in face of the Reagan adminstration's determination "to roll back communism."[33] This orthodox view concludes that the Cold War ended because Gorbachev recognized the futility of prolonging it.

One even more conservative interpretation declared the end of the Cold War and the demise of the Soviet State to constitute "The End of History."

> What we may be witnessing is not just the end of the cold war, or the passing of a particular period of postwar history, but the end of history as such: that is, the end point of mankind's ideological evolution and the universalization of Western liberal democracy as the final form of human government.[34]

But debate within the United States on the causes of the Cold War's end is neither so simple nor so conservative. Six months after these lines were written, an anonymous author (probably a high-placed government official) claimed that Gorbachev's supposed reforms were not reforms at all, but a fundamental critique of "the very basis of Soviet order and the historic matrix of what until now was called 'developed' . . . socialism." What we are seeing now, says the author, is the failure of economic *perestroika* alongside "the runaway success of *glasnost* and the progress of democratization and popular politicization."

> The false problem of how to restructure Leninism was now giving way to the real problem of how to dismantle the system, how to effect at last an exit from communism. *Perestroika* was not a solution, but a transition to this exit. . . . [C]ommunism is not reforming itself, it is disintegrating.[35]

The author concluded that the Soviet government could not produce an economically efficient communist system and, at the same time, democracy; nor could it bring about a transition from a party-

state with a planned economy to a free market system. The West's interest would be served best by slowing its arms buildup in order to reduce the arms burden on Moscow so that Gorbachev could concentrate on the domestic economy. Only in this way could a post-communist Soviet Union ease the transition into a future desirable to the West. Far from claiming an American victory, this asserts that the Soviet system collapsed of its own weight, and that the United States could accelerate East-West accord by reducing defense expenditures in order to enable the Soviet Union to do the same. In the conservative view, then, American policy forced the collapse of Soviet power. In the liberal view, the United States, by revising its policy, accelerated the collaspe of Soviet power brought on by its intrinsic weaknesses.

There are a number of variations on these conflicting analyses. One, for instance, argues that the Cold War ended because of a complex of factors on each side of the Iron Curtain. On the Western side there was a combination of coercive diplomacy and dramatization of Western values and quality of life to the Soviet Union's captive people, made possible partly through Gorbachev's reforms. And on the Soviet side there was the enabling charisma of Gorbachev's personality and gradual reduction in tensions made possible by "new thinking" and domestic transformation.[36] Another view recognizes the role of Washington's coercive diplomacy, particularly its deployment of INF weapons in Western Europe and subsequent offer to remove them, but insists that the strategy could not have worked without the fortuitous change in Soviet leadership.[37] In each of these interpretations, Gorbachev's role is indispensible, though not necessarily primary.

A broader conceptual view looks not at the Soviet-American competition for sources of ending the Cold War, but to the major trends of history at the time. It attributes the end of the Cold War to

---

[33] For the most specific and detailed study of the Reagan plan, see Peter Schweizer, *Victory: The Reagan Administration's Secret Strategy that Hastened the Collapse of the Soviet Union* (New York: Atlantic Monthly Press, 1994).

[34] Francis Fukuyama, "The End of History," *National Interest*, summer 1989.

[35] Z., "To the Stalin Mausoleum," *Daedalus*, winter 1990. For a summary of the paper, see *The New York Times*, January 4, 1990, p. A23 under the title "The Soviets' Last Crisis."

[36] Gerald Schneider, Thomas Widmer, and Deter Ruloff, "What Caused the End of the Cold War?" *International Interactions*, 1993, no. 4, pp. 323–342.

[37] Thomas Risse-Kappen, "Did 'Peace Through Strength' End the Cold War?" *International Security*, 1991, pp. 162–188.

(1) the fundamental change in the criteria of power in the 1990s, (2) the decline of authoritarianism as an alternative to liberal democracy (3) the illegitimacy of brutality as an instrument of government, and (4) the juxtaposition of these upon one another.[38] However one wishes to weigh the relative contributions of Moscow and Washington, it is only in the context of these historic forces that the Cold War could have ended.

It is for time and historians to resolve this debate. The question for the moment is how these recent international events have refined the American world view.

America and the New World Order

Paradoxically, the New World Order as introduced by President George Bush was born with the Persian Gulf War. It was while addressing first the United States Congress and then the United Nations General Assembly, both times on the subject of impending war in the Gulf, that he made his two seminal pronouncements. As we have seen, his timing was a product of Soviet-American diplomatic convergence on policy in the region, a capstone moment in the cascading events of two years. The war itself was to add another facet to the prevailing American mood about the post–Cold War environment: the fast and dramatically successful defeat of Iraq restored pride in the nation's military and its defense industries, and it went a long way toward resolving the post-Vietnam legacy of

seething unhappiness and loss of self-confidence. Consequently, by 1992, the American world view came to be refined by the addition of the following elements, each now supplementing the view as it evolved over centuries:

1. Cold War victory over communism, the only serious ideological challenge to the American ideal of global democracy
2. Cold War victory over socialism, the only serious economic threat to the American ideal of global capitalism
3. Cold War victory over the Soviet empire, the only serious geopolitical threat to the American ideal of a global consensus on economic competition
4. Cold War victory over the Soviet state, the only serious challenge to a world polity built on Western ideals
5. Cold War victory over Soviet military might to the extent of removing any serious threat of global or pan-European war
6. Restoration of self-confidence in the nation's power, both in absolute terms regarding the Persian Gulf victory and relative terms as the only real nuclear superpower after the decline of Soviet power

But in subsequent years the headiness of this combination has been blunted by countervailing factors:

1. Growing realization of the nation's insolvency as evidenced by annual deficits in budget and international trade
2. Disrputive structural change in the economy due to a decline in the defense industries, the products of which are in less demand both at home and abroad since the end of the Cold War
3. Growing recognition that the asymmetry in security affairs favors the United States, but the increasing symmetry in economic affairs does not
4. Growing concern that while the end of the Cold War has pacified great-power relations, the New World Order is far from stable

---

[38] Gaddis Lewis Smith, *The United States and the End of the Cold War* (New York: Oxford University Press, 1992), especially chapter 9, "Tectonics, History, and the End of the Cold War," pp. 155–167. For general treatments of the subject, see Coit D. Blacker, *Hostage to Revolution: Gorbachev and Soviet Security Policy, 1985–91* (New York: Council on Foreign Relations, 1993); Zbigniew Bryezinski, *The Grand Failure* (New York: Macmillan, 1990); H. C. D'Encausse, *The End of the Soviet Empire* (New York: Basic Books, 1993); and John B. Dunlop, *Rise of Russia and Fall of the Soviet State* (Princeton, N.J.: Princeton University Press, 1993).

5. Recognition that America's military power is peculiarly inappropriate to the kinds of conflicts that destabilize the post–Cold War international system

For those charged with formulating foreign policy, however, one towering antihistorical fact encompasses all of these: Virtually no one in contemporary public life had a mature political awareness the last time the United States was neither at war nor threatened with war from an Aggressor who, in both theoretical and real historical terms, has formed the dominant rationale for American foreign policy. Moreover, for almost half a century the Cold War confrontation was assumed to be a permanent condition of global politics, and the goal was less to end it (never assuming the collapse of either the Soviet empire or the Soviet state) than to regulate it. If there was but one aim that encapsulated Washington's Cold War policy, it was stability. The bedrock of U.S. foreign policy was to convert cold war to cold peace by stabilizing the global system. This was a basis that successive presidential administrations treated in their respective ways, but the common and familiar threat was passed one to the next. The common denominator, the starting point of debate, is now gone. Hence the burning policy questions of the New World Order: On what is American foreign policy now constructed? What comes of U.S. foreign policy when there is no enemy?

In the early post-Soviet years, the goals were stated simply as a by-product of the end of the Cold War: the global spread of both democracy and capitalism, to be achieved through a strategy of enlargement (presumably a rhetorical counterpoint to containment), with the emphasis on enlargement of nations with democratic market economies. In official pronouncements, democracy was on the march everywhere: in Russia and the lands of the former Soviet republics, in Eastern Europe, in Israel's recognition of Palestinian rights, and in the vastly expanded global political debate unleashed by the end of the Cold War. But there were countervailing trends also: ethnic-cleansing wars in the former Yugoslavia and Rwanda; the electoral trend back to conservatism and authoritarianism in Russia and Eastern Europe; the Russian war in Chechnya; and the renewal of harsh political repression in China. Furthermore, the goal of democratization stemmed from the assumption that a democratic world is a secure one because democracies do not go to war against one another. A study published in 1995 indicated, to the contrary, that while mature democracies may not war against one another, countries in the process of democratizing have a tenfold higher incidence of war than do authoritarian countries that have not commenced democratization. This is due to the temporary decline in central authority and accompanying instability that occur in the early stages of democratization.[39] A world of simultaneous democratizing movements may not, therefore, be intrinsically peaceful or conducive to long-term American interests.

The companion assumption was that with the end of Soviet-style socialism, capitalism would also overtake the world. Again there were evidences of this: securities exchanges cropped up in Russia, throughout Eastern Europe, and even in China; trade agreements expanded; the Russian president was invited as a nonvoting participant in the G-7 meetings (the economic summit arrangement of the seven largest capitalist states) in a "seven-plus-one" agreement; and Russian membership in the International Monetary Fund was openly discussed. But here, too, there were conflicting signs: post-socialist Russia saw its worst economic decline, with an estimated 40 percent of the population falling below the poverty line; Russia's need for the voluntary reintegration of its old partners contained elements of neoimperialism; and the Western-devised plan of recovery, the so-called Gaidar reform named for Yeltsin's prime minister, was praised in the West but seen as a new form of American neocolonialism

---

[39] Edward Mansfield and Jack Snyder, "Democratization and War," *Foreign Affairs*, May–June 1995, pp. 79–97.

in Russia.[40] And so, like the path to democracy, the road to global capitalism soon grew thick with obstacles.

Despite the hurdles, however, the goals of global democracy and capitalism remain in the forefront of American policy thinking. This is because from all ideological perspectives, democracy and capitalism serve both the interests and the values of foreign policy; both occupy the core of any world order satisfactory to the United States.

In pursuit of these goals and values, hard conservative and liberal lines were drawn in Washington. On the conservative side, the budget-reduction commitment of the 1994 Congressional election set the framework. With countless variations, its central theme included the following elements:

1. The trade and budget deficits and the cumulative national debt create circumstances in which the country cannot meet all of its foreign and domestic goals and, at the same time, reduce taxes and bring down deficits. Foreign objectives must, therefore, be secondary. (This is known as a "declinist" theory.)
2. The prospects for the world being thrust again into armed camps is sufficient to maintain high military budgets and preparedness. The end of the Cold War does not by itself protect American interests; only uninterrupted vigilence will. (This theory of national defense against international anarchy is known as "neorealist" theory.)
3. The nation's first responsibility is to itself by itself. Neither its interests nor their protection can be entrusted to international institutions. Thus the commitment to the United Nations and its principles should be minimized. Above all, American troops should never be placed under international command, and no

American troops should be earmarked to United Nations peacekeeping operations. (This is "nationalist" or "unilateralist" theory. Its principal variant recognizes the role of tightly controlled alliances.)
4. Except when American interests are materially threatened, its military power should be reserved and the impulse to intervene should be overcome. (In its extreme form, this is "isolationist" theory.)

The liberal side starts from an altogether different point. Rooted in twentieth-century traditions of Woodrow Wilson and Franklin D. Roosevelt, it proposes to use American power to advance civility and progressive international policy, to achieve humanitarian goals, and to structure international decision making in a quasi-parliamentary manner.

1. Even if the threat to American interests is minimal today, failure to defend them now may compound the danger in the future. (This is "activist" theory.)
2. Consistent with historic liberal internationalism, abuses of power are minimized by cooperative decision making and execution of policy. In a world order in which the United States is the only global superpower, it is more necessary than ever for it to pursue its policies multilaterally through the United Nations and other organizations than to risk becoming a world policeman, a global hegemon, or an arbitrary imperial state. The ideals of American constitutionalism should be imprinted upon the international community. (This is "multilateralist" theory. Its extreme variant is "constitutionalist" theory.)
3. The cost of maintaining international stability unilaterally is too great to bear alone, and so unilateralism and nationalistic enforcement of peace are beyond the nation's reach. One advantage of multilateralism is that it enables the United States to serve its function as a great power but to share the cost with others. (This is called "neointernationalism" or "assertive multinationalism," an expression credited to

---

[40] Compare Jeffrey D. Sachs, "Consolidating Capitalism," *Foreign Policy*, spring 1995, pp. 50–64, and Anders Aslund, "Russia's Success Story," *Foreign Affairs*, September–October 1994, pp. 58–71, with Georgi Arbatov, "A New Cold War?" *Foreign Policy*, summer 1994, pp. 90–104. Arbatov refers explicitly to both Sachs and Aslund in describing the failed Gaidar reforms and resulting Russian suspicion of Western intentions in designing the recovery plan.

Madeleine Albright, U.S. permanent representative at the UN.)

4. American foreign policy interests are inseparable from the goals of peace, prosperity, democracy, self-determination, and universal human rights. American power should be used in pursuit of them. (This is "humanitarian internationalist" theory.)[41]

In summary, the contemporary debate on the foundations of United States foreign policy is between those who rank international goals as secondary and would pursue them unilaterally, and those who consider global stability vital to domestic prosperity, and who prefer multilateral solutions. These camps correlate closely to those who attribute the end of the Cold War to the economic advantages of the American power position, and those who credit it to the popular power unleashed by *perestroika* toward Soviet adoption of superior Western political and economic values.

Tensions of this kind are the raw material of politics. But they are more pronounced in the aftermaths of long historical events such as the Cold War. In such circumstances, politics generates a feeling of anticlimax and disorientation. Civic discontent, distrust of the state, disaffection from politics, and dissatisfaction with ideology are common, as are wide swings in political orientation.[42] In the American case, they have traditionally recurred as isolationism and liberal internationalism. Following World War One internationalism enjoyed brief popularity before succumbing to the isolationism of the 1930s preceding Pearl Harbor. The internationalist urge after World War Two was spared the same fate by the rapid onset of the Cold War. In the post–Cold War period, the struggle is still on.

There are two immediate practical matters that these different orientations affect greatly. The first is establishing principles regarding when the United States will and will not intervene militarily in areas of unrest. Since the end of the Cold War this challenge has arisen several times, involving Iraq and Kuwait, Bosnia, Haiti, Somalia, and Rwanda. It has not arisen seriously in other circumstances: Angola, Liberia, Algeria, Azerbaijan, Georgia, and Mexico, all of which have seen varying degrees of internal warfare, and Chechnya, which has been through a war of secession against Russia. In all instances in which the United States has reacted, it has chosen the multilateralist route. But in each its motives differed. In Iraq-Kuwait the motive was economic and directly related to the cordial availability of vitally needed oil; in Somalia it was humanitarian; and in Haiti it was hemispheric tranquility and the spread of democracy. The problem is to articulate a cohesive foreign policy that serves as a reliable guide for action in the future. Failing that, the choices may eventually distill down to isolationism, nationalistic unilateralism, or imperial temptation.[43]

The second practical matter is the expansion of NATO, on which opinions differ greatly. NATO was established to prevent Soviet aggression in Europe. It was one of the prime instruments of Cold War containment. The Soviet Union was its *raison d'être*. Without the Cold War and the Soviet Union, two questions arise. First, what if anything is the role of NATO? Second, how do governments guarantee European peace on a post-containment, post-bloc, post-NATO-Warsaw-Pact continent? Because the former Soviet allies were out ahead of the NATO governments on this, a 1994 summit

---

[41] For a modified conservative statement by a leading contender for the Republican presidential nomination, see Robert Dole, "Shaping America's Global Future," *Foreign Policy*, spring 1995, pp. 29–43. And for a more theoretical and less partisan comparison, see Richard N. Haas, "Paradigm Lost," *Foreign Affairs*, January–February 1995, pp. 43–58. Haas's major contribution is the distinction between means and ends in foreign policy.

[42] Fashioned closely after Charles S. Maier, "Democracy and Its Discontents," *Foreign Affairs*, July–August 1994, pp. 48–64. The implications of these phenomena for domestic politics are unraveled in Daniel Deudney and G. John Ikenbergry, "After the Long War," *Foreign Policy*, spring 1994, pp. 21–35. For a study of the contemporary plight of liberal internationalism, see Stanley Hoffmann, "The Crisis of Liberal Internationalism," *Foreign Policy*, spring 1995, pp. 159–179.

[43] Robert W. Tucker and David C. Hendrickson, *The Imperial Temptation: The New World Order and America's Purpose* (New York: Council on Foreign Relations Press, 1992). This is a critique of President George Bush's foreign policy in light of his own world order ideals.

stalled the issue by offering consultation to all former Soviet republics (including Russia) and allies
under a Partnership for Peace. Eighteen months
later NATO adopted principles for expansion into
Eastern and Central Europe, though it admitted no
new members. Conservatives argue that NATO has
evolved into an instrument for expanding democracy and capitalism in Europe, and although the
Warsaw Pact is gone, Russia as a recovering great
power poses a permanent European boundary requiring a threshold level of defense. Liberals reject
the supposition that a military alliance can promote democracy and capitalism and conclude that
expanding NATO to Russia's former allies is nothing but neocontainment. If its real functions were
political and economic, then it should be extended
further and not anchored at the Russian border.
The peace of Europe needs new institutions built
on current realities rather than old.[44]

Such fundamental domestic disagreements call
into question the premise that in the post–Cold
War world American foreign policy operates without an enemy. Perhaps it is more nearly accurate to
say that as the nature of national power has
changed in the New World Order, so has the nature of conflict. For example, if one takes the view
that as a recovering great power Russia has to be
watched vigilantly, one is not necessarily predicting
war or a new cold war. But in view of the economic
and political upheavals that Russia continues to

encounter on its path to democracy and capitalism,
the potential for retrogression to authoritarian rule
and imperial politics is ever present. Is it a future
democratic Russia, a troubled democratizing Russia, or a Russia reverting to authoritarianism and
imperialism that awakens residual Western security
fears?

In the effort to understand and project the
conditions of the New World Order, this preoccupation with the further evolution of old conflicts
may lose its rationale. The new premise is that the
future of international conflict will center less on
nation-state or ideological disagreement, and more
on cultural differences. At a time at which the
West (including Russia, in this argument) is at the
peak of its power, political-economic assertion by
non-Western cultures poses a potential clash of civilizations in which the West will find itself pitted
against a half-dozen other cultures. Each of these
crosses national boundaries, stretches over vast ex-
panses of the globe, and desires to structure a world
order in non-Western ways. "With the end of the
Cold War, international politics moves out of its
Western phase, and its centerpiece becomes the interaction between the West and non-Western civilizations and among non-Western civilizations."
Because these non-Western civilizations do not
wish to undergo westernization *en route* to modernization, the "fault lines between civilizations will be
the battle lines of the future."[45]

Three of these non-Western civilizations are
important in forming the current American world
view. The first is the Japanese civilization, which is
unique to a single country. For historical reasons

---

[44] Fashioned closely after Michael Mandelbaum, "Preserving the
Peace: The Case Against NATO Expansion," *Foreign Affairs*,
May–June 1995, pp. 9–13; and a German view by Karl–Heinz
Kamp, "The Folly of Rapid NATO Expansion, "*Foreign Policy*,
spring 1995, pp. 116–129. Kamp argues that "Explaining to a
humiliated Russian military establishment that an extension of
NATO for the sake of stabilizing Russia's western periphery
would be a net gain for them, not another defeat, would probably exceed the ingenuity of even the most eloquent NATO ex-
pansionists" (p. 126). Also see a British view by Jonathan
Clarke, "Replacing NATO," *Foreign Policy*, winter 1993–94, pp.
22–40. Clarke proposes expanding the role of the Conference
on Security and Cooperation in Europe (CSCE) and enfolding
NATO's military role in it. This is very similar to the official
Russian view. Benjamin Schwarz, "The NATO Empire," *The
New York Times*, October 5, 1995, p. A29, calls the NATO expansion plan "the most significant and dangerous extension of
United States security commitments since the 1940s," that can
only exclude Russia from Europe.

---

[45] Samuel P. Huntington, "The Clash of Civilizations?" *Foreign
Affairs*, summer 1993, pp. 22–49. The quoted passages are from
pp. 23 and 22, respectively. For a critique of Huntington's thesis,
see Richard E. Rubenstein and Jarle Crocker, "Challenging
Huntington," *Foreign Policy*, fall 1994, pp. 113–128. See also
Graham Fuller, "The Next Ideology," *Foreign Policy*, spring 1995,
pp. 145–158, which criticizes the Huntington thesis on the observation that the clash of civilizations "is not so much over
Jesus Christ, Confucius, or the Prophet Muhammad as it is over
the unequal distribution of world power, wealth, and influence,
and the perceived historical lack of respect accorded to small
states and peoples by larger ones. Culture is the vehicle for expression of conflict, not its cause" (pp. 153–154).

dating to the first Western commercial contacts, Americans have inherited an abiding distrust of Japan. The nineteenth-century "opening" of Japan by an American fleet responded to both a demand for commercial access and the brutality of Japanese officials to sailors shipwrecked off Japan *en route* to Asian mainland ports. The Russo-Japanese War (1904–05), Japan's Twenty-one Demands on China (1917), the invasion of Manchuria (1931), and the unprovoked attack on Pearl Harbor (1941) are all reminders of Japan's ability to be an Aggressor, the *provocateur* in American foreign policy. While today's conflict centers almost exclusively on trade relations, Americans know that the disagreements are more fundamental than mere diplomatic sparring for advantage. To an important degree, the differences are cultural. But since both are mature democracies, it is assumed that conflict is manageable.

The second cultural confrontation that may be looming for the United States is with the Chinese. Presently we deal with China as a nation-state; but there are scores of millions, perhaps hundreds of millions, of "overseas Chinese" who in this generation or several before it have carried the ancient Chinese civilization into Eurasia, into the Himalayas, along the Asian and Southeast Asian coasts, and down the Pacific islands. Many of the Pacific Rim states are products of the Chinese civilization. In their modern development they have become as much a challenge to the United States economically as China has geopolitically. A mature fusing of these interests along cultural lines could form another Western–non-Western fault.

The third, and to most Americans currently the most menacing, is the Islamic civilization that stretches from North Africa, through the Middle East, up through the Balkan region, along the southern tier of former Soviet republics, into Eurasia, and on to Pakistan. Because of its size, its geographic stretch, its awakening energy, and its commitment to justice through *jihad* (holy war), its presence has become a major force in global politics. It has been linked to countless attacks on Western interests from car bombings in the Middle East to subway bombings in France, commercial aircraft explosions over Africa and Scotland, and the bombing of the World Trade Center in New York City. In 1995, a Muslim cleric and nine others were convicted of dozens of charges related to a terror campaign that included plans to bomb the United Nations, federal and city buildings in New York, and the tunnels connecting Manhattan Island with New Jersey.[46] The goal was to force a radical change in U.S. policy toward the Middle East, and toward Israel in particular. Within a few days of the convictions, the most radical Egyptian Islamic element, the one responsible earlier for the assassination of President Sadat and an unsuccessful attempt on President Mubarek's life, promised "maximum terror" to the United States in retaliation.

Since the inception of the New World Order, virtually every commentary on American foreign policy has reiterated the observation that Washington is searching for new foundations of policy, new paradigms, and new modalities. If anything was more unexpected than the rather abrupt end of the Cold War and the containment strategy that formed an unbroken policy rationale, it is the global chaos that followed. And that chaos has implications for the American view of the Developing Nations as well as elsewhere.

The Developing Nations

The end of the Cold War and the potential clash of civilizations have contradictory implications for United States foreign policy. During the Cold War, the American interests were easily articulated: (1) to maintain peace, ideological homogeniety, and open economic relations with the Developing Nations in the Western Hemisphere; (2) to maintain

---

[46] *The New York Times*, October 2, 1995, pp. A1 and B4–B5. For formal studies on the widespread character of the Islamic revolution, see as examples Andrew J. Pierre and William B. Quandt, "Algeria's War Against Itself," *Foreign Policy*, summer 1995, pp. 131–148; and a cluster of articles entitled "The Islamic Cauldron" in *Foreign Affairs*, May–June 1995; and Judith Miller, "Faces of Fundamentalism," *Foreign Affairs*, November–December 1994, pp. 123–143.

stability as was required to preserve open economic relations with Developing Nations elsewhere; and (3) to use economic and military aid to attract neutral Developing Nations to the Western side of the Cold War or, failing that, at least to prevent them from aligning with the Soviet Union. To those ends the United States spent billions of dollars annually, used military and economic rewards and punishments, and intervened in domestic and international affairs on a number of occasions, the largest in Korea and Vietnam. It is less well known that the overwhelming portion of direct economic aid went to a few places—Israel, Taiwan, South Korea, and the Philippines—both to safeguard them from encroachment and to build modern capitalist economies. Although building democracy was always a goal, it came only in the last few years to all but Israel.

These Cold War goals were fulfilled to a great extent. With the changed political background of the New World Order, however, Congress and the American taxpayer are much less inclined to perpetuate these costs. Aid to Developing Nations is, therefore, one of the issues caught in the debate between domestic primacy and declinism, on the one hand, and liberal internationalism, on the other hand. To put it differently, during the period in which the communist menace led to ideological pervasiveness and cohesion, the cost of foreign aid seemed reasonable, as it was the economic corollary of containment; but in the civic discontent and flight from responsibility that characterize the end of a historic cause, the cost of feeding children abroad is unreasonable as long as there are starving children right here at home.

On the other hand, the sources and nature of conflict after the Cold War impose new imperatives on the industrialized powers. In fact, the international political system is fraught with paradox: While the Cold War threatened nuclear destruction, the system was remarkably stable, even during the Korean, Vietnam, and Afghanistan wars; but the post–Cold War world, while free of nuclear obsession, is highly unstable. Moreover, the instability stems preponderately from the Developing Nations. Whether or not one accepts the "clash-of-civilizations" thesis, instability in the Developing Nations and the threat of major breakdown in relations between the rich nations and the poor are focal issues of world politics.

In some ways, the Developing Nations represent a political countertrend. The current tendency in the industrialized nations is to build institutions such as the European Union and the North American Free Trade Area that are above the nation and in which nationalism is subordinated to something higher. In rare instances, the higher institutions actually have supranational authority, that is, they can impose policies on their member states. Loyalty is partly transferred from the nation to the region, the multinational corporation, or to institutions that fulfill economic goals in place of the state. All of these weaken the state as an international actor.[47] In the Developing World, in contrast, the threat to state authority is not integration but fragmentation. It is the combination of domestic ethnic separation and transnational ethnic coalescence. This is a cultural phenomenon in which domestic order breaks down where statehood and nationality are not synonymous, and where nationality-cultural cohesion is substituted for state cohesion. This is a threat to the territorial state and existing diplomatic devices. Massive self-determination would be chaotic, as it would multiply the territorial complications. Redundant civil wars are no more desirable. To bridge this gap between statehood and nationality, one author proposes that the world order extend international status to nations and ethnocultural communities that are not synonymous with territorial states. This way fragmentation would be minimized, the rights of transnational ethnic groups preserved, and threats of civil war reduced.[48]

---

[47] Jack Citrin, Ernst B. Haas, Christopher Muste, and Beth Reingold, "Is American Nationalism Changing? Implications for Foreign Policy," *International Studies Quarterly*, March 1994, pp. 1–19.

[48] Gidon Gottlieb, "Nations Without States," *Foreign Affairs*, May–June 1994, pp. 100–112.

Within this evolving framework, however, the United States deals with certain unchanged realities. The Developing World, for example, contains nearly 70 percent of the global population, but produces less than 10 percent of its goods. Its deposits of metals, oil, gas, and gems and many of its crops are essential to the West. Yet many of its members have runaway population growth that consumes their economic advances, governmental corruption, civil disorder, both public and corporate mismanagement, chokingly excessive urbanization, and frivolous attitudes about weather-altering environmental policies (such as uncontrolled destruction of rain forests). Despite billions of American dollars given either directly or through international institutions for health, education, transportation, housing, nutrition, population control, and agricultural and industrial development, progress is painfully inapparent. Many of the Developing Nations participated in the expulsion of Taiwan from the United Nations and keep it out still; and many supported the General Assembly resolution that equated Israel with racism. Many are states with Cold War histories of having heaped the rhetoric of imperialism on the United States. Others participated in the OPEC conspiracy to upset world petroleum markets at enormous cost to the West. And still, in the common American view, their economic demands are unending, unreasonable, nonreciprocal, unruly, and a costly burden to the United States, both economically and politically.

The political problems of the Developing Nations are also disconcerting. In many of them, even in this hemisphere, political policy is so repressive that the immigration demand on the United States is causing a backlash, expecially in Florida, Texas, California, and New York, four of the pivotal states in presidential politics. Some municipalities are literally smothered by the cost of health, education, and welfare benefits to undocumented aliens. California voters adopted a referendum in 1994 limiting those benefits, though its implementation was blocked by the judiciary. The state and federal prison systems are disproportionately occupied by illegal residents. And virtually all illicit drugs are smuggled into the United States from the Developing World, where a combination of revenues and intimidation prevents governments from cooperating with the United States to stem the flow. In some places the United States is funding "alternative-crop" programs to induce the growers of drug plants to convert to other crops.

The problems are profound and the unhappy memories long, but stability in the Developing World remains essential to the United States. A satisfactory New World Order can neither be subject to repeated interruption of markets and sources of raw materials nor buffeted by genocidal civil wars. As adjusting to global strategies without the Soviet menace is proving difficult for the United States, so too is adjusting to a combination of the new and the old attributes of the Developing World.

The United States and Asia

Throughout this century the United States has been an Asian power. Beginning with its first commercial contacts with China in the 1840s, American intersts in Asia have grown steadily. Acquisition of the Philippines (independent since 1948) after the Spanish-American War (1898) marked the permanent establishment of American power in the western Pacific. Theodore Roosevelt first undertook to adjust the Asian power equation after the Russo-Japanese War (1904–05) by a settlement that gave prominence to neither. The more American interests grew in China during and after World War One, the more Washington's attention focused on Japanese power, but this was unable to prevent World War Two in Asia and the Pacific. In the global power structure of the Cold War, Asia became geopolitically essential to the United States because of (1) the Soviet foothold in Asia and the North Pacific from its eleventh-hour entry into the Asian war; (2) the communist victory in China; (3) American commitment to South Korea when invaded by North Korea; and (4) the decision to rearm Japan and promote its industrial recovery as an ally in Cold War policy. As the Cold War went on, the American goal was to establish a regional balance among itself, China, and the Soviet Union. At the end of the Cold War, when strategic considerations were less urgent, the balance of influence was among the United States, China, Russia, and Japan, with a wary eye to the economically powerful newly industrialized nations of the Pacific Rim.

China

The Chinese communist movement began in the 1920s. During World War Two it gained considerable steam to the point that there was a civil war within the war. Despite American aid and a variety of diplomatic efforts, the West-leaning nationalist government was defeated in battle by the communists and took flight to Taiwan in the closing days of 1949. This huge setback for the United States in its Cold War policy was underscored the following year when China intervened on the side of North Korea, preventing the defeat of the North Korean communists, forcing American-led UN troops back to the center of the peninsula, and freezing the political status quo to this day. China was branded by the UN General Assembly as an international outlaw and aggressor. Although at the time it was assumed that China was executing Moscow's policy in Asia, by 1960 it was clear that the movement of Mao Zedong was ideologically and politically independent.

The Korean armistice (there is still no peace treaty, and the dividing line is still defended on both sides) left as the most vexing Sino-American problem the status of Taiwan. Many powerful Americans had close ties to the nationalist government, which established itself as a Chinese government-in-exile on Taiwan, claiming to be reconstituting its forces for a return to the mainland. The communists insisted that the United States declare a "one-China" policy, that the nationalist representative at the United Nations be replaced by an appointee of the communist government, and that the United States stop dealing with Taiwan as a sovereign entity. Though the first and

second of these were achieved, the third was not, as the United States continued such policies as providing modern arms for Taiwan and playing a leading role in its defense.

Even after the historic visit of President Richard M. Nixon to China (1972) and the thawing of relations, U.S. policy was driven largely by conditions in the Washington-Moscow-Beijing triangle. With the failure of détente, for instance, Washington moved closer to China diplomatically and began sharing military information as a way of moderating Soviet policy. Dealings of this sort came to be known as "playing the China card." Wary of the potential consequences of this American tactic, China adopted a policy of equidistance, attempting to deal progressively with both Washington and Moscow, but without getting too close to either.

Major changes occurred in Sino-American relations during the decline of the Cold War. Perhaps the most important from the American vantage point was China's sale of Silkworm missiles to Iran, and later to Iraq and Syria, threatening the precarious power balances within the volatile Middle East. Also, when Chinese troops crushed a peaceful protest in Tiananmen Square, Beijing, in the spring of 1989, Americans were reminded of what butchers the Beijing communists were capable of being. The hope that as European communism lost its steel grip the same might happen in China was dashed, as the communists unabashedly and unapologetically used their might to destroy popular democracy. This open violation of human rights was added to American revulsion over Chinese population policy, which included forced sterilization, forced abortion, and infanticide of female babies.

To many Americans the principled response to these Chinese practices was to isolate China from the world community. But to many others, access to the huge and underserved markets of China was more important. One side argued that we should not have close relations with China until it improves its human rights record;[49] the

---

[49] See, for example, Robert L. Bernstein and Richard Dicker, "Human Rights First," *Foreign Policy*, spring 1994, pp. 43–46.

other that the benefits of normal economic relations will induce a better performance.[50] Others, taking a more practical view, argue that if the United States fails to enter into the competition, Japan will seize the full advantage, and by the time America gets in, it will be too late. Siding with the activists, President Clinton continued most-favored-nation trading status for China. Later he agreed to Chinese membership in the new World Trade Organization.

In 1995 and 1996 relations between the two countries fell to a new low. For its part, China test fired a long-range multiple-warhead missile, sold lesser missiles to Iran and Pakistan, stepped up the underground nuclear test series started in 1993, blocked continuation of UN peacekeeping in Haiti because of the Haitian government's pro-Taiwan leaning, and allegedly sold weapons-related nuclear technology to Pakistan. On the other side, Congressional conservatives eager to resume a "two-Chinas" policy, thus creating a sovereign Taiwan alongside China, forced President Clinton to over-rule the State Department and permit Taiwan's president to visit the United States on private business. (The Senate had already adopted a resolution to upgrade the Taiwan representative's status in the United States, and House Speaker Gingrich had publicly called for creating a UN seat for a Republic of China on Taiwan.) The Chinese reacted angrily, charging Washington with a violation of its diplomatic recognition of Beijing, temporarily recalling its ambassador, detaining two American military observers for being at an unauthorized site, imprisoning dissidents on the eve of Tiananmen Square's sixth anniversary, and trying for sedition (and then releasing) a Chinese-born naturalized American citizen.[51] As Taiwan's 1996 presidential election approached, Beijing conducted naval

maneuvers in the China straits and fired unarmed missiles into Taiwan's territorial waters. When it declared its willingness to resort to war should Taiwan declare sovereign independence, the U.S. sent two aircraft carriers to the China straits for the first time since the Vietnam War.

China has always been an enigma to Americans, who admire Chinese history and artistic culture, but cannot comprehend Chinese behavior. Americans know that as economic imperatives replace geostrategic goals in foreign policy, accommodation with China is essential to American competition, particularly so close to Japan. They also know that relations with Beijing are deteriorating at the same time at which American military presence in Asia is in decline. But it is clear that relations cannot be fully normal or even consistent until the United States does, at minimum, two things. It must determine whether the decoupling of human rights from trade is permanent, and it must decide conclusively at what price it will deal with Taiwan. The Asian component of the New World Order cannot be stabilized until these are done.

Japan

Few isolated events in the twentieth century are more memorable to Americans than the Japanese attack on Pearl Harbor (1941) and the two atomic bombings of Japanese cities by the United States (1945). The vividness of these recollections illuminates the degree of antipathy from which the two peoples have had to come to be allies. It is perhaps true that had the Cold War, and the Korean War especially, not driven them into an alliance of necessity, their contemporary problems might be worse than they are. For Americans, the modern history of Japanese-American relations is a mixed blessing: It is a success story ill rewarded.

When the occupation of Japan began in 1945, the aim was to construct a stable Japanese society that would be incapable of aggression in the future. Its massive war industries were to be broken up, and its industrial capacity limited. It was anticipated that these goals would take a long time to

---

[50] See, for example, James Lilley, "Freedom Through Trade," *Foreign Policy*, spring 1994, pp. 37–42.

[51] For a thorough review of events and exposition of problems and policy alternatives, see David Shambaugh, "The United States and China: A New Cold War?" *Current History*, September 1995, pp. 241–251. On the issue of Taiwan's independence and reentry into the United Nations, see Ross H. Monro, "Giving Taipei a Place at the Table," *Foreign Affairs*, November–December 1994, pp. 109–122.

achieve, but for a number of reasons General Douglas MacArthur, Supreme Commander of Allied Powers in the Pacific, accelerated Japan's independence and the end of occupation. In so doing, he prepared a constitution built on democratic institutions and included provisions that outlawed the acquisition of nuclear weapons and severely limited the deployment of forces. The onset of war in Korea in 1950 canceled virtually all of this vision. The first U.S. troops to land in Korea were transferred from Japan, and immediately American military planners recognized Japan as an ideal location for promoting Cold War strategies in Asia. Far from becoming a pastoral state, therefore, Japan was rearmed in alliance with the United States and became one of the cornerstones of U.S. defense policy.

But the relationship was not without irritants. The Japanese resented the continuous American presence, demanded that nuclear weapons be excluded from their territory, insisted on the return of Okinawa to their sovereignty, and limited the uses of Japanese territory for launching strikes against North Vietnam during that war. From the American side, the issues were different. Because of the exquisite defense provided by Washington, Japan was spared an enormous cost. While the United States was committing between 5 and 10 percent of its gross national product to defense, much of it bound for Japan, Tokyo never appropriated more than 4 percent, and probably never actually spent that much. The balance went into rapid, modern industrial and technological development. Huge industries reappeared, particularly in automobiles and electronics. While the United States was struggling to defend the Free World from communism, Japan was racing ahead, overtaking American production (often through patent infringement), capturing global markets at American expense, and even outselling American products within the United States. Meanwhile, it was protecting its own markets by excluding many American products and services.

Much of Washington's commitment to a fully developed global trade regime is a response to these problems. Similarly, much of its willingness to replace the General Agreement on Tariffs and Trade (GATT) with the World Trade Organization (WTO) and to give the latter authority to arbitrate trade disputes grew out of the constant Japanese-American trade controversy. In fact, in 1995 when the WTO almost got its first case, the subject was Japanese auto exports to the United States. On that occasion, however, Washington effectively blocked access to the WTO by declaring that if the matter were not settled diplomatically by a given date, it would impose huge import duties on luxury Japanese imports, virtually doubling the prices of high-end Acuras, Lexuses, and Infinities. Though the matter was settled at least temporarily, left on the table was the other half of the question, namely, opening Japanese markets to more products. In the orthodox American view, the trade imbalances produced by Japan's policies are retarding global economic development.[52]

The most important thing about this dispute is that it typifies the kind of conflict most likely to arise in the New World Order. From the American side, Japan's policies produce a cycle of economic events that hurts everyone but Japan. If Americans are denied the trading privileges in Japan that the Japanese have in the United States, then the United States will continue to have annual trade deficits that cannot be financed with goods. Consequently, American productivity is suppressed, existing jobs are lost and new ones are not created, and capital investment, industrial efficiency, and tax revenue all decline. The budget deficit is then accentuated, forcing the Treasury to borrow money by selling securities. To control inflation, interest rates are kept low, and so investors will seek high-yield investments elsewhere and American capital will flow out, deepening the payments gap. If, in contrast, U.S. government securities are sold at high rates, foreign investment capital will flow in, improving the payments balance. But now the

---

[52] For an official government statement, see Roger C. Altman, "Why Pressure Japan?" *Foreign Affairs*, May–June 1994, pp. 2–6. Compare Jagdish Bharwati, "Samurais No More," *Foreign Affairs*, May–June 1994, pp. 7–12, which presents American policy demands as punitive and in violation of free trade principles.

government's debt is held abroad, and when the securities mature capital will, once again, flow out. Throughout all this, the value of the dollar fluctuates against the stronger currencies, changing the prices of both imports and exports and forcing the government to use reserves of the strong currencies to stabilize the dollar.

Few Americans deal with these complexities, but most are sympathetic to Washington's blaming the nation's deficit problems on Japan's trade surplus. This is why Americans welcomed news of a 30 percent decline in the Japanese stock market in 1994, its unprecedented job layoffs, and the decline of its real estate market in 1995. Determined that the year 2000 will introduce "the second American century" as promised them by President George Bush, they take comfort in any sign of Japanese regression that seems to disprove predictions of "the Pacific century."[53]

Though all this seems very complicated, it is the daily fare of the global political economy. As economic politics supersedes strategic politics, the Japanese-American trading relationship stands as the first long-term test of the New World Order.

The Pacific Rim

While Americans concentrated on the Cold War, another precursor to the New World Order was evolving in the Pacific. In 1967, the governments of Malaysia, the Philippines, Singapore, Thailand, and Indonesia formed the Association of Southeast Asian Nations (ASEAN), and Brunei was subsequently admitted. (Preliminary arrangements have been made for Vietnam's membership in about 1997.) In 1989, the ASEAN governments combined with other Asian states (Japan, South Korea, China, Hong Kong, and Taiwan), two South Pacific nations (Australia and New Zealand), and two North American nations (the United States and Canada, with Peru, Mexico, and Chile joining later) to form the Asian-Pacific Economic Cooperation

(APEC) organization. Together these states form the Pacific Rim.

Behind this activity is the hope of cooperative economic development and regional free trade by the year 2020. From the American perspective, to be a party to this activity is to create an advantage that it does not have in the European Union, where it is an external party, and where the idea of a trans-Atlantic free trade area has not gathered force. The advantage of regionalism over bilateralism (that is, individual economic realtions with each of the participating states) is the evolution of common trade policy that the United States can influence through membership and leadership. Moreover, some of the members are among the "newly industrialized nations" with which the United States has problems it would like to resolve regionally. Taiwan and South Korea, the two models of U.S. foreign aid, are foremost among them.

The Pacific Rim nations are so disparate, so separated by other matters, so widely scattered, and so different in their stages of economic development that formal institution-building and regime-building are far in their future. There is little of catalytic value, for example, in having China in an organization with South Korea, which it does not recognize; Taiwan, which it claims as an integral part; and Hong Kong, which it will absorb in 1997! Furthermore, America's principal economic issues in Asia and the Pacific lend themselves for the moment only to bilateral resolution: All the power of the Pacific Rim nations cannot resolve the Japanese-American trade controversies. The Pacific Rim is, then, a nascent element in the New World Order, but bilateral relations with its more advanced members are crucial to America's role in the order now.

The Two Koreas

One of the bitter legacies of the Cold War is the division of Korea into a capitalist south and a hard-line communist north. Although it is reported to be near economic collapse, North Korea, even after the death of Kim Il Sung, prefers isolation from the global economy other than its relations with

---

[53] On the subject of Japan's ascendency, see Panos Mourdoukoutas, *Japan's Turn: The Interchange in Economic Leadership* (Lanham, Md.: University Press of America, 1993).

China. In fact, until a settlement in 1995, North Korea sought independent nuclear status as a way of avoiding the East German solution of being absorbed into—in contrast to "reunified with"—the south. And while it advocates a peace treaty ending the Korean War, it will negotiate only with the United States, not with South Korea. Furthermore, in agreeing to discontinue nuclear weapons research it will recieve reactors for generating electricity, but it will not accept them from South Korea.

If Americans see Iraq and Cuba as maverick states, they see North Korea as a passive enemy dangerous only to South Korea. Consequently, 25,000 American troops remain in the south more than four decades after the end of the Korean War. Reunification would, in the American view, remove one of the nagging problems willed to the New World Order from the Cold War and would give South Korea an opportunity for economic expansion, though at a very high cost.[54] On the other hand, South Korea's development already poses a number of trade problems for the United States, and so there are many Americans who see a non-belligerent division of the two Koreas as preferable to unification.

South Korea's meteoric economic rise has recently stalled, however. Throughout the 1980s, for example, its average annual growth rate was almost 10 percent; in the 1990s it is only about half of that. Inflation has soared, exports have declined, and deficits have expanded as wages and other production costs have risen. In the words of one observer,

> South Korea is no longer one of the robust Asian "tigers." It now has a "one-two-three" economy, struggling against the "three highs" and the "four shortages." One is for single-digit growth; two, for double-digit inflation; and three, for a triple-digit deficit. The three highs refer to high wages, high

interest rates, and high exchange rates for the won. The four shortages are in the areas of manpower, funds, technology, and social infrastructure. These factors have been responsible for soaring prices, sagging exports, and a growing balance of payment deficit.[55]

Under all these circumstances, some Americans wonder, can South Korea even afford reunification in the way it could have a decade ago? The cost to West Germany of reunification is a daunting reminder of how expensive it is for the richer half.

The United States and the European Union

The United States emerged from World War Two at an economic crest, partly because of the huge wartime industrial expansion and partly because the other large industrial economies of the world had been devastated. The transformation to a peacetime economy was assisted by the huge need for industrial products abroad. A further boost was provided by the Cold War. Fearful of potential Soviet aggression and concerned that the destitution of Western Europeans might lead to a surge of socialist sentiment, the Congress appropriated $14 billion for the European Recovery Plan, commonly called the Marshall Plan. The purpose was to rebuild the European consumer economies and thereby strengthen their constitutional governments. Meanwhile, Americans began a long period of direct private investment in Europe. The Cold War and the Korean War illuminated the importance of maintaining a mixed wartime-peacetime economy, and so government funds were poured into the defense industry even as private investment multiplied. American industrial wealth soared.

Subsequently, however, the American position has reversed in Europe just as it has in Japan. The maturation of the European Union comes after a

---

[54] For the economic consequences of reunification see John Y. T. Kuark, "Economic Impact of Korean Unification," *Decision Science Proceedings*, June 1993. It is estimated that the cost of German reunification to clean and provide modern infrastructure to the former East Germany was $400 billion in the first five years.

[55] Manwoo Lee, "The Two Koreas and the Unification Game," *Current History*, December 1993, pp. 421–425 at p. 423.

long period of economic integration under the European Economic Community. In its most fundamental form, this is a free trade area in which the members remove barriers to trade and capital transfer among themselves and establish common exclusionary practices with respect to nonmembers. The United States, of course, is a nonmember. This developed, furthermore, in an era in which Europe underwent massive reindustrialization, not merely recovering from the war in familiar industries, but launching into the new industries of the post-industrial (technological) age as well. Through fifty years of progress, the European Union has built elaborate institutions with limited supranational authority (that is, the Union as a whole can create obligations for the member states). In the area of international trade, it is by now accurate to say that through its organization, economic development, territorial expansion, and institutionalization, the European Union is now a superstate in world competition.

To Americans, the success of Europe is due in no small part to their own wartime and post-war generosity. Furthermore, from their own federal origins—the United States is a federation of fifty states, each of which still makes claims to sovereignty—they encouraged European unification as a basis of promoting peace (it seems to Americans that Europe has been at war forever) and prosperity (to make Europe less dependent on American taxpayers). And yet in international trade practice, Americans find Europeans thankless. European producers now fulfill most of the industrial needs of Western and Southern Europe, and where they cannot, they have made it expensive for Americans to do so. Their policies on subsidizing industry accelerate new product development above the norm of classical market economies. And subsidies reduce commercial prices, because manufacturers have less investment cost to recover. The European Airbus industry is a case in point. The subsidies its aircraft receive from public funds make it less expensive than comparable models built by Boeing and McDonnell Douglas, whose exports have declined sharply. They even compete so well within the United States that some domestic carriers are turning away from their traditional suppliers and purchasing Airbus products. To offset this price advantage, McDonnell Douglas has moved some of its manufacturing to new plants in China, where it takes advantage of low wages and high personal discipline. To the worker who has lost his or her job as a consequence, the culprit is not McDonnell Douglas, but Europe.

Another result of this kind of competition has been the urge "to get behind the tariff barriers." To avoid both transportation costs and tariffs on imported goods, American corporations have either bought or built production facilities in Europe, where they deal as though they were European. This is one of the main causes for the proliferation of transnational or multinational corporations, those that have corporate headquarters in one country but which operate in one or more others. It is a strategy in which American corporations build in Europe products for the European market. This is extremely lucrative for the manufacturer and its stockholders, but it has a number of negative characteristics. First, the employees of these so-called offshore subsidiaries or affiliates are not Americans but Europeans. Second, while the profits are eventually repatriated with positive effects on the balance of payments, the original capital cost is a drain from the United States. Uncontrolled, that could pose a treat to the gold supply that underwrites the value of American currency. Third, offshore operations are not subject to all aspects of American law and, in the view of some, are actually beyond the law. Tax liability on the sales of American goods produced abroad is a major complication.

In the New World Order, there are additional complications. For one, the emphasis on economic competition has spawned a demand that the European Union expand to include the states of Northern Europe. Clearly, as the tendency in the global economy is away from nationalism and toward multilateralism, more states will demand inclusion. In addition, the Westward turn of the former Soviet allies gives the European Union partners two large new advantages: new, open, underserved markets swinging rapidly to capitalism, and inexpensive

Presidents Yeltsin and Clinton share a laugh at a cryptic Yeltsin comment about the press, 1995. (*Source:* © AFP/Bettmann)

sources of labor. If the environmental horrors of the past can be overcome and modern production facilities constructed, the European Union will accelerate the economic recovery of Central and Eastern Europe at great long-term profit to itself. Americans are scrambling to take advantage of post–Cold War pro-American sentiment in Central and Eastern Europe to avoid being left behind in this unfolding process.

The United States and Global Stability

In its search for post–Cold War leadership strategies, the United States, in President Clinton's view, has "to drop the abstractions and dogma and pursue, based on trial and error and persistent experimentation, a policy that advances our values of freedom and democracy, peace and security."[56] Successful examples include restoration of an elected presidency in Haiti, humanitarian intervention in Somalia, NATO-coordinated air strikes in Bosnia, a 20,000-member portion of a NATO peacekeeping force in Bosnia, a multibillion-dollar loan to

Mexico to stimulate recovery from collapse of the peso, and successful diplomatic leadership in Bosnia, Northern Ireland, and the Middle East. In an effort to promote Russian democratization, Washington adopted a "Yeltsin-only" policy, attempting to strengthen the Yeltsin government despite the war in Chechnya and communist resurgence, and despite conservative chagrin at home. The decision to expand NATO toward Russia's boundaries displeased American liberals and caused divisions within NATO that were temporarily concealed by a concerted effort on the Bosnia crisis.

Consistent with the post–Cold War experience that the worst threats to peace arise from ethnic forces and poverty, the United States adopted a new intelligence strategy. In the words of one official,

> During the cold war, most security threats stemmed form state-to-state aggression, so most of the [intelligence] analysis was of factors that could produce state-to-state agression. Now we're focusing more on internal factors that can destabilize governments and lead to civil wars and ethnic strife. Now we're paying much more attention to early warning factors, like famine and the environment.[57]

---

[56] A Freedom House address as quoted in *The New York Times*, October 7, 1995, "Clinton Warns of U.S. Retreat to Isolationism," pp. A1 and A5 at p. A5.

[57] As quoted in "The Greening of U.S. Diplomacy: Focus on Ecology," *The New York Times*, October 9, 1995, p. A6.

The strategy includes an increase in scientific and social scientific studies in potential hot spots, and computer networks to speed the integration of information from other national and international sources. This job has been assigned to the Central Intelligence Agency (CIA).

Conclusion

The twentieth century has seen a radical alteration in the world position of the United States. It entered the epoch clinging to isolation but was forced twice in twenty-five years to intervene in European conflicts that threatened world stability. After 1945, it took up the challenge to play a permanent international role and twice more went to war, this time against spreading communism. Despite the détente that followed the Vietnam War, persistent confrontation of NATO and the Warsaw Pact, together with nagging problems in Central America and the Middle East, kept geopolitical strategy and military preparedness at the core of the foreign policy debate.

The 1980s brought the most remarkable spectrum of hopes and rhetoric. The decade began with the Soviet Union occupying Afghanistan and with martial law in Poland imposed on a liberalization movement. Soviet strength virtually throughout the world—in Europe, Asia, the Pacific, Africa, Central America, and the Caribbean—seemed ominous to Americans. The Reagan administration committed the nation to an extravagant but, to the majority, necessary arms program based on the continuing threat of the "evil empire." Meanwhile, relations with China were normalized, as new, forward-looking leadership welcomed foreign investment and commerce as methods of rapid economic development. On the economic front, a worldwide recession was followed by a recovery throughout the West and Japan that increased global trading competition, much to the detriment of the United States and its balance of trade.

In the early 1990s, attention had shifted largely from national security to economic competition as the foreign policy theme. The end of the Cold War and the demise of the Soviet Union had reduced global confrontation. Europe was partly demilitarized as troops were called home and whole generations of weapons were destroyed on both sides. The new Russia, its former Soviet partners, and its former Eastern European allies adopted reform policies that, to Americans, resembled Western-style democracy and capitalism. America had won the Cold War, and democracy and capitalism had triumphed over communism and socialism. Now the nation's economic woes were at the top of the foreign policy agenda.

Those difficulties focused on Japan, Western Europe, and the Developing World. The huge and chronic trade deficit with respect to Japan, the fear of a fortress Europe shutting out American goods after economic union, and the Developing World's trio of problems—need for financial aid, demand for preferential trading status, and staggering debt—all weighed heavily on Americans, who for a half-century had been accustomed to economic domination and uninterrupted enrichment. As security imperatives diminished, the national agenda turned to the American position in international commerce. The era of the United States as world policeman was over; but Americans were not content to be a declining power.

The shift to the primacy of economics in international affairs does not mean that security affairs are unimportant. Indeed, as we have seen, the New World Order is anything but tranquil. Since the end of the Cold War, the United States has had to make several decisions on whether or not to intervene in foreign hostilities. Those most heatedly debated regarded Bosnia, where the bombing of Serbian positions under NATO command and later the stationing of American troops for peacekeeping were matters of great public and partisan interest. In a 1995 speech designed to promote interest in the peacekeeping mission, President Clinton blasted his critics for their "isolationist backlash," and concluded: "Unilateralism in the world . . . we live in is not a viable option."[58] The unilateral

---

[58] As quoted in *The New York Times*, October 7, 1995, p. A5.

show of naval force as a symbol of commitment to Taiwan was an exception.

Nonetheless, without the Cold War, the cohesive motive of American foreign policy is gone. While global and domestic economic problems have bedeviled the United States in the 1990s, the underlying problem is to find a comprehensive rationale for the future. For the moment few things have been put in place. First, the basic goals are economic, and second, the modalities are more multilateral than they have been in the past. Bill Clinton defeated George Bush's bid for reelection in 1992 because of economic stagnation; both Houses of Congress fell to the Republican party in 1994 for the first time in a generation because of an immense demand for change in the national agenda. How the vision of the American role in the New World Order will emerge in establishing that agenda is unknown. Both America's wealth and U.S. leadership in the New World Order are at stake.

CHAPTER 4

The Perspectives of America's Principal Partners

The imbalance in the world's wealth tilts decidedly toward just eighteen northern hemisphere countries: the fifteen nations of the European Union,[1] Japan, Canada, and the United States. Among them passes fully two-thirds of all world trade, and their peoples have among the highest living standards. Except for a few states like Switzerland, these eighteen dominate world performance in nutrition, sanitation, education, health care, life expectancy, maternal and fetal health, industrial and technological innovation, savings and investment, GDP per capita, and many other social and economic indicators. In 1993 their combined GDP exceeded $17 trillion; all the rest of the world had less than $7 trillion. They also lead the world in political stability, even though their forms of government vary greatly. Since in the main (Austria is politically neutral) they also participate in the U.S.-centered defense structure, they also account for much of the world's defense spending. No matter how one describes the political structure of the New World Order—multipolar, unipolar, or nonpolar—these states wield great power in the aggregate. But as the declining years of the Cold War demonstrated, Japan, Europe, and Canada have economic and political destinies of their own that pull them in separate directions, often to the displeasure of the United States. The relationship among them is the constant struggle to balance interdependence with autonomy, common needs with individual goals, cooperation with competition. Often the outcome is conflict.

Japan

A paradox of forces shapes the Japanese world view. On the one hand, Japan is intensely nationalistic and has a proud history of cultural continuity and empire. Yet on the other hand, Japan removed itself entirely from world affairs from 1640 to 1854, when it was "opened" by threat of force by the American fleet of Commodore Matthew C. Perry. After the First World War, Japan was humiliated by the refusal of the Western powers to include in the Covenant of the League of Nations a declaration of racial equality. In 1945, under relentless firebombing and two atomic attacks, Japan was forced into surrender; and after six years of occupation by American troops, a peace treaty was arranged at the price of a series of military and

---

[1] Membership in the European Union (EU) can be dated from 1951 when the European Coal and Steel Community (ECSC) was founded, from 1957 when the European Economic Community (EEC) was founded, or from 1967 when the European Community (EC) was formed through the merger of the EEC with the European Atomic Energy Commission (EURATOM). The term European Union became official at the end of 1992 to mark completion of the final phase of the customs union aspects of European integration. This book uses 1957 as the initial date.

The original membership consisted of West Germany, France, Italy, Belgium, Luxembourg, and the Netherlands. In 1973 the United Kingdom, Denmark, and Ireland were added. Greece was admitted in 1981, and Spain and Portugal in 1986. Membership was increased to the current fifteen with the addition of Sweden, Finland, and Austria in 1995. (Norway was also offered admission, but it was defeated in a public referendum in November 1994.)

economic agreements. While these provided security during the Cold War era, they also compromised Japan's self-determination.

Despite these restraints, however, since the
Second World War Japan has undergone a remarkable economic rebirth. This island nation, which
fits a population half that of United States into a
territorial mass only the size of Montana, has
matched the United States in several economic
measures and exceeded it in some. Though its
growth rate has cooled in the 1990s, in twenty years
its gross domestic product skyrocketed from 20 percent of that of the United States to 67 percent. At
current rates of growth, it is entirely probable that
the Japanese GDP will exceed that of the United
States within a decade. (See Table 4–1 for some
competitive indicators, and Table 4–2 comparing
Japan's rate of growth with those of other principal
industrialized countries.) But to understand the
unique elements of Japan's world view, it is necessary first to explore the evolution of modern Japan.

The Opening of Japan

Like China, Japan fell into the covetous orbit of
American Manifest Destiny in the nineteenth century. As the China trade multiplied after 1844,
American merchants eyed Japan as an additional
source of Oriental goods and as a supply station and
refuge that would minimize the hazards of the long
Pacific journey. Already Americans had absorbed

the idea of this new land, and it had inspired their
missionary zeal: Popular tales about the Japanese
treatment of shipwrecked sailors had prompted
some Americans to brand the Japanese enemies of
humankind. After two unsuccessful diplomatic efforts, in the wake of expansionism in the Mexican
War and the acquisition of the Pacific coast, American nationalism and the idea of "opening" Japan
converged. The departure of Perry's squadron was
appropriately festive to the anticipated results, for it
was to mark the first time Americans would deal directly with the Japanese since the Napoleonic Wars,
during which a few Americans had carried on the
trickle of Dutch trade that Japan permitted. (Ironically, one of the sites of that trade was Nagasaki, the
second of the two cities destroyed a century later by
America's atomic bombs.)

In 1854, the Japanese entered reluctantly into
a treaty with the United States, seeing it as an
opportunity to learn industrial science. If the commercial treaty opened the door to Japan, the immediate evolution of Japanese-American relations
propped it wide. For by 1858, although Japan had
gained few concessions, Americans had acquired
most-favored-nation status (granting automatic improvement of trading conditions if Japan were to
offer more liberal terms to any other party), the
right of extraterritoriality (Americans charged with
crimes in Japan were to be tried in American courts
by American laws), and the rights to teach Western religions and to establish religious institutions.

TABLE 4–1

BASIC ECONOMIC INDICATORS FOR JAPAN
AND THE UNITED STATES

| | GDP | | | GNP/Capita 1993 | Avg. Ann. Growth GNP/Capita 1980–93 |
	1970	1993	Change		
Japan	$0.2 trillion	$4.2 trillion	21×	$31,490	3.4%
United States	1.0	6.3	6.3×	24,740	1.7

Source: World Bank, *World Development Report, 1995,* tables 1 through 3, pp. 162–167.

TABLE 4–2

COMPARISON OF AVERAGE ANNUAL GROWTH RATES IN THE INDUSTRIAL SECTOR FOR JAPAN AND PRINCIPAL TRADING PARTNERS

	1965–1980	1980–1993
Japan	8.5%	3.4%
United States	1.7	1.7
Britain	–0.5	2.3
France	4.3 $\Big\}$ 2.4 % = Avg.	1.6 $\Big\}$ 1.8 % = Avg.
Canada	3.5	1.4
West Germany	2.8	2.0[1]
Ratio	8.5/2.4 = 3.5×	3.4/1.8 = 1.9×

[1] Number reflects West German portion only.

Source: World Bank, *World Development Report, 1989,* from table 2, pp. 166–167; and *World Development Report, 1995,* from table 2, pp. 164–165.

As was the case in early Sino-American relations, then, the principal mark of these early dealings with the West was imbalance: Japan was assigned the obligations, while America gained the lucrative and enviable benefits.

Japanese Expansionism

As exploitive as the American presence might have been, it was not pervasive. As Japan became more aware of the Industrial Revolution elsewhere and commenced its own modernization, it was free to conduct its own foreign policy (except as its external interests were limited by its trade treaties with Washington and other capitals). Hence, despite a watchful eye from America, Japan was able to begin a quest for its own empire. Control of Korea, long an object of competition among China, Japan, and Russia, prompted the Sino-Japanese War of 1894–95, a war that Japan won because of its superior arms and modernization. Although Chinese interests were uprooted from Korea and Taiwan (Formosa), Japanese acquisitions on the Asian mainland were seized by Russia with the assistance of France and Germany. It was clear that if Japan were to achieve dominance in modern Asian, Western influence within the region would have to be restricted.

Peace was but a lull, as the Russo-Japanese War (1904–05) ensued, largely over competing claims to Manchuria and Korea. Again, however, a Western state's policy was to dominate the outcome. Having acquired the Philippines in 1898, the United States hoped that Asia and the Pacific would be stabilized by a Russo-Japanese stalemate. When Japan unexpectedly won decisive land and sea battles and appeared ready to seize eastern Siberia, President Theodore Roosevelt saw urgent need for a peace that would ensure the stalemate, as war apparently could not. While giving his assent in the Taft-Katsura Agreement of 1905 to Japanese control of Korea, Roosevelt urged moderation in Tokyo's other demands for indemnification. Because of his role, Japanese opinion blamed the unsatisfactory diplomatic outcome on the United States: U.S. policy had betrayed the Japanese victory. The flames of hostility were fanned by frequent reports of anti-Japanese racial violence in California and by American policies that excluded Asian immigrants. With Russia vanquished and

China quieted by Western colonialism, redress of grievances with the United States became the focal point of Japanese politics.[2]

The tenuous understanding that was achieved through a visit of the American fleet (painted white) to Japanese ports and through executive agreements concerning immigration and mutual respect for Pacific territories was broken by the First World War. When at the war's outset Germany vacated its China holdings, Japan moved swiftly to occupy them. Shortly thereafter, Tokyo issued to China the Twenty-one Demands (1915), which sought to enlarge Japan's influence throughout China. Because wartime diplomacy did little to resolve these issues, their persistence accentuated the mutual distrust. At the Paris Peace Conference, Japan—its economy vibrant, its navy among the world's most modern, and its national spirit running high—attached the China issue to a demand that the the League of Nations Covenant include a declaration of racial equality. Without it, Japan would not bow to President Woodrow Wilson's demand for a timetable for the return of Germany's former holdings to China. European states rich in non-white colonial holdings rejected Japan's demand. Western resistance prevailed, leaving the China question unresolved but, worse, leaving the Japanese more convinced than before of the untrustworthiness of Western intentions.

The breakdown of trust also sparked a division of Japanese opinion concerning the country's role in the post-war world. The civilian government and conservative elements readily subscribed to the Washington Treaties of 1922, which sought a permanent balance of interests in China and a restriction on naval armaments. But to expansionists and the military, they constituted surrender to a Western design to regulate Japan's influence in Asia. The military slowly became virtually self-governing, and

by 1931 the government denied that troops were moving into Manchuria even while the army was using a minor (and deliberately provoked) skirmish at Mukden as the pretext for a massive invasion of Manchuria and eventually of China, Asia, and the Pacific. To the expansionists this was a policy born of having been denied the prizes of conquest in 1885, 1905, and 1918. Consistent with this thinking were the decisions to withdraw from the League of Nations, to create the Greater East Asian Co-Prosperity Sphere, and to join the Axis Alliance (1940) with Germany and Italy. These moves were also necessitated by the imperfections of American neutrality and its tendency to favor China, and Washington's economic sanctions against Japan. Prevention, then, or at least delay, of American intervention in the Asian war required an aerial attack on the American fleet at Pearl Harbor, Hawaii, on December 7, 1941.[3]

The horrors of the Second World War in the Pacific climaxed with several events that apparently were indicative of Western attitudes toward the Orient. On the tactical front, as an alternative to invasion, the United States chose to firebomb Japanese population centers, a policy facilitated by the discovery of napalm (jellied gasoline); even worse, it used the only two atomic bombs in existence to devastate the industrial cities of Hiroshima and Nagasaki. Two political decisions also stand out in Japanese memories. First, at the Potsdam (Berlin) Conference, held a scant three weeks prior to the war's end, it was decided to force Japan into unconditional surrender and to reject an offer of surrender that had as its sole condition the preservation of the tradition of the emperor's sovereignty. (This condition was subsequently accepted, but only after the two atomic bombings.) Second, the Soviet Union declared war on Japan on the day of the second atomic attack, giving Moscow five days of belligerency and almost no combat, but a claim to reparations despite five years of formal Soviet-Japanese nonbelligerency.

---

[2] Raymond A. Esthus, *Theodore Roosevelt and Japan* (Seattle: University of Washington Press, 1966); Howard K. Beale, *Theodore Roosevelt and the Rise of America to World Power* (Baltimore: Johns Hopkins University Press, 1956), particularly chapter 5; and Charles E. Neu, *An Uncertain Friendship* (Cambridge, Mass.: Harvard University Press, 1967).

---

[3] Herbert Feis, *The Road to Pearl Harbor* (Princeton, N.J.: Princeton University Press, 1950.)

Ruins of Nagasaki after the atomic bombing in August 1945. (*Source:* © John Bennewitz/Black Star)

To the Japanese, the firebombings were an unnecessary and heinous attack on innocent civilian populations. These and the atomic bombings were wholly unnecessary in view of the offer to surrender on a single cultural condition. Because there was no strategic value to the use of atomic bombs, Japan already having reached virtual submission, these attacks are taken as evidence of the American intention to pulverize Japanese society or to demonstrate American strength to the Soviet Union at great and indiscriminate cost. The opportunism of the Soviet Union was seen with equal suspicion.

One haunting question pervades all of these arguments: Would the Second World War have concluded in this manner had Caucasian rather than Asian lives been at stake, Western civilization rather than Japanese?

During the occupation that followed, the Japanese were faced not only with national reconstruction, but also with the need for a revitalization of self-esteem under a victor whose intentions they did not trust even in good times.

The American Occupation

The prevailing international climate when Japan embarked on its program of restoration was one of utter turmoil. All Europe was in tatters; China was in the middle of a civil war; and the Soviet-American wartime rapport had broken down. Japan had to accept the United States as the sole occupying power, despite the intentions of the Allies to have a multilateral policy. It also had to acknowledge General Douglas MacArthur as the Supreme Commander of the Allied Powers in the Pacific, even though he personified the Allied conquest of Japan. In addition, the Japanese suspected the American estimate of a quarter-century to achieve the objectives of occupation: democratization, industrial restoration at a level below war potential, land reform and agricultural self-sufficiency, and the purging of war criminals and imperialists. Remarkably, nearly all these were achieved, or set in irreversible motion, in little more than three years. Within that time, MacArthur had authorized the drafting of a new constitution, and by the end of 1948, he and others were publicly calling for an expeditious end to the occupation.

But now the Japanese recognized that a prolonged occupation, if not oppressive, might be preferable to speedy independence. The Cold War was under way; Soviet-American talks on Korean reunification had broken down; and the ideological future of Asia seemed written in the forthcoming victory of Chinese communism. Independence would mean dealing with the Soviet Union, balancing the interests of two Chinas, accommodating American economic and military might when its right of intrusion was no longer acknowledged, and surviving on industries that would be long on productive capacity but short on raw materials and energy sources. Now was scarcely a propitious time for new Asian ventures.

Again, however, the decision fell to Washington, as Mao's victory and the Korean War altered Japan's place in the American world scheme. No longer did the United States look upon Japan as a pastoral and self-sufficient island kingdom but, rather, as a powerful, industrialized, and strategically located ally; an atomic fortress and haven for American investments; and a center of operations for American manipulation of Asian power. The cover of United Nations legitimacy in Korea could not conceal that in its decision to contain communism in Asia, Washington had summarily transformed the purposes, the timing, and the consequences of the Japan occupation.[4]

The Pacific Treaties and Japanese Prosperity

Amid these new circumstances, John Foster Dulles, later secretary of state, began to negotiate the Pacific Treaties of 1951. Dulles's zealous anticommunism, heightened by events in China and Korea, seemed to ensure a revised role for Japan; his insistence on a "peace of reconciliation" rather than a "peace of retribution"[5] created a cordial negotiating environment. It was clear from the beginning, however, that within this framework, the United States would require military, economic, and political conditions of Japan befitting its Cold War strategic agenda in Asia.

Of the four resulting Pacific Treaties, two pertained to Japan: a multilateral World War Two Peace Treaty and a Japanese-American Security Treaty. (The other two linked the Philippines, Australia, and New Zealand to American alliances.) In the Peace Treaty, Japan was obliged to sacrifice virtually all territories acquired since 1895. But from

---

[4] Frederick S. Dunn, *Peace-making and Settlement with Japan* (Princeton, N.J.: Princeton University Press, 1963).

[5] As a young man, Dulles had been a member of the American Peace Commission at the Paris talks leading to the Treaty of Versailles. He came away from the conference with the conviction that the peace would not last because it was punitive, thus forming the basis for his later strategy of negotiating a Japanese peace treaty based on reconciliation rather than retribution. See Townsend Hoopes, The Devil and John Foster Dulles (Boston: Atlantic-Little, Brown, 1973), especially chapters 2 and 7.

an economic standpoint, the arrangement was beneficial to Japan, because it was able to invest in economic revitalization capital that might have been squandered on security had Washington not been willing to support Japan's defenses. From 1950 through 1976, Japan's GNP multiplied 12 times, while that of the United States multiplied only 2.3 times and the average of those of the principal Western European countries about 3 times. From 1965 to 1980, the annual growth rate in Japan's GNP was 3.5 times the average of the United States, Britain, France, Germany, and Canada, and that from 1980 through 1993 was about twice theirs. Furthermore, as Table 4–1 indicates, Japan's GDP multiplied 21 times from 1970 through 1993, and that of the United States only about 6 times. Japan also gradually amassed huge trade surpluses, and the yen became one of the world's two most powerful currencies. By all measures except military might, therefore, Japan's status as a major power has been taken for granted for two decades.[6]

Japan from Recovery to World Stature: The Many Obstacles

While Americans look with envy upon Japan and its great economic miracle, Japanese are more likely to focus on the obstacles that had to be overcome, especially because most of them were external and often in conflict with Japan's goal of economic autonomy.

Trade with China   As Japan's industrial recovery proceeded, the absence of many vital resources—including fuel and most metals—made it dependent on foreign supply. China was rich in many of these and was in need of Japan's industrial products. The two seemed to be natural trading partners, each rich

in what the other needed. Until the end of the Vietnam War and the normalization of relations between Beijing and Washington, however, Washington's pressure prevented this relationship from maturing. The Japanese interpreted this as interference with national decision making and an affront to national economic growth. They also viewed it as a ploy to use containment of China as an instrument for restricting Japanese competition with American manufacturers. Furthermore, it was seen as a cause of unnecessary delay in normalizing Asian international relations, a delay from which Japan might suffer and for which it might be held responsible. Full diplomatic and economic activity did not commence until 1971–72, after which trade grew steadily as did Japanese investment in China's modernization. Table 4–3 shows the recent growth of Sino-Japanese trade and contrasts it with America's China trade.

Territorial Matters   Of the many territorial questions left over from the Second World War, none has been more symbolic to the Japanese than Okinawa. Even after the Pacific Treaties, this large territory, regarded by the Japanese as virtually a fifth home island, remained in American control, continuing as a major center for conventional and nuclear military strategies. Washington persistently rejected demands for the reversion of Okinawa to Japan, particularly as the Vietnam War underscored its strategic importance. The question was further complicated by powerful senatorial interests that insisted on restricting Japanese textile exports to the United States as a condition of reversion. Finally in 1972, amid global trade negotiations, American reassessment of its policy in Vietnam, and normalization of relations with China, Okinawa was returned to Japan by treaty, subject only to American rights under the Mutual Security Treaty of 1950.[7]

More recently the subject of Soviet—and then Russian—occupation of the Kurile Islands, a chain north of the home islands seized by the Soviet

---

[6] As examples, see Herman Kahn, *The Emerging Japanese Superstate: Challenge and Response* (Englewood Cliffs, N.J.: Prentice-Hall, 1971); Nobutaka Ike, *Japan: The New Superstate* (San Francisco: Freeman, 1973); Frank Gibney, *Japan: The Fragile Super Power*, rev. ed. (New York: Norton, 1979); and Panos Mourdoukoutas, *Japan's Turn* (New York: University Press of America, 1993).

[7] Chae-Jin Lee, "The Making of the Sino-Japanese Peace and Friendship Treaty," *Pacific Affairs*, fall 1979, pp. 420–445.

TABLE 4–3

GROWTH OF JAPANESE AND AMERICAN TRADE WITH CHINA

	UNITED STATES			JAPAN		
	China's Imports	China's Exports	Total	Total	China's Imports	China's Exports
1987	$4.8 billion	$3.0 billion	$7.8 billion	$16.5 billion	$10.1 billion	$6.4 billion
1988	6.6	3.4	10.0	19.1	11.1	8.0
1989	7.9	4.4	12.3	18.9	10.5	8.4
1990	6.6	5.3	11.9	16.9	7.7	9.2
1991	8.0	6.2	14.2	20.3	10.0	10.3
1992	8.9	8.6	17.5	25.4	13.7	11.7
1993	10.6	17.0	27.6	39.1	23.3	15.8

Source: International Monetary Fund, *Direction of Trade Statistics Yearbook, 1994.*

Union after World War Two, has moved to the center of the Japanese agenda. During the 1980s Moscow transformed these sparsely populated islands into a strategic fortress, installing long-range missiles with multiple nuclear warheads, raising troop deployments, and expanding naval facilities, especially for its Pacific nuclear submarine fleet. The territorial issue now merged with the vital security question of Japan's vulnerability to Soviet force or strategic blackmail, at a time at which confidence in the American security shield was low. In 1990, after the fall of the Soviet Union, Russian President Yeltsin proposed a five-part, multiyear program for settlement of this issue, but little has been done to date. One might think that the post–Cold War conditions would have diminished the importance of these bases, but there is no evidence that this has occurred. The reasons are apparently (1) consistent with the historic Russian need for warm-water ports in the Pacific, (2) the modernity of these facilities particularly as relates to the electronic C3I (command, control, communications, and intelligence), and (3) uncertainty regarding Russian long-range goals in the area, affecting not only Japan but China as well.

American Military Bases   A closely related issue was the status of American military bases on

Okinawa and elsewhere in Japan, authorized by the Security Treaty but popularly seen as symbols of compromised sovereignty and vestigial occupation. Most annoying was their continued use for servicing the American nuclear submarine fleet, a presence that the atomic-bomb-conscious population detested. Americanization of the Vietnam War heightened the urgency of these issues, as many Japanese feared their land would be targeted for retaliation against American actions. Finally two agreements were worked out. One removed nuclear weapons from Japanese territory and territorial waters, and the second required the United States to secure "prior consent" from Tokyo before launching military action from Japan. Still, the presence of bases is resented, and when three American servicemen were convicted of raping a twelve-year-old Japanese in 1995, public pressure resumed to close the bases permanently. Four decades after the end of occupation, the Japanese still feel the national humiliation of foreign interference.

The Nixon Doctrine   Resentment over military bases did not mean that the Japanese shunned American sponsorship of their national defense, or that they were willing to bear the cost themselves. Thus the ambiguity of Japan's place in the Nixon

Japanese police protecting U.S. serviceman. (*Source:* AP)

Doctrine (1970) sent a shock through Japanese domestic politics. In its search for methods of face-saving withdrawal from Vietnam, President Richard M. Nixon's administration considered noninterventionary paths to Western-oriented political stability in the underindustrialized world. The United States would no longer intervene in civil or regional wars, but it would provide arms and military information to help governments meet insurrections.[8] Though not included in the doctrine, the Japanese wondered what it might mean for the security of Asia and the Pacific. Would Japan need to remilitarize? Despite the Security Treaty, did the Nixon Doctrine and the American withdrawal from Southeast Asia portend reduced reliability in the American security shield?[9] Should Japan become a nuclear power? This last question was made more compelling when, in 1974, India tested a single nuclear weapon. Long the subject of heated

debate between those who abhor nuclear weapons and those who consider them a fruitful alternative to American domination, the matter was not settled until 1976, when the Japanese government signed the Nuclear Non-Proliferation Treaty, denying itself the nuclear option.

The First Nixon Shock Events quickened in 1971 when President Nixon announced his intention to visit China the following winter. This decision, made without consulting Tokyo, stunned the Japanese, who saw only contradiciton and illogic in a plan for Sino-American détente and continuing the Vietnam War. They suspected American motives in normalizing relations with China while forbidding Japan to do the same, particularly on trade. To make matters worse, if the United States ceased isolating China and enacted the Nixon Doctrine simultaneously, were the uncertainties for Japanese security multiplied? Anxiety over the future grew with each new American pronouncement. The path to independent policy, always obstructed by foreign interference, was now cluttered with unforeseen, unknown, and potentially menacing complications.

---

[8] Richard M. Nixon, *U.S. Foreign Policy for the 1970s*, report to the Congress by the President of the United States, February 25, 1971.
[9] Frank C. Langdon, "Japanese Reactions to India's Nuclear Explosion," *Pacific Affairs*, summer 1975, pp. 173–180.

The Second Nixon Shock Scarcely a month later, Washington announced an antirecessionary policy that included a ninety-day tariff surcharge of 10 percent on imports (with certain exceptions for Developing Nations and specially protected commodities). The Japanese interpreted this as an assault on the yen's value and on the Japanese automobile industry, already the leading edge of an export program that had eroded the American balance of trade. By this act the United States had directly and boldly intervened in Japan's domestic and international economic policies as a reprisal for success and had restricted Japan's global industrial competitiveness. Japan's post-war economic renaissance, supported by the United States as a way of controlling the Cold War Asian power distribution, had become too competitive. Once again, the setting in which Japan would have to design its regional and world roles was fraught with the uncertainty of unilaterally altered assumptions.

The Petroleum Crisis Caught in global recession and inflation, forced by Washington into a damaging currency revaluation, and once again conscious of their vulnerability to foreign economic decisions, the Japanese also saw domestic capital flow out to lucrative investment opportunities elsewhere. Their remarkable growth rate began to slide toward zero, and their enviable payments surplus dwindled. Now, in 1973, the Organization of Petroleum Exporting Countries (OPEC) threatened Japan with an oil embargo unless it either discontinued its relations and trading policy with Israel or offered technological assistance to the OPEC members. Even after the threat was withdrawn on the basis of an oil-for-technology agreement, the price of oil continued to rise intolerably, forcing Japan to petition the United States for a collective diplomatic offensive by the oil-consuming countries.

Japan's shortage of raw materials is nowhere more apparent than in fuel. At the time of the embargo, Japan ranked fourth in the world as an energy consumer and only twenty-third as a producer, much of that from nuclear sources. Replacements for OPEC oil were years off and depended on successful agreements and exploration with China, the old Soviet Union, Canada, South Korea, Taiwan, and Vietnam. With plans to expand electrical generation by a factor of twenty in a decade, the threat of embargo and the unchecked price increases in oil were particularly menacing. Though industrial and technological exports to the OPEC countries were increased, Japan's inability to compete with the United States and others in arms sales created a disadvantage that more than tripled its trade deficit with the Middle East in the following year.[10] This became a chronic problem for Japan, as the steady price increase in oil continued well into the 1980s, forcing Japan to enter into a multibillion dollar agreement with Canada and to purchase West Virginia coal mines.

Fortunately, the demand for oil has not risen as was predicted two decades ago. This is due partly to a national conservation program, partly to the use of other fuels (coal, gas, nuclear), but also partly to the general slowdown in incremental demand because of the more modest annual economic growth rate. Meanwhile, the relation of volume to price has also stabilized. Since 1985, Japan's oil consumption has risen 25 percent (or about 2 percent annually) and the price 14 percent (or about 1 percent annually), a clear advantage to a consumer of Japan's volume. As a hedge against the future, however, and always in search of ways of reducing dependence on the Middle East, Japan is involved in joint exploration with Vietnam, Canada, and China and is seeking ways to do the same with Russia. The importance of these alternatives is accentuated by public aversion to nuclear fuel, as shown in the response to a 1995 reactor accident and two efforts by government agencies to conceal it.

Burden-sharing in Defense Throughout the Cold War, one of the recurring themes of Japanese policy and of Japanese-American relations was dividing the cost of Japan's security. In one respect, this was an economic matter: Because the United

---

[10] Atef Sultan, "Japan Sells Hard to Make Up Oil Deficit," *Middle East Economic Digest*, December 5, 1975, pp. 5–9 and 29–30.

States largely bore the burden, the Japanese had more funds available for investment and economic growth, substantially altering their respective roles in the global economy. In another respect, it was a contradiction between Japan's notion of its role in the world, on the one hand, and the strategic realities of the Pacific, on the other.

Until 1976 Washington's repeated requests for Tokyo to accept a portion of this expense were rebuffed based on (1) the small strategic reach of Japanese interests in Asia, (2) a policy limited to tactical preparation for withstanding a conventional invasion, and (3) a constitutional prohibition on developing nuclear defenses. After a comprehensive study of defense needs, the Diet (parliament) adopted a policy in 1976 of limiting the defense budget to 1 percent of GNP annually. (Because of growth in the economy, this sometimes meant annual increases of as much as 9 percent.) A proposal of a 25 percent annual increase, made in 1979 by a Comprehensive National Security Study Group, was not adopted. But conditions changed markedly in the 1980s. The Soviet Union, angered over the Sino-Japanese Treaty of Peace and Friendship and responding to the arms buildup in Washington, invested heavily in military installations in the Pacific, especially in the Kurile Islands. By 1983 Moscow had deployed SS-20 missiles along with state-of-the-art Backfire bombers and nuclear submarines. Japan now became determined to have forces capable of denying Soviet submarines passage through the four main straits separating the home islands, and the Prime Minister promised to make Japan "an unsinkable battleship" in the Pacific.

To counter the potential Soviet threat, a new Japan Defense Agency study called for an annual military budget of 1.038 percent for the period 1986 through 1990, for a total five-year increase of $92 billion (American value). The purposes of the plan were three: (1) to improve the defense of airspace, protect vital sea lanes, and improve combat ability in coastal waters and beyond; (2) to improve Japan's C³I capabilities (communications, command, control, and intelligence) using intelligence satellites; and (3) to improve the ability to engage in sustained

TABLE 4-4

JAPAN'S LATE COLD WAR MILITARY MIGHT, I

	1986	1990
Fighter aircraft	306	320
Tanks	1146	1205
Submarines	14	16
Antisubmarine patrol aircraft	76	100

armed conflict. To meet these goals, the study called for four categories of expansion over a five-year period, as shown in Table 4-4. (Table 4-5 shows Japan's late Cold War military capability in broader terms.) Modest by Soviet and American standards, they were huge when measured against recent Japanese experience and the national vision of the necessities of security.[11] One critic summarized the antimilitary sentiment this way: "For the Japanese people, putting brakes on the expansion of their own country's military power has become Japan's international responsibility and thus a standard for national conduct."[12] Nonetheless, in the years following, Japan's defense expenditures rose as indicated in Table 4-6. Since annual percentage increases in expense are a combination of (1) flat percentage on GDP and (2) increase in the defense spending rate —the average annual percentage spending is compared with the average percent GDP increase. The conclusions become clear. First, despite the defense response to Soviet investment in the Kurile Islands, Japan held to or below its 1 percent ceiling on defense spending. (The numbers do not correlate perfectly for several reasons. Most important is that budget and expenditure are not always synonymous,

---

[11] For a review of the Japan Defense Agency White Paper and the statistical source for these passages, see Chuma Kiyokufu, "The 1986–90 Defense Plan: Does It Go Too Far?" *Japan Quarterly*, January–March 1986, pp. 13–18; and Bruce Roscoe, "Menace from Moscow," *Far Eastern Economic Review*, August 21, 1986, pp. 38–39.

[12] Odawara Atsushi, "No Tampering with the Brakes on Military Expansion," *Japan Quarterly*, July–September 1985, pp. 248–254 at pp. 248–249.

TABLE 4–5

JAPAN'S LATE COLD WAR MILITARY MIGHT, II

	1976	1986
SS-20 missiles	0	162
Backfire bombers	0	85
Divisions	31	41
Armed forces	300,000	370,000
Combat aircraft	2,030	2,390
Naval forces (vessels)	755	840

TABLE 4–6

CHANGE IN JAPAN'S DEFENSE SPENDING AND GROWTH OF GROSS DOMESTIC PRODUCT, CONSTANT 1988 VALUE

	Defense Budget	Increase	GDP Growth
1982	$21.3 billion		
1983	22.4	5.2%	2.7%
1984	23.5	4.9	4.3
1985	24.7	5.1	5.0
1986	25.9	4.9	2.6
1987	27.3	5.4	4.1
1988	28.5	4.4	6.2
1989	29.5	3.5	4.7
1990	30.3	2.7	4.8
1991	31.1	2.6	4.3

Source: SIPRI Yearbook, 1992, World Armaments and Disarmament, p. 261; and OECD, Economic Outlook, June 1995, p. A4.

especially when budget is based on GDP, which is always calculated in the future.) Second, as the New World Order set in, Japan's defense spending slowed slightly in dollar terms, but substantially in percentage of GDP (almost 40 percent).

The Problems of Economic Success The companion problem to burden-sharing in defense has been adjusting internationally to economic success. In relations with the United States, this has created by far the deeper and more enduring difficulties. From the American perspective, the long-term willingness to sponsor Japan's defense gave the Japanese an advantage in industrial and technological development that caused huge American balance-of-trade deficits, deepened by unfair and discriminatory practices that exclude American products from Japan. From the Japanese perspective, the national trade advantages result from enlightened management, improved worker productivity, wise and profitable investment, and a healthy relationship between the private sector and the government, particularly as represented by the powerful Ministry of International Trade and Industry (MITI). Another view holds that the imbalance stems from the United States having reduced taxes and invested in a huge military buildup in the 1980s, producing budget deficits that absorb into debt service what might otherwise go to economic productivity, and large consumer demand that can be met only by

imports.[13] A third view explodes the myth that Japan's economy continues to grow as it did in the years following World War Two and that, in fact, the gap has narrowed almost entirely.[14] (See Table 4–2.) The Japanese conclude from these arguments that American complaints about Japan's industrial investment advantage are unfounded.

Other data add to Japan's defense of its trade surplus relative to the United States. First, as is shown in Table 4–7, the United States also suffers trade deficits with other major partners. Second, compared with the rapidly industrializing economies of Asia, Japan's growth is very modest (see Table 4–8), and yet American trade with them is not particularly profitable either, as is shown in Table 4–9. The American problem, therefore, is not Japan, but the general competitive position of the United States. One sympathetic American observer agrees:

---

[13] Iida Tsuneo, "What Japan Can't Do About Trade Friction," *Japan Quarterly*, July–September 1986, pp. 252–255.
[14] Edward J. Lincoln, "Disentangling the Mess in US-Japan Economic Relations," *Brookings Review*, fall 1985, pp. 22–27.

TABLE 4–7

UNITED STATES TRADE, 1993, WITH MAJOR TRADING PARTNERS (OTHER THAN ASIA'S NEWLY INDUSTRIALIZING COUNTRIES)

Rank as U.S. Trade Partner	U.S. Imports	U.S. Exports	U.S. Balance
1. Canada	$113.6 billion	$100.2 billion	($13.4 billion)
2. Japan	110.4	48.0	(62.4)
3. Mexico	40.7	41.6	0.9
4. United Kingdom	22.4	26.4	4.0
5. Germany	29.5	19.0	(10.5)
8. France	15.7	13.3	(2.4)

Note: Taiwan and South Korea occupy the sixth and seventh ranks, and are shown in Table 4–9 with the newly industrializing states of Asia.

Source: International Monetary Fund, *Direction of Trade Statistics Yearbook, 1994.*

It is easier to accept such explanations as Japan's industrial plants were devastated by a world war, and it could therefore build modern facilities; Japan copied Western technology; Japanese companies undersell American ones because they dump goods. . . ; Japanese companies succeed because they are subsidized and protected by their government; Japanese workers receive low salaries; Japanese companies exporting to the United States violate antitrust and customs regulations.

It is more comfortable to overlook Japan's continued modernization decades after rebuilding from World War II, its effective organization, its genius in adapting technology, its patience in marketing, its disciplined work force. It is more comfortable not to ask how its businessmen could remain so zealous in selling goods in America if they were basically selling below cost. It is disquieting to admit that the Japanese have beaten us [Americans] in economic competition because of their superior planning, organization, and effort.[15]

In this age of extreme sensitivity to conditions of the global economy and threats of protectionism, however, a more commonly encountered attitude reflects the words of John Connally, a former governor of Texas and secretary of the treasury. He warned in 1979 that unless the Japanese open their markets more to American goods, they should "be prepared to sit on the Yokohama docks in [their] Toyotas and [their] little Datsuns and watch [their] own little portable TV sets because we have all of them we need."[16]

That a chronic imbalance exists is undeniable. Table 4–10 traces the history of this. But since Americans have insatiable hunger for Japanese goods—especially automobiles and consumer electronics—the emphasis in Japanese-American economic diplomacy is now clearly on Japanese imports from the United States. The urgency of this emphasis is underscored by the Trade Act of 1988, which requires the president to commence retaliatory policies against Japan if the trade balance

---

[15] Ezra F. Vogel, *Japan as Number One: Lessons for America* (Cambridge, Mass.: Harvard University Press, 1979), pp. 225–226.

[16] Speech in Jacksonville, Fla., on April 27, 1979, as quoted in the *Christian Science Monitor,* May 2, 1979, p. 7.

TABLE 4-8

COMPARISON OF AVERAGE ANNUAL INDUSTRIAL GROWTH RATES FOR JAPAN AND DEVELOPING ASIAN ECONOMIES

	1970–1980	1980–1993
Japan	4.0%	5.0%
Malaysia	8.7	8.2
South Korea	16.4	12.1
Singapore	8.6	6.2
Indonesia	9.6 } Avg. = 9.0	6.3 } Avg. = 8.2
Pakistan	6.1	7.2
India	4.5	6.2
China	8.9	11.5
Difference	225%	164%

Note: Unfortunately, this source does not report similar figures for Taiwan or Hong Kong.

Source: World Bank, *World Development Report, 1995,* table 2, pp. 164–165.

is not improved by the opening of Japanese markets to American goods. In 1990 negotiations, the United States sought agreements on supercomputers, earth satellites, wood and wood products, telecommunications equipment, construction services, pharmaceuticals, and agricultural products, all of which the U.S. government wishes to be able to market in Japan. The talks also included procurement processes that prevent foreign interests from selling directly to the Japanese government. The modest progress made was overshadowed by completion of the multilateral Uruguay Round

TABLE 4-9

U.S. TRADE WITH ASIA'S NEWLY INDUSTRIALIZING STATES, 1993

	U.S. Exports	U.S. Imports	Total	U.S. Balance
Taiwan	$16.3 billion	$26.3 billion	$42.6 billion	($10.0 billion)
South Korea	14.8	17.8	32.6	(3.0)
Singapore	11.7	13.1	24.8	(1.4)
Malaysia	6.1	10.9	17.0	(4.8)
Hong Kong	9.9	10.0	19.9	(0.1)
Thailand	3.8	9.0	12.8	(5.2)

Source: International Monetary Fund, *Direction of Trade Statistics Yearbook, 1994.*

TABLE 4–10

JAPAN'S TRADE WITH THE UNITED STATES

	Japanese Imports from U.S.	Japanese Exports to U.S.	Total Value	Japanese Balance
1971	$4.1 billion	$7.3 billion	$11.4 billion	$3.2 billion
1972	5.0	9.1	14.1	4.1
1973	8.3	9.7	18.0	1.4
1974	10.7	12.3	23.0	1.6
1975	9.6	11.3	20.9	1.7
1976	10.1	15.5	25.6	5.4
1977	10.5	18.6	29.1	8.1
1978	12.9	24.5	37.4	11.6
1979	17.6	26.2	43.8	8.6
1980	20.8	30.7	51.5	9.9
1981	21.8	37.6	58.4	15.8
1982	21.0	37.7	58.7	16.7
1983	21.9	41.2	63.1	19.3
1984	23.6	57.1	80.7	33.5
1985	22.6	68.8	81.4	46.2
1986	26.9	81.9	108.8	55.0
1987	32.0	85.0	117.0	53.0
1988	42.3	90.2	132.5	47.9
1989	48.3	94.0	142.3	45.7
1990	52.8	91.1	143.9	38.3
1991	53.6	92.2	145.8	38.6
1992	52.7	96.7	149.4	44.0
1993	55.9	106.9	162.8	51.0

Sources: This information is available in a variety of places, most importantly, the U.S. Department of Commerce, Survey of Current Business (monthly), The Economic Report of the President (annual), The Statistical Abstract of the United States (annual), and the International Monetary Fund, Direction of Trade Statistics Yearbook (annual).

negotiations of the General Agreement on Tariffs and Trade (GATT), which established a cornerstone of New World Order international trade. In addition to altering the global tariff structure, it created a new World Trade Organization empowered to mediate international trade disputes.

Pursuant to the Trade Act of 1988, after several warnings President Clinton announced in 1995 that unless there were a breakthrough on Japan's market restrictions by a specific date, he would impose import duties on luxury Japanese autos that would double their prices in the United States. Conservative Americans cheered; Europeans emphasized Washington's obligation to invoke the World Trade Organization (WTO) rather than provoke a trade war; and Japan held firm.

TABLE 4–11

AVERAGE ANNUAL GROSS NATIONAL SAVINGS AS A PERCENTAGE OF GDP FOR JAPAN, THE EUROPEAN UNION, AND THE UNITED STATES

	1982–1987	1988–1993	Difference
Japan	31.3%	34.1%	+2.8%
European Union	20.1	20.4	+0.3
United States	17.4	15.7	–1.7

Note: For the EU, 1993 is excluded.

Source: OECD, *Economic Outlook*, June 1995, annex table 27, p. A30.

TABLE 4–12

ANNUAL NEW WORLDWIDE FOREIGN DIRECT INVESTMENT FOR JAPAN AND THE UNITED STATES

	Japan	United States
1986	$15 billion	$14 billion
1987	20	28
1988	34	14
1989	44	29
1990	48	29
1991	31	29

Source: United Nations, *World Investment Report, 1992*, p. 16.

In the eleventh hour, enough concessions were arranged to defuse the confrontation and save the WTO from a neonatal catastrophe, but neither disputant gained much.

The data war progresses. Japan can demonstrate, for example, that while its share of world exports is stable, that of the United States is growing. As to exports themselves, the percentage of American annual growth is increasing, while that of Japan is actually declining steadily. Furthermore, export contribution to Japan's GDP is declining also, while that of the United States has begun to grow after a period of tiny losses. From the Japanese perspective, therefore, the United States is gaining ground globally if not specifically with Japan. The two sides agree that the problem is the import column: In the United States, about 16 percent of the value of all goods sold is imported; in Japan the comparable figure is more like 6 percent. The problem is disagreement on the cause. From the American perspective, Japan's imports are unnaturally low and would be higher were it not for a lack of reciprocity in public policy. But to the Japanese, it is due to inefficient American industries, fiscal policy that depletes the economy through obligatory debt service, and promiscuous consumer demand. The evidence for the last of these is that in Japan, gross national saving is about 33 percent of GDP, while in the

United States it is only 15 percent. These factors are summarized in Table 4–11.

In the middle of 1984, the U.S. dollar was worth about 155 Japanese yen, and for many years it was at or above 140. During that time the Japanese claimed that the artificially high dollar was itself a barrier to trade, because it made American goods unnecessarily expensive in foreign markets. By mid-1995 the value of the dollar had sunk to about 87 yen.[17] As it continued to drop, both the Federal Reserve and the Japanese central bank moved to prevent its further fall by buying excess dollars on the currency markets. Free market economic theory dictates that if price falls, demand and consumption will rise, and so U.S. goods should have sold better in Japan. Similarly, as the yen was now substantially more valulable than the dollar, Japanese goods should have risen in price in the United States and demand and consumption

---

[17] The slide in the currency against the Japanese yen was the subject of much debate in the United States. One side thought that the government's failure to strengthen the dollar (typically done by purchasing huge amounts on currency markets in order to drive up the price) would lead to a severe deterioration of American leadership in Asia. The other side saw the government's passivity as a useful means of making American products so attractive in price that the U.S.-Japan trade imbalance would be reduced by the Japanese importing more American goods. See, for example, a cluster of articles in *Foreign Affairs*, July–August 1995.

TABLE 4–13

AVERAGE ANNUAL GROWTH IN FOREIGN DIRECT INVESTMENT AND AVERAGE ANNUAL PORTION OF THE WORLD TOTAL FOR JAPAN AND THE UNITED STATES

	GROWTH RATE		PORTION OF WORLD TOTAL	
	1980–85	1986–90	1980–85	1986–90
Japan	22%	35%	10%	20%
United States	– 16	20	26	14

Source: United Nations, *World Investment Report, 1992,* p. 16.

fallen accordingly. The American interpretation of the dispute says that Japan's restrictive policies prevent these "laws" from operating, and the Japanese were weakened in their old argument.

Meanwhile, Japanese capital, too, continues to sink more deeply into the world's economies. Japan's foreign investment in 1970 totaled $3.3 billion and by 1979 had grown to about $31 billion, a tenfold increase. Tables 4–12 and 4–13 show the annual growth in Japanese foreign direct investment from 1986 through 1991 as compared with the United States. Note that in that period, Japan's share of the total invested globally doubled from 10 percent to 20 percent, and that its annual increase rose from a rate of 22 percent to 35 percent. Approximately half was in North America. Table 4–14 outlines the recent history of Japanese investment in the United States, and vice versa, and demonstrates the net Japanese position.

Such extraordinary economic success creates regional problems. As the dominant economic power of Asia, Japan cannot go unnoticed by its neighbors, many of whom have long memories of Japan's historical militarism, who are increasingly its economic competitors, and who are discomfited by the political liabilities associated with Japan's burgeoning private investment in the region. It might serve them one day to restrict the availability of fuel to Japan. This raises still a new security imperative in view of Japan's dependence on Middle Eastern oil: It could require more than a fivefold increase in naval strength to defend the 7500-mile sea journey from source to home.[18]

The perspective with which the Japanese entered the New World Order, therefore, is that of a nation of high economic development that remains dependent on the resources, markets, and stable economic policies of others in order to prosper. Most especially, the view is shaped by having arrived at the threshold of world power just when the methods of assessing power in international relations were changing rapidly. In production terms, Japan is powerful; in raw material terms, it is less autonomous than its competitors. In geopolitical terms, it has chosen a relatively small regional role, though in the new China-Russia-America interplay and the new economic conditions of Asia and the Pacific, it may have to rethink this. Given the primacy of economics in the New World Order, Japan is fully prepared for its role. But for its competitors, especially the United States, it may be too well prepared. Ironically, while the political conditions of the Cold War were a secondary imperative to Japan, its economic strength in the New World Order is a primary threat to its former protector. The Japanese know that to some Americans, Japan's economic might is "the next threat," that Japanese-American trade is "the new Cold War."

---

[18] Jay B. Sorenson, "Japan: The Dilemmas of Security," *Asian Affairs*, July–August 1975, pp. 363–370.

TABLE 4–14

JAPAN'S NET INVESTMENT RELATIVE TO THE UNITED STATES

	U.S. Direct Investment in Japan	Japan's Direct Investment in U.S.	Japan's Net
1980	$6.2 billion	$4.7 billion	($1.5 billion)
1985	9.2	19.3	10.1
1990	22.5	83.1	60.6
1992	26.2	96.7	70.5

Source: Statistical Abstract of the United States, 1994.

Japan's fears, in contrast, are at home and in the region. China's industrialization is growing at the world's fastest rate, and many of the products in which Japan previously dominated world markets now have competition from Taiwan, South Korea, and Singapore, where investment was subject to far less risk of political instability than today's China or much of the Developing World. At home Japan is battling signs of decline. The securities market lost a third of its value after 1990, though it has begun to recover. Real estate, once precious, is in a severe slump. A billion-dollar securities scandal at Daiwa in 1995 undermined the world's confidence in the Japanese banking system, impelling the United States—of all parties!—to pledge its financial support should there be a currency emergency. Declines in exports have forced factories to reduce production, and industries have had to abandon ages-old policies about protecting workers from economic recessions. Thus Japan has yet to find its way in the New World Order; but neither has the New World Order been especially good to Japan thus far.

Western Europe

Until half a century ago, world politics was Euro-centric. Europe was the center of the Industrial Revolution, home of the world's great financial capitals, site of the principal military and political rivalries, and the metropole from which vast empires were directed. Much of the world's population outside Europe, in Africa, Asia, the Mediterranean, and the Caribbean, was under European domination; Australia, New Zealand, Canada, and much of the Near East owed allegiance to one or another of the European powers. Even the American role in World War One, an intense but transitory plunge into global politics, did little to alter the fundamental structure of international politics. By refusing to join the League of Nations, the United States vested the management of international affairs in the European governments. Neither could the defeat of Germany and the realignment of old empires change the fact that world politics revolved around Europe.

But World War One set in motion certain inexorable trends. First, it gave Americans a new external vision and turned the economy into the world's most modern and productive. Second, Russia's participation in the war ended with the Bolshevik Revolution in 1917, which brought the Communist party to power and led to the creation of the Soviet Union. With a government dedicated to transforming a feudal society, massive industrialization, and the defense of state against capitalist encirclement, the Soviet Union meant change for Europe and the world. Third, in the wake of World War One, it was acknowledged broadly that imperialism and colonialism were major causes of war. The doctrine of national self-determination emerged and foretold the eventual collapse of the European empires.

In a real sense, then, World War One launched many of the forces that the Second concluded. World War Two left continental Europe in ruins, but American industry at unprecedented heights. As Western Europe launched its reconstruction with American help, the Soviet Union consolidated its Eastern European empire and set out to build an integrated regional economy and a fortress against capitalist encirclement. Eventually, as hostilities spread, the international power distribution was rearranged so that virtually all effective power clustered around either the United States or the Soviet Union. Europe was cordoned into the Soviet-allied Eastern sector and the American-allied Western sector. World politics was no longer Eurocentric but bipolar, a configuration in which, far from being the pivotal point of global relations, Western Europe was an object of conflict between the two nuclear giants.

The Cold War confrontation dictated that the United States act to preserve democratic polities and free market economies wherever possible, particularly in Western Europe. This policy, though usually expressed in ideological terms, had the firm support of American merchants and manufacturers (whose production surplus needed external markets) and American labor (which needed external buyers to maintain full employment). The investment community lent its support, too, confident that a reconstructed Europe would borrow American capital, and that a Western Europe staunchly defended from the Soviet menace would be a safe place for investment. Basic American Cold War policies, enunciated from 1947 through 1949, derived from the Soviet threat and from the convergence of all these domestic interests, and centered initially on the defense and reconstruction of Europe. These included the European Recovery Plan (the Marshall Plan) of 1947, in which Washington committed almost $14 billion to Western Europe's revitalization; the Truman Doctrine (1947), which proclaimed Washington's intention to resist the territorial advance of communism and on which

the containment policy was based; and the institutionalization of European-American defense in the North Atlantic Treaty Organization (NATO) in 1949. Each presupposed a prolonged threat of Soviet aggression.

As Europe neared full restoration and the uneasy European peace stabilized in the 1950s, however, trans-Atlantic strains began to develop. Most important among them were the economic consequences of the uniting of Europe, a process of economic consolidation for more successful competition with the United States and a revitalized Japan. As Western European states grew more interdependent after 1958, they asserted greater independence of the United States. Europeans saw no inconsistency between economic independence and security interdependence. Increasingly they found Washington's policy intrusive, particularly as the credibility of the unifying force—imminent Soviet aggression—deteriorated. France withdrew from the unified NATO command and forced the headquarters to move to Brussels in Belgium. (Not until 1996, when Paris reassessed its policies in relation to full European economic integration and twenty-first-century continental security alternatives—both in light of unified Germany's growing prominence—did it open a debate on France's full return to NATO.) American efforts to maintain the tenor of the trans-Atlantic partnership after the restoration of Western Europe fueled potential conflict among allies.

The Uniting of Europe

When the European Recovery Plan was launched in 1947, the United States encouraged common economic planning, an idea that took firm root by 1958. By then, the national economies of the region were rapidly reaching their recovery goals, and the fear of invasion from Eastern Europe seemed remote. The European governments were quick to realize, however, that with the American industrial head start and the recovery of Japan, their small individual economies were disadvantaged in world competition. Hence Western Europe seized upon the idea of a supranational economy by gradually integrating into one. Their regional economy would be stimulated by eliminating internal tariffs and by having common barriers to the goods of outside competitors.[19]

Originally six states (France, West Germany, Italy, Belgium, Luxembourg, and the Netherlands) created the European Economic Community (EEC), the European Coal and Steel Community (ECSC), and the European Atomic Energy Commission (EURATOM). Together they were called the European Community. Because of the substantial progress made since the initial acts, the aggregate is now called the European Union (EU). Consistent with its historical disdain for continental politics, Britian opted to establish a competing organization, the European Free Trade Area (EFTA), which encompassed virtually all noncommunist Europe outside of the EC. In 1963 London sought to leave EFTA and join the EC, but France, driven by President Charles de Gaulle's fervent wish "to de-Americanize Europe," vetoed the application because of Britain's "special relationship" with the United States. Britain (along with Denmark and Ireland) joined the EC ten years later when the community underwent its first expansion, to nine members. The current membership is fifteen (Spain, Portugal, Greece, Austria, Finland, and Sweden have been added, the last three from EFTA), and virtually all of EFTA now awaits admission. The reunification of Germany also adds to the community's geographic reach and aggregate economic performance. Other former members of the Soviet empire, particularly Poland, Hungary,

and the Czech Republic (the same ones that seek NATO membership) have already commenced talks with the European Parliament on EU membership once their economies are fully transformed from socialism and their reindustrialization is progressing. Slovenia was at a similar point, but the EU has subsequently declared that it has retrogressed.

Table 4–15 compares the populations, GDPs, and trade balances of the EU and its members with those of the United States and Japan in 1993; it paints a clear picture of the economic power generated by the integration of these fifteen economies. Moreover, the power was clear from the start, since the original six members had a combined GNP of more than half that of the United States. After three new members were added, the percentage rose to 83, and one more member brought it to 95. To the members, a common market of this magnitude, with free flow of goods within and protection against free external competition, was and is extremely beneficial. To an outsider, particularly the United States, which sees itself as having made all this possible, it was a form of ungrateful regional exclusivity. Today, however, as international trade has been regionalized and the United States has joined the trend through the North American Free Trade Agreement (NAFTA) with Canada and Mexico (1994), the challenge has become one of using global trade negotiations, such as the recently concluded Uruguay Round of GATT, to devise nondiscriminatory trade regimes.

The uniting of Europe is not exclusively an economic affair. On the political front, the members have created the European Commission, which performs transnational executive functions; the European Parliament, whose elected national delegates establish community policy; the Court of the European Communities, which adjudicates policy matters within the EU and between it and its members; and the European Court of Human Rights, which supersedes the jurisdictions of national courts on pertinent matters. The EU sends diplomatic representation abroad. Still, however, it cannot be said that on all issues there is a definable

---

[19] For a review of the historical passage from cooperation to competition with an essentially European perspective, see Ernst H. van der Beugel, *From Marshall Aid to Atlantic Partnership* (Amsterdam: Elsevier, 1966); and Henry A. Kissinger, *The Troubled Partnership: A Re-appraisal of the Atlantic Alliance* (New York: McGraw-Hill, 1965). For a study of European alternative strategies for effective global competition, see Alastair Buchan, *Europe's Future, Europe's Choices: Models of Western Europe in the 1970's* (New York: Columbia University Press, 1969). For an American interpretation sympathetic to the European, see Richard J. Barnet, *The Alliance* (New York: Simon and Schuster, 1983).

TABLE 4-15

BASIC INDICATORS FOR THE EUROPEAN UNION[1], THE UNITED STATES, AND JAPAN, 1993

	Population	GDP	Trade Balance
Austria	7.9 million	$182.1 billion	($8.0 billion)
Belgium	10.0	210.6	3.1
Denmark	5.2	117.6	7.2
Finland	5.1	74.1	7.7
France	57.5	1,251.7	9.9
Germany[2]	80.7	1,910.8	50.8
Greece	10.4	63.2	(13.1)
Ireland	3.5	43.0	8.8
Italy	57.1	991.4	35.3
Luxembourg	0.4	37.3[3]	
Netherlands	15.3	309.2	15.7
Portugal	9.8	85.7	(6.2)
Spain	39.5	479.0	(15.2)
Sweden	8.7	166.7	9.6
United Kingdom	57.9	819.0	(16.1)
European Union	369.0	6,741.4	89.5
United States	257.8	6,259.9	(166.4)
Japan	124.5	4,214.2	14.8

[1] Includes Austria, Finland, and Sweden, even though they were not admitted until 1995.
[2] Includes only former West Germany.
[3] Luxembourg's trade balance is included in Belgium's.

Source: World Bank, *World Development Report, 1995*, table 1, pp. 162–163, table 3, p. 166, and table 1A, p. 228; and OECD, *Economic Outlook*, June 1995, annex table 47, p. A50.

"Western European world view"; rather, there is a French world view, a German world view, and so on. This is also true of relations with the United States. One French observer put it this way:

In order to do a better job of analyzing the relations between Western Europe and the United States, one has to consider successively the dialogues between Bonn and Washington, London and Washington, Paris and Washington, all of which differ from one another. More precisely, it is desirable to separate two problems: (a) the attitude of the American government toward the European Community, or more generally, the effort to create a European unity; and (b) the attitude of the American government toward the different European governments in respect to the various problems posed. *There is no global dialogue taking*

Behind representatives of Britain, France, the United States, and the former Soviet Union—
the post-World War Two occupying powers—"Checkpoint Charlie," gateway between East
and West Berlin, is carried away, symbolizing German reunification.
(*Source:* © AP/Wide World)

place between Europe as an entity and the United
States.[20]

From the outset, however, the goal has been
economic independence through unity. The importance of this is redoubled in the conditions of the
New World Order when, simultaneously, removal

of the Soviet threat also kindles passions of security
independence from the United States.

International Trade

The original goal of Western European integration
was to improve competitiveness in international
trade. Performance figures indicate that it has succeeded. The four largest members of the community—Germany, France, Britain, and Italy—account
for more than a quarter of all world exports, compared to America's 12 percent and Japan's 9 or 10,

[20] Raymond Aron, "Europe and the United States: The Relations Between Europeans and Americans," in David S. Landes,
ed., *Western Europe: The Trials of Partnership* (Lexington, Mass.:
Lexington Books, 1977), p. 27. Emphasis added. Despite the age
of this statement, it remains almost entirely relevant.

though the EU has lost a little ground in recent years as American exports have improved. Moreover, as Table 4–15 indicates, the EU runs a healthy surplus in its trade with the world, though the balance is depressed by Britain's chronic deficit and the import needs of the three least industrialized members.

Table 4–16 illustrates the growth of EU trade with the United States. Total imports and exports are about $200 billion per year, contrasted with U.S.-Japan trade of $160 billion and U.S.-Canada trade of $200 billion. So while Japan ranks as America's second national trade partner, the EU as a trading bloc exceeds Japan considerably. This trade typically generates a small surplus for the EU, though it suffered two years of deep deficit in the early 1990s.

These consequences of Western European integration were entirely foreseeable, and the United States first prepared for them by adopting the Trade Expansion Act of 1962, which authorized the president to conduct negotiations for sweeping tariff reductions. The Kennedy Round of GATT talks achieved this goal, but not before Europeans accused the United States of attempting to manipulate their enviable trade surplus as retaliation against Europe's success. In 1964, as the American balance of payments began to sag alongside the balance of trade, President Johnson asked for a voluntary moratorium on exporting capital to Europe, another move seen as intended to depress Europe's steady growth. The ninety-day, 10 percent surcharge on tariffs applied in 1971 that so enraged the Japanese was taken by the European economic ministries as a step short of declaring a trade war. Washington, in turn, objected to European practices such as joint ventures in which governments were partners, artificially lowering prices and giving unfair advantage to European manufacturers. For twenty years, right through the 1980s, threats of trade war were exchanged frequently over everything from wine to commercial aircraft. Trans-Atlantic economic disputes centered on six factors:

1. The growing use of trade restrictions by governments in efforts to protect domestic industries from foreign competition within the domestic market.
2. The growing use of export subsidies by governments to promote domestic employment and to expand exports by reducing the apparent cost of production.
3. Frequent manipulation of domestic interest rates and adjustment of currency exchange

TABLE 4–16

EUROPEAN UNION TRADE WITH THE UNITED STATES

	EU Exports	EU Imports	Total	EU Balance
1987	$84.9 billion	$60.2 billion	$145.1 billion	$24.7 billion
1988	88.8	75.4	164.2	13.4
1989	88.8	86.6	175.4	2.2
1990	95.6	98.1	193.7	(2.5)
1991	89.4	103.1	192.5	(13.7)
1992	97.1	102.9	200.0	(5.8)
1993	101.4	97.0	198.4	4.4

Source: International Monetary Fund, *Direction of Trade Statistics Yearbook, 1994.*

rates to reduce domestic inflation and to make exported goods more attractive abroad by making them less expensive in comparison with similar goods produced in the host economy.

4. The emergence of national industrial policies in which the government becomes a "partner" in phasing out failing industries and in sponsoring new ones, in order to overcome in the world's markets those goods produced entirely by private investment in competitor economies.

5. Disagreement over the value of trade with the Soviet Union and Eastern European countries, with some (for example, the United States) attempting to use trade limitations as a means of political leverage, and others (for example, the EC) looking past ideological factors to trade as a means of expanding domestic employment and balancing trade performance.

6. The use of individualized national policies to take maximum short-term advantage of trade with the Developing World, whereas others have preferred taking less advantage while awaiting effective international management of the North-South trading axis.[21]

Despite a conservative turn in Britain, France, West Germany, and to a lesser degree, Italy and Spain, the EC governments dissented unanimously from the Reagan government's insistence that the evilness of the Soviet Union should prevent the West from trading with it. This, together with other American tendencies to disregard the European world view, was interpreted by Europeans as America's newfound unilateralism. By the end of 1985, fully 300 individual pieces of protectionist (trade restriction) legislation were before the U.S. Congress. But as evidence of the growing bilateral tendency toward reciprocal—even retaliatory—trade restraint, an Organization for Economic Cooperation and Development (OECD) study showed

that the amount of American industrial imports subjected to trade restriction rose from 6 percent in 1980 to 13 percent in 1983, and in the EU from 11 percent to 15 percent. The Tokyo Round of GATT negotiations (1979) had failed to head off the protectionist urge and to resolve issues of agricultural trade, and the Uruguay Round had yet to commence.

Like the Japanese, the Europeans throughout this period put America's problems at the American doorstep. The problem was not unfair economic practices in Europe, but labor inefficiency in the United States, the cumulative national debt that siphons valuable capital into debt service, borrowing abroad to cover overexpenditures, and outdated production techniques. In general, they thought, Americans live beyond their means; but the Reagan policy of increasing public spending and cutting taxes simultaneously did irreparable harm to America's competitive position in many fields, including electronics, machine tools, automobiles, and commercial aircraft. As if to add to its own woes, the United States had embargoed contracted grain sales to the Soviet Union in response to martial law in Poland and Moscow's armed intervention in Afghanistan, turning Moscow to European agriculture. With this the United States lost an advantage it had built carefully to balance lagging growth in manufactures exports. As 1992 approached, the year selected for completion of the European Union, the United States had left itself unprepared for the "competitive revolution."[22]

Profound changes in Europe and in the trans-Atlantic partnership accompanied the New World Order. Among the important ones are these:

Liberation from Security Obsession

With the threat of pan-European war gone, full attention could be turned to economic development, completion of the European Union, and adjustment to post–Cold War economies. The portion of GNP

---

[21] Adapted from Walter Goldstein, "Economic Discord in the Atlantic Alliance," in Robert J. Jackson, ed., *Continuity of Discord: Crises and Responses in the Atlantic Community* (New York: Praeger, 1985), pp. 183–199.

[22] George Taucher, "1992: A Competitive Revolution," *European Affairs*, winter 1989, pp. 53–60.

devoted to defense could be reduced and new priorities assigned to it.

Demise of Socialist Economies   After collapse of the Soviet empire and disintegration of the USSR, deliberate efforts were made throughout the former Soviet world to transform to market economies. This meant safe new places for investment, trade unrestricted by any notions of political morality the United States might try to impose on Western Europe, and new markets filled with people envious of Western Europe's prosperity. Hundreds of venture and joint venture opportunities arose almost immediately in everything from pharmaceuticals to power generation, welling and mining, environmental recovery, and management consulting. The transitional economies are treated elsewhere herein.

The Uruguay Round of GATT Negotiations   In progress since the mid-1980s, the globalization of the economy in the New World Order underscored the need for the Uruguay Round to get on with a new international trade regime by restructuring tariffs and other barriers to trade and creating machinery for dispute resolution. In the end, the Uruguay Round reduced average Japanese tariffs to 2.5 percent, American to 3.4 percent, and EU tariffs to 4.3 percent. It also terminated GATT and replaced it with a World Trade Organization with authority to arbitrate economic disputes between members.

Acceleration of Trade Regionalism   As the largest pioneer in regionalizing trade, the EU observed the success of the ASEAN nations, the development of the Pacific Rim as a coordinated economic development effort, NAFTA, the Caribbean Economic Community (CARICOM), and a free trade area among Argentina, Brazil, Paraguay, and Uruguay, and it viewed with growing concern China's potential impact on world trade. Some of the EU's historic advantages might now have corresponding disadvantages. Again, the Uruguay Round took on new importance to Western Europe, even though a dispute with the United States over agricultural subsidies delayed its conclusion.

Completion of the European Union   At the end of 1991, the EU members approved the Maastricht (Netherlands) Treaty that called for the completion of a unitary market by December 31, 1992, and laid out a program for further political integration by 1999. By "single market" was meant free flow of goods, labor, and capital; interchangeability of collegiate degrees; reaffirmation of common tariffs with respect to outside competitors; and a common currency and banking system. Though the treaty just barely scraped through the ratification process in (then twelve) member states, progress has been slow. The single market exists, however, in all but the banking and currency conditions, which have yet to be worked out. (On economic integration issues not directly related to trade, the EU partners are very far apart.) In practical terms, then, the post-Maastricht changes are minimal and have had little consequence for international relations.

The success of the European Union in the world trade arena has both enriched Europe and guaranteed its competitive position relative to the United States. The other issue that has fogged the route to full and equal competition is the American ownership of European production through direct foreign investment.

American Direct Investment in Europe

The uniting of Europe began at a time when American investors were seeking external opportunities and when, in an effort to improve efficiency, industries were becoming multinational. Because the European customs unions threatened their exports, American manufacturers wished to circumvent the tariff barriers presented by EFTA and the EC, by buying and building plants in European nations as foreign subsidiaries. These plants manufactured goods primarily for sale in Europe because they were free of import duties in European markets. Productivity increases were financed not with fresh

American capital, but from profit in Europe. But the initial investment caused a huge American capital outflow. The American balance of payments, already strained by military expenditures from the Vietnam War, slipped into severe deficit. President Lyndon B. Johnson responded with a voluntary restraints program in which American firms were asked to moderate their foreign capital expenditures. Nonetheless, by 1967 American firms controlled nearly 8000 foreign subsidiaries, nearly half of them in the EFTA and EC countries.[23] Of these, two-thirds were in Britain, France, Germany, and Italy. Unrestrained capital outflow prompted the imposition of mandatory controls in 1968.[24]

Table 4–17 demonstrates the volume of direct American investment in the combined EU economy. Measured by the extent to which America's total world direct investment is located in the EC, the facts are even more striking: In 1970, American direct investment in the EC totaled 27 percent of the worldwide amount; by 1978, the fraction had risen to 33 percent; and by 1988, to 39 percent ($126.5 billion out of a global total of $326.9 billion). But the total American investment in the EU countries took a dramatic jump at the outset of the New World Order, when it increased by more than 60 percent between 1988 and 1992. From the European perspective, in an age in which the net American investment position fell into deficit (more American assets owned by non-Americans than foreign interests held by Americans), U.S. investors were striking it rich through their direct investments within the EC.

For nearly thirty years the prevalence of American capital and the extensive American ownership of European production caused severe disenchantment among Europe's economic visionaries. France's President Charles de Gaulle, for instance, insisted that the only path to effective competition

---

[23] Raymond Vernon, *Sovereignty at Bay: The Multinational Spread of U.S. Enterprises* (New York: Basic Books, 1971), p. 141.
[24] U.S. Department of Commerce, *The Multinational Corporations: Studies in U.S. Foreign Investment, 1972* (Washington, D.C.: U.S. Government Printing Office, 1972).

TABLE 4–17

AMERICAN DIRECT INVESTMENT (TOTAL BOOK VALUE) IN THE EU

Year	Amount
1960	$5.9 billion
1965	11.4
1970	20.1
1973	31.3
1978	56.0
1982	77.7
1984	78.9
1988	126.5
1992	204.3

Note: Includes Austria, Finland, and Sweden, even though they were not admitted until 1995.

Source: Statistical Abstract of the United States for 1975, 1977, 1979, 1981, 1982/1983, 1986, and 1994; and U.S. Department of Commerce, *Survey of Current Business,* August 1988.

---

was the "de-Americanization of Europe." It was widely felt that continued American domination of European capital and production not only deferred equal competition but actually placed Europe in a position of dependency and colonization. This made a double blow of American retaliations for Europe's success. Furthermore, because American firms effectively penetrated the customs union, preventing Europeans from dominating their own markets, European profits were too small to stimulate the most efficient production. Consequently, the regional idea rapidly gave way to corporate demands for globalizing European industries. Following the American example, European industries originally considered the foundations of regional integration joined the multinational trend. Capital began to flow across the world from Europe, some of it stopping in the United States.

By the time the New World Order took root and as the EU approached its 1992 date for completion, the circumstances were very different. The enlarged EU had a bigger internal market than the United States and had enough industrial overcapacity to exceed the United States in trade volume and value. Paradoxically, American subsidiaries within the EU had kept down European unemployment during the recessionary 1980s, and much of Europe's export volume consisted of products that would otherwise have been made in the United States. All of this added to the tax revenues of the EU member governments. And the EU had a favorable balance of trade both globally and with the United States. Finally, Europeans were investing in the United States at unprecedented rates, significantly changing the net investment positions of the United States and the EU. The sense of colonization and exploitation diminished rapidly as the balance of economic power shifted favorably and decisively.

The European Union and Trans-Atlantic Defense

If the essence of the European Union is on regionalism, then the underlying postulate of the Western security system is Atlanticism. And if the United States relates to the EU in the economic sphere as a resentful competitor, then in NATO it is a dominant partner, unsure of its objectives but resistant to change in its stature. While the Europeans acknowledge the value of security interdependence, they deplore the political and economic consequences of imbalance.

Although it is an oversimplification, the history of the NATO era can be divided into three parts defined by changes in Washington's global military objectives. In the first, 1949 to 1974, the worldwide ring of American alliances stood against the spread of communism everywhere from Central Europe to Vietnam. During this time American defense budgets were high, partly because of the costs of maintaining the alliances. In general, trans-Atlantic relations were good, though the cost of the Vietnam War caused occasional acrimonious differences over cost-sharing within NATO. The European side of these disputes was critical of the American commitment in Southeast Asia, and European governments were unwilling to subsidize it

by paying a larger share of NATO. More severe skeptics lacked confidence in the American nuclear shield, fearing that Washington would either not use it in the event of a Soviet conventional attack, or would use it recklessly, in either case plunging Europe into war in order to prevent a direct Soviet-American nuclear exchange. For reasons of national stature and imperfect confidence in the American nuclear shield, Britain (1952) and France (1959) entered the nuclear club, and each retains a small nuclear deployment for purposes of "minimal deterrence."

The second period opened with the foreign policy reassessment that ended the American role in the Vietnam War (1974) and closed with the collapse of the Soviet empire and the disbanding of the Warsaw Pact, NATO's counterpart in Eastern Europe, in 1989. This was a period of great trans-Atlantic uncertainty and ambivalence embodied in (1) Washington's relentless pursuit of alliance politics and (2) efforts at confidence-building measures through the Conference on Security and Cooperation in Europe. In the first, the United States manipulated its NATO partners partly by threatening to withdraw troops over cost-sharing disagreements and then by massive buildup, especially in intermediate-range nuclear forces, in the 1980s, raising the specter once again of aggressive Soviet intentions. In the second, it used a pan-European forum (not limited to NATO or to the West) to build confidence that war would not occur. The contradiction of these two paths of logic and the divergence of European and American views over the arms buildup were described by one European observer this way:

> In the past, Europeans had tended to view nuclear weapons both as a means of last resort and as an alternative to expensive conventional defense. The United States, on the other hand, had increasingly come to regard nuclear weapons as an integral part of the military effort, designed to provide a spectrum of deterrence across the range of conceivable military contingencies. Both of these approaches were challenged by the missile controversy, and their

contradictions revealed: in Europe, the unreasonably high dependence on nuclear weapons for defense; in the United States, the impermissible slide from deterring to contemplating fighting a nuclear war.[25]

Throughout this period Europeans sought greater influence in strategic planning. The Eurogroup within NATO once debated, for example, combining the French and British deterrent capabilities as a means of having a European—as contrasted to NATO—deterrence policy. This middle period, then, was a rocky one for the security partners, with the Europeans frequently feeling like one of the principal pawns in a high-stakes Soviet-American game. When the EU-U.S. economic contest of the same years is factored in, it becomes plain that the 1974–1989 period contained a mixture of trans-Atlantic tension and the cooperation necessitated by circumstances. Americans were asking, "How much longer must we bear the cost of Western Europe's defense while we suffer increasingly from their economic competition?" For their part, Europeans were asking, "How can we reduce our reliance on the United States without emasculating the alliance to the point that the European power balance shifts to the East?" This was a time of dynamic tension between European regionalism and Atlanticism.

Quite obviously, even before 1989 the choice was never between NATO and no NATO, but between a security alliance fraught with conflict or one in which the costs of alliance were tolerable to all parties in military, political, and economic terms. In the words of one European, "The Western Europeans, suffering from perceived U.S. heavy-handedness, want a safety net and not a strait-jacket."[26] This was written on the eve of NATO's third period, one ushered in by the end of the Cold War. With the collapse of the Soviet empire,

disbanding of the Warsaw Treaty Organization, disintegration of the Soviet Union, and reunification of Germany, the "unifying enemy" that had held NATO together through crises large and small was gone. NATO's future was called into question, but in a larger context, namely, how to define—if at all—Europe's security needs and then how to provide for them. What are the proper new security roles of the United States, the former Soviet allies, and Russia in the Europe of the New World Order? These became practical rather than theoretical questions when Yugoslavia broke up and three of its parts—Serbia, Croatia, and Bosnia-Herzegovina—fell into brutal fratricidal wars. Ironically, NATO, established to meet the Soviet threat that never required a shot, saw its first combat in Bosnia.

Opinions differ regarding Europe's security needs. There are some who argue that the whole debate centers on the false assumption that there is or will be a threat to Europe's security. Others counter with the argument that internal threats such as those that struck the former Yugoslavia remain possible threats to regional security. A few see radical Islamic forces waging wars of terrorism, such as the 1995 terrorist activity in France in protest of France's tacit support of an Algerian government that will not yield to an elected Islamic successor, as an emerging security threat. Still others reject the notion that a diminished Russia poses no threat to the West, and claim that this Cold War remnant calls for Cold War–like preparedness in the form of a strong and enlarged NATO. German Chancellor Helmut Kohl, the strongest New World Order voice for complete economic integration within the EU, weds the security and economic questions by declaring that without integration, the EU nations will revert to war among themselves, and that the economic questions pending before the EU constitute war-peace issues for the next century.[27]

With no clear consensus on defining security needs, the debate has moved to method. It centers on two questions: (1) whether NATO or some

---

[25] Christopher Bertram, "Europe and America in 1983," *Foreign Affairs, America and the World* 1983 issue, pp. 616–631 at pp. 628–629.

[26] Peter Bender, "The Superpower Squeeze," *Foreign Policy,* winter 1986–87, pp. 98–113.

[27] "Kohl Casts Europe's Economic Union as War and Peace Issue," *The New York Times,* October 17, 1995, p. A10.

other institution should be the centerpiece, and (2) if NATO, how should it be configured? Among the current NATO members, Germany leads in the view that NATO should be phased out and the Conference on Security and Cooperation in Europe (CSCE) upgraded to a formal organization in which the Partnership for Peace concept is transformed into universal European membership. This view, shared by Moscow, recognizes fully the end of the East-West confrontation, gives Russia full status as a great European power, and eliminates the post–Cold War vision of NATO as perpetuating old conflicts. The United States takes the opposing view. It reasons that until Russia and its former allies have democratized and the transformation of their economies to capitalism is completed, NATO's role is unfinished. Further, those former Soviet allies that are progressing most rapidly deserve the shelter of NATO against any unforeseen Russian effort to reconstitute its empire. Consistent with this view, in 1995 NATO promulgated standards and criteria for expanding NATO amid speculation that Poland, Hungary, and the Czech Republic would be the first admitted in the near future.[28] Critics of this policy, some of them Western Europeans, argue that it does little more than redraw the Cold War lines of demarcation to places menacingly close to the Russian borders.

The practical consequences of these differences were made clear by a disagreement over maintaining peace in Bosnia. President Clinton committed the United States to contribute a force of 20,000 to a peacekeeping mission under NATO auspices. As a Cold War friend of Yugoslavia and long-time ally of the Serbs, Russia wished to take part in the operation but insisted that it be under UN auspices. The United States and NATO insisted that it was a regional matter subject to NATO and not the UN. If Russia were to take part, it would have to do so under a NATO command, something unacceptable to Moscow. It was later agreed, in a public attempt at harmony during the 1995 celebration of the United Nations' fiftieth

anniversary, that Russia would have an independent role.

Western Europe's world view is shaped, in summary, by a long history of imperial dominance and a shorter period of being the geopolitical center of one of the most intensely fortified military balances in history. Out of the ashes of World War Two it built an integrated economy capable of meeting the trade challenges of the United States and Japan. But in both the security and the economic realms, Western Europe has had to struggle continuously with the tensions of Europeanism and Atlanticism. The contradictions of economic independence and security dependence, the latter of which has often been masked as interdependence, remain central features of the European world perspective. Even in the New World Order, the United States dominates European security planning even though the conditions of European security have yet to be defined. The costs of economic independence have been high, as the United States clings to outmoded alliance politics to justify its intrusive hand in Europe.

Canada

If one indicator differentiates the relationship of the United States with Japan and Western Europe from that with Canada, it is proximity. Like its Asian and European counterparts, Canada shares an extensive economy and security relationship with the United States. But that relationship has the added features of a 3000-mile undefended border and a long tradition of intimate economic cooperation. Although until the end of the Second World War Canadian economic and political relations were closely tied to the United Kingdom, the predominance of the American economy since the war and the aggressive diffusion of American capital have reversed this course. At present, the trading relation between Canada and the United States reaches an annual value exceeding that of any other bilateral economic relation in history, and it continues to grow, jumping from $161 billion in

---

[28] *The New York Times*, September 29, 1995, p. A7.

1989 to $202 billion in 1993. Canada's trade with the United States comprises fully 72 percent of its global trade.

Canada's total economic capacity at present ranks eighth in the world by GDP and thirteenth by GNP per capita. Also, its capacity is increasing because of its vast mineral reserves. Supporting a population of only 29 million (11 percent that of the United States and only 23 percent that of Japan) in one of the world's largest territorial masses will enable Canada to preserve its natural resources longer than most nation-states can, although at the present rates of extraction the known petroleum and natural gas reserves will have been depleted within twenty-five years.

Despite these apparent foundations for national autonomy, the geographical closeness of the United States has fostered a pattern of investment, trade, and managerial control leading to what some call partnership and others label a colonial relationship. Still others are tempted to refer to an integrated Canadian-American economy, although such an observation ignores the asymmetry of benefits. The conditions that surround the effort to establish full economic, cultural, and political sovereignty out of this lopsided partnership govern the Canadian world perspective.

Domestic Influences Affecting the Canadian World View

Canadian domestic politics is divided along several firmly drawn lines. Most significant among them is the ethnic distinction between the dominant Anglo-Canadians and the French-Canadians, who are concentrated in Quebec Province. French-Canadians have long considered themselves a nation within a nation. Twice, in 1980 and 1995, referenda were conducted to determine whether or not Quebec should secede, each with a bitter debate between nationalists and separatists (also called unionists and sovereignists). All claims that separatism is extreme were dashed in the 1995 vote in which, with over 91 percent of eligible voters participating, the sovereignists lost by a margin of less than 1 percent. (The separatist premier of

Quebec blamed the loss on non-Francophone immigrants, insisting that a staunch majority of French-Canadians want their own nation.[29]) In their external outlook, however, even separatists are concerned for Canada's economic independence from the United States. As a self-proclaimed oppressed minority, they were unusually sympathetic to young Americans who emigrated to Canada rather than serve in Vietnam and whose criticism of American foreign policy and of the American establishment accentuated the appetite for Canadian autonomy even more than for Quebec's secession.

Anglo-Canadians have been slower to recognize the costs of economic ties to the United States, having for so long depended on American capital for industrialization. Those who inhabit the industrial heartland, however, which for the most part is centered close to the American industrial complexes along the Great Lakes, have developed a new self-consciousness regarding managerial control and are now eager to establish full Canadian economic sovereignty by reducing American ownership of the nation's industry. It is this geographic distinction that forms the second line of division among Canadians in determining their world outlook.

A third important line of difference in Canadian politics is that between the continentalists and the nationalists. The continentalists have resolved in their minds the partner/colony debate by preferring an economy closely tied to that of the United States for the maximum profit of Canada. This view is held most notably by mineral exporters whose profits are hurt by national policies that underprice their goods in the United States, and among those who reside at the industrial fringes, who believe that national investment policies favor the industrial heartland and retard the economic development of their own regions.

The nationalists, however—the growing number of Canadians who believe that American investment and ownership have already exceeded desirable levels—avidly support policies that safeguard Canada from further encroachment, policies

---

[29] *The New York Times,* November 1, 1995, p. A1.

that will reduce American industrial ownership of Canada. It is principally the convergence of this sentiment among the Anglo-Canadians who comprise the new entrepreneurial class (and who yearn for national scientific and technological development) with the more traditional French-Canadian nationalism that led to a reassessment of Canadian-American relations in the 1970s.[30] The goals were (1) to reduce foreign ownership of Canadian production, (2) to eliminate extraterritorial legal controls of foreign subsidiaries in Canada (i.e., to make them subject to Canadian law rather than the law of their ownership countries), (3) to improve ecological cooperation, and (4) to revise the security relationship. It is around these goals that the nationalists have their focus of the Canadian world view on the economic relationship with the United States. Nonetheless, "ambivalance concerning the choice of a proper balance between autonomy and integration has been a recurrent feature of Canadian foreign policy."[31]

As has been indicated, the trading relationship between Canada and the United States is the world's largest. Trade with the United States consistently comprises more than two-thirds of all Canadian trade. Table 4–18 summarizes the recent history of Canada's world trade, and Table 4–19 a quarter-century of Canadian-American trade. Together they underscore the success of Canada's trade not only in value, but in balance as well, which is consistently positive with respect to both the United States and the world. Note particularly the years 1982 through 1986. In 1982, the surplus

TABLE 4–18

CANADA'S WORLD TRADE

	Canada's Exports	Canada's Imports	Balance
1987	$98.2 billion	$90.3 billion	$7.9 billion
1988	117.1	110.0	7.1
1989	121.8	116.9	4.9
1990	127.2	120.3	6.9
1991	127.2	121.7	5.5
1992	134.4	126.1	8.3
1993	144.7	135.3	9.4

Source: International Monetary Fund, Direction of Trade Statistics Yearbook, 1994.

in trade with the United States doubled, and it nearly doubled again by 1986. In that year, the Canadian surplus accounted for 15 percent of the total U.S. trade deficit. It was about this time that Washington began pressing Canada for a new free trade agreement, and at which Canadians began to increase their imports from the United States. From 1986 through 1989, Canada's exports to the United States increased by approximately $17 billion while imports from the United States grew by $30 billion, thus gradually reducing the Canadian surplus in this trading relationship until 1990, when it shot up again.

Behind the Canadian trade surplus lurk a number of dangers. First among them is the threat of premature exhaustion of natural resources, though it is likely that more will be found in the vast but seasonally inaccessible Canadian north. Second is extreme reliance on a single partner for both import and export markets, which makes the Canadian economy vulnerable to economic fluctuations in the United States and subjects the value of the Canadian dollar to the extraordinary influence of another currency. Third are the external controls that attend foreign ownership of production and reliance on foreign capital for economic growth. More than anything else, objection to these controls dominates the sense of colonization. And fourth, because Canada's trade base is small compared with those of the United States, Japan, and

[30] Robert Gilpin, "Integration and Disintegration on the North American Continent," International Organization, vol. 28, 1974, pp. 851–874. See also John Sloan Dickey, "Canada Independent," Foreign Affairs, July 1972, pp. 684–699; and Gerald F. Rutan, "Stresses and Fractures in Canadian-American Relations. The Emergence of a New Environment," ORBIS, vol. 18, summer 1974, pp. 582–593. See also Foreign Ownership and the Structure of Canadian Industry: A Report of the Task Force on the Structure of Canadian Industry, January 1968, pp. 310–345.
[31] Michael B. Dolan, Brian Tomlin, and Harald von Reikhoff, "Integration and Autonomy in Canadian-United States Relations, 1963-1972," Canadian Journal of Political Science, June 1982, pp. 331–363 at p. 332.

TABLE 4–19

CANADIAN-AMERICAN TRADE AND THE CANADIAN BALANCE

	Canadian Imports	Canadian Exports	Total Value	Canadian Balance
1969	$9.5 billion	$9.8 billion	$19.3 billion	$0.3 billion
1973	16.5	17.1	33.6	0.6
1977	25.8	29.6	55.4	3.8
1978	28.4	33.5	61.9	5.1
1979	33.1	38.1	71.2	5.0
1980	35.4	41.5	76.9	6.1
1981	39.6	46.4	86.0	6.8
1982	33.7	46.5	80.2	12.8
1983	38.2	52.1	90.3	13.9
1984	46.5	66.5	113.0	20.0
1985	47.3	69.0	116.3	21.7
1986	45.3	68.0	113.3	22.7
1987	59.6	71.5	131.1	11.9
1988	70.4	82.0	152.4	11.6
1989	75.6	85.2	160.8	9.7
1990	75.3	95.4	170.7	20.1
1991	75.0	95.6	170.6	20.6
1992	79.3	103.9	183.2	24.6
1993	87.8	114.4	202.2	26.6

Source: Several issues, including 1994, of International Monetary Fund, *Direction of Trade Statistics Yearbook*.

Western Europe, it is unusually vulnerable to protectionism (tariffs and other trade barriers used to protect domestic economies against imported goods). To combat these susceptibilities, Canada has been an active partner in developing new international trade regulations.

The 1980s brought major changes to the Canadian-American trading relationship. In the opening years of the decade economic nationalism reigned, and both liberalized trade and U.S. ownership of Canadian production were highly unpopular. But a deep recession in 1981–82 caused a spike in unemployment to the extent that nearly half of

Canadians considered unemployment and economy-related problems the focal issues of the 1984 election. Seventy-four percent of Canadians thought that free trade with the United States was good for Canada; only 19 percent disagreed. While in 1980 only 30 percent thought that Canada should move closer to the United States in trade, by 1985 the number was 45 percent.[32] Simultaneously,

[32] Lawrence LeDuc and J. Alex Murray, "Open for Business?: Foreign Investment and Trade Issues in Canada," in Harold D. Clark, Marianne Stewart, and Gary Zuk, eds., *Economic Decline and Political Change: Canada, Great Britain and the United States* (Pittsburgh: University of Pittsburgh, 1989), pp. 127–139.

Washington became concerned about the chronic trade deficit with Canada, which by the mid-1980s appeared to be getting out of hand. Hence even while the global Uruguay Round of the GATT was in progress, the United States and Canada entered into a Free Trade Agreement on January 1, 1989. It calls for the complete elimination of tariffs between the two countries by January 1, 1998.[33] In 1993 the privileges of this free trade area were extended to Mexico in the form of the North American Free Trade Agreement (NAFTA).

NAFTA is a victory particularly for the continentalists, whose ultimate goal is economic integration with the United States. But NAFTA is less an integrating organization than it is a customs union, that is, it is what the European Union was in its infantile form as the European Economic Community. Thus it is a moderate gain for the continentalists. For the nationalists, it will probably represent a gain as well because it eliminates barriers in Canada's trade with the United States and Mexico without affecting ownership of production or flow of either capital or labor. It would become a loss to the nationalists only if the trade balance with the United States were to fall into deficit.

Against this regional background, the Uruguay Round, also concluded in 1993, is another victory for Canada, as it reversed the growing global trend toward protectionism. But with more than two-thirds of its trade conducted with the United States, and the new market opportunities created in Mexico through NAFTA, the new regional trade regime was the more important.

A secondary policy has been to expand trade with the Developing Nations. This has three principal benefits: (1) it opens new markets to Canada; (2) it helps Canada diversify its trade; and (3) it makes Canada less reliant on the United States. No country was more offended than Canada when, in response to the downing of two civilian aircraft

by the Cuban air force, President Clinton signed the Helms-Burton Act (1996) which purports to embargo trade with any nation that continues to trade with Cuba, one of the Developing World's principal buyers of Canada's exports. Helms and others have long considered Canada's Cuba trade an act of defiance against Washington to the extent that the unsuccessful Helms bill was nicknamed the Canada-Bashing Act of 1995[34] prior to the President's signing.

Direct Private Investment

During the lengthy period of British influence, private investment was mostly of the portfolio type—that is, the purchase of stocks and bonds on securities markets. As the era of American domination began, however, with investments rising from approximately $5 billion to $25 billion in twenty years, the pattern shifted to the purchase of Canadian firms and mineral deposits, and to construction of American subsidiaries in Canada. In the immediate post-war years and in the early years (1955–1965) of intense Canadian industrial development, government planning took for granted that this direct private investment was profitable. It brought needed managerial skills as well as capital into the country; it hastened industrialization and the ability to exploit natural resource reserves; it created profit and increased employment; and it generated public revenue as well as export surpluses. The rapid and sustained increases in the GNP and in per capita income seemed to prove the wisdom of an open policy on direct private investment from the United States.[35]

As Canadian economic nationalism began to rise, however, this policy was reappraised. Between 1964 and 1967, for example, Canadians who thought there was enough American capital in their economy rose from 46 percent to 67 percent

---

[33] For a summary of the agreement, see Harold Crookell, *Canadian-American Trade and Investment Under the Free Trade Agreement* (New York: Quorum Books, 1990), appendix B, pp. 161–205.

[34] *The Washington Post*, April 1, 1995, p. A17.
[35] For a history of foreign ownership in Canada, see Gordon Laxer, *Open for Business: The Roots of Foreign Ownership in Canada* (Toronto: Oxford University Press, 1989).

of those questioned. Clearly the population was aware of how much the partnership with the United States was decaying into colonial subordination. Table 4–20 dramatizes the basis for this fear, as three of Canada's largest and most important industries were owned almost entirely by foreign interests, U.S. investors predominant among them. By 1972, only 37 percent of Canadians polled felt that they shared with the United States an economic partnership, whereas 34 percent felt that they had become colonized. Only 34 percent felt that dependence on the United States was good for Canada; 53 percent thought it bad.[36] Table 4–21 summarizes direct American investment in Canada. It shows that while Canadian investments were becoming a smaller fraction of worldwide American investment, American ownership of Canadian industry actually doubled in value between 1978 and 1988.

After decades of satisfaction with the profitability of American investment, the national mood shifted. The Gray Task Force in 1972 focused as much on the costs of dependence as on its benefits. In a marked departure from traditional assumptions, the Gray Report concluded that most Canadian profit was actually drawn not from American investment capital but from the American corporations' ability to exploit Canadian resources.[37] If this were the case, then the wise course for Canada would be to distinguish between investment policy as a capital venture and foreign ownership, and thereafter to restrict foreign direct investment to a level below 50 percent ownership or control. As early as 1970, a plurality (although not a majority) of Canadians polled reported that they would approve a policy of restricting American ownership to

---

[36] For an extensive statistical study of Canadian attitudes toward American domination, see John H. Sigler and Dennis Goresky, "Public Opinion on United States–Canadian Relations," *International Organization*, vol. 28, 1974, pp. 637–668. For a briefer survey pertaining specifically to attitudes on foreign investment, refer to John Fayerweather, *Foreign Investment in Canada: Prospects for National Policy* (White Plains, N.Y.: International Arts and Sciences Press, 1973), pp. 13–72.
[37] Gray Task Force Report, *Foreign Direct Investment in Canada* (Ottawa: Information Canada, 1972).

TABLE 4–20

FOREIGN AND AMERICAN OWNERSHIP OF SELECTED CANADIAN INDUSTRIES, 1971

Industry	Foreign Ownership	American Ownership
Iron mining	86.2%	85.8%
Petroleum refining	99.9	72.0
Oil and gas wells	82.6	65.0

Source: Adapted from 1967 Report of Corporations and Labour Unions Return Act as quoted in the Report of the Standing Committee on External Affairs and National Defense, on investigation into Canada-U.S. relations ("The Wahn Report") and as produced in Malcolm Levin and Christine Sylvester, *Foreign Ownership* (Don Mills, Ontario: General Publishing, 1972), p. 74.

49 percent in any industry even if it meant a reduction in the national standard of living!

The Gray Report was followed only months later by an extensive government report on Canadian relations with the United States, major portions of which dealt with the question of whether asymmetrical interdependence with the United States automatically threatens Canada's economic sovereignty.[38] For both trade and investment policies, the report called for ways to ensure that the relationship with the United States would benefit Canada and Canadians. Thereafter, Parliament entertained a variety of proposals for screening foreign investments in accordance with the requirement that a project strengthen the Canadian economy without further deteriorating national control over economic activity. Recognizing that excessive nationalism might damage the economy by repelling useful investments, the government sought to run a delicate line between destructive nationalism and equally destructive continentalism.

---

[38] "Options for the Future," a statement on foreign affairs by Mitchell Sharp, Minister for External Affairs, published in a special edition of *International Perspectives* (Ottawa: Information Canada, autumn 1972).

TABLE 4-21

DIRECT AMERICAN INVESTMENT IN CANADA

	1970	1978	1985	1988	1994
U.S. worldwide investment	$75.5 billion	$168.1 billion	$232.7 billion	$326.9 billion	$612.1 billion
U.S. investment in Canada	21.0	37.3	46.4	61.2	72.8
Canadian investment as percentage of U.S. worldwide investment	28%	22%	20%	18.7%	11.9%

Source: *Statistical Abstract of the United States*, 1979 and 1982/1983; for 1985, 1988, and 1994, U.S. Department of Commerce, *Survey of Current Business*, August 1986, August 1989, and August 1995.

Efforts at reducing the amount of foreign (and particularly American) ownership resulted by 1979 in a decline to 28.5 percent ownership by foreign investors of all Canadian industry. Of that total, 75 percent continued to be American owned.

In autumn 1984, however, Canada's politics took a sharp conservative turn driven by the same economic factors that reversed opinion on trade. After more than a decade of liberal dominance, the Progressive Conservative party and Prime Minister Brian Mulroney took the reins of government, committed to the notions of free trade with the United States and a return to more open policies on American direct private investment in Canadian industry. During the election campaign, polls indicated that whereas in 1981 42 percent of Canadians thought foreign investment a national problem, now only 32 percent thought so.[39] The conservative American press hailed Mulroney's victory as the occasion of returning Canada from economic isolation and cheered him for not being "a prisoner of the out-dated, semi-socialist ideas that infected so many of his predecessors." Said the same source, "Smart U.S. businessmen and investors smell opportunity."[40] It is not by coincidence, therefore, that direct investment from the United States skyrocketed between 1985 and 1994 by 57 percent, and from 1970 through 1994 by 347 percent.

Natural Resources

Canada's richness in natural resources permits a favorable trade balance with the United States. Although fuel products comprise the bulk of these resources, Canada is also plentiful in ore deposits. The United States is the largest customer, to the extent that by exporting half of its annual gas and oil production, Canada fulfills about 6 percent of the total American demand. In 1971 the mining and refining industries were largely under American ownership, as is indicated by Table 4-20. Thereafter, with the combined effects of the Canadianization program and a National Energy Program designed to protect national fuel reserves in the wake of the 1973-74 OPEC embargo, the percentage of domestic control began to increase. Consequently, by 1979, approximately 63 percent (as compared with 83 percent in 1971) of the oil and gas industry was under foreign control, 47 percent (as contrasted with 65 percent earlier) in American hands.[41]

[39] Lawrence LeDuc and J. Alex Murray, "Open for Business? Foreign Investment and Trade Issues in Canada," pp. 127-139.
[40] Edwin A. Finn Jr. and Richard C. Morais, "Good Neighbors Again," *Forbes*, May 19, 1986, pp. 130-134. The cover proclaims: "Canada—Open for Business Again."

[41] Jock A. Finlayson and David G. Haglund, "Oil Politics and Canada-United States Relations," *Political Science Quarterly*, summer 1984, pp. 271-283.

But from the Canadian perspective, the statistics portray only a fraction of the story. Under foreign control, the profit from these enterprises contributes little to the Canadian economy but is repatriated to the United States. Moreover, the rate of production is determined less by Canadian public policy than by American demand and American corporate decisions. Of paramount importance is the tendency of Canadian fuel production to become enmeshed in American foreign policy. The OPEC threat of a total oil embargo in 1973 heightened Washington's interest in a continental oil policy that would formally subordinate Canadian national policy to joint Canadian-American determination. The growing demand for fuel in the United States, the steady increase of OPEC petroleum prices, and the increased reliance of the United States on external sources of fuel in the remaining years of the 1970s made the

attractiveness of Canada's riches even greater. Coupled with gradual depletion of Canada's reserves, such overtures continue to threaten Canadian autonomy, even though Canada's annual export volume of fuel to the United States is declining steadily, while its volume to Japan increases.

Ecological Preservation

Added to its concern for preserving its natural resources is Canada's long-standing determination to avoid environmental pollution. Its primary ecological issue is acid raid, precipitation that brings with it airborne industrial pollutants that stunt wheat and grain growth, kill freshwater fish stocks, and contaminate aquafers. (Figure 4–1 shows the acid rain pattern of North America as of 1986.) Because ecological pollution knows nothing of national boundaries, Canadians fear the continental

FIGURE 4–1 Acid rain sensitivity in the United States and Canada. The dotted sections are low in natural buffers and particularly sensitive to acidic precipitation.

Source: Canada Today / d'aujourd'hui (summer '86), vol. 17, no. 2, 1986, p. 12. Reprinted by permission.

consequences of Washington's failure to attack the acid rain problem forcefully. President Reagan disdained this issue, rebuffing even his friend Prime Minister Mulroney. President Bush paid rhetorical service to the issue but did little. Under pressure from the international community and consistent with the interests of Vice President Albert Gore, the Clinton administration sought modest advances, though its concern was more with weather-altering greenhouse gases and ozone-layer depletion than acid rain. The conservative Congress, in contrast, preferred to reduce environmental controls to stimulate economic growth.

Environmental preservation is an issue destined to plague Canadian-American relations indefinitely. Explosive population growth in the Developing Nations creates an export opportunity for Canadian farmers, but chemical pollution causes underproduction. The fields of immunology, toxicology, molecular genetics, and hydrogeology are amassing evidence of how carcinogenic and leukogenic chemical contaminants find their way into fresh water supplies and cause environment-related diseases. Extinction of species is related in some instances to the physical or chemical destruction of habitats. Some deforestation results from failure to recycle paper. A large portion of the world's aluminum lies forever in contaminated landfills. A continental relationship dependent on natural resource exploitation uncontrolled by the sovereign host and unenlightened by environmental imperatives is chronically destructive, but only Canada seems to understand.

Security

Although the principal Canadian-American links are currently economic, they were originally forged around the need for a continental defense policy during World War Two. That partnership was epitomized by including Canada in the Hyde Park Declaration of 1941, which agreed on a common production effort between the United States and Britain to meet wartime industrial and munitions needs. Later, Canada became an active member of NATO, although it declined to participate in the Inter-American Treaty of Mutual Assistance, the military wing of the Organization of American States. The continental radar defense system, NORAD, is a joint Canadian-American undertaking of long standing, as are several bilateral defense planning boards.

Despite this cooperation in common security matters, Canada has steadfastly refused to endorse American defense strategy in its entirety. Ottawa was one of the first Western capitals to break with Washington over both Korea and Vietnam; it sold wheat to China and the Soviet Union during the era of containment; it opened diplomatic relations with China during the Vietnam War (although at a point at which this act probably facilitated American withdrawal from Southeast Asia and aided Sino-American normalization); and while reducing its commitment to NATO, Canada became one of the main contributors to the United Nations' peacekeeping expeditions. One of the central tenets of Canadian defense policy is to distinguish between Canadian-American relations on continental and extracontinental matters.

This independent attitude results not simply from a different ideological view of the world or from disavowal of a global role. It rises, rather, from the will to conduct foreign policies from which Canada will prosper without the constraints of the American world view. It assumes that transnational economic relations are more effective governors of the international system than are ideological confrontations and arms races. Built into this policy is the realization that threats to Canadian security are extremely remote. Even before the end of the Cold War, Canada grew less responsive to what it considered excessive sensitivity in the United States to apparent threats to North America's security. Although the Mulroney government, as part of its review of Canadian-American relations, agreed to increase the defense budget by $2 billion per year for fifteen years, in constant U.S. dollars it never moved from the $9–10 billion range throughout the closing years of the Cold War and the beginning of the New World Order.

During the 1980s, Canadian-American security relations encountered unprecedented strain despite the close personal relationship between Prime Minister Mulroney and President Reagan. The anti-Soviet rhetoric of the United States and the escalation of the strategic arms race during the Reagan years deeply disappointed Canadians, the vast majority of whom deplored the strategic arms race and considered the Soviet Union to be modifying long before *perestroika* and *glasnost*. A public opinion poll taken in mid-1983 by the Canadian Institute of International Affairs revealed that while 51 percent of those polled continued to regard the Soviet Union as the principal threat to world peace, fully 21 percent had come to regard the United States as a greater danger.

A more specific source of friction occurred in 1983 over American testing of air-launched cruise missiles over Canadian territory. An initial agreement had been sought by the Carter administration, but it was not finalized until 1982. From mid-1983 to early 1984, when for the first time the missiles were transported across Canada fixed to the wings of an American bomber, public opinion rose in opposition to the tests. More than half of the Canadians polled on the tests opposed them. Court efforts to prevent the flight failed, and despite a great public outcry, the first flight was made in March 1984. These are strategic arms rather than theater arms, and Canadians were aware that in the event of a nuclear confrontation between the Soviet Union and the United States, cruise missiles would be launched against Soviet targets from American aircraft in Canadian airspace.

Consistent with its commitment to peace, Canada maintains a bare-bones military with a current funds budget of only about $10 billion (U.S.) annually. Furthermore, though Canada is a highly industrialized state, it has but a small arms industry and does not take part in the world arms export activity. It is a net importer of arms, using about 20 percent of its annual defense budget to purchase arms, almost entirely from the United States.

As one of the world's most productive states, Canada has all the ingredients of an independent and prosperous foreign policy and of continued national economic growth and autonomy. At present, however, neither of these goals is held in the tight control of Canadian decision makers, inasmuch as the resources and production facilities on which each relies are controlled by foreign interests, mostly American. Because this degree of external control raises the specter of foreign interference, the Canadian world view is one that is especially wary of the motives, needs, and machinations of its neighbor to the south, a neighbor that is friendly but rapacious; tolerant but ambitious beyond its means; libertarian in philosophy but determined that the foundations of its global supremacy will not be eroded. It is because Canada is so closely tied to those foundations and because its quest for autonomy is perceived by the United States to contribute to its erosion that the Canadian perspective of the international system is tinted by a growing sense of association with the dependent middle-ranking powers. Also, there is a commensurate sense of separation from the United States to the extent that Washington insists on those modes of interdependence that prevent Canada from achieving a full sense of autonomy in a world that it finds otherwise comfortably peaceful.

Nevertheless, in many respects Canada is the model New World Order country. It has a prosperous, environmentally sensitive industrial base; it has a demonstrated commitment to free trade; its foreign policies require little military support; it has consistently and repeatedly aided the United Nations in peacekeeping roles; relative to the size of its economy, it is a major contributor to the Developing Nations and especially to the least developed; its population growth is well controlled, with its liberal immigration policy accounting for more growth than does fertility; and its ambitions for international recognition are nondisruptive and noninterventionary. It has internationalist instincts consistent with the prescriptions of the New World Order. Its goal is to achieve full economic independence within the continental and Uruguay Round frameworks while preserving these assets.

CHAPTER 5

The Chinese Perspective

We have seen that national perceptions are not permanent. Just as events of the late 1970s brought about a reassessment of the American world position, so too did the Chinese attitude undergo major changes. From 1950 to 1976, the Chinese perspective was a product of Maoism, that is, of the leadership and domestic and foreign policies of Chairman Mao Zedong. After Mao's death and the rise of national leadership with a broader view of China's world position, new tolerances and aspirations revised national perceptions. But proving that old ideas die hard, in 1989 there occurred a partial reversal. Thousands of students demanding freedom of the press and exposure of government corruption used the global press coverage given Mikhail Gorbachev's historic visit to Beijing as an occasion for massive demonstrations in Tiananmen Square. Following Gorbachev's departure, units of the Red army were ordered to fire on the crowd. The Chinese government branded the demonstrators "antirevolutionary hooligans" led on by foreign, anti-Chinese forces, and after clearing the square, set about a nationwide sweep to arrest the leaders and restore ideological purity.

Nevertheless, for the most part, the world perspective of the People's Republic of China is based on a fusion of two great forces: a national force developed out of long history, and an ideological force of Marxism-Leninism-Maoism, both of which are important to understanding China's contemporary world perspective. The national force evolves from 2000 years of continuous history and culture. The infusion of communist ideology reshaped China's self-perception and the image of the country in the outer world. In the words of one Western observer, "China is an Oriental despotism first and a communist country second."[1]

China's history falls broadly into three periods: (1) the long classical epoch of imperial greatness (the "Middle Kingdom"), (2) a century of degradation and Western domination from 1840 to 1945, and (3) the modern period of national revolution and rebirth. It is impossible to understand China today without understanding these three periods.

The Middle Kingdom: Classical China

Classical China was a vast empire comparable to Rome's, but enduring many times longer. Most of the people under the direct sovereignty of the Middle Kingdom were ethnic (Han) Chinese, but with a multitude of regional, cultural, religious, and linguistic differences. Chinese were as different from one another as the European peoples, and their integration into a single political unit was a great feat of early social engineering.

One factor behind the central government system may have been that for its survival, China requires a huge irrigation network to control the twin

---

[1] George E. Taylor, "China as an Oriental Despotism," *Problems of Post-Communism*, Janaury–February 1995, pp. 25–28 at p. 25.

problems of flooding and drought that plague its rivers. The basic requirements of agricultural production depend on rigorous social controls to ensure the orderly development of hydraulic works throughout the vast territory. Perhaps because of their mutual water needs, the diverse lands of China joined politically.

This is not to suggest that ancient China was a fully integrated society. Local potentates ("warlords") wielded great regional power throughout Chinese history, and during long periods the emperor ruled only at their discretion. When the imperial center was weak, the warlords carved out zones of control and reduced the emperor to a powerless figurehead dependent on their armies. Only when the imperial court was strong, free of corruption, and skillful in building necessary coalitions could the warlords' power be reduced and could the central government rule effectively. In a sense, the empire was a syndicate of local organizations; tension always existed between the central and regional powers.

The emperor's authority was legitimized by the popular belief that he ruled by divine sanction as the Son of Heaven occupying the celestial throne. Emperors were dethroned throughout Chinese history, but this was explained as their having lost the mandate of heaven because of their enemies' success. Divine sanction had passed to the new rulers.

Official Chinese culture was conservative. It emphasized the Confucian virtues of obedience and filial piety, a system of moral obligations guiding all social behavior. Individuals derived identity mainly as members of the nuclear family or community, and through other group identities. Within these units every individual had some importance; outside them the individual was nothing.

The educational system emphasized knowledge of the classic writings. It was concerned more with the development of values than with the acquisition of functional knowledge. Advancement in society, to the extent that it depended on education, stemmed more from command of the ancient texts than from expertise.

All segments of Chinese thought, even reformist and revolutionary, were portrayed as conservative

and restorative of the principles in the venerated classics. Reforms were rationalized as reinterpretations of the great books, said to be more consistent with the original intentions of the texts than were existing practices. This system of reverence for the classical texts served as a stabilizing element in Chinese history. It encouraged a profound respect for literacy. Scholar-administrators were revered and powerful men, and the inventor of writing was deified. The nation was guided by the accumulated wisdom of a thousand years.

The Chinese believed themselves to be the center of world civilization, having relatively little contact with other peoples except weak states on the periphery of the empire. Many of these were periodically conquered by China during expansionist phases, only to regain independence when the warlord struggles reduced the emperor's ability to control the outlying regions. These historical expansions and contractions make it difficult to define the exact boundaries of the classical kingdom, complicating modern China's territorial claims.

Under China's tribute system, the rulers of the peripheral societies retained power by praising the superiority of the Chinese emperor with modest gifts and offerings of homage. This reinforced the Chinese national self-image as the Middle Kingdom at the center of known civilization. Non-Chinese were regarded as barbarians. A new envoy would arrive with a caravan of gifts and kneel before the Son of Heaven three times in the act of kowtow while presenting the tribute. This ritual set the tone for the entire relationship between China and other peoples, one not of equality but of dominance and submission. As China saw little need for the outside world, it sent forth few explorers, traders, or conquerors of its own.

The Century of Humiliation: The Meeting with the West

This stable, conservative, and self-confident Chinese society got a rude awakening when it came into contact with the European, Japanese, and American modernity. China was very poorly prepared for this experience, and the shock of it reverberates still.

The first Europeans entered China to spread Christianity and find trading opportunities, but they stirred relatively little interest. Elsewhere explorers had been revered as gods or at least as men of extraordinary power and inventiveness, but in China they were received as envoys from inferior civilizations. Early Chinese maps portray entities called England, France, America, Portugal, and so on as small islands on the fringes of a world with a huge China at the center. The advanced products of Europe that so dazzled other peoples were received unexcitedly in China. The Son of Heaven wrote to the king of England in 1793:

> The virtue and prestige of the Celestial Dynasty having spread far and wide, the kings of myriad nations come by land and sea with all sorts of precious things. Consequently, there is nothing we lack, as your principal envoy and others have themselves observed. We have never set much store on strange or ingenious objects, nor do we need any more of your country's manufacturers.[2]

Christian missionaries were tolerated but regarded as a nuisance.

China may not have been much interested in Europeans, but Westerners coveted China. By 1715 the British had established the first commercial base at Canton, and they were soon joined by French, Dutch, and American traders who, under close Chinese control, were confined to tiny enclaves and hampered by travel and other restrictions. Foreigners were required to deal exclusively with a government trade monopoly, and Chinese were forbidden to teach them languages. The traders grew increasingly unhappy with these restrictions, and their energetic representations were made to the emperor to no avail.

Perhaps the most serious problem for the traders was China's lack of interest in Western products. To buy from China they had to sell in exchange something that the Chinese wanted. The Europeans discovered that there was one major marketable product. That its open sale was encouraged may surprise the modern reader: The product was opium.

Opium had been known in China for many years, but as in Europe and America, its sale and use were prohibited. Before the Europeans stimulated the trade, opium addiction was a minor problem, partly because Chinese cultural traditions discouraged hedonism and antisocial behavior. But after the European trade reached its peak, in some communities as much as 50 percent of the population was addicted. The imperial government tried repeatedly to stop this traffic by decree, but with little effect. In 1729, at the time of the first decree, importation was approximately 200 chests of pure opium per year. By 1830, this had grown to about 19,000 chests, and by 1838 to 30,000. European persistence joined with ineffective decrees and corrupt Chinese officials to encourage growth of the drug trade.

The Opium War

This encounter with the West culminated in the Opium War in 1839, when a serious effort was finally made to halt the corrupt trade. Chinese forces ringed the commercial enclave, seized a huge quantity of opium, and drove the drug traffic out of Canton altogether. The British government, construing this as aggression against free international trade, promptly initiated a battle that ended in destruction of China's Canton forts and the Treaty of Nanking (1842). In military terms China's losses were minor. But a handful of barbarians employing the mere gadgetry of their inferior civilizations had humbled the great Chinese empire. One Chinese official asked the British, "Except for your ships being solid, your gunfire fierce, and your rockets powerful, what other abilities have you?"[3]

The Opium War was the first in a long series of national defeats that lasted from 1840 to 1945, the

---

[2] Quoted in John K. Fairbank and Ssu-yu Teng, eds., *China's Response to the West: A Documentary Survey* (Cambridge, Mass.: Harvard University Press, 1954), p. 19.

[3] Quoted in John Stoessinger, *Nations in Darkness* (New York: Random House, 1971), p. 14.

Century of Humiliation. During this time, the power of the celestial throne was destroyed and China found itself increasingly the victim of external enemies and of internal dissolution.

In the Treaty of Nanking, China was forced to give Hong Kong to Britain in perpetuity, to reopen Canton and the opium trade, to pay $21 million in reparations (equal to the entire American federal budget at the time), and most important in the long run, to give four more treaty ports to the Europeans. Treaty ports were put under the direct control of the Europeans; they were extraterritorial, meaning that even civil laws were to be enforced by European courts. In Cushing's Treaty (1844), the United States was granted similar rights. These unequal treaties produced many insults, including the lax treatment of Europeans convicted of crimes against Chinese and even a sign in a Shanghai park prohibiting Chinese and dogs.

China went into steady decline after the Opium War. In 1858, there was another skirmish in which British, French, American, and Russian negotiators, backed by thirty gunboats and 3000 troops, forced open eleven more ports to trade. Worse, for the first time they demanded access to China's interior, meaning penetration from the coastal areas into the vast heartland. Now all of China would be open.

The T'aip'ing Rebellion

Another step in the decline was the T'aip'ing Rebellion, a civil war that coincided with the American Civil War (1861–1865). In the American war about 400,000 died; in China the losses were closer to 20 million. The rebellion was a mass uprising led by a zealous Chinese Christian who believed that God whispered to him at night to redeem the nation. The T'aip'ings favored communal forms of social organization and production, a kind of peasant communism before Marx and Mao.

At first the Europeans looked interestedly on the rebellion, thinking that its Christian leadership might bring beneficial results. With European neutrality, the rebels almost succeeded in destroying

the Manchu Dynasty. But late in the struggle, the Western governments concluded that the fanatical zeal of the T'aip'ings might make them more difficult to deal with than with the corrupt officials of the imperial court, and so they helped the emperor quell the rebellion. The war ended with the imperial government weakened, the peasant movement destroyed, and the Europeans strengthened. The very power of the Manchu Dynasty to survive thereafter depended directly on foreigners.

China entered a period of self-criticism. How could it prevent total colonization? The policy of clinging to great traditions and refusing to acknowledge the inevitability of change had failed. China had scorned Western technology, but a handful of foreigners had reduced China to submission. This point was driven home in 1894 when Japan, which had met the Western challenge by adopting modern economic and industrial values, seized the Korean peninsula from China. In a mere quarter-century Japan had modernized its economic and military capacities while China had declined. The contrast was particularly humiliating.

The Boxer Rebellion

The first attempt at self-assertion was the Boxer Rebellion. The Japanese victory over China (1894–95), the spread of European commercial exploitation, and the growth of Christianity outraged national sensibilities, and some nationalists believed that the only recourse was a popular uprising against the white devils. In 1900, large numbers of young patriots joined a rebellion by the Society of Harmonious Fists (the Boxers). Attacks on Christian converts, missionaries, and especially European commercial and industrial interests aroused the outsiders to resistance. Here was a struggle between the Chinese, who felt that they were defending national independence, and the Europeans, who thought they were defending the rights of free trade and protecting their citizens. The Chinese were enraged by the unceasing advances of foreign profiteers and missionaries. The Europeans were enraged by the wanton acts of violence against

Western civilians and their Chinese friends. The United States demanded "speedy suppression of these rioters, the restoration of order, the punishment of the criminals and the derelict officials, and prompt compensation for the property destroyed."[4]

The Boxer Rebellion was counterproductive, stimulating foreign exploitation rather than stopping it. An eight-nation European force crushed the rebellion and looted the city of Peking (now Beijing, the national capital). Government collaboration with the Boxers destroyed the remnants of foreign cooperation. Westerners now proposed the wholesale dismemberment of China into spheres of influence under the control of the various foreign powers. But Britain and the United States opposed the spheres-of-influence concept and insisted on an Open Door policy. Under it everyone would share equally in the exploitation of China by dividing its territory and controlling many of its railroads, ports, and mines, and its foreign trade.

The Republic of China

Nevertheless, the revolutionary spirit spread and deepened. In 1911, a nationalist rebellion by followers of Dr. Sun Yat-sen, the father of modern China, succeeded in overthrowing the Manchu Dynasty, by then thoroughly discredited. But the revolutionaries seized a rump government. Real power went to the warlords, who filled the vacuum created by a weak center. Sun Yat-sen was quickly replaced by the most powerful of the warlords, Yuan Shih-k'ai, who suppressed Sun's Nationalist party, the Kuomintang (KMT). Sun fled the country, the party went underground, and the ideals of 1911 were temporarily defeated.

The Russian revolution in 1917 revived the cause of Chinese nationalism. From their lonely island in a hostile capitalist sea, Russian leaders looked with great interest on the possibility of a friendly China. In 1922, Lenin's government offered Sun Yat-sen substantial aid for his illicit party,

conceding that "the conditions necessary for the establishment of either socialism or communism do not exist in China." In exchange, Sun admitted the Chinese communists to the Kuomintang. Russian aid had reawakened hopes of national rebirth, and communist inclusion had boosted Soviet interest.

Upon Sun Yat-sen's death (1925), a powerful new figure rose in the Kuomintang leadership: Chiang Kai-shek. Chiang organized and led a successful Northern Expedition that destroyed or absorbed the power of the warlords, a major step toward unifying China. Chiang rewarded the communists for their participation in a united front against the warlords by turning on them in the middle of one quiet night in 1927, having them dragged from their beds and shot in the streets. He did not want competitors in the system of personal power he was to create. In one sweep, the membership of the Chinese Communist party dropped from 50,000 to 10,000.

Mao Zedong and the Communist Party

In 1928 a new figure emerged, a previously minor functionary named Mao Zedong. In five years of difficult organizing (1928–1933), he built a party of 300,000 and a Red army to oppose Chiang's. Mao's forces were no match for the huge nationalist army, however, and in 1933, 400,000 KMT troops killed 60,000 Red soldiers, still another defeat for revolution in China. The surviving elements of the Red army made the famous Long March across China to sanctuary in the mountains. No ordinary retreat, this was a 6000-mile forced march by 90,000 men and women, taking more than a year while evading KMT harassment on all sides. It was one of the great feats of military history and is memorialized in China's revolutionary literature and arts.

But successful communist evasion of KMT troops did nothing to rid China of foreign influences. While the struggle between opposing forces unfolded, foreign interests continued their rape of China. In 1931, Japanese troops invaded Manchuria by way of Korea (which Japan controlled) and

---

[4] Quoted in Edmund Clubb, *Twentieth-Century China* (New York: Columbia University Press, 1964), p. 27.

The 5-yuan bill of the Kuomintang government, dated 1935, is printed in English on one side, demonstrating the dominant position of foreign business in the Chinese economy.

achieved a foothold for further expansion through the so-called Greater East Asia Co-Prosperity Sphere, the Japanese term for their empire in Asia and the Pacific. Meanwhile the Soviet Union, hostile to the peasant foundations of Chinese communism—pure Marxism posits an industrial proletariat—doubted that the conditions for effective revolution existed in China. As a result, it considered limiting the growth of Japanese interests in China to be more important than influencing the outcome of the Chinese civil war. Right through World War Two, therefore, Soviet money, aircraft, advisers, and provisions were directed to the nationalists (KMT).

Disorder and administrative chaos followed the Japanese withdrawal in 1945. The Soviet Union, expecting the restoration of effective KMT control, lost no time in looting the industrial wealth of Manchuria abandoned by the Japanese. Whole factories were transported to Soviet territory. The Kremlin urged the Chinese communists to join a coalition with the KMT as the only available means of acquiring political power. This coincided with the American view, expressed in the mission of General George C. Marshall, that further interparty war would be useless and fratricidal, and that only a ruling coalition could acccelerate national recovery.

Mao rejected this strategy. He knew that the administrative structure of the KMT had been shattered and that popular support for Chiang had evaporated. In the nearly half-century-long struggle to free China from foreign control, national society had in fact disintegrated.[5] Furthermore, the communists had emerged from the world war in many areas as heroes of the anti-Japanese resistance. The seeming selflessness and wartime patriotism of the communist forces were contrasted in the public mind with the image of the Kuomintang as a self-seeking party of corrupt officials and landowners clinging to power and status. When the communists entered a village, they turned all land over to the peasants. When the KMT reentered, their initial act was often land repossession. The difference was not lost on the peasants.

In the civil war that raged from 1945 to 1949, the position of the KMT steadily declined. Whole divisions of Chiang's army, including officers, deserted to the Red army. To the end, the Russians continued to write off the communist cause as hopeless and continued their relationship with Chiang. But the fierce determination of Mao's forces led to the final rout of the KMT in 1949. Chiang fled with the remnants of his army to the island of Taiwan (Formosa), subdued the native people when necessary, and established a new but much-reduced dominion behind the shield of the

---

[5] James E. Sheridan, *China in Disintegration: The Republican Era in Chinese History, 1912–1949* (New York: Free Press, 1975).

U.S. Seventh Fleet, which for decades after 1950 protected the KMT from attack from the mainland. This was viewed by the communists as an unjustified intervention denying the Chinese people the right to complete their own revolution and preserving the insulting fiction of a rump government in exile. Nevertheless, with the flight of the KMT the Century of Humiliation was concluded, and China was reborn as a free and self-determined nation.

Modern China: Rebirth and Revolution

The world outlook of Communist China since 1949 has been deeply influenced by this history. Unlike other modern powers, China's soul has been seared by exploitation, humiliation, and oppression. The last remnant of the seemingly endless waves of foreign conquerors passed through China within the memories of the current leaders. The absolutely overriding consideration of post-revolutionary Chinese foreign and domestic policy has been the restoration and preservation of China as a powerful and independent nation invulnerable to external conquest and domination. This goal has required both objective and subjective changes, including the revival of self-confidence. But until the mid-1970s, there was full agreement among modern Chinese leaders concerning the paramount necessities of national defense and self-sufficiency. The enemies of China had to be kept at bay; and doing so meant deflecting the threats from the world's two most powerful and imperialistic countries: the United States and the Soviet Union.

In the ideological pragmatism that followed Mao's death, the Chinese approach to world affairs changed substantially and evolved rapidly. Between 1974 and 1977, for example, China adopted its own "three-world" theory of global politics. In the Chinese theory, the first world was the imperial world of the Soviet Union and the United States; the second was composed of all other developed states; and the third world was the Developing Nations, with China as the inspirational leader.[6] By 1978, however, as Sino-Soviet relations reached their lowest point and relations with the United States and the NATO countries improved rapidly, the Chinese world view became more Western oriented. The objective of this shift was to unite with anti-Soviet countries against the social-imperialist, an ideological adaptation in which the Chinese accepted the notion that even some socialist countries can have imperial ways. The early 1980s, which brought signs of a Sino-Soviet thaw and increasingly strained Sino-American relations, also saw the Chinese world view as becoming one of self-reliance and neutralism on East-West relations. This became known as the "equidistance" policy, one of promoting economic relations with both superpowers, but without getting too close to either.

This rapid evolution of the Chinese world view during the 1980s was a result of both domestic and international affairs. On the domestic front, there were three vital elements. The first was that internal Chinese politics took a conservative turn, causing the reshaping of domestic institutions along traditional Soviet-type lines. The second force was a desire to avoid dependence on the West, an alluring temptation at a time when Western technology seemed the correct answer to the Soviet military buildup in the Pacific. Third, relaxation of tensions with the Soviet Union was essential to the regional environment needed for China to succeed in its long-term four modernizations policy, a policy calling for the gradual modernization of agriculture, defense, science, and technology.[7]

The international stimuli to an evolving world view were even more complex. They included the

---

[6] Herbert S. Yee, "The Three World Theory and Post-Mao China's Global Strategy," *International Affairs* (London), spring 1983. One Chinese author ascribes the invention of this theory to Mao Zedong. See Huan Xiang, "On Sino-U.S. Relations," *Foreign Affairs*, fall 1981, pp. 35–53 at pp. 35–36. The author is vice president of the Chinese Academy of Social Sciences.

[7] See Edmund Lee (a pseudonym), "Beijing's Balancing Act," *Foreign Policy*, summer 1983, pp. 27–46.

Chinese leadership of the disparate Third World; continued Soviet military expansion in Asia and the Pacific; evolving economic and military relationships with Japan as well as with the United States and Western Europe; and anxieties over the political relationship with the United States. Given Washington's apparent interest in improving bilateral relations, the last of these was particularly vexing, especially because the United States refused to discontinue arms sales to Taiwan. Later, additional strain was added by Washington's protest over China's arms sales to the Middle East, an area in which virtually every other arms exporter in the world was profiting already. American condemnation of the use of arms in Tiananmen Square (1989) accentuated matters. A major confrontation may have been avoided when, in 1990, the Senate upheld by a narrow vote President Bush's veto of a bill offering Chinese students in the United States permanent sanctuary. No matter what else pressured Chinese foreign policy, it was clear that the relationship with the United States was an unreliable cornerstone. How ironic it was that the same event that caused the public Sino-American rupture—Tiananmen Square—occurred on the occasion of Mikhail Gorbachev's unprecedented visit to Beijing.

Throughout this evolution, however, the intensely nationalistic outlook of the Chinese communist leadership dictated an emphasis on defensive, China-centered priorities in international relations. We can infer the following hierarchy of priorities in the formulation of Chinese foreign policy since 1949:

1. Defense against external military attack or domination
2. Reintegration of outlying and alienated territories (particularly Tibet, Sinkiang, and Inner Mongolia)
3. Incorporation of Taiwan in the national administrative structure
4. Prevention of foreign nonmilitary interference in Chinese domestic affairs

5. Reestablishment of international respect, and the achievement of a leading role in regional and international affairs

Each of these principles requires brief elaboration.

National Defense

Defense of national territory and national values is, of course, the primary concern of any state. To the extent that a state feels its territorial integrity threatened, this concern becomes even greater. Since 1949 and until recently, China perceived itself as threatened by either the United States or the Soviet Union, and sometimes by both. Her geopolitical characteristics add to these woes. The 6000-mile land border separating China from the former Soviet Union (including Soviet-influenced Outer Mongolia) was the world's longest hostile border and was considered indefensible mile by mile. On the east, the Chinese navy cannot defend the seaward approaches on the Yellow Sea, the East and South China seas, or the Straits of Taiwan. Even the Indian borders on the southwest demand extensive defensive preparations, and they were fought over in 1972. Under these circumstances, China must rely for its defense on regional respect for the power and discipline of the massive People's army and on a growing nuclear deterrent. (Table 5–1 demonstrates China's nuclear deployment in 1990.) It is not difficult to understand the obsession of China's leadership with security and defensive preparations.

China's military modernization was hindered throughout the Cold War by its isolation from foreign sources of equipment and by its inability both to arm the nation in a modern way and to meet the other demands on the economy. Only during the brief period of Westward leaning in the 1980s was China able to acquire air defense radar equipment, transport helicopters, instruments for testing jet engines, communications systems, powerful computers, submarine tracking systems, range-finding instruments, and tank engines from the West. Despite a defense budget the size of West Germany's

TABLE 5–1

CHINA'S NUCLEAR DEPLOYMENT, 1990

Delivery System	Delivery Range	Number of Weapons
Airborne		
Type 1	1900 miles	
Type 2	750	200+
Type 3	250	
Land-based missiles		
Type 1	1750 miles	85–125
Type 2	3000–4400	20–30
Type 3	8100	10–20
Submarine-based missiles		
Type 1	1750–2050 miles	26–38
		Total 341–415

Source: SIPRI Yearbook, 1992, World Armaments and Disarmament, table 2.7, p. 81.

in percentage of gross national product, China's military modernity never could keep pace with the other Asian powers. The domestic arms industry matured later.

Reintegration of Outlying and Alienated Territories

During the Century of Humiliation, huge slices of Chinese territory were lost to hostile powers, as indicated in Table 5–2, through a series of unequal treaties. Despite early renunciation of these treaties by the Mao government and demands for return of these territories, more modern Chinese territorial concern focuses on the outlying and alienated areas within the current Chinese territory. Of particular concern are Tibet, Sinkiang, and Inner Mongolia.

The dynastic history of China and the longevity of its civilization conceal the fact that like most large nations, China has a number of national minorities within its population. These are particularly evident in the outlying and border areas of the territory, where distance from the governmental and cultural centers of China has resulted in the preservation of diverse languages, cultures, and national identities. Although small in numbers as part of the nation of more than a billion, these peoples occupy vast regions that could impose major new demands on Chinese defense and economic development if their inhabitants were to achieve independence from or incorporation into other nations.[8] The increasing number of

8 In the West, articles abound on China's potential and even forthcoming dissolution, partly for this reason. See as examples Edward Friedman, "China's North-South Split and the Forces of Disintegration," Current History, September 1993, pp. 270–274; Gerald Segal, "China's Changing Shape," Foreign Affairs, May–June 1994, pp. 43–58; and Jack A. Gladstone, "China's Coming Collapse," Foreign Policy, summer 1995, pp. 35–53. W. J. F. Jenner, The Tyranny of History: The Roots of China's Crisis (London: Allan Lane/Penguin, 1992), argues that China's inability to modernize and democratize is rooted in its culture of intolerance to difference, authoritarianism, and an educational system that omits critical thinking. He finds the only hope for the future in the coastal provinces, and he poses a dilemma between the nation being held back by the inner provinces or risking dissolution by allowing the coastal provinces to run far ahead of the rest.

TABLE 5–2

HISTORIC LOSSES OF CHINESE TERRITORY

Territory	Recipient	Year
1. Northeast Frontier Agency; Assam	Britain	after 1820
2. Left bank of Amur River	Russia	1858
3. Maritime Territory	Russia	1860
4. Tashkent Region	Russia	1864
5. Bhutan	Britain	1865
6. Sakhalin	Russia/Japan	after 1875
7. Ryukyu Islands	Japan	1879
8. Indochina	France	1885
9. Siam (now Thailand)	Independence	1885
10. Burma	Britain	1886
11. Sino-Burmese Frontier Region	Britain	1886
12. Sikkim	Britain	1889
13. Taiwan and the Pescadores	Japan	1895
14. Malaya	Britain	1895
15. Korea	Japan	1895 and 1905
16. Ladakh	Britain	1896
17. Nepal	Britain	1898

Russian-oriented Uigurs in Sinkiang, the province in which China has its most important nuclear weapons facilities, poses a threat to territorial integrity and defense modernization. Tibet, forcefully reincorporated in 1950, is subject to repeated rebellion in favor of national autonomy.

The Reincorporation of Taiwan

The reincorporation of Taiwan is a special issue, different from all other territorial demands. In fact, there is nothing in Chinese policy so sacred as the "one-China" principle: there is but one China, of which Taiwan is an integral part, and the government on Taiwan has no claim either to sovereign independence or to control of China. The right to govern China was determined when the communists ousted the nationalists in 1949. The government on Taiwan has no legitimacy in

international affairs, as confirmed by its removal from the United Nations in favor of a Chinese communist representative in 1971.

During the period of Sino-American normalization (1972–1978) and the early phases of formal diplomatic relations (1979), the Taiwan issue repeatedly upset the bilateral relationship. From the Chinese perspective, despite the good intentions of formal declarations, the United States continued a policy of duplicity in which it treated Taiwan as a separate state in political, economic, and military matters while formally acknowledging that it is part of a single China over which the Chinese Communist party holds sovereignty. American obligations are inscribed in three documents:

1. **The Shanghai Communiqué,** the formal joint statement that concluded President Richard M. Nixon's historic visit to China in 1972. In it the parties agreed that there is but one China, including

Taiwan, and that the Beijing government is its sole governing authority.[9]

2. **The Joint Communiqué on the Establishment of Diplomatic Relations** immediately preceding full diplomatic exchange on January 1, 1979.[10] Again the principle of one China including Taiwan was declared, as was acknowledgment of Beijing's exclusive governing right. Nonetheless, "Within this context, the people of the United States will maintain cultural, commercial and other unofficial relations with the people of Taiwan." Formal diplomatic exchange with Taiwan and the old military alliance were to be discontinued.[11] President Jimmy Carter abrogated the Mutual Defense Treaty, an act upheld by the Supreme Court as within presidential power in a lawsuit brought by angry members of the Senate. But the Taiwan Relations Act of 1979, in the Chinese view, embodies the duplicity of American foreign policy. It established a private institute to deal with Taiwan and preserved all U.S. rights that existed prior to the full recognition of Beijing including the right of the United States to provide Taiwan with "such defense articles and defense services as may be necessary to enable Taiwan to maintain a sufficient self-defense capability."[12]

The affront occasioned by the act itself was doubled when, during the first term of Ronald Reagan's presidency, the United States resumed arms sales to Taiwan. Presidents Bush and Clinton continued the practice.

3. **The U.S.-China Joint Communiqué of August 17, 1982,** which followed nine months of negotiations set off by the new arms sales to Taiwan. Once again, the United States pledged its support for a single China governed exclusively by Beijing, and repeated its intention "gradually" and "over a period of time" unspecified in the agreement to discontinue an independent military relationship with Taiwan.[13]

In 1991, in an effort to treat this problem proactively rather than reactively, Beijing released a statement of principles for the reincorporation of separated territories, including Hong Kong and Taiwan. One of these is the principle of one China with two systems, a guarantee that reincorporated territories will be permitted to retain their social and economic systems. This is a pledge against forced communization. Moreover, China has publicly reduced to five circumstances when it might force reintegration: a declaration of independence by Taiwan; Taiwan's development of nuclear weapons; a diplomatic drift on the part of Taiwan toward the Soviet Union (now presumably applicable to Russia); Taiwan's loss of internal control through succession in leadership of social pluralism; and Taiwan's failure to discuss the reunification issue for an intolerably long period.[14] Just how long this might be has not been defined.

An interesting potential test arose in the 1984 Anglo-Chinese agreement on the reunification of Hong Kong with China in 1997, with a guarantee to retain Hong Kong's social and economic

---

[9] For the official text of the Shanghai Communiqué, see *U.S. Department of State Bulletin*, March 20, 1972, pp. 435–438; and *Peking Review*, March 3, 1972, pp. 4–5. The latter is an English translation of the Chinese text but contains no significant variations that might have led to a misunderstanding of intent.

[10] For the official text of the Joint Communiqué on the Establishment of Diplomatic Relations, see *Weekly Compilation of Presidential Documents*, December 18, 1978, pp. 2264–2265. Although recognition did not take place until January 1, 1979, President Carter read the communiqué to the nation during a news conference on December 15, with the result that its publication bears an early date.

[11] For a careful study of the implications of the communiqué on American relations with both China and Taiwan, see John W. Carver, "Arms Sales, the Taiwan Question, and Sino-U.S. Relations," *ORBIS*, winter 1983, pp. 999–1035.

[12] For a brief history of the Taiwan Relations Act by one of its sponsors, see Jacob K. Javits, "Congress and Foreign Relations: The Taiwan Relations Act," *Foreign Affairs*, fall 1981, pp. 54–62. Senator Javits was the senior Republican on the Senate Foreign Relations Committee when the act was passed. For the full text of the Taiwan Relations Act, see *Congressional Record* (House Proceedings), March 26, 1979, pp. 6254–6256.

[13] For the full text of the August 1982 communiqué, see *U.S. Department of State Bulletin*, October 1982, p. 20. For a review of other irritating episodes in this problem, see Zi Zhongyun and Zhuang Qubing, "Sino-U.S. Relations: Opportunities and Potential Crisis," *Beijing Review*, October 14, 1985, pp. 21–24.

[14] This summary of the Chinese position on reunification is taken from Guo-cang Huan, "Taiwan: A View from Beijing," *Foreign Affairs*, summer 1985, pp. 1064–1080.

systems.[15] Beijing hopes to use this as a model to demonstrate to Taiwan that it is serious about its reunification principles. Indeed, Beijing has gone even beyond the Hong Kong example by assuring Taiwan that after reunification, it would be permitted to keep its separate local government, to retain its self-defense forces, and to undertake a limited independent international role. It has not said whether or not it would permit Taiwan to import arms.

For a brief time in connection with these happenings, China and Taiwan altered their rhetorical tone. In 1985, for example, during a commemoration of the fortieth anniversary of the end of the Second World War, a spokesperson for the Chinese Communist party publicly acknowledged the fruitful cooperation of the party and the KMT against Japanese aggression.[16] Less than a year later, China and Taiwan had their first political meeting in the history of their division. The occasion was Taiwan's desire to secure the return of a Boeing 747 cargo plane that had fallen into the hands of the Chinese government after its pilot had fled to the mainland for political asylum. The discussions resulted in an agreement under which the Chinese released the plane; more important, they marked Taiwan's first departure from its principle of no contact with the government in Beijing. Indeed, after concluding the Anglo-Chinese agreement on the future of Hong Kong, Beijing launched a comprehensive effort to increase contacts with Taiwan. Out of this came a surge in trade through the ports of Tokyo, Hong Kong, and Singapore.

In early 1988, Chang Ching-kuo, son of Chiang Kai-shek and president of the Republic of China for thirteen years, died and left his unfulfilled term of office to Lee Teng-hui. Although Lee had sat in the inner circle of the KMT for several years, unlike his predecessors he is a native-born Taiwanese, the first to head the government of the Republic. The political consequences of this event were potentially contradictory for the triangular relations among Beijing, Taipei, and Washington. For while the passage of power to Taiwan natives and away from the heirs of the Chinese civil war might soften Beijing's attitude on reunification, that same passage of power brought on Taiwanese demands for self-determination.[17]

Preventing External Nonmilitary Interference

Prevention of nonmilitary interference has been easier to achieve than the reincorporation of Taiwan will be. The traditional foreign interests were simply evicted after the revolution from their commercial and industrial positions. Foreign investments were expropriated, including, for example, $196 million in American holdings and larger amounts for other countries. Most remaining foreign residents were pressured to leave the country, and a deliberate policy of national isolation was adopted, a reaction in part to the isolation being imposed on China by the West.

There were some important exceptions to this curtailment of external interference, particularly involving the former Soviet Union and India. Soviet leaders took advantage of China's weakness immediately after the civil war to demand certain concessions in exchange for Soviet aid. These included the so-called mixed companies to develop Chinese oil and mineral resources, airlines, railroads, and other facilities. These gave Soviet personnel direct influence over and access to internal Chinese affairs. One form of Soviet behavior particularly disturbing to the Chinese was the covert support of Uigur separatist elements in Sinkiang. After 1955 the joint stock companies were phased out, but subversive activities in remote regions were more difficult to uproot, particularly during the darkest years of Sino-Soviet relations.

China perceives India to have interfered in Chinese internal affairs with regard to Tibet. One of the first acts of the People's Liberation Army in

---

[15] For a text of the agreement and an interpretive article, see "Joint Sino-British Declaration on Hong Kong," *Beijing Review*, October 1, 1984, pp. 14–15 and i–xx.

[16] Wu Jingsheng, "Reassessing the War in China," *Beijing Review*, August 12, 1985, pp. 13–22.

[17] Selig S. Harrison, "Taiwan After Chiang Ching-kuo," *Foreign Affairs*, spring 1988, pp. 790–808.

1950 was the repossession of Tibet. India, part of whose territory abuts Tibet, refused to recognize Chinese suzerainty and gave various forms of covert aid to Tibetan autonomists. In 1954, the Indian government seemed to recognize the Chinese claim in an agreement referring to "the Tibet region of China," but this did not settle the issue. In 1958, Prime Minister Nehru of India announced, and then under Chinese pressure canceled, a visit to Tibet to symbolize support for Tibetan nationalists. This was one element sparking a Tibetan revolt against China in 1959, a revolt quickly suppressed at a cost of 65,000 Tibetan lives. India allowed the shipment of supplies to the Tibetan guerrillas, and various dissident Tibetan elements fled to India after the revolt.

The issue of Indian interference is complicated by territorial issues on the remote Indo-Tibetan border in the Himalayan Mountains. This region is so desolate that it might seem to be of little interest to anyone. But a Chinese arterial road in Tibet passes through a portion of the area that each claims. Indian claims rest on a Sino-Indian treaty of nineteenth-century vintage. China views this document as an unequal treaty of a bygone era, without legal or moral force today, and rests its own claims on historical boundaries. This dispute led to a brief but bitter Sino-Indian border war in 1962, which resulted in a reaffirmation of the Chinese claims. Despite the remoteness of the territory, however, the dispute has never been settled.

China's Search for International Respect

The search for international respect was substantially rewarded between 1975 and 1985. Chinese interpreted the 1972 visit of President Richard M. Nixon, a confirmed anticommunist and Sinophobe, as a sign that their country could no longer be ignored and isolated and that their achievements had at last gained the world's respect. The seating of the Chinese delegation in the Security Council of the United Nations in place of the "Taiwanese" delegation institutionalized the new great power image. Finally, the establishment of formal

diplomatic relations with almost every major capitalist state, including the United States—for fully thirty years the chief impediment to China's drive for international respect and often its open enemy—culminated a patient and persistent quest for acceptance in the international community. By the end of 1985, China enjoyed diplomatic relations with 130 states, representing virtually every form of government in the spectrum, from communist to right-wing dictatorship.

China saw itself during this period as the antiimperialist supporter of Third World revolutionary movements. But from its isolated position and with its limited means, it distinguished its role from the social imperialist tactics of the Soviet Union. The official position of the Chinese government on intervention, even on behalf of revolution, was said to be purely Marxist, whereas the Soviet style of social imperialism was a dreaded departure from Marxism-Leninism. In the Chinese view,

> No Marxist would ever hesitate to state that communism will inevitably replace capitalism. . . . But Marxists also believe that it is entirely up to the people of a country to choose their own social system and it is futile for any outside force to try to do that on their behalf. Marxists always stand for peaceful coexistence among countries with different social systems; they do not stand for an "export of revolution." Particularly, they are opposed to any aggression or expansion carried out in the name of "revolution" or of "supporting revolution," and are opposed to the use of force or any attempt to use force as a means to settle differences arising from the difference of social systems and interests.[18]

The denial of aggressive intentions is central not only to Chinese diplomacy, but also to its fundamental notion of its own development. In the Chinese view, peace and economic development are interdependent. On the one hand, progress in development cannot be suspended in order to build military might. On the other hand, however, a strong China contributes to "the growth of the

---

[18] Huan Xiang, "On Sino-U.S. Relations," *Foreign Affairs*, fall 1981, pp. 38–39.

world's forces for peace."[19] On this basis China rejects its own growth as a hegemonic power, even regionally. One of the Eight Principles of China's diplomacy is "never seeking hegemony or succumbing to the pressure of hegemonism."[20] Furthermore, it is a fundamental tenet of Chinese foreign policy that the development movement has forever changed global politics to the extent that hegemonism cannot occur.

> A fundamental change has taken place in the pattern of post-war international relations owing to the rise of the Third World and the development of the Nonaligned movement. The days when a few big powers could dominate the world are gone once and for all.[21]

Perhaps in these words the Chinese government anticipated the end of the Cold War. In any event, we have seen how the forces of national history, Marxism-Leninism-Maoism, and the forces set free by the substitution of a pragmatic "seek-truth-from-facts doctrine" for "Mao's anti-intellectualism"[22] shaped the Chinese world view prior to the end of the Cold War.

China and the New World Order

As the world has entered into a transitional period, so has China. This vast land, the world's fourth largest (about half the size of Russia and only slightly smaller than Canada and the United States) supports a population of 1.2 billion people, 4.65 times that of the United States, 8 times

Russia's, and more than 41 times as large as Canada. In contrast to its size, however, its economic productivity is extremely low. While, on the one hand, China houses 21 percent of the global population, in gross national product per capita, on the other hand, it ranked ninety-ninth at $490 in 1993 against a world median of $1,140, $24,740 for the United States, and $37,320 for Luxembourg's all-time record. Throughout China's history, and particularly its modern era, the most daunting problem of government has been to harness the nation's natural attributes, including its population, into effective statehood. This has, at last, begun to occur. China today is classified economically as a low-income, developing exporter of manufactured goods with a low foreign debt that it manages easily.

Although the figures portray an economically feeble China, the steady march of progress is well along. The annual rate of increase in gross domestic product from 1980 through 1993, for example, was 9.6 percent compared with 2.7 percent for the United States and 4.0 percent for Japan. More dramatically, China's growth rate was the world's highest for that period, reaching 11.1 percent in 1993. Furthermore, while in 1970 the GNP was only $93 billion, by 1993 it was $426 billion, comparable to those of Brazil, Canada, and Spain. Industrial output grew in the same period from 38 percent of total output to 48 percent. From 1980 to 1992, manufactured goods as a portion of total exports leapt from 61 to 80 percent.[23]

Behind these successes is a complex economic development program that begins with pragmatic leadership and a realization that a severe domestic

---

[19] See the text of the Seventh Five-Year Plan in China, *Beijing Review*, October 7, 1985, pp. vi–xxiv, particularly p. xxiii.
[20] From "Eight Principles for China's Diplomacy," a speech by General Secretary Hu Yaobang, excerpted in *Beijing Review*, October 21, 1985, p. 7.
[21] Speech to the United Nations General Assembly on October 24, 1985, reproduced in *Beijing Review*, November 4, 1985, pp. 15–17 at p. 16.
[22] John King Fairbank, *China: A New History* (Cambridge: Belknap/Harvard, 1992), p. 417. One Chinese author goes considerably farther than this, as his title suggests: Liu Binyan, "The Long March from Mao: China's De-Communization," *Current History*, September 1993, pp. 241–244.

[23] The statistics in this section are taken from a variety of sources, but especially from *World Social Indicators in the 1990s* (New York: United Nations, 1994); *World Development Report, 1995* (New York: Oxford, 1995), published for the International Bank for Reconstruction and Development and the International Monetary Fund, especially the "Basic Indicators" tables; and *World Investment Report, 1992* (New York: United Nations, 1992), especially the "Annex Tables." Additional statistics come from Jan S. Prybyla, "All that Glitters? The Foreign Investment Boom," *Current History*, September 1995, pp. 275–279.

power struggle, even possibly disintegration, is probable without development of the consumer economy. The program consists of six principal parts. Three of them—trade, incentives to foreign investors, and external loans (numbers 3, 4, and 5 following)—comprise the policy of "opening up." They are summarized in Table 5–3.

1. **Population control.** One of the plaguing features of economic development is that population growth often consumes the benefits of economic progress. But in China, the 1972–1981 average annual population growth was 1.7 percent; from 1982 to 1991 it was 1.4 percent. This decline of 0.3 percent on a population base of 1.2 billion is a difference of about 3.6 million live births per year, which relieves the strain of adding an annual population increment equal to the current population of Puerto Rico.

2. **Domestic investment.** While controlling population, and thereby consumption, the Chinese government undertook a careful plan of investment from domestic sources. Whereas from 1970 to 1980 the average annual rate of increase in the domestic investment was 7.6 percent, from 1980 through 1993 it jumped to 11.1 percent, a 46 percent improvement.

3. **International trade.** One of the fundamental instruments of economic development is trade. It enables a government to use goods to underwrite imports rather than funds, a vitally important substitute because the country's currency may be of no value externally. An excess of exports over imports also provides the developing economy with reserve currencies, giving it the option to spend valued currencies, such as the German mark and the Japanese yen, in international markets. From 1978 through 1994, China's trade grew from $20 billion to $237 billion, a twelvefold increase, with exports growing faster than imports.

4. **Incentives to foreign investors.** Recognizing the benefits of direct private investment in a developing economy, something that orthodox Marxism-Leninism-Maoism always considered the pinnacle of imperialism, the Chinese government has taken two major steps to attract foreign direct

TABLE 5–3

CHINA'S FORMULA FOR ECONOMIC DEVELOPMENT

1. Controlling population:
   Result: decline in annual birth rate from 1.7% to 1.4%.

2. Investing domestic resources:
   Result: increase in average annual growth from 7.6% to 11.1%.

3. Expanding international trade:
   Result: twelvefold increase to $237 billion per year, with exports growing faster than imports.

4. Attracting foreign direct investment:
   Result: increased from a thirteen-year total of $51 billion contracted ($26 billion actually spent) to a three-year total of $251 billion contracted ($72 billion actually spent).

5. Securing external loans while controlling debt:
   Result: annual increase from $4.5 billion to 11.2 billion.

6. Reducing military spending:
   Result: reduced from 1983 to 1993 in fraction of gross national product (6.8% to 2.7%) and of total government expenditure (30.4% to 16.2%).

investment. In 1979, it took first steps toward "opening up" by adopting the Law on Joint Ventures using Chinese and foreign investment. Then, in 1991, it adopted a tax reform program. This created a flat tax (not graduated according to revenue value) on earnings from all foreign investments, offered temporary tax exemption for new investments, and provided a 40 percent tax refund on all earnings reinvested in China. From 1979 through 1991 total foreign direct investment attracted was $51 billion contracted and $26 billion actually spent. After the second legal reform in 1991, from 1992 through 1994 the amounts were $251 billion contracted and $72 billion actually spent.

5. **External loans.** Together with domestic investment and incentives to private foreign investors, China also sought external loan aid. From 1980 to 1993, loans jumped from $4.5 billion to $11.2 billion. By 1993 China's total external debt from all sources remained small by comparison with

Free Enterprise co-exists with
Communism in China.
(*Source*: Coco/Taiwan/Cartoonist
& Writers Syndicate)

other developing countries, measured as a percentage of both GDP and annual exports. It consisted of about $70 billion in long-term and $13 billion in short-term obligations. Much of this is financed by export growth, and so China is regarded as a good risk.

6. **Reduced defense spending.** The relative safety of the New World Order also enables China to devote a smaller percent of public revenue to national defense. Table 5–4 shows the comparisons using 1980 as the base year for an indexing system. Read this way: In the category of "active armed forces," by 1986–87 China had reduced its strength to 66.3 percent of the 1980 level, and by 1994–95 to 65.8 percent; etc. In addition, between 1983 and 1993 defense expenditure dropped from 6.8 percent of GNP to 2.7 percent, and from 30.4 percent of total government spending to 16.2 percent.[24] It is true, however, that China's defenses are modernizing rapidly, especially its missiles, and this is seen by some as a military buildup. Although China has no aggressive intentions, any attempt by Taiwan to declare its independence might result in its forceful incorporation into China. In Beijing's view, American duplicity on the status of Taiwan encouraged an independence movement to grow during Taiwan's 1996 presidential election campaign,

calling for a show of Chinese force as a reminder of Beijing's sovereignty over Taiwan.

In its development, China's economy is divided into approximately equal parts state control, collective, and private. Through the growth years, the private sector has been the most productive, the collective second, and the state-controlled portion continuously losing money. It is now safe to say, therefore, that while the term remains anathema, in both its internal and external strategies China's development is principally capitalistic. It is less evident that in the political realm China's development is democratic. Civil control remains a high value to the government more from historical continuity than from Maoism. While verbal dissent is common,[25] active, demonstrative dissent remains "counterrevolutionary." Commenting on the relationship between social order and economic liberalism, President Jiang Zemin said in 1995:

> We regard development as an objective, reform as the driving force and stability as the precondition.

---

[24] *World Economic and Social Survey, 1995* (New York: United Nations, 1995), p. 192.

[25] See, for example, the May 15, 1995, Petition, an appeal of forty-five scientists and intellectuals to the National People's Congress calling for greater political tolerance and release of the Tiananmen Square demonstration leaders from political imprisonment. Published in *Current History*, September 1995, pp. 264–265. For a general discussion of the prospects for democracy, see Merle Goldman, "Is Democracy Possible?" in the same issue of *Current History*, pp. 259–263.

TABLE 5–4

DECLINE IN CHINA'S MILITARY STRENGTH INDEXED TO 1980

	1980	1986–87	1994–95
Active armed forces	100	66.3	65.8
Main battle tanks	100	109.5	70.5
Combat aircraft	100	101.7	97.4

Source: United Nations, World Economic and Social Survey, 1995, p. 194.

Without political stability, we simply cannot undertake reform and opening-up, nor economic development. On the other hand, if we fail to make economic development our primary task, or if we do not undertake reform and opening-up, then there will be no economic development. Political or social stability will be out of the question.[26]

Because economic development is the people's will, where self-restraint breaks down, forced social order is required.

Consistent with the evolving conditions of the global system, the focal points of China's contemporary world view are (1) expanding its role as a global economic power and (2) promoting military and geopolitical subsystems that enhance Beijing as a regional power.

Beijing is keenly aware that Asia (including Japan and South Korea) will eventually surpass the European Union in global export competition. For purposes of both rapid development and being perceived as a major player in this growth, China places economic development first among its priorities, even if it requires some sharp breaks from Maoist orthodoxy. Not yet willing to go as far as Russia's break in economic philosophy from Marxism-Leninism, contemporary Chinese communism is creating a "socialist market economy," which it describes as a "leap" rather than a "break."

Integrated with the underlying socialist system, the new economic structure allows the market to play a primary role in resource allocation under state macro-control as well as to ensure that economic activities conform to the law of value and respond to changes in supply and demand. . . . A socialist market economy, as is now being built in China, is the very first and a totally new experiment of its kind in the history of social and economic development of mankind.

So while the basis is socialism, its modernization has required "important reform measures in the fields of fiscal, taxation, financial, foreign exchange, foreign trade, investment, pricing, circulation and enterprise systems." Furthermore,

Socialism, in essence, means emancipating and developing productive forces, eliminating exploitation and polarization of wealth and ultimately attaining common prosperity. Poverty is by no means what socialism stands for, nor is it realistic for everybody to attain affluence all at the same time. Hence, our policy is to allow and encourage some areas and some people to get rich first.[27]

All this reform has evolved since 1978, when pragmatism replaced old-line ideology in the form of the Four Modernizations. The companion of reform is opening-up, the process by which China dropped its self-imposed economic isolation and began exploiting the vicissitudes of East-West relations to its own economic benefit. This enabled it to purchase American military equipment one day and Soviet military jetcraft the next. And it enabled China to welcome foreign aid and foreign direct investment. The goal of doubling the GNP in the 1980s was exceeded, and Beijing is confident that plans for another doubling in the 1990s will also be reached early. While China's heartland remains rural and underdeveloped, the coastal provinces are modernizing at a record rate. Hong Kong, which rejoins China in 1997, will bring great wealth. Unification with Taiwan in the future would make China one of the world's economic giants.

---

[26] Jiang Zemin, "China's March Forward and the World," reprinted in Beijing Review, July 31–August 6, 1995, pp. 20–24 at p. 22.

[27] Jiang Zemin, "China's March Forward," p. 21.

As China takes aim on its economic future, it is also working out its political and security objectives for the post–Cold War world. In the words of one American observer,

> The People's Republic of China (PRC) has been one of the states most directly affected by the collapse of the [Cold War] world order. On the one hand, the demise of the Soviet Union enhanced Chinese security by eradicating the Soviet military threat, replacing the USSR with weaker states in Russia and in Central Asia, and creating a power vacuum in Asia that China attempted to fill. On the other hand, Beijing lost the leverage it had gained from its pivotal position in U.S.-USSR-PRC relations, faced increased competition for great power influence in Asia, and confronted new threats stemming from political and economic instability in Central Asia.[28]

In the prevailing Chinese view, the New World Order is built on one global superpower and four "subordinate powers." This basis leads to the structure shown in Figure 5–1, with the transactional content of the resulting political triangles determining global stability. China has important roles to play in the China-Russia-America and the China-Japan-America triangles. (One of the limits of this kind of visualization is that it overlooks a China-Japan-Russia triangle, undeniably one of the most important.) Thus China seeks improved relations with a weakened Russia, which would like to limit both Sino-Japanese and Sino-American relations, and with Japan, whose economic independence of the United States is one of the driving forces of Asia's economic autonomy. At the same time, however, Japan's refusal to acknowledge its guilt in World War Two or its atrocities against the Chinese in two wars (The Sino-Japanese War of 1894–95 and the Second World War from 1931 through 1945) is a major obstacle to reconciliation, and Russian military force in the Pacific needs balancing, if not by the United States then by China.

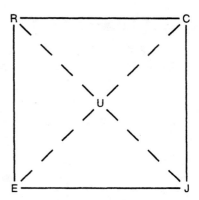

FIGURE 5–1   China's view of the post–Cold War world.

Note: R-Russia, C-China, E-Europe, J-Japan, U-United States.

Source: Xue Mouhong, "The New World Order: Four Powers and One Superpower?" *Beijing Review,* September 25–October 1, 1995, p. 19.

China and the United States

From the communist victory in 1949 to the end of the Vietnam War (1974), the United States was the foe of Asia's revolutionary aspirations. Its interventions in Korea and Vietnam, its policy of arming the dissident province of Taiwan, and its antirevolutionary diplomacy are all evidences of hostility. Moreover, now that China is modernizing industrially and is able to take part in international arms trade, the United States objects to its sale of missiles to the Middle East and to Pakistan. The United States criticizes China for not observing fully the Missile Technology Control Regime (MTCR) designed to prevent sale of anything but short-range missiles, and Transparency in Arms Tranfers (TIAT), a program with the goal of establishing a public registry of conventional arms sales.[29] Washington condemns China for underground nuclear tests in its own territory, yet sat by

---

[28] Roxane D. V. Sismanidis, "China and the Post-Soviet Security Structure," *Asian Affairs: An American Review,* spring 1994, pp. 39–58 at pp. 39–40.

[29] Roxane D. V. Sismanidis, "China and the Post-Soviet Security Structure," pp. 49–50.

quietly while France did the same thing in the South Pacific over the violent protests of the native people. And the United States is forever meddling in China's internal affairs, particularly on the matters of human rights and the status of Taiwan—always playing this "card" or that "card" in an effort to manipulate China.[30] So while the United States is crucially important to China's development and to Asian stability, it continues to address China in the hegemonic terms of the Cold War era.

One area in which this is unacceptable to China is the linking of economic assistance, broadly defined, to human rights. This problem has been accentuated by two unrelated factors: the Tiananmen Square incident of 1989 and the election of conservative majorities in both Houses of the U.S. Congress in 1994. Americans, it seems, cannot understand that civil order is a precondition of economic development, and that safeguarding it is not a communist aberration but is deeply rooted in the authoritarian traditions of Chinese political culture. This misunderstanding is magnified in an era in which one member of Congress after another proudly proclaims hatred of the Chinese government and supports a "two-Chinas" or a "one-China, one-Taiwan" policy. These create a political climate in which most-favored-nation trade status (i.e., trade conditions equal to the best granted to anyone) falls hostage to the misunderstanding of domestic policy. Ironically, in 1995 it was the big-business friends of these same conservatives who prevailed on the president to uncouple the two matters, as capitalist America's goals in the global economy triumphed for the moment over anti-Chinese and antirevolutionary hysteria.

But most damaging of all is the vexing problem of Taiwan. Despite diplomatic recognition and three historic communiqués that were intended from the Chinese perspective to clarify Washington's commitment to a "one-China" policy, American actions continue to endorse Taiwan's pretense of independent statehood. The infamous Taiwan Relations Act has become a virtual recognition,

within which Washington continues to sell modern arms, including F-16 combat aircraft, to Taiwan. Taiwan's efforts at readmission to the United Nations, this time as a separate entity rather than as China's representative, have been defeated (so far, without China's veto), but the effort of some conservative Developing Nations to create a study committee on the subject is viewed by Beijing as Taiwan-American dollar diplomacy of purchasing votes in return for development aid.[31]

Periodically this issue disrupts Sino-American relations, as it did in 1992 when, in the heat of an election battle that centered on economic recession, President Bush announced a multibillion dollar contract for F-16s for sale to Taiwan. Another flare-up occurred in 1995. Over China's protest, and probably fearful of conservative reactions if he refused, President Clinton permitted Taiwan's president to make a personal visit to the United States, the first by any Taiwan leader since recognition of the Chinese government in 1978.

It is precisely under the disguise of "unofficial" or "private" visits that Lee Teng-hui has traveled here and there in recent years in pursuit of so-called "vacation diplomacy" and "stop-over diplomacy" in an attempt to create "two Chinas" or "one China, one Taiwan" on the international front.[32]

In an address at Cornell University, Lee spoke forcefully about Taiwanese independence. One Chinese observer labeled the speech a "political hallucinogen for Taiwan independence,"[33] but the government reacted less metaphorically. The Chinese ambassador in Washington was called home, as was a high-ranking Air Force officer who was touring U.S. Air Force facilities. A previously jailed Chinese who had emigrated to the United States and then returned to China to conduct protests was arrested, tried, and convicted before being deported, and two American military officers were detained for being in "unauthorized places." More

---

[30] Xin Wei, "Another Wrong 'Card,'" *Beijing Review*, July 10–16, 1995, p. 18.

[31] *The New York Times*, September 21, 1995, p. A5.
[32] Chinese Foreign Ministry as quoted in *The New York Times*, May 24, 1995, p. A8.
[33] *Beijing Review*, August 14–20, 1995, p. 13.

The Chinese Red Army sweeps
Tiananmen Square in Beijing of
thousands of protesters for
democratic changes, spring 1989.
(*Source:* © Stuart
Franklin/Magnum Photos)

significantly, in an apparent show of how Beijing might treat a Taiwan declaration of independence following its presidential election of 1996, hastily planned war games were conducted in the straits that separate the island from the mainland, and unarmed test missiles were fired first in the vicinity of Taiwan and subsequently into Taiwan's territorial waters.[34]

Despite continued talk about a partnership for Asia's economic development,

> Instead of a partnership, some Chinese officials now suspect that the United States is developing a "containment" strategy against China with a military pact with Japan, weapons sales to Taiwan and the deployment of an anti-missile system in the Pacific that will neutralize China's strategic arsenal.[35]

---

[34] *The New York Times*, August 19, 1995, p. A1, and July 24, 1995, p. A2.

---

[35] *The New York Times*, May 23, 1995, p. A10.

The origin of this fear may have been a suggestion by a high-placed State Department official that long-term Sino-American adversity and a containment strategy might possibly occur. A spokesman for the Chinese Foreign Ministry made this comment:

> The current state of affairs in Sino-US relations has been created solely by the United States. What the US side should do now is to take effective action to completely remove the deleterious effects of Lee Teng-hui's visit to the United States and return to the right course of the three Sino-US joint communiqués.
>
> The Cold War containment policy, directed against other countries, has proven to be bankrupt and should be resolutely discarded. Any attempt by the United States to threaten China with containment, which runs counter to the trend of the times and turns Sino-US relations into a course of confrontation, is both dangerous and doomed to failure.[36]

The Chinese government did not permit these problems to deter it from its role in Asia's stabilization, however. During this period it joined the Nuclear Non-Proliferation Treaty (NPT) after condemning it for more than twenty years as a great-power device for monopolizing nuclear blackmail; it led the drive to extend the NPT for a second twenty-five years; and it assisted the United States in settling the question of North Korea's independent nuclear research and development.

China and Russia

In spite of their common revolutionary origins and communist convictions, the relationship between China and the old Soviet Union was never good. Stalin had a dim view of Mao's ability to defeat the KMT, and so he directed all his World War Two aid to the latter. If Mao expected major Soviet assistance after his victory in 1949, he was gravely disappointed. A mission to Moscow produced only

minor financial assistance. Stalin, a Marxist-Leninist who believed in the political destiny of the industrial proletariat, rejected the Maoist notion of agrarian communism. Furthermore, he denied the concept of multiple paths to communism. Perhaps most important, however, he was committed to a Soviet-centered communist world inconsistent with an independent movement the size of China's. Where Mao anticipated a lucrative alliance, Stalin saw ideological aberration and political challenge. It was not in his interest to sponsor Mao's experiment. This rocky start ended in a complete rupture in relations in 1956 from which the two parties never fully recovered during the Cold War, though there were productive occasions when one turned to the other in times of stress with the United States.

The end of the Cold War offered the first sustained opportunity since 1956 for a new mood in Sino-Russian affairs. The ideological disputes of old had lost their relevance. The long common border no longer required defense. Disintegration of the Soviet Union so changed the Russian priorities in Central Asia that conflict with China was unthinkable. Stripped of empire, cohesion, and land mass, and embarked on its own course of modernization and economic transformation, the new Russia was an opportunity for China, not a residual adversary. In addition, the many Russian-American arms agreements that gave the New World Order tangible meaning relieved much of the global strain to which China had been a third party. For Sino-Russian relations, the post–Cold War era introduced new goals and new policies.

Not all old ideas were discarded. For example, the notion of a Russian-American-Chinese triangle retains many of the "balancing" features of other forms of world order. China is well aware, for instance, that NATO's eastward expansion, so despised by Moscow, adds to the value of Russia's stable relations with China. Full knowledge of Moscow's goals adds, therefore, to China's options, such as purchasing modern military aircraft. In the 1996 Taiwan issue, for instance, China purchased 72 modern Russian fighter-bombers.

---

[36] As quoted in *Beijing Review*, July 17–23, 1995, p. 20.

There are barriers, though not political, to rapid development of a beneficial economic relationship even though the current quality of the relationship is at a historic peak. China's agricultural reform has not been as effective as its industrial modernization, and so it is not able to meet Russia's food needs. (The agricultural system handed down from the Soviet Union is notoriously underproductive.) The transformation of Russia's economy has created such income disparities that the consumer sector is unable to absorb much of China's export potential. And with few exceptions, Russia's petroleum and raw material deposits are at least the equal of China's, and with Western help they will be developed more efficiently. On the capital front, Russia's own need for investment absorbs all the capital it can accumulate, making Russia an unlikely partner in development.

Ethnic unrest in the former Soviet republics, especially on Russia's southern and eastern edges, is of concern to China. The sharp economic disparity between the coastal provinces and the interior coincides with ethnic division between the Han Chinese and scores of other ethnocultural populations elsewhere, some of which have historical links across China's borders. Thus unrest in the former Soviet republics presents a dilemma for Beijing: on the one hand, it would benefit from any successful Russian effort at stability, but, on the other hand, if the instrument for this were transformation of the CIS into a strong alliance, much of the stress taken from Sino-Russian relations by the New World Order could recur.

Pakistan and India also figure prominently in the China-Russia-America triangle. Chinese territorial disputes with India are one of Beijing's principal tactical concerns. But for reasons unrelated to China, India and Pakistan have been locked in a decades-old arms race, sponsored largely by the United States and the old Soviet Union. To minimize the Soviet role during the Cold War, the United States actually provided arms for both sides, and in 1993 it withheld a fully paid, billion-dollar shipment of aircraft to Pakistan because of sanctions imposed over a Sino-Pakistani aircraft agreement.

From the Chinese perspective, this perpetuates several imbalances within China's own continental sphere. First, it prolongs foreign intrusion in Asia's affairs. Second, it denies China the right to do exactly what the United States is doing in arms sales. Third, it enables the United States to weaken Pakistan relative to India, which is China's adversary. And fourth, it projects the image that China's regional strategic power is at American sufferance. Thus the withdrawal of the Russian component of these relations seems not to expand Beijing's options, but at least for now to restrict them.

At least for the short term, therefore, while Sino-Russian relations are warm and sympathetic, they are not very productive. The important thing, however, is that the stability offered by the Cold War's demise enables China to direct its attention and capital to development rather than to the geopolitics of Central Asia. In the longer term, it may have measurable effects on China's relations with both the United States and Japan.

China and Japan

Two major wars and a century of history have made China extraordinarily wary of Japan. The Japanese profited handsomely from the Century of Humiliation, and no people felt the atrocious power of Japanese militarism more than the Chinese. For their part, the Chinese, who have a history of lagging behind Japan in adapting Western inventiveness to their needs, look with envy on Japan's wealth and on its status as a major world power that commits less than 4 percent of GNP to military, all of it for defense.

With wariness and envy, however, goes need. China's development needs Japanese assistance and gets it. Japanese foreign direct investment in China follows only those of Hong Kong and Taiwan. (If that seems odd, remember that foreign direct investment is corporate money, not governmental.) Japan also provides governmental assistance, though in 1995 it announced that it would suspend its aid program over China's refusal to discontinue its underground nuclear test program. Coastal China has become virtually an open market for Japan's consumer goods, and for Japan to sustain its economic growth rate, it needs Chinese raw materials. The two, it seems, are natural economic partners despite their long and deeply troubled history.

During the Cold War, China resented the Japanese-American security arrangement because it prolonged the American military presence in Asia and the Pacific. At the end of the Vietnam War, the U.S. Navy abandoned its base there and Russia occupied it. Later, Washington moved out of its huge naval and air facilities in the Philippines. Although it scaled down its deployments in Japan, Okinawa remains part of the heartbeat of the American military establishment in Asia, as does South Korea. China is of two minds about this. On the one hand, a limited American presence contributes to regional stability at no direct cost to China. But, on the other hand, it also provides the means of a containment policy against China and a military cover for a Taiwan independence declaration. All of these features have to enter into China's defense planning. There are two undeniable benefits to the American military presence: First, it guarantees against a rebirth of the dreaded Japanese militarism; and second, it fills any vacuum that Russian adventurism might attempt to exploit.

Another Chinese advantage is the unending strain between Japan and Russia over Russian occupation of the Kurile Islands north of the principal home islands. These were seized by the Soviet Union under cover of its last-minute entry into World War Two in the Pacific, the same cover that enabled the Soviets to dismantle Manchurian factories and transport them to Russia for post-war reindustrialization. The Yeltsin government has acknowledged this as a barrier to normal relations with Japan, and in 1991 it proposed a long-term, five-stage program to resolve it. To date there has been no material progress. This is a division that China would like prolonged, because it blocks the way to any Moscow-Tokyo entente that might be disadvantageous to China.

Conclusion

In many respects the Four Modernizations campaign launched by China in 1978 anticipated a New World Order. Its pragmatic and gradual abandonment of ideological orthodoxy foreshadowed the break from the rigidities of the capitalist-socialist component of the Cold War. By the time the Cold War ended, China was already well on the road to industrialization using the same devices—aid, trade, foreign direct investment, and technical assistance—it had previously condemned as the formula by which the rich exploit the poor on a global basis. This not only accelerated China's development, but radically changed the tone of its leadership message to the rest of the Developing World.

The end of the Cold War and the collapse of Soviet power also presented China with new geopolitical options. Nuclear and conventional arms reduction, pacification of borders, and arms-backed power politics no longer dominate either China's policy imperatives or its choices for the expenditure of capital. But they also call into question China's own role in regional stabilization, especially with respect to the United States, whose military presence is, at the same time, resented, needed, feared, and suspected. The periodic recurrence of the Taiwan vexation and the related American duplicity maintain an insuperable barrier against trust. Just as the new Russia and the United States debate their respective roles in the New World Order, so too do China's leaders. Such is the price of fast-paced international dynamics.

CHAPTER 6

The Perspective of the Developing Nations

The realignment of world politics after the Second World War did not occur exclusively along East-West ideological lines. At the same time, the emancipation of the formerly colonized peoples of Africa, Asia, the Middle East, South and Central America, the Caribbean, and the South Pacific began to foretell the second major conflict of contemporary international relations: the North-South confrontation. In contrast with the ideological and military foundations of the East-West crisis, the North-South confrontation evolved principally over economic issues and secondarily over political and human rights issues.

"North-South confrontation" is something of a misnomer because many of the Developing Nations are actually in the northern hemisphere. Nonetheless, the confrontation between the wealthy world and the poor began to evolve early in the Cold War, though it took a quantum leap after 1956 with the explosion of newly independent states carved out of old, bygone empires. Together with a few older poor states, the newly independents formed the body known as the Less Developed Countries (LDCs). (Subsequently the same letters have been used to designate the Least Developed Countries.) With time they took on a false Cold War name: the Third World. This implied that they were independent of both West (First World) and East (Second World), though in fact many of them were closely tied to one or the other. In the New World Order this is a wholly inappropriate name, and so they are called now the Developing Nations or the Developing World. By whatever name, they are a loose coalition of geographically and culturally disparate nations that embrace more than half of the global population—China and India alone comprise 40 percent—but account for but a small fraction of the global economic output, most of it in raw materials. In general, their consumption exceeds their productivity, and with the continuation of rampant birth rates, their economic development is in uninterrupted jeopardy. Hence the gap between the rich and the poor is not closing but widening.

Although the unifying theme among the Developing Nations is the struggle for development, there are broad differences among the more than 120 members. Among the most significant for world order are the following.

Wealth No longer are all of them poor. In 1993 Israel, Kuwait, Qatar, Singapore, and the United Arab Emirates all ranked in the top twenty-three countries in gross national product (GNP) per capita, even after the devastation of Kuwait by Iraq in the Gulf War. Kuwait, Qatar, and the United Arab Emirates achieved their riches through the global oil demand and the multilateral policies of the Organization of Petroleum Exporting Countries (OPEC), but Singapore and Israel achieved them by industrialization. So the Third World consists of countries ranging in national wealth from utter poverty and infant industrialization (such as Bangladesh, Burundi, Sri Lanka, and Haiti) to substantial national wealth (such as the OPEC nations), but all are underdeveloped in some significant way.

Resources   The poor countries vary greatly in natural resource endowment. Some, such as the Sudan, lack many raw materials and are hampered in their development by the relative barrenness of the earth itself. Others, like Nigeria, are richly endowed and need only to find the social and political means to utilize their gifts. Others, particularly the petroleum countries, have already learned these lessons. Some developing states are not rich in mineral resources, but have unique agricultural circumstances. Cases in point are the coffee- and fruit-producing countries of Central America, the rice-producing states of East and Southeast Asia, and Cuba's sugar. South Africa is rich in gold and gems.

Population   Developing Nations also vary in the concentration of their human populations. Some are teemingly overpopulated; tiny Java (Indonesia) has more than one-third the population of the United States. Until recently population has been China's greatest problem, and it remains India's. Others are sparsely populated; oil-rich Libya is almost empty; and Tanzania cultivates only one-third of its arable land. Some are largely urban societies, concentrated in and dominated by the cities, many of which are beyond their capacities to provide basic necessities (e.g., Calcutta and Mexico City). Others are agricultural societies or even nomadic wandering cultures (e.g., Morocco). Some are huge in territory, such as India and Brazil. Others are countries of postage-stamp dimensions, such as most of the Caribbean countries, Cyprus, Mauritius, Luxembourg, Singapore and São Tomé and Principe.

Ethnic Divisions   The Developing Nations differ greatly in their ethnic composition and in the unity or diversity of their peoples. Some, such as Chile and Albania, have relatively homogeneous populations. Others are sharply divided into two or three ethnic groups among which there may be deep conflicts. Somalia, Rwanda, Liberia, the former Yugoslavia, and Nigeria are but a few that have had brutal civil wars in recent years over ethnic divisions, some of them genocidal wars aimed at eradicating rival groups. India is the extreme, with scores of languages and dialects symptomatic of an absence of cohesion that makes governing all but impossible; English, the former colonial language, is thus the official language. Religious differences make for additional complications, particularly when militancy arises. Northern Ireland, Lebanon, and several places with militant Islamic factions are illustrations.

Political Histories   The Developing Nations also have very different political histories. Most were colonies until recently, but others have not been subjected to direct foreign control for many centuries (Thailand). Some are ancient countries (Iran and China) with continuous cultures of thousands of years. Others are new political creations shaped by former colonial masters for their own administrative convenience (Nigeria), new federations of formerly separate peoples (Malaysia), products of war (Bangladesh), or successors to disintegrated states (former Soviet and Yugoslavian republics).

Modernizing and Traditional Cultures   Some peoples hew closely to ancient traditions, have a low consciousness of nationalism, and are concerned mainly with age-old problems of village and religious life (St. Lucia, Bolivia, Myanmar). In other societies, the traditional order is under challenge by a modernizing elite; some variety of participatory revolution is under way; and national identities are superseding antiquated principles of social organization (Angola, Trinidad and Tobago, Peru). Literacy rates vary widely in developing countries as do the roles of women, cultural and religious taboos, social mores, and dietary laws.

Governments   Governmental types include traditional ruling elites and monarchies (Morocco, Saudi Arabia), elected regimes on the Western democratic model (India, Egypt, post-apartheid South Africa), military juntas that have come to power by coup d'état (innumerable in Latin American history), revolutionary movements (China, Cuba, North Korea, Vietnam), and old-style despotic regimes (Iran, Dominican Republic under the Duvaliers, the Philippines under Marcos), many of which hide behind democratic facades. Some developing societies are stable because their governments are legitimate (Egypt, Costa Rica) and others because of state coercion (Iraq) or minimal civil liberties (South Korea). Others have highly ineffective governments that are constantly subject to change (Lebanon).

Economies Economies vary from those highly dependent on imports and exports (Taiwan) to others for which foreign trade is relatively secondary (Cuba); from societies in which income is distributed very unequally (Saudi Arabia) to highly egalitarian cases (North Korea); from primarily agrarian (Sri Lanka) or resource dependent (Kuwait) to substantially industrial (Singapore); from stagnation (Afghanistan) to rapid growth (Brazil); and from capitalist (Argentina) to socialist (Vietnam). Some developing economies are well diversified and by this means are protected against damaging fluctuations in world market prices of their exports. Others, in contrast, are disproportionately dependent on a single economic staple; nearly 100 percent of Saudia Arabia's, Kuwait's, and Oman's economies are in petroleum. This places them at the mercy of wild price adjustments (OPEC was founded both to prevent this and to make importers guarantee the price) and creates the long-term threat of resource exhaustion. Bolivia's tin and copper reserves have virtually been exhausted, increasing both the problems and the cost of development.

Indebtedness The Developing Nations also vary in the amount of external debt they carry. Some like China, Lebanon, and Namibia carry surprisingly little debt unlike others (Ethiopia, Argentina, and Syria) that are deep in debt and have difficulty managing it. Furthermore, debt is not necessarily related to income level or income structure, as low-income countries (China, Haiti) may have relatively little debt and some moderate-income Developing Nations (Brazil, Poland) may be struggling with debt.

All these differences notwithstanding, the UN Development Program classifies 127 nations as Developing Nations, of which 44 are considered the least developed. Assessments vary as to where on the development curve various states lie, but for rough comparison purposes, one can divide the total Developing World into imperfect categories according the scheme shown in Table 6–1. Clearly the great mass of Developing Nations does not enjoy the benefits of petroleum production and is not rapidly industrializing. For this huge fraction of the world's population, therefore, development has not progressed greatly.

To a large extent, then, the strength of the Developing World is not in its economic production, but in the force of its collective voice in the global political economy. Originally a loose coalition of noncompetitive states, by using the principle "unity in diversity" the Developing Nations successfully have forced their economic agenda onto the world stage, modified the dynamics of a power-oriented Cold War system, and partially shaped the New World Order.

The first fruits of Developing World solidarity occurred at Bandung (Indonesia) in 1955, at Cairo (Egypt) in 1962, and at the 1964, 1968, and 1972 conferences of the United Nations Conference on Trade and Development (UNCTAD). In all of these the Developing Nations progressed toward a common agenda involving a full spectrum of policies and aids to accelerate progress. These ranged from trade, loans, grants, and foreign investment to anti-imperial guarantees such as restraints on transnational

TABLE 6–1

THE DEVELOPING WORLD, 1996

Least developed states	44
Rapidly industrializing states	12
Petroleum-rich developing states	15
Other	71
Total Developing World	127

corporations, improved terms of trade (ratio of import costs to export profits), and protection of infant industries. In 1973 political and economic events converged to give the Developing Nations their first great success. At a summit meeting of Developing Nations in Algiers (Algeria), a formal agenda was adopted for the next UNCTAD meeting. Only months later OPEC (all the members of which are underdeveloped) declared an oil embargo on the industrial countries to force changes in their policies toward Israel and the Middle East. For the first time, the potential power of the Developing Nations had been dramatized, and at a moment that they were prepared diplomatically to press their case on the UN and its Development Program. Thereafter, the Sixth Special Session of the General Assembly launched the New International Economic Order and its Programme for Action.

This promising political triumph was followed by frustrating resistance from the industrial nations, which spent the next two years attempting to regain the initiative. Disappointment was particularly acute because this occurred during the Soviet-American détente, a time that seemed reasonable for refining global priorities. Some interpreted the industrial governments' participation in the Sixth Special Session as having been for the cynical reason of breaking the power of OPEC by playing it against the larger Developing World. Despite the early setbacks, however, analysts of the era regard the 1973–1975 period as important (and perhaps even prophetic of the New World Order) in that it saw the rapid maturation of the Developing World as a political force, foreshadowed many of the pivotal concepts of the international political economy for the balance of the century, and politicized the development issue permanently.[1]

The opposing moods were broken by Washington's abrupt reversal. In a 1975 address, Secretary of State Henry Kissinger announced that the United States was "prepared to engage in a constructive dialogue and to work cooperatively" on issues pertaining to the New International Economic Order.[2] This new tone pervaded opening statements at the Seventh Special Session, where the industrial states declared their intention to "turn away from confrontation" and approach the New International Economic Order with conciliation and responsiveness to the Developing World's initiatives. The North-South Dialogue had commenced.

The Seventh Special Session, the first phase of the North-South Dialogue, produced a carefully negotiated agenda for action, principally addressing problems of international trade and transfer of resources and technology. UNCTAD, the principal forum of the Developing World, transformed the compromise plan into an action agenda entitled "Trade and Development Issues in the Context of a New International Economic Order," summarized as follows:

I. An Economic Security System for Developing Countries

   a. Integrated Programme for Commodities—commodity market stabilization and price stabilization for the primary exports of the developing states.

   b. Improved Compensatory Financing Facilities—adaptation of the International Monetary Fund or establishment of a substitute organization to supervise stabilization agreements and provide compensatory export shortfalls resulting from international market instability.

   c. Debt Relief—improved mechanisms of channeling capital to the Developing World

---

[1] Karl P. Sauvant, "Toward the New International Economic Order," in Karl P. Sauvant and Hajo Hasenpflug, eds., *The New International Economic Order: Confrontation or Cooperation Between North and South?* (Boulder, Colo.: Westview, 1977), pp. 3–19.

[2] "Address by the Honorable Henry A. Kissinger, Secretary of State, before the Kansas City International Relations Council, Missouri, May 13, 1975," in *Issues at the Special Session of the 1975 UN General Assembly* (Washington: U.S. Government Printing Office, 1975). A more detailed background can be found in Catherine B. Gwin, "The Seventh Special Session: Toward a New Phase in Relations Between the Developed and the Developing States?" in Karl P. Sauvant and Hajo Hasenpflug, eds., *The New International Economic Order*, pp. 97–117.

and for reducing the indebtedness that hinders development.

II. Changing the Structure of International Economic Relations

   a. Reducing the Economic Dependence of the Developing Nations—expanding trade in manufactures, strengthening the technological base of the Developing World, and establishing a marketing and distribution system for primary commodities.

   b. Strengthening Trade and Economic Cooperation Among Developing Countries—reorientation of development strategy to one of collective self-reliance rather than dependence on the developed states, including thorough development of new international machinery.

   c. Global Management of Resources—including the establishment of new rules of international trade, reform of the international monetary system, and the development of strategies for the rational use of resources.[3]

By the end of the 1970s, then, UNCTAD had set an agenda designed to promote trade expansion, improve economic cooperation among developing states, restructure international debts, and promote economic integration among the Developing Nations in support of collective self-reliance.

Changed circumstances interfered with any real implementation of these principles. First, détente had ended, and Soviet-American relations deteriorated severely, with both political and economic consequences for the Developing World. Second, in its Four Modernizations program and equidistance policy regarding the nuclear superpowers, China had set out on a new diplomatic course with a broader focus than just the Developing World. Third, worldwide economic stagnation and recession had caused a sharp drop in export prices for the Developing Nations and inflation in import costs. The need to take on additional debt added to the weight of the Developing World's short- and long-term burdens. And fourth, instability in oil prices widened the economic gap not only between North and South, but between the oil-producing and the oil-importing members of the Developing World as well.

Amid these circumstances, an Independent Commission on International Development Issues, chaired by former West German Chancellor Willie Brandt, released *North-South: A Program for Survival*, noting that world conditions called not just for more aid, but for "new structures. What is now on the agenda is a rearrangement of international relations, the building of a new order and a new kind of comprehensive approach to the problems of development."[4] Consistent with the notion that the very survival of developing states was at issue, the United Nations opened the Third Development Decade (the 1980s) with a Conference on the Least Developed Countries, formally separating thirty-one (later thirty-six and now forty-four) countries encompassing more than 220 million people (equal to more than two-thirds of the U.S. population at the time) from the other Developing Nations for special aid programs. More than 80 percent of these are in Africa.[5]

But in the deepening worldwide recession in the early 1980s, commodity prices for the Developing World's exports had collapsed, causing an estimated loss of $21 billion between 1980 and 1982. Recession-induced protectionism in the industrial

---

[3] *Trade and Development Issues in the Context of a New International Economic Order* (UNCTAD/OSG/L/Rev.1), February 1976, pp. 8-33. Reprinted with minor adaptations from Karl P. Sauvant and Hajo Hasenpflug, eds., *The New International Economic Order*, pp. 39–62.

[4] *North-South: A Program for Survival*, The Report of the Independent Commission on International Development Issues Under the Chairmanship of Willy Brandt (Cambridge, Mass.: MIT Press, 1980), p. 18. In 1982 the commission reconvened to review its findings and recommendations, and it published a subsequent report, *Common Crisis—North-South: Cooperation for World Recovery* (Cambridge, Mass.: MIT Press, 1983). The commission found that since its first report, world economic conditions had worsened to the extent that emergency measures were needed to avoid such consequences as mass starvation.

[5] For evaluations of the conference, see Thomas G. Weiss, "The UN Conference on the Least Developed Nations," *International Affairs* (London), autumn 1983; and Thomas G. Weiss and Anthony Jennings, *More for the Least?* (Lexington, Mass.: D. C. Heath, 1983).

world shut Developing World goods out of the global market, and the post-war trend toward free trade seemed to be crumbling around Developing World aspirations. Resistance of the industrial nations, particularly the United States, thwarted the Developing World's goals at UNCTAD VI at Belgrade in 1983.

Now the United Nations directed its attention to Africa for several reasons. First, nowhere else had the pace of development been so slow. Second, a combination of rising ethnic tensions and uncontrolled arms importation had converted many African lands into powder kegs. Third, as a product both of poverty and of ethnic violence, refugees had begun to swarm across Africa, and with them famine and epidemic. The origin of AIDS, for example, has been traced to Zaire. The Special General Assembly Session on Africa (1986) produced a Programme of Action for African Recovery and Development for the period 1986 through 1990, founded on the assumption that "a stagnant and perpetually backward Africa is not in the interests of the international community." The plan called for $128 billion in investment, $46 billion from external sources and the remainder from the mobilization and reallocation of local resources. The emphases were on agricultural development and distribution, drought control (including harnessing water resources and reforestation), and human resources in the forms of training and improved working conditions.[6]

During the twenty-year period preceding the end of the Cold War, global attention to development had a plentitude of three items: rhetoric, planning, and money. Funds might have been much greater had Cold War priorities not exceeded development priorities in most of the industrial states, especially the United States and the Soviet Union. Ironically, the close of the Cold War has had little positive effect, because in place of Cold War priorities now are domestic problems. Conversion of Russia, the former Soviet republics, and Eastern European allies from a single integrated, planned economy into multiple independent

---

[6] *United Nations Chronicle*, August 1986, pp. 7–14.

Volcano of discontent.
(*Source:* Drawing by Eugene Mihaesco)

market economies has been traumatic for them, and for the Developing World as well. The ruins of the Cuban economy underscore the consequences of Moscow's loss of interest in its only permanent Cold War foothold within the Americas. The transitional economies of the former Soviet world are experiencing slow to negative economic growth rates (worse than minus 10 percent annually in Russia and the other former Republics), high inflation (over 35 percent per year) and unemployment rates, and sharply declining exports (almost 50 percent between 1985 and 1992). Under these conditions, there is little available for the Developing World. Moreover, as Russia attempts partially to reintegrate these economies voluntarily, its strategic need is regional development of transitional economies rather than global development in areas where geopolitical interests have evaporated.

The picture is different but equally discouraging in the United States. In the post–Cold War flight from international responsibility and the neverending search for a peace dividend, Americans have selected foreign aid for deep budgetary reductions. In wealthy conservative circles there is strong feeling that international spending in the New World Order is wasteful and, worse, unproductive because, this line goes, economic development elsewhere threatens the sale of American products both at home and in global markets. Among the broader population, a 1995 poll revealed, 75 percent think that the Washington spends too much on foreign aid and 64 percent want the amount reduced. Only 11 percent want the amount to remain at the current level, less than 1 percent of the federal budget, in contrast to the UN aim of having the industrial countries contribute 4 percent of GNP, which is many times higher than governmental budgets, to development.[7] From 1960 through 1990 U.S. aid declined from half of 1 percent of GNP to one-fifth of 1 percent, and its $4 per capita is the lowest among the major participants in global aid programs. Furthermore, unlike Japan and Germany, more than half of the annual American contribution goes not to economic development, but to military aid. In 1990, only 15 percent of a declining commitment went to the Least Developed Countries. In contrast, in the same year the European Community contributed two and one-half times as much total aid, two-fifths of 1 percent of aggregate GNP and 26 percent going to the Least Developed Countries. Japan's contribution was $1 billion less than America's, but one-third of 1 percent of GNP, $7 per capita, and 17 percent to the LDC.[8]

All evidence suggests that the commitment of the industrial states to the Developing World correlates directly to international and domestic economic circumstances at any time. Hopes were justifiably high during the détente period when the Developing Nations bound together and global tensions were less acute, then put on hold as the Cold War resumed in earnest in the 1980s, then dashed altogether when post–Cold War priorities turned elsewhere. What, then, have been the practical results of this lengthy effort?

There have, of course, been some smashing successes. Israel, Taiwan, South Korea, Singapore, Indonesia, and to a lesser extent Thailand, Malaysia, and the Philippines have made great strides toward industrialization and economic modernity. China, Brazil, Argentina, and Mexico are a notch or two lower. Vietnam and South Africa, having resolved their internal divisions politically, are poised for takeoffs. The oil-exporting states have done well financially, but income distribution and development of social capital have yet to benefit. Beyond these few, the vast bulk of the Developing World has made only the most modest progress, and this is as accurate for places like India, Pakistan, and Afghanistan as it is for virtually all of Africa.

This conclusion is backed by an abundance of statistical evidence. It is still true, for example, that 83 percent of the total world income belongs to only 20 percent of the global population. At the opposite extreme, the poorest 20 percent (more than 1 billion people) benefits from only 1.4 percent of global income. (See Figure 6–1.) In some categories there has been substantial improvement, including adult literacy, school enrollment, daily nutrition, life expectancy at birth, and child survival. Yet in 1990 there were still 1.45 billion people in developing lands without access to health services, 1.33 billion without safe water, and 2.25 billion (nearly half the world's population) without sanitation.

There is additional evidence from national economies. From 1980 through 1992, for example, Developing World trade grew in both imports and exports, and while the growth was at a steady rate, the percentage share of world trade dropped

---

[7] Program on International Policy Attitudes, University of Maryland College Park, January 1995. For a critical essay, see "The Intellectual Free Lunch," *New Yorker*, February 6, 1995, pp. 4–5.

[8] United Nations Development Program, *Human Development Report, 1992*, table 39, p. 198. Unless otherwise noted, financial and population statistics in this chapter are derived from the *Human Development Report, 1992*; UNCTAD, *Trade and Development Report, 1992*; United Nations, *World Economic Survey, 1992*; The World Bank, *World Development Report, 1995*; and United Nations, *World Economic and Social Survey, 1995*.

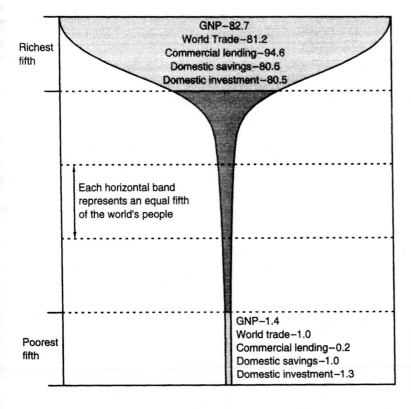

FIGURE 6–1 Global economic disparities.

Source: United Nations, *World Economic and Social Survey, 1995.*

alarmingly, meaning that the rich-poor gap related to trade deepened. (See Table 6–2.) The brightest part of this picture is that manufacturing exports rose substantially, and reliance on primary products declined accordingly. Still, however, both the volume and value of imports generally exceeded those of exports, meaning that terms of trade did not improve significantly. And the aggregate trade balance of the Developing World went from consistently positive from 1984 through 1991 to negative thereafter, meaning a net loss in trade. Add to that the cost of debt repayment, imported services, and private transfers, and the total annual transaction balance was negative throughout the period and worst after 1990. In 1993 alone the Developing World lost $109 billion in all its international dealings. The greatest losses were in Latin America, which averaged about 40 percent of the total in the worst years, and sometimes exceeded 50 percent.

The Developing Nations are also beset with high inflation rates that severely erode the value of their currencies. During the 1980s, when the industrial states had an aggregate annual inflation rate of 9.4 percent, the Developing World had a rate of 24.5 percent. The situation was worst in Latin America, as indicated by Table 6–3. Elsewhere, Uganda ran at an annual rate of 108 percent, Mexico at 73 percent, Sierra Leone 54 percent, Guinae-Bassau 53 percent, Ghana 44 percent, Somalia 43 percent, and Zambia 38 percent. Looked at annually rather than over a decade, the situation is far worse in some places. In Latin America, for example, the annual change in inflationary rate in 1989 was greater than 1000 percent, and in 1990 it was almost 1750 percent.

Finally, during the 1980s the Developing Nations combined had an average growth in GNP per capita of 3.4 percent, compared with the world rate of 3.2 percent and the industrial countries at 2.2

TABLE 6-2

DEVELOPING WORLD'S INCREASING VALUE BUT DECLINING SHARE OF WORLD EXPORTS

Year	Export Value	Percentage World Total
1980	$587 billion	29%
1985	494	26
1990	775	23
1992	907	25

Source: United Nations, *World Economic and Social Survey*, 1995, p. 310–311.

TABLE 6-3

LATIN AMERICAN ANNUAL INFLATION RATES, 1980–1989

Bolivia	392%
Argentina	335
Brazil	228
Peru	160
Uruguay	59
Ecuador	43
Paraguay	23
Chile	21
Venezuela	16

Source: United Nations Development Program, *Human Development Report, 1992*, table 24, pp. 174–175.

percent. But by excluding the high rates of Taiwan, South Korea, China, and Singapore, a more revealing picture emerges. More than a third of the individual countries actually had negative growth (i.e., real economic decline in GNP per capita), and another dozen had 1 percent or less in growth. Only fourteen had more than 14 percent (again excluding the rapidly industrializing countries), and most of them were in the Caribbean. The least developed countries averaged a loss of 0.7 percent, and the sub-Saharan African states a loss of 1.7 percent.

On balance, then, thirty years of bilateral and multilateral international development effort has been disappointing. Bringing down the Berlin Wall proved easier in the end that cracking the mysteries of persistent poverty and underdevelopment. There are two starkly different causal theories of underdevelopment. The conventional theory, favored in the traditional capitalism of the developing countries closely associated with the West (such as Brazil or Indonesia), ascribes poverty to internal conditions that prevent the poor countries from advancing rapidly. The radical theory, favored by revolutionary thinkers and the more militant voices in the Developing World (such as Cuba and Libya), blames poverty on international conditions of exploitation of the poor countries by the rich. The conventional theory sees the wealthy countries trying to help the poor lift themselves up by the bootstraps; the radical theory sees the rich countries profiting at the expense of the poor through rapacious foreign investment and structurally unequal trade.

The Conventional (or Capitalist) Theory of Development

According to the conventional theory, the process of economic growth and development has been arrested by low rates of productivity combined with high levels of social waste and inefficiency. The Western standard of living is high because workers with modern tools and technology produce a great deal in eight hours; with only primitive tools and methods, a comparable worker in the Developing World produces far less. On an American family farm, for example, a laborer may work more than one hundred acres, whereas three may be the limit in a Developing Nation. Furthermore, the American squeezes two or three times as much annual yield out of each acre by using advanced methods of fertilization, irrigation, and scientific farming. The result is that the American farmer is able to feed about fifty people rather than a family. The higher rate of agricultural productivity generates a surplus to be invested in industrial development, whereas retarded agricultural production in less developed countries slows economic growth and drains the labor force. By comparing annual rates of fuel consumption, generation of electricity, production of steel in tonnage, and so on, one can find many more explanations of the ways in which the industrialized countries use artificial means to enhance the efficiency of human labor and to stimulate capital formation through surpluses. This cycle of self-sustaining growth explains the expanding capitalization of modern economies, high personal consumption rates, and high standards of living.

The problem, according to the conventional theorist, is that economies reach this point of "takeoff" to self-sustaining growth only under conditions of rapid capital accumulation. But most of the Developing Nations have been able to achieve only modest rates of saving and investment because of poverty itself and various forms of waste and inefficiency. Even when surpluses are generated, they tend to be squandered on unnecessary forms of consumption rather than on growth-oriented investment.

Wastes that Retard Development

Population Growth Populations are growing much faster in the Developing World than elsewhere, as Figure 6–2 indicates. While the industrialized countries combined grew by less than 1 percent per year during the 1980s, Africa grew by 2.9 percent annually, and Latin America by 2.3 percent. It is estimated that by the turn of the century Latin America's population will have reached 538 million, 42 million more than was estimated ten years ago. Should this projection prove to have been accurate, Latin America's population will have grown by 225 percent in fifty years. Similarly, if the projection for Africa materializes (from 222 million in 1950 to 867 million in 2000, it will have increased by 290 percent in the half-century. Table 6–4 shows the population trend by region.

Developing Nations also have twice as much of their population under ten years of age as do the

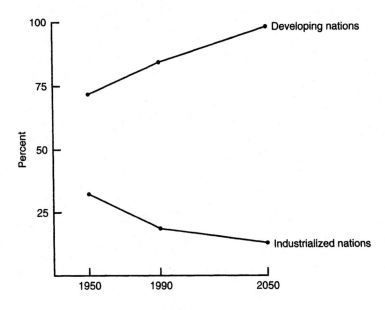

FIGURE 6–2 World population distribution, 1950–1990, and projected to 2050.

Source: United Nations, *Long-Range Population Projections,* 1992, p. 24.

TABLE 6–4

POPULATION GROWTH BY REGIONS

Region	1950	1970	1990	2000 (projected)	Multiple
Latin America	166 million	283 million	448 million	538 million	3.2
Africa	222	361	642	867	3.9
Asia	1,376	2,102	3,113	3,713	2.7
North America	166	227	276	295	1.8
Soviet Union/CIS	180	242	289	308	1.7
Europe	392	459	498	510	1.3

Source: United Nations, *Long-Range World Population Projections,* 1992, p. 24.

developed countries. Because infants and young children consume but do not produce, they act as a drain on economic growth. It is estimated that a country with a 3 percent population growth rate must invest 6 percent of its production each year just to keep up with the increase, without achieving any expansion of per capita income. The projected decline in Developing World annual population growth rate from 2.3 percent (1960–1990) to 2.0 percent for the remainder of the century will help, but it will not curb the problem in most places. Failure to do so will perpetuate an enormous burden. To make matters worse, as life expectancy rises, more older people continue to consume but cease producing. Economic growth is thus eroded at both ends of the population spectrum.

Four decades of efforts to relieve the population burden on the Developing Nations have been only modestly successful. Except for China, which has achieved a considerable drop in birth rate by means generally unacceptable to the rest of the world (mandatory sterilization, mandatory abortion, and allegedly, infanticide), those national birth rates that have dropped have done so only slightly. Birth control and family planning have not, on the whole, made a great impact. Many peoples consider large families a blessing, have religious objections to birth control, or are culturally ill suited to the regular use of birth control methods. The Vatican's condemnation of birth control goes a long way toward explaining Latin America's population plight.

Various medical innovations may achieve real breakthroughs in controlling population growth. Among these are long-term contraceptive implants for women, oral contraception for men, and chemical agents that prevent conception even if taken several hours after insemination. Meanwhile, in many countries the population growth is not being arrested, and one result is continued economic stagnation and declining per capita gross national product (GNP/capita). Current projections indicate that the problem is a long way from being solved: It is projected that by the year 2050, the global population will be double that of 1990 at more than 10 billion, and that 88 percent of it will reside in today's Developing Nations (Figure 6–2). One reason for this is that while in the industrialized world regular use of contraception runs at 70 percent, in the Developing World the rate is 41 percent, and below 10 percent in the Least Developed Countries and sub-Saharan Africa.

Excessive Urbanization   A generation ago, all the world's principal population centers were in the industrialized countries. New York, Tokyo, London, Paris, Rome, and Moscow led the list. Gradually, however, through both disparate birth rates and migration phenomena, other names began to appear on the list: Cairo, Mexico City, Rio de Janeiro, Buenos Aires, Seoul, Beijing, Calcutta, and Manila are examples. The United Nations estimates that by the turn of the century, all but three of the world's largest cities will be in the underindustrialized world. Mexico City, already in 1986 the most populous city with 18.1 million inhabitants, will have grown to 26.3 million. Table 6–5 shows the global urbanization trend and underscores the trend in the Developing World. It indicates that Developing World cities were burdened with a growth of almost 70 percent from 1960 to 1990, and that they will grow by another 22 percent in the remainder of this century.

This marked urbanization is a major obstacle to economic and social development. As urban populations grow, they require a variety of services, including jobs, housing, health care, education, water, sanitation, and waste removal, all of which require sophisticated planning, capital accumulation, and lead time. In the rapid urbanization of the Developing World, governments have not had the luxury of any of these. They have had to depend on external capital and resulting debt increases, but ability to cope with the problem has been minimal.

> Most cities in the developing world have ... become loci for the most degrading poverty, with vast throngs of people living on the margins of survival. Of every one hundred new households established in urban areas in developing countries during the second half of the 1980s, 72 were located in shanties and slums (92 out of every 100 in Africa). Today, an estimated 1.2 billion people—almost 23 percent of the world's population and 60 percent of the developing countries city-dwellers—live in squatter settlements, often shantytowns made from cardboard, plastic, canvas or whatever other material is freely available.[9]

These squalid conditions arise not only from population size, but from density as well, defined as the number of occupants per square kilometer (Table 6–6). This crowding phenomenon is responsible for contagion, addiction, crimes of violence, inequities of justice, and social predation. The risks are greater for women and children than for healthy men.

Thus the burdens of urbanization compound the phenomenon of economic development, rendering economic growth rates in absolute terms fruitless. If the benefits of growth must be squandered on public assistance, an overburdened criminal justice system, indigent medical care, and the like, they cannot be used for planned economic advancement by capital accumulation, investment, and taxation. They find their way into neither the public nor the private economy, and apparent economic gains are lost in a self-fulfilling system of declining economic capabilities.

Excessive Military Expenditure A third form of waste that erodes small economic advances is

---

TABLE 6–5

GLOBAL URBANIZATION TREND: PERCENTAGE OF TOTAL POPULATION LIVING IN CITIES

	1960	1990	2000
World	34%	45%	60%
Industrial Countries	61	73	75
Developing Countries	22	37	45
Least developed	8	20	26
Sub-Saharan Africa	15	31	38

Source: United Nations Development Program, *Human Development Report, 1992*, pp. 168–169.

---

[9] United Nations, *World Social Situation in the 1990s* (1994), p. 103.

TABLE 6-6

MOST DENSELY POPULATED CITIES IN THE DEVELOPING WORLD, 1988

City	Population/Square Kilometer
Calcutta (India)	88,135
Manila (Philippines)	45,839
Cairo (Egypt)	29,393
Mashhad (Iran)	21,132
Seoul (South Korea)	15,932
Buenos Aires (Argentina)	14,615
Casablanca (Morocco)	12,133
Amman (Jordan)	11,104
Guadalajara (Mexico)	10,286
Dhaka (Bangladesh)	9,930
Santiago (Chile)	9,878
New York City	8,722

Source: United Nations Development Program, *Human Development Report, 1992,* pp. 168–169 and 201.

military expenditure, on which many Developing Nations lavish their precious resources. From 1973 through 1982, for example, the oil-producing developing countries spent approximately $360 billion on military policy; the non-oil group spent an additional $374 billion. Together, their total military bill for the decade was $734 billion. From 1960 to 1989 the percentage of gross domestic product that went into arms rose from 4.2 to 4.6 percent, compared with a decline in the industrialized states from 6.3 to 4.9 percent. However, in 1990 the industrialized states' military expenditure was 28 percent of combined expenditures for health and education, whereas in the Developing World it was 169 percent.

Developing World defense spending generally reflects (1) the degree of regional instability (Table 6–7) and (2) ethnic conflict and other threats to domestic order (Table 6–8). Given the constant tensions in the Middle East during the 1980s, for example, much of the defense cost of the Developing World centered on Israel, Saudia Arabia, Egypt, Iran, Iraq, Jordan, and Syria. The Iran-Iraq war ran the total way up. Other regional hot spots accounted for large shares of Developing World arms spending in the 1980s as well: China and Taiwan, India and Pakistan, North and South Korea. During the course of the Afghanistan War, the Soviet Union shipped more than $8 billion to the Afghan government. States that maintained high military expenditures during the 1980s in face of threats to domestic order include Chile, Honduras, Libya, Ethiopia, South Africa, Mozambique, Zimbabwe, and Angola. Some of the military costs of Iraq and Turkey are directed against their own Kurdish populations.

TABLE 6-7

DEVELOPING WORLD EXPENDITURES TO MEET EXTERNAL THREATS, 1982–1991

Country	Expense	Avg. Annual GDP
Israel	$52.6 billion	14.6%
Syria	27.7	13.8
Jordan	6.0	13.4
Egypt	47.2	5.9
Iran	78.0	3.1[1]
Iraq	179.6	24.6
Saudia Arabia	184.3	20.2
Kuwait	13.8	6.8[2]
United Arab Emirates	19.8	6.6
North Korea	17.8	11.0[3]
South Korea	68.4	4.9
China	not listed	not listed
Taiwan	58.2	6.4
India	84.0	3.4
Pakistan	27.4	6.7

[1] Iran's GDP not reported after 1986.
[2] 1991 excluded, both columns.
[3] Figures reported 1981–86 only, both columns.

Source: SIPRI Yearbook, 1992, World Armaments and Disarmament, adapted from pp. 259–268.

TABLE 6-8

DEVELOPING WORLD EXPENDITURES TO MEET INTERNAL THREATS, 1982–1991

Country	Expense	Avg. Annual GDP
Angola	$ 7.1 billion	20.3%
Chile	14.1	7.6
Ethiopia	5.3	9.7*
Honduras	3.2	5.3
Lybia	28.2	12.9
Mozambique	0.3	10.6*
Nicaragua	3.9	17.4*
Peru	10.9	5.3
South Africa	35.7	4.3
Zimbabwe	4.9	6.2*

*Adjusted for date discontinuities.

Source: SIPRI Yearbook, 1992, World Armaments and Disarmament, adapted from pp. 259–268.

With the exception of the momentary spike in military spending in the Middle East caused by the Iraqi invasion of Kuwait and the war that followed, the new decade brought a general decline in global defense spending, and it was reflected in the Developing World as in the former Cold War adversaries. These trends show most dramatically in the decline in international trade in major conventional weapons (see Table 6–9). In subsequent years, the total commitment to arms has declined steadily.

The cost of maintaining the Soviet-American strategic arms race so captured the world's attention that the debilitating cost of arming the Developing World is often overlooked. But for advocates of the conventional theory of development, the military costs of the Developing World were every bit as wasteful as was the nuclear balance of terror. Critics of American defense spending are fond of reciting the number of hospitals, schools, modern farms, medical discoveries, and social programs that could be supported by the money spent on a new

generation of missiles. Advocates of the conventional theory of development are equally quick to claim that were it not for the military investment in the Developing World over the last two decades, social and economic development might have been accelerated immeasurably. It seems ironic to them that so much should have been wasted on arms, only to have the same governments coming back to the Western capitals and international institutions requesting still more funds for development.

But those who associate arms costs with forgone development opportunities look beyond the Developing World and concentrate on the world's total commitment to arms. To one, idle arms are as destructive to development as deployed weapons are to global tranquility. "[T]he ever increasing accumulation of destructive machinery would come to be seen as even more perverse [than war itself]— an arsenal which kills people even without being used because it eats up the money without which people are condemned to death through starvation."[10] Others explore what the reallocation of national and international resources from arms might do for development. One such study projected the availability of additional funds for international economic development from 1980 to 2000 using two major indices: per-year baseline contributions to development by industrialized countries and additional contributions resulting from the reduction in military expense commitments. In Figure 6–3, line A results from a linear projection from 1980 to 2000, with the industrialized countries making a standard contribution of 0.35 percent of their annual GNP to Developing World growth. Line B makes a similar projection, this time factoring in an additional 15 percent contribution throughout the 1980s and an additional 25 percent contribution throughout the 1990s resulting from the reduction in arms spending. Line C deals only with baseline (pre-arms-reduction) contributions, but using a figure of 0.7 percent of annual GNP throughout the

---

[10] Willy Brandt, *Peace and Development* (London: The Third World Foundation, 1985).

TABLE 6-9

RISE AND FALL OF DEVELOPING WORLD ARMS IMPORTS

Year	Total	Latin America	Africa	Asia	Middle East
1982	$43.4 billion	$4.0 billion	$5.6 billion	$6.7 billion	$13.7 billion
1983	44.0	4.6	4.1	7.8	14.9
1984	42.7	4.3	4.4	7.7	14.3
1985	39.3	2.3	3.9	9.6	11.8
1986	41.9	2.1	4.0	11.6	12.3
1987	45.9	2.3	3.2	12.3	15.9
1988	39.3	1.0	2.3	12.8	9.8
1989	38.2	1.4	2.0	15.2	5.8
1990	29.0	1.2	1.3	9.4	6.8
1991	22.1	0.8	0.1	7.5	4.7

Note: The horizontal columns do not equal the "total" column because some parts of the Developing World are not included.

Source: SIPRI Yearbook, 1992, World Armaments and Disarmament, p. 308.

1980s and 1.0 percent throughout the 1990s. Finally, line D uses the baseline assumptions of line C but then adds contributions resulting from 15 percent arms reductions in the 1980s and 25 percent in the 1990s. Because the values are based on 1970 (not adjusted for inflation or changes in currency values), the magnitude of the differences is difficult to appreciate. Nonetheless, the essence of the argument is that as one moves from the minimalassumption of line A to the maximal assumption of line D, the value of investment in development multiplies by a factor of approximately 12.[11]

The study cited in the preceding paragraph was concluded eight years before the New World Order.

More recent studies show that "there is considerable disillusion about the peace dividend."[12] For Americans, the "peace dividend" was to have been tax reductions following the end of the Cold War, and they lost it to the realization that the 1980s arms buildup was done on borrowed money that multiplied the national debt. To liberal internationalists, the "peace dividend" was to have been the reallocation of former defense funds to international development, and they lost it to the economic plight of the former Soviet empire and a conservative-led withdrawal from America's international commitments.

Luxury Consumption   In many poor countries, the abysmal poverty of the masses contrasts sharply with the astronomical wealth of a handful of landlords, maharajas, princes, or industrial barons. The

[11] For a thorough econometric analysis of the impact of the Developing World's own arms expenditures on development, see Sasdet Deger, *Military Expenditure in the Third World Countries: The Economic Effects* (London: Routledge and Kegan Paul, 1986). The authoritative, comprehensive source of annual arms statistics is the *SIPRI Handbook* series. (SIPRI is the Swedish International Peace Research Institute.)

[12] A comprehensive review is found in United Nations, *World Economic and Social Survey, 1995,* chapter 13, "Assessing the Peace Dividend Resulting from the End of the Cold War," pp. 189–224.

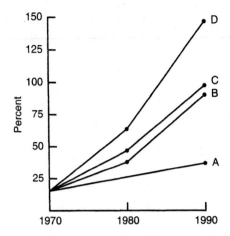

FIGURE 6–3 Potential added investment in Developing World growth through reduction in worldwide arms expenditures, 1970–2000.

Source: United Nations Centre for Disarmament, *The Relationship Between Disarmament and Development, 1983,* p. 94.

stratification (unequal distribution) of wealth is much sharper in the Developing World than in the wealthy nations. For example, in Colombia the top 5 percent of the population gets 42 percent of the income. (In the United States, the top 5 percent of the population gets 16 percent of the income.) In more than half the developing countries, less than 10 percent of farms have over half the cultivatable acreage.

It might be thought that concentrations of wealth could be invested in economic development. But the rich throw away much of this potential through luxury spending on automobiles and baronial estates instead of putting it to development purposes. And not all luxury expenditures benefit single individuals. Sometimes poor nations use precious funds to create false impressions of their economic condition. Sometimes in the name of religion—as in massive temples and shrines—and sometimes in more secular forms—such as massive public works projects that are of secondary value to society—these choices severely strain public budgets. Perhaps the most striking modern example is in the Ivory Coast, where a Christian

leader of a non-Christian people has squandered hundreds of millions of dollars to construct a full-size equivalent of the Vatican in the African desert. More recently, international aid projects, both intergovernmental and through international organizations, have sought to prevent this sort of waste by monitoring the uses of domestic public revenues as a condition of providing external assistance. The recipients often regard this as an unwarranted interference in domestic affairs, but to the conventional theory of development, this is neither more nor less than a prudent control on the distribution of scarce resources.

Official Corruption Luxury spending by individuals often crosses over into corruption and abuse of public authority. Although this is by no means a creature of the Developing World (after all, the United States lost both a vice president and a president to corruption in the 1970s; several high Italian and Japanese officials have been forced from public life amid scandals; and in 1995 the Secretary General of NATO was under indictment for crimes allegedly committed while he was an official in the Belgian government), the scarcity of wealth means that corruption will have a much deeper consequence for a developing economy. In the United States, more than 90 percent of the taxes that are due (after loopholes) are successfully collected, but some Developing Nations have an actual collection rate below 50 percent. The state treasury—one of the main instruments of development—is thus depleted by tax evasion. In addition, allotments from the treasury are eroded by the corruption of project administrators at every level. A flood of resources put into the pipeline at one end can come out the other end reduced to a trickle. Sometimes corruption takes the form of "legitimate" expenditures such as luxury cars for officials and inflated expense accounts.

The two most exceptional instances of public corruption and its consequences for developing economies have occurred in lands greatly favored by American foreign military and economic aid. They involve the Shah of Iran and former

Waste in the Developing World: The Yamoussoukro basilica rises in the open land of the Ivory Coast at a cost of more than $200 million. (*Source:* © CRI Barry Iverson/TIME Magazine)

President Ferdinand Marcos of the Philippines. Each received billions of dollars from the United States in military and economic development aid. Each eventually fell ignominiously at the hand of revolutionary public opinion, the shah to a fundamentalist revolution and Marcos to exile after attempting to rig a presidential election that he had lost to the wife of his assassinated political rival. After the shah's fall, Iranian officials claimed that fully $24 billion of public funds, most of it U.S. aid, had been exported by the shah, most of it to the United States, for his own wealth. And upon the fall of Marcos, revelation followed revelation regarding his property holdings in the United States and elsewhere, Swiss bank accounts, lavish shopping sprees, political favoritism in the use of aid funds, and so on, all totaling many billions of dollars. In 1995, a Swiss court ordered one bank to return to the Philippines government some $22 billion stashed away by Marcos. One can but wonder how different might be both the politics and the economies of these two countries had corruption not so dramatically stolen investment capital.

Management Inefficiency The management of a thriving economy is an enormously complex affair both economically and politically. In addition to tax revenue, economic managers must arrange for finance, negotiate loans at tolerable interest rates, marshal human resources, establish priorities, create infrastructures, train personnel for industrial functions, make judgments about risks and probable profits, induce investments from internal and external sources, ensure economic efficiency and productivity, and perform thousands of other integrated functions. Modern economies are far too complicated to be guided by an "invisible hand" or other self-regulator. Instead, countless well-trained specialists are needed both for creation and coordination. Just as a musician must know the scales before sight-reading Beethoven, so must a growing economy develop around trained and dedicated specialists. In realizing this, the developing countries have for four decades sent their most promising young scientists and managers to the industrialized world for education and training. Many of these have gone either to the United States or Western Europe for training in capitalist economics or to the Soviet Union or China for training in socialist economics. The objective is to improve the speed and efficiency of economic development without incurring additional dependence on or interference by foreign interests.

The long-range costs of inefficient planning and economic implementation are illustrated dramatically in the spending binge carried on by the OPEC countries from 1974 to 1978. During that time, they spent more than $400 billion on development projects, and Western observers estimate that more than half of it may have been wasted.

> Immediate social and political consequences of rapid development were already evident: inflation, unsound organization, an excessive building boom, a large influx of foreigners, an adverse impact on agriculture and traditional industries and often a lopsided distribution of wealth. These problems, in turn, led to a weakening of established social and political values, accompanied by disappointment and resentment.[13]

The OPEC countries are not unique in this regard. All the Soviet money poured into Cuba during the Cold War did little to promote development; instead it produced a dependency that has the economy in shambles now that the gift rubles are gone. In China's case we have seen the zealous intrusion of ideology in development; the Cultural Revolution was a misbegotten and mismanaged event that set China's development back a decade. And in converting the former Soviet economies to capitalism, the most pressing concern other than capital is that there is no post-socialist managerial class to manage the transition. Tempting as it may be, therefore, to think of development as primarily a money problem, it is clear that it cannot be achieved without skillful mangement.

These, then, in the view of the conventional theory, are the principal obstacles to development. We turn now to the ingredients of its preferred remedy: foreign economic assistance.

Foreign Economic Assistance

With exceptions, the Developing Nations are typically low-income agrarian societies that devote the greater portion of their economic activity to subsistence production. Industrial development and agricultural mechanization are the keys to economic expansion, but circumstances prevent domestic capital accumulation for the requisite investment. The basic solution, in the conventional view, is to find new sources of capital. The answer is external, in the industrialized countries, where the ingredients exist in excess. They are four in number: (1) aid, (2) trade, (3) direct investment, and (4) technical assistance.

Foreign Aid   Foreign aid is a transfer of publicly held or publicly guaranteed resources to one or more developing countries, either in the form of direct funding or in commodities and goods subsidized by the donor country. It can take the form of outright grants or of long-term, low-interest loans. It may come directly from a single country (called bilateral aid) or from an international organization or other funding consortium that has use of the funds of several donor states (called multilateral aid). When loans are involved, they may be made on a short-term basis (usually for not more than one year), on an intermediate basis (usually for one to ten years), or for the long term (ten or more years, usually twenty-five but sometimes as long as forty years). Because of the length of time for repayment and the favorable interest rates, developing countries usually prefer long-term loans to the others.

When the United Nations initiated the first Development Decade (1960–1970), its goal was for each developed country to achieve a level of 1 percent of GNP per year for development aid. Later, when UNCTAD became the voice of the Developing World, the goal was scaled down to a more modest 0.7 percent. During the peak of OPEC's power in the 1970s, three of its members—Kuwait, Saudia Arabia, and the United Arab Emirates—greatly exceeded those goals, their ten-year averages ranging from 5 to almost 7 percent. (Much of this was in the form of oil subsidies to Developing Nations to protect them from the shock of the price increases aimed at the industrialized states.) As OPEC declined in the 1980s, so did its members' individual aid programs. By 1993

---
[13] Quoted from Robert Stobaugh and Daniel Yergin, "Energy: An Emergency Telescoped," *Foreign Affairs, America and the World* 1979 issue, pp. 562–595 at pp. 564–565.

the total OPEC contribution to development was less than 15 percent of its 1980 level, totaling only $1.5 billion.

Of the Western lenders, only Norway, Sweden, and the Netherlands met the UNCTAD goal on a ten-year-average basis from 1971 to 1981. None met the United Nations Development Program (UNDP) goal. Conspicuously absent from these observations are the wealthiest capitalist states: the United States, Japan, Britain, France, West Germany, Canada, and Italy. To be sure, many of them contributed large dollar amounts, but none reached the goals established. Table 6–10 indicates the sizes of contributions in selected years.

In the United States, the popularity of foreign aid has always been associated with specific purposes. The $14 billion Marshall Plan was intended to ensure Western Europe's recovery from World War Two at a time when the American population was largely of European origin, and to help contain communism. President Kennedy's Alliance for Progress was to bring prosperity and tranquility to this hemisphere. Aid to Taiwan was a reflection of communist victory in China, and assistance to South Korea a natural economic sequel to military intervention following the North Korean attack. Aid to Israel is explained by the composition of the American electorate and a moral commitment to Israel's survival. But Africa is a continent on which Americans in general have found little to which to give their tax dollars. And more generally, with the decline of the Cold War and the new economic competition from Taiwan and South Korea, they began to wonder even about the old commitments. Complacent over their self-declared Cold War victory and passively confident that the Soviet threat is gone, they are reluctant to assist Russia's twin conversions to capitalism and democracy. And still deeply divided over NAFTA, they are unhappy with President Clinton's loan to Mexico to prevent the collapse of its economy following the sudden and huge loss of the peso's value. Weary of international commitments, post–Cold War Americans find little of value in foreign aid. Traditionally a budget cutter's target, foreign aid is the more so in

TABLE 6–10

GOVERNMENT ASSISTANCE TO DEVELOPMENT, 1992

Government	Percentage of GNP	Amount
Norway	1.16%	$1.27 billion
Sweden	1.03	2.46
Denmark	1.02	1.39
Netherlands	0.86	2.75
Finland	0.64	0.64
France	0.63	8.27
Canada	0.46	2.52
Switzerland	0.45	1.14
West Germany	0.39	7.58*
Belgium	0.39	0.87
Australia	0.37	1.02
Italy	0.34	4.12
United Kingdom	0.31	3.24
Japan	0.30	11.15
United States	0.20	11.71

*This was a budgeted amount for the former West Germany prior to reunification.

Source: World Bank, *World Development Report, 1995*, p. 196.

the U.S.'s current wave of conservatism and the unpopularity of international commitment.

American opinion is not alone. Total international assistance reached its peak in 1992, when the sixteen principal industrial participants offered a total of almost $61 billion. But the following year, it declined to $54.5 billion, and fifteen of the sixteen reduced their commitments. (Japan's tiny increase was the only exception.) A large part of what Germany appropriated went not to Developing World projects, but to the recovery of the former East Germany. Whereas Soviet aid formerly went in large quantities to Cuba, Angola, Afghanistan, and Syria, Russian funds now are going almost exclusively to domestic economic recovery and conversion, and to stimulating the voluntary reintegration of the CIS and Central European

UN Peacekeepers in Somalia.
(*Source:* © Reuters/Bettmann)

economies. The Russian and German changes alone constitute multibillion dollar losses for the Developing World.

There are other trends that buffet the Developing World. The gap between the rich and the poor is expanding rather than narrowing. The Cold War's close dislodges a major incentive for the industrial states to provide funds. Ethnic unrest makes many Developing Nations bad risks from a purely economic viewpoint. Growing global sensitivity to polluting industries and deforestation practices, especially as they may relate to severe weather changes (including draught, ozone depletion, greenhouse gases, and global warming), impose new lending criteria that may limit direct economic impact. And the speed with which the industrial age has yielded to the technological threatens to make the developing economies the more obsolete despite their modest advances. There is no evidence that more aid is on the horizon to meet these needs, and no confidence that even if there were, it could address the last of them. As Table 6–11 indicates, the Developing World's share of "new product" export, broadly defined as technological, is high and growing; but as is so often the case with this aggregation of disparate economies, the benefits are limited to a handful of rapidly industrializing members. Note that in the respective years, the Developing World's shares of world exports in all manufactured goods were 12, 16.1, 18.5, and 22.0 percent, respectively. Hence those who took part in new-product export were doing considerably better than those who were not.

Not all capital that flows to the Developing World comes from individual governments. Large volumes also come from international institutions such as regional development banks (five such banks had total commitments of $12.8 billion in 1994), the specialized agencies of the United Nations ($3 billion committed in 1994), and the World Bank Group including the International Bank for Reconstruction and Development (the World Bank), which had $27.2 billion in commitments in 1994. But with a single exception (one subsidiary of the World Bank raises funds through its own investment program), these institutions acquire their funds from their members and dispense them according to their members' wishes. Often the voting procedures are weighted to the largest donors, whose political agendas may dominate the organization's lending pattern. The principal interest of the regional banks is stimulation of trade and

TABLE 6–11

DEVELOPING WORLD EXPORT OF NEW PRODUCTS AS PERCENTAGE OF WORLD TOTAL

Product	YEAR			
	1980	1985	1990	1993
Office machinery; data processing	2.7%	6.3%	14.7%	21.9%
Telecommunications equipment	10.7	11.6	24.1	32.9
Electronic components	23.6	24.3	27.7	32.2
All new products	11.5	12.5	22.0	28.2

Source: United Nations, *World Economic and Social Survey,* 1995, p. 173.

economic stability; of the UN agencies, specific programs such as population control, child welfare, refugee relief, or disease control; and of the World Bank, large infrastructure projects such as water, power, and transportation that may take many years, even decades, to deliver their impact on the economy.

Another source of capital is banks and other private financial institutions. Their interest rates tend to be the highest, their terms short, and the projects they support specific. The lender may assume the full risk, in which case the rate is higher, or it may be guaranteed against loss by a government. In this way governments increase the pool of development capital without having to charge it to current accounts. With debt restructuring in recent years (discussed later), the total Developing World's debt to transnational commercial banks dropped from $289 billion in 1987 to $219 billion in 1991.[14] In the same year, however, the total debt of the non-oil-producing Developing World to all

sources—public and private, bilateral and multilateral—was $918 billion. The trap here, of course, is that bank loans have to be paid in regular installments with interest. Too often, Developing Nations cannot meet these obligations and have to borrow money to pay for existing loans. This constitutes "forced borrowing."

While the availability of external capital is essential to development, it carries grave risks. Just as important to the Developing Nations, therefore, is international trade.

Foreign Trade   It is for more than poetic reasons that foreign aid and foreign trade are considered by the conventional view to be the principal ingredients of modernization. Because self-sufficiency is impossible in most economies, acquisition of foreign sources of goods (imports) and foreign markets for the export of products are essential elements in economic expansion.

In fact, foreign trade plays several important roles in a developing economy, one of which relates directly to foreign aid. Because of interest, every dollar of aid must be repaid with a dollar plus in cash, and because domestic funds are scarce, the best source of repayment is income from exports. Export trade, then, is an important source of new capital. The certainty of export markets is also important in determining the volume of a product that will be produced, which in turn determines its selling price in both domestic and foreign markets. Price helps determine competitiveness in world markets. Finally, exports are essential in maintaining the developing economy's trade balance. While accumulating a capital debt by borrowing foreign money, a developing economy cannot afford also to amass a trade deficit (value of imports exceeding value of exports). Part of a development strategy, therefore, must be to produce for export in sufficient quantities and at competitive prices so that the external sale of goods will at least equal imports in value. The more export value exceeds import value, the easier it is to service financial debt and the faster to accumulate capital for development.

---

[14] United Nations Center on Transnational Corporations, *Transnational Banks and the Indebtedness of Developing Countries* (1992), pp. 2–3.

Although export potential is an extremely complicated issue, it can be simplified as depending primarily on (1) annual production growth and (2) production growth per capita. The first is straightforward: Is the country able to increase annually the amount it produces? The second is more complicated, because it relates production growth to population and domestic consumption. If, for example, a population remains stable and production grows, then more goods ought to be available for export. If, on the other hand, production remains the same and the population grows, then the per capita production has declined; and if domestic consumption simply remained the same per capita, there would be less available for export.

The critical elements, then, are four in number: (1) annual change in population, (2) annual output change, (3) annual change in gross domestic product per capita, and (4) annual change in imports and exports. We have already seen that population growth is the chronic enemy of the Developing Nations. As for output, UNCTAD's estimates for the industrialized and the developing economies are summarized in Table 6–12.

Even making allowances for the skewing of these figures by China and the most rapidly industrializing states, it is apparent that the Developing World is making substantial progress in economic output as measured by annual growth.

But what happens when population is factored into output growth? The resulting computation is annual increase in gross domestic product per capita, as shown in Table 6–13. (In the Developing World, GNP and GDP are virtually identical.) Here we see where the Developing Nations lose the advantage of their economic investment. The picture is clarified even more by dividing the Developing World into parts that we can correlate directly with population increase. Contrast, for example, China's growth rate and population program (without casting judgment on methods) with those of Africa and Latin America.

Now that we have looked into export potential, we turn to the statistical evidence of trade itself. The three issues that measure the transformation of potential to real gain (or loss) are (1) relation of exports to imports in volume, (2) relation of exports to imports in value, and (3) price changes for exports and imports that determine terms of trade and actual profit (or loss). Clearly, if the value of exports exceeds that of imports, there is a real capital gain when exports increase. If, on the other hand, the relationship of export value to import value is reversed, then only huge increases in exports will overcome the difference. Moreover, if price fluctuations alter the value of imports, exports, or both, then changes in volume may or may not compensate for changes in value.

TABLE 6–12

AVERAGE ANNUAL GROWTH IN ECONOMIC OUTPUT

	1980–85	1985–90	1990–95	1995–2000
Industrial Economies	2.4%	3.2%	2.1%	2.8%
Developing Economies	1.9	3.4	4.1	4.3

Source: UNCTAD, *Trade and Development Report*, 1992, p. 33.

TABLE 6–13

ANNUAL GROWTH IN GNP/CAPITA

	1975–84	1985–94
Industrial Economies	2.1%	2.0%
Developing Economies	1.7	2.0
Latin America	0.7	0.5
Africa	0.3	–1.0
West Asia	–2.3	–2.8
South and East Asia	3.7	3.9
China	6.2	8.3
Mediterranean	1.9	–1.4

Source: United Nations, *World Economic and Social Survey*, 1995, p. 299.

As to volume of exports, we know that the Developing World's annual rate of export growth from 1985 through 1995 was considerably greater than that of the developed market economies, averaging 9.3 percent annually versus 5.3 percent. In the same period of time, the value of its exports rose at an average annual rate identical to that of the developed market economies, but if you exclude the first two years of the period, its annual growth exceeded the developed world's by 12.3 percent to 9.0 percent. Annual percentage volume and value increases are shown in Table 6–14. Unfortunately, only in South and East Asia (including China) did export reliance on primary products (agriculture, raw materials, and fuels) drop sharply and export of manufactured products increase correspondingly. In Africa, West Asia, and Latin America primary products continue to comprise virtually all exports except for

rare circumstances like the Brazilian aircraft and munitions industries.

The final index for understanding the Developing World's trade position is the relation of export prices to import prices. These partly determine the value of trade, and they are reflected in the value figures cited in Table 6–15 together with the terms of trade they dictate. These data differ greatly from those for volume and value growth, as it is clear that import prices are rising much more steeply than export prices, producing negative—unfavorable—terms of trade in every year except one in the eleven-year period.

To assess the trade position of the aggregate Developing World, it is necessary now to deal with GDP/capita, volume, value, and price structure. (UNCTAD reports that imports equaled exports, and so there is no difference there to factor in.) Compare the following:

TABLE 6–14

ANNUAL CHANGE IN EXPORTS

	1985	1986	1987	1988	1989	1990	1991[1]	1992	1993	1994[2]	1995[3]	Avg
VOLUME												
World	3.7%	5.5%	5.0%	8.8%	7.3%	4.4%	5.6%	5.7%	5.3%	9.4%	7.1%	7.5%
Developed Market Economies	4.7	2.4	4.4	8.7	7.4	5.1	3.8	4.4	3.0	8.4	6.5	5.3
Developing Economies	1.0	17.5	7.5	10.0	8.9	4.6	11.3	9.6	11.7	11.8	8.6	9.3
VALUE												
World	1.3	9.5	16.7	13.8	8.1	13.5	2.3	7.0	–0.2	12.0	11.5	16.3
Developed Market Economies	3.4	16.1	16.6	14.4	7.1	15.3	2.0	5.9	–3.0	11.3	11.3	9.1
Developing Economies	–3.0	–6.8	20.2	15.6	13.1	11.2	5.4	10.3	7.7	13.7	13.3	9.2

[1] 1991 and beyond reflect German unification.
[2] 1994 estimated.
[3] 1995 projected.

Note: For the 9-year period 1987–1995, the average growth in trade value for the Developing Nations was 12.3%.

Source: United Nations, *World Economic and Social Survey, 1995*, pp. 315–316.

TABLE 6–15

ANNUAL CHANGE IN TRADE PRICES AND TERMS OF TRADE
FOR DEVELOPING NATIONS

	1985	1986	1987	1988	1989	1990	1991	1992	1993	1994[1]	1995[2]
Export Prices	3.2%	–16.7%	12.2%	5.6%	3.9%	6.7%	–4.9%	0.3%	–3.8%	1.8%	4.5%
Import Prices	–2.0	3.8	11.6	6.1	1.3	7.5	–1.3	1.4	–2.9	2.6	5.2
Terms of Trade	–1.3	–19.8	0.6	–0.5	2.6	–0.7	–3.7	–1.1	–1.0	–0.8	–0.6

[1] 1994 estimated.
[2] 1995 projected.

Source: United Nations, *World Economic and Social Survey, 1995*, pp. 316–317.

Positive Accomplishments

1. Maintained share of world total exports
2. Increased total volume
3. Increased total value
4. Achieved better export prices
5. Improved share of "new products"

Negative Accomplishments

1. Continued growth in population
2. Declined in GDP/capita
3. Suffered higher import prices
4. Suffered deteriorating terms of trade

Despite the substantial advances made in trade during this period, its value for accumulating investment capital was minimal because of unfavorable conditions both internally and externally. Remember, however, that because of the vast dissimilarities among the Developing Nations, what is true of the group may have little relevance to any single country. In trade as in investment and development of human capital, the disparities are huge. There is, for instance, literally no comparability between Taiwan and any of the Least Developed Countries in economic or social terms as there is none between China's recent surge and the chronic stagnation of sub-Saharan Africa.

Foreign Direct Investment The third principal remedy of the conventional theory of development is foreign direct investment, in which foreign governments and corporations actually enter the developing economy and create and operate production facilities. This differs from portfolio investment, which is the purchase of stocks, bonds, and other financial assets. A company such as General Motors may sell shares to portfolio investors and use the revenue for direct investment in a developing economy, say, by building a stamping plant in Indonesia.

Table 6–16 indicates the magnitude of foreign direct investment from 1980 to 1990 and compares investment flow to developed economies and developing. From the perspective of the Developing World, while the amount is substantial, the ratio of preference is clearly deteriorating in favor of the industrialized economies. As a measure of production, Developing World affiliates of American corporations rarely account for more than 10 percent of the total exports of overseas affiliates everywhere. And in the 1986–1989 period, only eight developing economies relied on foreign direct investment for more than 10 percent of all capital formation: Nigeria, Guatemala, Hong Kong, Papua New Guinea, Botswana, Seychelles, Singapore, and Swaziland.[15] In 1993, only six Developing Nations

---

[15] United Nations, *World Investment Report, 1992*, p. 61.

TABLE 6–16

FOREIGN DIRECT INVESTMENT INFLOWS

	Avg. 1980–85	1986	1987	1988	1989	1990
To Developed Economies	$37.2 billion	$64.1 billion	$108.0 billion	$128.6 billion	$165.4 billion	$152.0 billion
To Developing Economies	12.6	14.2	25.0	29.7	29.8	31.8

Source: United Nations, *World Investment Report, 1992*, pp. 311–312.

had net capital flows (net of inflows and outflows) in excess of $2 billion:

China	$25.8 billion	Malaysia	$4.3 billion
Argentina	6.3	Thailand	2.4
Mexico	4.9	Indonesia	2.0

This suggests that from an external investor's perspective, South Korea, Taiwan, and Singapore are saturated and unlikely to yield high dividends to additional foreign direct investment.

Advocates of increased foreign investment enumerate the following advantages of foreign capital:[16]

1. **Jobs.** Most positions created by foreign firms go to indigenous workers. For example, U.S. multinational enterprises operating in the developing countries employ more than 3 million locals, as against only 25,000 American nationals located abroad.

2. **Technology.** The foreign firm brings the most advanced methods and technologies, acting as an agent for the transfer of new knowledge. This spills over to local subcontractors as production is integrated in the local economy.

3. **Import substitution.** Foreign investment often helps the balance of payments of a developing nation by enabling it to produce for itself what it once imported.

4. **Market access.** The foreign firm brings international market connections conducive to a continued inflow of capital and the expansion of export opportunities.

5. **Efficiency.** The profit incentive is keyed to cost reduction and the maximum use of resources. The foreign investor has a natural motive and the managerial skills to organize local people and information in the most cost-effective and productive way.

6. **Demonstration effect.** Local enterprises may be induced to utilize the techniques and management ideas of the efficient foreign branch to maintain their competitive position.

7. **Planning.** International investors are in an excellent position to assess the comparative advantages of local production in world markets, and they may aid in the identification of ideal lead sectors for planned national economic development.

For all these reasons, the politically more conservative voices in the Developing World reject the isolationist course of a closed door to Western capitalism.[17]

Technical Assistance   A fourth form of international aid to the developing countries is technical assistance. Most of the world's research and development is conducted in the rich countries. If the

---

[16] Roberto Campos, "Economic Policy and Political Myths," in Paul E. Sigmund, ed., *The Ideologies of the Developing Nations* (New York: Praeger, 1967), pp. 418–424.

[17] Harry G. Johnson, "The Multinational Corporation as an Agency of Economic Development," in Barbara Ward, Lenore D'Anjou, and J. D. Runnals, eds., *The Widening Gap* (New York: Columbia University Press, 1971), pp. 242–251.

results of technological advances are to reach beyond the privileged peoples, means must be found to facilitate the transnational migration of knowledge, or technology transfer. Examples of technical assistance include the Atoms for Peace Program, under which the United States has given small atomic reactors and fissile materials to more than fifty countries to meet electrical power needs; the arid zone research program, under which the United States supports research on desalination of sea water by advanced means; and most significant of all, scientific advantages in agriculture known as the Green Revolution, which brings to Developing Nations modern cultivation techniques and new seed strains that dramatically increase farm productivity.

Using the new methods of the Green Revolution, the output of grain cereals (rice, corn, wheat) can be multiplied without any expansion of acreage or labor force. For example, high-yielding dwarf variety wheat, pioneered in Mexico, has a genetic potential double or triple that of the best yielders among older, tall-strawed varieties. With American help, this advance has been introduced, along with the necessary supporting improvements in fertilizer, insecticides, weed killers, irrigation, and machinery, on the Indian subcontinent with spectcular results. India increased its wheat production by 80 percent in four years, Pakistan by 60 percent in two. These two nations have long been known as major food-deficit sufferers, dependent on charitable imports. Now they are approaching not only self-sufficiency but even surplus and a capacity for export. Similar results have been seen in the rice crops of the Philippines and Sri Lanka. These advances not only overcome chronic agricultural deficiencies; they also stimulate the excess production that can be exported to raise investment capital and relieve problems with trade and payments problems.

There are, however, some costs that must be accounted for in the balance sheet of the Green Revolution. The intensive use of chemical fertilizers and insecticides raises ecological issues that are now familiar in the wealthier nations. Fish and wildlife are endangered, and the runoff carries excessive nutrients and poisons to the oceans, whose ability to sustain pollution is not infinite. The vulnerability of the new strains to disease requires increasing dosages of insecticide, with the long-term danger that new insect varieties will develop that are resistant to all known poisons.

There are also social problems associated with the Green Revolution. Advanced agriculture is based on the substitution of capital for labor to pay for machines, seeds, fertilizer, insecticides, and irrigation systems. As agriculture becomes capital intensive rather than labor intensive, small farmers are squeezed out. Agricultural employment may be reduced as productivity increases. Thus, the effect of the Green Revolution is to widen class disparities rather than to narrow them, increasing the characteristic stratification problem noted earlier. It may also promote urbanization, as farm employment dwindles. The initial beneficiaries of the Green Revolution may be the already prosperous rather than the suffering poor. But advocates of the conventional theory argue that the flood of benefits will inevitably trickle down to the lower classes and that the solution to maldistribution is rational planning rather than forgoing the potential benefits of new methods.

The benefits of technical assistance are not limited to the agricultural sector. In industry, computers and advanced electronic equipment have been transferred to the developing countries to improve productivity and to expand industrial potential. Computers have also been introduced to improve managerial efficiency and education. Advances in chemical technology have enabled many of the oil-rich developing countries to improve their own refining capabilities, thus permitting them to deliver finished products rather than crude oil to industrial consumers.

Furthermore, both governments and international organizations such as the United Nations make technical experts available to the developing countries. Faced with technical problems in management, industry, finance, or agriculture, developing countries can call upon foreign personnel for assistance. These persons are part of the network by which technology is gradually transferred to the Developing World from the industrialized centers.

The technological revolution, a product of a handful of industrialized countries, holds two benefits for the underindustrialized nations. First, it provides the instruments of technology to improve management, manufacturing, communications, transportation, and the like. Second, because wages are lower than those in the industrialized countries, the manufacture of technological goods offers opportunities for employment in parts of the Developing World in which political stability invites foreign plant construction. Indeed, this has become so common that many technology corporations in the United States, Japan, and Western Europe import virtually all their own manufactures, thus depriving their domestic labor forces of countless job opportunities. We have already seen, however, that this phenomenon is limited to a few Developing Nations, and so it does not spread the employment benefits very far.

The Radical (or Dependency) Theory of Development

The radical theory of development disagrees fundamentally with the foregoing view regarding both the causes and cures of underdevelopment. To the conventional theorist, the cause is internal inefficiency, and the cure is outside help from the developed states. To the radical, the cause is international exploitation by exactly these developed "friends," and the cure is a fundamental change of international relations between the poor and the rich. The very medicine proposed by the conventional theorist—technical assistance, foreign investment, trade, and aid—is considered the root of the disease by the radical, for whom investment, trade, and aid are extractive mechanisms that systematically siphon away the wealth of the developing countries.

The two schools disagree on basic assumptions regarding global inequality. To the conventional theorist, the rich are ahead of the poor because of dedicated effort and managerial skills. To the

radical, the Western peoples achieved their advantage "not by the laws of the market, but by a particular sequence of world conquest and land occupation."[18] It follows from the conventional view that when the poor make up the gap in productive skills (with the help of foreign aid and so on), the economic gap will close. It follows from the radical view that only cutting the international relationship will end the unjust division of the world's wealth.

The conventional view posits an essential similarity between the development problems of the poor today and those successfully mastered by the now-rich states in earlier periods. It says in effect, "Just as the United States and Europe developed yesterday and Mexico and Singapore are developing today, so will you, the late starters, develop tomorrow." Development is portrayed as a linear process in which every economy passes through certain known stages of economic growth.[19]

Radical analysis rejects this portrayal of the developing countries. The economies of the big capitalist states started as largely autonomous markets under domestic control, although international trade and investment were conducted within careful limits. The economies of the Developing World, however, enter the modern development epoch as mere subsystems of global capitalism, having long ago been penetrated by foreign interests and been made economic satellites of the dominant states of the North. The global system consists of a "center"—Europe, America, and Japan—and a "periphery"—the dependent economies of Latin America, Africa, and Asia. The basic economic institutions

---

[18] See Ward et al., eds., *The Widening Gap*, pp. 152–164, where the two views are eloquently contrasted. For major expressions of the radical theory, see Samir Amin, *Unequal Development* (New York: Monthly Review Press, 1976); and Paul Baran and Paul Sweezy, *Monopoly Capital* (New York: Monthly Review Press, 1966). See also Barbara Ward, *The Radical Economic World View* (New York: Basic Books, 1979). Gunnar Myrdal, *Against the Stream: Critical Essays on Economics* (New York: Vintage, 1972), presents some challenging critiques of the conventional theory of development.

[19] Walt W. Rostow, *The Stages of Economic Growth* (London: Cambridge University Press, 1960), is the standard source for this view.

of the dependencies were formed in response to the insistent demands of the industrial world, rather than in relation to local needs and interests. The typical dependency economy is geared to the export of commodities needed by the industrial center and the import of products from the center. This is known as the pattern of foreign-oriented development, in which external rather than domestic influences shape the society, economy, and political structure.

What produced this lopsided and unnatural development, so heavily dependent on foreign interests? In the earliest period, it was caused by massive raw material hunger on the part of the industrial nations. The underdeveloped regions, subdued and controlled by the superior military force of the center, were reduced to being cheap suppliers of raw materials, useful mainly for their wells, mines tea, or rubber. Cuba became a sugar plantation, Bolivia a tin mine, the Arab world an oil field, Southeast Asia a rubber plantation, Gabon (in Barbara Ward's phrase) "a faint appendage to a mineral deposit." In many cases, local impulses to produce industrial goods for home consumption were quelled by the dominant foreigners, as the dependency was needed as a secure market for exactly these products from the center. Thus foreign domination served to channel economic activity into a high degree of forced specialization.

In most of the developing nations, one main export item accounts for a much higher portion of foreign sales, unlike the export pattern in the rich nations. It is fair to say that the typical developing country is a one- or two-product exporter, whereas the typical developed nation has a diversified economy. Venezuela exports 90 percent oil; Colombia depends on coffee; Cuba has not escaped sugar dependence; and two-thirds of Chilean exports are copper. Should the mineral be exhausted (as is happening in Bolivia) or a cheaper source be found for the national product (such as the seabed), or should changing consumer preferences reduce demand, dependent economies could be destroyed. In other words, highly specialized economies are dangerously subject to the vicissitudes of the world market.

The Terms-of-Trade Problem

Despite the growth in the Developing Nation's manufactured exports, the export commodities in which they specialize tend to be primary products—minerals, fuel, and crops taken more or less directly from the earth, with minimal processing. The principal exceptions, as we have seen, are in East and South Asia, and all are listed in Table 6–17. This commodity composition of trade adversely affects developing economies. One reason is the tendency of primary product export prices to fluctuate substantially and sometimes extremely in the world market. When large portions of an economic activity and a labor force are tied to export products that are so unstable in the world market, resulting wild boom-and-bust cycles may be socially hazardous and detrimental to orderly economic development. Furthermore, development economists consider this kind of price decay with respect to industrial products an intrinsic inequality in trade

TABLE 6–17

MOST INDUSTRIALIZED DEVELOPING NATIONS, 1993, IN MANUFACTURING AS PERCENTAGE OF GNP

Greater than 35%	China		
30–34	Zimbabwe		
25–29	Singapore	South Korea	Thailand
20–24	Argentina	Brazil	Ecuador
	El Salvador	Indonesia	Mauritius
	Mexico	Peru	Philippines
	South Africa	Vietnam	Zambia
17–19	Costa Rica	India	Jamaica
	Morocco	Tunisia	Turkey
	Uruguay		

Reference:
   Germany = 27%
   Japan = 24%

Note: This source does not list either Taiwan or Hong Kong, each of which is probably around 30%.

Source: World Bank, World Development Report, 1995, pp. 166–167.

between the industrialized world and the Developing World.[20]

The relationship between world prices for primary products and those for industrial products is at the heart of the terms-of-trade problem for the developing economies. Defined as export value divided by import value, terms of trade becomes a measure of the extent to which international trade assists in the development of a national economy. On balance, the Developing Nations conduct their most disadvantageous trade with the developed market economies because in the terms of that trade, primary products are exported at unstable and declining world prices, whereas industrial produce is imported at stable and increasing prices. Nonetheless, trade with the developed market economies continues to be a larger part of the aggregate trade, thus annually accentuating the terms-of-trade dilemma. As a consequence, billions of dollars have been drained out of the Developing World simply by loss of value relative to industrial goods. It is significant that this drain results not from explicit imperialism or exploitation but, rather, from the quiet operation of market laws seemingly beyond anyone's control—so-called objective world market prices.

Productivity Increases   The terms-of-trade factor puts the poor states in a position that cannot be compared with that of the rich states in an earlier period. The now-advanced states achieved rapid increases in productivity during their "takeoff" stage, and these are regarded as the key to their success. But today, the primary price decay erodes productivity gains. Malaysia, for example, increased its rubber exports almost 25 percent from 1960 to 1968—from 850,000 to 1.1 million tons—while significantly reducing its plantation labor force. This is a notable gain in productivity. But its income

from rubber sales declined by about 33 percent during these years, as prices fell. In effect, productivity increases were passed along to foreign consumers in the form of lower prices, rather than to Malaysian workers in the form of higher wages and living standards. The terms-of-trade problem can be a treadmill on which it is necessary to run faster and faster just to stand still.

Inelastic Demand   Explanations of this phenomenon are based on the disadvantages of primary products against those of finished goods. One is the relative inelasticity of demand for primary goods—only so many bananas will be consumed no matter how many are produced, tending to reduce prices after the market is saturated.

Unorganized Labor   Another factor is the position of labor in the Developing World compared with that of the industrial countries. Workers in the advanced states are relatively well organized into trade unions and can command a share of the gains from productivity increases. The comparative weakness of labor organizations in the developing economies, however, allows productivity gains to be taken by management in the form of profits or to be passed on to consumers in the form of lower prices. Productivity gains in the center are taken at home, but productivity gains in the periphery tend to flow away—to the center—in the form of lower prices or in profits remitted to foreign owners. The deck is stacked in favor of the already developed world, and mere productivity advances of the type advocated by the conventional theorists will not change the unfavorable rules.

The Radical View of Foreign Investment

Although the conventional theorist views the multinational corporation as an agency for the transfer of capital and technology for the advancement of developing countries, the radical theorist sees it as an instrument of foreign control extracting exorbitant profits. United States investment, for example, increases its capital annually in both the

---

[20] Two classics developing this view from different perspectives are the United Nations Conference on Trade and Development, *Towards a New Trade Policy for Development* (1964), universally known as the Prebisch Report; and Arghiri Emmanuel, *Unequal Exchange: The Imperialism of International Trade* (New York: Monthly Review Press, 1972).

developed and the developing economies, but the annual earnings yielded to American investors in the Developing Nations greatly exceed those in the indusrialized economies. Table 6–18 illustrates this fact, showing that earnings on investments in the developing economies (measured as a percentage of total investment) in the 1970s were more than two times as great as in the developed economies. The gap narrowed considerably in the 1980s due to global economic conditions and the politics of oil. In the current decade, the gap has widened again: investments in the Developing Nations yield about twice the percentage return as they do in developed economies. The greatest advantage continues to be in exploiting primary products.

In the radical theory of development, these findings indicate an accelerated rate of economic penetration and exploitation of the Developing World by the developed nations in the guise of direct private investment. Because earnings gained on these investments are returned to the industrialized economies rather than left as investment funds in the host economy, American and other Western investors are actually decapitalizing the underdeveloped.

Another objection to foreign capital is its effect on the social and class structure of the host society. The foreign firm is at first typically an isolated enclave of modern economics in a sea of underdevelopment, but eventually a network of subcontractors extends the patterns of dependency outside the company gates. Often the multinational guest dwarfs all local enterprises. The sales revenue of the United Fruit Company, for example, exceeds the entire national budgets of countries such as Panama, Nicaragua, Honduras, Guatemala, and El Salvador. The pure economic power of such an entity opens the doors of the middle and even the top strata of the official bureaucracy and creates at the same time a dependent class of local merchants and bankers. In addition, the foreign firm develops a special relationship with certain privileged sections of the labor force, sometimes by paying wages slightly above the depressed local rates. United States firms in northern Mexico, for example, can pay wages well above the local average, but a

TABLE 6–18

AMERICAN INVESTMENT EARNINGS IN INDUSTRIALIZED AND DEVELOPING ECONOMIES AS PERCENTAGE OF TOTAL INVESTMENT

Year	Industrial Economies	Developing Economies
1970s (average)	11.5%	25.8%
1980s (average)	13.3	16.6
1992	7.6	16.5
1993	8.8	15.5
1994	8.9	14.6

Sources: Annual editions of the Statistical Abstract of the United States; and Survey of Current Business, August 1989 and June 1995.

fraction of wages for comparable work in southern Texas. Local workers are co-opted by the competition for these prized jobs. In effect, foreign capital creates satellite classes whose interests are tied to the *dependencia* syndrome. Mexico's attraction to the North America Free Trade Agreement (NAFTA) hinged largely on exploiting this, and the objections of American labor were based on the fear that jobs would "move south" for exactly this reason.

Objections to Foreign Aid

For several reasons, even foreign aid is regarded with suspicion in the radical theory. First, most foreign aid consists not of simple grants but of interest-bearing loans that must be repaid. The typical developing economy runs a chronic payments deficit because of the unfavorable balance of trade and the drain of excess profits to foreign firms. Borrowing foreign aid to make up the gap in current bills leads to mounting indebtedness and simply defers the day of reckoning, accumulating losses to be repaid in some future golden age. Borrowing from Peter to pay Paul (or "rolling over" the debt) does not break the pattern of dependency but reinforces and perpetuates it. Throughout the 1980s Developing Nations made annual payments on principal and interest payments that averaged about 150 percent of their annual export value. No matter how much their exports improved, their debt deepened. Table 6–19 shows the 1993 annual debt obligations of selected Developing World debtors compared with 1980. (For 1980, the given figure for each country is the sum of payment due on principal and interest payment.) Only Mexico and Morocco have shown significant improvement, and most of the rest are locked more firmly in the debt trap. The consequence is that the value of their exports for accumulating development capital is eroding severely, deepening their dependence on foreign capital and adding still more to their debt burden. To the radical theorist, therefore, aid begets not capital but new layers of debt.

Alternative Futures

Throughout the development era (1960 to the present), the debate regarding international economic development has been conducted principally between the traditionalists (who focus on modernization strategies) and the radicals (who concentrate on global practices that perpetuate dependency). But new approaches to the problem have been suggested. One argues that neither of the two dominant theories can explain the late development of some countries, because economic advancement is not necessarily tied exclusively to economic factors. This observation leads to the conclusion that disparate paths to development must consider such local sociological factors as traditions, motives, attitudes, and religious influences on traditionalism and modernism.[21]

A second effort at expanding the debate begins with the premise that in each developing state, class formation, capital formation, and the formalization of state authority take place at different times and at different rates. Furthermore,

TABLE 6–19

ANNUAL DEBT OBLIGATION OF SELECTED DEVELOPING NATIONS AS PERCENTAGE OF EXPORTS

	1980	1990		
Total		Due on principal	Interest	Total
Uganda	21.0%	143.6%	25.6%	169.2%
Algeria	34.8	76.9	15.0	91.9
Bolivia	56.1	59.4	16.0	75.4
Peru	64.4	58.7	23.8	82.5
Argentina	58.1	46.0	25.3	71.3
Zambia	34.0	32.8	14.8	47.6
Nicaragua	35.7	29.1	15.9	45.0
Morocco	49.7	31.7	13.0	44.7
Uruguay	29.4	27.7	16.5	44.2
India	13.5	28.0	14.8	42.8
Indonesia	20.5	31.8	11.0	42.8
Mexico	74.7	31.5	10.5	42.0
Zimbabwe	5.3	31.1	10.5	41.6
Turkey	42.9	28.3	13.1	41.4
Colombia	27.6	29.4	10.1	39.5

Source: World Bank, *World Development Report, 1995,* pp. 200–201 and 206–207.

contemporary conditions render some of these states authoritarian, others nationalistic, and some dependent on external economies. The conclusion is that social interests and state policies influence dependency. They multiply development possibilities and create a variety of change patterns that neither the traditional theory nor the dependency theory can explain.[22]

A third observation notes that in addition to the world's economic center and its periphery, there exists a semiperiphery of developing economies

---

[21] Ogura Mitsuo, "The Sociology of Development and Issues Surrounding Late Development," *International Studies Quarterly,* December 1982, pp. 596–625, trans. David Olson.

[22] Michael Bratton, "Patterns of Development and Underdevelopment: Toward a Comparison," *International Studies Quarterly,* September 1982, pp. 333–372.

that are already fairly industrialized or are industrializing rapidly. For them, development is led by manufactured exports rather than by agricultural or other primary export products. As a result, there are different paths to development that are not recognized by either of the dominant theories.[23]

Viewed through the lenses of modern history, it becomes apparent that routes to development other than aid, trade, and technical assistance have been tried.

The Chinese Model

Some voices in the developing countries, such as the ruling party in Tanzania and the Maoist groups in Latin America, find a useful example for the poor nations in the Chinese experience. Before the communists took power, China's industrial and commercial sectors were thoroughly penetrated by foreign influence, to the extent that the national currency was printed in English on one side. As late as 1935, foreigners controlled 95 percent of China's iron, three-quarters of its coal, half of its textile production, and most of its shipping, public utilities, banking, insurance, and trade. Most industrial workers were employed by foreign firms, and the Chinese social structure showed many of the typical symptoms of what we now call the dependency syndrome. The corrective steps taken by the communists after 1949 were harsh, but they succeeded in cutting the ties of dependency and putting China on a self-reliant path of rapid development. China in effect virtually sealed its borders to capitalist trade and investment and adopted an economic policy of isolation and autarky for twenty years.

Could the Chinese example of the closed door and almost total self-reliance be imitated by other developing countries? Probably not. China is a world in itself, a nation of more than a billion people providing a huge internal market with diversified resources and productive potentials. The thirty countries of sub-Saharan Africa taken together have less than 25 percent of this population base; individually, most developing countries are much smaller. Most economists agree that the cost of isolationism to a small country would be a substantially reduced rate of growth, if not economic collapse. Historians and political theorists seem to agree that the rule of Chinese communism is consistent with a centuries-long authoritarian tradition that always had one form or another of social and political structure, all of them involving power. These underlying conditions are not, in the main, present in today's developing countries, and so the model is not applicable. To the extent that the Chinese model was used by North Korea or Cambodia, it has been a total failure. To the extent it was used in Vietnam, it has been abandoned.

Perhaps the most telling evaluation of the Maoist model is that since it was largely abandoned fifteen years ago, China has made greater strides toward modernization than it did in the centuries before. The new method is akin to the standard Western model, including mutilateral aid, some bilateral aid, and much foreign direct investment. China remains highly authoritarian in social policy, but rather liberal in economic policy. It seems, therefore, that the China model to which some looked a decade or two ago is no longer in place.

Regional Integration

Another alternative is consolidating small economies within a region into a single large one. Present experiments in economic integration among Developing Nations include the East African Common Market, the Arab Common Market, the Central American Common Market, and the Latin American Free Trade Association. Degrees of integration range from the free trade area (where tariffs on trade among members are eliminated), through the customs union (where a common external tariff is added to the free trade area), to the common market (where labor and capital as well as goods and services are permitted to move freely).

---

[23] James A. Caporaso, "Industrialization in the Periphery: The Evolving Global Division of Labor," *International Studies Quarterly*, September 1981, pp. 347–384.

Later steps in economic integration may include monetary union (a common currency and banking system), the merger of tax systems, and finally a single regional budget including a shared defense budget.

Each stage of economic integration has political costs as well as benefits, and inevitably some elites will gain from a merger while others will lose. The success of Developing Nations in achieving regional integration is partly a function of the relative strengths of these forces not only nationally, but transnationally as well. Unless domestic elites find sympathetic counterparts in the other participating nations, behavioral barriers will prevent integration. Institution-building is a complex process in any circumstances, but it is most difficult when social and political forces are unable to unite across national boundaries.

Another obstacle to regional economic integration is the fear that the costs and benefits of cooperation will be distributed unequally. Experience has shown that without special preferential measures favoring the less developed members of a group, the benefits of integration are likely to be concentrated in the more advanced countries, while a disproportionate share of the costs will be borne by the less advanced ones. In theory, this inequality could be relieved by asymmetrical tariff policies providing a higher degree of protection for a prolonged transition period for the less developed states, as well as directly subsidizing their development in key sectors. But in practice, even the more advanced members of a regional grouping tend to experience developmental strains, and national priorities rather than mutual interests tend to prevail. Moreover, the economic systems of neighboring states may have a limited potential for integration. States whose previous economic development was geared to the export of highly specialized products to the developed countries may find difficult the expansion of trade with fellow developing countries. The noncomplementarity of developing economies explains their tendency to concentrate the volume of trade on distant, more advanced partners rather than on their neighbors.

Another obstacle to integration is the national pride of newly independent countries and the mutual hostility of some adjoining states. Integration requires a sacrifice of unrestricted autonomy in favor of joint decision making, and this in turn requires mutual trust and a willingness to accept a shared fate.[24] Many developing peoples, especially those that gained independence within the past two decades, seem to prefer a go-it-alone strategy. Indeed, intra-African economic integration has declined rather than ·increased since the collapse of the colonial empires, and dependence on the center paradoxically has increased. During the colonial period, integration was forced on diverse neighbors by their European masters, such as the French-imposed West African Customs Union and the Equatorial African Customs Union. Britain established a common market, a common currency, and common railways and other services in the East African colonies of Kenya, Uganda, and Tanganyika. Since independence, however, these cooperative arrangements largely have been dismantled. The lines of commerce and communication from most developing nations thus flow not to their neighbors but to the nations of the center, like spokes to a hub. This is especially true of the former French empire, the former members of which are held in close economic alliance with France by two multilateral treaties.[25]

Commodity Producer Cartels

In reality, many developing countries seem destined to be primary product exporters for years to come. Means of quickening the pace of economic development will have to be found within the

---

[24] D. C. Mead, "The Distribution of Gains in Customs Unions Between Developing Countries," *Kyklos*, vol. 21, pp. 713–734; R. F. Mikesell, "The Theory of Common Market as Applied to Regional Arrangements Among Developing Countries," in R. F. Harrod and D. C. Hague, eds., *International Trade Theory in a Developing World* (New York: Macmillan, 1963), pp. 205–229.
[25] Dharam P. Ghai, "Perspectives on Future Economic Prospects and Problems in Africa," in Jagdish Bhagwati, ed., *Economics and World Order* (New York: Macmillan, 1972), pp. 265–266.

present framework of commodity specialization. For this reason, some governments are looking for agreements among producers of primary products to regulate and improve the world prices of their commodities.

The outstanding example of success for such producer groups is OPEC, which succeeded in raising the world price of crude oil more than 900 percent between 1973 and 1982. Petroleum exporters with large populations, such as Nigeria and Indonesia, suddenly had the capital resources to finance development at a greatly expanded pace. Exporters with small populations, such as Saudi Arabia, Kuwait, and the United Arab Emirates, bought rags-to-riches luxuries and accumulated huge and unprecedented financial surpluses with which to influence other countries, even the great powers. The entire world watched as Saudi Arabia, once described as "rushing madly from the eleventh century into the twelfth," banked a $30 billion surplus in one year, while Great Britain, on whose empire the sun was never to set, was at its feet.

Oil is, of course, a very special commodity in international trade, and it has enormous political power. As the lifeblood of modern industrial society, any substantial halt in its flow could topple the great industrial economies of the West, and more so Japan, which is almost totally dependent on imported fuels. For a decade after 1973 it was an open secret that gaining leverage over OPEC was the first priority of American eocnmic foreign policy. A second oil embargo would have been a uniquely potent weapon to the West's disadvantage in the North-South Dialogue.

Oil's monetary value is its second noteworthy attribute. The revenue from trade in oil makes minuscule that of all other raw materials and fuels combined, and oil trade has a more profound impact on the balances of payments of the industrial states than do all other forms of trade, industrial and agricultural. From the West's vantage point, the balance-of-trade issue is magnified by the small populations of some of the OPEC states, because their import needs are small in relation to their export volume. This contributes to balance-of-trade

deficits among OPEC's customers. For the United States, for example, oil imports alone added $10 billion to the trade deficit of 1979 and $14 billion more in 1980. In contrast, from 1970 through 1981, Saudi Arabia multiplied its currency reserves by 5000 percent, Kuwait by 2400 percent, and the United Arab Emirates by 3500 percent, all from cash remitted to cover the unbalanced trade.

The pattern of dependency between North and South, at least insofar as fuel was concerned, was reversed during the glory days of OPEC. OPEC's experience seemed to demonstrate that a Developing Nations cartel in a primary product badly needed by the industrial economies would be a most advantageous route to economic development. This sentiment continued even though a series of external circumstances and internal disagreements caused OPEC to lose control of the world petroleum market in the mid-1980s, declining from its peak influence in 1980, and OPEC has been a minor force since the Desert Storm War of 1991. Table 6–20 correlates daily production with value of exports from 1970 through 1994 (estimated). It shows that from 1970 to 1980, production increased by 14 percent, but the value of exports rose by 1826 percent! This was all due to increases in the price per barrel. After 1985 the relationship between production and price stabilized in reflection of the declining power of the cartel.

Nevertheless, to the extent that OPEC succeeded in advancing its goals, the question remains whether the cartel experience can be duplicated by other producer groups. Members of the Intergovernmental Committee of Copper Exporting Countries, the Union of Banana Exporting Countries, the International Tin Council, and at least a dozen other commodity groups hope so, but professional observers disagree on their prospects. Five conditions determine whether a cartel will be durable and effective.[26]

---

[26] Adapted from Steven D. Krasner, "Oil Is the Exception," *Foreign Policy*, spring 1974, pp. 68–90.

TABLE 6-20

OPEC OIL: RELATION OF VOLUME[1] TO VALUE[2]

	1970	1980	1985	1988	1989	1990	1993	1994
Volume	23.3	26.6	15.8	19.7	21.4	22.9	24.7	24.9
Change	—	14%	(41%)	25%	7%	7%	8%	1%
Value	14.5	279.3	128.9	86.4	111.2	144.7	126.0	116.1
Change	—	1826%	(54%)	(33%)	29%	30%	(13%)	(8%)

[1] Millions of barrels produced per day.
[2] $ millions in current value.

Source: United Nations, *World Economic and Social Survey, 1995*, pp. 344–345.

1. **Price elasticity of demand.** Demand must be relatively unresponsive to price. If a commodity is important to consumers, and substitutes are not readily available, then price increases can be imposed without a severe loss of sales. This is the case with oil, and it is also believed to be true of minerals such as copper and aluminum and some foods such as coffee. Other products, such as natural rubber and bananas, have a more elastic demand and cannot increase in price without also curtailing sales.

2. **Limited number of producers.** A relatively small number of producers controlling a relatively large share of total world exports in a commodity is ideal for collusion. This condition is met by at least eight major commodities in which the top four developing economies produce over half of world exports. Moreover, there must be high barriers to entry against new producers—that is, it must be difficult for new competitors to break into a market by underselling the cartel price. This also is true for many commodities, whether because of the limits of raw material sources, climatic and soil conditions, the start-up costs of production, or other factors.

3. **Shared experience of producers.** Producing states must be aware of their interdependence and be willing to cooperate and act as a limited economic coalition. This condition also is met by producers of several commodities, although in other cases the necessary basis of shared values is less evident.

4. **Consumer resistance.** The probability of a cartel's success will decline if consumers are organized for effective resistance. In the petroleum market, the position of the major oil companies is believed to have facilitated collusion among the exporting countries. But other commodity markets lack such vehicles, and the probability of resistance may be higher.

5. **Ability to take a long-term perspective.** Cartel members must be prepared to accept short-term costs for long-term gains. The market may contract severely as buyers resist the inflated price and draw down their inventories. The oil-exporting states were in a good position to curtail production, as they could live for some time on the substantial capital reserves previously accumulated. Also, the production of oil is not labor intensive, and relatively few workers were idled by the deliberate slow-down. Countries with small financial reserves and high proportions of the labor force dependent on export production are in a poor position to pay the short-term costs of cartelization. The temptation to cheat may be irresistible to the poorer cartel members, who will be able to take advantage of the situation by price shaving. In no other commodity are

producing countries in as strong a position to accept short-term costs as in oil.

Is cartelization of other primary commodities, then, probable or improbable? The evidence is ambiguous, but some Western observers believe that the developed world will face "one, two, many OPECs,"[27] and some Developing World leaders believe that cartels are the best opportunity for the developing economies truly to redress global inequalities. Should this become a common pattern, especially as natural resources approach exhaustion, some fear widespread economic warfare.

Others call for cooperation between the producing and the consuming states to raise the income of the primary producers with minimum disruption to the international economy. Developing World spokespersons believe that the global redistribution of wealth is long overdue and that increases in prices of exports of developing countries will be a principal means of achieving it. The rich countries have become used to a terms-of-trade structure that must be changed, and they are finding the transition painful. This is not a sufficient reason to perpetuate old patterns and deepen the dependency to which the Developing World is subjected.

Russia may be expected to support the Developing World on this issue. It is the world's leading producer of petroleum and capable of being a substantial exporter. The change in the price of oil achieved by OPEC resulted in direct gains to the USSR of about $2 billion per year in export earnings. Russian-American joint ventures have already commenced to try to develop Russia's oil-exporting potential. As a major producer of other primary products as well, Russia would be strengthened by further revision in the terms of trade particularly

related to the NATO allies and Japan, the world's major raw materials importers.

The Developing Nations and the New World Order

As the world turned its attention from the Cold War, there was a renewed concern that the 1980s had been a dismal decade for most of the Developing World. For the Least Developed Countries in particular, "the 1980s can be considered in general as a period of set-backs." So declared the Second United Nations Conference on the Least Developed Countries in its *Paris Declaration and Programme for Action for the 1990s*.[28] To reverse the losses of the preceding decade, the conference report, later adopted by the General Assembly, called on the industrialized states to raise their donations to the Least Developed Countries to within a range of 0.15 and 0.2 percent of gross domestic product per year. For coordinating purposes, it recommended that aid be funneled through the United Nations and other multilateral agencies. It also called for commodity price stabilization to improve income from trade, and for a number of internal reforms including population control.

On the broader issue of development, the 1990s have been years of heightened recognition of the constituent problems and of multilateral debate, but progress has been difficult to measure. Four major world conferences addressed specific aspects of development:

> *The United Nations Conference on the Environment and Development* (1992) at Rio de Janeiro focused on specific environmental issues such as deforestation, desertification, ozone depletion, greenhouse gases, and their weather-altering consequences.

---

[27] See especially C. Fred Bergsten, "The Threat from the Third World," *Foreign Policy*, summer 1973; and his "The Threat Is Real," *Foreign Policy*, spring 1974.

[28] UNCTAD, *Paris Declartion and Programme of Action for the Least Developed Countries for the 1990s* (1992).

The United Nations Conference on Population and Development (1994) at Cairo dealt with the controversial problem of population control as a device for ensuring the value of increases in exports and in gross domestic product per capita.

The United Nations Conference on the Status of Women (1995) explored proposals regarding women's rights in general, but with a particular goal of including women in productive roles in Developing Nations.

The World Conference on Human Settlements, Habitat II (1996) at Istanbul looked at general issues of housing, but concentrated on the social and economic consequences of uncontrolled urbanization in the Developing Nations.

In preparation for this activity, the General Assembly charged Secretary-General Boutros-Ghali to submit a comprehensive agenda for development, which he did in 1995.[29] To the frustration of the Developing World, neither the agenda nor the several world conferences produced anything significantly tangible.

Once again as they had in the 1970s, the Developing Nations seized the initiative. Concerned that the United Nations, structured as it was around the political realities of the Cold War, was inadequate to meet their needs in the New World Order, the Developing Nations called for, among other things, a restructuring of the organization to reflect more accurately the new political realities, including a revision of the Security Council membership.

The Developing Nations themselves have carried out two important changes in the early years of the New World Order. First, with very few exceptions, they have embraced the conventional route to development, that is, aid, trade, technical assistance, and foreign direct investment. Those that are new to it have undertaken it with care not to fall into the debt trap, though they are in danger of overheating their economies and suffering setbacks. Second, despite the continued conflict in places such as Angola, Rwanda, Mozambique, and Sri Lanka, the orgy of spending on imported arms seems to have been stemmed. (This is not true of China, Taiwan, India or Pakistan.) Technically, this should improve economic conditions, provided that the industrialized countries are as willing to provide credits for the purchase of vitally needed items as they were to underwrite arms exports a decade ago. One of the tests of the New World Order will be the record in this important regard.

The voice of the Developing Nations has been restored from the disappointments of the 1980s. Absent the Cold War, they have a new opportunity to influence the priorities of the industrialized states, especially as the United States adjusts itself to an entirely different style of global leadership, an adjustment that is still in progress, and while Russia determines how it will peform its role as a great power when its greatness has been diminished severely. But progress is not measured in units of oration or exhortation. As the century wound down to its final thirty-six months, the Developing World in general and the Least Developed Countries in particular remained unable to convert lofty global intentions into material progress.

---

[29] Boutros Boutros-Ghali, *An Agenda for Development, 1995* (New York: United Nations, 1995).

CHAPTER 7

Power

The previous chapters have been concerned with values, perceptions, and goals of key actors in today's international system. This section focuses on the instruments of foreign policy and the ways that systems of international relations constrain states in their goals. We will move from the level of actors to that of systems and interrelationships.

The Nature of Power

What is power in international relations? We may define it broadly as the ability of an actor on the international stage to use tangible and intangible resources and assets in such a way as to influence the outcomes of international events to its own satisfaction. This definition points out some of the important features in the relationship of influence among actors. First, power is the means by which international actors deal with one another. It implies possession, specifically a collection of possessions to create an ability. Second, power is not a natural political attribute, but a product of material (tangible) and behavioral (intangible) resources, each of which has its unique place in the totality of the actor's power. Third, power is a means of achieving influence over other actors who are competing for outcomes favorable to their objectives. And fourth, the rational use of power is an attempt to shape the outcome of events in a way that will maintain or improve the actor's satisfaction with the international political environment. The

derived satisfaction measures the degree to which the national policymaking elite perceives its objectives to have been served by the prevailing international norms.

These characteristics of power suggest others. It is important, for example, to think of power as having an instrumental character: Power is a means to an end, an instrument for achieving objectives, but not an end in itself. Possession of power is meaningless if its application cannot deliver results that enhance the wielder's self-interest. Furthermore, power is relative rather than absolute. When two states compete over an objective, their abilities to exert power may be roughly equal (a symmetrical power relationship) or severely unequal (an asymmetrical power relationship). So it is important when assessing power to ask, "Powerful relative to whom or to what?" We know, for example, that in 1990 Iraq was sufficiently powerful to overrun Kuwait, but the same Iraqi weapons were virtually impotent in the face of the modern counteroffensive launched by an American-led UN coalition only months later.

Moreover, the use of power may have diminishing returns. In South Vietnam, for example, the United States used virtually all military means short of nuclear weapons to subdue North Vietnam, yet, despite all its firepower, failed. The North Vietnamese and Viet Cong, infinitely less powerful militarily, exploited both national will and deteriorating American support for the war to achieve politically what they could not gain militarily: governmental self-determination and the expulsion of

185

American forces. The diminishing returns of American firepower, together with the superior intangible resources available to North Vietnam, redressed the apparent asymmetry of their relationship. Some forms of power are impotent indeed!

Vivid as military examples may be, not all power relationships are measured in armaments. In fact, it should be said categorically that power is not force, and the ability to exert power is not limited to forceful situations. Indeed, international actors exercise their power unceasingly; yet so rarely, given the huge volume of international transactions, do they resort to force that it is considered an aberration of the normal power relations between states. Force resides at the extreme end of a continuum of choices available for manipulating events to satisfactory outcomes.

At the other extreme of that continuum is persuasion, or the achievement of goals by the power of reason. Regrettably, it is appropriate only in situations in which two or more actors have similar objectives, or in which one asks but a small alteration in the policy of another in an event that is not crucial to the latter. Beyond these rare cases, the achievement of influence depends on the relative availability of positive and negative sanctions to affect the behavior of the other party. Positive sanctions are rewards or inducements to concur in a particular policy. One government, for example, may offer a major concession to another for its support on an unrelated issue, such as the United States offering to cancel certain Egyptian debts in exchange for Cairo's assistance against Iraq. When such enticements fail, the same government may resort to negative sanctions—punishments or deprivations—to alter another's policy. It may threaten to rupture diplomatic relations, to discontinue trade, or any of countless other deprivations. Or in situations crucial to its satisfaction, an actor can threaten or use force. Force, then, is the result of an escalation in the power relationship between actors.

Choice among these methods of exerting power depends on several factors in the relationship of the parties. Foremost is the importance of the outcome. A government will not threaten nuclear war over issues of marginal importance. In addition, the choice of methods depends in part on the access that one actor has to another. Specifically, if the relationship includes a general agreement on international satisfaction, then persuasion and rewards will normally be adequate. Equally important, however, is the degree of similarity in the respective interpretations of the specific issue. For example, since the Second World War, the United States and Britain have enjoyed an extraordinarily high degree of mutuality on general issues of international satisfaction. Yet they broke sharply over the British role in the Suez War of 1956, with the United States resorting to diplomatic embarrassment—public withholding of concurrence—to alter British policy. In some cases the problem has another dimension, one in which one government is simply unable to reach another. This was particularly true in the Cold War years when in order to exert power over America's allies, the Soviet Union had to contend with American responses; and in dealing with the governments of Eastern Europe, the United States was faced with Soviet counteractions.

In all of these situations, one actor has power over the other when it enjoys a superior power position relative to the issue at hand, although not necessarily an asymmetrical advantage on all issues. In all cases diplomatic effectiveness is linked to the capabilities that underlie policy. In cases of ultimate confrontation, it is linked to the state's military capabilities.

The Ingredients of Power Potential

Power is a mixture of capabilities derived from both domestic sources and international activities. Furthermore, power comes from three sources: natural, sociopsychological, and synthetic. The importance of each varies according to the type of international transaction and the choice of power exercise that has been selected as a matter of national policy. Obviously the greater the degree of conflict and the more coercive the intentions, the more intricate will be the combination of power ingredients brought to bear.

Natural Sources of Power

Among these, geography is one of the more important, and it was regarded classically as the most important single ingredient of power. Although long-distance warfare has reduced their importance, geography and territorial position are nonetheless among the most enduring determinants of national power. They determine the extent of the land mass, which affects both the ease (size) and the difficulty (length of hostile borders) of national defense. The vast extent of the Russian land mass frustrated and devoured invading armies throughout history, causing the defeat of Napoleon in 1812 and that of Hitler nearly 150 years later. But just as sheer size can multiply defensive capabilities and reduce vulnerability, so too can lengthy borders be detrimental to strategic planning and military costs. Both China and the Soviet Union, for example, which share the world's longest border, spent billions of dollars in border defenses over nearly a half-century. Similarly Israel, surrounded by boundaries easily traversed by hostile tanks and infantry and further weakened by its tiny size, is severely hindered in national defense by the natural aspects of geography. In contrast, the United States is protected by 3000 miles of ocean on the east and 6000 on the west, separating it from pre-missile-era antagonists. (The Pearl Harbor Memorial is, of course, an ever-present reminder that Hawaii is the exception.)

It has been demonstrated that the frequency of wars correlates with the number of borders a nation shares, an observation that has led to the theory of geographic opportunity.[1] It was once fashionable in the study of international relations to search for simple geopolitical laws that delineated national power for all time. Three prominent examples are

1. Sir Halford Mackinder's heartland formula in 1904: "He who rules Eastern Europe commands the Heartland of Eurasia; who rules the Heartland commands the World Island of Europe, Asia, and Africa; and who rules the World Island commands the World."[2]
2. The dictum of Alfred T. Mahan, a late-nineteenth-century American admiral, that control of the seas is decisive in the global balance.[3]
3. Attempts to explain the sweep of Russian imperialism as a search for warm-water ports open in winter.

No one doubts of the importance of seapower, warm-water ports, or control of Eastern Europe in world history, but the effort to derive immutable geopolitical laws from historical observation is a fallacious approach to the study of international power. No monocausal theory can account for the richness of military and political geography. This is not, however, to deny the importance of special geopolitical assets such as the Suez and Panama canals, the Persian Gulf, the Dardanelles, and the Straits of Malacca, Hormuz, and Gibraltar. Even in the age of missile warfare, strike aircraft that fly undetected, and ubiquitous surveillance satellites, all of these convey economically and militarily important benefits.

But even geographic features of power are not limited in their significance to security. Just as warm-water ports may house major naval facilities, so too do they facilitate international trade, support oceanic and suboceanic research, and provide other services vital to national enrichment. By the same token, territorial size not only figures in the

---

[1] James Paul Wesley, "Frequency of Wars and Geographical Opportunity," *Journal of Conflict Resolution*, vol. 6, no. 4, December 1962, pp. 387–389.

[2] Sir Halford Mackinder, *Democratic Ideals and Reality* (New York: Henry A. Holt, 1919), p. 150.
[3] Alfred T. Mahan, *The Influence of Sea Power upon History* (Boston: Little, Brown, 1890).

equation of national defense, but also determines in part the resources that will sustain a population at peace and contribute to the national economic well-being. Any of these factors may play a major role in national cohesiveness, the stature of the nation in the international community, and in general, the satisfaction of the population with international events and its ability to foster that satisfaction.

Second among the natural sources of power, then, are the state's natural resources. There is no doubt that plentiful natural resources helped create the superpower status of the United States and the Soviet Union during the Cold War, and such may someday do the same for China and Brazil. Nations rich in raw materials are less dependent on the outside world and hence less vulnerable to negative sanctions (blockade, boycott, and so on), to interruptions in trade, and to wild price fluctuations. And they are better able to apply both positive and negative sanctions to opponents by extending or withholding their wealth. Ultimately, resource wealth may be used to expand the military potential of the state and to mobilize the highest negative sanctioning (warmaking) capability.

An extraordinarily instructive example of the ability of natural resources to affect world politics, even to the point of altering its course, is found in the recent policies of the underindustrialized oil-producing states. From 1973 to 1983, through rapid and very large increases in the price of crude petroleum, and by acting collectively through the Organization of Petroleum Exporting Countries (OPEC), most of these states accumulated such huge trade surpluses and reserves of foreign currencies ("petrodollars") that they were able to finance rapid development and to throw the international monetary system into upheaval, loosening its former imperialistic patterns. In addition, the coincidence of these events with Arab-Israeli war in 1973 enabled the Arab members of OPEC to use the threat of oil embargo and the actual reduction of petroleum exports as an instrument to force many industrialized states to alter their political and economic policies in the region.

The importance of natural resources does not, however, offset the fact that many poorly endowed nations are powerful and many richly endowed countries are weak. Japan, for example, imports most of its critical raw materials and yet has been one of the most important economic and military powers of the twentieth century; Indonesia, with huge reserves of minerals, has played an insignificant role on the world stage. A nation that effectively mobilizes its economic and industrial capacities may adjust to a scarcity of raw materials by importing primary products and exporting finished goods, by stockpiling reserves, or by inventing synthetic substitutes for otherwise precious ingredients of economic or military might.

A third natural component of power is population.[4] In general, large populations are capable of a variety of social functions and services: promoting industrial vitality, maximizing use of resources, and supporting large military establishments, among others. Yet there are dramatic exceptions to the rule that size and power are directly correlated. Indonesia, for example, with 150 million people, or India (850 million) cannot be ranked in modernity and power with Germany (78 million) or Japan (124 million). Table 7–1 reveals the disparity between population size and economic modernity as a measure of power. The contribution of population to power depends not exclusively on size but on the social, economic, and psychological consequences of size as well. Among these qualitative factors are level of technical skill, productivity per capita, level of social and political development, and effective coordination of human and material resources. Unskilled, starving, and ineffectively governed populations such as that of India cannot marshal into effective power their other resources. China, where population has traditionally obstructed power development, has only recently begun to coordinate its human resources for effective state development.

---

[4] For a good general theoretical background, see Katherine Organski and A. F. K. Organski, *Population and World Power* (New York: Oxford University Press, 1960).

TABLE 7-1

DISPARITY BETWEEN POPULATION AND ECONOMIC MODERNITY AS A MEASURE OF POWER, 1993

POPULATION			ECONOMIC MODERNITY	
Rank	Millions		GNP/Capita	Rank GNP/Capita
1	1,178	China	$490	104
2	878	India	300	117
3	258	United States	24,740	7
4	187	Indonesia	740	90
5	156	Brazil	2,930	48
6	149	Russia	2,340	56
7	125	Japan	31,490	3
8	123	Pakistan	430	106
9	115	Bangladesh	220	125
10	105	Nigeria	300	116
11	90	Mexico	3,610	41
12	81	Germany	23,560	9
13	71	Vietnam	170	132
14	65	Philippines	850	84
15	64	Iran	NA	51
16	60	Turkey	2,970	52
17	58	Thailand	2,110	60
18	58	United Kingdom	18,060	20
19	58	France	22,490	11
20	57	Italy	19,840	17
21	56	Egypt	660	94
22	52	Ethiopia	100	134
23	52	Ukraine	2,210	58
24	44	South Korea	7,660	32
25	40	Spain	13,590	25
26	40	South Africa	2,980	47
—				
30	29	Canada	19,970	15

Read this way: India has the second largest population in the world but ranks only 117th in gross national product per capita with an average annual income of $300, whereas Canada, only 30th in population, has an average annual income of almost $20,000, ranking 15th in the world.

Luxembourg and Switzerland have tiny populations, but rank first and second in GNP/capita. The Arab OPEC states are also small in population but high in economic measures. They are omitted because size is the principal criterion of this list.

Note geographic distribution of the largest countries. Of the top seventeen, nine are in Asia, all but one (Japan) classified as underdeveloped. Of the top twenty-six, seventeen are underdeveloped.

Source: World Bank, *World Development Report, 1995,* tables 1, 3, and 1A.

Social and Psychological Components of Power

Just as population size has significance for power, so too do the images, attitudes, and expectations of peoples. Among the most critical is national self-image, which contributes acutely to the concept of rightful national role in international affairs. Ideas, even when perverse, govern foreign policy in large measure. Such slogans, for example, as "White Man's Burden," "Manifest Destiny," and "World Police-man" not only express a mood about national expectations, but also form a social framework for setting national policy. Such policies may, indeed, be more indicative of mood than of rational choice.

Images of others are equally important in the policymaking framework. When national peoples hold the governments and peoples of other nation-states in high regard, their attitudes toward foreign relations reflect tolerance and forbearance; when they view the second party with mistrust, suspicion, or fear, their expectations about foreign relations are reactive at best. Social-psychological research has amply demonstrated that demands on foreign policy stem significantly from perception and from attitudes that peoples hold toward others. We have seen in Part I of this book the important link between perceptions, on the one hand, and foreign policy, on the other.

All these images of self and others contribute to yet another component of power: public support and cohesion. Support of government and popular unity are critical morale factors in national power. Internal divisions consume political and military resources needed to secure domestic cohesion, and they pose the danger of a fifth column—a dissident domestic faction unifying itself with a foreign enemy. For example, some Ukrainian separatists joined the Nazi invaders of the Soviet Union in the hope of liberation from Russian domination. A relatively unified population such as Israel's, on the other hand, is capable of great exertions. Popularity and political legitimacy are difficult to measure, and they do not correlate any better to democratic than to authoritarian governments. What counts in conflict is the effective disposition of the population to mobilize

resources and undertake sacrifices proportionate to the perceived importance of the outcome. Thus unity and public will are the indispensable catalysts for transforming potential power into useful power.

Final among the social determinants of power is leadership, though the quality of leadership is the most unpredictable component of national power. Leadership orchestrates the other components, defines goals in realizable ways, and determines the path of strategy.[5]

China's communist revolution exemplifies the extent to which a change in leadership alone can mobilize the other latent energies and capacities of a nation, transforming it from the weak victim of a succession of international predators to a self-sufficient power able to exercise considerable influence in foreign affairs. The same population with the same territory and endowment of natural resources can be weak and disunited, or strong and dynamic, depending on the quality of leadership.

Sometimes the rise of a unique individual at a particular moment catalyzes other historical forces to change the trend of events. Napoleon, Bismarck, Hitler, Franklin Roosevelt, de Gaulle, Lenin, Castro, Gandhi, Churchill, Mao, Mandela, de Klerk, Gorbachev, Sadat, Benazir Bhutto—these were visionary and charismatic leaders who changed the global power equation and the course of history, irrespective of their individual ideological leanings. Leadership cannot create power out of air but can dip into untapped reserves of national creative energy. Sometimes a single statesperson makes the difference.

The Synthetic Components of Power

In addition to the natural and sociopsychological determinants of power, there are some that are

---

[5] Substantial scholarship exists on the extent to which leadership personality determines the selection of strategies (including war/no-war decisions). See particularly Harold D. Lasswell, *Psychopathology and Politics* (Chicago: University of Chicago Press, 1930); and *Power and Personality* (New York: Norton, 1948); and a quantitative study by Lloyd S. Etheredge, *A World of Men: The Private Sources of American Foreign Policy* (Cambridge, Mass.: MIT Press, 1978).

synthetic. These involve the skillful use of human and other resources so as to coordinate, develop, and ready the state to put its power into motion. Most important among them are industrial capacity and military preparedness.

Industrial capacity is virtually synonymous with major-power status in the twentieth century, especially in the post–Cold War era, in which national power is measured at least as much by economic capability as by military might. Contemporary prosperity and modern war both require sophisticated manufacturing capability and huge economic resources. The victory of the Allied powers in the Second World War, for example, may be traced to the ability of Soviet and American assembly lines to turn out artillery pieces, tanks, and aircraft in greater numbers than the German and Japanese factories. As the economic costs are staggering, especially in an age in which technological hardware replaces older equipment, the correlation of national rankings in gross national product (GNP) to military ranking (see Table 7–2) is revealing.

Quantitative studies of power and capability have tended to confirm the importance of industrial capacity as the single most important determinant of power.[6] One found that the wealthier state or coalition won thirty-one of thirty-nine international wars from 1815 to 1945, suggesting that an advantage in industrial capacity brings victory in four of five cases.[7] This reduces the warmaking function from heroic exploits of the brave to mundane statistical comparisons among the number of ironworkers, ball bearing output, efficiency of the airframe industry, and so forth. Military might today depends as much on the managers and engineers as

TABLE 7–2

TEN PRINCIPAL MILITARY POWERS AT THE END OF THE COLD WAR BY EXPENDITURE, 1988

	Military Expenditure	Rank in GNP
United States	$267.8 billion	1
USSR	260.0	2
France	29.1	5
West Germany	28.2	4
United Kingdom	26.1	6
Japan	21.6	3
Italy	15.2	8
Saudi Arabia	15.0	< 10
China	11.0	7
India	8.8	12

Sources: For military expenditure, *SIPRI Yearbook,* 1989, pp. 183–187, expressed in constant dollars and exchange rates based on 1986 U.S. values. (Soviet and Chinese figures are SIPRI estimates and have a high degree of uncertainty. American intelligence sources place Soviet military expenditures as much as 50 percent higher.) For GNP, *Statistical Abstract of the United States,* 1989, p. 822.

on the generals. Nonetheless, as we have seen previously, superior unity and will can overcome vastly greater industrial output even in warfare, as in the case of the Vietnam War.

Power and War

As has been emphasized, the exercise of power in international relations takes many forms, springs from a myriad of capabilities, and is constrained by a number of limitations and countervailing factors. Yet a state desperate to defend its satisfaction level or to disrupt the prevailing satisfaction distribution may, upon exhaustion of other appropriate means of exercising power, resort to war. When diplomacy, economic bargaining, persuasion, extension of both positive and negative sanctions, and all other peaceful means fail, governments may resort to actual force. While most initial war acts are undertaken by the party intent on altering the prevailing

[6] F. Clifford German, "A Tentative Evaluation of World Power," *Journal of Conflict Resolution,* vol: 4, no. 1, March 1960, pp. 138–144; Rudolph Rummel, "Indicators of Cross-national and International Patterns," *American Political Science Review,* vol. 68, no. 1, March 1969, pp. 127-147; Bruce Russett, *International Regions and the International System* (Chicago: Rand McNally, 1967); and Harvey Starr, *War Coalitions* (Lexington, Mass.: D. C. Heath, 1973).
[7] Steven Rosen, "War Power and the Willingness to Suffer," in Bruce Russett, ed., *Peace, War, and Numbers* (Beverly Hills, Calif.: Sage, 1972), pp. 176–178.

order, some may begin with the intent of protecting that order before aggression occurs. In either event, the purpose is to redistribute global or regional political values and resources using war as the ultimate arbiter of competing interests. In an anarchical global system of sovereign states, the only restraint on such behavior is the aggressor's own material and strategic assessments.

We may conceptualize war, then, as a distribution mechanism making allocations of scarce goods to competing parties. The two sides make mutually exclusive claims to a given position or resource (such as a piece of territory or control of the instruments of state), and war decides who is to get what. The decision rule that operates in making a settlement is to award to each side a share of the disputed values that corresponds to its relative war power. War establishes a ratio of power between the contestants, and political bargaining allocates the prize according to this formula. Thus it is a useful reminder that war has been defined as politics by other means, and politics as the study of who gets what, when, and how.

Cost Tolerance

To war each party brings two essential elements: strength as described herein, and cost tolerance. The latter is the extent to which each party is willing to suffer deaths, deprivation, and destruction of its own assets in defense or pursuit of its objective. The party inferior in strength, yet superior in cost tolerance, may paradoxically be more powerful than a strong opponent less willing to suffer. This was precisely the case in Vietnam, where the physical might of the United States vastly exceeded that of the communists, yet the total power equation was nearly even or tilted to the weaker side. Ho Chi Minh predicted, "In the end the Americans will kill ten patriots for every American who dies, but it is they who will tire first." This was also the model in Algeria forty years ago, where commitment of the nationalists enabled them to withstand the immense power of France longer than the less committed French were willing to accept much

A rebellious Sikh instructs a small child on the handling of a pistol during occupation of an Indian holy place, 1988. (*Source:* © AP/Wide World)

lower costs inflicted by the Algerians. A study of forty wars found that almost half of them were won by the party that suffered more.[8]

Revolutionaries in particular, who consider themselves fighting the might of global imperialism, have put special emphasis on the idea that courageous hearts can compensate for the opponents' superior strength. The power of the anti-imperialists is their willingness to die. Arab commandos call themselves fedayeen—"the sacrificers," and an Irish revolutionist said, "It is a question which can last longer, the whip or the back."

---

[8] Steven Rosen, "War Power and the Willingness to Suffer."

This phenomenon has been labled "the stimulus of blows,"[9] and it is credited with having hardened the British against German air attacks during World War II. More recently, it has been applied to American bombing of North Vietnam.

> So far from terrorizing and disrupting the people the bombings seem to me to have stimulated and consolidated them. By the nature of the attacks so far, civilian casualties have not been very great, but they have been enough to provide the government of the Vietnam Republic with the most totally unchallengeable propaganda they could ever have dreamed of. A nation of peasants and manual workers who might have felt restive or dissatisfied under the stress of totalitarian conditions had been obliged to forget their differences in the common sense of resistance and self-defense. From the moment the US dropped its first bomb on the North of Vietnam, she welded the nation together unshakeably.[10]

The revolutionary's conviction that the will to resist can overcome immense disparities in material strength is often questioned by orthodox strategists. To a claim that communist cost tolerance in Vietnam was a bottomless pit, for example, Henry Kissinger is said to have replied, "Every pit has a bottom." Although it is evident that in their devotion to a cause the revolutionaries may survive overwhelming odds, it is clear that Kissinger was also right: More often than not, the weaker party will yield. The nation with a superior industrial capacity starts with a long lead in war power.

Starting and Ending Wars

Overrating your own power means relatively underrating your opponent. In the First World War, for example, both the French and the Germans expected quick victories within a matter of weeks; both were disappointed. In Vietnam, each side long

believed that the other would eventually yield, so that victory was purely a matter of time. The communists seemed to have in mind the example of Algeria or their own victory over the French in Vietnam, whereas the Americans based their policy on the model of post-war Greece and Malaya, where guerrillas had been defeated.

We noted earlier that the function of a war settlement is to allocate values in proportion to war power. Because the two parties have different pictures of the power ratio in advance of the fighting, they propose different settlements to each other. Each considers that the other is offering too little. Washington reasoned in Vietnam, "Why should we accept a communist-dominated coalition government when they will be unable to force one on the battlefield?" The communists reasoned, in contrast, "Why should we give up our political goals as the Americans demand when the trend of battle is sure to favor us?" The disparity in power perceptions ensures conflicting political demands.

The reverse phenomenon is underrating yourself and overrating your enemy. While a government is not likely to initiate war while thinking itself the underdog, underrating oneself can lead to prolonged arms races. Throughout the decade of the 1980s, for example, the official position in Washington was that Moscow was edging ahead of the United States in nuclear weapons deployment, thus requiring billions of dollars annually to accelerate the growth and sophistication of the American arsenal. When first the Soviet empire and then the USSR itself crumbled at the end of the decade, the West was surprised to learn of the dilapidated status of Soviet military power and the chaotic condition of its military. The Central Intelligence Agency (CIA) was soundly criticized by the Congress for its failure to foresee the Soviet collapse. Yet at the end of the decade, the national debt had tripled, unneeded military hardware had to be scrapped, thousands of career military people were let loose into an economy depressed by the abrupt halt in military manufacturing, and nuclear warheads fell to the possession of several newly independent Soviet republics, raising the specter

---

[9] Arnold Toynbee, A Study of History (London: Oxford University Press, 1934), vol. 2, pp. 100–112.
[10] James Cameron, Here Is Your Enemy (New York: Holt, Rinehart and Winston, 1966), p. 66.

of nuclear proliferation. Yet the excesses of self-underestimation were heralded as the basis for "winning the Cold War": Huge growth in American defense spending had brought the Soviet Union to its knees not militarily, but through the Soviet defense industry's inability to compete.[11]

When war does erupt, and providing it is not fought to the point of virtually total victory (as was World War Two), it typically ends when the parties arrive at a common picture of their relative power and a common assessment of appropriate settlement claims. There is negotiating on these questions within each nation as well as between nations, and the domestic debate may result in acceptance of lesser terms than are popularly anticipated. Leaders making peace on less than perfect terms must sell both the settlement and their version of the battlefield situation to their own people. The Persian Gulf War is a case in point. Saddam Hussein, who took his nation to a war with no gains and much destruction, promoted his military loss as a political victory over the Western imperialists and the lackey United Nations. And former President George Bush, under whose leadership the United States–led coalition liberated Kuwait and drove Iraqi troops back across its borders, has been called upon ever since to explain why the war was not carried to completion with a major attack of Baghdad and the capturing of Hussein himself.

One of the functions of international mediation is to help national leaders find domestic support for imperfect settlements. (President Bush argues that the final acts anticipated by many Americans were not mandated by the resolutions of the UN Security Council under which the coalition waged war.) When a significant portion of the politically aware population believes that the leadership is making a needlessly unfavorable settlement, the basis may be molded for a subsequent adverse political reaction. One of Hitler's main

appeals was the claim that the nation had been sold out in 1918 and his demand that the Versailles treaty be repudiated as a document of shame. A stable settlement means that the agreement, however unfavorable, must be accepted as realistic.

Wars end when mutual rejection of claims is not worth the costs of continued fighting to one side or both, in light of the available strategic estimates. As the power estimates of the two sides become congruent, their offers of settlement converge. In Vietnam, the United States at first offered the Viet Cong a deal that amounted to its dissolution as a political force, and the Viet Cong offered to preside over the dismemberment of the Saigon regime. As the two sides' optimistic hopes of decisive victory were frustrated, they came closer together.

The immediate function of war, then, is to provide empirical evidence to adjust divergent assessments of relative power and permit the parties to develop similar perceptions of reality on which to base a settlement. The purpose of fighting is not ordinarily to destroy an opponent completely (the "Carthaginian peace") or to deprive it of residual strength and render it helpless and defenseless. Wars seldom go this far. It is not usually necessary to destroy an opponent to change its opinion or values or to cause it to abandon its objectives. The Second World War, which was fought almost to an unconditional surrender, is a notable exception. It fell short of total surrender because the Japanese emperor's status was preserved. Japan was to have been made a "pastoral state," self-sufficient but unable to rearm. Germany was divided and occupied. The condition of both halves of Germany changed with the onset of the Cold War, and that of Japan was changed when the Korean War altered American defense strategies in Asia.

Wars begin with a determination on the part of each combatant to convince the opponent of its version of the power ratio. The ideal strategic goal in war is to bring the enemy's power estimate to the point at which it will agree to the settlement that one seeks. When the compromising is

---

[11] Peter Schweizer, *Victory: The Reagan Administration's Secret Strategy that Hastened the Collapse of the Soviet Union* (New York: Atlantic Monthly Press, 1994).

done on the battlefield and at the negotiating table, the settlement terms will inscribe the power ratio for the moment. And whether or not those terms will be able to maintain the peace over time will depend on both their accuracy and the subsequent evolution of the power ratio between the parties.

Measuring War Power

How do we determine which of two adversaries is the more powerful? How can decision makers reasonably estimate their national power potential in relation to a certain opponent, to chart a strategic course in the face of many uncertainties? One observer noted that in war "all action must . . . be planned in a mere twilight, which . . . like the effect of fog or moonshine, gives to things exaggerated dimensions and an unnatural appearance."[12] Systematic planning requires reasonably reliable bases on which to estimate the probabilities that a given course of action will have a predictable outcome.

Even purely physical capabilities for war are exceedingly difficult to estimate. Simple magnitudes of hardware must be assessed. How many X-type tanks equal a Y piece of artillery, and under what conditions of development? Obviously, opinions will vary. Even the gross defense expenditures of an opponent may be difficult to estimate. It has been shown, for instance, that during the Cold War different methods of computation by reliable analysts yielded estimates of Soviet defense expenditures as a percentage of U.S. defense expenditures ranging from 28 percent to more than 100 percent for the same year.[13]

Army Medical Examiner: "At last a perfect soldier!" (*Source:* Antiwar cartoon by Robert Minor, 1915)

And if measuring physical items is difficult, far more challenging is the effort to measure matters of human potential: political leadership, military leadership, cost tolerance, public impact of propaganda, manipulation of images, military training, speed of weapons development, the value of momentary advantage, resistance, determination, and so forth. Hitler could not have appreciated in advance the tenacity of French resistance, nor Lyndon Johnson the cost tolerance of North Vietnam.

The application of quantitative analytical techniques and the use of computers have improved the science of predicting complex social and political phenomena in answering the question, "What is the probable outcome of a war between State A and State B?" Far more than a scholar's game, this quest has been a statesperson's obsession. During the early years in Vietnam, Secretary of Defense Robert McNamara employed a battery of computer techniques and quantitatively trained social scientists to measure the probable

---

[12] Karl von Clausewitz, *On War* (Baltimore: Penguin, 1968), p. 189, originally published in 1832.

[13] Lynn Turgeon, "The Enigma of Soviet Defense Expenditures," *Journal of Conflict Resolution*, vol. 8, no. 2, June 1964, pp. 116–120. For a comprehensive study of the problem of estimating, see John Prados, *The Soviet Estimate: U.S. Intelligence Analysis and Russian Military Strength* (New York: Dial, 1982).

outcomes of alternative strategies for victory in limited war. Although the attempts at prediction all failed miserably, the drive for new and better answers continues.

The most common starting point in compiling measurable and comparable indices is the relative GDP of the involved parties, as this is a bulk statement of any nation's economic activity. But even this is not entirely reliable. Different economic systems place different values on similar activities; the separation of goods from services in the economy may lead to distortions; and gross quantitative economic activity says absolutely nothing about the ability of respective states to activate their economic capacities and populations for war. Hence these internal factors must be measured alongside economic data. One suggested formula is

$$\text{internal component of power} = \frac{\text{gross national product}}{\text{population}} \times (\text{population}) \times (\text{tax effort})$$

where the tax effort is the computed relation of the tax capacity of the economy (based on GDP) and the willingness of the government to exert pressure to extract enough to wage war effectively. It is also suggested that the external component of power be expressed as

$$(\text{foreign aid accumulated}) \times (\text{tax effort of the recipient})$$

The total measurable power of the state, then, should be the sum of these two formulae, and by tabulating these indices for two or more combatants, a rough measurement of probable outcome should emerge.[14]

Still, however, the emphasis is on the tangible aspects of power. One improvement on this attempts to include motivation and situational specificity:

$$P_p = (C + E + M) \times (S + W)$$

where P_p is perceived power; C is the critical mass of population and territory; E and M are economic and military capabilities, respectively; S is strategic purposes; and W is the will to pursue national strategies. Simply stated, power is the product of physical and psychological capabilities. A 1975 study assessed each of these and produced a global assessment of real power capability. Despite the superior physical position of the United States, the behavioral determination of the Soviet Union at that time not to be subordinated to the United States gave the Kremlin a decided edge in real power (by an index nearly twice that of the United States).[15]

At each stage of strategic analysis, opinions diverge over whether optimistic or pessimistic assessments are warranted. Alternative pictures of any situation confront decision makers with a range of power ratios from which they must choose. Should President Lyndon B. Johnson have listened to the Joint Chiefs of Staff in 1965, who told him that the communists could be defeated in Vietnam within two years, or to the CIA, which gave him a much gloomier prediction?

Research findings are highly contradictory about whether statespersons generally decide on optimistic estimates or darker ones. One study found that social groups tend to overrate themselves and underrate their opponents,[16] but an-

---

[14] A. F. K. Organski and Jacek Kugler, "Davids and Goliaths: Predicting the Outcomes of International Wars," *Comparative Political Studies*, July 1978, pp. 141–180.

[15] Ray S. Cline, *World Power Assessment: A Calculus of Strategic Drift* (Washington, D.C.: Georgetown University, Center for Strategic and International Studies, 1975). See also David A. Baldwin, "Power Analysis and World Politics: New Trends Versus Old Tendencies," *World Politics*, January 1979, pp. 161–194. Baldwin summarized several studies of power comparability, critiqued their weaknesses, and identified their valuable contributions.

[16] Bernard Bass and George Dunteman, "Biases in the Evaluation of One's Own Group, Its Allies, and Opponents," *Journal of Conflict Resolution*, vol. 7, no. 1, March 1963, pp. 16–20.

other found quite the opposite: that the "armed services inevitably overstate the military capabilities of the opponent."[17] Still a third study found that aggressors sometimes recognize the potential superiority of their opponents, perceiving this edge more clearly than do the defenders, but take the risk that it will not be effective.[18] The inconclusiveness of this evidence underscores the subjective component in framing assumptions about going to war.

It is likely that a full study of strategic planning in past wars would show that decision makers tended to use optimistic rather than pessimistic assumptions if both were based on equally plausible information. Effective leadership will concede critical objectives only when there is no reasonable hope of successful struggle. The rational strategy for mobilizing public will and forging national unity is to use the more optimistic estimates, provided that they are equiprobable with pessimistic alternatives.[19]

Ordinarily, optimistic planning is based not on wild fancy but on seemingly reasonable estimates, such as the expectation of the Joint Chiefs in 1965 that the North Vietnamese could not withstand strategic bombing or the deployment of a half-million well-armed American troops.[20] Doubters

may offer gloomier projections, but they cannot prove their case over the optimists. The final decision is always in some measure a leap of faith. Hitler bet that the British and French would not intervene over Czechoslovakia; he was right. Secretary of State Dean Acheson and President Harry S Truman bet that the Chinese would not intervene in Korea; they were wrong. Certainty is much easier looking back than for the decision maker forced to rely on advance projections!

Avoiding War

In this discussion of power, we have studied threat or use of force as the ultimate means of influence. The dilemma is that nations continue to find military capabilities useful and necessary instruments of diplomatic action (as evidenced by the volume of international arms trade and the frequency of war as demonstrated in Table 7–3), even while technological changes make the use of violence ever more horrible and cataclysmic. In ancient and medieval warfare, a battle might have raged all morning between two mercenary armies, paused, and then resumed with equal ferocity in the afternoon, leaving at the end of the day losses of perhaps twenty men and a donkey. In trench warfare, on the other hand, the gain or loss of a few hundred yards might cost ten thousand lives. This form of fighting accounts for the dramatic increase in casualties in conventional warfare during the first quarter of the present century (see Figure 7–1). Modern nuclear warfare has the potential to tower above these numbers, as exemplified in the 100,000 deaths in a few moments from the atomic bombings of Hiroshima and Nagasaki in 1945. Recent advances in both explosive might and delivery accuracy would enable a missile-launched thermonuclear war targeted to major population centers to kill millions of people instantly. Indeed, one of the great complications in predicting conflict behavior in the modern era results from the fact that fundamental arms developments that

---

[17] Samuel Huntington, "Arms Races," in Carl Friedrich and Seymour Harris, eds., *Public Policy 1958* (Cambridge, Mass.: Harvard University Press, 1958). "In 1914, for instance, the Germans estimated the French Army to have 121,000 more men than the German Army, the French estimated the German Army to have 134,000 more men than the French Army, but both parties agreed in their estimates of the military forces of third parties."

[18] Bruce Russett, "The Calculus of Deterrence," *Journal of Conflict Resolution*, vol. 7, no. 2, June 1963, p. 97.

[19] While not designed for this purpose, there are some elements of this in Donald Kagan, *On the Origins of War and the Preservation of Peace* (New York: Doubleday, 1995).

[20] Estimating North Vietnam's strength and whose estimates to accept remains one of the controversial issues surrounding the war. For an equally controversial retrospective, see Robert S. McNamara, *In Retrospect: The Tragedy and Lessons of Vietnam* (New York: Times Books, 1995), and a passionate rejoinder by Louis G. Sarris, "McNamara's War, and Mine," *The New York Times*, September 5, 1995, p. A17.

TABLE 7-3

CIVIL AND INTERNATIONAL WARS (116), FROM 1945 TO 1995, WITH STARTING DATES

Syria–Lebanon	1945	Israel–Arab states	1973
Indonesia	1945	Iraq (Kurdish)	1974
China	1945	Cyprus	1974
Malaya	1945	Angola	1975
Indochina	1946	Timor–Indonesia	1975
Greece	1946	Lebanon	1975
Madagascar	1947	Spanish Morocco	1976
India–Pakistan	1947	Somalia–Ethiopia	1977
Kashmir	1947	Ethiopia (Eritrea)	1977
Philippines	1948	Syria–Lebanon	1977
Israel–Arab states	1948	Libya–Egypt	1977
Hyderabad	1948	Iran	1978
Burma	1948	Nicaragua	1978
Korea	1950	Vietnam–Laos	1978
Taiwan	1950	Chad	1978
Tibet	1950	Zaire	1978
Kenya	1952	Rhodesia (Zimbabwe)	1978
Guatemala	1954	N. Yemen–S. Yemen	1979
Algeria	1954	Uganda–Tanzania	1979
Sudan	1955	China–Vietnam	1979
Cyprus	1955	Vietnam–Kampuchea	1979
Sinai	1956	Nicaragua	1979
Hungary	1956	South Africa–Angola	1979
Suez	1956	USSR–Afghanistan	1980
Lebanon	1958	Iran–Iraq	1980
Cuba	1958	El Salvador	1980
Vietnam	1959	Peru	1980
Himalayas	1959	W. Sahara	1981
Rwanda	1959	Britain–Argentina	
Laos	1959	(Falkland Islands)	1982
Congo	1960	Israel–Syria–PLO	
Colombia	1960	(in Lebanon)	1982
Cuba (Bay of Pigs)	1961	South Africa	1982
Goa	1961	Sudan	1982
Angola	1961	Kampuchea–Thailand	1983
Yemen	1962	Sri Lanka	1983
West New Guinea	1962	U.S.–Grenada	1983
Portuguese Guinea	1962	Sudan–Libya	1983
Algeria–Morocco	1963	Mozambique	1984
Cyprus	1963	Turkey–Iraq (Kurdish)	1984
Malaysia	1963	India (Sikh)	1986
Somalia–Kenya	1963	Mozambique–Zimbabwe	1986
Zanzibar	1964	Colombia	1989
Thailand	1964	Panama	1989
Mozambique	1964	Romania	1989
Dominican Republic	1965	Azerbaijan–Armenia	1990
India–Pakistan	1965	Liberia	1990
Indonesia	1965	Iraq–Kuwait	1990
Biafra	1966	Rwanda	1990
Israel–Arab states	1967	Desert Storm	1991
Czechoslovakia	1968	Somalia	1991
Malaysia	1969	Haiti	1991
El Salvador	1969	Serbia–Croatia	1991
Chad	1969	Bosnia	1991
Northern Ireland	1969	Georgia	1992
Ethiopia (Eritrea)	1970	Tajikistan	1992
Cambodia	1971	Moldova	1993
Bangladesh–Kashmir	1971	Mexico (Zapatistas)	1994
Burundi	1972	Russia–Chechnya	1994

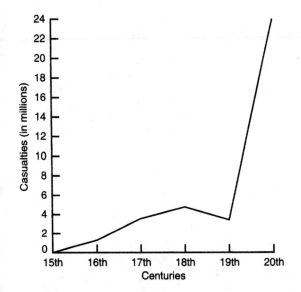

FIGURE 7–1 War casualties in Europe, 1500–1925.

Source: Pitirim Sorokin, *Social and Cultural Dynamics*, vol. 3 (New York: Bedminster Press, 1962), originally published in 1937.

once took up to 500 years may now take only 5 years.[21] Consequently, managers of power must be concerned not only with enmities and magnitudes, but also with all the destabilizing effects of rapid strategic change.

Clearly, controls must be established over the use of force, both to prevent the outbreak of war and to limit its scope and intensity once begun. Since World War Two, three basic approaches to the control of force have dominated both practical foreign policy and the theoretical literature:

1. War prevention through regional and global balances of power between quarreling states, so that resorting to war is made unprofitable, even though disagreements continue.
2. War prevention by balance of terror, a variant of the balance-of-power concept, in which technologically developed adversaries have the capability for mutually assured destruction through finely targeted instantaneous warfare. Aggression is deterred by the certainty of intolerably destructive retaliation. With the end of the Cold War and of the Soviet-American nuclear arms race, the importance of this alternative in strategic thinking has declined sharply.
3. War prevention by further institutionalization of mediation and other means for nonviolent conflict resolution, ultimately including a central peacekeeping authority and the disarming of nation-states.

Because the first two ideas address the practical problem of deterrence in a world of heavily armed states acting autonomously, they have enjoyed primacy in the debate on conflict control. In the New World Order, however, in which the nuclear arms race is removed and the global military distribution virtually is unipolar, the balance-of-terror alternative has lost much, if not most, of its former importance. Hence the contemporary emphasis is on replacing the deterrence models of international relations with one built on intergovernmental institutions capable of establishing and enforcing an equitable distribution of values. To some observers, this is an impossible dream. To others, who look beyond unstable peace to the survival of humankind and improvement of its condition, it is the endurance of the nation-state system that is the impossible dream. If, since World War Two, national governments have given us two new wars per year, why must one presume that the costly pursuit of peace through competition is superior to the quest for peace through cooperation?

---

[21] Herman Kahn, *On Thermonuclear War* (Princeton, N.J.: Princeton University Press, 1960). There is, of course, a limit to this rate of change. Today, although there may be no end of technically achievable ideas for war and defense, the level of sophistication of these ideas requires substantial time for implementation. The same factor multiplies the cost of each successive generation of weapons.

"Land Day," a day of protest by Israeli Arabs and Palestinians against the Israeli expropriation of Arab lands. Begun in 1976 when six people were killed by the Israeli army, it has continued ever since. (*Source:* Jonathan Lurie/Impact Visuals)

Conclusion

Any discussion of power must explore the range of options available to states, from persuasion to war. Industrial production, weapons, psychological motivation, natural resources, leadership, and so on all enter into regional and global power equations. Yet in the New World Order, presuming optimistically the continued absence of a polarized standoff between giants or alliances, power will be defined increasingly in economic terms. Similarly, national security will be sought principally through economic competitiveness. While the traditional instruments of power will continue to exist to some unpredictable extent, nonmilitary means of persuasion will supplant the traditional resort to threat of force.[22] In the past, economic strength has been a route to national military power; in the future, it will be the essence of power.[23]

---

[22] See John M. Rothgeb Jr., *Defining Power: Influence and Force in the Contemporary International System* (New York: St. Martin's, 1993), for a comprehensive study of the nonmilitary instruments of persuasion in international politics.

[23] For a comprehensive study of the relationship of economic to military power from 1500 to 2000, see Paul Kennedy, *The Rise and Fall of the Great Powers* (New York: Random House, 1987).

CHAPTER 8

Balance of Power

Historians, diplomats, and students of international relations often assert that the only way to keep peace is through a careful "balance of power." What do we mean by this commonly used expression? It connotes not only military and deterrent capabilities but also the entire structure of power and influence that governs the relations of states. Balance of power encompasses all the political capabilities of states—coercive and pacific—by which the delicate balance of conflict without war is maintained.

Meanings of "Balance of Power"

Among laypersons and scholars alike, the expression "balance of power" has many uses. Consider four uses in these sentences:

1. There is a balance of power between India and Pakistan.
2. The balance of power favors the United States.
3. The balance of power has shifted in favor of Israel.
4. Britain was the crucial actor in the nineteenth-century balance-of-power system.

Clearly, there are several different meanings here. The first statement implies that equilibrium exists between two parties. Further, the relations of the respective parties with outside states are nearly equal, thus preventing disequilibrium by the unilateral addition of external strength. In short, the equilibrium in the relations between India and Pakistan exists because neither has significantly more power or influence; neither can distort the balance. Figure 8–1(a) shows the situation that exists; (b) shows the maintenance of equilibrium by the equal use of influence on outside states.

The second statement carries a sharply different implication. To say that the balance favors one party over the other is to introduce a disequilibrium (Figure 8–2). Here the United States holds the upper hand over some other party and is able to rely on greater military, diplomatic, and other resources. Throughout the Cold War, for example, the United States and the Soviet Union, although perhaps not absolutely equal in military potential, had practical equivalence. Yet the United States had a vast edge in influence and in ability to work its will with economic resources, and was "favored" by the balance of power.

Now consider the third sentence: The balance of power has shifted in favor of Israel. This connotes either a shift from equilibrium to disequilibrium or a shift in predominance from one party to the other (Figure 8–3). Acquisition of a new weapons system by Israel might have a major impact on the Middle Eastern balance, as might a change in the country's stature by a diplomatic victory. Recognition by West Germany, for example, improved Israel's access to military and industrial goods and gave it a new and powerful friend.

The fourth statement implies still a different meaning, which cannot be illustrated by the simple balance beam. The balance-of-power system was a

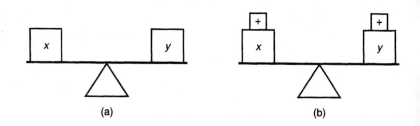

FIGURE 8–1   (a) Two-part
equilibrium. (b) Equilibrium
maintenance.

specific historical event in a Eurocentric world from
the nineteenth century to the outbreak of the First
World War. In that system, states behaved in certain ways (described next), with one state conserv-
ing its influence solely to maintain equilibrium.

In summary, then, in place of a concise definition of "balance of power" we may say that it is a
concept of many meanings, particularly equilibrium, disequilibrium, and shifts in dominance, as
well as a particular historical systemic principle.
This chapter will examine the various ideas behind
. the term. It is particularly concerned with balance
as a system of keeping peace.[1]

Balance of Power
as an Analytical Device

All structural systems of world politics share certain
assumptions:

1. In international relations, the potential for
   conflict is permanent.
2. Because it is permanent, the goal of a balance
   is not to eliminate power but to control and
   manage it.
3. Power is not absolute, but is quantitatively relative to the power of others.
4. Power is achievable by the aggregation of natural, sociopsychological, and synthetic resources.

5. Except in abnormal circumstances, power is
   an instrument of the state rather than a self-
   standing possession.

In light of these observations, the balance of
power can be presented as an analytical concept for
exploring the practical effects of equilibrium and
disequilibrium in world politics and for assessing
the consequences of power shifts. It becomes an analytical device rather than a form of advocacy, prescribing no particular model(s) for world peace.
Instead, it searches out the conditions of order and
disorder in international relations, concentrating
on the sources and consequences of balance and
imbalance.

The role that a state plays in a global or regional balance of power is determined by its capabilities and intentions. In its external relations, a
government makes rational and calculated determinations of the costs and benefits of specific policies as related to specific objectives. From these
formulae it sets the course of foreign policy, and by
them it determines the state's role in the balance of
power. "Will we attempt to enlarge our power, or
are our present interests served in the international
system by the power that we presently command?"
"Do our relations with a neighbor require that we
alter the existing balance?" Or, "Is our neighbor altering the balance to our detriment, and must we,
therefore, increase our power potential?"

This distinction between power and power potential is an important one in the balance-of-power
concept. Many states have considerable potential
power but have little effect on global or regional
balances. Hence the balance-of-power theory must
take into account the stages of power readiness.
The possession of adequate resources of power is

---

[1] For thorough discussions of the several, and often confusing,
meanings of "balance of power," see Inis L. Claude Jr., *Power in
International Relations* (New York: Random House, 1962), particularly part 1; and Ernst B. Haas, "The Balance of Power: Prescription, Concept, or Propaganda?" *World Politics*, vol. 5, 1953,
pp. 442–477. A third useful source is Hans J. Morgenthau, *Politics Among Nations*, 4th ed. (New York: Knopf, 1967), pp.
161–163.

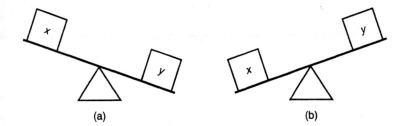

FIGURE 8–2
(a) Disequilibrium favoring y.
(b) Disequilibrium favoring x.

potential power. When these are developed, coordinated, and supplied with the will to use power, then the state possesses mobilized power. And when the developed resources are applied to actual situations, the state commands active power (or kinetic power).

The lowest stage of readiness (potential power) gives to a state little more than a passive role in the balance of power. More powerful states are only minimally moved by the actions of the potentially powerful, preferring to acquiesce in the prevailing norms of the international system.

Command of mobilized power, in contrast, enables the state to be a significant participant by contributing to the stability or instability of the balance. The balance of power is concerned mainly with the balance of mobilized power.

Force—the extreme utilization of mobilized power—is used to alter the power balance drastically

and rapidly. A state may wish to correct a disequilibrium by force or to upset a power balance to its advantage. Perhaps the most illustrative use of active power in the balance-of-power theory is the preemptive war. This is warfare in which State A anticipates an attack by State B. Rather than wait for an orderly escalation of hostilities, A destroys B's capability before B has a chance to start the fighting. A has preempted B by an anticipatory attack depriving B of altering the balance of power, and in the course of events A may have done so itself. Israel's purpose in attacking Arab military airfields in 1967 was preemptive. Under threat of attack itself, Israel wanted to strike at Egypt and Syria in a selective manner to diminish their capability to alter the balance.

Preventive war has similar balance-of-power connotations. This is a type of selective attack undertaken against an enemy state considerably

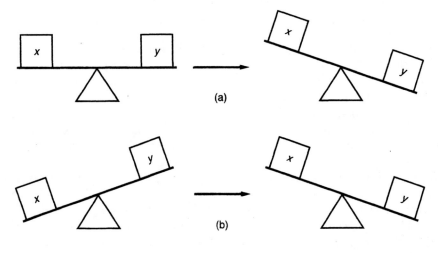

FIGURE 8–3
(a) Equilibrium shift to disequilibrium.
(b) Disequilibrium shift to opposite disequilibrium.

before that state has effective military potential. Long before China was a nuclear power, for example, people openly mused on the efficacy of preventive attacks on Chinese installations to delay nuclear development and prolong its weakness. Japan's attack on Pearl Harbor in 1941 was a different type of preventive war, conducted to deprive the United States of retaliatory strength as Japan undertook further territorial quests in Asia and the Pacific. Israel's attack on an Iraqi nuclear plant in 1981 was designed to prevent its enemy from gaining a huge strategic advantage in the regional balance. The only real difference between preemptive and preventive war is the time element; the effects for the balance of power are identical.

In the traditional study of international relations, it was assumed that the balance of power was determined exclusively by military relativities. More modern concepts of international relations, in contrast, recognize that relative military preparedness is not the sole determinant of the balance of power. The tendency now is to distinguish between military power, on the one hand, and the overall ability to command international influence, on the other. Thus, a major component of the balance of power is economic potential.

Modern Japan is a case in point. Since the end of the Second World War, Japan has not been a significant military power. Its defense is firmly tied to American strategic policy. Despite this military inferiority, Japan has assumed major-power status by virtue of its enormous economic revitalization.

Western Europe is another illustrative case. During the Cold War, despite its reliance on the trans-Atlantic security arrangement, Western Europe achieved major-power status through its ability to compete in world trade aided by a unified international economic policy. Through economic union and restoration, Western Europe acquired a role in the global balance disproportionate to its military strength. In the New World Order, in which the military portion of the balance has been downgraded, this unified economic might makes Western Europe one of the three great trading competitors, together with North America and Japan.

The Middle Eastern example of forced change in the global power balance through economic means between 1973 and 1983 is even more striking because its impact was so sudden and so profound. By tying their oil export policy to economic development and to political objectives concerning Israel, the Middle Eastern oil-producing states were able to force policy changes on virtually all Western industrialized countries and Japan. While still developing industrially, their vast petrodollar reserves substantially affected economic relations throughout the nonsocialist world. And the threat of a petroleum boycott was sufficiently menacing to Japan, Western Europe, and the United States that it was one of the most fruitful instruments of foreign policy available anywhere. Consequently, this capability forced a change in the regional and global power balances virtually without a military component.

Having now considered the fundamental issues of equilibrium, disequilibrium, and change in balance-of-power theory, we will turn to some alternative structural models.

Structural Models of Balance of Power

Although balance-of-power theory does not prescribe a preferred model of global or regional stability, it does facilitate description of the principal power configurations that have existed in the past 150 years. It also enables us to demonstrate graphically the power relations of major states and groups of states, whether globally or regionally.

These models are of no greater value than to depict roughly power configurations as they existed in the past. They attempt to freeze time in the sense of describing relations in fixed position, rather than to explain the dynamic flow of relations among international actors. In this sense, these models are static; and they are as artificial as is a tinker-toy model of a molecule that demonstrates the ideal configuration of its major components while ignoring the dynamic flow of subatomic

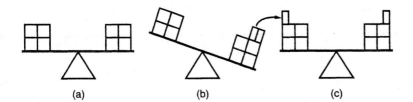

FIGURE 8–4   Adjusting the equilibrium.

particles that either maintain or change the basic shape. The international system is as dynamic as that molecule, and any attempt to reduce it to fixed form necessarily diminishes its vitality. Nevertheless, because such descriptive models are typically referred to as indicators of major-power configurations, they are instructive despite their static character. Despite the crude simplicity of the geometric models, then, we are reminded that "politics is not geometry."[2]

The Nineteenth-Century Balance-of Power System

Historians of the balance-of-power system (dated from the end of the Napoleonic Wars in 1815 until the outbreak of the First World War in 1914) identify the underlying conditions. They note that it could have existed only among several nation-states in a fairly well-defined territorial area. Although it was an interstate system, it was not global. The system could not have worked except among participants relatively homogeneous in political culture, who had rational means of estimating one another's power (wealth, military potential, and so on).[3]

In retrospect, this international system seems to have resulted from several basic assumptions about states' previous behavior. First, each state would attempt to maximize its power for its own purposes. Second, as a consequence, when states accumulated power and their interests (such as

imperial interests) collided, there was potential for international conflict. Third, to enhance their respective power potentials, like-minded states entered into alliances, and so alliance competition rather than state competition characterized the system. Fourth, because each state placed a high value on equilibrium, it was necessary for some state or states periodically to change alliances for the purpose of adjusting any disequilibrium that might evolve.

Early historians of the balance-of-power system assumed that this adjustment process was automatic, as shown in Figure 8–4. An existing equilibrium (a) is upset (b) by the addition of a new participant or by a major technical development that adds to the weight of one coalition. In (c), equilibrium is restored by the transfer of one state from one alliance to the other. Later historians, however, rejected the automaticity theory, arguing that the process was, at best, semiautomatic, and conducted through such things as vigilance, alliances, intervention, mobility of action, reciprocal compensation, preservation of participants, coalitions, diversion into colonial expansion, and war. More important than these, however, is the concept of The Balancer, a specific state that changes allegiances expressly to maintain the balance as shown in Figure 8–4.[4] The introduction of this concept means that the adjustment process is less than semiautomatic; rather, it is manual.

The Balancer must have special characteristics. If a weak state were to take on this role, or a

[2] John Lewis Gaddis, *The Long Peace* (New York: Oxford University Press, 1987), p. 221.
[3] Edward V. Gulick, *Europe's Classical Balance of Power* (Ithaca, N.Y.: Cornell University Press, 1955), chapter 1.

[4] The means of balance are derived from Edward V. Gulick, *Europe's Classical Balance of Power*, chapter 3, and George Liska, *International Equilibrium* (Cambridge, Mass.: Harvard University Press, 1957), pp. 36–37.

state that favors disequilibrium, the function of manual balance would hardly have been served; so The Balancer must be an effectively powerful state, one whose strategic options enable it to influence the entire system. Moreover, it must be a state that not only favors equilibrium, but demands for its own purposes that equilibrium be safeguarded.

Advocates of this model universally identify Britain as having been The Balancer. Britain's assets as The Balancer included its geographic location (which spared it from common boundaries with other powerful European states), its apparent interest in equilibrium as the most favorable climate for its imperial policies, and its great mobility of action.[5]

Despite these modern refinements, this entire scheme has many skeptics. One critic, for example, challenges the assumption that power is the foremost national value. He also denies that nations are static and unchanging from within, insisting that through industrialization, improvements in governmental efficiency, and so on, states increase their potential power. These changes are not adjustable through the presumed mechanics of the balance of power. Third, because states are often tied to one another through economic, political, or psychological bonds, the freedom to switch alliances for no other purpose than balance is uncharacteristic of history. He interprets British policy as motivated by self-interest, not as fulfilling the self-appointed role of The Balancer. In fact, he denies that any state in the nineteenth century preferred equilibrium to advantageous disequilibrium. Finally,

he concludes that imbalance of power is the characteristic pattern, particularly since the Industrial Revolution (which occurred during the 1815–1914 period), with major states and their respective coalitions actually trying to maintain disequilibrium.[6] Another observer concludes that balance-of-power systems are rare in history rather than "a natural form of international relations." He cites only three: the city-states of ancient Greece and Italy, and the period under discussion here.[7]

Nevertheless, the premise holds that in multiparty international systems favoring equilibrium, there must be some implicit rules of behavior. Based on his studies of the nineteenth-century system, one theorist identifies these:

1. Participants will increase their capabilities, but they will accept the responsibility to negotiate differences rather than fight.
2. Because increase in capabilities is the prime motive of foreign policy, states must be willing to fight, if necessary, rather than to forgo further development.
3. When at war, states will be prepared to terminate fighting rather than to upset the foundations of equilibrium by eliminating a major participant.
4. Every participant intent on equilibrium will contest any tendency to dominance by any state or coalition.
5. Because the system is built on states' power, participants must constrain tendencies toward supranational organization or organizations

---

[5] This presentation follows the tradition of treating the entire balance-of-power century as having had a relatively unchanging political system. Recently, however, it has been suggested that the period 1815 to 1914 actually consisted of three distinctly different balancing mechanisms, all governed by many of the same assumptions but necessitated by different relationships and dominated by different parties and different balancers. They were 1815–1878 (Britain The Balancer, the most effective of the three experiments); 1878–1890 (Germany The Balancer, ingenious but not inherently stable); and 1890–1914 (Britain The Balancer, a desperate effort at maintaining order). See Gordon A. Craig and Alexander L. George, *Force and Statecraft: Diplomatic Problems of Our Time* (New York: Oxford University Press, 1983), chapter 3, "Balance of Power, 1815–1914: Three Experiments."

[6] A. F. K. Organski, *World Politics*, 2nd ed. (New York: Knopf, 1968), pp. 282–299. A contrasting view aggregates two principal assumptions of the balance-of-power system (alliance bonding and capability distribution across individual nations) into one ("bloc concentration") and then examines changes in the power distribution of the system to reestablish equilibrium when one or more states tend to move it into disequilibrium. The study concludes in favor of the balance-of-power hypothesis for the years 1824 to 1914. See Richard J. Stoll, "Bloc Concentration and the Balance of Power: The European Major Powers, 1824–1914," *Journal of Conflict Resolution*, March 1984, pp. 25–50.

[7] Henry Kissinger, *Diplomacy* (New York: Simon and Schuster, 1994), particularly chapters 1 and 4. The author rejects the notion that in its role in power poitics, Britain preferred balance to a power distribution advantageous to its own imperial objectives.

that would alter the sovereign status of the system's participants.

6. Each participant must be willing to permit defeated major actors to restore their positions, and they must encourage lesser actors to achieve the status of full participants. All major parties must be treated equally as acceptable role partners.[8]

These rules have a pragmatic basis: If the system is to be viable, the participating states must be viable. We shall return subsequently to the question of whether multipartite systems such as this or limited-bloc systems (such as bipolarity) tend toward greater stability.

The Tight Bipolar Balance

The nineteenth-century balance-of-power system involved political relationships that ended with the First World War. Thereafter, international stability was not governed by the factors we have discussed. Other systems of power balance emerged, particularly after the Second World War. It is necessary, therefore, to explore the military relations of other balance-of-power systems in order to understand the contemporary distribution of power.

Although the First World War had begun the process of restricting the number of major powers, the prostration of Western and Central Europe and of Japan after the Second World War ensured that for the foreseeable future, world politics would center on Washington and Moscow rather than on London, Tokyo, and Paris. To this was added the spread of nuclear weapons and the threat of instantaneous and catastrophic warfare. But there was also a third critical development: the intense ideological hostility between the two principal powers, which opened an era of conflict, distrust, competition, and misperception. This was the essence of the Cold War.

These three factors together—the two-part division of power, the advent of atomic warfare, and unprecedented ideological rivalry—resulted in an international system of tight bipolarity, one in which virtually all the world's effective power was encompassed in two competing blocs. The institutional structure was that of two formal alliance systems, dominated by the Soviet Union and the United States, respectively. (A few states such as Finland and Switzerland chose not to participate.)[9]

A tight bipolar international system may be said to have existed from 1946 to 1955, a decade that saw such momentous events as the breakdown of the wartime coalition, the emergence of the Soviet Union as a second nuclear power, the establishment of NATO and the Warsaw Pact, the Berlin Blockade, the accession to power in China by Mao Zedong, and the Korean War. With the exceptions of the Cuban Missile Crisis (in which American threats caused the Kremlin to withdraw missiles from Cuba) and the Vietnam War, most of the defining events of the Cold War occurred in these years. The Soviet alliance system was largely regional, especially after its close ties to China broke in 1956. The American alliance structure, in contrast, was global (and remains so despite the collapse of the South East Asian Treaty Organization (SEATO) after the Vietnam War), and developed as follows:

1947, Organization of American States (the "Rio Pact," or the Inter-American Treaty of Reciprocal Assistance) (twenty-two members)

1949, North Atlantic Treaty (fifteen members)

1951, Security Treaty with Japan (bilateral)

1951, Security Treaty with Australia and New Zealand (trilateral)

1951, Mutual Defense Treaty with the Republic of the Philippines (bilateral)

---

[8] Morton A. Kaplan, *Systems and Process in International Relations* (New York: Wiley, 1957), p. 23; and also Kaplan, "Balance of Power, Bipolarity and Other Methods of International Systems" *American Political Science Review*, vol. 51, 1957, pp. 684–695.

[9] This definition varies from Kaplan's, which defines tight bipolarity as a system in which "non-bloc member actors and universal actors either disappear entirely or cease to be significant." ("Balance of Power, Bipolarity and Other Models of International Systems," p. 693.) Kaplan denies, however, that a tight bipolar system has ever existed.

The height of the Cold War, 1953. In the United Nations General Assembly, Ambassador Andrei Vishinsky of the USSR accuses the U.S. of acting like a "master race" in trying to push through a proposal on the makeup of the Korean Peace Conference. American ambassador Henry Cabot Lodge and British ambassador Sir Gladwyn Jebb listen resignedly to the familiar invective. (*Source:* © AP/Wide World)

1953, Mutual Defense Treaty with the Republic of (South) Korea (bilateral)

1954, Southeast Asia Collective Defense Treaty (eight members)

1954, Mutual Defense Treaty with the Republic of China (Taiwan) (bilateral)

Altogether, these treaties and the institutionalized alliances that they created encompassed some forty-four nations including the United States, with several states belonging to more than one. In addition, the United States had bases agreements and status-of-forces agreements with Spain and Libya (the latter agreement no longer exists), so that the United States was involved in some level of military activity with no fewer than forty-six different governments on every continent. Solidarity was furthered by the alliances sponsored by London, including the Central Treaty Organization and its military prerogatives in its colonial areas, particularly in Asia and the Mediterranean (for instance, Malta). Combined, the Anglo-American alliances and the Soviet alliances involved in excess of sixty states and almost half again as many non-self-governing areas. Compare this with the 1955 membership of the United Nations, which was only seventy-six nations, sixteen of which were not admitted until 1955. Thus at the start of 1955, while the United Nations had a membership of only fifty-nine distinctly different sovereign states (Ukraine and Byelorussia were parts of the Soviet Union, but had separate voting status, making the total voting membership sixty-one), the Anglo-American and Soviet alliances together encompassed more than sixty states. The universality of the alliance systems should be self-evident.

Furthermore, because of (1) the threat of massive warfare and (2) the extraordinary dependence of the alliance members on Washington and Moscow both economically and militarily, adherence to the alliance was extreme and deviations rare. It is for these reasons that we describe this power distribution as tight as well as bipolar.[10] (See Figure 8–5)

The operating characteristics of tight bipolar balance differed markedly from those of the nineteenth-century system. The basic assumption here was that international equilibrium was a second-best objective; the principal aim was to belong to the dominant coalition. Furthermore, the system presupposed that all effective power was included in the major blocs, or poles, and so there was no powerful state dangling free to play the role of Balancer. Indeed, the objective of this power pattern was to anticipate the defeat of the other coalition should it breach the frontiers of one's own members. It was for this reason that the ruling American political-military strategy of this era was massive nuclear retaliation, though it is doubtful that the threat was ever taken seriously. More likely, the balanced conventional strengths of the European alliances ensured stability through this

era. Nevertheless, the philosophy of tight bipolarity renders massive retaliation quite logical as a strategic foundation. This model of international order is maximally hostile.

The Loose Bipolar Balance

In the mid-1950s, a number of fundamental changes occurred in the international system. The two superpower alliance systems began to loosen, with internal conflicts and losses of confidence appearing in each bloc, and dependencies began to dissipate. In the Soviet sphere, events took several paths. Eastern European dissatisfaction with Soviet control, foreshadowed a few years earlier in East Germany, climaxed with the brief Hungarian revolt of 1956. Coupled with Nikita Khrushchev's campaign to de-Stalinize the Soviet Union and Eastern Europe, this event resulted in increasing demands for quasi-independence among the Soviet satellites, despite forceful suppression by Soviet troops. The politics of the Soviet sphere came increasingly to be identified as polycentric, suggesting reduced Soviet control over the states within its orbit. At the same time (1956) Moscow formally discontinued diplomatic and economic relations with Beijing, broke off foreign aid, withdrew its technicians, and left China to develop alone. This went well beyond polycentrism. Contrary to one of the basic notions of American foreign policy, namely, that communism was monolithic (all directed from the center), it was now clear that versions of communism could exist independently without increasing threats to international peace. This accelerated the loosening of bipolarity.

The American bloc began to crack also. Latin America, increasingly disenchanted with Washington's sporadic paternalism, began to consider itself a member of the Developing World despite its formal ties with the United States. Fidel Castro's seizure of power in Cuba under the Marxist banner brought the first serious challenge to ideological solidarity in the Western Hemisphere. In Western Europe, successful reconstruction led gradually to resentment of American economic and trade

---

[10] For a study suggesting that the power distribution be described in terms of symmetry and asymmetry, regardless of the number of major blocs, though especially in two-bloc systems, see Wolfram F. Hanreider, "The International System: Bipolar or Multibloc?" *Journal of Conflict Resolution*, vol. 9, September 1965, pp. 299–308. Hanreider provides alternative diagrams for depicting perfect and actual tight bipolarity.

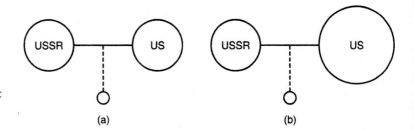

FIGURE 8–5   (a) Perfect tight bipolarity. (b) Actual tight bipolarity, 1946–1955.

(a)   (b)

domination. Charles de Gaulle's demand that Europe be de-Americanized threatened to dilute the potential effectiveness of the United States in facing the Soviet Union across Europe. Strategic policy in NATO led to other resentments and suspicions, with some Europeans doubting the credibility of the American nuclear umbrella, while still others feared that careless American responses to Soviet threats might unnecessarily embroil Europe in war. To make matters worse, the unpopularity of Washington's nuclear strategy in Asia after the Korean War and resistance to Washington's efforts to prevent Sino-Japanese trade grew to the point that widespread rioting accompanied the 1960 renegotiation of the defense alliance, forcing the cancellation of a state visit to Tokyo by President Dwight D. Eisenhower.

Outside of the blocs another critical change was taking place. Beginning in 1957, although more markedly after 1960, the number of nation-states burgeoned. In 1960, seventeen states were admitted to United Nations membership, every one of them newly independent. A world that had been revolutionary in several respects now added a new dimension—a sudden and unprecedented increase in the number of national actors. These new states, bound only by poverty, underdevelopment, and racial difference from the dominant white nations, were courted by both the United States and the Soviet Union, each seeking territorial advantage (especially if economic oportunity or natural resources were involved) and new adherents to its ideology. Most of the new states, however, preferred assistance with as little political cost as possible. This growing group of nonbloc actors further loosened global bipolarity.

In addition to the polycentrism of the Soviet sphere and the beginning of decentralization among American allies, the emergence of the Third World further loosened global polarity because it presented many nonbloc actors. Figure 8-6 shows the resulting loose bipolarity. Diagrammatically, the differences between this and the tight bipolar model are the presence of nonbloc actors and the splintering in the two main blocks. Yet the structure is still basically bipolar with respect to effective power relations. Only two bloc actors are portrayed as relating directly to the fulcrum. Each of the others either arises from a major bloc or is tied to one for power purposes, yet it may not be thoroughly allied.

For bloc members, the behavioral norms in tight and loose bipolar systems were essentially the same. Members pledged to prepare to eliminate the opposing bloc but preferred to fight small wars rather than large. Members agreed to strengthen their own bloc internally and to resolve differences by negotiation rather than open conflict. The threat of total destruction led to a tacit agreement not to provoke war between the dominant members of opposing blocs.

But for the dominant members, the Soviet Union and the United States, there was an added objective in loose bipolarity—namely, to maintain optimum tightness under conditions that encouraged fragmentation. The mechanisms for this function were like the normal rewards and punishments by which powerful states influence the less powerful: economic rewards and deprivations, offers and withdrawals of military supply beyond that needed for the state's contribution to bloc security, and so on. Force was used in extreme cases: the Soviet

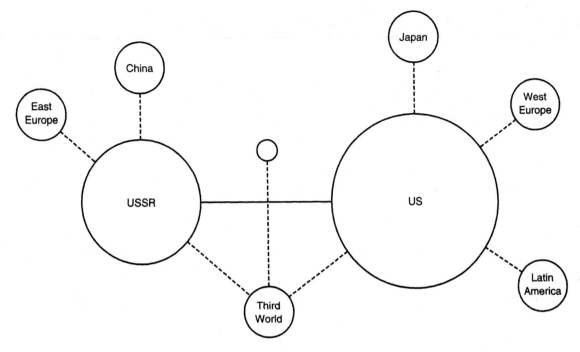

FIGURE 8–6 Loose bipolarity, 1955–1965.

Union in Hungary in 1956 and the United States in Cuba in 1961 and in the Dominican Republic in 1965. In addition, the dominant states used the institutionalized alliances to prolong the perception of threat by playing to the self-aggrandizing behavior of pertinent elites, such as national military commands. In this sense, threat perception became an important aspect of dominant-member political strategy in the loose bipolar system.

The norms of nonbloc actors were considerably different. Their basic role was as a ground for peaceful competition of the major powers and blocs. Their conflicts were internalized (Nigeria and Biafra), carefully circumscribed (Rhodesia and Zambia), or submitted to global settlement (Congo). They resisted great-power intervention when it threatened to bring in the other major power or result in subordination. The wars in Vietnam and Afghanistan, the last great interventionary wars of the United States and the Soviet Union, respectively, violated these rules, but it remains important that neither became militarily involved in the other's war.

The Incipient Multipolar Balance

For decades it was anticipated that in the normal course of events, bipolarity would yield to multipolarity, with the quasi-independent blocs becoming independent power poles. Some observers have argued that such a situation existed almost thirty years ago. But passage to multipolarity was stalled by a number of factors, and eventually shattered by the collapse of the Soviet Union.

During the 1970s and 1980s, it was thought that the world order was evolving into a six-center multipolar structure: North America, a united Western and Northern Europe, the Soviet Empire including Eastern Europe, Japan, China, and the geographically diffuse Developing World. To be sure, even during this period these centers often overlapped and were variously interdependent in many ways. NATO, for example, continued to bind the United States and Western Europe despite growing economic and trade friction between them. Similarly, Latin America was militarily tied to the United States and dependent on it in world trade, yet in its economic policy and debt problems strongly allied with the Developing World. Japan, too, was wholly reliant on the United States for national security, but repeatedly at the edge of trade war as its trade surplus skyrocketed and its markets remained almost closed to American products and services. Figure 8–7 shows this configuration.

Nonetheless, several circumstances prevented the linear passage from loose bipolarity to multipolarity. First, the progress toward political integration of Western Europe stumbled on a number of occasions over internal matters (such as monetary union) and external influences (such as renewed dependence on NATO following resumption of the Soviet-American arms race in the 1980s). Second, China's advancement suffered a number of setbacks

in economic planning and in global recognition, prompted principally by a dismal record in human rights and military exports, including modern rockets, to Iran and Iraq. Third, the power of the developing countries to influence the international order centered almost entirely on the oil-rich states, at a time at which nuclear and synthetic substitutes as well as conservation reduced the susceptibility of the West to OPEC's leverage. And fourth, the trade competition between North America and Japan, and between North America and Europe, fell so badly out of balance that the principal trading partners locked in conflict that the transition could neither explain nor control.

By far the most momentous events occurred in Eastern Europe and the Soviet Union, beginning with the Polish demand for democratic government. Tolerance of this movement by Mikhail Gorbachev's Soviet government became a tacit renunciation of the Brezhnev Doctrine, the principle under which Soviet forces had intervened in previous democratic movements in Eastern Europe.

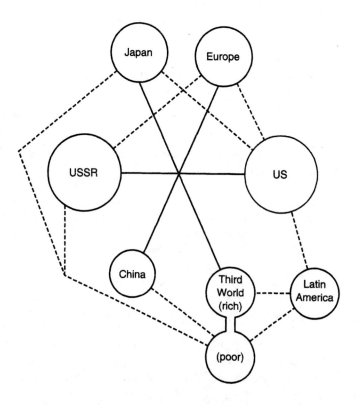

FIGURE 8–7   Incipient global multipolarity, 1965 to 1991.

(This doctrine said that the solidarity of the Socialist Commonwealth is more important than the politics of any of its parts, and must be preserved even if by force.) In 1989, Hungary became the first open Eastern European country since the Second World War by tearing down the barbed wire at its Austrian border; and the formerly illegal Polish Solidarity labor movement managed to establish the first noncommunist government in Eastern Europe in almost forty-five years. By the middle of 1990, communist governments had either collapsed or been replaced in East Germany, Poland, Hungary, Czechoslovakia, Bulgaria, and Romania (where civil war accompanied political events). Furthermore, the Berlin Wall, for more than three decades the most vivid symbol of a divided Europe, had been opened both politically and physically, followed by the opening of the Brandenburg Gate and the removal of the famous Checkpoint Charlie; and the two Germanys and the four occupying powers (United States, Soviet Union, Britain, and France) had agreed to the reunification of Germany and its membership in the North Atlantic Treaty Organization. By the middle of 1990, then, the Cold War in Europe had ended and the process of reuniting Europe had begun, only thirty months before the anticipated economic union of the European Community members.

If the collapse of communist governments in Eastern Europe was a revolutionary event, then the dissolution of the Soviet Union immediately thereafter was even more so. The "captive states" of Lithuania, Estonia, and Latvia demanded political independence and removal of Russian armed forces. Ukraine and Belarus (formerly Byelorussia), incorporated in the Soviet Union after World War One, created local governments and declared their independence of Soviet control. One by one the less well-developed Soviet Socialist Republics peeled away. Gorbachev, under whom all this change occurred, gave way to Boris Yeltsin, who consolidated his power only after bombarding the parliament building to bring an attempted coup to its knees. And as all this occurred, the United States and Moscow were dismantling nuclear weapons and delivery systems, embarking on joint ventures to accelerate Russia's transformation to a market (capitalist) economy, and cooperating in the United Nations on matters that the norms of an earlier day would have required their opposition, such as the peace movement in the Middle East and the military conquest of Iraq in the Desert Storm War. Even the brutal Russian war against insurgent Chechnya had little dampening consequences for Russian-American relations.

History continues its march. The liberated countries of Eastern Europe, sensing the economic disparities with Western Europe, now look to the West for their economic future; and still fearful of conservative resurgence in Russia, particularly in

The destruction of Pershing missiles, the backbone of the American intermediate-range nuclear force in Europe, after the U.S.-Soviet agreement to eliminate the weapons. (*Source:* © AP/Wide World)

light of the war in Chechnya, they seek membership in NATO. Simultaneously, as the European
Union solidifies, the United States, Mexico, and
Canada have launched the North American Free
Trade Area, a customs union and barrier-free trade
consortium not unlike that of Western Europe
(though it is limited entirely to trade, and does not
extend to labor markets, currencies, etc.). And gone
are the nuclear arms race, European battleline, and
the Cold War with all its classic, inflammatory
rhetoric: "containment," "capitalist encirclement,"
"communist menace," and so forth.

With all these changes and more, the structural characteristics of world politics no longer tend
toward multipolarity. For one thing, there is now
only one military giant, the United States. Alliances are in many respects vestigial political
structures, as power is now defined more in economic than military terms. In the absence of competing military coalitions as a global phenomenon
(they still exist in some regions), the concept of a
balance itself is gone. These, then, are the characteristics of a New World Order, not of the long-
anticipated multipolar phase of an older world
order. Contrary to a twenty-year assumption, loose
bipolarity evolved not into multipolarity, but into
a balance between the politics of competition and
the politics of collaboration without threat of
global war. Here, there is no Balancer and no en-
forcer. The equilibrating functions of a classical
balance of power are conducted with economic
rather than military weapons. Furthermore, when
potentially devastating events have occurred, such
as in the breakup of Yugoslavia and the ethnic-
cleansing civil war in Bosnia-Herzegovenia, the
principal interested powers have favored multilateralism to nationalistic solutions. Specifically, Russia and China have cooperated in the decisions of
the United Nations Security Council to endorse
both multinational peacekeeping missions and
NATO aerial bombardment of Bosnian Serb military installations to stop the killing.

This is not to imply that force will never again
occur on a global scale, but that it will not be characteristic of interstate relations as long as the new

system survives. The technological knowledge to
build better and better weapons will not evaporate,
nor will aggressive tendencies or opportunities.
And if this chapter demonstrates nothing else, it
shows that there is no more an end to political evolution than there is to the evolution of species.[11]
The world could drift into a new structural system
in the next decade as well as it did in the last, and
all the suppositions about the New World Order
could perish with the change. Meanwhile, force
will be a subglobal phenomenon, more often than
not with the larger states and coalitions acting in
diplomatic concert and multilateral response teams
across their vestigial alliances.

In a prescient study published in 1984, one observer examined the power theory of international
relations in light of the fundamental changes in the
preceding quarter-century. He found six causes of
change in traditional interstate power relations: (1)
accelerating resource scarcity; (2) increasing demand for redistribution of the world's wealth; (3) a
decline in governmental authority to maintain
order and cope with internal and external transformation; (4) a tendency away from loyalty to the
nation-state ("subgroupism"); (5) fragmentation of
intergovernmental relations even within alliances;
and (6) transnationalization of an increasing number of issues previously the preserve of governments
("cascading interdependence"). Together with the
improved ability of individuals to understand public policy and to force change in it, these factors
have led to the simultaneous disintegration of the
old order and integration into a new one, through a
"patterned chaos" of sociopolitical relations within
and among states. It is these dynamics that form
the framework of structural models of the world
order, that determine the pace, quality, and progress

---

[11] Though this argument addresses specifically international
change and, therefore, possible international change resulting
from unpredictable domestic phenomena, it explicitly departs
from the view that with the end of totalitarianism, liberal
democracy will be the final stage of ideological evolution and
will foster unprecedented stability. See Francis Fukuyama, *The
End of History and the Last Man* (New York: The Free Press,
1992).

of interstate relations, and that determine whether or not marked structural change will occur in the world order.[12]

In fact, marked structural change has occurred, and it is so profound that the balance-of-power notion is virtually obsolete, at least in global military terms. Of the New World Order it has been written that

> . . . balance of power politics will not be the defining feature of interactions among great powers in the coming decades, since the nature of states and the nature of the international system differ fundamentally from those [of the prior world order]. Because the great powers of the future will be nonunitary actors focusing primarily on maximizing wealth and acting not simply within a system of states . . . , they will no longer engage in balancing alliances but will settle conflicts and enhance their security through negotiation and compromise rather than through the use or threat of force.[13]

But one task remains before turning to modern concepts of national and international security, namely, to evaluate the Cold War world order—the era of tight bipolarity, loose bipolarity, and incipient multipolarity—as one of stability or instability.

The scholarly debate on this question occurred principally during the period of loose bipolarity, as fragmentation of alliances, the growing Developing World, and the strained credibility of mutually assured destruction by nuclear war all imparted their marks on world politics. One observer concluded, for instance, that bipolarity was principally stabilizing for four reasons: (1) the influence of dominant states was so great that major conflict could not develop beyond their control; (2) interbloc competition was such that there was an infinite variety of subject matters through which the domi-

nant members could control conflict within and between blocs; (3) the constancy of pressure to avoid major war ensured that crises would occur at lower levels of world politics; and (4) constant pressure and major-power domination enabled the blocs to sustain disruptive changes that might otherwise have resulted in wider warfare. These factors argue that the tighter the bipolarity, the more stabilizing it will be.[14]

In coming to the opposite conclusion, another study examined multipolar systems over time. It observed that bipolar systems limit peaceful transaction, accentuate antagonism, and promote degeneration and instability. It rejected the supposition of those who look for peace through controlled crisis and mutual fear, and it found the increased interdependence of broad-ranging international transactions in multipolarity a more stabilizing political environment.[15]

Yet a third conclusion was drawn from an empirical study of twenty-one actual historical situations. Its author found that multipolar systems experience war more frequently than do bipolar ones, with more violence, more participants, and more casualties. Bipolar systems, on the other hand, produce less frequent, shorter, and less costly wars. From this he concluded that only a single-nation-dominant world order, while rare, is the most stabilizing.[16]

Can any sense be made of these conflicting conclusions, all from leading students of the subject, though writing long before the end of the Cold War? Perhaps the missing link is that the Cold War world order had characteristics so different from its predecessors that the lessons of history fell short in predictive power. No former system of world order

---

[12] James N. Rosenau, "A Pre-theory Revisited: World Politics in an Era of Cascading Interdependence," *International Studies Quarterly*, September 1984, pp. 245–305.

[13] James N. Goldgeier and Michael McFaul, "A Tale of Two Worlds: Core and Periphery in the Post–Cold War Era," *International Organization*, spring 1992, pp. 467–491, p. 469.

[14] Kenneth N. Waltz, "The Stability of a Bipolar World," *Daedelus*, vol. 93, summer 1964, pp. 881–909. See also R. N. Rosecrance, "Bipolarity, Multipolarity, and the Future," *Journal of Conflict Resolution*, vol. 10, 1966, pp. 315–317.

[15] Karl W. Deutsch and J. David Singer, "Multipolar Power Systems and International Stability," *World Politics*, vol. 16, 1964, pp. 390–406.

[16] Michael Haas, "International Subsystems: Stability and Polarity," *American Political Science Review*, vol. 64, 1970, pp. 98–123.

in modern times had such all-inclusive alliance structures. None occurred in the face of such rapid growth in the sorts and sophistication of military hardware. None had scores of thousands of nuclear weapons on land, at sea, under the sea, and in the air to remind the dominant states that war would be tantamount to annihilation, for none had been preceded by any military event with such profound meaning as the atomic bombings of Hiroshima and Nagasaki in 1945.

Perhaps even an event as profound as the end of the Cold War cannot in the short term resolve the theoretical debate on whether bipolar systems or multipolar systems are the more stable. Nonetheless,

it is apparent that while economic and other international phenomena tended toward multipolarity as the Cold War evolved, the threat of nuclear war remained principally bilateral. No one thought seriously that France or Britain would engage in nuclear war without the United States, and no one took seriously the threat of China sustaining an independent nuclear offensive. Based, then, on the bilateral character of the Cold War's strategic component, one observer has concluded that the post–World War Two global system was founded on basic political realities that required no elaborate international political management. This, he concluded, made of the Cold War the era "the long peace."[17]

---

[17] John Lewis Gaddis, *The Long Peace*, especially chapter 8, "The Long Peace: Elements of Stability in the Post-war International System." For a similar theme from different perspectives, see Charles Kegley, ed., *The Long Postwar Peace* (New York: Harper-Collins, 1991).

CHAPTER 9

International Security

The historical practice in the study of international relations has been to consider military affairs and security either from national or alliance perspectives, or to postulate a single global security system through the military dominance of a few major powers. During the Cold War, for example, volumes were devoted either to "national security" or to the "East-West confrontation." The emphasis on national security underscored the urgency of individual, nationalisitic priorities, and dealt with broader geopolitical issues as by-products of national security. The most ambitious interpretations assumed that national defense required a distant military reach, and all friendly governments that fell within it benefited. These circumstantial combinings, often consummated in formal alliances, were presumed to be competing "security systems." While they varied greatly in most respects, their common threads were (1) a shared sense of security emergency and (2) military interdependence, often severely unbalanced. The vast network of American alliances, backed by weapons of mass destruction, theories of deterrence, and second-strike capability, was understood to be Washington's response to potential Soviet aggression against American interests almost anywhere, interests so varied and so widespread that their defense required extending the security shield to disparate societies abroad. From the Soviet perspective, the threat posed to Marxism-Leninism by capitalist encirclement required a regional security system in Eastern and Central Europe, and opportunistic *quasi*-alliances elsewhere to undermine the encirclement wherever possible. Within its sphere of interest, then, the Soviet Union created and maintained a competing security system, and equipped itself diplomatically to erode the American shield at such distant points as Syria, Nicaragua, Cuba, North Korea, the former North Vietnam, and so forth.

In contrast to this interpretation of Cold War security as an impasse of competing security systems, others saw it as having evolved into a single global system that prevented wars between and among major powers by the presence of destructive power so great, as seen at Nagasaki and Hiroshima in 1945, as to exceed the cost tolerance of all rational political systems. The inclusion of virtually all industrialized nations and much of the Developing World in the dominant alliance systems globalized the strategic and tactical reaches of the two nuclear giants to the extent that challenges to their military balance were impractical if not impossible. A disaffected power such as China had no opportunity to disrupt the basic global balance. However the power distribution might have been defined in political or economic terms, the capabilities of the United States and the Soviet Union fostered a bipolar military structure in which mutual deterrence evolved into a single global security system. The recurrence of both civil and international wars throughout the Cold War, many of them involving the United States or the Soviet Union indirectly and some of them directly, reveals the limits of this interpretation; but advocates of this interpretation of the Cold War security system insist that because

in none of these did two major powers fight one another, their viewpoint shows the system's essential
value. (Chinese intervention in the Korean War
after American involvement is the exception,
though it occurred early in the Cold War and at a
point at which China was a nascent power save for
the enormity of the People's Army.)

Whether one views the Washington-Moscow
nuclear confrontation as having been a threat to or
a guarantor of the Cold War peace, it has come to
an end. Nuclear delivery systems are being demolished or disarmed, and nuclear warheads are being
decommissioned. But the end of the Cold War has
diminished both Russian and American ability to
prevent war in many places. Furthermore, modern
conventional (nonnuclear) military technology is
available virtually everywhere, as the sale of arms
has become a staple of international commerce.
Given these unanticipated consequences of the Cold
War's end, the search is on to find the ingredients
of international security in the New World Order.

"International security" is a difficult concept to
define. To assume that it is the total of multiple national security systems is to ignore that what is one
nation's security may be another's threat. India, for
example, may feel secure from Pakistan, but the latter may feel threatened by the former. Iraq is fear-
less of Israel, but regards the United States as a
menace to its security. It cannot be said, therefore,
that international security is comprised of the addi-
tive consequences of various national security systems. The focal point of national security is the
individual nation with little regard for others.

Nor is there any basis for arguing that, at present, there exists a "global security system." In the
words of one author, the concept of global security
presumes "a common definition of security worldwide and sets of values, rules, and principles not yet
existing."[1] Perhaps the closest thing to universal security values is the Charter of the United Nations
but, as we will see subsequently, the practical
management of presumed universal norms in the

Security Council exemplifies their unreliability.
The end of the Cold War, profoundly important as
it is, could not have eliminated all differences in a
world of diverse cultures, varying ambitions, competing political philosophies, and vastly divergent
levels of satisfaction with the global distribution of
wealth and political influence.

We are left, then, with twin problems: first, to
define "international security" as something different from both national security and global security;
and second, to identify the tangible ingredients
that embrace international security in a manip-
ulable system of politics, policymaking, and supportive technology. Given the complexities of
international relations, the first of these must be
solved within modest limits, as utopian applications of the New World Order idea are of no practical value, as was emphasized in Chapter 1.

With these thoughts in mind, we define international security as a generally held confidence
that the world will not be plunged into war; that
the security interests of major powers are sufficiently globalized and compatible to prevent or
minimize regional warfare through multilateral
means; and that the world's tolerance for genocidal
civil wars has diminished to the point that politically controlled multilateral intervention is a
higher value than honoring the ancient sovereign
prerogatives of states that have no legitimate sovereign authority. After having set the stage by exploring the security legacy of the Cold War era, we
will return to this definition and explore the ingredients by which it is managed in the New World
Order.

The Cold War as Prologue

The international security system that evolved during the Cold War consisted of three principal parts:
(1) the mutual deterrence policies of the United
States and the Soviet Union that prevented cataclysmic global war; (2) carefully managed regional
conflicts (e.g., the Middle East, the two Koreas)
that, while occasionally hot, were prevented from
threatening general world security; and (3) the

---

[1] Helga Haftendorn, "The Security Puzzle: Theory-building and
Discipline-building in International Security," *International
Studies Quarterly*, March 1991, pp. 3–17 at p. 4.

evolution of neutral UN peacekeeping as a substitute for great-power imposition of peace under the original terms of the charter. We will concentrate at present on the Soviet-American confrontation, which was a nuclear-age adaptation of balance-of-power theory universally referred to as the Balance of Terror.

At the heart of both Soviet and American policies was the doctrine of strategic deterrence, under which each deployed thousands of nuclear weapons in its strategic triad (airborne, land missile, and submarine delivery systems) to signal to the other that in the event of attack (first strike), it would have enough strategic reserve to conduct massive retaliation as a second or responsive strike. This was a concept of mutually assured destruction (appropriately referred to as MAD). Missiles were targeted at population centers (countervalue strategy) and at military installations (counterforce strategy). To improve the ratio of firepower to delivery cost, both Washington and Moscow developed missiles with multiple warheads of two types: multiple reentry vehicles (MRVs) aimed at a single target, and multiple independently-targeted reentry vehicles (MIRVs) in which the rocket was a stage for releasing nuclear warheads to several targets simultaneously. By the time the Cold War ended, the United States had 1957 delivery vehicles in active deployment carrying 13,000 nuclear warheads, and the Soviet Union had 2474 vehicles packing 11,562 nuclear warheads. Delivery capability was measured in "throw weight" and explosive power in equivalent tonnage of TNT.

To protect its strategic weapons, the United States placed its ground-launched missiles in hardened (inpregnable) underground silos, kept nuclear-equipped B-52 bombers in the air around the clock, increased its reliance on its swift and silent nuclear submarine fleet, and built antiballistic missile defenses. (The Strategic Defense Initiative, or Star Wars, introduced by President Ronald Reagan was an unexecuted plan to extend the antimissile defenses to outer space.) The Soviet Union developed similar techniques, and added to them the mobility of railroad mounting. Generation followed generation of missiles on both sides, and to

modernize the warheads the United States conducted 910 nuclear tests and the Soviet Union 636 by the end of the Cold War. For each, most were conducted after the Partial Nuclear Test Ban Treaty of 1963 (579 for the United States and 451 for the Soviet Union). Meanwhile, France conducted 172 tests, Britain 41, China 31, and India 1. These states together remain the "nuclear club," though several other governments are believed to have or to be nearing nuclear capability. (This will be discussed subsequently.)

Variations in the intensity of the Cold War enabled Moscow and Washington partially to limit the growth in strategic arms. Eight examples stand out:

1. **Partial Nuclear Test Ban Treaty, 1963,** prohibited signatories, including the United States and the Soviet Union, from testing nuclear devices in the atmosphere. Tests were subsequently conducted underground.

2. **Nuclear Non-Proliferation Treaty, 1970,** prohibited nuclear signatories, including the United States and the Soviet Union, from supplying materials or technologies to nonnuclear states for the purpose of developing nuclear weapons, and prohibited nonnuclear signatories from accepting such materials and technologies.

3. **Anti-Ballistic Missile Treaty, 1972,** limited Soviet and American antiballistic missile defenses to two sites. The implicit agreement behind this formula was that second-strike capability is a better deterrent than first-strike capability, so that some of it should be protected from attack. But because second-strike missiles can also be used for first strike, they should not all be protected.

4. **SALT I, first Strategic Arms Limitation Treaty, 1972,** placed absolute quantitative limits on intercontinental ballistic missiles (ICBMs), deployed nuclear warheads, and MIRVS, but did not limit theater weapons. (Long-range missiles aimed at Soviet targets from the United States were limited, but shorter-range missiles designed for Europe's defense were not.)

5. **SALT II, second Strategic Arms Limitation Treaty, signed in 1978 but never ratified by**

the U.S. Senate, would have extended limits on first-strike ICBMs, but foundered in part over differing interpretations of the impact on European theater weapons.

6. START I, first Strategic Arms Reduction Treaty, negotiations began in 1981 but were not consummated until after the end of the Cold War. The linguistic change from SALT to START is important, because the goal of SALT was to put quantitative limits on weapons growth, while START was designed to reduce the existing ceilings.

7. MBFR (Mutual and Balanced Force Reduction) Talks, began in 1983 on the reduction of conventional (nonnuclear) forces in Europe, but were not consummated until after the end of the Cold War.

8. INF Treaty, 1987, reduced Soviet and American intermediate-range nuclear forces in Europe. These were the "theater weapons" that had been omitted from SALT I and complicated ratification of SALT II.

Meanwhile, while the balance of weapons production and weapons limitation was proceeding, governments were amassing chemical and biological stockpiles designed to do everything from eradicate populations to incapacitate troops temporarily. All this was at a staggering cost that, on the one hand, stimulated national economies, but on the other hand, squandered natural resources, drained scarce financial resources from quality of life and desperately needed international economic development, and left a legacy of nuclear and chemical contamination that will require careful handling for thousands of years. Moreover, not all weapons-grade radioactive material is accounted for in either the United States or the former Soviet Union, introducing serious issues of nuclear weapons proliferation by irresponsible governments and the possibilities of both nuclear blackmail and nuclear terrorism. The financial cost of nuclear demobilization has never been estimated. Nor is there an accurate measure of the costs to nature, human health, and the planetary environment from contamination. The complexity of the political, ideological, and economic issues that follow the Cold War pales when compared with that of the probable long-term health and environmental issues.

International Security in the New World Order

The end of the Cold War presents the third opportunity of the twentieth century to create a reliable international security system. Efforts following World War One were hampered by a combination of fatal weaknesses including (1) distrustfulness of multilaterialism, as exemplified principally by the American refusal to join the League of Nations; (2) a punitive peace that encouraged the resurgence of German militarism and the rise of Nazi totalitarianism; (3) Japanese militarism and a cultural belief in destiny through conquest; and (4) Western fear of the Marxist-Leninist challenge to capitalism and constitutional democracy. World War Two was followed by a second effort at multilateralism through the United Nations, this time strengthened by improved measures for collective response to aggression and by enthusiastic American participation consistent with Washington's determination to remain a global power. The intrusion of the Cold War, heightened by the Soviet Union's second nuclear achievement and the global dimensions of the East-West standoff, plunged the world into a system of competing alliances that fostered peace through threat and mutual deterrence rather than through cooperation.

In each post-world-war era, therefore, circumstances encouraged a retreat to national security. The relevant combination of factors today is altogether different, offering an unprecedented—though hardly perfect—opportunity to build an international security system with appropriate diplomatic and technological instruments, and with the necessary political controls (and economic limitations) to prevent a worldwide security autocracy in the militarily unipolar environment. The ingredients for pursuing such a goal are several.

TABLE 9–1

U.S. NUCLEAR ARMS REDUCTION UNDER START I, IN NUMBER OF WARHEADS DEPLOYED

	Cold War Maximum	START I Requirement
Land-based (ICBM)	2,450	1,300
Sea-based (SLBM)	5,312	3,456
Air-based (bombs)	5,238	2,864
Totals	13,000	7,620

Source: SIPRI Yearbook, 1989, p. 12, and SIPRI Yearbook, 1994, p. 294.

TABLE 9–2

RUSSIAN NUCLEAR ARMS REDUCTION UNDER START I, IN NUMBER OF WARHEADS DEPLOYED

	Cold War Maximum	START I Requirement
Land-based (ICBM)	6,860	3,200
Sea-based (SLBM)	3,602	1,696
Air-based (bombs)	1,100	1,068
Totals	11,562	5,964

Source: SIPRI Yearbook, 1989, p. 15, and SIPRI Yearbook, 1994, p. 294.

Dismantling the Strategic Arms Race and Nuclear Confrontation

The foremost precondition of structuring a new international security system in the post–Cold War world is eliminating the defining military characteristics of the Cold War itself. We already have seen that progress had been made in this regard in the diplomatic process of transition. Concluding the INF agreement on intermediate-range nuclear forces in Europe was a signal achievement, followed in importance by opening the MBFR talks on theater conventional weapons and the START I talks on Soviet and American strategic weapons. Since the end of the Cold War, the MBFR talks have resulted in the Treaty on Conventional Forces in Europe (CFE Treaty, 1990), START I has been concluded (1991), and START II has been signed (1993) and ratified by the U.S. Senate, but has not been approved constitutionally by the Russian government.

Because strategic weapons were the core of global deterrence, we look at them first. We have seen already that at the end of the Cold War, the United States had in active deployment 1957 delivery vehicles (combined strategic aircraft, submarines, and intercontinental ballistic missiles) carrying a total of 13,000 nuclear warheads. The delivery systems were of various geographic ranges, many exceeding 10,000 miles, and the warheads of

varying explosive power up to 457 kilotons. The Soviet Union had 2474 combined delivery vehicles carrying 11,562 warheads with ranges of up to 8000 miles and explosive power of as much as 1.5 megatons, or about three times as great as the maximum of American weapons. The goal of START I was to place absolute limits on the number of deployed warheads. Table 9–1 demonstrates the consequences for American strategic deployment, bringing the total down to 7620, a decline of 40 percent. Table 9–2 does the same for Russia, which eventually took control of all former Soviet strategic weapons in countries made independent by the breakup of the Soviet Union. It shows a reduction from 11,562 warheads to 5964, a reduction of 48 percent.[2]

START II continued the trend of absolute reductions, with results as shown in Tables 9–3 and 9–4. The treaty called for deployed American and Russian nuclear warheads both to be reduced to about 3500. Moreover, START II also aimed for a

---

[2] Strategic disarming of the former Soviet Union was complicated by the fact that the dissolution of the USSR resulted in four independent nuclear states: Russia, Belarus, Ukraine, and Kazakhstan. By agreement among them, Russia took responsibility for all strategic weapons, and by the end of 1995 Russia had completed their removal or destruction from Belarus, Ukraine, and Kazakhstan. The process had begun within Russia. By a Washington-Moscow agreement, the United States began purchasing the nuclear components of the decommissioned weapons.

TABLE 9–3

U.S. NUCLEAR ARMS REDUCTION UNDER START II, IN NUMBER OF WARHEADS DEPLOYED

	START I Maximum	START II Requirement
Land-based (ICBM)	1,300	500
Sea-based (SLBM)	3,456	1,728
Air-based (bombs)	2,864	1,260
Totals	7,620	3,488

Source: SIPRI Yearbook, 1994, p. 295.

TABLE 9–4

RUSSIAN NUCLEAR ARMS REDUCTION UNDER START II, IN NUMBER OF WARHEADS DEPLOYED

	START I Maximum	START II Requirement
Land-based (ICBM)	3,200	1,005
Sea-based (SLBM)	1,696	1,696
Air-based (bombs)	1,068	798
Totals	5,964	3,499

Source: SIPRI Yearbook, 1994, p. 295.

return to single-warhead missile defenses, or elimination of MRVs and MIRVs; Tables 9–3 and 9–4 indicate the goal was almost reached for both ICBMs and submarine-launched ballistic missiles (SLBMs). Figure 9–1 summarizes the quantitative and qualitative goals of both START I and START II as compared with late–Cold War deployment levels.

Early in 1996 the U.S. Senate ratified the START II treaty, but its status in Russia remains in doubt. The resurgence of Russian nationalism in 1995 and 1996 led to the removal of the pro-Western and pro-reform foreign secretary and his replacement by a hard-line communist nationalist. General political disarray and the revised popularity of communism, as shown in the parliamentary elections of late 1995, accentuated concerns that Russia will decline to conclude START II.[3] Although many Russians agreed that START II was in danger in Moscow, their explanation centered on Western provocation that accounted for Russian political behavior. Writing specifically for an American audience in 1996, Mikahil Gorbachev, the former Soviet premier and president whose policies led to

the end of the Cold War and disbanding of the Warsaw Pact, offered this analysis:

> The problem is the American double standard: a demand for disarmament while disrupting the balance of power by pushing NATO's ill-conceived plans to march toward Russia.
>
> Expanding NATO's umbrella, including its nuclear weapons, to cover Poland, the Czech Republic, Slovakia and Hungary—moving NATO's frontiers some 400 miles closer to Moscow and the Russian heartland—is seen as a fundamental violation of Western guarantees after Russia dissolved the Warsaw Pact and agreed to German reunification.
>
> Many in the West see NATO as benign. But Russians see it as something that didn't change with the end of the cold war—as a war machine that is trying to take advantage of our troubled political and economic situation. The fear, realistic or not, is that the West or some politicians in the West want to deliver a coup de grace to the Russian Federation and eliminate forever a Russian challenge to United States dominance.
>
> The result, of course, is that Russian defense officials are loathe to endorse any new cuts in their missile forces. Not surprisingly, the Russian Parliament may refuse to ratify START II. . . .
>
> . . . Already the friction over NATO and START II is undermining what is left of Russia's confidence

---

[3] See John W. R. Leppingwell, "START II and the Politics of Arms Control in Russia," *International Security*, fall 1995, pp. 63–91. This paper was written before the 1995 Russian parliamentary elections, in which nationalistic fervor over such issues as Russia's world and European roles gave a major victory to the Communist party.

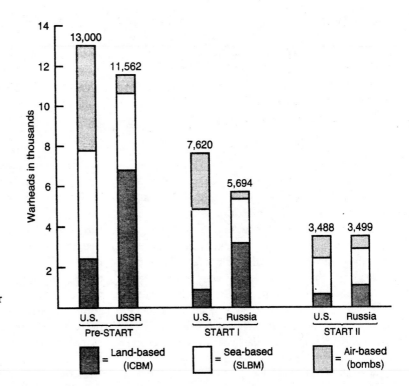

FIGURE 9–1 Cold War, START I, and START II nuclear deployments, United States and USSR/Russia.

Source: SIPRI Yearbook, 1989, pp. 12 and 15, and *SIPRI Yearbook, 1994,* pp. 294–295.

in the West and helping our ultra-nationalists in their bid for presidential power.

    There is a real danger that we'll restart the arms race. I wouldn't be surprised if the nuclear-security card [were] resurrected in the coming elections in both Russia and the United States. . . .[4]

Clearly, therefore, the early post–Cold War euphoria over bilateral nuclear arms reduction has fallen victim to a deteriorating political climate directly—and perhaps causally—related to subsequent disagreements over the Russian role in Europe's post-Soviet power equation. Because a resurgence of the East-West nuclear arms race would erode confidence in global peace, its shadow is the foremost threat to international security in the New World Order.

Even short of that, however, the drift toward power politics as usual in the late 1990s has consequences untenable to international security in the post–Cold War setting. As the Russian-American gap has widened, Moscow unexpectedly has renewed ties with China, at first in general diplomatic and economic relations[5] and shortly thereafter in an agreement to complete the long-delayed sale of seventy-two advanced fighter aircraft.[6] The announcement was made during a period of severe strain between Beijing and Washington over Taiwan's attempts to establish an independent international identity, prevention of which is the first priority of Chinese policy. In the following section we will deal with this matter from the East Asian regional perspective.

---

[4] Mikhail S. Gorbachev, "NATO's Plans Threaten START II," *The New York Times,* February 10, 1996, p. A15.

[5] Steven Erlanger, "An Old Flame Heats Up: Miffed at the U.S., Russia Flirts with China," *The New York Times,* December 29, 1995, p. A4.

[6] *The New York Times,* February 7, 1996, p. A1.

For the moment, however, it is important that Moscow's decision is symptomatic of the New World Order's weakening foundation, and an indication of willingness to resume the historic balance-of-power policies by playing once again the venerable China card.

Stabilizing the Incendiary Regions

The second assumption of the New World Order's international security system is that the global objectives of the major powers are compatible enough to ensure stability in places threatened with regional wars. Foremost among these is the European theater, where the the most crucial regional race in conventional and tactical nuclear arms has occurred since the late 1940s. But equally important to long-range peace and stability are the Middle East, where there have been five major regional wars and one multiparty civil war (Lebanon) since World War Two, and Asia, where India and Pakistan, North and South Korea, and China and Taiwan all maintain warlike postures.

Europe With the conclusion of the Intermediate-range Nuclear Forces (INF) Treaty (1987) and progress in the MBFR talks, important advances were made toward the military stabilization of Europe before the end of the Cold War. But as tensions eased, the pace of discussions quickened. The Treaty on Conventional Forces in Europe (CFE), signed in 1990, entered into effect after ratifications in 1992, and added to it was the Concluding Act of the Negotiation on Personnel Strength of Conventional Armed Forces in Europe (also called the CFE 1-A Agreement).

Unlike the START agreements, which are entirely bilateral[7] and limited to long-range strategic

weapons, the goals of CFE involve the daily issues of immediate territorial defense for virtually all countries from the Atlantic Ocean to the Ural Mountains, the so-called "impact area" of the CFE Agreement. Many of these were formerly members of the Soviet Union reliant on Moscow for security; and others, formerly cornerstone members of the Warsaw Pact, now covet membership in NATO, once the enemy alliance. Yet the arithmetical calculations of the CFE Agreement resemble the geopolitical landscape of the Cold War. The Western side consists of the United States and its historical NATO allies; and the Eastern side consists of Russia, the former Warsaw Pact allies (called the Budapest Group because of the location of intra-Eastern prenegotiations), and former members of the Soviet Union now included in the Commonwealth of Independent States (CIS), in the CFE context referred to as the Tashkent Group. This ignores substantial political realignments that occurred in the wake of the disbanding of the Warsaw Pact, especially within the Budapest Group. Nonetheless, the result with respect to conventional weapons is found in Table 9–5. (The total for the Russia/Tashkent Group, and the Budapest Group is supplied for post-CFE comparison with NATO.) All of these goals were to have been achieved within forty months of ratification and were thus to have been completed in late 1995. Note that the Eastern reductions are far steeper than are the Western and that in two critical categories, fixed-wing aircraft and helicopters, Western post-CFE ceilings are actually higher than the pre-CFE deployment levels.

Table 9–6 presents the pre-CFE troop personnel holdings and the post-CFE ceilings. Note that NATO post-CFE ceilings are higher than the number of troops deployed before the agreement. (This includes only troops dedicated to NATO and does not include, for example, all U.S. armed forces.) The national contributions are altered substantially, however. Germany, France, Turkey, and Britain, for example, have substantial reductions, but the U.S. has a potential increase of 75,000 troops. On the Eastern side, there is a small total reduction with Russia, Belarus, and Ukraine leading the way (a

---

[7] The START agreements do not affect Britain, France, or China. As of 1994, Britain was estimated to have had deployed 100 nuclear bombs and 100 SLBM warheads; France 80 bombs, 384 SLBM, and 48 land-based warheads; and China 150 bombs, 24 SLBM, and 110 land-based warheads. It was not known if China had deployed MIRVs. See *SIPRI Yearbook, 1994*, pp. 298–302.

TABLE 9-5

CONVENTIONAL FORCE REDUCTIONS IN EUROPE, 1995

Group		Tanks	ACVs	Artill.	Aircraft	Helos.	Total
Budapest	pre-CFE	11,861	13,215	11,777	1,838	183	38,874
	post-CFE	6,850	10,000	6,825	1,649	500	25,824
Russia/Tashkent	pre-CFE	17,932	27,737	12,801	6,512	1,364	66,346
	post-CFE	13,150	20,000	13,175	5,150	1,500	52,975
Total	pre-CFE	28,793	40,952	24,578	8,350	1,547	105,220
	post-CFE	20,000	30,000	20,000	6,799	2,000	78,799
NATO	pre-CFE	23,424	39,159	19,353	4,901	1,636	88,473
	post-CFE	19,142	29,822	18,286	6,662	2,000	75,912

Note: ACVs = armored combat vehicles;
     Artill. = artillery pieces;
     Helos. = helicopters.

Source: SIPRI Yearbook, 1993, pp. 608–609.

total of 256,000). But take the Budapest Group as a subset:

Country	Pre-CFE Holdings	Post-CFE Ceiling	Change
Czech Republic	110,010	93,333	–16,677
Hungary	76,226	100,000	+23,774
Poland	273,050	234,000	–39,050
Slovakia	55,005	46,667	–8,338
Totals	514,291	474,000	–40,291

This group has a reduction of 7.8 percent under CFE, smaller than the 9.7 percent reduction for the entire Eastern side of the balance. Moreover, should NATO subsequently admit these nations, or should they fail to side with Russia and the Tashkent Group in any confrontation, then the Western side is strengthened by 474,000 troops, an amount larger than the French army.[8] Given both

the deeper cuts in absolute military strength than the West through both the START and CFE agreements, and insistent that Central European power not shift to the Western side through political realignment, Moscow announced in 1993 this modification in its pledge not to use nuclear weapons first:

The Russian Federation will not use nuclear weapons against any non-nuclear-weapon State Party to the Treaty on the Non-Proliferation of Nuclear Weapons, except in the event of an attack on the Russian Federation, its territory, armed forces or allies conducted by a State of this kind that is linked by an agreement of association with a nuclear-weapon State or that acts together with, or with the support of a nuclear-weapon State in carrying out such an attack.[9]

These caveats notwithstanding, the combination of strategic arms reduction and the INF and CFE reductions in Europe has resulted in sharp reductions in annual defense expenditures. In the United States, for example, where annual defense spending for NATO alone had been rising at a

---

[8] To reduce budget deficits, a requirement of including the franc in determining the value of the future common European currency, France announced in early 1996 additional unilateral troop reductions. It also announced that it would discontinue nuclear testing and nuclear weapons manufacture, that it would eliminate its domestically unpopular land-based nuclear arsenal, and that it would abandon the military draft. See The New York Times, February 22, 1996, p. A1, and February 23, 1996, p. A3.

---

[9] The statement is reprinted in many places including The United Nations and Nuclear Non-proliferation (New York: United Nations, 1995), Document 42 at p. 174.

TABLE 9-6

MILITARY PERSONNEL LIMITATIONS IN EUROPE, 1995

	NATO GROUP		RUSSIA/BUDAPEST/TASHKENT GROUP		
	pre-CFE	post-CFE	post-CFE	pre-CFE	
Belgium	76,088	70,000	NR	7,101	Armenia
Canada	4,077	10,660	NR	NR	Azerbaijan
Denmark	29,256	39,000	100,000	143,865	Belarus
France	341,988	325,000	104,000	99,404	Bulgaria
Germany	401,102	345,000	93,333	110,010	Czech Rep.
Greece	165,400	158,621	40,000	NR	Georgia
Italy	294,900	315,000	100,000	76,226	Hungary
Netherlands	69,324	80,000	NR	NR	Moldova
Norway	29,500	32,000	234,000	273,000	Poland
Portugal	39,700	75,000	230,000	244,807	Romania
Spain	177,078	300,000	1,145,000	1,298,299	Russia
Turkey	575,045	530,000	46,667	55,005	Slovak Rep.
U.K.	288,626	260,000	450,000	509,531	Ukraine
United States	175,070	250,000			
Total	2,667,154	2,790,281	2,543,000	2,817,248	

Note: NR = Not Reported.

Source: SIPRI Yearbook, 1993, pp. 614.

steady 5 to 6 percent, from 1987 through 1993 it declined almost uninterruptedly in amounts ranging from less than 1 percent to more than 10 percent. Moreover, the 1992 U.S. National Defense Funding Plan for the period 1994 through 1998 called for an aggregate reduction in total military spending of 19.6 percent, using constant prices.[10] Meanwhile, NATO's combined military expenses dropped steadily from 1987 through 1993, enough to effect a full 1 percent drop in fraction of gross domestic product. And the combined NATO equipment expense dropped annually from 1988 through 1993, for a total decline of over 39 percent.[11]

The military situation in Europe, it becomes clear, is in a state of flux. What in the late 1980s appeared to be a linear path to stability has deteriorated into an intra-NATO dispute about the organization of European security and the future status of at least four former members of the Warsaw Pact (Hungary, Poland, the Czech Republic, and Slovakia), and into an East-West dispute about the security of the Russian Federation's borders, the decline in Russia's military strength, and the resumption of balance-of-power politics spilling over from Europe to Asia.

Asia From an economic perspective, no region has prospered more from the New World Order than Asia. The much-envied progress of Japan, South Korea, Hong Kong (which reverts to China

[10] *SIPRI Yearbook, 1994*, pp. 395 and 403.
[11] *SIPRI Yearbook, 1994*, pp. 394 and 401.

in 1997), Taiwan (which China claims), and Singapore now has spilled over to Vietnam, Indonesia, Malaysia, Thailand, and the Philippines. For the first time in modern history, China is poised to become a major economic power and participant in world trade, even in advanced goods. Many Asian countries have become havens for foreign direct investment, as political stability and trained work forces make manufacturing profitable there. As a consequence, Asian imports in recent years have tended away from primary commodities such as agricultural products and natural resources, and toward manufactures including electronic and other engineering products. But Asia is not without its storm clouds.

War between China and Taiwan has been a repeated but unlikely probability since 1950, when the vanquished forces of Chiang Kai-shek took refuge to the island, leaving China proper to Mao Zedong's communist forces. Throughout the Korean War (1950–1953) and for more than a decade thereafter, Chinese invasion was deterred by the presence of the U.S. Navy and hundreds of thousands of American air, sea, and land troops in South Korea, Japan, and the Philippines. Through persistent diplomatic efforts, Washington and Beijing have sidestepped the long-term question of Chinese sovereignty over Taiwan (which calls itself the Republic of China) by agreeing on a one-China policy in which Washington recognizes only the People's Republic of China (China proper) and conducts economic and military relations with Taiwan through agreements that are presented as commercial rather than intergovernmental. China covets Taiwan's economic prowess, but bristles at Washington's open defiance of its political sensitivity over such things as the sale of modern fighter aircraft to Taiwan.

Remarkably, the circumstances of the New World Order have worsened this delicate situation. Taiwan's wealth has gained it favors in some sectors of the Developing World, where small coalitions now annually sponsor the creation of a United Nations seat for Taiwan, thus abandoning the one-China notion for a two-Chinas or a one-China,

one-Taiwan policy of international recognition. (In 1996, China prevented the extension of UN peacekeeping in Haiti because of Haiti's Taiwan leanings.) In its first fully democratic presidential election (1996), the Taiwanese elected a president who is not a nationalist Chinese, but a native Taiwanese who claims Taiwan's historical sovereignty over the island irrespective of competing interpretations of the Chinese civil war. Conservative politics and anticommunist sentiments in the United States, spawned by China's dismal human rights record and hostility to popular Taiwan, have made it difficult for presidents not to drift with many of Taiwan's friends toward implicit recognition of sovereignty. But the potential crisis deepened in 1995 and 1996 after Taiwan's leader, presumably traveling as a private citizen, visited the United States with the State Department's blessing in spite of Chinese protests. Thereafter, China cracked down on political dissenters, detained legitimate American military observers, increased military production, threatened to resume nuclear testing, conducted military maneuvers in the straits between China and Taiwan, and announced that they would invade Taiwan if it were to declare sovereign independence. The appearance of two U.S. aircraft carriers in the straits for the first time since the Vietnam War was a signal to Beijing that its pre-Taiwan election war games would not be permitted to undermine Taiwan's democratic development. The long-delayed sale of seventy-two advance fighter aircraft by Moscow to Beijing in early 1996 accentuated the instability of the area and, from the American perspective, resumed the process of manipulating regional power distributions in a way more appropriate to the Cold War than to the New World Order.

Also capable of military flare-up is the lingering hostility between the two Koreas. In contrast to North Korea, where succession from the cult of Kim Il Sung brought not liberalism but near economic collapse (furthered by Russia's loss of interest in supporting North Korea after 1992), South Korea gradually has democratized as part of the public demand associated with economic modernization.

Many in the South fear that a military adventure may be the only thing that would re-awaken nationalistic pride in the North. This fear was heightened in 1994 and 1995 when it became known that North Korea's nuclear research program was advancing rapidly, and though the government claimed that it was for the purpose of generating electricity only, evidence mounted about the potential for producing weapons-grade plutonium. Through combined UN and U.S. intevention, the program was discontinued in return for an agreement to provide peaceful nuclear reactors. Unlike the China-Taiwan situation, the standoff between the two Koreas seemed to have stabilized as the decade entered its latter half. Undoubtedly this was due in part to both Russian and Chinese neutrality on the matter.

The third Asian hot spot, again of long standing, is India and Pakistan, which have been locked continuously in territorial dispute since the late 1940s. Throughout the Cold War, the United States and the Soviet Union maintained a dangerously high-level military balance between the two. Even after the Cold War, India remained the largest importer of foreign arms in the world, having spent $10.5 billion (U.S. value at 1990 constant prices and exchange rates) from 1989 through 1993. For the same period of time, Pakistan was the ninth largest arms importer in the world and seventh largest in the Developing World, with $3.6 billion.[12]

The situation worsened in 1996 when the United States presented evidence that India had resumed its nuclear research program, presumably fearful of China's Taiwan-related military enhancement. Almost immediately thereafter, Washington accused Beijing of transferring nuclear technology to Pakistan. This raised the specter of regional nuclear tripolarity potentially involving 40 percent of the world's population, with China and India having a combined population of more than 2 billion.

South Korean soldier guards border with North Korea. (*Source:* © AP/Wide World)

In this context, the sale of modern fighter aircraft to Beijing by Moscow was seen not only as part of the budding Taiwan crisis, but as a way of diverting American attention from Europe by stirring the broader Asian cauldron.

Given all of these trends in South and East Asia in the latter half of the decade, one author's assessment of the future, written in 1993, becomes disturbingly prophetic. His analysis is summarized as follows:

1. The East Asian power balance is up for grabs.
2. If economic liberalism in East Asia is not accompanied by democratization, the end of the Cold War could prove destabilizing for the region.

---

[12] *SIPRI Yearbook, 1994,* p. 485.

3. It is not Japan but China that, over time, is most likely to disturb regional equilibrium.
4. The United States cannot stabilize the region militarily except at an intolerable cost.
5. The U.S. commitment in the region, especially to Taiwan, is dangerously vague and invites conflict and miscalculation.[13]

In light of the events that followed these observations, it is clear that East and South Asia's stability has declined, and that while the New World Order has profited greatly the region's economic situation (especially East Asia), one of the tenets of the post–Cold War international security system—that the interests of major powers are compatible enough to prevent regional wars—is in grave danger there. Indeed, this region may more than any other reveal the incompatibilities of major-power interests.

The Middle East For fifty years the Middle East has commanded the world's attention because of the fundamental differences between Israel and its Arab neighbors over land rights in the religiously historic region. From the Arab perspective, what has been at stake more than anything else are the territorial survival of the Palestinian people and preventing Israel from claiming the Holy City of Jerusalem. After the most recent (1973) Arab-Israeli war, however, Israel occupied territory it had seized in the Sinai Desert, the Gaza Strip, the West Bank region of the Jordan River, and the Golan Heights. In its peace agreement with Egypt in 1977, it gave up its Sinai holdings, but the others remained controversial until recently. Decades of terrorism, threat of war, political assassination, espionage, and retaliatory Israeli forays into Lebanon against terrorist camps began to abate only in 1989 when Israel and the Palestine Liberation Organization (PLO) opened their first public peace talks.

The first stage resulted in 1995 in Israel granting limited self-rule to Palestinians in Gaza and in the West Bank region of the Jordan. Talks began between Israel and Syria in 1996 regarding the Golan Heights. The 1995 assassination of Israeli Premier Yitzhak Rabin by a young Israeli opposed to further peace talks and land cessions threatened the process less than did the antipeace terrorism of Hamas, which resumed in 1996. The mid-1996 election of the conservative Benjamin Netanyahu as Prime Minister further threatened the process. His platform included canceling the policy of land for peace, and one of his early acts was to announce resumption of building Israeli settlements in the occupied territories.

Ending the Cold War was an integral part of settling Arab-Israeli differences. Presidents George Bush and Mikhail Gorbachev were instrumental together in arranging the first formal peace conference (at Madrid, Spain) after secret discussions had begun in Oslo, Norway. Furthermore, the end of the Cold War spelled the end of a long-standing Soviet relationship with Syria, through which Soviet policies had been pursued in the region at the price of arming Syria. The general reduction of tensions, the withdrawal of the Soviet Union from its historic commitment to Syria, and a growing desire for peace despite mutual intolerance and strongholds of violent antipeace sentiment on both sides enabled the peace process to advance. In this period, Egypt's and Jordan's defense expenditures dropped; Israel's stabilized, but at a rate of merely half of that in 1983; and Syria's increased.[14]

Elsewhere in the Middle East, however, the consequences for the New World Order are less promising. Iran, greatly weakened by its 1980 war with Iraq, continues to use the ready availability of modern arms to rebuild its forces. Iraq's 1990 invasion of Kuwait, provoking the 1991 Desert Storm War, was the first major aggression of the post–Cold War era, though it occurred at such a

---

[13] Richard K. Betts, "Wealth, Power and Instability: East Asia and the United States After the Cold War," *International Security*, winter 1993–94, pp. 34–77 at p. 37. The paper does not discuss the South Asian situation addressed here.

---

[14] *SIPRI Yearbook, 1992*, p. 260.

Yasir Arafat, left, pays a condolence visit to Yitzhak Rabin's widow after the assassination of the Israeli Prime Minister. (*Source:* © The Bettmann Archive)

transitional moment that the Iraqi government may have underestimated the Soviet Union's untested commitment to a markedly revised world order. Nonetheless, the world remains concerned with Iraq's recovery in arms; its spotty cooperation with UN inspectors on its nuclear, biological, and chemical weapons programs; its international arms purchases; and the bellicose behavior of its government. Recently, in an attempt to accelerate its economic recovery from war, Iraq has proposed a limited relaxation of the global boycott against its products so that it might export small quantities of oil to earn foreign exchange for food and medical products. Whether or not these discussions will lead to agreements that pacify Iraq's regional policies is not known yet.

We conclude this section by returning to the pertinent characteristic of the New World Order's international security system, namely, the extent to which major-power interests are compatible and able to prevent regional wars. On balance it appears at this stage of the new order that this tenet fits the Middle East best among the incendiary regions of the world, that evolving conditions place it in peril in East and South Asia, and that its applicability to Europe will be unsteady until Russia and NATO

agree to a regional security regime that threatens neither.

Multilateral Pacification of Civil Wars

A third major tenet of international security in the New World Order is that genocidal civil wars are so intolerable to the global community that politically controlled multilateral intervention, for humanitarian purposes only, is preferred to the alternative of respecting the sovereign independence of states that are without legitimate civil authority. One of the by-products of the sovereign equality of states is their independence from external political intervention and from violations of their territorial integrity, principles endorsed emphatically by the UN Charter. But in the modern era, need these principles preclude properly constituted multilateral efforts to save populations from disease, starvation, and torture provided the purpose is not to impose political settlements on combating forces?

In a discussion of preventive deployment in his *Agenda for Peace, 1995,* Secretary-General Boutros-Ghali wrote as follows:

American forces in Saudi Arabia prepare for Iraq's chemical weapons by conducting military preparations in protective equipment. (*Source:* © AP/Wide World)

The Organization must remain mindful of the carefully negotiated balance of the guiding principles annexed to [the pertinent General Assembly resolution of 1991]. Those guidelines stressed . . . that humanitarian assistance must be provided in accordance with the principles of humanity, neutrality and impartiality; that the sovereign territorial integrity and national unity of States must be fully respected in accordance with the Charter of the United Nations; and that, in this context, humanitarian assistance should be provided with the consent of the affected country and, in principle, on the basis of an appeal by that country.[15]

Elsewhere in the text he describes peacekeeping as "hitherto" having required the consent of all concerned parties, suggesting a movement to qualify the consent requirement.[16] And in a third place, discussing the rapid evolution of peacekeeping in the New World Order, he noted as follows:

There are three aspects of recent mandates that . . . have led peace-keeping operations to forfeit the consent of the parties, to behave in a way that was perceived to be partial and/or to use force other than in self-defence. These have been the tasks of protecting humanitarian operations during continuing warfare, protecting civilian populations in designated safe areas and pressing the parties to achieve

---

[15] Boutros Boutros-Ghali, *An Agenda for Peace, 1995* (New York: United Nations, 1995), p. 50.

[16] Boutros Boutros-Ghali, *An Agenda for Peace, 1995*, p. 45.

national reconciliation at a pace faster than they were ready to accept.[17]

While acknowledging that consent-based peacekeeping and specially mandated use of force for purposes other than self-defense are inconsistent diplomatically and not undertaken interchangeably, he nonetheless endorsed the nonconsent mandates for limited purposes. Unfortunately, the two places in which they have been attempted were two of the low spots in the history of UN peacekeeping: Somalia and Bosnia.

In the wake of the Cold War there has been unleashed a list of civil wars without precedent, most of them in the Developing World. The list includes Haiti, Somalia, Rwanda, Burundi, Liberia, Angola, Algeria, not to mention the former Yugoslavia, Chechnya, Georgia, Moldova, Armenia, and others. There is little prospect that third parties would be interested in directing the United Nations toward humanitarian intervention in the Russian Federation or Russia's so-called near abroad, the new states resulting from dissolution of the Soviet Union. Moreover, Moscow certainly would use its Security Council veto to forestall such an initiative. But if the world is to respond effectively to the victims of Developing World civil wars, especially those that have genocidal facets, the types of mandates suggested by the secretary-general must be part of the multilateral diplomatic arsenal of the New World Order, despite their questionable contributions in Bosnia and Somalia. Only in the multilateral setting of the United Nations are there sufficient political checks and balances to prevent abuses.

Arms Proliferation

A critical material precondition of international security in the New World Order is stabilization of the arms climate. Throughout the Cold War, and particularly after OPEC used international petroleum pricing to erode the trade balances of the major industrial countries, trade in conventional arms became a staple of international commerce. In addition, as the East-West confrontation spread to the American and Soviet client states, international arms transfers were regarded as an essential element in maintaining regional power balances in Asia, Europe, the Middle East, Central America, and North Africa. By the end of the Cold War new competitors entered the market, particularly Brazil and China, which were marketing everything from automatic weapons and aircraft to surface-to-air and antiship missiles.[18] East European nations, heirs to late Soviet Cold War arms, entered the competition as well. Russia, awash in decommissioned and never-deployed materiel, took its own place in the international arms bazaar. Sophisticated military jet aircraft, shoulder-launched surface-to-air missiles, automatic weapons, concealable plastic explosives, small and large ammunition, and many more instruments of war fell easily into the hands of not only governments, but insurgent movements, terrorist organizations, and soldiers of fortune as well. All this contributes directly to the frequency of war and violence in the post–Cold War era. In addition, the spread of nuclear knowledge and technology threatens many of the power balances in the world's incendiary regions.

Conventional Arms Proliferation and Nonproliferation

International arms transfers generally are understood to occur under three types of national policy. *Industrial arms transfers* are licensed for the purpose of profiting or supporting domestic arms industries, and they are a matter of economic policy. *Restrictive arms transfers* are designed to stabilize the import regions and to reduce the probability of regional conflict. *Hegemonic arms transfers* comply with the

---

[17] Boutros Boutros-Ghali, *An Agenda for Peace, 1995,* p. 15.

[18] On China's arms sales, see Richard A. Betzinger, "Arms to Go: Chinese Arms Sales to the Third World," *International Security,* fall 1992, pp. 84–111.

selling parties' desires to enhance their political and strategic positions in the importing region.[19] One variant is *antihegemonic arms transfers*, conducted for the purpose of interfering with the overseas strategic position of a third party.

In one study, ninety arms transfers were studied, thirty-four for the United States, thirty for France, and twenty-six for West Germany during the period 1950–1976. On balance, American policy was found to be hegemonic, French industrial, and West Germany restrictive.[20] It is probable that if the study were done using more recent transfers and extended to include China, Russia, and Brazil, it would be found that in New World Order conditions, hegemonic motives are in sharp decline, restrictive motives on the slight increase, and industrial motives rampant even for some of those, including the United States and Russia, whose policies previously were hegemonic. Chinese arms sales would probably be found to be a combination of industrial and antihegemonic, as a central goal of Chinese foreign policy has been to break the hegemonic influences of the United States and the Soviet Union/Russian Federation. American aid to Afghan rebels was for the purpose of reducing Soviet hegemony, and Moscow's to the Nicaraguan Contras to weaken the United States in its own hemispheric sphere of influence. Brazil's arms exports almost certainly would be found to be industrial. In early 1996 the British government was rocked by a scandal in which an authoritative report found cabinet members guilty of deceiving the Parliament and the public over arms sales to Iraq just prior to the 1990 invasion of Kuwait.[21] The purpose could not have been either restrictive or hegemonic.

For purposes of world order, the importance of this analytical scheme is that it helps to understand when arms trade is stabilizing and when it is not. Restrictive arms transfers are calculated to improve stability directly, and hegemonic to do so through third-party manipulation under larger security umbrellas. In the Middle East, for instance, the Arab-Israeli conflict was stabilized by a constant rebalancing of forces by outside parties interested in such things as the stability of oil prices. Industrial arms transfers, in contrast, are without regard to stability. Under the conditions of the New World Order, as more arms transfers derive from industrial motive, the threat of their having destabilizing consequences increases.

Figure 9–2 depicts the global trend in conventional arms trade from 1984 through 1993, and it shows clearly that as the Cold War abated and the hegemonic arms policies of the United States and the Soviet Union declined, total world arms trade dropped sharply. But Table 9–7 expands the picture. It demonstrates the trend in international arms sales to the Developing Nations as a percentage of gross world arms transfers. It shows that gross arms sales to the Developing World have declined at about the same pace as global arms sales, and that the financial commitment of the Developing Nations to new arms is on the decline in the post–Cold War era. But it also shows that well over half of all international arms sales continue to go to the Developing World. To be sure, some of this goes to wealthy nations such as Saudi Arabia, Kuwait, Taiwan, and Israel. Nonetheless, much goes to far poorer lands such as India, Egypt, and Pakistan, as shown in Table 9–8. Moreover, much goes to nations of questionable commitment to regional stability such as Iran, North Korea, and Turkey.

Table 9–9 aggregates the annual arms sales of the six principal sellers for the post–Cold War years 1989–1993 and shows the amount of each seller's total that went to the Developing World in price and in percentage of the world total. The result is striking, as it reveals that in the first five post–Cold

[19] This analytical scheme is attributed to SIPRI, *The Arms Trade with the Third World* (London: Paul Ecek, Ltd., 1971).

[20] Gregory S. Sanjian, "Great Power Arms Transfers: Modeling the Decision-making Processes of Hegemonic, Industrial, and Restrictive Exporters," *International Studies Quarterly*, June 1991, pp. 173–193.

[21] *The New York Times*, February 16, 1996, p. A1.

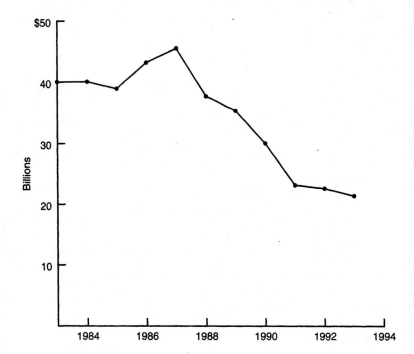

FIGURE 9–2   Global conventional arms transfers, 1984–1993, in $U.S. billions, 1990 constant value.

Source: Adapted from several editions of *SIPRI Yearbook,* especially *SIPRI Yearbook, 1994,* p. 457.

War years, these six parties alone shipped $67.3 billion in arms to Developing Nations, almost 56 percent of their global sales.

We have already seen that the East and South Asian region is, if anything, less stable in the post–Cold War order. Part of the evidence comes from data about the region's combined arms imports and arms production. Table 9–10 lays out both of these for East Asia alone for the 1984–1993 period, with the left-hand column showing arms imports and the right-hand showing regional arms production. Note that both are in constant U.S. dollar value pegged to 1990, so that the absolute growth in production is understated and the apparent decline in imports overstated.

From a global perspective, striking as these findings are, the real facts are undoubtedly worse. These figures include only those arms contracts that are public. They do not include clandestine arms transfers, or sales to parties other than governments. How many insurgent movements have been armed through channels that do not report their

munitions contracts? How many of Africa's post-Cold War civil wars would have been less brutal had arms not been available so readily? Would the fate of the post-Yugoslavia peoples have been more merciful had there been arms embargoes against all parties instead of just the Bosnian Muslims?

These facts and questions illuminate the fragility of an international order in which arms sales driven increasingly by economic motive overshadow humane rationality. The effort of the United Nations to curb this corrosive feature of the New World Order by establishing a voluntary annual registration of arms transfers can contribute little to stability if profiteers are unwilling to place peace on a higher plane.

Nuclear Arms Proliferation and Nonproliferation

Alongside the vast spread of conventional arms in global concern is nuclear proliferation. The mutual deterrence regime constructed by the United States

TABLE 9–7

ARMS SALES TO THE DEVELOPING WORLD (1990 CONSTANT VALUE)

Year	Global Arms Sales	Sales to Developing World	Developing World as % of Global Total
1984	$40.5 billion	$28.9 billion	71.4%
1985	39.0	26.4	67.7
1986	43.0	28.0	65.1
1987	46.0	31.0	67.4
1988	38.0	23.1	60.8
1989	36.5	21.4	58.6
1990	30.0	17.9	60.0
1991	23.0	12.7	55.2
1992	22.5	11.7	52.0
1993	22.0	12.4	56.4

Source: Adapted from *SIPRI Yearbook, 1994*, p. 510.

and the Soviet Union during the Cold War contributed mightly to "the long peace," and it was neither threatened nor accentuated by the independent nuclear capabilities of France and Britain. India discontinued its nuclear program for decades after its first test explosion. China joined the nuclear race late. By the mid-1980s it was assumed broadly that Israel had developed nuclear capability, and South Africa was known to have manufactured nuclear weapons. At about the same time, Iraqi and North Korean nuclear ambitions became known. A decade later the United States charged Beijing with supplying nuclear technology to Pakistan. By the latter half of the 1990s, therefore, it appeared that the world was headed for a nuclear club of ten, including the current four, with a disturbingly unfamiliar regional pattern:

Asia—China, India, Pakistan, North Korea (with South Korea under the American nuclear umbrella)

The Middle East—Israel and Iraq (following the Desert Storm War, in which Iraq demonstrated its ability to reach Israeli population centers with intermediate-range missiles)

Due to its economic collapse, North Korea agreed to discontinue its nuclear program in return for peaceful reactors to stimulate its industrial economy, and the Iraqi program was terminated and subjected to UN inspection and surveillance as part of the agreement that terminated the Desert Storm War. Nonetheless, it was in an atmosphere of heightened tension that the signatories to the Nuclear Non-Proliferation Treaty (NPT) met in 1995 to determine the treaty's subsequent duration, as required by its original text.[22] Tensions were heightened still more by China's resumption of nuclear testing and France's announcement that it would do the same by the end of the year. While signatories to the NPT, China and France continued underground testing because neither belonged to the

---

[22] For a thorough background on the issues facing the conference, see J. B. Poole and R. Guthrie, eds., *Verification 1995: Arms Control, Peacekeeping and the Environment* (Boulder, Colo.: Westview, 1995), especially chapters 1–21.

TABLE 9–8

MAJOR POST–COLD WAR ARMS PURCHASERS IN THE DEVELOPING WORLD (1990 CONSTANT VALUE) USING TOTAL EXPENSE 1989 THROUGH 1993

World Rank	Country	Five-year Total	
1	India	$10.5 billion	
3	Saudia Arabia	8.0	
4	Turkey	7.7	
5	Greece	6.3	
6	Afghanistan	6.3	(none after 1991)
8	Egypt	4.6	
9	Pakistan	3.6	
10	China	3.4	
11	Israel	3.1	
12	South Korea	2.9	
13	Thailand	2.8	
14	Taiwan	2.7	
15	Iran	2.6	
17	United Arab Emirates	2.5	
21	Kuwait	2.3	
24	Iraq	1.9	(none after 1990)
27	North Korea	1.7	(none after 1992)
35	Syria	1.1	

Note: The numbers are not consecutive because of the world ranks of some industrialized nations.

Source: SIPRI Yearbook, 1994, p. 485.

Treaty on the Limitation of Underground Nuclear Weapon Tests (signed in 1974, entered into force in 1990).[23]

By the time the Review and Extension Conference of the Parties to the Nuclear Non-Proliferation Treaty met, the treaty had 171 signatories, including Belarus, Kazakhstan, and Ukraine, which had sacrificed the nuclear weapons they had inherited from the dissolved Soviet Union. Prominent among the missing were Israel, India, and Pakistan. China took the view that Russian-American interest in nonproliferation relates not to international security, but to their refusal to abandon their global dominance. Siding with a number of Developing Nations (including Mexico, Indonesia, Venezuela, and Egypt) that preferred repeated extensions of twenty-five years in order to avoid freezing the world permanently into a division of nuclear haves and have-nots, China broke from the rest of the nuclear club in not advocating an unconditional and indefinite extension of the NPT.[24] Finally, it was agreed to extend the treaty through 2020. In mid-1996 India, long opposed to nuclear testing but fearful of China's and Pakistan's weapons developments, blocked completion of a global comprehensive nuclear test ban treaty.

The urgency of expanding the nuclear nonproliferation regime conceptually was underscored less than a month after the conference when 5 tons of Russian surplus zirconium were found in New York City and 2 tons in Cyprus. (Zirconium is a necessary element in the construction of nuclear weapons.) The purpose and destinations of the shipments were either not known or not made public, but their existence pointed out the ease with which such materials are found in international markets. Perhaps in awareness of just this phenomenon, one writer had argued two years earlier that the traditional approach to nonproliferation had become obsolete, and he called for a global policy of "antiproliferation." Given the dispersion of military capabilities following the end of the Cold War, he argued the inadequacy of traditional nonproliferation because

> it no longer encompasses all significant dimensions of the proliferation problem or the full range of policy responses. Antiproliferation strategies for the future must look beyond the traditional emphasis on denial alone, to include new diplomatic and military

[23] For a summary documentary history of the nuclear nonproliferation regime, see *The United Nations and Nuclear Nonproliferation* (New York: United Nations, 1995).

[24] *The New York Times,* April 19, 1995, p. A16.

TABLE 9–9

MAJOR POST–COLD WAR (1989–1993) ARMS SUPPLIERS TO THE DEVELOPING WORLD: SALES (1990 CONSTANT VALUE) AND PERCENTAGE OF GLOBAL TRADE

Supplier	Global Total	Export to Dev. World	Sales to Dev. World as % of Global Total
United States	$56.6 billion	$26.4 billion	46.6%
USSR/Russia	35.4	22.1	62.4
Germany	8.7	2.8	32.2
France	7.8	5.3	67.9
UK	6.6	5.0	75.8
China	5.7	5.7	100.0
Total	$120.8	$67.3	55.7%

Source: SIPRI Yearbook, 1994, p. 484.

elements that emphasize coping with a world in which proliferation is slowly progressing, and manipulating the balance of incentives and disincentives this process creates for more cooperative approaches to problems of international security.[25]

One might argue that the American guarantees of assistance in peaceful uses of nuclear fuel given to North Korea in exchange for abandonment of its own nuclear initiative was just such an incentive.

Rapid Response

If stabilizing the arms environment is the most important material precondition of the contemporary international security system, then the capacity for rapid response to armed crisis is the most important tactical precondition. In a sense this has been true since World War Two, as American troops and equipment have been forward-positioned uninterruptedly on and under the Atlantic, Pacific, Arctic,

and Indian Oceans, and in bases in much of the world. Indeed, the American response to North Korea's invasion of the South in 1950 would have been very different had the requisite forces not been available in Japan.

But the contemporary circumstances differ markedly. Where once American troops stared down a sworn enemy across identified frontiers from Korea to Berlin, today's crisis may not involve an enemy at all, particularly if it is in the Developing World. This is precisely why the passage from Cold War to New World Order brings with it the concept of international security in place of the preidentified imperatives of national security. To a degree previously unknown in this century, contemporary security is security without preconceived enemies. This is, of course, not true to the total exclusion of national security priorities, as the debate over the future of NATO, concern over Russia's perceived manipulation of the Asian power balance, and Washington's unreduced determination to deter North Korean aggression attest. But the common concern for regional stability and the growing trend of multilateral humanitarian intervention in

---

[25] Brad Roberts, "From Nonproliferation to Antiproliferation," *International Security*, summer 1993, pp. 139–173 at p. 173.

TABLE 9-10

EAST ASIAN ARMS IMPORTS (1990 CONSTANT VALUE) AND PERCENTAGE OF TOTAL GLOBAL IMPORT AND PRODUCTION

Year	Imports	Imports Plus Production as % of Global Total
1984	$5.3 billion	12.4%
1985	6.3	15.9
1986	5.8	13.7
1987	5.3	11.5
1988	6.9	17.7
1989	6.2	16.5
1990	4.9	16.1
1991	4.6	19.4
1992	5.3	23.4
1993	4.6	21.1

Read as follows: "In 1992, East Asian governments imported $5.3 billion in arms, but their combined arms imports and weapons production reached a post–Cold War record 23.4% of the world's total."

Source: SIPRI Yearbook, 1994, p. 552.

genocidal civil wars, particularly those that do not involve the salient and proximal interests of major powers, are unique features of the New World Order that call for new rapid-response strategies in the interest of international security.

The legal and tactical precedents for these new strategies are found in the lessons of UN peacekeeping. First, for many years a number of nations, including Sweden, India, Ireland, Australia, and Canada, maintained "standby agreements" with the United Nations under which contingents of their national defense forces were trained and earmarked for peacekeeping service. Once the Security Council voted to establish a peacekeeping mission, these troops, equipped for peacekeeping rather than combat, could be called on as the response of the United Nations. This planning increased greatly the speed and efficiency with which the UN's presence could arrive in the crisis area,

because there was no need to waste precious time negotiating with governments over deployment and equipment details. This practice needs to be expanded in the New World Order, particularly with respect to limited humanitarian intervention in genocidal Developing World wars.

Second, because the principles of peacekeeping include political neutrality, the permanent members of the Security Council were excluded from participation on the assumption that their global strategies and alliance structures ensured their partisan interests in virtually all crises. Under conditions of the New World Order, this premise is less valid. Moreover, knowledge among combatants that great-power force as well as great-power influence lies behind multilateral intervention, particularly nonconsensual intervention, may have a salutary impact on decision making. Hence excluding the major powers from the globalization of rapid-response preparations needs a thorough reconsideration.

Third, in considering the future of peacekeeping, the secretary-general has introduced the concept of "preventive deployment," under which UN-sponsored forces would be deployed to a troubled area before violence erupts.

> In inter-State disputes, when both parties agree, I recommend that if the Security Council concludes that the likelihood of hostilities between neighbouring countries could be removed by the preventive deployment of a United Nations presence on the territory of each State, such action should be taken. The nature and tasks to be performed would determine the composition of the United Nations presence.
>
> In cases where one nation fears a cross-border attack, if the Security Council concludes that a United Nations presence on one side of the border, with the consent only of the requesting country, would serve to deter conflict, I recommend that preventive deployment take place. Here again, the specific nature of the situation would determine the mandate and the personnel required to fulfil it.[26]

---

[26] Boutros Boutros-Ghali, *An Agenda for Peace*, 1995, p. 51.

Sikh members of the Indian paramilitary forces look for separatist Kashmiri militants in the countryside, 1993. To fight the militants, who began the armed struggle in December 1989, India has sent more than 150,000 troops to the Kashmir region located on India's northwestern border with Pakistan. (*Source:* AP/Wide World)

Because this applies only to two-party disputes, its application to civil wars is uncertain. If one assumes the legitimacy of nonconsensual humanitarian intervention subsequent to the onset of fighting, however, then in situations of incipient civil war the same principle can apply to preventive deployment.

Fourth, as we shall see later, international organizations are not sovereign entities, and thus they depend on their members for any power they are able to wield. And just as the United Nations has no army or air force personnel, neither does it possess military materiel. It doesn't even have a budget for acquiring it, nor is it likely to, because the member states insist on preserving the organization's dependence on them. To bridge this gap, the secretary-general proposes that

[a] pre-positioned stock of basic peace-keeping equipment . . . be established, so that at least some vehicles, communications equipment, generators, etc., would be immediately available at the start of an operation. Alternatively, Governments should commit themselves to keeping certain equipment, specified by the Secretary-General, on stand-by for immediate sale, loan or donation to the United Nations when required.

Member States in a position to do so should make air- and sea-lift capacity available to the United Nations free of cost or at lower than commercial rates, as was the practice until recently.[27]

And fifth, as a sequel to preventive deployment and peacekeeping, the secretary-general recommends that the United Nations adopt a policy of peace enforcement in which troops would, if necessary, be equipped more heavily than in peacekeeping. The purposes would be to enforce peace terms once they are established, and to assist in the process of reconstructing government and society under democratic principles.

The political checks and balances of the Security Council make it the best, if not the ideal, place to institutionalize these principles. But in the early days of the New World Order, despite the resurgent popularity of multinationalism, governments are reluctant to extend the prerogatives of the United Nations, even under tight political controls. This is accentuated by a wave of political conservatism and the primacy of domestic economic priorities, particularly in the industrialized West, since the end of the Cold War. (During the 1996 Republican

---

[27] Boutros Boutros-Ghali, An *Agenda for Peace, 1995*, p. 60.

presidential primaries, for example, several of the candidates bashed the United Nations and multinationalism, and ad hominem attacks on Secretary-General Boutros-Ghali were frequent. Robert Dole, for instance, publicly accused the secretary-general of attempting to infringe the sovereignty of the United States by advocating a stronger role for multilateralism; and as part of his isolationist theme, Patrick Buchanan declared derisively that American foreign policy is not the business of "Bou Bou Ghali." Buchanan also pledged that "When I raise my hand to take the oath of office, the New World Order will come crashing down.") This explains in part Washington's reluctance to undertake the post-Dayton Accords operation in Bosnia under a UN mandate and to turn to NATO instead. NATO's anti-Soviet success during the Cold War made it far more popular with nationalists than the United Nations. Furthermore, in the debate over NATO's future, it was useful to find it a specific role, particularly one that would compel Russia to play a secondary role in the new Europe behind a NATO whose motives it suspected, and one that would exclude China from decision making regarding Europe.

Nonetheless, American strategy is changing in other respects. In successive announcements in late 1995 and early 1996, for example, the Pentagon announced a multibillion-dollar contract for the largest transport aircraft in order to improve the rapid-response capability of American forces. It then announced the cancellation of an order for B-2 bombers on the grounds that the expense was unjustified by the changing nature of international conflict. Looked at most optimistically, one might see this as starkly symbolic of an evolution from Cold War national security strategies to New World Order international security strategies. Perhaps more realistically, however, this change recognizes the reduction of American troop strength in NATO, the probability of being compelled to reduce strength in Okinawa, and the simple economic calculus of maintaining full-time troops abroad as against mobilizing them from reserve units and delivering them efficiently to trouble spots when needed.

While the very concept of "international security" is elusive, we have attempted here to identify and analyze some of its important characteristics, and to assess them in the contemporary context. As has been emphasized throughout this book, the New World Order is neither a utopian claim nor a fully and consistently peaceful historical passage. It is, instead, an analytical basis for dissecting and understanding the post–Cold War international system and the evolutionary opportunities presented to world politics. The reader will understand, therefore, why the international security aspect of the New World Order is in its own very early evolutionary stage.

CHAPTER 10

Principal Causes of War

One of the most pressing matters in the field of international relations is the causes of war. Why are international political controversies so often violent? The pages of international history are saturated with blood, and the moralist may ask fairly why people condone in war behavior that they would not tolerate in peace. Is war an international disease of the human social system, a collective insanity, a malfunction like falling down the stairs? Is it the product of conspiratorial behavior by certain interests and groups? Or is war a rational and functional, if horrible, component of the international system? Whatever it is, we know that it is an integral part of every system of world politics that has ever evolved or been designed. In this chapter, we shall review fifteen theories of the cause of war, summarized in Table 10–1, that have emerged from the growing field of conflict and peace research.

Although war typically is regarded as a political phenomenon, it springs not only from political events but also from economic motives, from ethnic and racial conflict, from cultural and anthropological differences, from individual personalities, and sometimes from psychopathology. A comprehensive study of the causes of war necessarily carries one into the literatures of politics, economics, history, philosophy, psychiatry, social psychology, anthropology, psychology, and other pertinent fields of study. In keeping with the central concept of this book, then, this chapter seeks to present not a single cohesive theory of the cause of war, but a comparative review of the several principal theories.

Scientific research on war is based on two critical assumptions. First, there are patterns and regularities in conflict behavior that can be identified systematically. If this assumption is not true—that is, if war behavior is idiosyncratic or unique from case to case—then research of this kind is unproductive. Second, in a decentralized system of sovereign states, anarchy reigns, and only countervailing power can deter war. Scholars of different orientations and tastes will find a list of fifteen causes of war far from comprehensive, for there is scarcely a limit to the ways in which international (or intrasocietal) violence can be categorized. Nonetheless, the categories that follow are based on this definition of "war": an organized conflict of major armed hostilities between social groups and nations. This definition enables us to consider internationally significant civil wars as well as international wars, the distinction between which has eroded in the last half-century.

1. Power Asymmetries

The condition most feared among governments as a cause of war is the power asymmetry—that is, an unfavorable tilt in the distribution of power. There is widespread conviction that whatever other impetuses to war may be present, a careful equilibration of power among antagonists will tend to prevent war, whereas a disequilibrium will invite aggression. The maintenance of international peace requires that technological and other gains on each of two

---

TABLE 10-1

FIFTEEN THEORIES
OF THE CAUSE OF WAR

1. Power asymmetries
2. Power transitions
3. Nationalism, separatism, and irredentism
4. International social Darwinism
5. Communications failure because of misperception
6. Communications failure because of technical irony or error
7. Arms races and the security dilemma
8. Internal cohesion through external conflict
9. International conflict through internal strife
10. Relative deprivation
11. Instinctual aggression and sociobiology
12. Economic and scientific stimulation
13. The military-industrial complex
14. Population limitation
15. Conflict resolution by force

---

sides be matched and kept essentially even. A vacuum of power, such as that created by unilateral disarmament, destabilizes international relations and encourages military ventures. Proponents of this Realpolitik believe that occasions and issues for conflict always exist and that the immediate cause of warfare is usually a failure to balance power symmetrically. The operating principle of this doctrine is "If peace is your goal, prepare for war." Hence, the U.S. Air Force boasts that "peace is our profession," and the MX missile was sold to the American people with its $30 billion price tag as the Peacekeeper missile.

In conflicts in which one side seeks a major redistribution of values while the other wishes to preserve the status quo—that is, when there is a clear distinction between the offense and the defense— peace may be preserved by a certain kind of asymmetry. An advantage to the defensive party will more reliably deter aggression than will a close balance. Conversely, an overbalance in favor of the

offensive party will make war more likely. Thus, in the clear offense-defense case, peace is more nearly ensured by superiority of the nonrevolutionary (or "predatory") antagonist. For example, Winston Churchill argued in his iron curtain speech at Fulton, Missouri, in March 1946, that Soviet aggression would be stopped only by Western military superiority: "The old doctrine of a balance of power is unsound. We cannot afford, if we can help it, to work on narrow margins, offering temptations to a trial of strength." However, power asymmetries are inherently dangerous and tend to produce aggressive policies even when the favored state was previously peace loving and defensive.

Asymmetries pertain not only to different levels of industrial capacity, population, and other physical elements of war potential, but also to the more variable and volatile political elements. Of special importance is the ability to attract and retain allies willing to pool resources for mutual security. During the Cold War only two states, the United States and the Soviet Union, were able to act alone in most contingencies, and even for them there are many political and strategic advantages in allied action. For lesser powers, it is vital to cement alliances to prevent asymmetries. Israel's dependence on the United States and Syria's on the Soviet Union in the same period is a classic example.[1]

Another important factor is will. Even very good capabilities and solid alliances can result in asymmetries if a party declines to fight. Conversely, a state with limited resources and support may be able to prevent asymmetry by showing a resolute determination to utilize its capacities fully. To prevent power asymmetries, it is not necessary that all possible pairs of states be balanced perfectly, but only that potential aggressors know in advance that the costs of overcoming resistance will outweigh the benefits. Thus, the asymmetry of power is one cause of war that can be controlled.

---

[1] The role of alliances in maintaining symmetries has been the subject of voluminous research. See, as a contemporary example, John A. Vasquez, *The War Puzzle* (New York: Cambridge University Press, 1993).

2. Power Transitions

One special adaptation of the theory that power asymmetries produce international conflict is the power-transition theory of war. Its unique feature is that it concentrates not on existing asymmetries but evolving asymmetries—upsets in the international balance produced by rapid advantageous development among states inclined to challenge the international status quo established and protected by dominant states. The assumption underlying this thinking is that the international political system is dynamic, that there are fluctuations of power at the highest, intermediate, and lower ranks.

This theory postulates that states are differentiated by their relative power capabilities and by their satisfaction or dissatisfaction with the prevailing international system. Thus, in addition to the dominant states (during the Cold War the United States and the Soviet Union), some are powerful and satisfied (Britain, Germany, France, Japan, Canada); others are powerful and dissatisfied (China); still others are powerless and satisfied; and others are both powerless and dissatisfied. Similar relationships exist within regional settings. In the Middle East, for example, Israel and Egypt are powerful and satisfied; Syria and Libya are powerful and dissatisfied; Jordan is relatively powerless but satisfied; and Lebanon is powerless and dissatisfied.

The power transition is characterized by sudden and significant challenges to the status quo that result from rapid internal development in power capabilities. Whether they are a result of rapid social mobilization or of sharp advances in national economic capability, the roots of the challenge are in internal national development. Should the events occur in a state satisfied with the prevailing international or regional system, they are unlikely to be disruptive. But should they occur in a state that was not a party to the establishment of the prevailing norms and prefers to replace them, the development will be viewed by the dominant states as a challenge. Conflict will result, and war

may follow from hegemonic thrust. By the same token, if the development occurs gradually, the prospect of accommodating it to the existing system will be brighter than if it occurs at revolutionary speed.[2]

Although the United States and the Soviet Union never fought war directly, the Cold War was an example of the power-transition theory. At the close of World War Two, many of the satisfied nations (for example, Britain and France) were in ruins, and the dissatisfied nations that had attempted through global war to replace the prewar system (Germany and Japan) were occupied by the conquering powers. The United States was the sole surviving dominant nation, determined to restore the political and economic systems of the prewar international system. The Soviet Union, socialist rather than capitalist, used its post-war geographic advantage and rapid economic and thermonuclear development to challenge Washington's exclusive right to restore the system. It was this rapid development, filled with economic, military, and geographic credibility, that led to the measures and countermeasures later labeled the Cold War.

One variant of the power-transition notion is that of the power cycle. This postulates that as a state's capability, power status, and international

---

[2] The most influential work on the power-transition theory is by A. F. K. Organski and his collaborators. See particularly A. F. K. Organski, *World Politics*, 2nd ed. (New York: Knopf, 1968), chapters 7 and 8, and *Stages of Political Growth* (New York: Knopf, 1965); also A. F. K. Organski and Jacek Kugler, *The War Ledger* (Chicago: University of Chicago Press, 1980). See also Michael D. Wallace, *War and Rank Among Nations* (Lexington, Mass.: D. C. Heath, 1973). Wallace deals with quantitative studies of international status and status redistribution as causes of war. For an analysis that attaches the power-transition theory directly to economic cycles, see Raimo Vayrynen, "Economic Cycles, Power Transitions, Political Management and Wars Between Major Nations," *International Studies Quarterly*, December 1983, pp. 389–418. Jack S. Levy, "Declining Power and the Preventive Motivation for War," *World Politics*, October 1987, pp. 82–107, argues that a power in decline will fear the consequences of that decline and provoke war in an effort to forestall them. Lars-Erik Cederman, "Emergent Polarity: Analyzing State-Formation and Power Politics," *International Studies Quarterly*, December 1994, pp. 501–533, introduces the notions of "predatory" nations and "hegemonic takeoff" to the power transition theory.

political role change, there are specific points at which perceptions, miscalculations, or overreactions to international events may trigger war. The most likely point is when the state is at its peak as a power entity, principally because of rapid economic development. The second, in an urgent need to adjust international conditions as the state begins to slip in status, is at the point when the state's decline is detectable and its prospects for resurgence are recognized internally as minimal. The third most likely point is just before reaching the peak. And the least likely point is before the state begins its assent.[3]

Our principal concern here is with international power transitions and international wars. But the same two can occur at the domestic level. Civil wars may have high casualty rates, cause millions to flee as refugees, spread starvation and disease, invite foreign intervention, and so forth. Recently scholars have begun to analyze the ethnopolitical causes of civil wars. They have shown that between 1987 and 1994, seventy different domestic ethnopolitical crises arose (ten in Europe, six in the Middle East, twenty-eight in Asia, twenty-three in Africa, and three in Latin America and the Caribbean), resulting in 4 million deaths and 27 million refugees. Moreover, most of these crises erupted when the states were themselves in internal power transition characterized usually by new state formation, political revolution, or efforts to democratize autocratic regimes.[4] Other studies concentrate specifically on domestic religious strife and its spillover into politics,

sometimes resulting in international crisis.[5] The triumph of religious fundamentalism in Iran changed the face of world politics substantially for twenty years; France is embroiled politically in a religion-generated state crisis in Algeria; Indian forces attack Sikh mosques; and Protestants and Catholics in Northern Ireland reached a stage of semi-peace in 1993 and a fitful accord in 1995 after more than seventy years of fighting. The force of international power transitions, rooted in culture and often more specifically in faith, may indeed alter the course of history.

3. Nationalism, Separatism, and Irredentism

Nationalism is a collective group identity that passionately binds diverse individuals into a people. The nation becomes the highest affiliation and obligation of the individual, and it is in terms of the national we-group that personal identity is formed: "I am a Canadian." From Hitler's celebration of the Volk to de Gaulle's near-mystical belief

---

[3] Charles F. Doran, "War and Power Dynamics," *International Studies Quarterly*, December 1983, pp. 419–441.
[4] Ted Robert Gurr, "People Against States: Ethnopolitical Conflict and the Changing World System," *International Studies Quarterly*, September 1994, pp. 347–377; and *Minorities at Risk: A Global View of Ethnopolitical Conflicts* (Washington, D.C.: United States Institute of Peace, 1993). Also see Ted Robert Gurr and Barbara Harff, *Ethnic Conflict in World Politics* (Boulder, Colo.: Westview, 1994); F. Wilmer, *The Indigenous Voice in World Politics* (Newbury Park, Calif.: Sage, 1993); R. D. Kaplan, "The Coming Anarchy," *Atlantic Monthly*, February 1994, pp. 44–76; and Charles William Maynes, "Containing Ethnic Conflict," *Foreign Policy*, spring 1993, pp. 3–21.

[5] M. Juergensmeyer, *The New Cold War: Religious Nationalism Confronts the Secular State* (Berkeley: University of California, 1993). On February 8, 1995, Mr. Newt Gingrich, Speaker of the United States House of Representatives, declared that the United States will not tolerate "Islamic totalitarianism." (Speech excerpted in Mr. Gingrich's voice on WCBS-AM, New York, the following morning.) For a debate on whether or not Islam poses a threat to Western security, see Leon T. Hader, "What Green Peril?" *Foreign Affairs*, spring 1993, pp. 27–42, and immediately following, Judith Miller, "The Challenge of Radical Islam," pp. 43–56; and a similar debate with an international flavor is found in "The Muslims Are Coming: A Real World Menace, or Just a Bogeyman?" *World Press Review*, May 1994, pp. 8–13. See also Ghassan Salame, "Islam and the West," *Foreign Policy*, spring 1993, pp. 22–37; and Judith Miller, "The Faces of Fundamentalism," *Foreign Affairs*, November–December, 1994, pp. 123–143. Tetsuya Sahara, "The Islamic World and the Bosnian Crisis," *Current History*, November 1994, pp. 386–389, concludes that conservative Islamic governments (e.g., Saudi Arabia) as well as moderate (e.g., Turkey) and radical (e.g., Iran) have all taken active roles in the Bosnian crisis because "Muslims tend to identify the fate of [Muslims in] Bosnia with their own, and to see this war as a symbol of their own destiny."

in the French, the most powerful elements of the political spectrum seem to agree that the ethnic nation is the highest form of identity.

This curious and compelling identification with one group tends to produce conflicts with others. A 1969 research team enumerated 160 disputes having significant likelihood of resulting in large-scale violence within fifteen years. This large inventory fell broadly into the following classifications:

1. Nationalist conflicts, including disputes between ethnic, racial, religious, and linguistic identity groups perceiving themselves as peoples
2. Class conflicts, including issues of economic exploitation
3. Other conflicts not characterized primarily by clashes between identity groups or classes

Significantly, nationalist and ethnic conflict accounted for about 70 percent of the cases, whereas class and other conflicts divided the balance. Indeed, nationalism appears to be a potent factor in the causal chain to war, accounting for more bloodshed than any other cause.[6]

The disputes identified in 1969 were reviewed fifteen years later in 1984, revealing that serious civil strife occurred in more than thirty cases at least once, and international conflict with significant damage and death occurred in twenty-three.

In recent years, the main link between nationalism and war has been the survival of separate identities among populations whose geographic distribution differs from the international boundary lines. Peoples who do not feel that they belong to a country tend to feel an infringement of basic human rights in a world of nation-states. Populations submerged in other peoples' countries (Algerian Muslims), populations divided among two or more countries (Kurds), and populations denied the control of the governments of their own

countries (black South Africans) tend to rebel against these denials. But territorial and political rearrangements often cannot be achieved without armed conflict between the deprived or oppressed groups and other interests. Thus the link between nationalism and war today operates most importantly through militant territorial and political demands organized around certain principles of ethnic, linguistic, religious, and racial we-group identities.

Although this chapter attempts to draw fine lines between the several theories of wars' cause, several of these theories overlap. In this section, for example, discussion focuses on nationalistic causes of war, and section 11 addresses sociobiological explanations. One theory relates these two by arguing that over long stretches of time and in view of specific environmental circumstances including threat to security, social evolution may result in ethnic cohesion oriented to conflict.[7] If true, this would help to explain defensive nationalism among ethnically homogeneous peoples.

Two key forms of nationalist militancy predominate in modern war. These are the separatist form and the irredentist form. In the separatist form, a nationalist group attempts to secede from an existing state to form a new one. In the irredentist form, an existing state lays claim to a territory and population group presently subsumed within another state. These forms are illustrated in Figure 10–1.

Separatism and War

Most of the world's approximately 190 nation-states incorporate substantial minority populations. Even after prolonged periods of apparent assimilation among other groups, many minorities continue to think of themselves as separate and distinct (see Table 10–2). This feeling of distinctness becomes a

---

[6] Steven Rosen, ed., *A Survey of World Conflicts* (Pittsburgh: University of Pittsburgh Center of International Studies Preliminary Paper, March 1969).

[7] R. Paul Shaw and Yuma Wong, "Ethnic Mobilization and the Seeds of Warfare: An Evolutionary Perspective," *International Studies Quarterly*, March 1987, pp. 5–32.

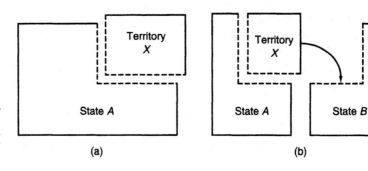

FIGURE 10-1 (a) The separatist model. Territory X secedes from State A to form new State X. (b) The irredentist model. State B claims Territory X from State A.

separatist movement when a formal demand is made for territorial secession to form a state or, short of this extreme, for a considerable measure of internal autonomy from control by the existing political order. These separatist demands usually are resisted by the incumbent authorities because of the threat perceived to the state's political and territorial integrity. In this way, conflicts over separatist demands become common causes of war.

Minority movements take on added significance for the study of international relations when outside powers intervene. Often, one comes to the aid of the threatened government, while another lends its support to the restive minority. The various factions in the internal dispute become clients of outside sponsors motivated by their own interests. Foreign intervention is particularly important when a neighboring state allows its territory to be used as a sanctuary and staging area for guerrilla forays and political organization by the dissident population. This is seen by the threatened government as subversion and tends to lead to intergovernmental conflict.

Irredentism and War

Nationalist and ethnic disputes have still greater significance for international relations in their irredentist form. Virtually all the world's populated land surfaces are by now identified with the delineated territory of particular nation-states. But in many cases, the historic demarcation of boundaries

(mainly through war and conquest) ignored natural lines of division between different peoples. Thus political lines often are not congruent with ethnogeographic regions, and in many places one people straddles a border between two states. Irredentism is the struggle of such a people for reunification,[8] and the irredenta is a territory where a portion of the ethnic nation resides that is regarded as lost or stolen.

The irredentist territorial claim normally evokes resistance from the state, because its territory would be reduced in the event of a successful claim. The challenged state often can base its own claim on historic ties and treaties regarded as legally binding. There is a fog of claims and counterclaims, and the stirring patriotic call of one side is a threat to the other. Even the most barren piece of territory is regarded as a sacred part of the national patrimony, and seldom does a border move a hundred yards in any direction without the spilling of human blood.

---

[8] The term referred originally to the late-nineteenth-century struggle of Italian patriots to redeem or reincorporate into Italy certain neighboring territories having a predominantly Italian population. As the term is used here, the impetus for reunification can come from the separated population (irredenta), the main body, or both. Both separatism and irredentism assume that the restive population is geographically well contained, and thus that adjustment of boundaries will resolve the drive for self-identity. In a pioneering article on the subject, Gidon Gottlieb points out that this may not be the case, and that it may be necessary to recognize sovereignty or semi-sovereignty of groups within states: "Nations Without States," *Foreign Affairs*, May–June 1994, pp. 100–112.

TABLE 10–2

SOME SEPARATIST AND AUTONOMIST MOVEMENTS

Recent wars of secession

1. Nigeria: struggle by Ibos for a separate Biafra; unsuccessful
2. Pakistan: secession of East Pakistan to form Bangladesh; successful
3. Sudan: black secessionists versus Arab state; unsuccessful
4. Chad: Arab secessionists versus black state; unsuccessful
5. Iraq: Kurds; unsuccessful
6. Ethiopia: Arabs of Eritrea, supported by Arab states; unsuccessful
7. Oman: Dhofar region; unsuccessful
8. Congo: Katanga; unsuccessful
9. Russia: Chechnya; unresolved

Other separatist movements

1. Spain: Basques; Catalans
2. Yugoslavia: Croatians; Albanians; Serbs; Muslims
3. Uganda: Bugandans
4. Puerto Rico: Independista movement
5. France: Brittany; potentially Basques
6. United Kingdom: Ulster Catholics; Welsh; Scots
7. Indonesia: minorities in Moluccas, Sumatra, Celebes
8. Russia: Latvians; Estonians; Lithuanians; Ukrainians
9. Sri Lanka: Tamils
10. Switzerland: Jura

11. Canada: French of Quebec
12. China: Sinkiang; Tibet
13. Myanmar: Karens; Kachins; Shans; Chins; Mons; Arkanese
14. Pakistan: Baluchis
15. South Africa: Namibia (Southwest Africa)
16. Czech Republic: Slav minority

Multiple secession movements

1. Kurds from Iraq, Iran, Turkey, and Former USSR and Russia
2. Bakongos from Zaïre, Congo, Cabinda, and Angola

Strained federations

1. Lebanon: Moslems versus Christians
2. Guyana: Blacks, East Indians, and others
3. Ghana: northern versus coastal tribes
4. Mauritius: Hindu, Creole, Moslem
5. Surinam: Creole, East Indian, Japanese
6. Rwanda and Burundi: Watutsi versus Bahutu
7. Belgium: Flemings and Walloons
8. India: many minorities
9. Mexico: Chiapas (Zapatistas)
10. Russia: Chechnya, Ingushetia

Resistance to irredentist claims occurs when

1. An existing state would cease to operate as an independent entity.
2. One or more states would lose territory (both India and Pakistan lost territory in the establishment of Bangladesh).
3. Irredentism would reunify two halves with different political ideologies (the post-war reunification of the two Vietnams; the possible reunification of the two Koreas, and the reunification in 1990 of the two Germanys).
4. One population occupying the irredenta fears that it would be a disadvantaged minority in

the case of reunification (Protestants in Northern Ireland; the Turkish population in Cyprus).

In all of these cases, some group stands to lose in the event of successful irredentism.

Issues in Separatist and Irredentist Conflicts

Economic Consequences Although territorial issues of separatism and irredentism begin as ethnic questions, they also entail profound economic and natural resource issues. When Hitler seized the

Quebec nationalists rally for independence from Canada, 1995.
(*Source:* © Robert Galbraith/Sipa Press)

Sudetenland from Czechoslovakia in the name of 3 million Sudeten Germans, he also seized 70 percent of Czechoslovakia's iron and steel, 86 percent of its chemical industries, and 70 percent of its electrical generating capacity. Similarly, British support for the self-determination movement in Kuwait and Brunei is related to their oil wealth, and Belgian support for the Katanga secession attempt in the Congo was keyed to the copper deposits of that region. The secession of Biafra would have taken from Nigeria not just the Ibo people but also much of its national resource base and industrial capacity. Thus, nationalist disputes are also international economic issues.

The Moral Dilemma Aside from economic issues, separatist and irredentist movements pose a moral dilemma for the international system. National self-determination is a cardinal value, and many concerned observers support struggling peoples seeking their own places in the sun. But the immense complexity of ethnogeography means that the world cannot possibly accommodate each splinter group with its own territory. All African states, for example, include members of tribes that straddle international borders. If each national group were given its own country, thousands of economically nonviable units would result. The fifty states of Africa, with a total population less than half that of India, are already too fragmented. When the Ibos sought secession from Nigeria, they were supported by only a few outside states (notably Tanzania, Zambia, Gabon, and the Ivory Coast), despite the moral appeal of their position. Pan-Africanists hold that the real future of the continent is in regional amalgamation and federation, not further "Balkanization." In addition, wholesale border revisions probably could not be achieved without an unacceptable amount of conflict and warfare among interested states.

Colonial Boundaries Many frustrated minorities blame their problems on past imperialism. Borders violate ethnic lines primarily because they reflect the points at which advancing armies stopped or deals between big powers were reached. They rarely reflect natural lines of human settlement. In many less developed regions, precolonial societies simply did not have officially drawn boundaries. When the Europeans came, they drew lines that seemed administratively, economically, and politically convenient in Paris, London, Berlin, and Lisbon, but that often ignored tribal and ethnic lines. Unified peoples were splintered, and incompatible tribes and groups often were lumped together. This was not just chance, but a calculated policy of divide and conquer. Many peoples have permanent problems as a consequence of past colonialism.

Unresolved and unresolvable irredentist and separatist issues are threats to the territorial interest of many nations (see Table 10–3). Nationalist conflicts may be latent and seemingly forgotten for prolonged periods, suddenly to emerge with renewed vigor as group identity reawakens. Recollections of lost territory tend to simmer beneath the political surface, and it is a simple matter for a jingoist leader or a demagogue to stir them up and ride to power on a nationalist tide. A latent irredentist or separatist feeling is a potent chemical reaction waiting for the right catalyst and is always, therefore, a potential cause of war.

Nation-State Disintegration

Before the disintegration of the Soviet Union in 1992, General Secretary Mikhail Gorbachev's *perestroika*, or restructuring, had awakened nationalistic identities among non-Russian peoples incorporated into the Soviet Union after the Bolshevik Revolution of 1917. Sporadic episodes of Armenian nationalism had been frequent since the death of Josef Stalin forty years before, but more recently expressions of nationalism had arisen among Azerbaijanis and Uzbekistanis, and from the Moldovan people annexed from Romania. All demanded varied forms of political and linguistic independence.

The ravages of civil war in Iraq. (*Source:* © Pierre Emmanuel Pessemier/Sygma)

TABLE 10–3

SOME IRREDENTIST MOVEMENTS

Claims to whole states

1. Tibet was reincorporated by China.
2. Togo has been claimed by Ghana on grounds of Ewe reunification.
3. Mauritania is regarded by some as part of Morocco.
4. French Somaliland (now Afar-Issa of Djibouti) has been claimed by Somalia.
5. Israel is regarded by Arab nationalists as a land stolen from the Arab nation.
6. Kuwait has been claimed by Iraq (no longer).
7. Gambia was carved artificially out of Senegal by the colonial power.
8. Cyprus is regarded as part of Greece by Greek Cypriots.
9. Taiwan is claimed as part of China.
10. Goa is claimed as part of China.
11. Armenia was incorporated into the Soviet Union (now independent).
12. Estonia, Lithuania, and Latvia were annexed by the Soviet Union (now independent).

Divided states with different political orientations

1. North and South Korea
2. East and West Germany (now resolved)
3. The two Yemens
4. The two Vietnams (now resolved)

Claims to parts of states

1. United Kingdom is threatened by IRA demands that Northern Ireland (Ulster) be reunited with Ireland.
2. Algeria is threatened by Moroccan claims in Spanish Sahara, rich in phosphates, and Tindouf, rich in oil.
3. India is threatened by Pakistan's claim to Kashmir.
4. Kenya is threatened by Somali nationalist claims to the Northern Frontier District.
5. Guyana faces territorial claims by Venezuela and Surinam.
6. Italy has negotiated territorial claims by Austria and former Yugoslavia.
7. China has extensive claims against the former Soviet Union, Mongolia, and other states.
8. Malaysia has resisted Indonesian and Philippine claims to Sabah.
9. Germany, under Hitler, laid claim to regions of Czechoslovakia, Poland, and Austria on grounds of Aryan reunification.
10. Japan claims Kurile and Sakhalin Islands occupied by Russia.
11. Peru and Ecuador have territorial dispute at borders.
12. Argentina continues to claim Falkland Islands after war loss to Britain.
13. Palestinians, Lebanese, and Syrians claim territories occupied by Israel.

Moreover, the Baltic states annexed to the Soviet Union in 1939—Estonia, Lithuania, and Latvia—used the occasion of *perestroika* and Gorbachev-supported liberalization in Poland, Hungary, and East Germany to express continuing discontent with Soviet control. Unlike its official toleration of the growth of noncommunist power in Eastern Europe, the Kremlin reacted initially to the Baltic peoples with implicit threats against "the virus of nationalism." But as the weakness of the Soviet state became more apparent and the passion for independence more irresistible, fully fourteen republics formerly integral to the Soviet Union became independent in an almost continuous ring from Estonia in the far northwest to Tajikistan, Krygyzstan, and Kazakhstan on the border of China. Lost to the empire were some of its most advanced regions: Armenia, Georgia, Ukraine, and Belarus.

The tragic story of Yugoslavia since 1992 is one of greater loss of life but less extensive territorial division. Serbs, Croatians, and Bosnian Muslims have all claimed their share of the former state, with the Serbs gaining most. Only the Muslims,

Faces of War: Bosnia, 1995.
(*Source:* © ITN-Sipa Press)

deprived of the requisite armaments by a United Nations embargo, have been unable to consolidate their claims.

4. International Social Darwinism

International social Darwinism is the belief that societies, like biological species, evolve and advance through competition, resulting in the survival of the fittest and the elimination of the weak. The social Darwinist sees the war of each against all as a cruel necessity for the progressive advancement of civilization. International relations is, in this perspective, the arena of combat between whole peoples where the global destiny of humanity is determined. The role of war is to pass the reins of power from the weak and decaying to the strong and dynamic.

In recent years, this philosophy has most often been associated with fascism. In advancing war as a positive aspect of fascism, Benito Mussolini declared: "Fascism sees in the imperialistic spirit—that is, in the tendency of nations to expand—a manifestation of their vitality. In the opposite tendency, which would limit their interests to the home country, it sees a symptom of decadence."[9] Moreover, "fascism above all does not believe either in the possibility or the utility of universal peace. It therefore rejects the pacifism which masks surrender and cowardice." And "war alone brings all human energies to their highest tension and sets a seal of nobility upon the peoples who have the virtue to face it."[10]

Carried to its logical conclusion in Nazism, the fascist philosophy views societies as biological entities united by blood ties. Two principles link Nazism with war: the principle of race and the principle of territory. Nazism, according to Adolf

---

[9] Quoted in S. William Halperin, *Mussolini and Italian Fascism* (Princeton, N.J.: Van Nostrand, 1964), p. 152.
[10] Benito Mussolini, quoted in Reo M. Christensen et al., *Ideologies and Modern Politics* (New York: Dodd, Mead, 1971), p. 70.

Hitler, "by no means believes in equality of the races, but along with their difference it recognizes their higher or lesser value. . . . Thus, in principle, it serves the basic aristocratic ideas of Nature." Moreover, because population expands but living space (Lebensraum) is limited, races must compete for territory. "Nature knows no political boundaries. First she puts living creatures on this globe and watches the free play of forces. She then confers the master's right on her favorite child, the strongest." The higher races must not agree "in their pacifistic blindness to renounce new acquisitions of soil," or they will leave mastery of the world to "the culturally inferior but more brutal and more natural peoples." Hitler was deeply suspicious of international law and diplomacy—"a cozy mutual swindling match"—and frankly set out "to promote the victory of the better and stronger, and demand the subordination of the inferior and weaker in accordance with the eternal will that dominates this universe."[11]

As these passages suggest, international social Darwinism glorifies conflict and focuses on incompatibilities among groups. It offers an appealing and simplistic account of history, providing a perfect rationalization for aggression. And, of course, it raises many questions for social theory.

Is race the basic human unit or only a biological accident that is promoted and distorted by corrupt politics? Is competition the basic law of nature, or are the most important human achievements attained mainly by cooperation and mutual effort? Do nations in fact face a shortage of living space, or are the most densely populated nations (for example, Japan) often the most prosperous? (It is interesting to note here that of the estimated 25 million square miles of arable land in the world, only about one-sixth is under cultivation.) Are people pressing outward from overcrowded population centers, or is the trend toward urbanization and concentration increasing while rural population is declining? Is the creative height of civilization reached in war or in peace?

Whatever the answers to these questions may be, and despite the fact that Nazism is now nearly dead, the philosophy of international social Darwinism is alive and well. Its sharpest critics are the Marxist-Leninist theorists who build their theory on dialectical materialism and believe that all war is a social phenomenon rooted in class differentiation across national boundaries. So to them, international social Darwinism is one of many attempts on the part of bourgeois theoreticians to substitute biological, psychological, and other factors for the social-class basis of war.[12]

5. Communications Failure Because of Misperception

Another cause of war treated extensively in the conflict literature is the theory of communications failure. As we have found, national leaders and national peoples perceive one another through ideological lenses and with stereotypical images, with the result that their communication, whether formal or informal, may be distorted.[13] Several attempts have been made to identify and even to quantify the specific forms of misperception that interfere with communication. Among those that have attracted the most interest are a diabolical image of the adversary, a virile self-image, a moral self-image, a selective inattention to critical events and signals, an absence of empathy for the

---

[11] Adolf Hitler, *Mein Kampf* (Boston: Houghton Mifflin, 1943), pp. 134–157.

[12] For a collection of papers by Soviet authors, see *Problems of War and Peace: A Critical Analysis of Bourgeois Theories* (Moscow: Progress Publishers, 1972), trans. Bryan Bean, particularly part II, "The Origins and Essence of War."

[13] See, for example, H. C. J. Duijker and N. H. Frijda, *National Character and National Stereotypes* (Amsterdam: North Holland, 1960); and O. Klineberg, *Tensions Affecting International Understanding* (New York: Social Science Research Council, 1950), Bulletin 62.

opposing party's problem(s), military overconfidence, a leader's self-perception, a leader's perception of his or her counterpart's character, perception of the adversary's intentions, perception of the adversary's power and capabilities, military overestimation, and military underestimation.[14]

The perceptual distortions that result from these phenomena cause selective reception of messages and signals, and mutual misperception of intentions.[15] For example, potentially threatening messages from another government may be more salient or perceptually prominent than are cooperative or conciliatory statements. Listeners hear what they expect to hear, as in the theory of cognitive dissonance. The images that nations have of one another not only fail to match the realities they are supposed to represent, but these images are also highly resistant to change—even when evidence and experience contradict fixed expectations. (See Chapter 1 for a more detailed treatment of this process.) Communications failure and exaggerated fear contribute to escalatory processes by multiplying the consequences of international tensions.

As the speed and precision of modern weapons have increased the need for improved communications, so too should the communications revolution have assisted the world's leaders to convey their intentions better. There is no shortage of technical devices for these purposes: hotline telephone connections between the White House and the Kremlin, communications satellites that transmit information around the world in seconds, computers that communicate with one another over great

distances, and so on. The difficulty, of course, is that as technical aids have become more sophisticated, leaders have become more, rather than less, wary of the spoken intentions of one another. Furthermore, international communications tend to be public statements concealed in political messages. It is not uncommon, for example, for the president of the United States to deliver a message to an adversary abroad, such as Saddam Hussein of Iraq, in a State of the Union speech, but in a combative tone designed for domestic purposes that may risk distorting the message in Baghdad.

Although the technical aspects of international communication have become modernized, the strategic aspects have become more complicated. This is particularly true in regard to the language of escalation. Only in its final stages does the escalation of international events involve such things as deploying troops, making decisions regarding tactical nuclear weapons, or mobilizing alliances. The earlier, equally critical, phases are largely verbal and symbolic. Often their form, designed as much for domestic political consumption as for international communication, may make de-escalation all but impossible. Threats, deliberate distortion of images, propaganda, public rejection of settlement proposals, legislative condemnation, domestic mobilization, economic restructuring, and political positioning among the loyal opposition— these and hundreds of other events, all carrying messages of intractability to the adversary, precede actual preparation for combat. As patriotism begins to run high in public opinion polls, the difficulty increases of conducting more informative and accurate communications through diplomatic channels. Governments may simply lose the ability to communicate effectively to the adversary or to place strategic trust in the messages that are being received from abroad.[16] Instead they head straight

---

[14] For a review of the literature and extensive reference to original sources, see Jack S. Levy, "Misperception and the Causes of War," *World Politics*, October 1983, p. 76.

[15] See Anatol Rapoport, "Perceiving the Cold War," in Robert Fisher, ed., *International Conflict and Behavioral Science* (New York: Basic Books, 1964); also Kenneth Boulding, *The Image* (Ann Arbor: University of Michigan Press, 1956); and Karl W. Deutsch and Richard L. Merritt, "Effects of Events on National and International Images," in Herbert Kelman, ed., *International Political Behavior* (New York: Holt, Rinehart and Winston, 1965).

[16] For a classical treatment of escalation and its role in political communications, see Herman Kahn, *On Escalation* (New York: Praeger, 1965).

at each other as if they were two drivers playing Chicken, each determined to force the other off the road by sheer resolve of purpose. But unlike the two drivers, neither can remove its steering wheel and throw it onto the highway to signal its inability to change course. Lacking a last-minute communications display, the two collide in combat.

Communication is by nature a two-way undertaking and is thus subject to distortion at both the originating and recieving ends—or with either the sending or the receiving party. Consequently, international messages and their interpretations are subject to all the perceptual variation that we have studied. And just as communicators are driven by their own perceptions of both the subject matter and the receiver, there are domestic political circumstances that may shape (or misshape) messages. It has been argued, for example, that for lengthy historical eras such as the forty-five-year Cold War, international communication may have been distorted by a combination of bureaucratic stasis and the urge for self-preservation in elite foreign policy circles. These, it is postulated, led to conceptual lag, or the failure to revise and modernize policy based on evolving circumstances.[17]

6. Communications Failure Because of Technical Irony or Error

Not all communications failures in international politics are rooted in psychology. Many result from the contradictory purposes to which communications technologies are put, and still others are caused by human error or misjudgment or technical failure at a crucial time.

There is a great irony in the contemporary communications revolution with respect to international relations: Rather than improving communications between adversary governments, the revolution has been used to introduce precision warfare, to transform major powers into planetary powers by giving them military strength without occupation in distant lands, and to introduce new methods of concealing one's own strengths while improving the ability to detect another's. Together with sensing devices and computers, communications advances have produced a "transparency revolution" in which the competition for arms superiority is between the visible and the hidden. Thus, rather than enhance international communication for peace, the revolution has brought strategic competition to an unstable and dangerous condition. Whether or not the next generation of advances will emphasize mutual detection and verification rather than further competition in invisibility remains to be seen.[18]

Unquestionably the most tragic example of failed communications in recent international relations was the Soviet destruction of a civilian Korean airliner over the Sea of Japan in September 1983. Apart from unanswered questions of why the plane was off course and over Soviet territory, the inability of the United States, the Soviet Union, and Japan (all of whom were monitoring conversations between the Soviet pilot and his command base) to avoid tragedy astonished the world. The Soviet Union claimed that because the plane had previously intersected paths with an American intelligence craft, they were unable to determine whether the intruder was the American spy craft or the civilian liner. (Later they claimed that they knew it was the Korean plane but that they had evidence it was conducting a spy mission over Sakhalin Island under the cover of civilian aviation.)

---

[17] Richard A. Barnet, *The Roots of War* (New York: Atheneum, 1972).

[18] For a pioneering discussion of the transparency revolution and its impact on international communications, see Daniel Deudney, *Whole Earth Security: A Geopolitics of Peace*, Worldwatch Paper 55 (Washington, D.C.: Worldwatch Institute, 1983), particularly pp. 20–32.

Whatever may have been the real Soviet motive in firing an air-to-air missile, however, we know that several communications opportunities were missed.

1. The plane was nearly out of Soviet airspace when fired on and had thus been followed for sufficient time to have enabled either Japanese or American officials to intervene by communicating with the Soviet Union or for Soviet officials to have made international inquiries about the known locations of civilian craft in the vicinity of Sakhalin.
2. Translation difficulties between Japanese intelligence and the National Security Agency of the United States delayed a real understanding of the pending crisis longer than tolerable under the speed-of-sound flight of the Soviet interceptors.
3. There is no evidence that the Korean pilot was contacted by accepted international signals with the message that he was off course and in forbidden airspace.
4. There is speculation, although no hard evidence, that the plane was off course precisely because of an error in operating a navigational computer or because of an electronic failure within the computer.
5. The communications hotline between the White House and the Kremlin was never activated.

All these failures of communication, and failures to use to best advantage the most sophisticated communications electronics ever known, demonstrate the precarious condition of international relations when military or intelligence events occur at speeds greater than the speed of the human link in a communications chain. In this case, inefficient use of intelligence data resulted from (1) recent escalation of the Cold War, (2) the unexplained location of the Korean flight, (3) the earlier intersection of the civilian craft with an intelligence plane, (4) the Soviet eagerness to make a fire

or no-fire decision before the plane left Soviet airspace, and (5) delays caused by slowness in translating Soviet air-to-ground communications first into Japanese and then into English. Despite the speed-of-light communications capability among the three parties, it was actually the speed-of-sound chase seven miles above ground that determined that 269 persons would die. In August 1986, it was announced that a telephone hotline connecting Tokyo, Moscow, and Washington had been established in the hope of averting another such disaster in this strategically sensitive part of the world where private, military, and intelligence interests so often intersect.

7. Arms Races and the Security Dilemma

Another theory of the outbreak of war links it to runaway arms races that become strategically unstable and politically uncontrolled. Here, hostile nations lock into a cycle of mutual fear (a process called hostility reaction formation), in which each side believes itself to be threatened by the other. The defensive preparations of one are taken as evidence of offensive intentions by the other, who then arms in response. Each seeks a margin of superiority, leading to qualitative and quantitative competition in armaments and organized forces. This contest results in the security dilemma: Although one or both sides in a bilateral conflict may wish to have peace, the means by which they seek to secure it tend to destabilize the environment and reduce the prospects for peace. Another version of this argument says that arms competition up to some indefinite point may contribute to stability but that an incremental buildup beyond that point both diminishes the stability and fosters security that is inversely related to incremental cost. In either instance, the basic concept of the security dilemma has generated several new mathematical approaches to the study of military power and war that conclude that arms actually contribute to insecurity.[19]

Many American liberals contend that excessive military preparedness causes war. On the other side, conservatives tend to favor the adage *Si vis pacem, para bellum* ("If you want peace, prepare for war"). Do armaments cause wars or prevent them? Despite the volumes of scientific studies devoted to this question, the results are inconclusive.

But arms invariably exist in a political and security context, and so the role of arms races in international conflict is linked closely to the issue of power symmetries or asymmetries. If an arms race has a stabilizing effect because it results more in symmetry than in asymmetry, then it is not likely to be an immediate cause of war. If, on the other hand, the race tends toward asymmetry because of superior acceleration on one side, then war-related temptations may be irresistible. Hence it is not the mere existence of the race that influences the outcome, but its comparative characteristics.

For more than four decades, the Soviet-American strategic arms race achieved a remarkable stability, with neither side tempted to a first nuclear strike. But a simple faith in the fact that the race never erupted in war does not necessarily mean that further escalation of the competition would have added to either security or stability. The difficult problem for analysts and diplomats alike is that the actual strategic and political conditions under which stability deteriorates dangerously are unknown. It is probable that the numbers of weapons on the respective sides are a less important indicator of stability than they once were, despite the sometimes simple arithmetic of arms reduction talks. Accuracy, penetrability, and preservation of second-strike capability all seem to be more crucial to determining stability. As a result, it is the

weapons systems that introduce new capabilities, rather than those that add to familiar capabilities, that seem the most threatening to stability. It is for this reason that the American plan of deploying electronically controlled defensive weapons in space so markedly raised the stakes in the Soviet-American discussions in the 1980s.

It was not exclusively in Soviet-American relations, however, that these destabilizations may have consequences. In the many regional arms races to which Washington and the Kremlin contribute—from the Arab-Israeli arena to the two Koreas and the upheaved nations of the Persian Gulf—the unbalanced introduction of new weapons systems could have revolutionary consequences. This underscores the conclusion that arms races alone do not determine outcomes; it is the stabilizing or destabilizing characteristics of those races that are the critical factors.

Arms races, like communication failures, are seldom the root cause of conflict. The decision to maintain extremely high military expenditures most often reflects a prior condition of discord and conflict with an opponent. Arms races and exaggerated fears may inflame an existing conflict, but they seldom create one. The distinction should be underscored, however, between arms races as causes of political conflict and arms races as causes of war. Arms, after all, expand the alternatives for dealing with conflict as a result of either rational or irrational decision making. In particular, perceptions of armed strength between adversaries may result in preventive war (armed conflict to prevent another party from expanding its decisional alternatives or its armed might) or preemptive war (armed aggression undertaken in anticipation of aggression from the other party and launched to beat that party to it).

8. Internal Cohesion Through External Conflict

Another theory sees war as the product of policies designed to promote internal group cohesion through

---

[19] One of the earliest was Lewis Richardson, *Arms and Insecurity* (Pittsburgh: Boxwood, 1960). For more recent expressions, see Bruce Bueno de Mesquita, *The War Trap* (New Haven, Conn.: Yale University Press, 1981); and Stephen J. Majeski, "Expectations and Arms Races," *American Journal of Political Science*, May 1985, pp. 217–245.

the unifying effects of outside conflict—the process of drawing together to face a common enemy. Bismarck's calculated provocation of three external wars from 1866 to 1871 to integrate the German states is the classic example of wars fought purposely. Secretary of State William Henry Seward's fruitless proposal to President Abraham Lincoln that the United States precipitate international warfare to reunite the nation and avoid civil war exemplifies the same tactic. There exists an extensive literature that demonstrates the relationship of external conflict to internal cohesion at all levels of social interaction.[20] In international relations, the implication of this theory is that resort to warfare may be preferable to internal dissolution.

Despite the apparent weight of this theory, however, most scientific studies conclude quite differently. If internal conflict tended to be externalized in foreign wars, it is hypothesized that there should be a statistical relationship between the frequency of internal and external conflict. But in the most careful quantitative research, no clear and consistent relationship has been found,[21] although one study demonstrated a slight relationship.[22]

---

[20] Anthony de Reuck and Julie Knight, *Conflict in Society* (Boston: Little, Brown, 1966), p. 32; D. Kahn-Freund, "Intergroup Conflicts and Their Settlement," *British Journal of Sociology*, vol. 5, 1954, p. 201; Georg Simmel, *Conflict and the Web of Group Affiliations* (Glencoe, Ill.: Free Press, 1955); Lewis Coser, *The Functions of Social Conflict* (Glencoe, Ill.: Free Press, 1957), pp. 104–106; and Robert North, Howard Koch Jr., and Dina Zinnes, "The Integrative Functions of Conflict," *Journal of Conflict Resolution*, vol. 3, September 1960, pp. 355–374.

[21] Rudolph Rummel, "Testing Some Possible Predictors of Conflict Behavior Within and Between Nations," *Peace Research Society (International) Papers*, vol. 3, 1963, p. 17, and "The Relationship Between National Attributes and Foreign Conflict Behavior," in J. David Singer, ed., *Quantitative International Politics* (New York: Free Press, 1968); Michael Haas, "Social Change and National Aggressiveness: 1900–1960," in Singer, p. 213; Raymond Tanter, "Dimensions of Conflict Behavior Within and Between Nations, 1958–1960," *Journal of Conflict Resolution*, vol. 10, no. 1, March 1966, p. 46; and Samuel P. Huntington, "Patterns of Violence in World Politics," in Huntington, ed., *Changing Patterns of Military Politics* (New York: Free Press, 1962), pp. 40–41.

[22] Jonathan Wilkenfeld, "Domestic and Foreign Conflict Behavior of Nations," *Journal of Peace Research*, vol. 1, 1968, pp. 55–59.

9. International Conflict Through Internal Strife

In contrast, one may observe that in the twentieth century many international military encounters have resulted from domestic dissolution. To a very large extent, in fact, the distinction between civil and international war has been blurred, particularly as a result of frequent external intervention.

Illustrations abound. At the close of World War One, when Russia was destabilized by the Bolshevik Revolution and the civil war that followed, American troops landed in Russia to assist the White Russian army in defeating the Bolsheviks and returning the government to non-Marxist-Leninist elements more sympathetic to the West and to capitalism. The Vietnam War, fought almost continuously from 1950 to 1973, involved first French (supplied in large measure by the United States as part of the Asian anticommunist strategy that led to American intervention in Korea) and, later, American intervention. In 1984, the United States intervened indirectly in Nicaragua to bring down the Cuban-oriented leftist Sandinista government there and in El Salvador to protect the pro-American government from falling to leftist insurrectionists. In each of these civil wars, direct American or Cuban intervention was possible at any time.

Governments often claim that they are forced to intervene militarily in their client states because of destabilization caused by adversaries. The Soviet Union, for example, justified its interventions in Czechoslovakia (1968) and Poland (1981, with martial law rather than invasion) in part on the allegation that the United States and its NATO allies had, through propaganda and economic relations, created domestic instability that threatened the solidarity of the socialist commonwealth. In the case of Czechoslovakia, intervention resulted in the Brezhnev Doctrine, which proclaimed that the Warsaw Pact would not permit any political or economic change in an individual Eastern European state that would threaten the cohesion of the alliance. This does not differ greatly from the Theodore Roosevelt Corollary to the Monroe Doctrine that dominated inter-American relations from 1907 to 1932. Roosevelt's corollary attempted to stabilize South America, Central America, and the Caribbean under American influence by simply declaring Washington's willingness to use force if necessary to prevent the further establishment of European influence in the hemisphere. This led to American interventions in Venezuela, Colombia, and Mexico, to name only a few major examples. The Reagan Doctrine of the 1980s declared Washington's aim to regain governments recently lost to communism.

Many twentieth-century interventions have followed revolt against imperialism and colonialism. Not only is this a major theme of Marxist international relations theory, but it also is observable in a number of concrete instances. The Boer War, for example (1898–1900), was a British imperial action designed to consolidate its rule in South Africa, which was mineral rich and strategically important to British shipping lanes from the South Atlantic to the Indian Ocean. At the same time, as China was being divided into sectors for Western and Japanese economic dominance, military occupations and forceful defeat of local opposition became common.

It has been argued that foreign intervention occurs when domestic strife threatens to establish governments hostile to the economic aspirations of specific external countries. For example, it has been claimed that the motive for American intervention in Vietnam was not simply ideological or geopolitical but economic and neoimperialist as well. This thesis claims that by 1960 the United States had determined to protect from Soviet or Chinese-oriented influence all Third World territories having significant deposits of minerals and other raw materials critical to America's dominance in the emerging technological age.

The preceding examples vary in kind, but they all illustrate that external intervention in the domestic strife of nations, particularly economically

less developed ones, has become so common and frequent as to have blurred the distinction between civil and international war in current history. In the early years of the New World Order, however, there has seemed to be a preference for multilateral approaches to civil war, particularly in Rwanda, Somalia, and Bosnia. There was no intervention in Liberia. Time will reveal whether or not the revised global conditions will reverse the historical trend toward individual state intervention in civil wars.

10. Relative Deprivation

The concept of relative deprivation is especially useful in describing the origins of internal wars. It maintains that political rebellion is most likely when people believe that they are receiving less than their due. To achieve greater benefits or to relieve the frustration of denial, groups may turn to aggression and political violence.[23]

This differs from simple common sense in one important respect: The objective or absolute conditions of poverty and oppression do not lead directly to rebellion, but rather, the subjective or psychological response to these conditions is determinant. To illustrate, studies of rebellion and revolution find that violence most often occurs when conditions are beginning to improve rather than when they are at their worst point. The beginnings of improvement after a long period of deprivation trigger a revolution of rising expectations. Hopes rise more rapidly than realities, and an aspiration gap results, as shown in Figure 10–2. Careful statistical studies

---

[23] See especially Ted Gurr, *Why Men Rebel* (Princeton, N.J.: Princeton University Press, 1970). Also Crane Brinton, *The Anatomy of Revolution* (New York: Vintage, 1965); James Davies, "Toward a Theory of Revolution," *American Sociological Review*, vol. 27, no. 1, February 1962; and Peter A. Lupsha, "Explanation of Political Violence: Some Psychological Theories Versus Indignation," *Politics and Society*, vol. 2, no. 1, fall 1971.

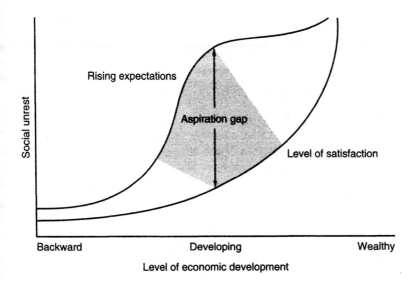

FIGURE 10–2   Level of economic development: The aspiration gap and rebellion potential (shaded).

have found that violence has tended to increase during the transitional period from traditional to modern society, as predicted by the theory of relative deprivation. The shaded portion in the figure shows the general relationship between violence and level of economic development.

For the full duration of the Cold War, civil wars were more frequent in the Developing World than in already developed states. The developed countries experienced only sporadic incidents of riot-scale violence in their own territories. But in Korea, Vietnam, Nigeria, Bangladesh, Indonesia, Colombia, Algeria, Cambodia, Laos, Zaire, Angola, Mozambique, Guinea-Bissau, Chad, Sri Lanka, Lebanon, Nicaragua, Trinidad and Tobago, El Salvador, Haiti, Uganda, China, Sudan, Yemen, Iran, Iraq, and India, the dead numbered in the tens and hundreds of thousands and even in the millions. In the highly publicized violent events in the developed countries, however, the dead numbered only in the tens of hundreds: in the United States (the African-American revolution), Northern Ireland, Spain, French Canada, Belgium, Portugal, and Czechoslovakia. To explain this disparity between rates of violence in developed and less-developed

countries, the theory of relative deprivation and the aspiration gap is attractive.[24]

However, several objections arise. Rich countries have engaged in many hostile confrontations outside their own borders, usually in the territory of dependent developing client states. This displacement of violence to the developing countries may have been a Cold War privilege conferred by the unequal distribution of influence in the international system. Also, Marxist critics have argued that there is an essential unity in the global revolutionary movement and that even revolutions in

---

[24] Many governments have increased expenditures for the use of force against internal upheaval much more dramatically than they have for international stability or war. From 1966 to 1975, for example, police expenditures in Africa rose by 144 percent, while appropriations for armies rose 40 percent. See Morris Janowitz, *Military Institutions and Coercion in the Developing Nations* (Chicago: University of Chicago Press, 1977). For an empirical debate on whether lack of freedom—as contrasted to lack of material goods, food, or welfare—causes wars, see R. J. Rummel, "Libertarianism and International Violence," *Journal of Conflict Resolution*, March 1983, pp. 27–71, which draws an affirmative conclusion; and Jack Vincent, "Freedom and International Conflict: Another Look," *International Studies Quarterly*, March 1987, pp. 103–127, for negative findings.

remote parts of the world are challenges to the worldwide system of imperialism. Modern struggles occur in the periphery rather than in the center because of the imperialists' relatively weaker hold in outlying regions. The overbalance of violence in the developing countries is, in the Marxist view, a transient historical phenomenon from which causal inferences should not be drawn too hastily.

Another objection to this theory of political violence concerns the separation of physical bloodshed from other forms of abuse. The isolation of violence as the dependent variable in many studies ignores the fact that physical conflict exists on a continuum with other forms of harm, such as systematic oppression, imprisonment, and political denial. Such institutional violence can be quite as painful as physical abuse, and it can continue over much longer periods of time. Singling out rebellious violence alone as a social disease ignores the everyday suffering of millions of people and may result in false theories and vacuous remedies.

The violence pattern has changed since the end of the Cold War. Civil wars and armed rebellions have continued to plague the Developing World, with new outbreaks of violence in Somalia, Haiti, Rwanda, Burundi, Liberia, Mozambique, and Mexico. But the demise of the Brezhnev Doctrine and of the Cold War sent shock waves through the former Soviet Union and its external empire. Civil wars in Romania and Georgia are less well known than Boris Yeltsin's 1994 decision to fire heavy artillery at the Russian Parliament Building as a last resort in putting down an attempted coup d'état. Russia's war in Chechnya is a response to a secessionist movement. And the breakup of the former Yugoslavia sparked multiple wars, the most severe among them in Bosnia.

11. Instinctual Aggression and Sociobiology

One of the most popular theories of war among laypersons is the idea of an instinct of aggression—the blood lust that is depicted in so many lurid movies and magazines. In the aggression theory, the root of war is seen as a vestigial instinct of bellicosity that has survived from our animal roots. Many observers have concluded that people like to fight and that at least in part, international conflict has its basis in male competitiveness (machismo) and even direct sadism. The outbreak of war is thus traced to biological proclivities and to individual and collective psychopathology.[25]

It is quite evident that people enjoy violence; otherwise television and the movies would not be so full of it. But there is much controversy concerning the relationship between aggressive impulses and the decision to go to war. One major study of twenty-five wars found that the decision to go to war was "in no case . . . precipitated by emotional tensions, sentimentality, crowd behavior, or other irrational motivations."[26] As organizations become more bureaucratic, controls are put on personal impulsiveness and deviance. Decisions made by groups are more likely to approximate rational choice than are decisions made in similar situations by individuals.[27]

On the other side, several theorists view aggression as a dominant impulse triggered by political

[25] William McDougall, "The Instinct of Pugnacity," in Leon Bramson and George Goethals, eds., *War: Studies from Psychology, Sociology and Anthropology* (New York: Basic Books, 1964), pp. 33–44; Edward Glover, *War, Sadism, and Pacifism* (London: Allen and Unwin, 1933); Elton McNeil: "Psychology and Aggression," *Journal of Conflict Resolution*, vol. 3, no. 3, September 1959, pp. 195–293; "Personal Hostility and International Aggression," *Journal of Conflict Resolution*, vol. 5, no. 3, September 1961, pp. 279–290; "The Nature of Aggression," in McNeil, ed., *The Nature of Human Conflict* (Englewood Cliffs, N.J.: Prentice-Hall, 1965), pp. 14–44.

[26] Theodore Abel, "The Element of Decision in the Pattern of War," *American Sociological Review*, vol. 6, 1941, p. 855.

[27] See O. G. Brim, ed., *Personality and Decision Processes* (Stanford, Calif.: Stanford University Press, 1962). For an important view on the other side, see Harold Lasswell, *Psychopathology and Politics*, 2nd ed. (New York: Viking, 1960). Lasswell found a tendency for psychopathological individuals to go into public life out of proportion to their numbers in a group, displacing and rationalizing private disturbances in terms of the "public interest." For a review of literature on this question, see Brent Rutherford, "Psychopathology, Decision-Making, and Political Involvement," *Journal of Conflict Resolution*, vol. 10, no. 4, December 1966, pp. 387–407.

disputes that provide the necessary rationalization for violence. As Albert Einstein said, "Man has within him a lust for hatred and destruction. . . . It is a comparatively easy task to call this into play and raise it to the level of a collective psychosis."[28] Bertrand Russell claimed: "War is accepted by men . . . with a readiness, an acquiescence in untrue and inadequate reasons."[29] Naturally, this opinion is more convincing to those who reject the official rationale but must account for the persistence of their opponents in adhering to it.

Systematic studies distinguish between realistic and nonrealistic conflicts.[30] In a realistic conflict, the cause of struggle is rational disagreement over goals. In a nonrealistic conflict, the immediate issues are merely a pretext for fighting, and the real purpose of the combatants is violence itself. When we have both an instinct of combativeness and a disagreement over political issues, we have a chicken-and-egg problem of deciding which is the real cause. Are the political issues only rationalizations to justify violence and to permit the relaxation of normal inhibitions against bloodshed that are applied unless reasons of state are involved? Or is it the reverse—leaders facing realistic disagreements with opponents take advantage of the aggressiveness of their followers to arouse a spirit of national struggle? Is aggressiveness a cause of war or only a consequence of it?

No final answer to this question has emerged from conflict research, but it is a reliable maxim that the aggressive urge is important only insofar as it is translated into ideology. Sheer blood lust plays a relatively minor role, but aggressive and demanding definitions of political situations are commonly behind warlike disputes. If the aggressive urge distorts perceptions and magnifies perceived threats (the Cold War, for instance), it is a

causal contributor to war. Research thus tends to disprove the crudest forms of the aggression theory and to support the more complex and subtle forms.

There is, however, a substantial research literature on the nature and function of the aggressive urge and its relation to political violence. Much of it focuses on animal behavior for clues to human aggression. In the best known of these reports, Konrad Lorenz examined the logic and functions of aggression in a variety of animal species. He found that aggression is useful in many ways: for self-defense and protection of the young; for forcing territorial spacing over the available food area, preventing depletion in one location; or for mate selection through male rivalry, leading to the upward evolution of species.

What, then, keeps aggressive behavior within tolerable and useful limits and prevents it from destroying the species altogether? A second factor exists alongside the aggressive urge. This is a built-in inhibition against the use of violence, present in every species whenever aggression occurs. The inhibition is triggered biologically when the victim of an attack gives an appropriate signal of submission. The intensity of the inhibition in each species is proportional to its innate lethality—the stronger the natural weapons of the species, the firmer the inhibition. The supposedly vicious wolf, for example, is quite incapable of continuing an attack on another wolf once the victim signals submission by exposing a vulnerable section of its neck. The dove, on the other hand, supposedly as peaceful as the wolf is warlike, is actually quite vicious. Having poor equipment for aggression, it has little inhibition against aggression and has been known to pluck apart another dove ruthlessly over a forty-eight-hour period, disregarding signals of submission.

Lorenz extended this theory to an explanation of human aggression. He reasoned that people lack teeth, claws, poison, and other natural weapons of great power. Hence the corresponding level of their inhibition is relatively moderate, but they have used their brains to develop artificial weapons that greatly enhance their lethality. Their programmed

[28] From a letter to Sigmund Freud in James Strachey, ed., *The Standard Edition of the Complete Psychological Works of Sigmund Freud*, vol. 22 (London: Hogarth, 1964), pp. 199–202.

[29] Bertrand Russell, *Why Men Fight* (New York: Bonibooks, 1930), pp. 5–6.

[30] Lewis Coser, *The Functions of Social Conflict* (New York: Free Press, 1957).

inhibitions are exceeded by their unprogrammed potential for destruction, and they are able to release their aggression with relatively little restraint. Aerial bombardment, long-range artillery, and other remote-control weapons interfere with the passing of signals that would restrain the attacker. Thus humans, according to Lorenz, have upset nature's balanced design, and their aggressive urge threatens to destroy them.[31]

Among humans' inhibitions, of course, is the power of rationality, and that is accompanied by the ability to institutionalize critical decision making such that the instinct of aggression of one or a few people need not result in society-wide violence. In all social relations, one must distinguish between individual aggressiveness and the social organization of violence. Lorenz's work attempts to build a bridge between the two. On the individual level, modern science has made some small contributions to understanding. For about thirty years there has been a sporadic attempt to link criminal aggression with specific genetic defects, but with inconclusive results. More recently, studies of lower primates that demonstrated a biochemical basis to power seeking have been confirmed in humans.[32] Researchers have found a high statistical correlation among (1) levels of whole-blood serotonin, (2) three characteristics of the Type A personality (aggressiveness, competitiveness, and drive), (3) distrust, and (4) self-confidence. Whether or not these studies will subsequently explain an individual's fighting instinct, as contrasted with social aggressiveness, is a question of interest to theorists of war.

Cultural Differences and Aggression

Are some countries and cultures more aggressive than others? Many historians and social scientists have attempted to match degrees of aggressiveness with different national characters. Germany, for example, has been identified as a country with a cultural background particularly conducive to authoritarianism and the use of force, as reflected in prevailing child-rearing practices, the martial quality of German music, and other cultural attributes.

Nineteen hundred years ago, Tacitus gave this classic account of the German propensity to war:

> Many noble youths, if the land of their birth is stagnating in a protracted peace, deliberately seek out other tribes, where some war is afoot. The Germans have no taste for peace; renown is easier won among perils, and you cannot maintain a large body of companions except by violence and war.... You will find it harder to persuade a German to plough the land and to await its annual produce with patience than to challenge a foe and earn the prize of wounds. ... When not engaged in warfare, they spend some little time in hunting, but more in idling, abandoned to sleep and gluttony. All the heroes and grim warriors dawdle their time away, while the care of the house, hearth, and fields is left to the women, old men and weaklings of the family. The warriors themselves lose their edge. They are so strangely inconsistent. They love indolence but they hate peace.[33]

This opinion accords with the views of many observers of German behavior during the first half of the present century.

But is there a scientific basis for the opinion that different cultures have varying propensities to political violence? Careful studies disagree on the answer. Some relate various cultural attributes to the occurrence of aggressive behavior, taking the frequency of violence as an indicator of the cultural propensity for war.[34] Others doubt that the frequency of violence and war is attributable to culture. A more important factor may be the number of common borders that a country shares with

---

[31] Konrad Lorenz, On Aggression (New York: Harcourt Brace Jovanovich, 1966); see also Robert Ardrey, The Territorial Imperative (New York: Atheneum, 1966).

[32] Douglas Masden, "A Biochemical Property Relative to Human Power Seeking," American Political Science Review, June 1985, pp. 448–457.

[33] Tacitus, On Britain and Germany (Baltimore: Penguin, 1948), pp. 112–113.

[34] For example, Tom Broch and Johan Galtung, "Belligerence Among the Primitives," Journal of Peace Research, 1966, pp. 33–45; and Quincy Wright, A Study of War, (Chicago: University of Chicago Press, 1942) pp. 9, 10, and 20.

other nations. This is the theory of "geographical opportunity"—the more borders, the more wars.[35] Another factor unrelated to aggression is the territorial distribution of ethnic groups. As we have seen, multiethnic countries have more opportunities for conflict than do homogeneous populations, and thus more incidents. Against these and other factors, purely cultural variations in aggressiveness may be a weak explanation for warlike behavior. At least one study concludes that there is no good evidence for a cultural propensity to aggressiveness:

> Although culture patterns may be fruitfully compared in terms of their ways of handling and expressing hostility/aggression, it is essentially meaningless to describe one culture as more or less hostile/aggressive than another in any absolute terms, since no external criterion exists that is not in some sense arbitrary.[36]

In general, one may say that the present evidence for cultural propensities to war is inconclusive.

War-Peace Cycles

Another strand of aggression research is the search for cycles of violent behavior. Does the amount of violence in human society ebb and flow in patterns? Is there a "war curve"?

Quantitative research into this matter varies in its conclusions. Some older studies pointed confidently to validating the war-peace cycle. One found a trend of an upswing in the level of violence about every twenty-five years, with a twenty-year cycle prior to 1680 and thirty years the apparent cycle after that. Another hypothesized that the observed cycle of war is caused by patterns in social psychology. After a war, memories of suffering are vivid, and so further fighting is avoided. As time passes, unpleasant memories fade or are repressed, and "the themes employed in the descriptions of the last great war shift from 'horror'-dominant to

'glory'-dominant." War is then romanticized again until a new opportunity arises to satisfy violent needs. There is a parallel rotation of decision makers every twenty to twenty-five years, and the new leaders, it would appear, need to have their own war. This seems to assume that "the opportunities for employing violence are always present."[37]

More recent quantitative studies of war reject the notion of periodicity. Some go the additional step of disproving the war-weariness hypothesis that armed conflict engenders images that forestall the next war. One study concludes, for example, that there is no statistical support for the contention that great-power wars are followed by periods of predictable length during which none of the participants will engage in another war. It also concludes that there is no relationship between the intensity and the ruinousness of war, on the one hand, and the length of time before the outbreak of another war, on the other hand.[38] These conclusions and others like them would seem to indicate that the frequency of war is not primarily a function of culture or of time, but of political conflict. War cannot be understood apart from politics.

12. Economic and Scientific Stimulation

Another theory of war concerns its economic functions. Both war and the threat of war have accelerated scientific discovery, technical innovation, and industrial development. It is said that a major external economy of war is this great industrial spin-off. Sluggish economies may be stimulated by the creation of artificial demand: "The attacks that have since the time of Samuel's criticism of King Saul been leveled against military expenditures as

[35] James Paul Wesley, "Frequency of Wars and Geographical Opportunity," *Journal of Conflict Resolution*, vol. 4, December 1962, pp. 387–389.

[36] R. T. Green and G. Santori, "A Cross Cultural Study of Hostility and Aggression," *Journal of Peace Research*, vol. 1, 1969, p. 22.

[37] Frank Denton and Warren Phillips, "Some Patterns in the History of Violence," *Journal of Conflict Resolution*, vol. 1, no. 2, June 1968, p. 193. A similar conclusion positing fifty-year cycles is found in Oswald Spengler, *Decline of the West* (New York: Knopf, 1926), vol. 1, pp. 109–110.

[38] Jack S. Levy and T. Clifton Morgan, "The War-Weariness Hypothesis: An Empirical Test," *American Journal of Political Science*, February 1986, pp. 26–49.

waste may well have concealed or misunderstood the point that some kinds of waste may have a larger social utility."[39] There is little doubt, for example, that the Great Depression of the 1930s ended for America only with the onset of the Second World War. Military demands put Americans back to work and primed the pump of economic recovery. Today, with economic pump priming managed principally through public spending and government manipulation of interest rates, increases or decreases in military spending may be crucial factors in most industrialized nation-states.

Nevertheless, even if high levels of military spending can be shown to be good for the corporate economy, it does not follow that war is good for business. Major wars tend to produce side effects such as inflation, the tightening of credit, and the interruption of international trade and financial flows—all of which harm the largest corporations. The New York Stock Exchange averages declined in response to escalation in Vietnam and Cambodia and recovered their losses only with the de-escalation of the war.[40] Even firms specializing in the production of military hardware did not flourish during the Vietnam years. United States defense profits ran at substantially higher rates from 1961 to 1964 than from 1965 to 1972. Thus we are led to the paradoxical conclusion that defense spending might be good for the capitalist economy, but war definitely is not. Perhaps the perfect combination from a profit viewpoint is a prolonged state of controlled international tensions (such as the Cold War) with high military spending but without the actual outbreak of war. A high and sustained level of multiregional conflict inviting huge

international arms sales was one of the most profitable components of military business throughout the Cold War. And while the 1990s peace movement in the Middle East might portend an eventual reduction in arms sales there, the Iran-Iraq War and the Persian Gulf War both accelerated arms sales in that region.

Even if warlike policies were clearly and unambiguously favorable to business, it would not follow automatically that governments would act in these interests. It was shown in 1935 that financial and industrial elites had played a relatively secondary role in the expansionist policies of the imperialist states. Investors supported governments interested in expansion for other reasons, but the political elite used the business groups, rather than the reverse.[41] Another study found that economic causes figured directly in less than a third of the wars from 1820 to 1949 and that they have been more important in small wars than in large wars.[42] The results in studies such as these often depend on the way that the question is posed and the measures that are used for key variables.

Apart from the well-known relationship between conflict and arms innovation, the role of scientific stimulation in causing war is less well understood. Clearly, a government with an economic advantage over its adversary in materiel, ability to sustain long logistical lines, and the like may be tempted to provoke a war of conquest. And a technological advantage may diminish prospects for strategic security, as could have been the case with the American Strategic Defense Initiative, because it might have given a new dimension to the Soviet-American nuclear arms race. But probably the most important consequences of scientific stimulation for peace are regional. First, as the technological

[39] Arthur Waskow, *Toward the Unarmed Forces of the United States* (Washington, D.C.: Institute for Policy Studies, 1966), p. 9. Also David Bazelon, "The Politics of the Paper Economy," *Commentary*, November 1962, p. 409; and Michael Reich, "Military Spending and the US Economy," in Steven Rosen, ed., *Testing the Theory of the Military-Industrial Complex* (Lexington, Mass.: D. C. Heath, 1973), pp. 85–86. See also John Nef, *War and Human Progress* (Cambridge, Mass.: Harvard University Press, 1950).

[40] See Betty Hanson and Bruce Russett, "Testing Some Economic Interpretations of American Intervention," in Steven Rosen, ed., *Testing the Theory of the Military-Industrial Complex.*

[41] Eugene Staley, *War and the Private Investor* (Garden City, N.Y.: Doubleday, 1935). See also Kenneth Boulding and Tapan Mukerjee, eds., *Economic Imperialism* (Ann Arbor: University of Michigan Press, 1962); and Steven Rosen and James Kurth, eds., *Testing the Theory of Economic Imperialism* (Lexington, Mass.: D. C. Heath, Lexington Books, 1974).

[42] Lewis Richardson, *Statistics of Deadly Quarrels* (Pittsburgh: Boxwood, 1960). Contrast John Bakeless, *The Economic Causes of Modern War* (London: Yard, 1921).

transfer in arms and other goods destabilizes regional power balances, the threat of war through asymmetries arises. Second, as aspiration gaps are widened because of the disparity between the promise of technology transfer and the actual performance, internal forces may grow violent through visions of relative deprivation.

But these details of and speculations about the roles of economy and science in promoting war should not obscure the basic theoretical issue at hand. Economic factors play a part in virtually every theory of war except those based wholly on psychological factors. Furthermore, the purpose of war is to bring about by force a redistribution of resources (territory, population, industry, raw materials, wealth). Economic development stimulates not only competition but lust and covetousness as well. One of the potential means of avoiding war, therefore, is the peaceful redistribution of wealth to reflect the distribution of power so that war will not be invoked for forceful redistribution. One quantitative study shows that when both sides in a conflict have adjusted their economies to a war footing, the probability of war can be measured by each party's understanding of the other's balance of consumption utility and war disutility, and the clarity with which these are revealed in the diplomacy of the prewar conflict phase.[43]

13. The Military-Industrial Complex

One issue of special interest in the debate over the causes of war is that of the military-industrial complex. Powerful domestic groups within the major states that have vested interests in military spending and international tension use their influence to promote antagonistic relations among nations, according to this theory. These domestic groups that comprise the military-industrial complex include (1) professional soldiers, (2) managers and, in the capitalist states, owners of industries deeply engaged in military supply, (3) high government officials whose careers and interests are tied to military expenditure, (4) legislators whose districts benefit from defense projects, and (5) the scientific and engineering research communities, including universities and colleges, where research depends heavily on government financial support.

These core members of the military-industrial complex are supported by associated and lesser groups such as the veterans and military service associations who do defense-related research. These groups occupy powerful positions in the political structures of the major states, and they exercise their influence in a coordinated and mutually supportive way to maintain optimal levels of war preparation and to direct national security policy. According to proponents of this theory, the influence of the military-industrial complex exceeds that of any opposing coalitions or interests.

This complex rationalizes high levels of military spending with an ideology of conflict, such as the mythology of the Cold War. This ideology may be a deliberately manufactured deception to mislead the public, or it may be a militaristic false consciousness that arises spontaneously with high military spending. Whether or not the complex is a conscious conspiracy, it requires an ideology of international conflict to guarantee its position within the society's political and economic structure. To the conventional theorist, arms races are caused by realistic conflicts and a cycle of mutual fear between opposing states. To the military-industrial-complex theorist, the external threat is merely a necessary projection for the self-aggrandizing activities of domestic military-industrial complexes.

In its classic (Cold War) formulation, this theory applied to both capitalist and socialist states.[44] In the latter, the professional military combined with the managers of state defense industries and the related functionaries within the Communist

---

[43] Degobert L. Brito and Michael D. Intriligator, "Conflict, War and Redistribution," *American Political Science Review*, December 1985, pp. 943–952.

[44] C. Wright Mills, *The Causes of World War III* (New York: Ballantine, 1958), and *The Power Elite* (New York: Oxford University Press, 1956).

party apparatus, the ministries, and bureaucracies. There was a natural and effective alliance of interests among Soviet heavy industry, the armed forces, and the conservative wing of the Communist party, forged on "their understanding of the interdependency that exists between security, heavy industry, and ideological orthodoxy." Without it, harm would befall the career interests and social positions of both the professional military elite and some of the most highly paid civilian personnel in the country. Thus despite state ownership of production facilities, the USSR also had a military-industrial complex interested in the continuation of international conflict.[45]

The theory of the military-industrial complex is far from flawless. It fails to account for the decline in percentage of national production devoted to defense in both the United States and the Soviet Union in the early 1970s and in the New World Order of the 1990s. The U.S. defense budget in constant dollars (that is, discounting inflation) declined in 1973 to a level comparable with that of the 1950s, and the decline in both constant dollars and percentage of the gross national product (GNP) continued throughout the decade. (In 1995, critics of defense reductions claimed that unless funds were added to the Pentagon's request, the level would fall to pre–World War Two levels as percent of gross domestic product and of the federal budget.) This occurred even as the cost of designing and building military technology increased, although some of the cost was offset by the decrease in the military population after the Vietnam War. Several congressional battles over military procurement have resulted in the elimination of entire weapons systems. For a brief period, several aerospace industries faced bankruptcy, one of which (Lockheed) had to be rescued by the government. In many ways, then, the defense sector shows signs of decline and weakness rather than the omnipotence attributed to it by military-industrial-complex theorists, at least in the United States

(which alone accounts for about 40 percent of the entire world's military expenditures).

The last gasp of the Cold War saw a marked increase in military spending in the United States, predicated on the theory that to force the Soviet Union into a new and ever more expensive competition for arms would expose the weaknesses of the Soviet economy, take advantage of a trend toward democratization, and hasten the end of the Cold War itself. Historians will for ages debate the role of this strategy in ending the Cold War, but it is likely that the consequent decline in defense expenditures illustrates one important feature of arms races: The recession that followed in the United States was more a structural readjustment in the economy than a familiar economic cycle. Parts of the nation previously rich in defense industries, most notably California (Hughes Aircraft and others), Long Island, N.Y. (Grumman Aircraft), Connecticut (Electric Boat, maker of the nuclear submarine fleet), were all deep in recession long after the rest of the country enjoyed such economic growth that the Federal Reserve raised long-term interest rates seven times in twelve months.

But even when the defense sector expands rather than shrinks, other doubts still apply. The theory of the military-industrial complex assumes that political behavior is motivated essentially by private interest rather than public good or national interest. At the core of the theory, critics charge, is a crude and simplistic economic determinism. Careful studies of international events generally find a much more complex pattern of motivation behind national policies. Particularly in warlike conflicts, where the highest values of life and death and national survival are at issue, behavior tends to be guided by principled conviction rather than by crude self-interest.

The theory of the military-industrial complex gains plausibility if ideology is considered alongside self-interest and conflict behavior. Behavior may be determined by convictions, but where do these come from? Perhaps self-interest sets the frame for broader values and perceptions. If so, military-industrial dependency might produce a conflict-filled world view.

---

[45] Vernon Aspaturian, "The Soviet Military-Industrial Complex: Does It Exist?" in Steven Rosen, ed., *Testing the Theory of the Military-Industrial Complex.*

14. Population Limitation

One of the precursors of Hitler's theory of Lebensraum is the theory of population expansion and war suggested by Sir Thomas Malthus. In his *Essay on the Principle of Population* (1798), Malthus argued that there is an innate tendency for population to expand geometrically, while food resources expand only arithmetically. Thus, "the power of population is infinitely greater than the power in the earth to produce subsistence for man." Because population must be proportioned to food supply, there must be controls on population growth. One of these is war.

This theory of war as a control on surplus population growth still remains attractive to laypersons, although not to conflict researchers. The rate of global population expansion is much greater now than in Malthus's time. Indeed, more people have lived since 1900 than in the sum of human history before that date! And this number will multiply well into the next century. Some observers, echoing Malthus, predict cataclysmic wars and famines in the future to dispose of surplus population.

This theory does not accord with the facts, however. Wars have in general taken very few lives when measured as a percentage of populations, even when the deaths have been in the millions. Only the most exceptional wars have taken more than 5 percent of the populations of the warring parties; more than half of all wars end with battle losses under one-half of 1 percent (see Figure 10–3). Even during the Second World War, the loss rate did not significantly depress populations. The losses of the North and South Vietnamese, staggering as they were, were lower than the birth rate, and so the population continued to grow.[46] These figures do not sustain the Malthusian view of war as a significant population-limiting device. In addition, the technology of the Green Revolution now promises to multiply the capacity of the earth to produce food geometrically—finally putting to rest the theory of Malthus unless, of course, we include nuclear war in the analysis. But an atomic cataclysm would destroy arable land as well as population.

15. Conflict Resolution by Force

We have saved for last the most general and comprehensive theory: war as a device for conflict resolution. In the general theory, conflict exists when two or more groups make mutually exclusive claims to the same resources or positions, and war is a means of allocating scarce values to resolve the conflict. War, in this view, is a rational instrument of decision, and war policies are decided by a logical computation of costs and benefits.

The claim of rationality is controversial. Conflicts can be decided by arbitration, elections, courts and tribunals, administrative decisions, direct negotiation, and compromise—even the flip of a coin. How is it rational to spill blood when nonviolent means are available?

The answer lies in the importance of the issues typically involved in warlike disputes. Every nation or movement has a few core values that cannot be compromised and many shell values that it would also like to satisfy but are not vital. Secondary interests can be compromised with an opponent, but leadership is obligated to defend core values by all available means—including, if necessary, violent defense. War is the *ultima ratio*—the last resort. In the words of Walter Lippmann, war is "the way in which the great human decisions are made."[47]

The image of the armed forces and military policy has been depreciated in the United States and other countries, partly as a consequence of the unpopular wars in Vietnam, Yugoslavia, Afghanistan, and Chechnya. (The brief infatuation with

---

[46] See Steven Rosen, "War Power and the Willingness to Suffer," in Bruce Russett, ed., *Peace, War, and Numbers* (Beverly Hills, Calif.: Sage, 1972).

[47] Walter Lippmann, "The Political Equivalent of War," *Atlantic Monthly*, August 1928, pp. 181–187.

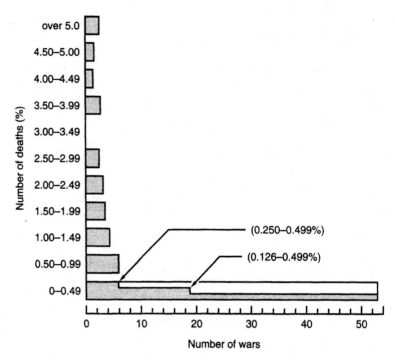

FIGURE 10–3   Percentage of population lost in battle deaths in major international wars.

military technology and nationalism that attended the Persian Gulf War among Americans was a major exception, and it owed principally to the disproportion between huge victory and very small casualty rate.) At the same time, most people reject absolute pacifism and retain a belief in the "just war." For example, on May 24, 1969, the World Council of Churches resolved: "All else failing, the church and churches would support resistance movements, including revolutions, aimed at elimination of political or economic tyranny which makes racism possible." Although most people value nonviolence, they evidently value other things even more and are willing to pay the exorbitant price of human lives in their pursuit of core value objects.

Conclusion

Many of the theories that we have reviewed imply that the cause of war can be found in conspiracies, irrationality, hidden motives, and the influence of certain elites. One is attracted to the conclusion that calm and thoughtful people who are not involved in the munitions industry or the military high command, who are not particularly aggressive or greedy or sinister, who neither hate the enemy unreasonably nor willfully misunderstand it, and who detest the idea of war as a waste of life and treasure do not make wars, but are led or duped into them.

But most wars involve very real incompatibilities between the basic moral objectives of the two sides, and it is historical fact that ordinarily the population of each side deliberately and without any element of crowd irrationality supports the carefully formulated policy of the leadership. In their zeal to eradicate war, political scientists cannot ignore the nonconspiratorial and quite rational processes in social life that turn the peace loving into warriors. It is the behavior of these people that is at the core of the theory of war as a rational instrument of conflict resolution.

CHAPTER 11

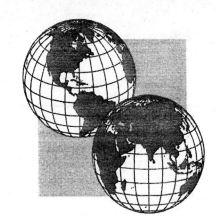

The International Political Economy

A ny discussion of power in international relations is likely to leave the impression that most of the content of world affairs relates to conflict and military preparedness. In fact, however, the principal interactions of governments and peoples are economic, although to be sure, in areas like international arms sales, power politics and global economics converge. Even in intergovernmental relations, however, the frequency of economic transactions and events greatly exceeds the number of military events. And in the broader universe of international relations involving public organizations, corporations, individuals, and other nongovernmental actors, economic transactions comprise the great majority of activities. This is why this book has not distinguished between the political and the economic content of international relations. Not many years ago it was thought that international politics was for the political scientist, and international economics for the economist. But today, just as it is faulty to present global politics from a single national perspective, so too is the study of international relations insufficient if it is restricted to politics unenlightened by economic content. This part of the book, then, deals not with technical economics and econometrics, but with the economic motives, activities, and policies that cross the boundaries of national politics.

What, then, is the international political economy? Simply stated, it is the global interaction between politics and economics. This simple premise recognizes the essential reciprocity of politics and economics.

> On the one hand, politics largely determines the framework of economic activity and channels it in directions intended to serve the interests of dominant groups; the exercise of power in all its forms is a major determinant of the nature of an economic system. On the other hand, the economic process itself tends to redistribute power and wealth; it transforms the power relationships among groups. This in turn leads to a transformation of the political system, thereby giving rise to a new structure of economic relationships. Thus, the dynamics of international relations in the modern world is largely a function of the reciprocal interaction between economics and politics.[1]

The international political economy, then, is "the reciprocal and dynamic interaction in international relations of the pursuit of wealth and the pursuit of power."[2] In the Cold War era wealth and power were more easily distinguished than they are in the New World Order, in which substitution of economic security for nuclear confrontation is the crux of world politics.

Economic aspects of the international system have been a dominant force since the Industrial Revolution. As distances have become shorter and

---

[1] Robert Gilpin, *U.S. Power and the Multinational Corporation* (New York: Basic Books, 1975), pp. 21–22.
[2] Robert Gilpin, *U.S. Power and the Multinational Corporation*, p. 43.

competition keener, the need for markets and inexpensive skilled labor, not to mention such other driving forces as raw materials and sources of energy, has stimulated volumes of international political implications. The quest for development in the post–World War Two era added another impetus, as did the central political-economic antipathy between the capitalist West and the socialist East throughout the Cold War. Although these problems stem from economic issues, they nevertheless fuel the international political system. To regulate these relations, the world has created an elaborate international economic system, much of which has become institutionalized (i.e., it is organized around formal intergovernmental institutions) since the United Nations was formed. Such agencies as the International Monetary Fund, the International Bank for Reconstruction and Development, the General Agreement on Tariffs and Trade and its new (1995) World Trade Organization, the Organization of Petroleum Exporting Countries, the Organization for Economic Cooperation and Development, the United Nations Conference on Trade and Development, and dozens of others

contribute to the orderly regulation of the international political economy. Yet other aspects remain conspicuously unorganized: economic intervention in the Developing World, political-economic subversion, and international arms trade, to mention only a few.

Goods pass daily between nations, and payments are adjusted through systems of international credit. But international trade is a source of more than profit; for as nations compete for natural resources, labor, capital, and profits from world markets, they collide with one another's interests. Despite the closeness of Japanese-American relations since the Second World War, for example, the great success of Japan's technological growth has threatened American sales throughout the world, eroded profits within the United States, and made Japan so nearly self-sufficient industrially as to need fewer and fewer American goods. In the final decade of the Cold War era, severe strains developed as a result of these factors, but the need for a close security relationship made the situation politically manageable. One of the principal problems facing the New World Order is the potential consequences of

A symbol of the failed East European economies falls into history with the Cold War. (*Source:* Peter Kneffel/Photoreporters, Inc.)

Japanese-American economic hostility unmoderated by the former security imperative.

Economic relations between states are strained by more than trade. Throughout the Cold War, for example, East-West trade was hampered by ideological differences and the difficulty of setting meaningful price comparisons between capitalist and socialist economies. Even within the capitalist world, however, price comparisons and currency values impose severe strains on international activity. Domestic inflation, international trade volume, and the numerical ratio of a state's exports and imports all affect the value of that state's currency. For twenty years after the Second World War, the American dollar and gold were regarded as the most precious media of exchange. Now, however, the decontrolled value of gold (which went from $35 to as high as $900 per ounce in a five-year period, only thereafter to drop to $300 and then rise again) provides little stability to international business; and the value of the American dollar has slipped, despite two official devaluations, to the point that central banks prefer to hold German marks or Japanese yen. (In the summer of 1984 the dollar was worth 155 yen, but by the summer of 1995 it was worth only 87.) For all these reasons and more, a comprehensive understanding of international relations requires that international trade and the international organization of money be considered as sources of international conflict as well as sources of global stability.

In the New World Order the normal peacetime issues of commerce and trade play larger roles in foreign policy and international interaction than ever, because the void left by strategic obsession has been filled by the quest for economic security. The spread of industrial capability, the onset of the technological era, huge increases in international trade volume, fluctuation of national currency values, foreign aid, protection of national economies from foreign-made goods, domination of international economic activity by transnational corporations—these and other characteristics of the contemporary international political economy ensure that economic topics often dominate

front-page news. Theoretical refinements, counterarguments, and mathematical treatments important to the economist are left aside here in favor of concentrating on a few essential principles particularly important to the student of politics, many of which have been touched upon elsewhere without having been flagged as uniquely economic topics.

1. Conflicting economic philosophies as a basis for the Cold War (Chapters 2 and 3)
2. Discussion of capitalist imperialism (Chapters 2 and 3)
3. Interallied economic competition as a source of tension (Chapter 4)
4. Economic aspects of China's power growth (Chapter 5)
5. Economic development in the underindustrialized countries (Chapter 6)
6. Economic components of national power (Chapter 7)
7. Technological bases of modern arms competition (Chapter 9)
8. Economic causes of war (Chapter 10)
9. Economic causes and effects of international integration (Chapter 16)
10. The transnational corporation as a global actor (Chapter 16)

In addition, this part explores two of the dominant issues in the international economy: trade and the international monetary system.

These twelve topics together suggest the breadth and variety of the global political economy as well as the variety of players in it.

National Politics and Global Interdependence

As "the pursuit of wealth and the pursuit of power" indicates, the most fundamental characteristic of the international political economy is competition. Whether through their governments or by direct action, individuals and groups of individuals (through organizations or corporations) use the international economy to increase their power and wealth. When this is done through government, it is seen as a national goal achieved through foreign policy. When it is done privately, it is known as transnational activity, though it may occur under the legitimacy or even the protection of governmental policy. Indeed, most such activities are governed by public policy. Trade, for instance, occurs within the context of governmental and intergovernmental policies; but these, too, take their shape from normal political give-and-take. Materials deemed sensitive to national security are traded only under special license. And although trade is for the most part a bilateral matter, third-party interests may intervene occasionally. In the early 1980s, for example, President Ronald Reagan attempted to prevent Western Europe from becoming dependent on the Soviet Union for natural gas by refusing to grant trade permits to American corporations or their European subsidiaries to sell gasline and pumping equipment to the Soviet Union. And in 1987, after it was revealed that a subsidiary of Japan's Toshiba company had sold submarine propeller-boring equipment to the Soviet Union, the U.S. Senate adopted a resolution calling for a two-year ban on imports of all Toshiba products. This was because of fears that quieter propulsion would make Soviet submarines more difficult to detect, and that improved detection equipment for the United States would cost $30 billion. From the American perspective, a Japanese company's pursuit of wealth had a high price for the American pursuit of power and security. And in a third example, in 1996, when Cuban Jets downed two unarmed private planes, President Clinton signed the Helms-Burton Bill. This not only intensified economic sanctions against Cuba, but also purported to extend the sanctions to any nation that trades with Cuba. Technically, this means that Americans cannot trade with Canada!

The literature of American history regarding the public-private nexus and the simultaneous pursuit of wealth and power grows steadily. Three examples stand out. First, one of the most compelling

explanations of the American decision to intervene in World War One is that American economic interests in England and France—both war and nonwar related—had to be preserved from German victory. Second, it is widely believed that behind the apparent altruism of the Marshall Plan —under which $14 billion was invested in rebuilding Western Europe after World War Two—lay such motives as reconstructing capitalist economies for short-term American profit and reconstructing constitutional democracies for the preservation of American power in Europe against the threat of Soviet communist expansion. And third, a popular antiestablishment explanation of the American intervention in the Vietnam War (and in general in the Third World from 1948 into the 1970s) was that it was to safeguard American access to natural resources for industry in general and the arms industry in particular.

Such interpretations are not unique to American historical revisionism. Indeed, from ancient times, conquest has more often than not been motivated by such economic imperatives as securing arable land, gaining warm-water ports for year-round use, and controlling natural resources ranging from timbers to oil and metals. France's intervention in the American Revolution was designed to deprive Britain of using North America's natural riches (such as shipbuilding timbers) to pursue its European policies, and France's subsequent sale of the Louisiana territory to the United States was to provide badly needed capital for the Napoleonic Wars. The Monroe Doctrine was an American statement of hemispheric hegemony intended to prevent the spread of European imperialism from Africa and the Middle East to Latin America and the Caribbean. Soviet expansion into Eastern Europe and its unsuccessful efforts to control southwestern Europe after World War Two were designed partly as a defense against capitalist encirclement and economic strangulation as predicted by Marxism-Leninism. All these are examples of national politics in the global political economy. So too are corporate acquisitions in foreign lands; direct private investment abroad; manufacture of goods abroad to avoid higher labor costs at home; creation of international debt by the private acquisition of foreign governmental securities; changes in OPEC price and volume policies, with all their consequences for Western industries and trade balances; laws restricting the import of foreign goods; secret arms sales to Iran during its war with Iraq, and diversion of the profits to assist the antigovernment Contra forces in Nicaragua (in violation of U.S. law); and thousands of other events that take place hourly. As examples of either governmental or private political-economic activity, they also illustrate the simultaneous pursuit of wealth and power and the conflicts that may result.

Another of the characteristics of the New World Order is globalization of the economy, as described in Chapter 1. In political terms, its corollary is the extension of world politics into every aspect of economic transaction. Gone are the days when trade regimes were concerned almost exclusively with raw materials, agriculture, and manufacturing, and when the issue was principally barriers to trade. Today, add financial and information services, equity in market penetration, patent tampering, illicit copying, economic espionage, cartels, massive customs unions, and the opening of huge underserved markets in Russia and its former Cold War empire, where free trade and market development have replaced rigid barriers and central planning. Billions of dollars are exchanged weekly by currency speculators trading electronically around the globe, gaining and losing margins here and there as they trade currencies against one another within the daily fluctuation ranges. New securities markets have arisen in Russia, Central Europe, and even China, creating new wealth and new economic classes that demand more of governments. Some of the previously underindustrialized nations have joined the high stakes of global trading in manufactured goods from computer chips to superships, from rolled steel to locomotives. South Korea, Taiwan, the Philippines, Singapore and Indonesia, dependent on foreign aid

only a quarter-century ago, are all major traders today. And if the European Airbus is a threat to the United States in megacraft, then Brazil is their counterpart in short-haul transport.

Cooperative (Reciprocal or Symmetrical) Interdependence

The magnitude of the global political economy indicates the extent to which peoples and nations are interdependent. For example, Indonesians welcome the construction of factories by American and Japanese corporations because they create jobs, attract technology, provide export products for earning foreign exchange, and generate public revenue. All these contribute to Indonesia's economic and social development and domestic tranquility. If any party loses in this arrangement, it is the unemployed American worker whose job may have gone to Indonesia in the decision to build there rather than in Atlanta or Chicago. The U.S. government, for its part, enjoys some gains and sustains some losses. On the positive side, corporate income rises and, with it, its federal tax bill. On the negative side, the import of the company's Indonesian-produced goods contributes to the balance-of-payments deficit, and individual income taxes are lost. Perhaps the most important consequence, however, is that Indonesia's development removes it from the list of capital-starved nations dependent on American (and other) support and, in the Cold War era, reduced the prospect that Indonesia would gravitate into the Soviet political orbit. On balance, then, in the simultaneous pursuit of wealth and power the advantages are roughly reciprocal.

Provocative (Nonreciprocal or Asymmetrical) Interdependence

Not all international political-economic activities are so well balanced. Indeed in recent years, the concept of global reciprocity has come erroneously to have almost exclusively a positive value in describing the political economy, regardless of the participating parties' relative strengths, wealth, size, or international standing. Although the example of the American factory in Indonesia is one of cooperative or reciprocal interdependence, there are many contemporary instances of exploitative or nonreciprocal interdependence. In our discussion of economic development (Chapter 6), for instance, we contrasted the conservative and radical viewpoints. Whereas the traditional argument focuses on direct private investment and stimulated trade as helping develop an unindustrialized economy, the radical view sees them as extensions of exploitation. Trade may well be stimulated, but at terms dominated by the industrial states, yielding cumulative debt that surpasses annual export increases. Thus although some benefits accrue to the developing economy (jobs, public revenue, improved social stability), the economic benefits to the industrialized partner are far greater and more stable. This conclusion applies to all forms of imperialism (political and economic domination) and neoimperialism (economic imbalance and exploitation in the presence of apparent political independence), though each may contain some interdependent characteristics.

In modern history, no people have seen exploitative interdependence to a greater extreme than have the native people of South Africa. Conquered by Europeans at the turn of the century, they have transformed their nation's economy under white domination. Today the South African economy is the most vigorous in sub-Saharan Africa, as a result of direct Western private investment in both mining and manufacturing. And it is virtually free of international debt. After decades of cooperative interdependence between the white minority and U.S. and European interests, a decade ago pressure started to mount in America and Europe to recognize that behind the country's economic growth resided a racial majority enslaved in its homeland, restricted by apartheid (absolute racial separation) to squalid living conditions, to entrance to commercial areas only by permit, to

restricted use of public transportation, and to virtually no health and educational facilities. This majority was prohibited altogether from holding public office or voting in national elections. Under cover of the Sullivan principles—a code of morally permissible business activity in South Africa that used benefit to the black majority as one of its legitimacy criteria—American and Western European corporations had continued to earn great wealth from South Africa. But as the unwillingness of the white minority to loosen its stranglehold became more apparent, the legitimacy of those principles diminished. One company after another abandoned its South African holdings, under a number of pressures, including the divestment by hundreds of American colleges and universities of all their stock holdings in companies conducting business in South Africa. Many countries applied trade sanctions for more than five years. Finally, in the early months of the New World Order, the de Klerk government repudiated apartheid, released long-incarcerated political prisoners including Nelson Mandela, and organized presidential and legislative elections free to blacks and whites alike. The results included the election of Mandela as president, discontinuation of all sanctions, the return of investment capital, and the return of cooperative international relationships.

With the exception of the domestic complexities of the South African situation, these examples of both cooperative and exploitative interdependence are based wholly on bilateral situations. But while most of the world's daily transactions are bilateral, many of them have important consequences for third parties. Even cooperative interdependence may, as a result, have adverse effects that have to be weighed outside the bilateral advantages. The Middle East provides an instructive case in point. The formal peace between Israel and Egypt occurred at the time at which OPEC enjoyed its greatest power. Egyptian-Israeli peace gave the United States an opportunity to adjust its relations with Egypt, Saudi Arabia, and other moderate Middle Eastern countries at a time when oil imports were the most important factor in both the burgeoning American balance-of-trade deficit and a sharp rise in domestic inflation. One of Washington's responses to this combination of opportunity and crisis was an extensive arms agreement with Saudi Arabia by which the latter received large shipments of the most current military technology, including AWACS aircraft, the world's most sophisticated airborne early-warning defense system. For its part, Saudi Arabia kept up the flow of oil to the United States and its allies and continued to exercise a moderating influence over OPEC. Despite this interdependence, the arrangement led to a severe, although reparable, disruption in American relations with Israel, specifically, in the Israeli view, because the arrangement threatened the always-delicate regional military balance. Again we see the interplay of power and wealth, with the United States adding to Saudi Arabia's power in order to continue the pursuit of its own wealth, seen by Israel as a potentially adverse regional adjustment in the power column.

Because the pursuit of wealth may influence power distributions, the concept of provocative interdependence may have a domestic variant. Events in the Philippines and in South Korea illustrate this point. Because each was vitally important to the American defense perimeter in the Pacific, the U.S. government and American corporations for decades sponsored economic development through aid and direct investment. In each case the result was middle class expansion and improved distribution of wealth. In the Philippines, the middle class developed a growing dissatisfaction with the government of Ferdinand Marcos, regarding it as corrupt and despotic, rejecting court findings that close associates of Marcos were innocent in the death of his most prominent political rival, and charging the government with political fraud and embezzlement of inestimable amounts of public money. (In 1995 a Swiss court awarded to the democratic government of the Philippines several billion dollars previously hidden there.) Thus it was the redistribution of political forces nourished by

American aid and investment that brought down the Marcos government in 1986.

In South Korea, the twin avenues of American-sponsored industrialization and democratic access to higher education contributed to a redistribution of political forces and a growing disenchantment with an antidemocratic military government in the mid-1980s. A rapid growth in the middle class, rising per capita income, and growing sentiment for reunification with the North (accompanied by substantial anti-Americanism around the presence of American armed forces) all contributed to growing demands for political liberalization. A South Korean population restive for democracy came to regard the traditional cooperative interdependence as an instrument for sustaining a nondemocratic government (and to some, an unnecessary division of the two Koreas) and was provoked to violence in demand of national political transformation. The story of the democratization of Taiwan is quite similar, the first popular election of a president having occurred only in 1996.

These multiple forms of interdependence suggest yet another condition of the global political economy: the influences of political stability, orderly change, and revolutionary change on political-economic activity. As the definition of the international political economy indicates, the interaction of politics with economics influences the international and domestic distribution of both material wealth and political power. Thus the conditions of stability and change are important to determining the frequency, quality, and effects of political-economic transactions.

A few contrasting illustrations will illuminate this point. First, because of political stability in Indonesia, American and Japanese firms are eager to construct plants there and to take advantage of high productivity and relatively low labor costs. Their presence assists in reaching the next stage in modernizing the nation, as we have seen. Political change is orderly and controlled; the government enjoys a high degree of legitimacy; there is a sense of advancement toward the national goals and personal aspirations; and the security and profitability of foreign investment are ensured by domestic conditions.

A second and contrasting example is Pakistan. A young nation with a history of political violence and little success in coalescing disparate ethnic and political elements around vitally important national goals, Pakistan has been unable to attract the kind of foreign investment to spur its development. It has been relatively unsuccessful in using international aid, from either other countries or international organizations, to develop the kind of economic infrastructure (transportation, trained labor, financial networks, and so forth) required for economic modernization.

Yet a third class of example is found principally in Latin America, although also in Africa, and is seen in industrializing states (such as Argentina) as well as in those that depend on a few primary products (coffee, copper, fruit) to fuel their economies (e.g., Nicaragua). During the Cold War many of the Third World countries went through rapid and broad swings of political control. Since World War Two, Argentina has gone from fascism to democracy and then to military rule before a return to democracy. Nicaragua has passed in a short time from a despotic right-wing dictatorship to a Soviet-backed military state without a socialist economy, and then to a peaceful democracy. Chile passed by constitutional means from a moderate government to an elected socialist government that was destroyed by a combination of domestic and international elements, possibly including the Central Intelligence Agency of the United States, and then fell to right-wing military control before its return to open elections. Many peoples of the Developing World are accustomed to one coup d'etat after another in which a group, often military, seizes the reins of government simply by taking over its offices and its official radio, killing or imprisoning its officials, and securing the loyalty of the armed forces. In all these instances, the prospects for the continued profitability of industrial development are slim, and nations choosing these political paths

find themselves consigned to a role in the international political economy characterized by poverty, debt, adverse terms of trade, and perpetual exploitation.

A fourth variety of interdependence that illustrates the impact of change on political-economic stability has recently arisen in the New World Order, one related directly to the changing ideological landscape. As Russia's post-Soviet reforms progressed and state economic planning was supplanted by market forces, the old Western adversaries granted Moscow access to the formal institutions of the global economy, including the World Bank. But as political and economic reform faltered under the weight of rampant inflation, unemployment, and shortages of consumer goods, communism enjoyed a renewed popularity. The 1995 parliamentary elections awarded a majority of seats in the lower house to Communist candidates, and the prospects of the reformist Boris Yeltsin being reelected president in 1996 dimmed. For his part, Yeltsin tried to accommodate the Communists by replacing his economic and foreign ministers, both reformists, with familiar hardliners. For their part, the Western powers not only accelerated a loan of $10 billion (American value) to the Russian government, but did so virtually unconditionally, in stark contrast to their dealings with the Developing Nations. This act was considered almost uniformly in the West, in the Developing World, and within Russia as a thinly-veiled attempt by the capitalist powers to intervene in Russian domestic politics by easing a protracted economic crisis and refocusing attention on Western-oriented reform in the crucial twelve weeks preceding the presidential election. The ultimate goal was to derail the communist revival and all that it might have meant both for political and economic relations between Russia and the industrialized, capitalist nations and for the New World Order.

At this point we may summarize the basic characteristics of the global political economy. It consists principally of (1) the dynamic interaction of politics and economics; (2) the simultaneous pursuit of wealth and power; (3) the intermingling of public activities, focused first on power and second on wealth, with private activities, centered first on wealth and second on power; (4) global interdependence, whether it be cooperative (balanced, reciprocal, or symmetrical), exploitative (imbalanced, nonreciprocal, or asymmetrical), or provocative (as measured by primary international consequences or by primary domestic consequences and secondary international results); and (5) domestic conditions of political-economic stability and change that influence behavior in the global political economy. Underlying all these is the constant exchange of domestic politics and its spillover onto the global scene.

The International Political Economy: An Annotated Outline

The following material is organized as an annotated outline of the principal components of the global political economy, accompanied by a series of descriptive notations or explanations. It begins with a fundamental distinction, namely, that between the policy domain of the political economy and the material domain. Each of these is subdivided into its major components, and these in turn are segregated into specific political-economic activities, with notations about the relation of the public and private sectors. In instances in which these are discussed at length elsewhere, there is but a brief annotation here. Other activities are introduced in greater detail. Table 11–1 summarizes this material.

Certain cautionary notes are in order. First, although any outline imparts a sense of descending logic, all the elements here are interactive. The policy and material domains depend on each other all the time and are not as distinct in content or logic as they may appear. Visually, if the outline were constructed in a circle, the ends would meet, and there would be no real beginning or end; and if the entire outline were arranged as a sphere, both the vertical and horizontal boundaries would disappear.

Second, the outline is intended to be illustrative rather than exhaustive. Moreover, more than half the items identified are discussed elsewhere in this book, most of them in considerable detail. Their repetition here is to highlight the ways in which they affect the political economy when removed from their individual contexts as elements of national power or problems of contemporary diplomacy. The addition of new items both shows their places in the global political economy and provides a place to introduce them as subjects in international relations that have not been touched on elsewhere.

Third, in capitalist economies such as that of the United States, there is a tendency for power to be pursued at a more macroscopic level than is wealth. Many interests converge to form the national interest and determine foreign policy. Some of these are wealth-seeking interests that differ greatly in kind and source. Hence the pursuit of power is primarily a public-sector matter even when it is inextricable from the wealth of the government's constituent. Foreign policy seeks wealth only to the extent that disparate wealth-seeking interests can gain the protection of foreign policy. In capitalist economies, then, governmental participation in the global political economy is primarily for the pursuit of power and secondarily for the pursuit of wealth. For the private sector, wealth is the primary objective and enhancement of governmental power the secondary. Domestically, the private sector contributes to the power of the state to gain protection to pursue wealth internally and externally. Because of these two discretely different roles, this outline emphasizes the power seeking of the public sector and the wealth seeking of the private sector. It is, then, an outline distinctly influenced by capitalist political-economic philosophy, as is the political economy of the New World Order.

TABLE 11-1

AN OUTLINE OF THE INTERNATIONAL POLITICAL ECONOMY

I. The Policy Domain: Public-Sector Primacy

A. The pursuit of power

   1. Expansive activities

      a. military aid and arms sales

      b. hegemonic policies

      c. intervention and aggression

      d. covert activities

      e. space policies

   2. Protective activities

      a. military modernization

      b. alliance policies

      c. maintenance of political stability

      d. securing of boundaries

      e. espionage

      f. export controls

   3. Regulated activities

      a. law of the sea

      b. laws of war

      c. regulation of aggression: United Nations Charter

B. The pursuit of wealth

   1. Expansive activities

      a. economic aid

      b. international trade and technical assistance

      c. imperialism and neoimperialism

      d. intervention and aggression

      e. international integration

      f. primary-products diplomacy

   2. Protective activities

      a. national restraints on trade

      b. preservation of natural resources

      c. labor controls

      d. fiscal and monetary policies

   3. Regulated activities

      a. international trade

      b. international debt

      c. customs unions

      d. codes of conduct

II. The Material Domain: Private-sector Primacy

A. The pursuit of wealth

   1. Cooperative activities

      a. exchange of goods and services

      b. educational and cultural exchange; tourism

   2. Competitive activities

      a. utilization of Developing World resources

      b. technological development

      c. competition for talent

      d. exploitation of global money markets

B. The pursuit of power

   1. Cooperative activities

      a. maintenance of profit-oriented ideology

      b. responsiveness to economic needs of national government

      c. responsiveness to economic needs of allied governments

      d. expansion of employment for government power

   2. Competitive activities

      a. international trade in arms

      b. protection of world markets and natural resources

      c. maintenance of advantageous terms of trade

Fourth, the policymaking bodies of the international global economy are national governments and intergovernmental organizations, which promulgate policy, international law, and other regulations of interstate activity. And it is governments alone that, through domestic politics, determine how their individual and corporate constituents will interact with the global system. Those constituents, on the other hand, are the subjects rather than the creators of policy, and they use those policies and regulations to guide their participation in the global political economy. Consequently, it is the public sector that plays the primary role in the policy domain, and the private sector that is the primary actor in the material domain. Again, however, these roles are not mutually exclusive. To protect its goals in the material domain, a wealth-seeking interest participates with governments in the policy domain; and to sustain the growth of the economic sources of national power, governments assist their corporate constituents in their material-domain activities.

The Policy Domain

Except on matters wholly anarchical, the international political economy operates under a vast complex of rules, policies, and regulations produced by governments and intergovernmental organizations. Some of these have virtually global application, and others are more narrowly multilateral, bilateral, or individual. All these together comprise the policy domain of the political economy, as they form the policy structure for the simultaneous pursuit of wealth and power.

Governments both seek and use power in expansive ways. The use of military aid and the sale of arms are devices by which governments extend their influence abroad, acquire military and economic uses of foreign territories, and attempt to influence orderly political change for maximizing the profitability of investment by their domestic constituents. When geopolitical, economic, or military interests are threatened, governments may resort to the whole spectrum of coercive measures to ensure favorable outcomes—intervention, support of revolutionary or resistance forces, aggression, and so on.

Sometimes, however, the scope of conflict expands beyond a single nation or region. From ancient times, imperial forces have sought to control whole sectors of the globe. The great empires of antiquity were built on the notion of complete domination of vast regions, as were the empires of the nineteenth and twentieth centuries. And during the Cold War, the United States and the Soviet Union regarded virtually the entire globe as within one or the other of their vast protectorates. On the one hand, this was little more than a modern application of traditional hegemonic military policy; but on the other hand, it was related to wealth as well. Whatever other motives may have driven American policy during that era, wealth, capitalism, natural resources, access to markets, and countless other economic issues were always close at hand. And for the Soviet Union, capitalist encirclement, economic strangulation, and deprivation were threats from a capitalist-dominated global political economy that required military vigilance and expansionism. Moreover, for both sides the perceived military imperative begot technologies that found their way into global commerce; protections granted to distant peoples affected the global flow of goods and services; neoimperialism ruled even in the presence of rising expectations; and military deployments controlled the pace of political change and, with it, the redistribution of political and economic power.

In addition to their expansive policies, states also pursue protective policies. Alliance behavior is a classical form of this, as are controls on foreign labor and exclusion of foreign goods to protect domestically produced goods from competition. Many take particular exception to goods that enjoy governmental subsidies that bring large profits even at low prices. On the other hand, states may seek to protect their own resources by outlawing export, thus guaranteeing them into the future for their exclusive use. States generally forbid one another's military aircraft from crossing their territories, and they may include commercial craft under the same ban. Even close allies may require permission to launch military strikes from their territory because of fear of reprisal. Restrictive immigration policies are generally protections, usually related either to financial limitations or minimizing causes for domestic strife. (This does not intend to hide that some restrictive immigration policies are simply for the purpose of racial or ethnic exclusion.) Fiscal policy may also be used protectively. Interest rates,

GARAGE SALE : RUSSIAN STYLE

(*Source:* © Jim Bush)

in particular, are manipulated by central banks not only to control domestic inflationary and deflationary trends, but to alter the international flow of investment capital. If, for example, American interest rates are low and German high, American investors are likely to send their capital to Germany for higher profits. If American rates rise, domestic capital is more likely to remain at home and German capital to be lured in.

States also pursue regulatory policies, particularly in the economic sphere. Their purpose is not to tie their own hands, but to maximize comparative advantage and to avert the kinds of competition that have led to war. One of the first stimulants of Western Europe's economic integration was

controlling the historic Franco-German coal competition, so that the European Coal and Steel Community was one of the seminal institutions of European union. Additionally, except where size, wealth, or temporary global conditions invite economic domination, the most reasonable goal is to fare as well as possible in as many markets as possible and in as many commodities as possible. This recognizes the legitimacy of competition rather than the goals of economic hegemony, and the value of regulation in place of anarchy. In its most powerful days (1973–1983), the Organization of Petroleum Exporting Countries promulgated policies that were a mixture of expansive and regulatory. From an external perspective, their controls were expansive, with volume declining and price rising, disrupting the industrial economies, upheaving the world currency markets, and forcing changes in Western policies toward the Middle East. But from an internal perspective they were regulatory, because all participating members were bound to restrict themselves to the export quotas set for them and to the price per barrel, even if demand might otherwise have forced the price still higher.

Substantial progress was made in regulatory policy in the Cold War era, but today it is accelerating as it must in a global political economy that virtually defines the world order. In place of inexhaustible hegemonic expansionism, the New World Order stresses economic security through cooperation, regulation, and elaborate political-economic regimes. Elsewhere we will look into the GATT trade negotiations, the activities of UNCTAD on behalf of the Developing States, the new popularity of vast customs unions, and the extreme of international integration, all alternatives to great-power domination of the international political economy. These are not idle experiments, but formal attempts at finding new modes of peaceful competition. To be sure, the New World Order is not a grand constitutional scheme to which everyone has suddenly subscribed. It is more the merger of a variety of forces—not just the end of the Cold War—the cumulative effects of which have provided a markedly changed political-economic atmoshpere in which to promote regime-building.

The Material Domain

We turn now to the material domain, in which the private actor is the main player in the simultaneous pursuit of wealth and power. As was indicated earlier, the private sector uses the international political economy to enhance its wealth and contributes to the pursuit of power through the international political economy by assisting the national government in enhancing its influence on this sphere. It is from this protective power that the private sector gains economic advantage.

Because private commerce is naturally competitive, there is little formal cooperative activity in the pursuit of wealth in the material domain. The limits of competition have already been established in the policy domain. What little additional cooperative activity there is results from cooperative interdependence and consists of peaceful international trade, sponsorship of educational and cultural exchanges, tourism, and such informal

Iraqi forces left Kuwait's oil fields ablaze.
(*Source:* © Reuters/ Bettmann)

arrangements as may exist among chambers of commerce, labor unions, or conspiracies to violate patent laws, antitrust laws, and the like.

In the main, the activities of the material domain are competitive and are more typically out of balance than in balance. It is in the pursuit of material-domain wealth that the private sector of the industrialized nations conducts exploitative interdependence with the Developing Nations with respect to primary products, food, and even semi-manufactures. It is here that corporations take advantage of relatively cheap labor, often to the benefit of the host people, but always to the profit of the corporation. Direct private investment in the Developing World is almost invariably more profitable for American corporations, for example, than is similar investment either at home or in other developed economies.

Among the industrialized countries, one of the main manifestations of competition is the search for talent. After World War Two, the American economy was so far ahead of Europe that much of the best European scientific and business talent left Europe for North America, introducing the "brain drain" phenomenon. Although the re-awakening of pan-European pride has reduced the frequency of this flow, there continue to be episodes of it. The most recent was in the early 1980s, when the American economy recovered from the global recession faster than did others. Investment in American manufacturing greatly outpaced investment in Europe, creating a sudden spurt of opportunity in the United States that did not exist until a few years later in Europe. During that time there was a minor brain drain. (Although no reverse brain drain has occurred, advocates of continuing to build Stealth bombers and strategic submarines based their argument partly on the need to retain the requisite talent and keep it sharp.) The same phenomenon has not occurred among the Japanese, whose national pride has been invested steadily in domestic economic development. The consistent trend of that development has not created vacuums of opportunity, as have occasionally occurred in Western Europe. Those Japanese who do reside in the United States for long periods typically work in Japanese corporate offices or in subsidiaries of Japanese corporations. Unlike their European counterparts, they are not expatriates.

A billboard depicts Vietnam old and new.
(*Source:* © Reuters/ Bettmann)

Relocation of exceptional talent has been an intermittent problem for the Developing World. After World War Two, a first generation of young people went abroad to study engineering, science, medicine, education, and other specialized professional fields and returned to become the national intelligentsia. The return rate was very high. Subsequently, however, because of the frustrations of development, more young people sent to Western Europe, the United States, Eastern Europe, Russia, and China for higher education have attempted to remain in their host countries. Their success in achieving their wishes has been determined by the host country, its economic circumstances, and its visa conditions.

Without question, the area of keenest competition in the material domain is technological development. The electronics revolution, the computer age, demand for improved military technology, and the economic spinoffs of space exploration all have combined to create fierce competition in the discovery, development, and commercial exploitation of technological products. And what the electronics revolution has done in engineering competition, the genetics revolution has replicated in the biochemical and pharmaceuticals industries.

In the pursuit of wealth within the material domain, the private sector plays a direct and independent role. In the pursuit of power, in contrast, its role is less direct, working through governments and intergovernmental organizations. This is a symbiotic and mutually beneficial relationship, in which the private sector provides the economic wherewithal by which the government develops its power and, in return, the government offers the protection of its power to the private sector in the further pursuit of wealth in the world political economy. The private sector provides jobs that foster public revenue and political stability for the growth of state power. It also responds to the government's economic needs by readjusting production and conducting product-oriented research for both the military and civilian economies. Underlying all this is the goal of perpetuating the symbiosis with

government and, thereby, preserving the profit-oriented ideology for application in the global political economy. In socialist economies, the distinction between the policy and material domains remains, but government is the principal actor in both, because private ownership of the means of production does not exist.

In its purest form, this is all a formula for economic nationalism and in a bygone world was exactly that. In the last quarter-century, however, two phenomena have joined to negate this. The first is the rise and maturation of transnational corporations, the giant production conglomerates that have headquarters in one country but production and distribution faciles in two or more countries. These are major instruments in the globalization of the economy, technololgy transfer, global distribution of wealth, employment and standard-of-living patterns, capital transfers, market penetration, and so forth. Because they operate in multiple countries, they are able to take advantage of what the law permits in each and, consequently, are virtually beyond the reach of any single government. In the view of one writer, "the main creators and controllers of technology have increasingly become large, multinational corporations with more global reach than global responsibility."[3] If, as has been suggested, these entities are the "new sovereigns," then there is in motion a downward relocation of sovereignty from the nation-state to the transnational corporations. Their credo is not nationalism, but corporatism.

The second of these phenomena is the economically integrating region, the largest and most significant being the European Union, which unites the economies of fifteen countries. Such entities greatly enhance the competitiveness of the individual economies, take advantage of multina-

---

[3] Paul Kennedy, *Preparing for the Twenty-first Century* (New York: Random House, 1993), p. 47. For a prophetic study that has stood the test of time, see Richard J. Barnet and Ronald E. Muller, *Global Reach: The Power of the Multinational Corporations* (New York: Simon and Schuster, 1974).

A Central American cartoon sees the United States as Japan's economic satellite. (*Source:* © Arcadio/Costa Rica/Cartoonists & Writers Syndicate)

tional labor pools, facilitate the movement of goods within the region by eliminating trade barriers, and pledge the members to treat outside competitors in a common way. They represent an upward relocation of sovereignty from the nation-state to the "region state"[4] with multinational authority. Their credo, therefore, is neither nationalism nor corporatism, but suranationalism.

Conclusion

The contemporary study of international relations recognizes the crucial interplay of politics and economics and of the public-private nexus in market economies. Moreover, it acknowledges the extent to which international behavior is guided by domestic politics, domestic economic imperatives, and the international objectives of dominant economic elites within nations. For these reasons, scholars have in the last decade or so begun to explore the concept of the global political economy as one of the fundamental elements of international relations. Here we have defined the global political economy, outlined its essential elements and illustrated them with specific activities that characterize the political economy.

Two of the dominant issues within the subject of the international political economy are international trade and the international monetary system, each built upon economic theory but important to the conduct of global political relations. The next two chapters deal with these subjects in greater detail.

---

[4] Kenichi Ohmae, "The Rise of the Region State," *Foreign Affairs*, spring 1993, pp. 78–87. Kenichi finds the modern nation-state dysfunctional from an international economic perspective, and considers the region state better suited for entry into the international economy.

CHAPTER 12

International Trade

Few international activities occur more frequently or with greater regularity than trade in goods and services. The hailing ports of trade vessels in the world's great harbors and countries of origin of cargo aircraft at major airports convey a sense of the distance and variety of places between which trade takes place. One need spend only a few hours watching commercial barges passing between Detroit and Windsor, Ontario, to appreciate the billions of dollars in trade value that crosses the international boundary annually. More than any other activity, international trade underscores the interdependence of nations despite their political disagreements.

Today as yesterday, interdependence in the trading environment is far from just one-for-one exchange of goods and services. Historically, trade was closely related to territorial conquest. Ancient empires expanded partly to secure goods unavailable within the realm; and if the owners of such goods resisted unequal exchange, that is, if the stronger party exploited foreign goods at a discernible disadvantage to the lesser party, territorial conquest was a likely consequence. Although we tend to think of a trading relationship as one of equality and reciprocity over relatively brief periods of time, the concept was actually born of inequality.

In modern times, this notion is illustrated in a number of ways. The great European explorations that resulted in the discoveries of sea routes to the Far East and the settling of the Americas were financed not as scientific adventures but as searches for trade routes. Later those routes were used to exploit the lands and peoples thus encountered. By the same token, the efforts of a small number of economic powers to carve China into spheres of economic influence early in the twentieth century were an extension of the concept of unequal trade, providing cheap and exotic goods for the West with little regard to the economic betterment of the exploited peoples. A broader application of the principle is found in the massive colonization of Africa, Latin America and the Caribbean, the Middle East, the Pacific, and Asia by a handful of economic powers, even in places in which political independence was presumed to have developed.

Even before the Industrial Revolution, the major powers recognized their dependence on foreign supply. North American timbers, for example, were essential to the growth of Britain as the world's leading naval power. But industrialization multiplied the need for foreign goods, at first mainly natural resources. Ores and fuels led the list and, in fact, continue to. Then urbanization and the decline of agricultural workers gave rise to the need for foods, particularly grains, dairy products, and meats. The growth of the textile industry led to demands for greater supplies of cotton and wool. By then, however, the number of industrially productive countries had begun to grow, and the concept of reciprocity evolved as a critical element of international trade.

But the Industrial Revolution and its aftermath had other consequences as well. The first was excess production. As industrialization progressed, more units of industrial goods were produced than could be consumed by the domestic economy. Rather than reduce production and with it both efficiency and profit, manufacturers turned to other countries as potential markets. In some they were the only source of the goods in question; in others they competed with domestic manufacturers or with other exporters, sometimes with both. And whereas in some instances they extracted large cash profits, in others they used their industrial exports as the means for purchasing primary products or other manufactured goods. Whether such exchanges constituted equal trade or exploitation of foreign markets depended on value equity. As we saw earlier in our discussion of international economic development, the conventional theorists tend to see such exchanges as bilaterally beneficial when they result in capital for investment; but the radical theorists of development look upon this early system of trade as the foundation of a global economic structure that perpetuates the exploitation by the rich and the dependence of the poor.

The second major consequence of industrialization and trade was competition. The drive to elevate profits took a variety of paths, among them the constant effort to control the costs of production. This meant, among other things, attempting always to widen the gap between the price of industrial goods and the prices of the primary goods from which they were made. With this, trade between the industrial exporters and the primary goods exporters became imbalanced. But in many industries, the cost of production is controlled more by the price of labor than of primary goods, and so the manufacturers attempted to minimize the number of employees and their wages and to maximize their productivity, often through brutal labor practices. Gradually governments intervened, imposing on industry laws designed to humanize working conditions: child labor laws, laws governing female employees, fair labor practices, minimum wages, workers' compensation and unemployment benefits, standards for health and safety in the workplace, and so on. And at other times labor itself intervened by organizing to influence the terms and conditions of employment. All these drove up the cost of production, often as the gap between the price of manufactured and primary goods became increasingly advantageous to manufacturers. Now industries began to relocate; for example, the American textile industry abandoned the northern states and moved to the South, leaving many of the boomtowns of the Industrial Revolution (such as Lawrence, Lowell, Fall River, and New Bedford in Massachusetts and Providence and Pawtucket in Rhode Island) virtually prostrate economically. Others sought cheaper supplies of labor outside their own countries, constructed plants abroad, exploited local labor conditions, and began to import their own products.

With this practice was born the multinational (MNC) or transnational corporation (TNC), the entity that has its headquarters in one country but manufactures its product in at least one additional country. Today the web of the TNC encompasses the world. Consider General Motors as an example. Motors Trading Company, one of its subsidiaries, uses foreign currency reserves and both primary and manufactured goods to buy other primary goods in areas whose local currencies are of little value in the international market. These goods are then shipped to other GM subsidiaries around the world. For instance, motor casings made in one country may meet in another country transmissions made in yet another country, and these and other parts may be shipped to Canada for assembly, after which the finished automobile is imported into the United States and sold as a domestic product. Meanwhile, an auto from the same assembly line may be shipped to another foreign market and booked as an American import. In other industries, few if any units are manufactured in the United States, yet their American labels identify their country of origin because of the location of the maker's headquarters.

These are just a few of the complexities of global trading. They arise not from economic theory but are the natural consequences of their histories. In subsequent pages we shall explore international trade at greater theoretical depth. But before doing so, it is useful to look briefly at the magnitude of world trade. In 1963, nearly two decades after the end of World War Two, total world exports stood at $154 billion (in 1963 dollars). It was not until 1977 that this amount crossed the $1 trillion mark, and by 1980 it was nearly at the $2 trillion level. After a substantial decline in the recession of 1981–1983, this amount again approached $2 trillion in 1984. In 1987, the total exceeded $2.5 trillion, and by 1993 it had risen to $3.8 trillion. Figure 12–1 illustrates this dramatic growth in world exports.

Why Nations Trade

At the simplest level, a nation will import a commodity that it does not produce and export one that it produces beyond its own need. For example, a nation that lacks fuel will import oil and gas, whereas another nation, which produces more automobiles than it needs (because they are cheaper individually when produced in large numbers), will export the excess. If all nations imported and exported different items, if there were a perfect international division of labor in the production of goods such that competition were absent, and if all participants kept constant both their need (demand) for imported goods and their production (supply) for export, then a perfect natural regulation of international trade would result. But with modern innovation and global demands for improved living standards, such circumstances are as unlikely as a single, rigidly regulated and centrally directed world economy. In fact, most nations engage in international trade in a vast array of goods even while their own corporations attempt both to control domestic markets and to produce goods at internationally competitive prices.

Furthermore, many nations import goods that they themselves also produce in large numbers; some goods might be both imported and exported! A standard example is the United States, which was until 1980 the world's largest producer of cars, trucks, and buses but which is also the largest export market for Japanese cars and the German

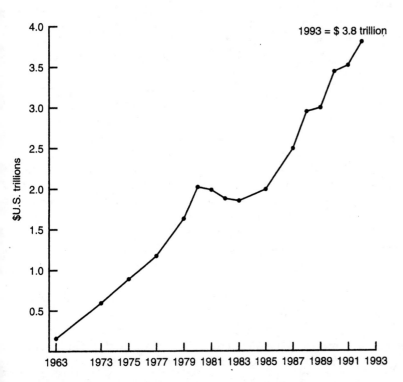

FIGURE 12–1 Total annual world exports, 1963–1993.

Source: International Monetary Fund, *Direction of Trade Statistics Yearbook,* various issues.

Volkswagen. In the latter case, the German producer was in danger of falling behind the American demand and of losing its share of American market to Japan, and so it purchased an abandoned automobile production facility in Pennsylvania, modernized it, and commenced to produce VW cars in the United States. Meanwhile, American manufacturers were finding production costs in the United States so high that they were producing automobiles abroad and selling them in the home market as American goods: Fords made in Canada and England, Buicks made in Italy, Mercurys made in Germany, and Dodges made in Japan. (The 1975 Mercury Capri, which was sold to Americans as an American product, called attention to the need for unleaded gasoline by the command "Achtung!" on a sticker over the tank cap.) Now Nissan and Honda produce automobiles in Tennessee and Mazda in Michigan on property almost adjacent to Ford's gigantic Rouge River facility; Ford and Toyota have joined forces to produce the Nova in California, as did General Motors and Toyota on the Geo.

If all this seems comical, it is nonetheless vitally important to international relations, for when VW produces in the United States, German workers lose jobs while Americans gain them; and the establishment and management of the production facility represent huge financial transactions for Germany, which must export funds to the United States. On the other hand, the external production of autos by American manufacturers represents a loss of jobs for Americans as well as a large capital export. In addition, when producing overseas, American manufacturers spend capital and production costs abroad (thus producing no tax revenues at home) and bring home (repatriate) only their profits.

Obviously, the real circumstances of international trade are unlike the simple example with which we started. In the modern context, then, the theory of international trade begins with a question: Why, if a nation can produce a given item at home, should it import from abroad? Imports, after all, erode domestic jobs and demand for domestic goods. Beyond a certain point, the growth of

imports might even lead to the collapse of domestic firms and the loss of employment for an entire labor sector. It is well known, for example, that the production of color television sets in the United States has halted almost entirely, with the loss of thousands of jobs. Similarly, imported shoes, steel, textiles, radios, and hundreds of other products have flooded the American market, devastating whole industries and geographic regions. In such circumstances here and elsewhere, demands for protectionism have become common, so that external goods are either excluded or made artificially expensive by high tariffs. Everyone agrees that we should import what is unavailable at home, but why allow imports to threaten domestic production and employment in areas of self-sufficiency? Even though "free trade" has an appealingly democratic ring, what justification can there be for the potentially calamitous effects of imports?

The answer to these vexing questions actually lies within them, namely, in the emphasis on imports and to the point of ignoring exports. If, indeed, imported goods supplant domestic products and replace domestic jobs, so do exports create jobs and make possible the production of more than can be consumed at home. In addition, production on a mass scale improves efficiency, circulates capital, and reduces prices. So while imports in one commodity may have harmful consequences, vibrant exportation of other products will offset the losses. To appreciate the comprehensive effects of trade, therefore, one must look at both imports and exports, and at a full range of production sectors rather than one or two in isolation. While the displacement of workers may be personally tragic, the goal of international trade is to balance imports and exports nationally, using whatever combination of primary and agricultural products, manufactures, and services may be necessary.

Before looking at the notion of an international trade balance, it is instructive to return with this new perspective to a question posed earlier: Why do nations trade at all? Part of the answer is found in the comparative prices of goods in two countries. If the price of autos produced in Country A is significantly lower than for those produced in

Country B, and if the cost of transporting them from A to B is less than the production cost difference, it will be sensible for B to import automobiles from A because of the lower price. But given the impact on employment in B, it will be of far greater advantage to B to import A's autos if in return B is able to produce and transport some other commodity, such as computers, at a lower price than A can build them. This is the beginning of a rational exchange between the two: A's autos for B's computers. (This ignores, of course, matters of perception and personal taste. While the United States could still be numerically self-sufficient in autos, many Americans prefer the fuel efficiency of Japanese cars, the social panache of a BMW or Mercedes, the safety features of Saabs and Volvos, or the sporting image of a Porsche.)

Although this situation is considerably more complex than the primal circumstances used earlier, it is still atypical of international trade. Such reciprocal advantage is quite rare, especially given the broad array of goods that nations produce and demand. Moreover, it is common that one country in a trading partnership may be more productive and more cost-efficient in several, or even all, of the goods that might be exchanged. Even under these circumstances it may be rational for them to maintain a bilateral trading relation. To explain this paradox and to lay the foundation for a deeper understanding of international trade, it is necessary to go beyond isolated examples and to introduce the basic theory of comparative advantage that underlies the global exchange of goods and services.

The Theory of Comparative Advantage

The Ricardian theory of comparative advantage, named for the eighteenth-century classical economist David Ricardo, holds that the general welfare of two or more countries will be higher for all if free trade among them is permitted than if each attempts to restrict trade or trade produce only for itself. This will be true even if some countries are absolutely more efficient in the production of all goods than the others are and even if, hypothetically, each country could produce everything for itself.

To understand this essential principle, imagine a two-country, two-commodity world consisting of only the United States and Taiwan and only two products, automobiles and wheat. Assume also that American labor is absolutely more efficient in the production of both items: it takes an average of one person-year to produce a car in the United States compared with two person-years in Taiwan, and one person-year to produce 1000 tons of wheat in the United States compared with four person-years in Taiwan. Finally, make the simplifying assumption that these direct labor costs represent all the factors of production in each country and, for the moment, assume a world without money in which there is a direct barter exchange of goods.

At first glance, it might—incorrectly—appear that the United States will be in a better market position as a producer. But this impression is immediately corrected when we consider the *comparative* production advantages in the two countries, as reflected in their internal barter rates of exchange. In the United States an automobile, which represents one person-year of labor, will be worth exactly 1000 tons of wheat, because each thousand tons also contains one person-year. However, in Taiwan the internal barter rate of exchange will be different. There, it will take two automobiles to buy 1000 tons of wheat, because the two person-years contained in a Taiwanese automobile is only half of the four person-years it takes to produce 1000 tons of Taiwanese wheat.

The comparative advantage of each country is inherent in this difference of the barter rates of exchange—one car equals 1000 tons in the United States, compared with 500 tons in Taiwan. Both sides will gain if there is a trade of American wheat for Taiwanese cars. For example, if the American wheat producer offers the Taiwanese car producer 750 tons for an automobile, the American will be spending less wheat than would be needed to buy an American car—750 compared with 1000 tons— and the Taiwanese will be receiving more wheat for a car than he would in a home trade—750 compared with 500 tons. Clearly there is a mutual advantage in the trade.

Note, however, that the opposite exchange does not work. The American car producer wants at least 1000 tons of wheat per automobile, because this is the price at home. But the Taiwanese producer of wheat will not be willing to accept such an exorbitant price, because 1000 tons at home will net two cars. Therefore, the exchange of American cars for Taiwanese wheat does not work. Only the exchange of American wheat for Taiwanese cars is sensible.

In this example, there is likely to be a thriving trade in American wheat for Taiwanese autos at 750 tons of wheat per car because this barter rate of exchange is advantageous for both sides. Is there a loser? As trade grows, the short-term loser will be the American producers of cars and the Taiwanese wheat farmers. Neither will be able to export, and it is to be expected that both will lose shares in their domestic markets as their products are undersold by foreign competition. The American producer was able, for example, to buy 1000 tons of wheat for each automobile before international trade, but in the changed market a car brings no more than the Taiwanese price in wheat: 750 tons. The industrialist might profit, in fact, from leaving the car business to produce wheat instead, because one person-year of labor will produce 1000 tons, with which to buy a Taiwanese car and still have 250 tons of wheat. By remaining in the automobile business the industrialist produces one car per year and has no wheat at all.

The advantage of free trade will be clearer after considering two economies as a whole. Imagine that there are 100 workers in each country and that workers are freely transferable between industry and agriculture. Assume further that in each country workers are in the pretrade situation, evenly distributed between the two production sectors. This picture is presented in Table 12–1.

Now assume that a certain volume of American wheat is exchanged for Taiwanese autos at the barter rate of 750 tons of wheat per auto—an exchange rate we know to be advantageous to both sides. Assume also that as a result of the trade,

TABLE 12–1

TOTAL OUTPUT WITHOUT TRADE

	Number of Workers (A)	Output per Worker/Year (B)	Total Production (A × B)
U.S. wheat	50	1000 tons	50,000 tons
U.S. autos	50	1 auto	50 autos
Taiwan wheat	50	250 tons	12,500 tons
Taiwan autos	50	0.5 auto	25 autos

there is a growth in U.S. wheat production, which now supplies both the home and foreign markets, and contraction of the U.S. auto industry, which loses part of the home market and is unable to export competitively to Taiwan. Correspondingly, there is a decline in the Taiwan wheat sector and a growth in the Taiwan auto sector. Reallocation of the work forces in the two countries will occur away from the declining industries and into the growing ones. Table 12–2 represents the result.

With the same number of workers and the same output per worker per year (labor productivity rate), the total world production of both products increases significantly when each country specializes in the line of production in which it is *comparatively* more efficient (even though the United States is in our example *absolutely* more efficient in both production sectors). Before trade (Table 12–1), the combined production of wheat was 62,500 tons, and the combined production of autos was 75 units. With trade and its accompanying reallocation of the work forces, the combined production is 67,500 tons of wheat and 80 autos. By having each country concentrate in the area of its comparative advantage, and permitting free trade between the two at the mutually advantageous rate of 750 tons = 1 car, the final supply of goods in both countries is significantly higher in every area than it was before trade. That is, the result of free trade increases the aggregate standard of living for both partners, and conversely, a refusal to trade would result in a lower standard of living for both.

TABLE 12–2

THE GAINS OF FREE TRADE

	Col. A	Col. B	Col. C	Col. D[1]	Col. E[1]	Col. F	Col. G	Col. H
	No. of Wkrs.	Output per Wkr./Yr.	Total Prod. (A × B)	Minus Exports	Plus Imports	Net Supply (C–D+E)	Supply Before Trade from Table 12–1	Gains of Trade (F–G)
U.S. wheat	65	1,000	65,000	12,750		52,250	50,000	+4.5%
U.S. autos	35	1	35		17	52	50	+4%
Taiwan wheat	10	250	2,500		12,750	15,250	12,500	+22%
Taiwan autos	90	0.5	45	17		28	25	+12%

[1] Assumes trade at the barter rate of 750 tons wheat = 1 auto.

This is the powerful economic principle behind the call for free trade. With all its problems and dislocations, a free flow of goods, under normal conditions, has the potential to enhance the welfare of all countries. The results illustrated by Tables 12–1 and 12–2 could be extrapolated to apply to any number of countries and any number of products. This is precisely what is intended to happen in contemporary world trade, as the rules of the game lean inexorably toward the free flow of goods.

The Problems of Free Trade

Despite the attractiveness of the Ricardian free-trade argument, free trade is not without practical problems. Trade provokes a variety of conflicting interests that must be reconciled for the international political economy to function smoothly and profitably. It is important to differentiate, therefore, between problems that are sensibly resolved or regulated by a free trade program and those for which such a program might be counterproductive. Recall also that the extension or withdrawal of free trade can be used as an instrument of power in world politics. Governments may use free trade as a means of strengthening friendly governments and may discontinue trade individually or through collective sanctions to weaken hostile governments. Clearly, the philosophy of free trade is not entirely divorced

from higher political principles and objectives in international relations.

Most frequently, objections to free trade arise from workers, managers, and owners in industries adversely affected by imports, who quite naturally wish to protect their jobs and investments by reducing the price advantages of imports or banishing them altogether. Italy and France have sparred over red wine trade. French farmers have protested the agricultural policies of the EU by dumping fresh vegetables. The American textiles industry has sought protection against Chinese and South Korean imports. The United States and Japan are in chronic conflict over automobiles, computers, and other consumer electronic products, much of the dispute centering on the contradiction between open American markets and restricted markets in Japan. The AFL-CIO and the United Auto Workers lobbied vigorously against NAFTA, fearing the loss of industrial jobs to low-paid Mexican workers who labor under inferior environmental conditions. Typically, advocates of protection call for some or all of the following instruments.

1. **Tariffs, import surcharges, or other import taxes,** all of which are designed to increase the imported goods' prices relative to domestically produced competitors. If a Japanese car normally sells in the United States for $200 less than a comparatively equipped American-made car, then an

General Motors workers demonstrate against recent layoffs. Many people feel that international trade agreements like NAFTA encourage companies to seek cheaper labor in less-developed countries at the cost of American jobs.
(*Source*: Donna Binder/Impact Visuals)

import tax of $300 on the Japanese model should cause an increase in sales of the American product and a decline for the import, omitting personal tastes and other subjective factors. But these barriers to trade are not taken lightly, and they often evoke tariff retaliation. Such action and reaction can result in trade warfare or tariff warfare, which is antithetical to the concept of free trade. To prevent this, the major trading nations have used bilateral, regional, and global negotiations to arrange regulatory trade regimes under international treaty law.

These have the twin goals of stimulating international trade and minimizing the prospect of disruption of trade relations. NAFTA and the EU are the most encompassing regional experiments, and the many rounds of GATT negotiations, most recently the Uruguay Round, are the outstanding nongeographic example.

2. **Preferential tax treatment for domestic production.** One of the major reasons that imports threaten domestic producers is differences in the rate of investment for modernization in different countries. Outdated production methods lead to uncompetitiveness by elevating prices. Thus modernized production gains the advantage in international trade, and it may undersell products made in the country with older methods. The logical response is modernization but at a heavy capital cost, and at a time when the value of a weak competitor may seem a risky investment. Often, therefore, industries appeal for tax incentives to lower the cost of modernization. If it is the corporation's taxes that are reduced, then more funds are available for reinvestment. If the taxes due on stockholders' earnings (in the United States, called capital-gains taxes) are reduced, then the incentive to invest in the corporation's future is increased. Either way, the government—or the tax-paying public—has subsidized the industry in its return to competitiveness.

3. **Public subsidy of domestic production.** As an alternative to tax relief, a government may consider the loss of competitiveness so threatening to stability or prosperity that it provides a direct subsidy, or subvention, to the industry. Often this is in the research and development stages, and it is designed to reduce capital costs and, therefore, inherent risks. Less frequently, governments opt to become partners in production, contributing public funds to production. The result of both alternatives is to reduce the price of the final product, because the manufacturer has less cost to recover. Americans object that Boeing and McDonell Douglas are being undersold both internationally and in the United States by the European Airbus, and that the competition is made unfair by

the direct financial participation of European governments.

4. Import restrictions including prohibition. Whatever combination of remedies might be sought, import restrictions almost invariably are included. These simply prevent or limit subsequent importation of the threatening commodity by limiting or revoking import licenses. These are unilateral acts without compromise. Reasonable as they might seem in light of urgent domestic circumstances, they are highly destructive of international relations. Their impact on employment, investment, and fiscal policies in the target countries is swift and profound, whence the risk of provoking economic retaliation and subsequent escalation. Imagine the impact on Japan if the United States were to prohibit importing automobiles, and the chaos that would likely follow in Japan and internationally.

5. Advertising restrictions. This more subtle means of alleviating threats from imports works against the foreign competitor not by locking out its product, but by altering the terms of competition once the product is imported. Although foreign goods may be permitted to enter the country, advertising restrictions may prevent their effective sale. Their availability is obscured, and obscurity causes the few who are aware of the product to suspect it. A product that is barred from dealing with public perceptions is not likely to fare well in a consumer economy.

6. Product regulation. This is a deterrent to sales competition that involves the strict stipulation of standards of production and product quality required for import. Restraints related to standards of production are rare. The concept was invoked in 1994 and again in 1995 when the United States considered denying China most-favored-nation trade status because of its use of slave prison labor. Much more often, governments base restraints on product standards. This is commonly applied to food imports, generally using public-health standards as the ostensible rationale. Pharmaceuticals may be treated the same way. (Many foreign-made drugs are prohibited from the United States.) In the automobile industry, protection was given temporarily to American manufacturers by suddenly raising the environmental control standards, an act that rendered thousands of imports unsalable and required redesigning and retooling abroad. The secondary benefit of this device is that recovering competitiveness carries a capital cost, and lacking tax relief or public subsidy, it will be reflected in the price of the new product, immediately affecting its competitiveness in the import market.

Generally speaking, these restraints on trade apply only to bilateral relations. But as economic regionalism spreads, they will occur increasingly in interbloc relations, or between trading blocs and individual external trading partners. Already the EU and the United States have had many trade disputes, one of which nearly derailed the Uruguay Round. This is the major reason that GATT gave way to the new World Trade Organization, which has authority to mediate and adjudicate trade disputes.

To assess the merit of a protectionist case, it is necessary to consider whether the competitor's advantage is from real comparative efficiency or is an artifact of unfair and unnatural advantages conferred by its government. If there is a real comparative advantage in Ricardian terms, it is unwise to restrict imports solely because they cost less. Indeed, that the import is cheaper provides the rationale and advantage of free trade, and denying cheaper goods to one's people solely because they are foreign only inflates prices irrationally. The more rational response is to allow the foreign goods in and to devise measures to divert some of the gains of trade to expanding export industries with real comparative advantage. For example, advocates of free trade often propose government aid to workers displaced by imports to retrain them for work in industries of comparative advantage. As the economies of regional scale replace the trade of individual nations, proposals of this type will be more frequent and more urgently needed. But they will still have significant problems. Workers' ages and barriers to geographic relocation (e.g., spouses' obligations, depressed selling markets in real estate in areas of high worker displacement) will often mean that retrained workers will still not find appropriate work.

Realistically, it is unlikely that perfectly logical free trade, unfettered by restrictions and protectionism, lies ahead. Instead, the potential gains from unrestricted trade testify for it, but the painful adverse effects balance the debate. Thus there is a tug-of-war, both nationally and internationally, between those who stand to gain and those who stand to lose from free trade, and the overall trade regime that exists at any moment represents the balance of power between these two forces. This controversy is well known to students of American economic history, who have observed wide fluctuations between periods of liberal trade and periods of protectionism.

Furthermore, the gains themselves are elusive. In Japan, the huge annual positive trade balance adds to the nation's wealth through overproduction for export purposes, corporate profit, employment, tax revenue, and more technical devices such as the multiplier effect of money. In contrast, the more the United States exports, the more it imports, and its trade deficit is chronic. The villain, then, is on the import side of the balance sheet, but it is the public's taste, not government policy, that demands imports. Moreover, while the AFL-CIO opposed NAFTA in defense of its members' security, the U.S. government was concerned about how to make up the hundreds of billions of dollars that would be lost in tariff revenues under the combined new restraints of NAFTA and the Uruguay Round of GATT.

Despite these difficulties, there is at present a broad consensus among governments about the value of free trade. Still, however, a few categories of protectionism survive. One is the problem of an infant industry, one that has just started in a country and must compete with the imports of a mature firm in another country. For example, in the first years of automobile manufacturing, a new firm in a developing country can hardly expect to match the efficiency, quality, and cost-effectiveness of a huge, mature foreign producer, even at home. The new firm will lag indefinitely in many categories of business success: scale of production; capital accumulation from profit; competitive sales and service networks; plant engineering; product engineering; work-force training; and so forth. During this period of infancy it may be rational and consistent with the national interest to restrict imports to assist the fledgling producer by guaranteeing it the domestic market. If it does not have to compete with cheaper foreign products in the early years, it may eventually realize its own comparative advantage as a domestic producer and even as an exporter competing in world markets with established foreign producers. It is partly for this reason that the South Korean government declared years ago that it would never permit Japanese autos to be sold in South Korea.

Although the infant industry argument is rational, two dangers should be recognized. First, the new industry may never become fully competitive and may demand preferential treatment long beyond its infancy. In such a case, indefinite restrictions on imports can no longer be justified strictly on economic terms, with respect either to the domestic economy or any sensible regime of free international trade. Second, once an industry is created it becomes a political fact and possesses a reality of its own. In effect, an inefficient industry may bear the seeds of its own perpetuation even if it never realizes a comparative advantage. For these reasons the infant-industry argument, properly applied, should pertain only to those lines of production in which there is a reasonable expectation that eventually a comparative advantage will accrue. It is not rational to apply this argument for protection to any and every industrial endeavor. Too often, particularly in Developing Nations and those in the second industrial rank, new projects are undertaken for reasons of national pride or in the absence of adequate business judgment, rather than in reasonable anticipation of long-term comparative advantage.

Another special class of protectionist argument applies to strategic industries. Here the domestic suppliers recognize that they have a permanent comparative *disadvantage*, but one offset by higher national interests that preclude dependence on foreign sources. For example, if it is judged that the supply of a vital product could be interrupted by international conflict, that the long-range commitment of the external supplier is uncertain, or that the political relations with the supplying government are adversely affected by overdependence, then the country in need may wish to be self-sufficient even at a higher economic cost. Israel commenced an expensive fighter aircraft industry at a time when it was uncertain of the American commitment to its security.

Strategic self-sufficiency is often a compelling argument in a world of conflict, though it loses its appeal in the New World Order in which economic security is the principal driving force. Even previously, however, it was an argument that lent itself to gross overextension in practice. For example, radio manufacturers have been known to demand protection on the ground that the military applications of their products must be protected; watchmakers produce chronographic instruments for the army; and agricultural interests point out that an army marches on its belly. It behooves the policymaker to raise a skeptical eyebrow when every interest group wraps its self-interest in the sacrament of the national flag. Even in the area of arms production, it is by no means self-evident that dependence on foreign producers is ipso facto against the national interest. The strategic value of self-sufficiency must be weighed against the larger interests of the economy, which are also strategic concerns. If a country sacrifices all other interests to pursue absolute strategic autarky, it may weaken rather than strengthen its international position. Conversely, a nation such as Japan or Canada, which accepts its dependence on foreign producers of many strategic goods, may enjoy a favorable international position. Moreover, defense is not the only criterion; at some point, an obsession with

strategic needs may unduly sacrifice other needs of the people, including their aspiration to the improved standard of living that often comes with freer trade. Whether or not protection of a particular strategic industry is a rational choice will be determined by the sober consideration of all these factors.

A third class of special protectionist argument applies particularly to the Developing Nations struggling to escape the shackles of underdevelopment. It concerns the effort to diversify production so that the country's development pattern need not rely shakily on only one or two primary products. Diversification aims for a healthier balance of production and of export potential, which both diminishes reliance on too few commodities and enables the developing economy to adapt to fluctuations of international demand. The older, prediversification pattern of single- or dual-commodity dependence in exports while importing an array of goods from industrialized nations, often termed foreign-oriented development, is now recognized as pernicious in most cases and adverse to the long-range interests of most developing countries, however powerful the short-run economic logic might have seemed. For this reason, many Developing Nations protect a limited number of domestic industries, irrespective of the normal calculations of comparative advantage.

Although diversification contains a number of obvious symbolic attractions, it may not always correspond to the real enlightened self-interest of a country. It is unlikely that many of the world's poorest countries can achieve competitive production efficiencies in the thousands of product lines that they consume and in which they rely on imports at present. Some infant industries may be deserving of protection, but attempts to replicate in small populations industrial miniatures of a world economy are not rational. (Most of the world's poorest 100 countries have populations of less than 6 million, and half of them have populations of less than 1 million each.) Most either will fail miserably or will be forced by economic inefficiencies to charge their domestic customers far higher prices than would be required by imports. The result of such uncontrolled diversification will be to lower rather than to raise the aggregate economic level. Selective diversification, on the other hand, will carefully apply the infant-industry argument to the protection of a few especially promising sectors.

The final class of justifiable protectionist argument applies to countries that suffer chronic trade imbalances. This is a situation in which, year after year, a country's imports have a higher monetary value than its exports do, resulting in a form of chronic debt from trade. Typically this type of debt leads to unemployment, as jobs lost to imports are not made up by employment created by exporting industries. Moreover, such a situation weakens a nation's currency relative to those of countries with stronger trade positions. Here protection against imports may be seized as a partial corrective, but it is not the principal solution. The principles of international monetary exchange, discussed in the next chapter, take over where simple barter fails.

Balance of Trade

Crucially important to a nation's trade is its balance of exports against imports. Rarely are import and export values identical. Ideally, export value will be the greater, as a surplus indicates a vibrant economy and strengthens the country's currency internationally. Deficits, on the other hand, suggest structural economic weakness or dependence on foreign supply, and they are costly to economic stability and currency value.

During World War Two and the years that followed, the industrial position of the United States assured it of large annual trade surpluses. More recently, however, a chronic deficit has set in. It has become popular to blame this on Japanese trading policies and on export subsidy programs of the European Union. The United States has gone to the brink of trade war with each on a number of issues. But in reality, the problems are far more complex. The following are the major reasons for the

upheaval of world trade from the American perspective.

1. **The enormous success of Japan's export industries, particularly automobiles, but other industries as well, including electronics and computers.** This success, coupled with the Japan's import restrictions, makes it difficult for the United States to balance its trade with Japan despite a steady increase in exports. In an almost unbroken climb from 1975 to 1987, the U.S. deficit in its trade with Japan reached a record $58 billion before falling by a third in the early 1990s and then shooting up once again to $51 billion in 1993. Figure 12–2 depicts this trend in that imbalance.

2. **Growth of the combined economic might of the European Union nations and their uniform import policies.** This strength results in part, in the American view, from unfair subsidy practices in which governments underwrite the costs of capital modernization in order to reduce the cost of industrial production. Whereas between 1972 and 1982 American industrial subsidies ran at a nearly constant rate of 0.5 percent of gross domestic product (GDP), in the European Union the average annual subsidy was approximately 2.5 percent of GDP.[1] Table 12–3 traces the recent EU-U.S. balance. It does not appear to substantiate the American objections to EU trade: in five of the seven years it was the United States that enjoyed the surplus. In 1991, the American surplus in its trade with the EU was almost $25 billion, offsetting more than half of its deficit with Japan ($39 billion) in the same year.

3. **OPEC's temporary strength combined with the dependence of the capitalist industrial states on Middle Eastern oil.** From 1974 to 1980, and to a declining extent thereafter, the cost of oil has had an immense inflationary effect on the Western economies and a severely detrimental consequence for their trade balances. OPEC's life has had three distinct chapters. The first, from

---

[1] International Monetary Fund, *Trade Policy Issues and Developments*, July 1985, p. 31.

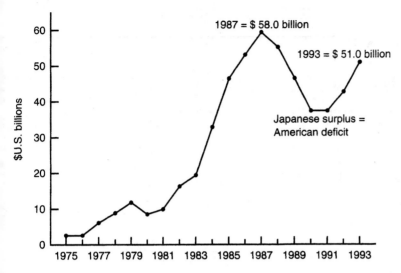

FIGURE 12–2 Japanese-American trade imbalance, 1975–1993.

Source: International Monetary Fund, Direction of Trade Annual; U.S. Department of Commerce, Business Statistics, 1982 (supplement to the Survey of Current Business), November 1983, pp. 75–79. For 1987 and after, International Monetary Fund, Direction of Trade Statistics Yearbook, 1988 and 1994.

1973 to 1981, was a period of enormously rich ascendency. The second, 1981–1986, saw OPEC's decline. The third, from 1986 to the present, has been a period of stabilization because of a number of factors, including a leveling of the world demand for oil, effective production controls, and moderate price increases. We will return to this subject later.

4. **The mounting export success of the industrializing Asian states, four of which—Hong Kong, Taiwan, Singapore, and South Korea—are often called the Dynamic Asian Economies (DAEs).** Their imports invaded American domestic markets in the 1970s and 1980s and created additional competition in distant markets. To this were added the products of Malaysia, Thailand, Indonesia, and China in the 1990s. The competition includes everything from footwear to computers, from Chinese textiles to Korean automobiles. Table 12–4 demonstrates the U.S. trade balances with these countries. (China is treated separately later.) The pattern is one of unbroken deficit, but its characteristics are changing. Between 1987 and 1993 the deficit relative to the four DEAs has declined by 60 percent and the total by 34 percent, but the deficit with respect to the three younger economies has risen by 162 percent. It becomes more alarming to view this performance against the American

trade deficit with Japan (Figure 12–2). In 1987, the record deficit was set in trade with Japan ($58 billion), the deficit with the countries in Table 12–4 was almost $42 billion, or 72 percent as high as the deficit with Japan. In 1990, when the deficit with Japan dropped to $38 billion, the deficit with the industrializing Asian economies was still 57 percent as high. By 1993, the deficit with Japan was again up to $51 billion, and that with the states in

TABLE 12–3

EUROPEAN UNION'S TRADE WITH THE UNITED STATES (BILLIONS)

	EU Exports	EU Imports	EU Balance	Total Value
1987	$82.9	$66.7	$16.2	$149.6
1988	84.6	79.4	5.2	164.0
1989	85.7	91.2	(5.5)	176.9
1990	96.5	105.0	(8.5)	197.0
1991	87.7	112.5	(24.8)	200.2
1992	95.3	111.0	(15.7)	206.3
1993	98.5	103.6	(5.1)	202.1

Source: International Monetary Fund, Direction of Trade Statistics Yearbook, 1994.

TABLE 12–4

UNITED STATES TRADE BALANCES WITH THE INDUSTRIALIZING ASIAN ECONOMIES

	1987	1988	1989	1990	1991	1992	1993
Hong Kong	($6.5 billion)	($5.1 billion)	($3.9 billion)	($3.2 billion)	($1.6 billion)	($1.2 billion)	($0.1 billion)
Singapore	(2.3)	(2.5)	(1.8)	(2.1)	(1.4)	(2.0)	(1.4)
Taiwan	(19.0)	(14.2)	(14.3)	(12.3)	(11.0)	(10.6)	(10.0)
South Korea	(9.9)	(9.9)	(7.0)	(4.9)	(2.2)	(3.8)	(3.0)
Subtotal	(36.7)	(31.7)	(27.0)	(22.5)	(16.2)	(17.6)	(14.5)
Malaysia	(1.2)	(1.7)	(2.0)	(2.1)	(2.4)	(4.1)	(4.8)
Indonesia	(2.9)	(2.5)	(2.6)	(1.8)	(1.7)	(1.9)	(3.1)
Thailand	(0.9)	(1.5)	(2.3)	(2.6)	(2.7)	(3.9)	(5.2)
Subtotal	(5.0)	(5.7)	(6.9)	(6.5)	(6.8)	(9.9)	(13.1)
Total	(41.7)	(37.4)	(33.9)	(29.0)	(25.0)	(27.5)	(27.6)

Source: International Monetary Fund, *Direction of Trade Statistics Annual*, 1994.

Table 12–4 54 percent as high. The important point is that even if American trade with Japan were to stabilize at a deficit of about $50 billion, there remains the likelihood of a growing deficit with other Asian countries. When China reaches its full export potential and India, Pakistan, Vietnam, and the Philippines accelerate theirs, Asia's competition with the United States will be all the keener.

5. **Declining worldwide dependence on American agricultural and seafood products.** Although the growing world population continues to demand more food production, agricultural improvements elsewhere in the world have reduced the demand for American produce. For example, American fruits and vegetables have been replaced on the world market by the produce of Latin America, Southern Europe and Israel; meats by those of Brazil and Argentina; the Northern European countries, Japan, and Russia have gained dominance in providing sea products. Japan has profited handsomely from its export aquaculture industry. Finally, the world demand for American grains has become sporadic as the Green Revolution has improved yields elsewhere.

As a result of these and other factors, the United States went in a short time from being the dominant Western trading nation to having a chronic trade deficit. But it is not alone. With the exceptions of Japan, Germany, and the Arab OPEC countries (notwithstanding the Iran-Iraq War and the Desert Storm War), few major players in world trade have consistently enjoyed surpluses. Table 12–5 summarizes the recent annual trade balances for some of the countries that enjoy perennial surpluses.

The Resurrection of Protectionism

Not surprisingly, surplus nations want to preserve their surpluses and deficit nations to overcome their imbalances. Accordingly, when the post–World War Two international system was structured around the United Nations, economic issues were addressed in detail. The International Monetary Fund (IMF) was established to deal with currency matters, and investment capital was made available through the International Bank for Reconstruction and Development (IBRD, also called the World Bank). In the trade realm, original

TABLE 12–5

AVERAGE ANNUAL TRADE BALANCES OF NATIONS WITH SUSTAINED BALANCE-OF-TRADE SURPLUSES, RELATED TO THE PHASES OF OPEC'S EVOLUTION

	1974–1980	1981–1986	1987–1993
Germany	$16.3 billion	$16.8 billion	$44.3 billion
Japan	0.5[1]	23.2	83.2
Saudi Arabia	31.1	27.7	11.1
United Arab Emirates	6.1	9.8	6.5
Kuwait	8.4	4.3	2.2[2]

[1] Due to the oil crisis, Japan actually had four deficit years in this seven-year period ranging from a low of $2.1 billion in 1975 to a high of $10.9 billion in 1980. It has never had a deficit since.
[2] Kuwait had small deficits in 1991 and 1992 as a result of war with Iraq and Iraq's final act of igniting most of Kuwait's oil wells.
Source: International Monetary Fund, *Financial Statistics Yearbook* and *Direction of Trade Statistics Yearbook*, multiple issues.

proposals included a World Trade Organization (WTO), but in 1950 the idea was withdrawn by the United States, which found it ill-suited to evolving conditions and inappropriate for the kinds of trading structures being established, especially in Soviet Eastern Europe and in Western Europe, where the precursor to the European Union was already in progress. In its place was put a temporary arrangement, the General Agreement on Tariffs and Trade (GATT). Despite its temporary status and lack of institutional structure, GATT became the main vehicle for multilateral trade negotiations. Most modern trading relations, particularly among the market economies, are conducted under its terms. Importantly, when in the judgment of the participants the terms were inadequate, lengthy trade negotiations were established under the aegis of GATT. In the 1960s, when the United States was particularly concerned about the mounting strength of Western Europe, the so-called Kennedy Round of GATT negotiations was initiated. Over a period of seven years, it produced a 35 percent across-the-board reduction in tariffs on manufactured goods. In the 1970s, with the United States still concerned about Europe and growing fearful of Japanese competition, another round, termed the Tokyo Round, was undertaken, with the result of additional tariff cuts of 31 percent.

Despite these substantial achievements toward free trade, in the 1980s there were calls for protectionism unprecedented in the post-war political economy. There were several reasons. First, America's chronic deficit position popularly was attributed to the illegal or unfair trading practices of Japan, South Korea, Western Europe, Taiwan, and others. Even when the practices were marginally legal, the White House adopted the view that free trade is free trade only when it is fair trade to all.

Second, the structure of global trade was changing rapidly. Agricultural trade, for example, was growing rapidly but moving away from traditional patterns. For the United States, agricultural trade was in a sharp decline because of both new international competition and carefully protected markets in Japan and Europe. GATT negotiations had never successfully opened agricultural trade as it had industrial trade. Furthermore, in the last two decades, the global trade in services—financial services, data services, and the like—has risen to as much as 20 percent of the annual global exchange. Such trade was wholly unregulated by GATT or the negotiations undertaken in its name.

Third, GATT's dispute settlement machinery increasingly was inadequate and moved very slowly. For instance, accusations of illegal practices often were not resolved for years, leaving the charged party to continue its practices and the aggrieved to suffer its frustration.

Fourth, GATT permitted protectionist practices under certain specific circumstances. It had, for example, a Generalized System of Preferences (GSP) under which all participating industrialized nations offered common preferences to Developing World exports. But another exception gave vague preferences to nations suffering chronic balance-of-trade deficits. When a participant as large as the United States fell into chronic deficit, domestic forces began to demand that the government avail itself of these passages. One protectionist measure after another was introduced in Congress, but only two of significance found their way into law. One obligated the president to inform the Congress periodically whether or not specific countries had discontinued illegal or unfair trade practices, a review that could potentially result in subsequent protectionist legislation. The second called upon the White House to review periodically the most-favored-nation status of China to determine whether or not extra import duties should be placed on China's exports to the United States. To date the most-favored-nation status has been maintained though, because of China's questionable human rights record, it has been a subject of bitter controversy.

Fifth, the electronics revolution coincided with the growth in export strength of the newly industrializing Asian nations, whose explosion upon the world trading scene severely undermined the export status of the traditional industrialized market economies, none more than the United States. Because the competition centered on manufactures new to world markets, particularly computers and consumer electronics, there arose in the 1980s a "new protectionism" demand in the United States and elsewhere. In a sense, everyone wanted to protect the same infant industries.

Given the contemporary circumstances, governments began to use a combination of GATT-justified and national means to protect their markets from unfavorable international trade. In the 1980s alone, they took hundreds of protectionist actions. Consequently, by 1985 the European Community had protected itself in one way or another from 41.9 percent of its trading partners' exports. Japan had achieved the same with 8.7 percent of its contracting parties' exports, and the United States with 15.1 percent.[2] Not surprisingly, the three leading proponents of free trade, all allies but also fierce competitors, led the world in contemporary protectionism.

In addition to such international agreements as GATT, American foreign trade is regulated by the Trade Act of 1974, Section 301 of which empowers the president to act on petitions submitted by American corporations that charge foreign interests with unfair practices against the United States. Between 1975 and 1986, fifty-seven such petitions were submitted, resulting in twelve American trade retaliations. A measure of the increased demand for protection is that fifteen additional cases were pending at the end of 1986.[3] Most of these involved Japan, Western Europe, and South Korea, but one notable exception focused on the Canadian lumber industry. This one was not acted on.

This enormous growth in tensions impelled the GATT partners to turn once again to multilateral negotiations, this time the Uruguay Round that ran from 1986 through 1993. The length is explained partly by the number of new disputes that arose during the negotiations, again ranging from Japanese auto exports to European agricultural policies. With additional tariff reductions, settlement of the agricultural problems, and completion of the General Agreement on Trade in Services (GATS), the GATT participants established the long-awaited International Trade Organization (ITO), gave it the strong dispute resolution authority that GATT had lacked, and dissolved GATT.[4] The limitations of the Uruguay Round, however, were highlighted by yet another Japanese-American dispute over automobiles in 1995, when the two narrowly averted a trade war bilaterally after the United States declined to submit its claim to the ITO.

The Special Case of Petroleum Trade

While the world's fossil fuel reserves are dwindling, the energy demands of the industrialized countries rose steadily through the 1980s, after which the

---

[2] For extensive details, see International Monetary Fund, *Trade Policy Issues and Developments*, July 1985, table 7, pp. 104–105.

[3] *Economic Report of the President, 1987,* p. 132.
[4] For a summary of the accomplishments of the Uruguay Round, see *Economic Report of the President, 1995*, pp. 205–214.

growth in demand slowed considerably. (At present the fastest rate of growth is in Asia, where the newly industrializing economies have increasing energy needs.) Much of this comes from the petroleum-rich Middle East, where their suppliers drive the production and pricing policies of the Organization of Petroleum Exporting Countries (OPEC). From 1974 through 1982, OPEC increased the price of crude petroleum an average of twice a year, eventually raising the price per barrel from slightly over $3 to about $34. Not until early 1983 did OPEC unity begin to crumble. At that point moderate members advocated stable prices and controlled productivity, and the more radical members demanded price increases and uncontrolled production. The result was the first moderate price decreases in a decade. Note in Table 12–6 the performance of the OPEC trade balance beginning in 1975, the year after OPEC's maturation, and then the drop in 1983 and stabilization thereafter.

This stabilization was set askew in mid-1990 by Iraq's conquest of Kuwait, its threatened invasion of Saudi Arabia, and the Desert Storm War that followed. Before withdrawing from Kuwait, Iraqi forces ignited most of the local oil wells, putting Kuwait temporarily out of oil trade. United Nations sanctions against Iraq, including a global trade embargo, removed Iraqi oil from the world market as well. Contradictory messages went out from both Iran and Saudi Arabia about increasing production to meet the import gaps in Japan and the United States particularly. Iraq vetoed the calling of an emergency meeting of OPEC to review production and price schedules. Iraq's sudden reconciliation with Iran in order to redeploy troops from the Iran border (and occupied territory) to the Saudi Arabian and Jordanian borders raised fresh questions about Iran's willingness to assist the West on the eve of a new holy war. Prices rose immediately. Throughout the West, national energy policies were reviewed hastily, nuclear debates once apparently closed were reopened, and the public cry for conservation of fuels echoed the winter of 1973–74. Oil was once again at the center of the global economic stage as President Bush announced that the Iraqi menace in the Persian Gulf posed an economic threat to a way of life in the West.

For most industrialized countries, oil represents the largest single negative item in the balance of

TABLE 12–6

JAPAN'S TRADE DEFICIT WITH OPEC

1973	($3.4 billion)	1983	($24.8 billion)
1974	(11.9)	1984	(27.5)
1975	(10.8)	1985	(26.0)
1976	(12.5)	1987	(16.7)
1977	(12.9)	1988	(16.9)
1978	(11.3)	1989	(22.2)
1979	(20.5)	1990	(29.4)
1980	(31.9)	1991	(24.3)
1981	(26.8)	1992	(21.5)
1982	(28.1)	1993	(21.0)

Source: International Monetary Fund, *Direction of Trade Statistics Yearbook,* various issues.

TABLE 12–7

OIL AS A PERCENTAGE OF TOTAL AMERICAN IMPORTS

	Total Value of Imports	Value of Petroleum Imports	Petroleum % of the Whole
1970	$39.9 billion	$2.9 billion	7.3%
1974	103.7	26.6	25.6
1978	176.0	42.3	24.0
1982	247.6	61.2	24.7
1984	334.0	57.5	17.2
1986	365.2	34.4	9.4
1988	477.4	39.6	8.3
1990	498.3	62.3	12.5
1992	536.5	51.6	9.6
1993	589.4	51.5	8.7
1994	655.6	54.0	8.2

Source: Economic Report of the President, 1989 and *1995.* Figures for 1994 are projected from third quarter actuals.

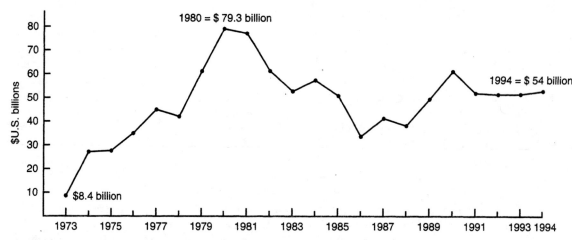

FIGURE 12-3   U.S. import costs for petroleum and petroleum products, 1973–1994, in $U.S. billions.

Source: Economic Report of the President, 1989 and 1995.

trade. Table 12–7 shows the extent to which petroleum and petroleum products have dominated American imports for two decades. The center column, "Value of Petroleum Imports," is also shown graphically in Figure 12–3. To avoid misunderstanding these observations, remember two important things: (1) not all oil is imported from OPEC nations (Canada is a major supplier to the United States); and (2) the cost of oil has been subject to wide variations in OPEC prices, at which virtually all the world's oil is sold, so that the figures are influenced simultaneously by price and volume.

In addition to appreciating the cost of oil and oil products as a function of total import value, it is useful to show it in relation to overall annual trade performance. Figure 12–4 plots oil imports as a percentage of the annual trade deficit. The graph shows clearly that in every year since OPEC first flexed its muscles, the value of annual American oil imports has exceeded the total trade deficit. The record high year was 1973, in which the cost of petroleum imports was 6.5 times the entire trade deficit. The low year was 1986, when the trade deficit grew so high that the portion attributable to oil was only 22 percent. (There was actually a small trade surplus in 1975, for which reason the graph

falls to the base line.) Look now at Figures 12–3 and 12–4 together. They show that from 1973 to 1978 the annual cost of imported oil rose steadily, although those exports as a fraction of the annual trade deficit declined. Then in 1980, both the price and oil's part of the trade deficit spiked to their high records, after which both declined almost at the same rate until 1987, when both rose once again. But the entire period of decline was marked by huge increases in the annual deficit, with the result that while oil imports declined by less than half ($79.3 billion in 1980 to just over $30 billion in 1986), oil's portion of the total deficit dropped dramatically, from 253 percent in 1980 to only 22 percent in 1986. So although the importance of oil remained a very substantial American economic problem, other serious problems, such as the chronic trade deficit with Japan, began to overshadow it.

Because Japan is nearly totally reliant on foreign fuel, the OPEC maturation was just as threatening to Tokyo. Contrary to common opinion and to its government's own prediction, Japan's consumption of imported energy did not skyrocket from 1974 to 1981; it remained almost identical. But given the huge price increases during those

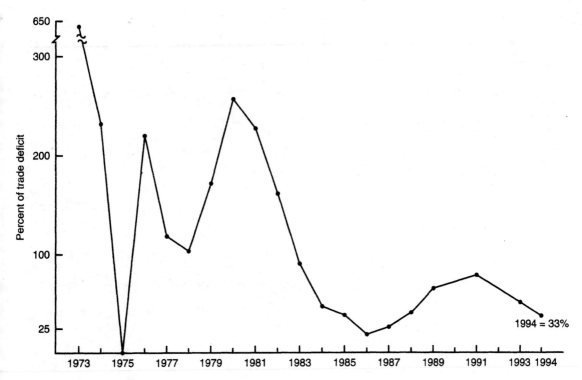

FIGURE 12–4 U.S. oil imports as a percentage of the annual trade deficit, 1973–1994.

Note: Read this graph as follows: In 1994, the value of American petroleum imports was equivalent to 33 percent of the nation's balance-of-trade deficit. In 1980, in contrast, the value of petroleum imports was equivalent to two and one-half times the balance-of-trade deficit.

Source: Economic Report of the President, 1989 and *1995.* For 1994, the figures for the year are projected from the actual performance through the first three fiscal quarters.

years, the cost of maintaining even a steady supply of fuel was staggering and had a severely detrimental influence on Japan's trade balance with OPEC, as Table 12–7 suggests. Even in the era of stabilization, however, Japan's trade deficit with respect to its fuel suppliers is a stark contrast to its overall balance-of-trade surplus. To Tokyo, this is nothing but the price of the industrial overproduction that yields huge profits in the export markets.

Our interest here is not simply in the troubling facts of global petroleum trade but in their consequences for the global political economy. From the American and Japanese perspectives, OPEC's strength for seven years was nearly crippling. Almost by itself, in the United States it sent the domestic inflation rate soaring to record heights, with interest rates following. At the same time, industrial productivity declined, creating both a loss of confidence in the economy among investors and consumers and a demand for durable goods that could be met only by foreign production and imports. The Japanese took a reciprocal view: They adjusted their pattern of oil consumption, established a national policy giving industrial consumption first priority, and multiplied their industrial production. In this way they were able greatly to increase their exports of manufactures and thus to offset their trade deficit with OPEC even during the years of its greatest ascendancy. As the United States emerged from recession, the dollar gained strength in world markets, with the result that American goods became increasingly costly. Hence, as Japan's trade surplus widened, that of the United States continued to slide even after OPEC lost its control of the world oil trade. This, in turn, led to demands of protectionism in the United States, particularly with respect to Japan.

Another consequence of OPEC's impact on world trade, as we have seen, was the vast growth in international arms sales. One thing that was in demand among the OPEC states and readily available from the industrial economies (except Japan) was military equipment. For the United States and France particularly, arms sales were a way of offsetting the OPEC trade advantage. Furthermore, because of the Western interest in balancing power between Israel and the Arab states, arms sales to one had to be matched by similar sales to the other. Consistent with its own trade needs and Cold War interests in the region, the Soviet Union played an independent role. Oil riches drove this trade, but it is questionable that an effective balance was maintained. Two major wars in the region in a few years, though neither involved Israel (which stayed out of the Desert Storm War despite being struck by a few Iraqi missiles), suggest that the arms trade was more reckless than intended.

OPEC has recently been buffeted by a number of strong winds with cumulative effects. These include the decline of OPEC cohesion after 1986, the slow recovery of Iran from its war with Iraq, the exclusion of Iraqi oil from world markets as a result of its invasion of Kuwait, world stability in demand for oil, the new political relations of the West with the moderate Arab OPEC countries, and disaffection of non-Arab members from the membership. Among them they have stripped OPEC of its cartel characteristics. The ability to use political cohesion to monopolize world oil trade is no longer.[5] In the early years of the New World Order, then, the major competing economic forces are not faced with the threat of disruption that lurked

---

[5] Vahan Zanoyan, "After the Oil Boom: The Holiday Ends in the Gulf," *Foreign Affairs*, November–December 1995, pp. 2–7.

This Japanese oil tanker is heading for the Straits of Hormuz on its way out of the Arabian Gulf. Japan imports nearly all of its petroleum. A liter of gasoline in Tokyo costs three times more than in New York City. (*Source:* Reuters/Corbis-Bettmann)

throughout the 1970s, but this means political and economic adjustment in the Middle East, too.

Russia and Central Europe

During the Cold War, East-West trade was a controversial issue. In the most contentious years of containment, trade isolation of the Soviet Union was almost a cardinal rule. Washington's European partners grew less rigid about this, first by opening trade with the Soviet allies and later by liberalizing their trade with the Soviet Union itself. During and after détente, the United States joined the Europeans in the idea that using trade deprivation as a political instrument should be replaced by using mutual trade as a potential route for intercultural understanding and improved international tolerance. In essence, this view interpreted trade as a functional instrument, one with which to build trust and confidence. This general revision of thinking was accentuated by the growing Western European tolerance of socialism and communism and by the growth of Eurocommunism. Moreover, the trans-European policies of Germany, commencing with Konrad Adenauer, and of French Gaullism became a suitable rationale for trade between East and West Europe, although more with the smaller satellite states than with the Soviet Union itself. Finally, in addition to détente and pan-Europeanism, the Sino-American political thaw of the 1970s was accompanied by vigorous Western and Japanese overtures to China to trade industrial products for natural resources.

By the mid-1970s, then, East-West trade was growing quickly, but it was not to grow at a steady pace. The Carter administration reacted to the imposition of anti-Solidarity martial law in Poland and to the Soviet invasion of Afghanistan with retaliatory trade policies; and throughout most of two Reagan administrations, the notion of the Soviet Union as the "evil empire" was used to prevent technological trade with the East. Moreover, until the launching of *perestroika* in the late 1980s, there was little export potential in Eastern Europe beyond what was required by the common production and distribution system among the participating states.

Table 12–8 details the Western trade of the Soviet Union. In the year immediately preceding *perestroika* (1987), the Soviet Union exported to the entire world $37.2 billion in goods and services, and imported $44.9 billion, a worldwide trade deficit of $7.7 billion. Barely a third of Soviet exports went to the West; almost all of that third ($13.6 billion) went to Western Europe. The amount of trade with the United States (as well as with Japan, which is not included in the table) was tiny by major-power standards. Most of Soviet trade, then, was within the Council for Mutual Economic Assistance (COMECON) or with the Developing World, including importantly in this period Cuba, Nicaragua, Syria, and India.

From 1979 to 1987, Soviet trade with the EC remained stable, involving about $14 billion of Soviet exports and $11 billion of Soviet imports annually. In the same period, trade with the United States was stagnant. This resulted from a 1980 recommendation of the President's Export Council, an excerpt from which follows.

> As to the Soviet Union, the Council recommends that the process of normalizing trade relations, which was broken off by the Soviet invasion of Afghanistan, be resumed only if and when there is significant improvement in U.S.-U.S.S.R. relations. Meanwhile, the U.S. should continue non-sensitive trade as circumstances make appropriate, while indicating a willingness to increase trade and resume normalization steps if and when the Soviet Union changes its policies to a peaceful cooperative course.[6]

Soviet-American relations for most of this period of Presidents Carter and Reagan and Soviet General Secretaries Brezhnev, Andropov, Chernenko, and Gorbachev resulted in little to warrant the repeal of this recommendation. With *glasnost, perestroika,* and the end of the Cold War, however, events began to unfold rapidly. At the Malta Summit in 1989, President Bush announced publicly his agreement to explore immediately Mikhail Gorbachev's proposal that the United States grant most-favored-nation trade status to the Soviet Union. The status was subsequently granted.

The trading pattern of Eastern Europe followed closely that of the Soviet Union, although the volumes are much smaller. Most of the trade of these nations occurred within COMECON, that is, among themselves and the Soviet Union itself, in a commonly planned production and distribution system. Table 12–9 reveals what little trade these nations had with the United States and the EC members. Trade with the United States was minimal, and that with the EC amounted to no more than one-third of exports or imports for any member of the

---

[6] President's Export Council, *The Export Imperative*, December 1980, vol. 1, p. 104.

TABLE 12-8

DIRECTION OF SOVIET TRADE WITH THE WEST (BILLIONS)

	WORLD			U.S.			EC		
	Exp.	Imp.	Bal.	Exp.	Imp.	Bal.	Exp.	Imp.	Bal.
1979	$26.6	$30.9	($4.3)	$0.8	$4.0	($3.2)	$10.5	$9.9	$0.6
1980	32.4	38.8	(6.4)	0.4	1.7	(1.3)	13.9	11.9	2.2
1981	33.2	42.6	(9.4)	0.3	2.7	(2.4)	14.0	10.2	3.8
1982	34.1	40.7	(6.6)	0.2	2.9	(2.7)	15.8	10.0	5.8
1983	33.3	39.9	(6.6)	0.3	2.2	(1.9)	15.4	12.2	3.2
1984	33.8	38.6	(4.8)	0.6	3.6	(3.0)	16.5	10.9	5.6
1985	31.1	38.7	(7.6)	0.4	2.7	(2.3)	14.5	10.4	4.1
1987	37.2	44.9	(7.7)	0.4	1.6	(1.2)	13.6	11.7	1.9
1988	49.5	62.6	(13.1)	0.6	3.0	(2.4)	13.8	13.3	0.5
1989	50.2	66.7	(16.7)	0.7	4.7	(4.0)	14.9	15.1	(0.2)
1990	49.6	64.9	(15.3)	1.1	3.4	(2.3)	19.4	21.1	(1.7)

Source: International Monetary Fund, *Direction of Trade Statistics Yearbook, 1986, 1988,* and *1991.*

group (Czechoslovakia, with Hungary trailing close behind) except Yugoslavia, communist but always independent of the Soviet Union. Eastern European trade with Japan was no greater than that with the United States.

Needless to say, the end of the Cold War had a profound impact on these trading relations.

The commitment of Russia and its East European neighbors to abandon planned economies and develop market economies in an environment no longer threatened with war opened vast new opportunities. Despite severe and sometimes devastating inflation (Table 12–10), Western investment capital began to flow into Russia, the Council of

TABLE 12-9

DIRECTION OF EASTERN EUROPEAN TRADE, 1989 (BILLIONS)

	WORLD			U.S.			EU		
	Exp.	Imp.	Bal.	Exp.	Imp.	Bal.	Exp.	Imp.	Bal.
Poland	$13.5	$10.3	$3.2	$0.4	$0.2	$0.2	$4.1	$2.8	$1.3
Czechoslovakia	14.1	14.1	—	0.1	0.1	—	3.6	3.7	(0.1)
Hungary	9.7	8.9	0.8	0.3	0.2	0.1	2.4	2.5	(0.1)
Romania	11.2	9.0	2.2	0.6	0.2	0.4	2.8	0.5	2.3
Bulgaria	2.8	5.2	(2.4)	0.1	0.2	(0.1)	0.5	1.8	(1.3)
Yugoslavia	13.5	14.9	(1.4)	0.7	0.8	(0.1)	5.2	5.9	(0.7)
Totals	64.8	62.4	2.4	2.2	1.7	0.5	18.6	17.2	1.4

Source: International Monetary Fund, *Direction of Trade Statistics Yearbook, 1991.*

TABLE 12-10

ANNUAL INFLATION INCREASES

	1993	1994	1995	1996
Bulgaria	64%	125%	60%	30%
Czech Republic	21	10	9	8
Hungary	22	19	27	16
Poland	35	32	23	18
Romania	295	137	45	35
Russia	840	226	102	60
Slovak Republic	23	13	10	8

Note: Projections for 1995 and 1996.

Source: OECD Economic Outlook, June 1995, p. 112.

Independent States, and the former Soviet allies from governments, private corporations, and international institutions. Russia and Ukraine quickly became two of the top four recipients of U.S. government economic aid. (Israel and Egypt are the others.) Table 12–11 displays the rapid accumulation of debt. Amid the enormous problems of transition, productivity recovered rapidly, as shown in Table 12–12. With it, so did trade.

As Table 12–13 indicates, Russia's trade leapt in the post-Soviet era to over $31 billion in 1992 and then virtually doubled in 1993. In each year Russia enjoyed a small surplus, an important factor because it indicates a cautious policy of not accumulating trade debt while taking on short-term and long-term capital obligations. Trade by the other CIS states remains very small, in virtually all cases less than $1 billion. In Central Europe, however, trade has begun to grow, but as is shown in Table 12–14, at a cost of modest annual deficits. This is generally ascribed to the fact that the economic transition of the old Soviet allies is in some respects more difficult than for Russia, because Russia and the CIS countries, all formerly part of the Soviet Union, occupied a favored status in the COMECON machinery particularly with regard to the location of factories. Russia also has a brisk

TABLE 12-11

POST–COLD WAR RUSSIAN AND CENTRAL EUROPEAN DEBT

	1989	1990	1991	1992	1993	1994
Russia						
Long-term official	$2.2 billion	$7.5 billion	$13.3 billion	$13.7 billion	$25.0 billion	$32.0 billion
Long-term private creditors	33.5	40.5	41.6	52.0	46.5	47.5
Short-term	18.2	11.8	12.6	13.0	7.9	9.0
Other	—	—	—	—	3.7	3.9
Central Europe						
Long-term official	25.9	31.4	43.5	38.2	39.3	42.0
Long-term private creditors	37.3	40.1	39.8	37.2	42.5	42.1
Short-term	17.3	17.7	15.4	12.3	11.1	8.6
Other	2.2	2.2	2.1	8.6	8.5	11.2

Source: United Nations, World Economic and Social Survey, 1995, p. 335.

TABLE 12-12

PERCENTAGE ANNUAL PRODUCTIVITY INCREASES

	1993	1994	1995	1996
Bulgaria	-4.2	0.0	2.0	2.0
Czech Republic	-0.9	2.6	4.0	5.0
Hungary	-0.8	2.5	1.0	3.0
Poland	3.8	5.0	5.5	5.0
Romania	1.3	3.4	3.0	4.5
Russia	-12.0	-15.0	-5.0	2.5
Slovak Republic	-4.1	4.8	5.0	5.0

Projections are given for 1995 and 1996.

Source: OECD Economic Outlook, June 1995, p. 115.

TABLE 12-13

POST–SOVIET RUSSIAN TRADE

	Exports	Imports	Balance
1992	$15.7 billion	$15.5 billion	$0.2 billion
1993	29.4	28.5	0.9

Source: International Monetary Fund, Direction of Trade Statistics Yearbook, 1994.

TABLE 12-14

POST–COLD WAR CENTRAL EUROPEAN TRADE BALANCES

	Hungary	Poland	Romania	Czechoslovakia
1989	$0.8 billion	$3.2 billion	$2.2 billion	$0.2 billion
1990	1.0	5.4	(3.4)	2.2
1991	(0.7)	(0.5)	(0.9)	0.4
1992	(0.4)	(0.6)	(1.1)	(0.7)
1993	(3.8)	(4.5)	(1.4)	***

*** Czech Republic   (0.4)
　　 Slovak Republic   (1.0)

Source: International Monetary Fund, Direction of Trade Statistics Yearbook, 1994.

trade in natural resources that are unavailable in Central Europe.

The Industrializing Asian Economies

Thirty years ago "made in Taiwan" was a euphemism for shoddy goods and trinkets. Today a close examination of almost any electronic product is likely to reveal that all or part of it was manufactured in an industrializing Asian state, even if it bears a Western product label. In those intervening three decades, the Dynamic Asian Economies (DEAs) of Taiwan, South Korea, Singapore, and Hong Kong evolved into major competitors in thoroughly modern, high-quality goods. Their annual productivity increases are among the highest in the world. Standards of living, especially in the urban regions, have catapulted. Hong Kong and Singapore, virtually city-states, are saturated with capital and industrial installations.

Their success is not limited to industrial exports, however. Hong Kong follows only Tokyo as a financial capital of Asia; a standard item in any financial news report is "Hong Kong gold," the price on the Hong Kong commodities market. Similarly, Taiwan and South Korea have become proficient in civil engineering and construction, and they are providing stiff competition in contract bidding for highways, harbors, airports, and electricity generation in developing Asia. South Korea's Halla Group of industries, as just one example, is building seaports, airports, freight-handling systems, locomotives, ships, and turbine generators for China and other Asian states, and provides millions of cubic meters of concrete annually for Asian construction. China's massive Two Gorges proposal, which will change the course of the Chang River and increase hydroelectric power production, will be one of the largest civil engineering undertakings in the world. In an earlier day most of the lucrative business would have gone to American, European, and perhaps Japanese contractors. Today, however, Korea, Taiwan, and Hong Kong will be in the thick of the competition.

The twenty-first-century sequel to the DEAs' success will almost certainly be in Malaysia, Indonesia, and Thailand. These are all politically stable places that now attract investment capital that once flowed to the DEAs. Multinational corporations (MNCs) looking for stable environments with well-trained work forces and congeniality to investment-driven, export-oriented development find these profitable places to be. Table 12–15 combines the four DEAs with these three countries to demonstrate their combined trading activity in 1993. To emphasize their ability to compete in manufactured goods as contrasted with the primary products on which they formerly relied, Table 12–16 lays out their respective growths in manufactured exports, notes their average annual productivity growth rates, and gives comparable figures for the United States and Japan as points of reference.

China's recent global trading pattern indicates the extent to which China has abandoned isolation on its path to economic modernization. From 1979 to 1988, China's global exports and imports each

TABLE 12–15

DIRECTION OF TRADE, ASIAN INDUSTRIALIZING ECONOMIES, 1993, IN BILLIONS

	Exports	Imports	Balance	Total Value
Hong Kong	$135.0	$138.6	($3.6)	$273.6
South Korea	83.5	81.4	2.1	164.9
Singapore	74.1	85.4	(11.3)	159.5
Taiwan[1]	50.3	49.6	0.7	99.9
Malaysia	47.1	45.7	1.4	92.8
Thailand	36.7	46.1	(9.4)	82.8
Indonesia	36.8	28.3	8.5	65.1

[1] The United Nations bows to China's claim that Taiwan is a province of a single China. Hence United Nations data, including those of the IMF, omit Taiwan as an independent statistical center, though in some instances they include "Taiwan Province of China" as part of Asian statistics. The information here is restricted to Taiwan's trade with the United States, Japan, South Korea, and the European Union.

Source: International Monetary Fund, *Direction of Trade Statistics Yearbook, 1994.*

TABLE 12–16

MANUFACTURED GOODS OF THE INDUSTRIALIZING ASIAN ECONOMIES, AS PERCENTAGE OF EXPORTS, 1970 AND 1993, WITH PERCENTAGE GROWTH IN GNP PER CAPITA, 1980–1993

	MANUFACTURED EXPORTS		
	1970	1993	Avg. Annual Percent Growth, 1980–1993
Singapore	31%	80%	6.1%
Hong Kong	96	93	5.4
South Korea	76	94	8.2
Taiwan	76	93	NA
Malaysia	8	65	3.5
Thailand	8	73	6.4
Indonesia	1	53	4.2
United States	70	82	1.7
Japan	94	97	3.4

Source: World Bank, *World Development Report, 1995,* tables 1 and 15.

approximately tripled, as did its trade with the United States, the European Union, and Japan. (See Table 12–17.) The pattern is one of steady growth although, ironically, not the growth anticipated in 1979 following formal diplomatic relations between Washington and Beijing. During the same period, ideological differences with the Soviet Union prevented Sino-Soviet trade from developing. Again ironically, Mikhail Gorbachev was visiting Beijing in May 1989 to begin the process of normalizing relations between the two capitals when, presumably taking advantage of the worldwide press coverage of the Gorbachev visit, demonstrations began in Tiananmen Square that resulted two weeks later in bloodshed and subsequent repression. Though for years following the Tiananmen event there was popular talk of isolating China because of inferior human and civil rights policies, Table 12–17 makes it clear that no such thing occurred. One cannot rule out, of course, the possibility that China's external trade might have grown faster had it not been for this factor.

Nonetheless, between 1989 and 1993 China's exports nearly doubled, as did its total trade. Its exports to the United States multiplied almost four times, and those to the EU and Japan doubled.

Increased imports from the industrialized world had adverse consequences for the trade balance. Two important observations emerge. First, China's trade is booming, a reflection of its rapid economic transformation. Second, it is booming particularly in industrial products. Old predictions that China would remain dependent on industrial imports in exchange for primary products simply have not held since the change in policies twenty years ago. In those two decades, China's Four Modernizations have progressed to the point that in the realm of trade, a major new competitor has emerged. The current goal is to rival the United States, Japan, and the European Union in economic might by the middle of the next century. At present, however China's import needs generate a trade deficit with all categories of trading partners (Table 12–18).

From a political perspective, China's growth as an economic competitor is not comparable with the DEAs'. Taiwan's and South Korea's growth were, after all, seeded and nourished by the United States, and while harmony is not ever-present, it is the norm. The same applies to Hong Kong and Singapore. But the modern history is not the same with China. Geopolitical containment was the cornerstone of Washington's strategy throughout the

TABLE 12–17

DIRECTION OF CHINA'S TRADE WITH THE WEST, IN BILLIONS

	WORLD			UNITED STATES			EC			JAPAN		
	Exp.	Imp.	Bal.	Exp.	Imp.	Bal.	Exp.	Imp.	Bal.	Exp.	Imp.	Bal.
1979	$13.7	$15.7	($2.0)	$0.6	$1.9	($1.3)	$1.7	$3.4	($1.7)	$2.8	$3.9	($1.1)
1982	21.9	18.9	3.0	1.8	4.3	(2.5)	2.2	2.2	0	4.8	3.9	0.9
1985	27.3	42.5	(15.2)	2.3	5.2	(2.9)	2.3	6.2	(3.9)	6.1	15.2	(9.1)
1988	47.5	55.3	(7.8)	3.4	6.6	(3.2)	4.7	8.2	(3.5)	8.0	11.1	(3.1)
1989	52.5	59.1	(6.6)	4.4	7.8	(3.4)	4.9	9.1	(4.2)	8.4	10.5	(2.1)
1990	62.1	53.3	8.8	5.3	6.6	(1.3)	6.0	8.4	(2.4)	9.2	7.7	1.5
1991	71.9	63.8	8.1	6.2	8.0	(1.8)	6.8	8.4	(1.6)	10.3	10.0	0.3
1992	84.9	80.6	4.3	8.6	8.9	(0.3)	7.6	9.8	(2.2)	11.7	13.7	(2.0)
1993	91.0	103.1	(12.1)	17.0	10.6	6.4	11.7	14.4	(2.7)	15.8	23.3	(7.5)

Source: International Monetary Fund, *Direction of Trade Statistics Yearbook*, various issues.

TABLE 12-18

DIRECTION OF CHINA'S TRADE, 1993, IN BILLIONS

Destination	Exports	Imports	Balance	Total Value
World Total	$91.0	$103.1	($12.1)	$194.1
Industrial World	47.8	54.4	(6.6)	102.2
Developing World	42.9	47.4	(4.5)	90.3
Non-oil Developing World	40.2	44.7	(4.5)	84.9

Source: International Monetary Fund, *Direction of Trade Statistics Yearbook, 1994.*

Cold War, and economic containment is proposed today as a solution to the Chinese economic potential.[7] Under the operating rules of the New World Order, however, it is apparent that China cannot be excluded.

Conclusion

International trade is one of the principal measures of global interdependence. At the same time, the tone in which it is conducted says much about not only the international economy, but the political economy as well. As economic issues have superseded geopolitical strategies as the driving force of global politics, trade—the external economy of every state—measures the dimensions, the security, the reliability, and the equity of the New World Order. Equitable trade regimes are every bit the modern analog and successor of arms reduction agreements only six years ago, and trading partnerships the replacement for military alliances. But

trade also cuts directly to the heart of many sensitive domestic subjects such as employment, public revenue and resulting services, capital accumulation, and both domestic and foreign investment. Each of these invades domestic politics and eventually foreign policy. The relations of the political to the economic and of the international to the domestic are indelible.

More than any other interstate activity, trade underscores the realignment of actors in the international system. The expansion of the European Union to the Nordic states and the likely expansion into the former Soviet-allied states end ideological confrontation just as the fall of the Berlin Wall, the death of the Warsaw Treaty Organization, and the reunification of Germany ended strategic confrontation. The rush to regionalism is consolidating continents in unprecedented ways. Post–World War Two economic designs to stem the growth of communism have generated extraordinary economic power in Germany and Japan, and in South Korea and Taiwan. With all these structural changes, the United States finds its economic leadership challenged as at no time since World War One. The essence of these changes is that while economic capability has traditionally been an important factor in the global power distribution, now it is the most important. But the United States, accustomed to leadership in both the economic and geopolitical spheres, finds the military basis of its geopolitical leadership minimally relevant to the New World Order, and its economic leadership slipping to Japan, the European Union, and the Dynamic Asian Economies. The subsequent evolution of these trends will determine, more than any other single factor, the durability of the New World Order.

---

[7] For a similar conclusion arrived at differently, see Kenneth Lieberthal, "A New China Strategy," *Foreign Affairs,* November–December 1995, pp. 35–49.

CHAPTER 13

International Monetary Exchange

While it is handy to discuss international trade in terms of a steady flow of offsetting imports and exports, such perfect reciprocity rarely exists. Even if a nation's trade with a single partner were in perfect balance, its trade with the world would not be. Typically, a nation may have an export surplus with respect to some trading partners and an import surplus with respect to others, putting its total trade in surplus (higher total export value than import value), deficit (higher import value than export value), or balance (equal import and export values). A nation's annual trade performance and its multiyear trend are important indicators of its economic condition, irrespective of its standard of living.

The discussion of international trade in Chapter 12 emphasized the importance of trade value rather than trade volume. (Although volume units were used in the hypothetical example of wheat and autos in Taiwanese-American trade, certain assumptions were made in advance with regard to the value of labor and produce.) Needless to say, given the complexities of international trade, simple barter is rarely if ever used. Value is measured in monetary units, and because of social and economic differences among countries, national currency units have different absolute values. As a result, their values have to be compared with one another. To an American, for example, a dollar is worth a dollar (although with inflation it purchases less even in the domestic market than it did earlier). To an Italian, a hundred lira are worth a hundred lira, and to a Briton, a pound is worth a pound. But when an American dollar is offered in Canada, it may bring anywhere from 90 cents to 1 dollar and 30 cents Canadian. In London, it will draw about 1.5 pounds sterling, and in Rome, a cascade of lira. Hence, while a dollar is worth a dollar, it is also worth a specified amount in foreign currencies.

The same is true of all national currencies: A national unit has a price in international exchange, and the price may vary frequently, perhaps even daily, and sometimes violently. (A catastrophic drop in the value of the Mexican peso in 1995 required a multibillion-dollar American loan to prevent an economic disaster for Mexico and a severe disruption in trade within NAFTA.) Goods are traded internationally according to the prevailing relative values of the currencies of the importing country and exporting country.

Currency values change constantly. In a stable and unchanging relationship, they fluctuate in only small amounts. But in a dynamic complex of trading relations among nations, fluctuations can be extreme, and divergences of value can be dramatic. These changes will be influenced by such factors as volume activity, different rates of capital investment, different degrees of productivity, variations in incentives, domestic inflation or deflation, and the like. From 1979 to 1983, for example, the American dollar became steadily less valuable in international finance, while the German mark and the Japanese yen gained in value. It gradually took more American dollars to purchase German and Japanese goods because it took more dollars of lower value to purchase marks or yen of higher value. Then in 1984, the value of the dollar suddenly rose again, more nearly equating the values of the three currencies. At that point, German and Japanese goods became relatively less expensive for Americans, and American goods became relatively more expensive for people spending marks or yen. In 1986, the fall of the dollar resumed, and the dollar hit record low values against the yen in 1995. (From the summer of 1984 to mid-1995, the value of the dollar against the yen fell by 44 percent.) This resulted once again in a relative rise in the price of Japanese goods for American consumers and a reduction in the cost of American goods on international markets. The rule that emerges is a simple one: As a currency rises in value relative to others, the price of goods originating in the country of that currency will rise; and as it loses relative value, those prices will fall.

This simple rule has profound political economic consequences. International economic activity is, after all, designed to strengthen the domestic economy and to contribute to domestic political stability. If changes in currency values have far-reaching effects on relative import and export values, both the economic and the political goals of global activity may be undermined. If, for example,

the rise of the dollar's value makes American-built machinery so expensive internationally that consumers turn to German or French imports, then the machine tool industry in the United States will be adversely affected. Fewer units will be exported, and because the overall production level was set with the assumption that exports represented productivity in excess of domestic demand, buyers at home will not be able to consume those units that are no longer exported. Results: Production goes down; investment is curtailed; income is reduced; employees are released; and plants may be closed. But the ramifications run still deeper: The loss of income results in reduced bank deposits, a decline in capital accumulation, and a reduction of investment in other industries. Meanwhile, both the industry and the unemployed workers pay less to tax revenues—the source of public investment—commensurate with their lost income. In fact, the workers may now draw subsistence from public welfare, thus not only eliminating them as taxpayers but also transforming them into financial liabilities for public revenue. Hence, as public revenue declines, public expense rises, and changes are forced on the distribution of the public treasury. The variation in currency value has now resulted in social and economic changes at home. The domestic

Inside Fort Knox.
(*Source:* © Fred Conrad/Sygma)

political consequences will depend on the intensity of the change and on public reaction to it, but they could range from mild changes in political alignment to revolution. Almost invariably, one of the consequences is hostility to foreign goods and a demand for protectionist measures.

Fortunately, such dire consequences are rare because of the adjustments available to the seller. If it is currency value that erodes competitiveness, then the seller can reduce the price to protect the competitive position. This may mean less income from exports, but theoretically this should be made up in volume. This explains how both Germany and Japan can sustain large trade surpluses despite the enviable value of their currencies. It also explains why currency-related trade influences on international trade usually have transitory rather than lasting consequences.

Return now to the simpler level of international trade, and consider this question: Does it pay for an American to buy an Italian car priced at 1 million lira rather than an American car priced at $15,000, assuming the quality of the two products to be identical? Or does it pay for the Italian consumer to buy the American car at these prices? The questions cannot be answered without knowing the exchange rates between the two currencies. Americans do not ordinarily carry lira to the market, nor Italians dollar bills. The exchange rate is, therefore, the instrument through which the price system of one country is related to the price system of the other. At one level, the exchange rate might stimulate American interest in Italian products and dissuade Italians from buying American. But at a different level, the exchange rate might reduce American interest in Italian goods and increase attractiveness of American products in Italy. At some intermediate point, the exchange rate might result in mutual trade: Some Italian goods would be less expensive for buyers in both countries, while other American products would be advantaged in both markets. The exchange rate determines the price of each country's goods in the other's markets.

Now take another example. Suppose that on some hypothetical Day One the German mark and the American dollar are exchangeable one for one.

Suppose also that identical automobiles are made in the two countries such that the American model will sell in Germany for $20,000 and the German model will sell in the United States for $20,000. (For simplicity's sake, ignore transportation and import charges.) Now suppose that subsequently, because of a variety of national and international factors, the mark becomes twice as valuable as the dollar. Because it would now take two dollars to buy one mark, it would take two of the American models to purchase (or trade for) one German. If one is exchanged for one, Germany will be owed the cash value of a second in order to get its full value from the trade, because trade is measured in value. Without such a payment, Germany will have suffered a trade deficit in the transaction; but to compensate Germany's trade balance by making a payment of $20,000, the United States must incur a payment deficit of $20,000. The point is that the only thing that changed in this example was the value of the mark relative to the dollar.

Although dollars, marks, yen, francs, and pounds sterling exchange easily, the same is not true of all currencies. In fact, most of the world's national currencies have little or no value in international markets. They are not "backed" by gold or other precious metals, and they may be unspendable. These are termed "nonconvertible currencies," because merchants cannot convert them easily into the internationally valued currencies. In the example of German-American unbalanced auto trade requiring cash settlement, the German manufacturer will not accept settlement in Haitian gourdes or Ghanan cedis or Albanian leks. If he or she cannot get marks, he or she will demand the mark equivalent in another convertible currency, and the stronger the better, preferring yen to American dollars, but dollars to many other currencies. In actual practice, of course, the payment will be a check drawn on an American bank and presented to a German bank, which will handle the conversion to marks. But if this trade were with Malawi rather than the United States, the German bank might refuse a check valued in kwachas, leaving the merchant high and dry. Thus the trade would occur only if the government of Malawi were able to guarantee that it holds in reserve enough convertible currency to convert the buyer's check into something transactable in Germany.

Convertibility is a matter of intergovernmental recognition. It stands to reason that governments will not want to risk stockpiling currencies that lose value because of uncontrolled inflation in their countries of origin. Nor will political instability and the threat of severe devaluation endear a currency to other governments. Furthermore, different socioeconomic systems use different criteria in setting the values of their currencies. The Soviet ruble, for example, was worthless in the West because its value was unrelated to its marketability. In its transitional economy of the post–Cold War era, Russia is attempting to gain both stability and convertibility by using a $6 billion ruble-stabilization loan from the International Monetary Fund (IMF), and by setting a trading range for the ruble on open markets.[1] If the trading value falls below the range, the stabilization fund will be used to buy rubles at a higher-than-market price to restore its minimum value. Until Russia can demonstrate its ability to do this without continuous IMF support, the ruble will not be generally accepted abroad, and it will remain a nonconvertible currency.

Similar progress will be required of those former Soviet allies that covet EU membership. And it will be required of China and the Dynamic Asian Economies before their currencies are fully convertible. It has long been speculated that the South Korean won would become the next convertible currency, but this has yet to occur. The reasons include uncertainty of the country's ability to sustain its economic growth, the ill-defined relationship with communist North Korea, and anxiety regarding the fate of productivity should the two reunite.

An extraordinary problem arises with respect to the planned single currency of the EU. More than twenty years ago, the European Currency Unit (called the E-note or the ECU, and often written as ₤) was introduced as a quasi-currency for settling national accounts. Its value was and is determined by the actual values of a basket of member-country currencies. In the intervening years it has gained limited legitimacy as an expendable currency even though its distributor, the European Monetary Institute (EMI), forerunner of what will eventually be the European Central Bank, lacks monetary sovereignty. Under the terms of the Maastricht Treaty on European Union, a comprehensive monetary system is to be created in stages, the final of which will be in 2002. (This is a revision from the original Maastricht Treaty, which had set the date as 1999. In 1995, because of continent-wide anxieties over a hasty move to monetary unity, the EMI recommended the extended timetable.) One of the provisions is a single currency for the members that meet the criteria of having annual budget deficits of no more than 3 percent and accumulated debt of no more than 60 percent of GDP. (At the end of 1995, only Germany and the Netherlands met these tests.) Their currency values are to be frozen in 1999 and replaced in 2002 by the ECU at a value determined by the combined frozen rates. Numerous problems arise in this scheme, many of which have caused Europeans to have second thoughts about the next phase of integration. From an international perspective, however, the problem is that a fixed-rate currency has no place in a global monetary system based on fluctuating rates. Outside of the EU, therefore, the ECU will need to find its value against each of the other convertible currencies.[2]

These everyday phenomena of the global political economy comprise little more than the crust of an enormously complex system of trade and payments. In the preceding chapter we dealt with trade and balances of trade. Here we launch into the far more complex—and, to some, the more mysterious—aspects of international economic life, seen not from the perspective of the foreign traveler but from the macroeconomic viewpoint of

---

[1] *The New York Times*, July 6, 1995, p. D1.

[2] For a comprehensive history and discussion of theoretical and legal problems involved in creating a common currency, see Hercules Booysen, "A Future Currency ECU: The Problem of Succession and the Private Law Implications," *Journal of World Trade*, September 1994, pp. 83–98. On the work of the EMI on the currency matter, see *The New York Times*, November 15, 1995, p. D7.

Money exchange on a Moscow
Street.
(*Source:* © AP/Wide World)

governments. As material interdependence has increased the importance and volume of international trade, so too has the global exchange of
goods and services strained the machinery by
which nations balance their accounts with one
another.

The International
Monetary System

Among the most important characteristics of the
global political economy is the international monetary system. It is a web of international organizations, national policies, bilateral and multilateral
agreements, currency markets, and business behav-
iors of governments, corporations, and individuals.
Here we will be concerned principally with the
intergovernmental portion, which is designed to
aid national governments in regulating international economic behavior, encouraging international economic activity, and facilitating the
balances of national trade and payments. In the
preceding chapter, the discussion of the General
Agreement on Tariffs and Trade (GATT) was our

first encounter with the international monetary
system.

Before World War One, the world operated almost exclusively on a gold standard of exchange.
National currencies were fixed in value at some
percentage (or multiple) of gold's value. When a
nation's trade fell into deficit, the balance was
made up by payment in gold, either by the physical
transfer of gold blocks or by accounting between
central banks. In the interwar period, as international trade reached new heights and the dollar
exceeded all other currencies in desirability,
gold and the dollar together ruled the international monetary system and gradually became almost interchangeable. But as dollars were shipped
to Europe for recovery and reindustrialization,
the debt burden of the European governments
mounted. With this history in mind, much of the
nonmilitary diplomacy late in World War Two addressed the post-war configuration of the monetary
system, with all parties seeking official safeguards
against a repetition of the debt crisis of the interwar years.

Out of this diplomacy came the Bretton
Woods system, named for the 1944 conference in

New Hampshire at which the outline of the new monetary system was introduced by Washington. Complex and intricate by the standards of the 1940s, today it seems remarkably simple in its original design. Indeed, because of its simplicity, this system was unable to endure all the problems of the post-war global economy and required major changes in the 1970s. Its main components are the International Monetary Fund (IMF) and the International Bank for Reconstruction and Development (IBRD, or the World Bank). In 1956, in an effort to stimulate private investment in the Developing Nations, the newly created International Finance Corporation was affiliated with the IBRD, as was the International Development Association (IDA). The role of the IDA is to provide loans at subsidized rates to the Developing Nations. Today it deals more specifically with the Least Developed Countries. Because only the IMF is directly involved in settling national accounts, our attention here will be limited to that.

The International Monetary Fund

The Bretton Woods system was designed to achieve two things: (1) a standardized code of behavior for international trade, finance, and payments, and (2) a source of borrowing for nations with temporary balance-of-payments deficits. Consistent with the informal practice of the later interwar years, the IMF was based on the principle of a gold-exchange standard in which the dollar was equated with gold at $35 per ounce, and the U.S. government guaranteed to exchange dollars for gold at a ratio of one to one. All other currencies were given fixed rates relative to gold and the dollar and were allowed to rise or decline in market price by a maximum of 1 percent. If market forces changed a currency's value more than this, the country of its origin was pledged to draw on its reserves (originally gold and dollars, but later including other convertible currencies) to purchase the excess of its own currency on the international exchange at a price within the plus or minus 1 percent band. Changes in par value (formal revaluation) could be made only with

permission of the IMF upon the satisfactory demonstration of a fundamental disequilibrium between the current par value and the international economic forces affecting the currency.

This concept of equilibrium is central to the theory of the IMF, for it appears not only in the standards for revaluation but also in the quota system for borrowing, in the voting system, and in the borrowing machinery. Upon entering the fund, each government was given a quota based on the global ranking of its trade and other factors related to its economic stability and currency value. This quota then dictated three important factors: the distribution of voting rights, the obligation to store financial reserves with the fund, and the magnitude of borrowing rights. Voting rights were weighted by quota (proportional voting), thereby giving the greatest power over the international monetary system to the economically strongest nations, especially the United States. And because voting was used to determine currency values, borrowing rights, and subsequent changes in the fund's reserve holdings, this was one of the most important political decisions underlying the post-war international monetary system.

The assignment of a quota determined how much of its reserves a government would store with the IMF. Once this was established, 25 percent of the total was submitted to the fund's accounts in gold and the remainder in the national currency. Thereafter, upon sustaining a (presumably short-term) balance-of-payments deficit, the government could go to the fund to borrow back some of its reserves. It was limited to borrowing 25 percent of its quota per year for a maximum of five years, and its first 25 percent increment had to be its own gold deposit. In subsequent years, its borrowing would be not in its own currency but in convertible currencies (originally U.S. dollars) that were more desirable to international creditors than was the debtor's own. Repayment was to be within five years of each annual borrowing and was made by buying back from the fund the debtor's own currency, by depositing convertible currencies presumably gained by the strengthened trade enabled by the borrowing. At the end of the repayment cycle, the fund would again hold no more than 75 percent of the country's quota in its own currency.

With a number of policy changes, the IMF dominated the international monetary system from 1947 to 1970. Among the most important changes were the establishment of the two-tier gold system in 1968 and the introduction of the Special Drawing Rights (SDRs) in 1970. Both were responses to declining international financial reserves in the face of an enormous increase in international trade and the resulting disequilibria. The two-tier gold system, invented primarily as a means of protecting the American gold supply—recall that under Bretton Woods the United States was obliged to exchange dollars for gold, and the glut of dollars in Europe was evolving into a demand for gold exchange—maintained the value of gold at $35 per ounce among the central banks but permitted it to fluctuate by market forces outside official circles. The SDR, sometimes called "paper gold," was a wholly new invention and will be discussed later. Despite these important adaptations, by 1971 the Bretton Woods system was strained beyond repair. Consequently, the first fundamental changes in the post-war international monetary system were introduced.

By 1971, the global economy already was undergoing major structural changes. Although OPEC's meteoric rise was still ahead, trade and exchange between the Developing World and both the Soviet Union and the West had already begun to alter some of the Bretton Woods system's assumptions. In addition, both Europe and Japan had recovered fully from the economic ravages of World War Two and rapidly were invading America's reserve domains in international trade. The European Economic Community (EEC) was beginning to challenge the United States and, furthermore, used its customs-union characteristics to diminish the access of American goods to West European markets. Japan's export industries were beginning to threaten American exclusivity elsewhere.

In an effort to overcome the West European import barriers, American companies began constructing manufacturing plants in Europe, unleashing a vast flow of private capital out of the United States. And in contrast to the Bretton Woods assumption that balance-of-payments deficits would be temporary, some nations, including the United States, fell into chronic debtor status. The SDRs and the two-tiered gold system notwithstanding, world reserves relative to trade continued to dwindle. The dollar shortage of the early Bretton Woods years evolved into a dollar glut, with such an abundance of dollars in foreign markets, especially in Western Europe, that their real value declined despite the artificiality of the fixed-rate system of currency values. As European treasuries sought full value for their dollars, they demanded American gold, which was falling into dangerously short supply (because of the gold backing requirement ensuring that for every dollar of circulating currency there would be a gold reserve of at least 20 cents). The international monetary system was in crisis.

This crisis was addressed by the dominant members of the IMF in Washington in 1971, and the result of their deliberation was the Smithsonian Agreement. The fixed-rate system of currency values was abandoned in favor of freely fluctuating rates, and the United States was released from its obligation to exchange dollars for gold at a one-to-one ratio. The official value of gold was raised to U.S. $38, a device for effectively devaluing the dollar by about 9 percent. Other currency values also were changed officially before going to market fluctuation, the most important among them being the German mark, at the time the most desirable of the convertible currencies. Subsequent changes have introduced the so-called managed float system, a combination of valuing currencies by both market forces and government policy (by purchasing excess currency). The separation of gold from the dollar was a formal departure from the gold-exchange standard established by the Bretton Woods system and effectively placed the Western world on a dollar system, with all currencies valued in relation to the American currency. Because the dollar now fluctuates, sometimes wildly, a practice has emerged of periodically adjusting the dollar value of an SDR and then presenting currency values and certain international economic statistics in SDR-equivalent values.

The Smithsonian Agreement is broadly regarded as the triumph of monetarism in the international global economy, that is, the recognition of the superior role of adjusting monetary policy to resolve the disequilibria of international payments. The system continues to evolve. Throughout the 1980s, for example, there was a series of intergovernmental meetings (variously called G-5, G-7, and G-10 meetings, depending on the number of participants), some of them hastily, and even secretly, called to deal with urgent matters of adjustment. In 1986 and 1987, when, after a period of high valuation, the American dollar once again fell

precipitously, the finance ministers met several times to determine methods either to stabilize the dollar or to stem its fall at a level at which it would contribute positively rather than negatively to the U.S. balance-of-trade deficit. Once again we come to the interrelation between trade and payments, and between the international political economy and the forces of domestic politics. In the 1990s the G-7 heads of state have conducted annual economic summits amid much heraldry, but their agenda has been as much political as economic. President Boris Yeltsin, who demands expansion to G-8, has been invited as a partial participant on two occasions, and so the Russian press now refers to the G-7 1/2 or the G-7 plus one.

The importance of currency valuations cannot be overstated. The value of a national currency

Annual summit of the G-7 heads of state (1995), with Russian President Boris Yeltsin as participating guest. (*Source:* Jacques Longevin/Sygma)

relative to others not only will have direct consequences for international activity, but may have major domestic impacts as well. In the era of fixed rates, governments whose currencies were artificially *under*valued resisted revaluing upward, for fear of diminishing the profitability of trade. Meanwhile, countries with artificially *over*valued currencies objected to revaluing downward, because devaluation typically is viewed either domestically or globally as a sign of economic decline. Fluctuating rates, whether by free or managed float, overcome these difficulties; but in return, they increase the burden on policymakers to apply monetary and political policies to adjust currency values to levels that will maximize the value of international trade and minimize the effects of international disadvantage on the domestic economy.

National Accounts

Having studied both international trade and the international monetary system, we now turn to the concept of national accounts, of which both trade and payments are important parts. In simpler days, national accounts consisted almost entirely of the import and export of goods, services, and funds. Today, however, fluctuating currency rates have introduced international currency speculation, with billions of dollars changing hands electronically across the world. Transnational corporations move capital around the globe, creating both capital deficits for the home accounts and improved overseas assets. Governments use their reserves for anticipating future payments needs and for purchasing their own currencies from foreign central banks in order to control their values. They may also buy other currencies to affect their values. In 1995, for example, when the American dollar reached its historical low against the yen, both Washington and Tokyo purchased dollars on the open market to raise their value. Much more rarely a government may dump a foreign currency onto the market, hoping that abnormal abundance will depress its value. Unless this is done by agreement,

it is a hostile act, as it forces a temporary devaluation on an unwilling government.

These complexities notwithstanding, we begin with the assumption that the comprehensive balance of a nation's accounts is a product of the import and export of goods, services, and funds, both public and private. Foreign payment for a load of exported tractors brings a financial benefit, and so the sale contributes positively to a payments balance. Paying for a similar imported load contributes negatively. But if domestic funds are spent abroad, as in an investment, the economy is deprived of them, contributing negatively to a payments balance. When those funds are returned, however, they contribute positively to the domestic payments balance. A simple rule of thumb will help sort out some of the first-order confusions of these differences: *Goods going out contribute positively, but funds going out contribute negatively; and goods coming in contribute negatively, whereas funds coming in contribute positively.* The reason for this apparent contradiction is that exchanges are viewed in terms of value. The sale of tractors means receipt of payment. If that payment comes from another country, it represents a net addition to the domestic account. Conversely, when investment capital is sent abroad, the action represents a net reduction in the domestic account. Only when that investment begins to profit, and only when the earnings from the investment or the proceeds of its subsequent sale are returned to the domestic economy, does it enter the books as a net increase in the domestic account.

As recently as a decade ago, this simple rule and its direct consequences told most of the story of national payments balances. In the modern globalized economy, however, statements of payments balances include many other factors. The older notion that the current account (composed of the balance of goods, services, and long-term capital movements) accurately states a country's payments condition no longer holds. Today the annual payments statement adds to these such things as net reserve position (in gold, foreign exchange, SDRs, and IMF credit), short-term capital movements, and liabilities constituting the foreign reserves of other countries. Table 13–1 is a simple organization of the contributing factors, identifying the activities that are typical of the public and private sectors. The right-hand column aggregates these activities into the specific categories of payments accounting. We will review each of those here and then explore how the IMF actually follows and states national balances.

The Public Sector

The simplest public-sector influences on the national balance are the payment or collection of fees, debt, and the interest on debt. For the collector, the influx of the payment means a net positive increase on the national account; for the payer, the outflow of funds represents a withdrawal from the national account. Foreign aid has much the same reciprocal influences: The lender withdraws funds and ships them away, and the recipient has a net positive increase in its cumulative capital resources. (For this reason much foreign aid is extended in credit, thus both keeping the cash in the lender's accounts and ensuring that purchases will be made in the lending country rather than elsewhere.) Also relatively simple is the payment of direct expenses abroad, or the payment by foreigners of direct expenses in a host economy. The stationing of American troops in South Korea, for example, is extremely costly for the United States and represents a continuous outflow of funds. From the South Korean perspective, however, those funds are spent in the local economy for food, housing, education, entertainment, and the like. This is a constant stimulus to the South Korean economy, providing not only individual livelihoods, but savings and capital accumulation as well. This is every bit as valuable as the capital gained from a balance-of-trade surplus, and more valuable than development loans, because it does not have to be repaid and carries no interest. (Note that this ignores potential political costs.)

The international sale of public securities has become one of the major devices of international exchange in the last two decades. Because the annual expenditures of many governments exceed their revenues, it has become common to increase cash resources by selling public securities. In the past, most of these were consumed at home. Millions of Americans, for example, own savings bonds, one of the simplest forms of government security. More recently, however, as gaps between the national budgets and tax revenues have increased (the U.S. national debt doubled between 1981 and 1986), government securities have been sold more frequently and in unprecedented amounts. Today a declining percentage of this paper is bought by domestic consumers, and more by foreign financial institutions. This, in fact, virtually is guaranteed by setting long-term interest rates at levels attractive to foreign investors whose domestic economies are returning lower rates. These sales represent short-term capital inflow for the United States and outflow for Japan, Germany, or the Netherlands. In the longer run, however, they are a costly device. At maturity (or earlier) the United States must buy back the security at its face value, and in the meanwhile it may have paid out interest equal to the face value. After the initial capital flow resulting from sale and purchase, the benefit accrues largely to the national account of the purchaser.

The final device available to the national government is the enhancement of its reserves. It is true, of course, that all the foregoing are instruments for increasing government reserves. But it is more accurate to say that they all are means of improving a government's net capital position. The distinction is that net capital is for current investment, whereas reserves are intended as savings in specific forms to be used subsequently to meet payments problems. The means by which governments do this are, specifically, acquiring gold at advantageous prices; acquiring and/or saving diverse reserves of convertible currencies; minimizing credit obligations to the IMF; and maintaining a balance between net increases in capital outflow and anticipated revenues from capital investment and foreign aid.

Given the fluctuations of the global economy, a government's reserve position is crucial to both its liquidity and its solvency. Before Bretton

TABLE 13–1

FACTORS INFLUENCING NATIONAL BALANCES

	Positive Influences	Negative Influences		Balancing Factor
Balance of Trade	1. Export of goods	Import of goods	1.	} Net trade position
	2. Export of services	Import of services	2.	
Balance of Payments				
1. Public sector	1. Collection of debt	Payment of debt	1.	
	2. Collection of fees	Payment of fees	2.	
	3. Collection of interest on debt	Payment of interest	3.	} Net cash position
	4. Direct expenses paid by foreigners	Direct expenses abroad	4.	
	5. Receipt of foreign aid	Payment of foreign aid	5.	} Net capital position
	6. Sale of public securities abroad		6.	
	7. Preservation of IMF credit	Use of IMF credit	7.	
	8. Preservation of SDRs	Use of SDRs	8.	} Net reserve position
	9. Acquisition of gold	Loss of gold	9.	
	10. Currency-strengthening policy	Currency-weakening policy	10.	
2. Private sector	1. Import of capital	Export of capital	1.	
	2. Repatriation of capital		2.	} Net capital position
	3. Repatriation of foreign earnings		3.	
	4.	Purchase of foreign public securities	4.	
	5. Corporate expenses of foreigners	Corporate expenses abroad	5.	
	6. Personal expenses of foreigners	Personal expenses abroad	6.	} Net cash position
	7. Collection of interest	Payment of interest	7.	
	8. Collection of foreign debt	Payment of foreign debt	8.	
	9. Successful currency speculation	Unsuccessful currency speculation	9.	Net reserve position
	10. Reinvestment of foreign earnings abroad		10.	Postponement of effect

Woods, reserves consisted entirely of gold and foreign currencies. (Table 13–2 shows the world distribution of gold reserves, and Table 13–3 deals with currency reserves.) The advent of the IMF changed that, first with the invention of fund credit as previously described, and later (1970) with the addition of the SDRs. Unlike ordinary fund credit, the SDR represents a recognition that balance-of-payments problems can be chronic. The SDR is an artificial unit of credit that the IMF allocates to a government. The Fund may, upon satisfactory demonstration of a chronic payments problem, authorize a government to use SDRs to borrow convertible currencies from the treasuries of other members. The SDR's own value is based on the values of a "basket" of dominant currencies—the American dollar, the German mark, the British pound, the French franc, and the Japanese yen. Thus, as is the case with individual currencies, the SDR's value is subject to fluctuation; but because it is based on several currencies simultaneously, whose values frequently change with respect to one another, these fluctuations are small compared with those experienced by some individual currencies. SDR distribution is shown in Table 13–4 and IMF credit distribution in Table 13–5.

Once authorization is granted to use SDRs, each participating country is required to accept them in exchange for convertible currencies up to a level of twice its own SDR allocation. Although SDRs are not literally currency and cannot be spent for commodities, they have the effect of expanding governmental payment capabilities by making convertible currency reserves available. Their creation has been regarded as "a genuine breakthrough in monetary thinking,"[3] and it has contributed considerably to easing the currency reserve problem of countries with chronic trade deficits.

The importance of SDRs as reserve units is underscored by the degree to which their total value grew in only fifteen years. When the units were first

TABLE 13–2

GOLD RESERVES, 1993, IN MILLIONS OF TROY OUNCES

World	913	United States	262.0	(29%)
		Germany	95.2	
Industrial		Switzerland	83.3	
Countries	771	France	81.9	
		Italy	66.7	
Developing		Netherlands	35.0	
Countries	142	Belgium	25.0	
		Austria	18.6	
		United Kingdom	18.5	
		Portugal	16.1	
		Spain	15.6	

Source: International Monetary Fund, *International Financial Statistics Yearbook*, 1993, pp. 50–53.

distributed in 1970, they totaled only 3.124 billion units. But by the end of 1985, the total amount had risen to 18.2 billion, 14.9 billion of which were held by the industrialized countries and only 3.3 billion by the combined developing countries.[4] By 1993, their total value had declined to 14.6 billion units and the distribution changed. These figures indicate both the extent of the industrialized world's reliance on expanded reserve assets and the degree to which the chronic debtors in the international payments scheme are industrialized rather than developing countries.

For most of the post-war years, international financial statistics were kept and expressed in $U.S. billions. Today, however, with fluctuating exchange rates and the dollar's unreliability, the IMF expresses such statistics in value equivalents of the SDR. Hence, its value with respect to the dollar or any other currency has become a matter of

---

[3] Fritz Machlup, *Remaking the International Monetary System* (Baltimore: Johns Hopkins University Press, 1968), p. 34.

[4] See William J. Byrne, "Evolution of the SDR, 1974–85," in John Adams, ed., *The Contemporary International Economy*, 2nd ed. (New York: St. Martin's Press, 1985), pp. 340–350.

TABLE 13-3

INTERNATIONAL CURRENCY RESERVES, IN BILLIONS

	1970	1975	1980	1985	1990	1993
Industrialized Countries						
United States	$0.6	$0.1	$7.9	$11.7	$36.7	$30.2
Germany	8.5	19.4	34.9	35.5	44.3	52.9
Japan	3.2	9.1	16.9	20.3	48.8	64.6
OPEC Countries						
Saudi Arabia	0.5	18.2	16.3	12.5	6.0	4.1
Kuwait	0.1	0.7	3.7	4.2	1.1	2.9
Venezuela	0.5	6.2	4.4	8.1	5.8	6.2

Source: International Monetary Fund, *International Financial Statistics Yearbook,* 1993, pp. 58–61.

TABLE 13-4

SDR DISTRIBUTION EXPRESSED IN SDR VALUE UNITS

	1970	1975	1980	1985	1988	1993
Industrialized Nations	2.6	7.2	8.9	14.9	17.6	11.4
Developing Nations	0.5	1.5	2.9	3.3	2.6	3.2
Total	3.1	8.7	11.8	18.2	20.2	14.6

Source: International Monetary Fund, *International Financial Statistics Yearbook,* 1993, pp. 42–43.

importance. When the SDR was established, it was equated with gold. Their relative values were expressed as one to one, or as SDR/$U.S. = 1.0 and, conversely, $U.S./SDR = 1.0. As both the dollar and the basket of currencies have fluctuated, however, the equivalence has changed, with the SDR consistently more valuable than the dollar. By mid-1995, the dollar had gotten so weak that an SDR was worth $1.4925. This is another way of saying that in twenty-five years, the convertibility of American dollars for SDRs dropped by 50 percent.

In sum, then, national financial reserves in the current global economy consist of fund credit, SDRs, foreign currencies held in reserve, and gold at the official rate. Table 13–6 depicts the evolution of the U.S. reserve position for the years 1970 to 1993. Note particularly the following features of Table 13–6: (1) the American gold stock has remained almost perfectly stable for twenty three years, after a substantial fall in the 1960s[5]; (2) only

after OPEC began its slide from power did the United States once again begin to amass foreign currency reserves; and (3) the greatest increase in the net U.S. reserve position has been through the devices of the IMF, in both traditional credit and SDRs. The huge growth in currency reserves is recent.[6]

The Private Sector

The private sector's contributions to the national payments account are considerably easier to understand, even though they include currency speculation and the purchase of foreign public securities. Corporate and personal expenses paid by foreigners, or the payment of such expenses received from foreigners, play the same role as do the payment and receipt of direct expenses by governments. And the payment or receipt of interest on a foreign debt is identical to the corresponding category in the public sector.

The other categories all relate to private investment, either directly into industry or into securities portfolios. Sending investment capital abroad represents an account deficit, even though it also creates a net investment advantage and a potential long-term capital gain. It is an immediate capital

---

[5] Though the gold supply has been stable in the last decade, the capital outflow of the 1960s resulted in a reduction of gold reserves from 442 million Troy ounces to the current 262 million.

[6] For a general comment on the inadequacies of the IMF in the current international economy, see Zanny Minton-Beddoes, "Why the IMF Needs Reform," *Foreign Affairs,* May–June 1885, pp. 123–133.

TABLE 13-5

FUND CREDIT DISTRIBUTION EXPRESSED IN SDR BILLIONS

	1970	1975	1980	1985	1988	1993
Industrialized Nations	6.6	7.7	10.7	25.2	19.5	28.3
Developing Nations	1.0	4.9	6.1	13.5	8.8	4.5
Total	7.6	12.6	16.8	38.7	28.3	32.8

Source: International Monetary Fund, *International Financial Statistics Yearbook,* 1993, pp. 46–47.

improvement in the recipient country. This relationship lasts only until the profits from the investment are repatriated or until the investment is sold and the original capital and profit are returned home, now representing a net capital advantage to the home economy and a net deficit to the host.

In recent years, the net American position on U.S. investment abroad and foreign investment in the United States for all categories—direct private investment (construction of plant, and so on), indirect private investment (purchase of stocks and bonds), and public securities (sale and purchase of government securities, a major means by which governments borrow money)—has reversed; and in the mid-1980s, the United States went from being the world's largest creditor to the world's largest debtor. In a subsequent section, "The World Debt Crisis," this is demonstrated numerically.

Not all money invested abroad represents additional capital outflow. Foreign investments, like investments at home, appreciate regularly. The annual earnings may be reinvested (for example, an American-owned manufacturing plant in Spain is enlarged using funds from annual earnings) or repatriated (returned home) to be distributed to stockholders. How much will be reinvested and how much repatriated will be determined by such issues as tax policies in the home and host countries, corporate priorities, competition, long-range planning, and so forth. Or foreign earnings may be moved to another foreign site for investment or reinvestment.

Fluctuating currency values introduced a whole new profession to the realm of international finance, that of the currency speculator. As we have seen, a currency unit that has a value of $100 today may rise to $110 next year or fall to $70. The wise speculator will buy currencies that are low but climbing in value. The speculator is a student of gross economic trends: interest rates, economic stability, employment trends, political stability, and other factors influencing currency values. A thorough knowledge of these trends will tell him or her when to buy a currency, just as if buying the stock of IBM or Boeing, in the expectation of selling it later as its value increases.

But not all currency speculation is for such a long term. Unlike the stock markets where trading takes place in public, the global currency market is a network of computerized private selling floors,

TABLE 13-6

U.S. NET RESERVE POSITION

	1970	1975	1980	1985	1988	1993
SDRs	$0.85 billion	$2.33 billion	$2.61 billion	$7.29 billion	$9.64 billion	$9.02 billion
IMF Credit	1.94	2.21	2.85	11.95	9.75	11.80
Foreign Exchange	0.63	0.08	10.13	12.86	17.36	41.50
Gold	11.07	11.60	11.16	11.09	11.06	11.05
Total	$14.49	$16.22	$26.75	$43.19	$47.81	$73.37

Source: International Monetary Fund, *International Financial Statistics Yearbook,* 1993, p. 739.

worldwide telephones, and satellite communications. The selling rooms are in New York, Hong Kong, Zurich, London, Tokyo, Rome, and a few other places. In one of these, a currency may be selling for $1.03 and in another only $.97. In the latter a trader may buy 10 million units and then alert his or her correspondent in the former to sell 10 million units. The transfer from one city to another around the world takes place by a computerized transaction, and if the sale works out, the two traders will have made for their client a half-million dollars in a few moments. And because these transactions frequently take place in magnitudes of hundreds of millions or even billions of dollars, the profits are often multiples of a million. In fact, it is no longer uncommon for the trader to make several million dollars in commissions on such activities. From an international perspective, while these funds are in foreign hands, they represent a net liability for the country of origin and a net increase in the reserves of the country in which they are deposited.

These, then, are the basic components of a nation's balance of payments, the net of all flows inward and outward that have monetary value. The many parts are regularly brought together by governmental agencies and by such international organizations as the World Bank and the IMF. Table 13–7 uses the IMF format to show the national balances of the United States, Japan, and Saudi Arabia. Note that section G shows how reserves are used to bring the national account into balance annually. The table serves both as an example of how this accounting is presented and as statistical information about changes in the global economy. (The lines are numbered so that the text can refer more easily to some of the table's important features.)

We look first at the format. Note the following features:

1. Line 1 is a statement of the current account balance, consisting of the balance of trade in goods and services and net income from investment

earnings. This portion of the current statement is identical to the types of net trade figures used in the preceding chapter. The contributing parts are listed on lines 2 through 8, each of which provides useful detail on trade.

2. Line 9 states the capital account balance, the net of lines 10 through 12, dealing with long-term capital principally in the forms of direct and portfolio investments. (Direct investment goes immediately to production, such as constructing a plant, equipping an oil field, and so forth. Portfolio investment is the purchase of stocks, bonds, and other financial securities.)

3. Line 13 sums sections A and B and presents the so-called basic balance, the sum of the current and capital account balances.

4. On line 14, short-term capital flows are added to the equation, and then small adjustment items are added on line 15.

5. Line 16 adds all the preceding items and presents the so-called official settlements balance. Lines 17 and 18 factor in other small adjustments.

6. The summary balance, which adds all the preceding items, is presented on line 19. It is at that point that the actual intergovernmental settlements are made. Note that section G on line 20 is, in every case presented, the reciprocal of line 19. The reason for this is that whereas line 19 indicates a government's total surplus or liability for the period in question, line 20 is a statement of the manner in which the adjustment was made. The following detail on lines 21 through 25 indicates the various amounts taken from (or added to) the different reserve resources to bring the entire account into balance.

7. Finally, because it is now customary to present these accounts in SDR value rather than in billions of American dollars (because of the relatively greater stability of the SDR than of the dollar), lines 26 and 27 state the SDR value of the national currency for the period in question. For example, in 1980 it took 1.3015

TABLE 13–7

AGGREGATED BALANCES EXPRESSED IN BILLIONS OF SDRs

	UNITED STATES			JAPAN			SAUDI ARABIA			LINE
	1980	1986	1991	1980	1986	1991	1980	1986	1991	
A. Current account	1.5	145.4	–3.7	–8.3	85.8	72.9	32.9	–11.3	–25.8	1
Merchandise exp.	172.4	223.4	416.0	97.4	205.6	306.6	77.4	20.1	48.2	2
Merchandise imp.	–192.0	–368.4	–489.4	–95.8	–112.8	–203.5	–19.6	–17.1	–26.1	3
Services: credit	90.8	72.3	145.7	24.2	23.5	44.7	8.7	2.7	3.0	4
Services: debit	–64.0	–73.2	–113.2	–32.9	–35.5	–85.0	–25.9	–20.3	–38.6	5
Income: credit	—	88.3	143.3	—	30.2	143.9	—	11.3	8.9	6
Income: debit	—	–71.9	–114.0	—	–23.2	–121.2	—	–0.7	–0.9	7
Other	–5.8	–14.9	–31.1	–1.2	–2.1	–12.5	–7.7	–7.8	–20.2	8
B. Capital account	—	81.9	2.9	—	–132.1	31.4	—	4.4	26.4	9
Long-term capital	–6.5	15.4	–15.7	1.8	–14.3	–29.4	–21.0	1.0	26.4	10
Direct investments	–1.8	71.6	–27.2	–1.6	–102.0	35.5	–2.5	3.5	—	11
Portfolio investments	2.2	–5.1	13.7	7.2	–15.8	22.2	–18.1	—	—	12
Other	–6.9	—	—	–3.8	—	—	–0.5	—	—	—
Total A & B (basic balance)	–5.1	–63.6	–0.75	–6.4	–46.3	104.3	11.8	–7.4	0.6	13
C. Short-term capital	–21.1	13.9	–20.7	12.7	58.6	–103.2	–8.8	–0.2	–0.6	14
D. Net errors/omissions	19.2	15.9	–1.1	–2.4	2.5	–7.7	–0–	—	—	15
Total A–D (official Settlements balance)	–6.2	–33.8	–22.6	4.5	14.8	–6.6	0.7	–7.6	0.1	16
E. Exceptional financing	0.9	–0–	—	–0–	—	—	–0–	—	—	17
F. Liabilities constituting foreign reserves	11.5	33.5	16.8	–0–	—	—	–0–	—	—	18
Total A–F (summary balance)	6.2	–0.3	–5.76	4.5	14.8	–6.6	3.7	–7.6	0.1	19
G. Change in reserves	–6.2	0.3	5.76	–4.5	–14.8	6.6	–3.7	7.6	–0.1	20
Monetary gold	0.1	0.1	—	–0–	—	—	–0–	0.2	—	21
SDRs	–0–	–0.25	–.18	–0.8	.14	.47	0.1	2.3	.5	22
Fund reserve (IMF)	–1.3	1.5	–.37	0.8	.14	–1.68	0.6	1.0	1.1	23
Foreign exchange	–5.1	–0.9	6.31	–4.5	–15.1	7.83	3.1	6.4	–1.2	24
Use of fund credit	–0–	—	—	–0–	—	—	–0–	—	—	25
Conversion	U.S.$/ SDR=									26
	1.2754	1.2232	1.4304							27

Note: "Direct investments" go directly into another economic activity, such as constructing a manufacturing plant, whereas "Portfolio investments" are purchases of stocks, bonds, and other securities.

Source: International Monetary Fund, *International Payments Statistics,* 1992.

American dollars to purchase an SDR unit. To convert any figure in the 1980 column for the United States into billions of American dollars, then, because the table is expressed in billions of SDR, merely multiply that number by 1.3015. For 1991, the figure is 1.4304.

Turn now from the format itself to its practical meaning. There are countless conclusions that can be gleaned from a review of the actual figures. For instance, the current account for the United States has gone from a slight positive to a huge negative, and then a modest negative. The cause of the precipitous fall was the balance of trade deficit (the sum of lines 2 and 3), and the reason for the reversal was improvement in the service and investment income credits. Japan, whose huge balance-of-trade surpluses we saw in the last chapter, loses its advantage in service and income losses. The same is true for Saudi Arabia.

The tabular format belies the diplomatic and political complexity of all these transactions but, at the same time, indicates to some extent the degree to which we are misled about some of these things. In the United States, for example, there is so much concern over the deteriorating international trade position that little attention is given to the remarkable stability of the overall balance of payments. But behind even this contradiction lies an important political-economic conclusion: Despite the relative balance-of-payments stability, the international trade picture persistently presents an image of declining American competitiveness in both the basic industries and the more modern manufactures, calling into question such profound things as future employment patterns in the United States, loss of domestic production and commensurate dependence on uncertain foreign supply, and major swings of capital into the United States for portfolio enrichment but out of the United States for direct investment in industries elsewhere that will accentuate the loss of jobs at home and American dependence on foreign manufactures. In this cycle of events, the modern transnational corporation is the paradoxical element: Even though it invests directly in other economies and thus provides employment abroad at the expense of employees at home, and even though its products are imported into the United States as part of the net balance-of-trade deficit, it nonetheless produces substantial portfolio wealth for both American and foreign investors.

The World Debt Crisis

Resourceful as the managers of the international monetary system may have been, a succession of unforeseen events between 1980 and 1995 shook the global economy. Among them were the following.

1. A worldwide recession in the 1980s that, among other things, caused the first decline in Japan's annual GNP since 1948 and drove the American balance-of-trade deficit to a record $174 billion in 1987

2. The struggle to stabilize industrial economies in the West and Japan amid uncertainty about OPEC's future strength

3. Political instability in Asia including a threatening conflict among China, Vietnam, and Cambodia, the Soviet war in Afghanistan, strife between Pakistan and India, civil war in Sri Lanka, and rumblings of disruption between the Koreas

4. An elevation in Cold War tension, a massive spurt in the nuclear arms race that doubled the U.S. national debt

5. The Iran-Iraq War that disrupted world oil markets

6. The Iraqi invasion of Kuwait and the Desert Storm War that followed, threatening the petroleum-driven basis of Western life

7. Growing competition with the Dynamic Asian Economies, causing a loss of confidence in international investment, particularly in the Asian Developing Nations

8. The emancipation of Eastern Europe and the collapse of the Soviet Union, both followed by the launching of transition from communism to free market economies

9. The interest of the West in accelerating the capitalization of Russia and the other transitional economies, with capital normally bound for the Developing Nations diverted there

10. The beginning of chronic inability of Poland, Mexico, and many less well developed states to meet the obligations on their international debt

11. Enlargement of the European Union, completion of its single-market goals, the creation of NAFTA—the rapid and extensive regionalization of international trade

12. The passage of the United States from the foremost creditor nation to the largest debtor

Because most of these issues have been addressed previously, this section will concentrate on Developing World's debt crisis, the transitional economies, and the evolution of the American global position, all of which have profound effects on the global system.

The Developing World's Debt Crisis

The cost to Argentina of the Falkland Islands War and the exposure of Poland's economic weaknesses after the Soviet imposition of martial law awakened the world to the impending debt crisis of the Developing World. These events did not cause the crisis, but they did bring it to light. The crisis itself can be understood only in the context of a sluggish global economy, the economic consequences of political instability both regionally and between the superpowers, deteriorating terms of trade for Developing World exports (including oil), demand by overcommitted lending institutions for repayment, and the depletion of national credit reserves in the IMF.

The Developing World debt crisis charged onto the global scene in 1982, when the aggregate external debt of Developing Nations exceeded $680 billion. At the time, fourteen countries had the greatest difficulties. Brazil and Mexico led the list of debtors with outstanding amounts of $92 billion and $87 billion, respectively, after which the amounts dropped sharply: Argentina's foreign debt was $39 billion. The geographic distribution of the debt was also alarming, with approximately $283 billion of the total attributed to only six Latin American countries, out of a total of $330 billion owed by the entire region. The total Third World debt was rising by about $40 billion per year and reached $875 billion by early 1988, of which $325 billion was owed to private-sector sources and the balance to governments and international organizations. By 1993, the combined external debt of just twenty-one Developing Nations reached almost $1.1 trillion (Table 13–8) despite a decade of debt-reduction strategies. The debt of the entire Developing World was considerably higher: $1.52 trillion.[7]

More alarming than the aggregate figures, however, is the relationship of debt to economic development. Among the states in Table 13–8, total external debt in 1993 was equal to 52 percent of GNP; out of each $100 worth of goods and services created, $52 was owed to foreign creditors. (If the highest six are removed, the figure is still 26 percent.) Moreover, because theoretically exports provide development capital, the relationship of debt to exports is important. We see that in 1993, average debt was 2.15 times the value of exports among these nations. This means that if these nations had imported nothing and used all the proceeds from exports to pay their debt, they would have retired less than half of it. Not all of this debt was due in a single year, however, and so the relationship of exports to annual debt service (annual principal and interest payment) is the crucial measure. It turns out that in 1993, these states had an average scheduled payment of more than a quarter of their combined exports. This means that just to meet the annual obligation, they would have to enjoy a 27 percent balance-of-trade surplus. Worse, the situation has intensified since 1980 for the group, though it has improved or remained stable for eleven of the countries. The conclusion is that in most of the Developing World, exports cannot keep up with annual debt service and cannot, therefore, provide accumulated capital for further

---

[7] United Nations, *World Economic and Social Survey, 1995*, p. 340.

TABLE 13-8

TWENTY-ONE PRINCIPAL DEVELOPING WORLD DEBTOR NATIONS, 1993

Rank	Country	Total Debt	Debt as % GNP	Debt as % Exports	DEBT SERVICE AS % EXPORTS 1980	1993
1	Brazil	$132.7 billion	26%	296%	63%	24%
2	Mexico	118.0	33	176	48	32
3	India	91.8	29	225	9	28
4	Indonesia	89.5	59	195	14	32
5	China	83.8	18	84	4	11
6	Argentina	74.4	29	417	37	46
7	Turkey	67.9	38	216	28	28
8	South Korea	47.2	13	46	20	9
9	Thailand	45.3	37	92	19	19
10	Egypt	40.6	71	171	15	15
11	Venezuela	37.5	63	211	27	23
12	Philippines	35.5	60	173	27	25
13	Nigeria	32.5	110	NA	4	NA
14	Pakistan	26.1	39	205	18	25
15	Algeria	25.8	51	206	27	77
16	Vietnam	24.2	162	569	NA	14
17	Malaysia	23.3	37	43	6	8
18	Morocco	21.4	73	232	33	32
19	Iran	20.6	NA	106	7	7
20	Chile	20.6	45	160	43	23
21	Peru	20.3	46	385	45	59
Total		$1,078.9	—	—	—	—
Average		—	52%	215%	25%	27%

Source: World Bank, *World Development Report, 1995,* tables 20 and 23.

development. For the entire capital-importing Developing World, the ratio of annual debt service to exports improved considerably from 1985 to 1994, dropping from 23.5 percent to 14.2 percent.[8]

[8] United Nations, *World Economic and Social Survey, 1995,* p. 340.

The Developing World debt problem is, then, two crises in one. First, debt severely erodes the effort to improve economic performance through exports. And second, throughout the industrialized world and the network of financial international organizations, governments, corporations, and agencies await payment of interest and principal needed

TABLE 13–9

DEVELOPING WORLD DEBT RESTRUCTURINGS AND RESCHEDULINGS

Year	PUBLIC SOURCES		PRIVATE SOURCES		TOTAL	
	Number	Amount	Number	Amount	Number	Amount
1984	14	$3.8 billion	26	$91.3 billion	40	$95.1 billion
1985	22	6.5	14	23.2	36	29.7
1986	19	12.2	12	72.7	31	84.9
1987	17	13.0	19	89.7	36	102.7
1988	15	9.4	10	79.7	25	89.1
1989	24	18.6	4	6.8	28	25.4
1990	17	6.1	5	5.4	22	11.5
1991	14	44.3	0	0.0	14	44.3
1992	16	12.5	1	NA	17	12.5+
1993	10	3.4	1?	0.2	11?	3.6
1994	3	14.0	1	0.2	4	14.2

For 1993, it is assumed that one rescheduling occurred with a private bank because a dollar amount is listed.

Source: United Nations, *World Economic and Social Survey, 1995,* pp. 342–343.

to meet their own obligations, in a global environment in which the prospect of timely repayment seems to decline steadily.

For the developing country unable to meet its payments, several options are now available. The oldest is simply to borrow more money to meet current debt, but this method is notorious for both postponing the inevitable and making it more damaging. Debt restructuring and rescheduling are far more popular in the Developing World and have become so among the lending nations because they are desirable alternatives to default. Rescheduling is a device by which the creditor and the debtor agree to a new schedule for payment of interest and principal. Restructuring is analogous to what overextended families do in the United States. The debtor government and the creditor look at all the transactions between them and consolidate them into a single repayment schedule. Table 13–9 summarizes debt restructuring and rescheduling for the

years 1984–1994. The numbers need no explanation, because their magnitude speaks volumes about the extent of the debt crisis for both debtor and creditor. It should be pointed out, however, that both the number of revisions and the amount of debt involved have been in steady decline since 1987 and steep decline since 1991, suggesting that at least for the time being, banks and lender governments are nearing the limit of their willingness to postpone repayment.

From the creditors' perspective, three major methods have been used to come to grips with unpaid debt aside from rescheduling. The first is a series of attempts by the IMF to ease the crisis using their special capabilities. Political wrangling in the United States between conservatives, who wished to expand the IMF's credit capacity, and liberals, who thought the extension of credit a bailout for American banks and a device for deepening the Developing World's dependence on banks, prevented the

IMF from making a major contribution. Furthermore, the IMF rejected a proposal for a joint operation with the World Bank to have been called the Debt Adjustment Facility. The Facility's role was to have been to serve as a body for purchasing Developing World debt at discount prices and contributing the savings to the debtor. This is similar to a collection agency that pays an unpaid creditor a fraction of the debt's value, then attempts to collect whatever it can from the debtor. The difference is that while the collector in such a scheme keeps any profit, in the case of the Debt Reduction Facility the difference would have been subtracted from the debt owed. The World Bank did, however, create a Multilateral Investment Guarantee Agency, which guarantees private investors against certain types of losses. The purpose of this mechanism is to discourage private investors from exiting the Developing World credit business.

The second approach is that of the private banks themselves. Convinced by 1987 that some Developing World debt would never be paid, some began the process of preparing for large losses by establishing set-aside programs. These are programs in which profits are placed in reserve (rather than paid out to stockholders or used for other investments) to be used to balance defaults in the future. In the first such moves Citicorp, Bank of America, J. P. Morgan, and Manufacturers Hanover moved simultaneously to create this protection using $4.6 billion. Later in the year, Citicorp added $3 billion to its set-aside account, and the Bank of Boston began its own program with $200 million.

The third major approach, one that is American rather than multilateral, is the Brady Plan (named for its author, Treasury Secretary Nicholas Brady). Unlike its predecessor, the Baker Plan (named for former Treasury Secretary and later Secretary of State James Baker), the Brady Plan assumes that most Developing World debt will never be repaid at full value. The other central features are these:

1. Although all thirty-nine Developing World debtors that have previously resorted to rescheduling are eligible to participate, its main target is the six or eight principal debtors to banks.

2. It addresses not the entire external indebtedness of these countries, but only that portion that is owed to banks.

3. To be eligible to participate, a debtor must show substantial progress toward economic reform, a standard often used by the World Bank as well. The plan calls on the IMF and the World Bank to supervise economic reform.

4. Because it is assumed that most Developing World debt will never be repaid at full value, the plan is based on a discount, or secondary market, principle. Table 13–10 shows the U.S. bank-related indebtedness of the seven original targets of the Brady Plan in 1989, listing their debt to American banks at full value and at discount market value. The final column identifies the discount value as a percentage of the full value.

Although the Brady Plan has limitations (for example, it addresses only part of the debt; and it is concerned only with American banks), it was heralded as a progressive partial solution of the Developing World crisis. It provides incentives for banks to liquidate debt at discount prices without suffering stock market value, and it encourages the Developing World governments to practice sound fiscal policies, seek noninflationary market adjustments, and provide incentive for capital to remain at home rather than to seek larger profits abroad. It "denationalizes" criteria for sound economic practices by having the IMF and the World Bank provide the criteria and supervision. It attempts to secure investment guarantees from the World Bank and the IMF. And it hopes to lure Japanese capital into the general problem of Developing World debt relief. Because debt reduction was in occasional practice prior to announcement of the Brady Plan, it is not original to the plan. But as a comprehensive package, the Brady Plan is seen as a new and

TABLE 13-10

MID-1989 MARKET VALUE REDUCTION APPROACH TO DEVELOPING WORLD INDEBTEDNESS TO AMERICAN BANKS (BRADY PLAN)

Country	Debt	Market Value	Market Price (% of face value)
Bolivia	$ .9 billion	$ .1 billion	10%
Chile	11.2	6.6	61
Costa Rica	1.5	.2	14
Ecuador	5.5	.8	14
Mexico	63.8	24.1	38
Philippines	10.5	4.8	46
Venezuela	22.6	8.2	37
Total	116.0	44.8	39

Source: World Bank Debt Tables as adapted from Jeffrey Sachs, "Making the Brady Plan Work," *Foreign Affairs*, summer 1989, pp. 87–104 at p. 91.

promising device for bringing debt, at least to the private sector, into line.[9]

The Developing World's debt has been a major feature of the international political economy for four decades, but the serious pursuit of progressive solutions has been with us for only about one. Among the most important economic phenomena of the last decade has been realization in public policy—not merely in individual minds—that the magnitude of debt is such that repayment is almost certainly out of the question. The trick, of course, is to reduce debt burden in the Developing World without transferring it to taxpayers and institutional creditors, whether public or private. Despite recent efforts at easing the burden, Developing World debt remains "a long-term economic and political barrier to development that is slowly strangling world economic growth."[10] This fact poses itself as one of the foremost challenges to the New World Order.

The Post-Soviet Transitional Economies

During the Cold War era, COMECON (Council for Mutual Economic Assistance, also called CMEA), the economic integrating instrument of the Soviet sphere, consisted of the Soviet Union and its East European allies. Despite their different stages of development, all had communist governments and socialist economies. And while some, especially the Soviet Union, Poland, Czechoslovakia, East Germany, and Hungary, conducted modest extra-bloc trade, their trade was essentially among the members. With the change in the political geography of the region, there is profound economic change as well. Whereas Russia was bound with fourteen other Soviet Socialist Republics into the USSR, today Moscow's concern is to achieve voluntary economic and security integration through the Commonwealth of Independent States (CIS) with the fourteen post-Soviet states that it calls "the near abroad," though there is little expectation that the Baltic states (Estonia, Latvia, and Lithuania) will participate. And in place of the generally pliant East European allies, there is no longer an East Germany, as the two sectors have reunited as a single member of both NATO and the EU; Czechoslovakia has divided politically—though not economically—into the Czech Republic and Slovakia; and Yugoslavia has been torn by civil war into five parts.

---

[9] For a partial text of the Brady speech that outlined the plan, see *The New York Times*, March 11, 1989, p. A37. The summary here leans heavily on Jeffrey Sachs, "Making the Brady Plan Work," *Foreign Affairs*, summer 1989, pp. 87–104. For a view that sees the Brady plan as little more than an American refinement of practices already well established, see Benjamin J. Cohen, "A Global Chapter 11," *Foreign Policy*, summer 1989, pp. 109–127. Cohen calls for a more radical approach to debt reduction along the lines of Chapter 11, the American bankruptcy code.

[10] Christine A. Bogdanowicz-Bindert, "World Debt: The United States Reconsiders," *Foreign Affairs*, winter 1985–86, pp. 259–273 at p. 259.

TABLE 13-11

GROWTH RATES OF THE TRANSITIONAL ECONOMIES

	1991	1992	1993	1994	1995
CIS including Russia		(8.0%)	(18.3%)	(12.0%)	(16.3%)	(11.5%)
Eastern Europe	(11.3)	(4.7)	1.0	8.0	5.0
Baltic States		(31.6)	(14.4)	1.9	2.8

Figures for 1994 are preliminary, and for 1995, projections.

Source: United Nations, *World Economic and Social Survey, 1995,* p. 300.

From an economic perspective, virtually all of the newly independent nations and the former allies have embarked upon transition from socialist to market-driven economies.

The trauma has been considerable for all of them. High inflation and unemployment, severe environmental degradation, deteriorating production plants, lack of noncommunist management experience and training, and total inexperience with price structures based on market value rather than government control—these and dozens of other factors have combined to make the transition very difficult, though not uniformly so. Perhaps because of their long Westward orientation and their pre–World War Two industrial histories, Poland, Hungary, and the Czech successors have fared best. Table 13–11 shows the trend in GDP from 1991 through 1995. For a review of CIS and East European external debt, see Table 12–11 in the preceding chapter.

Unlike the Developing World, however, the transitional economies have controlled their external debt relative to GNP and exports, and their debt service obligations relative to exports. Table 13–12 demonstrates these features of their recovery. There are other facts pertaining to Poland, one of the countries in which the debt problem was so severe that it signaled the crisis in the early 1980s. In 1987, Poland ranked sixth among the top debtors globally. Since then, its debt has risen by only $2 billion, and the ratio of debt service to exports has

TABLE 13-12

EXTERNAL DEBT RATIOS OF THE TRANSITIONAL ECONOMIES, 1993

Country	Total Debt	Debt as % GNP	Debt as % Exp.	Debt Service as % Exports
Russia	$81.3 billion	25%	162%	5%
Ukraine	3.6	3	22	1
Belarus	1.0	3	35	<1
Georgia	0.6	16	113	3
Poland	45.3	50	229	9
Hungary	24.8	67	213	39
Bulgaria	12.3	119	231	9
Czech Rep.	8.7	27	46	7
Romania	4.5	16	74	6
Slovak Rep.	3.3	29	42	8

The others are either not reported by this data source or insignificant for the purpose here.

Source: World Bank, *World Development Report, 1995,* tables 20 and 23.

dropped by half and its world rank as a debtor has declined to ninth.[11]

The United States as a Debtor Nation

When World War One broke out in Europe in 1914, American investors gradually provided the financial wherewithal for France and Britain to carry on the fight, even during the official period of American neutrality (1914 until the American intervention in 1917). Indeed, some have argued that the United States might not have been drawn into war had it not needed to rescue those investments. Be that as it may, from that time forward the

---

[11] For an early assessment of the transitional economies by the U.S. government, see John P. Hardt and Richard F. Kaufman, eds., *East-Central European Economies in Transition* (Armonk, N.Y.: M. E. Sharpe, 1995), prepared for the Joint Economic Committee of the Congress of the United States.

United States was continuously a creditor nation, providing capital, both public and private, for the peacetime and the wartime sustenance of other countries. The Lend-Lease Program through which Washington armed the wartime allies, including the Soviet Union, throughout World War Two, and the Marshall Plan that financed Western Europe's post-war recovery are major examples of massive public efforts to provide capital for the maintenance and survival of strong market economies abroad. The history of private capital parallels that of the use of public revenue for these purposes.

In 1986, however, this historical continuity came to an end amid extraordinary circumstances. On the one hand, despite a conscious policy of lowering the dollar's value to improve the trade deficit, the stock market rose to one record level after another. While personal wealth was being amassed through portfolio investment, the nation was growing poorer. Moreover, the attraction of the stock market drew unprecedented amounts of foreign private capital out of other countries while, simultaneously, the U.S. government sought to balance its books by selling public securities in huge amounts, thus doubling the national debt in six short years. By the end of 1986, the net capital position of the United States in the combined public and private sectors had been reversed; and for the first time in seventy-two years, the United States had become a debtor nation. Depending on one's political perspective, either because of or despite both domestic fiscal policy and international monetary policy, the United States had fallen to a position in which its debt was, for the first time, being financed by foreign interests.

Many of the trends continued into the 1990s. The domestic gap between rich and poor widened just as it did in the international arena. The Dow Jones average climbed relentlessly through both the 4000 and 5000 marks in 1995. Bank and telecommunications mergers were announced weekly in astronomical figures—billions where they used to be millions. But layoffs struck every industry and at every level of employment. AT&T offered

retirement incentives to 78,000 people in 1995 in expectation of either retiring or laying off more than 20,000. Wage increases stopped their upward climb, and tens of millions of people were employed in capacities far below their abilities. College graduates found barriers where once there were open doors, and it became conventional wisdom that graduates of the 1990s would be the first in American history to have a standard of living lower than that of their parents. For the first time, the interconnection between the global economy and the standard of living of Americans at home became a matter of outspoken public concern.

The trend toward American indebtedness is measured by a combination of interrelated economic performances:

1. The annual domestic budgetary deficit and resulting cumulative national debt, only of indirect concern here (as pertains to currency value, productivity, etc.).
2. Annual balance of trade, studied in detail in the preceding chapter.
3. Accumulation and depletion of financial reserves related to the annual balance of payments, discussed in the preceding pages.
4. Net investment position, or the inward and outward capital flows generated by American direct and portfolio investments abroad and foreign investment in the United States. Foreign ownership of American production and annual capital outflows related to payment of interest and dividends on debt are secondary concerns in this balance.
5. Foreign purchase of U.S. government securities, a measure of national dependence on international "subsidies," an indicator of long-term financial obligation and interest payment.

The reversal of the net investment position is a new phenomenon. In 1981, the balance between

---

[12] U.S. Department of Commerce, *Survey of Current Business*, carries a full annual assessment of the net U.S. investment position in its June and August issues.

American investments abroad and foreign investment within the United States reached its peak, and only six years later it had become a deficit. Since 1987, foreign interests have been investing more in the United States than have American investors in other countries, even though the overseas assets of Americans continue to grow.[12] All this is summarized in Table 13–13. But to understand this, we need to see how direct investment and portfolio investment, both entering and leaving the U.S., result in the nation's deficit position.

Direct Investment. For decades Americans have been investing abroad in manufacturing, mining and drilling, and agriculture. During the 1960s, as European economic integration gained steam, American manufacturers were especially eager "to get behind the tariff barriers" by establishing European affiliates so as to sell in Europe without having to pay import duties that would make their goods uncompetitive. The huge capital outflow that resulted was regarded as an economic crisis in the United States, and a program of voluntary restraint was followed by mandatory limits on the export of capital. But as the multinational corporation

became the main engine of manufacturing productivity, capital began to pour out once again.

This kind of capital outflow is a two-edged sword. On the one hand, it advances the American status as a creditor nation and it brings back a steady flow of capital from earnings. But on the other hand, as we have seen, it contributes negatively to the national balance of payments; and unless it is made up by positive influences elsewhere in the national accounts system, it has to be made up at year's end by depleting reserves. (In the actual case of the United States in the 1960s, the cost was a reduction of the national gold supply from 442 million Troy ounces to 262 million, about 41 percent. At the official rate of $35 per ounce, this is $6.3 billion. At a current market rate of around $400 per ounce, it would be more in the vicinity of $65 billion.) The chronic deficit in merchandise trade strains the current account, though trade in services and income from foreign investments provide some improvement. The answer, then, is in the capital account by encouraging a capital inflow.

Table 13–14 shows the balance of American direct investment abroad against foreign direct investment in the United States. It tells us that while both continue to climb, foreign direct investment in the United States is growing at a faster rate, thus

TABLE 13–13

NET INVESTMENT POSITION OF THE UNITED STATES

Year	U.S. Assets Abroad	Foreign Assets in U.S.	Balance
1980	$936.3 billion	$543.7 billion	$392.5 billion
1985	1,304.0	1,171.1	132.8
1987	1,637.1	1,648.2	(11.1)
1988	1,784.1	1,918.6	(134.5)
1989	1,979.3	2,229.7	(250.3)
1990	2,066.4	2,317.5	(251.1)
1991	2,131.7	2,486.8	(355.1)
1992	2,142.2	2,657.9	(515.7)
1993	2,393.6	2,938.9	(545.3)
1994	2,477.7	3,158.6	(680.8)

Source: U.S. Department of Commerce, *Survey of Current Business*, June 1995, p. 60.

TABLE 13–14

CAPITAL FLOW RESULTING FROM U.S. NET DIRECT INVESTMENT POSITION

Year	U.S. Direct Investment Abroad	Foreign Direct Investment in U.S.	Balance
1980	$396.2 billion	$125.9 billion	($270.3 billion)
1985	387.2	231.3	(155.9)
1987	493.3	313.5	(179.8)
1988	515.7	374.3	(141.4)
1989	560.0	436.6	(123.4)
1990	622.7	468.2	(154.5)
1991	655.3	487.2	(168.1)
1992	666.3	492.3	(174.0)

Source: Statistical Abstract of the United States, 1994, p. 807.

narrowing the gap and offsetting more and more of the capital outflow, which in 1992 was almost $100 billion less than it had been twelve years earlier.

Direct foreign investment in the United States takes many forms. Honda Accords, Toyota Avalons, and some Mazda models are all manufactured in the United States. Real estate, including Manhattan's Rockefeller Center, is a favorite target as are agribusiness, resort complexes, restaurants, and athletic facilities.

Portfolio Investment   Portfolio investment (Table 13–15) presents a much more dramatic picture. Here we see that in the same twelve-year interval, international trade in investments went from a virtual balance to a surfeit of foreign investment in the United States of almost $300 billion. In this category, then, the United States is a debtor rather than a lender but, at the same time, the greater inflow than outflow of capital has a positive impact on the national account too. Stated the other way around, the capital account has come to the rescue of the current account to create a payments balance despite a huge and chronic balance-of-trade deficit, but at the cost of making the United States a net debtor nation.

Foreign Purchase of U.S. Government Securities   This is the third debtor problem in the area of capital flow. It has become virtually habitual for the United States to operate on a budget richer than the government's revenues, and so public securities are routinely auctioned. When this practice began after World War Two, Americans bought most of these securities. But as the domestic market neared saturation and the net capital position of the United States began to decline, interest grew in attracting overseas capital. Because the trade surpluses of Japan, Germany, and other countries were creating considerable capital wealth, there was plenty of money to attract provided it could be pried away. The device for this was setting interests rates higher than they were in the capital-rich places. If Japanese fixed-rate securities were selling at 4 percent interest, offering 25 percent better—a 5 percent rate—on a billion-dollar investment by a wealthy Japanese bank would be ample inducement. The result appears in Table 13–16. Five-eights of a trillion dollars in U.S. government securities were held in 1993 by foreign interests, more than half of it by other governments and the balance by private financial institutions.

TABLE 13–15

CAPITAL FLOW RESULTING FROM U.S. NET PORTFOLIO INVESTMENT POSITION

Year	U.S. Investment Abroad	Foreign Investment in the U.S.	Balance
1980	$62.5 billion	$74.1 billion	$11.6 billion
1985	112.8	207.9	95.1
1987	153.7	341.7	188.0
1988	176.6	392.3	215.7
1990	229.3	469.0	239.7
1991	294.2	556.3	262.1
1992	327.4	617.3	289.9

Source: Statistical Abstract of the United States, 1994, p. 807.

TABLE 13–16

U.S. GOVERNMENT SECURITIES HELD BY EXTERNAL INTERESTS

Year	Held by Other Governments	Privately Held	Total
1985	$138.4 billion	$88.0 billion	$222.4 billion
1986	173.3	96.1	269.4
1987	213.7	82.6	296.3
1988	253.0	100.9	353.9
1989	257.3	166.5	423.8
1990	287.9	162.4	450.3
1991	307.1	189.5	496.6
1992	323.0	224.9	547.9
1993	370.9	254.1	625.0

Source: Economic Report of the President, 1995, p. 393.

As is the case with both direct and portfolio investment, the consequences are mixed. On the beneficial side, these sales help finance the budget deficit and the cumulative national debt, and they figure positively in the payments balance as capital inflow. But on the negative side, they obligate the U.S. government to interest payments and they must someday be paid off, both of which represent capital outflows. In principle they violate the rule that one should not borrow to cover debt, because the long-term problem is compounded thereby. They are also a sign of severe dependency: The U.S. government cannot operate without foreign "subsidy." Hence this dependency not only contributes to the debtor status of the United States; it mortgages a measure of national solvency indiscriminantly to the highest bidder.

We have now examined all of the international aspects of the American debtor status. One observer concludes that American economic policies

> have contributed not only to our economy's interdependence with the rest of the world, which is perfectly healthy, but to its dependence on outsiders, which is not. The necessity to finance part of the U.S. budget deficit with foreign capital; the necessity, over the last two years, for foreign central banks to acquire more than $150 billion to support our currency; our trade deficit and growing foreign debt; the steep increase in domestic assets sold abroad to finance our deficits—all of these factors, and more, have created a dependence on the policies of other sovereign governments and private interests that affect every U.S. domestic issue.[13]

Conclusion

Even though we think of the international system principally in political terms, much that fuels global politics is economic in nature, especially as new imperatives supersede the geopolitical preoccupations of the Cold War era. Trade, exchange, currency values, international investment, payments balances, surpluses and deficits, competition, economic development, barriers to trade, protectionism—all these lie prominently beneath the surface of political rhetoric daily. One can even go so far as to argue that the Cold War might not have occurred had it not been for the determination of two very different economic systems, capitalism and socialism, to rid the world of one another. Although surely not every international event is economic, there is scarcely one that has neither economic content nor economic consequence.

It is for this reason that this section is entitled "The Logic of the International Political Economy" rather than simply the "International Economy." The purpose is less to convey volumes of economic data than to clarify the inseparability of the economic from the political in international relations, especially in the New World Order.

Until recently, the only two isolated events that changed the course of the international political economy in this century were the Bolshevik Revolution and Soviet Marxism-Leninism in 1917, and the Keynesian adjustments to capitalist economics after the financial crash of 1929. Today, however, the rush of economic events is spellbinding. Among them, the most notable are (1) the inadequacies of economic development and the debt problem of the Developing World; (2) the evolution of the United States into a precarious economic condition as the world's largest debtor after years of having been the mainstay of global economic stability; (3) the political collapse of communism in Eastern Europe with all the unknown consequences for international economics; (4) the gradual development of free enterprise alongside planned socialism in China; and (5) the approach of complete economic integration within the European Union in this decade. The late 1990s promise to students of the international political economy a laboratory of unprecedented excitement, and to the New World Order problems that nothing as simple as Cold War arms races will be able to resolve.

---

[13] Felix Rohatyn, "America's Economic Dependence," *Foreign Affairs, America and the World* 1988–89 issue, pp. 53–65 at pp. 54–55.

CHAPTER 14

International Law

As the preceding section has stressed, certain economic mechanisms accompany day-to-day international transactions. These are intended to adjust the relations among states as they compete for natural resources, markets, development opportunities, and national enrichment. These adjustments contribute to the pacification of international practice and do their part to promote order in a global political system that, in their absence, would succumb to self-assertion and disruption for national purposes.

But other relations among nation-states are not subject to such mechanisms. Adjustments of payment balances have little bearing on the ability of the nuclear powers to destroy the planet; and currency revaluations, although helpful in stabilizing relations, offer little toward offsetting nuclear arms races, aggressive intervention, or border clashes. Specifically, because power is a relative concept (power with respect to what?), some international actors will always be able to threaten others with coercion, enslavement, or destruction. Whenever states are unwilling to exercise self-restraint (or autolimitation), there are but two alternatives for ensuring international stability: holding other states hostage to the threat of superior force, or submitting to collective means for making international decisions and enforcing compliance. This chapter deals with the second of these alternatives by exploring one specific method that, for over three centuries, has been practiced by governments with differing amounts of enthusiasm and varying degrees of performance: international law. The succeeding chapters continue that examination by looking at other practical methods: international organization, international integration, and transnational participation. How do legal and organizational processes in the international system promote a more stable world order?

The Nature of International Law

Well-ordered domestic societies have complex legal systems with specific organs for making, adjudicating, and enforcing laws. The state has the authority to call individuals to account for their behavior relative to the law. Laws are made on their behalf; they can be summoned to court against their will. Legal regulations are enforced whether or not an individual likes them.

The international system is not so well ordered. Because only the nation-state is sovereign, it is not subject to the decisions of external institutions in the way citizens are to the institutions of their societies. No legislative body exists above the state, no international court has the capacity to compel behavior, and there are few organs to execute international regulations. If a parallel between the domestic legal system and the legal attributes of the international system is lacking, just what is international law?

No student need feel alone in skepticism about the existence or the nature of international law. It is a matter that scholars and governments have been debating for centuries. The debate among scholars is in the realm of jurisprudence (science of law), within which countless interpretations have been offered. It will be useful to look into two theoretical interpretations that differ vastly: positivism and neorealism.

Positivism

Positivist theory is based on an analogy between domestic law, with its rules and institutions, and the international setting. It understands the law to be a system of rules (norms) that specify the rights and obligations governing the external behavior of states. Positivist theory holds law to have a consensual basis—that is, states become subject to rules only by voluntary consent. These two concepts are summarized in an opinion of the Permanent Court of International Justice, to which France and Turkey voluntarily submitted the Lotus case for decision in 1927.

> International law governs relations between independent States. *The rules of law binding upon States therefore emanate from their own free will* as expressed in conventions [treaties] or by usages generally accepted as expressing principles of law and established in order to regulate the relations between these co-existing independent communities or with a view to the achievement of common aims. *Restrictions upon the independence of States cannot therefore be presumed.*[1]

The progressive development of an international legal order depends, accordingly, on convincing governments that their relations are best protected by mutually arranged norms with which they will comply consistently and voluntarily.

---

[1] PCIJ Series A, no. 10. The emphasis has been added to illuminate the twin positivist principles of rule orientation and consent.

Neorealism

At the other end of the theoretical spectrum is the neorealist school. It denies that rules are at the center of a legal order and argues instead that policy and values are the foci. Hence this theory is said to be policy oriented and value oriented. Because international relations are in constant change, regulatory law must be a process of decision making in which all states and international agencies participate, with the content of the law changing at every moment. Because there are no fixed rules, international law is "a constitutive process of authoritative decision." The law is what the policies of the contributors make it, and it is imposed on the world by power of the actors in accordance with the values they wish the law to promote and defend. When major actors dispute the outcomes of the constitutive process or when they disagree on the values to be promoted, then international law is identified with the foreign policy of that state whose value objectives most nearly approximate the pursuit of human dignity. This highly subjective standard is a product of the Cold War.[2]

The political uses to which these two theories can be put by governments are as different as are the doctrines themselves. If a government accepts the positivist definition, it will presumably regulate its behavior by existing treaties and other agreements, and it will expect other governments to regulate their actions by formal norms as well. In this way governments will be able to predict one another's actions and will have solid ground on which to question one another's motives. Compliance or

---

[2] For statements of the neorealist theory, see Harold D. Lasswell and Myres S. McDougal, "Jurisprudence in Policy-oriented Perspective," *Florida Law Journal*, vol. 19, 1967, pp. 486–513; Myres S. McDougal, "The Comparative Study of Law for Policy Purposes: Value Clarification as an Instrument of Democratic World Order," *Yale Law Journal*, vol. 61, 1952, pp. 915–946; Myres S. McDougal, "International Law, Power and Policy," *Recueil des Cours*, vol. 82 (The Hague: Academy of International Law, 1953), pp. 133–259; Harold D. Lasswell, Myres S. McDougal, and W. Michael Reisman, "The World Constitutive Process of Authoritative Decision," *Journal of Legal Education*, vol. 19, 1967, pp. 253–300 and 403–437, in two parts.

noncompliance with formal agreements communicates the intentions of governments.

If, however, a government prefers the neorealist interpretation of international law, it will shun the reliability of formal agreements and justify its behavior on the claim that its value objectives are superior to those of its adversary, that its foreign policies more nearly approximate the goals of human dignity. In this way, declarations of foreign policy become international law. One neorealist author, for example, argues that the Truman Doctrine "has gradually evolved . . . into a kind of common law of international order, a prudent rule of reciprocal safety."[3] The doctrine was announced in 1947 as a unilateral policy of the United States for restraining the growth of international communism. It was an instrument of containment undertaken by the United States against the Soviet Union. The neorealist sees it otherwise.

No government accepts either view of the law exclusively. In fact, for most powerful states, the choice of legal interpretations depends on the facts at hand. A safe rule of thumb emerges: Governments will seek to maximize their rights (neorealist interpretation) and minimize their obligations (positivism), but they will attempt to minimize their adversaries' rights (positivism) and maximize their adversaries' obligations (neorealism). When governments have genuine concerns for legal interaction, they will speak as positivists; but when they have politicized concerns for the law, they will come forth as neorealists.

The Sources of International Law

Think again about the analogy of international law to domestic law. Rules arise from constitutions, formal legislation, custom, and court decisions. Such institutionalization exists in the international system

to a far less authoritative degree. From where, then, do the norms of international law come?

The authoritative statement of the sources of international law is found in Article 38 of the Statute of the International Court of Justice, the permanent judicial organ of the United Nations. The statute lists the sources as (1) international conventions (treaties) in force between parties, (2) international customary rules, (3) general principles of international law, and (4) such subsidiary sources as prior judicial decisions and the writings of the highly qualified publicists.

Treaties, bilateral and multilateral, are the most logical primary source. Whether a convention be one of codification (formalizing into written agreement practices already accepted through custom) or of a legislative character (creating new rights and obligations), it represents the maximum explicit consent of the signatories. Much of the business of early-twentieth-century intergovernmental organizations was the codification of existing principles and customs. Only in the last half-century has the bulk of legislative international law been added to treaty law.

Custom, until recently the largest component of positive law, is the practice of states. It is generally held that usage becomes an international legal norm when it has been repeated over a period of time by several states, when they have generally acquiesced in such behavior by one another, and when governments begin to act in certain ways out of a sense of legal obligation. In this manner, most of the international laws of the high seas originated, as did the laws of diplomatic and consular privileges and immunities, and the rules governing neutrality and international commerce, to mention only a few.

General principles of international law are less clearly defined, partly because it is difficult to demonstrate widespread acceptance and partly because the distinction between a firm principle and a customary rule is obscure. Nevertheless, there are general principles that can be readily identified. Many of the amenities of international relations are general principles that arise out of the theory of

---

[3] Eugene V. Rostow, *Law, Power, and the Pursuit of Peace* (Lincoln: University of Nebraska Press, 1968), p. 43. (Also published in a paperback edition by Praeger.)

sovereignty. Other general principles emerge from the necessity for sovereign equality, including the principle of legal equality and the expectation of fair treatment of one another's nationals.

Subsidiary sources are still less specific and merit last place among the sources of international law. In judicial tests of legal rules, the rules themselves must undergo interpretation. The business of courts is to interpret the law and apply it. In international adjudication, rules may be interpreted by national courts, standing international tribunals, panels established to deal with specific problems, or international courts, among them the International Court of Justice (ICJ). In most national systems, courts are bound by the rule of stare decisis, meaning that what the court has previously decided is the law and is precedent binding on courts. International tribunals generally subscribe to the same principle, and the decisions of such courts contain references to former cases, just as the decisions of American courts do in domestic cases. The ICJ, however, while using its prior decisions and those of other courts, is not bound so firmly by precedent. Unlike other tribunals, the ICJ may interpret the legal significance of declarations and resolutions of the political organs of the United Nations. This is especially the case in its advisory jurisdiction, which enables the ICJ, upon request from the UN organs, to render constitutional interpretations that may have political effects on member states.

Viewed from a big-power standpoint, the most significant example of this action was embodied in the advisory opinion *Certain Expenses of the United Nations* (1962).[4] Because the Soviet Union and other governments had refused to pay their apportioned shares of financing UN peacekeeping operations in the Middle East and the Congo, the General Assembly requested clarification of its authority under the charter to bill members for such expenses against their will. The court dealt with the legitimacy of the operations themselves, rendering a constitutional interpretation on the limits of UN authority. It favored an expansive

view. Out of this controversial decision an argument has arisen that the charter contains implied powers of UN organs over and above the explicit ones.[5] The contrary view holds that the most effective contribution the ICJ might make to the progressive development of international law is through the cautious use of advisory jurisdiction—that the court might thus earn the trust of states, which might then be more willing to submit to it their bilateral disputes.[6] Time and practice will determine which of these views is the more nearly accurate. For the time being, however, the *Expenses* case reveals the potential political impact of international judicial activity.

The Sanctions of International Law

How is international law enforced without international government or police? Merely to posit the existence of international law is not to prove the international system capable of legal regulation. We must demonstrate the extent of states' willingness to comply with legal norms. What, then, is the compelling force of international law, and by what mechanisms is it presumably enforced? Is international law "law, properly so called," or is it merely "positive international morality" that lacks the enforceability necessary to make it law?[7]

---

[4] International Court of Justice, advisory opinion of July 20, 1962, found in *ICJ Reports*, 1962, pp. 151–180.

[5] Rahmattullah Khan, *Implied Powers of the United Nations* (Bombay: Vikas Publications, 1970). For a demonstration of use of implied powers by the secretary-general, see Hugo Caminus and Roberto Lavelle, "New Departures in the Exercise of Inherent Powers by the UN and OAS Secretaries-General: The Central American Situation," *American Journal of International Law*, April 1989, pp. 395–402.

[6] Leo Gross, "The International Court of Justice and the United Nations," *Recueil des Cours*, vol. 120 (The Hague: Academy of International Law, 1967), pp. 313–330.

[7] This is the classic distinction made by the English positivist John Austin. For other expressions and discussions of the argument, see particularly Westel W. Willoughby, *Fundamental Concepts of Public Law* (New York: Macmillan, 1924), pp. 224 ff., and "The Legal Nature of International Law," *American Journal of International Law*, vol. 2, 1908, pp. 357–365; and Hans Kelsen, "The Pure Theory of Law and Analytical Jurisprudence," *Harvard Law Review*, vol. 55, 1941, pp. 44–70.

Any form of law has as its incentives a variety of normative, utilitarian, and coercive sanctions. An individual may drive an automobile lawfully out of fear of penalty (coercive sanction), or as a matter of personal safety (utilitarian sanction), or as a contribution to orderly social coexistence (normative sanction). Likewise among states, compliance with rules of law is rather consistent and is grounded in normative and utilitarian motives. Governments generally do regard reciprocal behavior as mutually beneficial and often are sensitive to international pressures. They wish to avoid reprisals and embarrassing declarations and resolutions brought on by improper behavior, except when perceived needs exceed the risk of external criticism or sanction. Furthermore, states rarely enter into formal international agreements unless they intend to benefit through compliance. Nor do they acquiesce in custom over the long run without anticipating benefits. It is not at all extraordinary, then, that states should normally comply with their voluntary obligations.

Coercive sanction takes over where all else fails. Indeed, the necessity for coercion occurs only when a state departs from its normal pattern of behavior under existing rules, when a behavior pattern is devoid of legal restraint, or when a state does not participate in what other nations consider to be law. When a state is not party to agreements that contain generally applicable normative or utilitarian sanctions, its external behavior may be controllable only through the threat of coercion.

Coercive theories abound in international law. Some theorists claim that norms are not legal norms unless they are capable of coercive enforcement by some political entity juridically superior to the actor; unless international law is enforceable by some power above the sovereign state, it is not really law. Others go so far as to define law in terms of its enforceability: Only if violation of a norm elicits a coercive response can that norm be interpreted as a legal rule.[8] It is the response that defines the character of a norm, not the content. Hence law is a statement of coercibility.[9]

Among the coercive measures that states utilize are a vast array of forceful and nonforceful acts. Nonforceful acts are referred to as retorsions, which are reciprocal, punitive acts of retaliation. If one state should take steps to restrict the imports of another, the victimized state may respond by freezing the assets of the first state held in the banks of the second. In general, such acts are proportionate, so as to minimize the likelihood of escalation.

Retaliatory acts in response to forceful violations, and which would themselves be illegal except as proportional retaliations, are called reprisals. Because such acts are military in kind, it is difficult to measure and to maintain proportion. The law requires, nonetheless, that a reprisal be equivalent to the original violation. A few familiar acts of reprisal are American bombing raids of North Vietnam in response to attacks on American destroyers in the Tonkin Gulf in the summer of 1964; Israeli air strikes on guerrilla sites in Lebanon after the latter government's failure to prevent terrorist activities; American air strikes on Libya in retaliation for state-sponsored terrorism; American bombardment of Iraqi targets for violation of the Desert Storm armistice accords; and NATO bombings of Bosnian Serb military installations for persistent shelling of civilian populations in UN-declared "safe zones."

The ultimate sanction in international relations is war. War is a political instrument, not always undertaken to destroy, but to deprive the target state of the ability and will to violate international norms further. The threat of war, then, may deter states from aberrant behavior, and the use of war as a response to prior actions is punitive reprisal. But in either case, the major intention of a state undertaking responsive warfare is to force political submission.

---

[8] See Hans Kelsen, "The Pure Theory of Law and Analytical Jurisprudence," p. 58; "The Pure Theory of Law," *Law Quarterly Review*, vol. 50, 1934, pp. 474–498; and *General Theory of Law and State* (Cambridge, Mass.: Harvard University Press, 1949), pp. 51–58.

[9] The coercive theory of law is not, however, universally accepted. For major exceptions, see Gerhart Niemeyer, *Law Without Force: The Function of Politics in International Law* (Princeton, N.J.: Princeton University Press, 1941); and Michael Barkun, *Law Without Sanctions: Order in Primitive Societies and the World Community* (New Haven, Conn.: Yale University Press, 1968).

Collective Sanctions in International Law

Traditionally, responses to illegal behavior have been left to aggrieved states. Indeed, international law includes a doctrine of self-help, which permits each state to launch punitive responses to illegal or other noxious acts. Although the doctrine of self-help (a by-product of absolute sovereignty) tries to provide international politics with formal and legal means for sanction, abuses or excesses often contribute to international anarchy. Primarily for this reason, twentieth-century international organizations have striven to replace unilateral sanctions with collective sanctions. But by their very nature, international institutions have severe limitations (discussed in detail in the next chapter).

Intergovernmental organizations are political creatures. Because they are comprised of national governments, they derive their operating funds from their members; their powers and procedures are results of political compromises among the members; and every action that they take is on behalf of the members and results from the members' agreements and compromises. Governments form and join these organizations principally to improve their means of advancing their own international goals, not for limiting their policy flexibility. From the point of view of international law, therefore, international organizations are the sum of their powerful parts, with little political will of their own. When international law is made, its content reflects struggle and compromise; when it is violated, the consequence of the violation is determined by the same kind of struggle and compromise; and when it is enforced by the organization, it is enforced to the extent that the members wish collectively.

From these common observations emerge several caveats regarding the capacity of an international organization to make and enforce law.

1. Like any other bilateral or multilateral agreement, law sponsored by any intergovernmental body is the product of the participating governments.
2. In both making and enforcing law, an intergovernmental organization cannot exceed the political will of the member states.
3. Under the auspices of the organization, the member states at most will agree to enforce the law sponsored by that organization.
4. Law is not self-contained policy; every use of it is a result of a group political decision.

These observations arise not from an esoteric theory of international organization, but from the fact that all international law is based on the consent of the participating states.

When the League of Nations was established after the First World War, an effort was made to create machinery for collective sanctions in the sole instance of a government's decision to undertake war. Chapter XI of the League's Covenant inscribed the principle that "any war or threat of war . . . is hereby declared a matter of concern to the whole League." This concern was to be activated by the decision of the Council—meaning, of course, the member states of the Council—to act under Article 16:

> Should any Member of the League resort to war . . . it shall *ipso facto* be deemed to have committed an act of war against all other Members of the League, which hereby undertake immediately to subject it to the severance of all trade or financial relations, the prohibition of all intercourse between the nationals of the Covenant-breaking State and the State, and the prevention of all financial, commercial or personal intercourse between the nationals of the Covenant-breaking State and the nationals of any other State, whether a Member of the League or not.

The covenant further authorized the council to recommend to states what military forces they should contribute for the implementation of Article 16.

These principles of the League of Nations were greatly expanded in the Charter of the United Nations. Chapter VII of the charter, entitled "Action with Respect to Threats to the Peace, Breaches of the Peace, and Acts of Aggression," authorizes the Security Council to determine the existence of a threat to international stability and to recommend either peaceful measures for its resolution or coercive acts short of force. Ultimately, however, Article 42 authorizes the Security Council to call on states to use armed force on behalf of the organization:

> Should the Security Council consider that measures provided for in Article 41 would be inadequate or have proved inadequate, it may take such action by air, sea, or land forces as may be necessary to maintain or restore international peace and security. Such action may include demonstrations, blockade, and other operations by air, sea, or land forces of Members of the United Nations.

This principle of all against one—the entire world against the aggressor—is termed collective security. This differs both from self-help, which is a doctrine of unilateral action, and from collective self-defense, which is an alliance arrangement by which a group of geographically or ideologically cohesive states agree that an attack on one shall be considered an attack on all.

Because the United Nations is not a government and must depend on separate nation-states for military forces, much of Chapter VII is devoted to the means by which such forces are to be placed at the disposal of the Security Council. Fifty years after its founding, however, the organization is still reliant on the political limitations of Article 48, which provides that "the action required to carry out the decisions of the Security Council for the maintenance of international peace and security shall be taken by all the Members of the United Nations or by some of them, as the Security Council may determine." Note that in empowering states, it may empower groups of states. Nonetheless, by exercise of the veto power, any one of the five permanent members of the Security Council can prevent others from answering the call or can guarantee itself against a retaliatory obligation. (For precisely these purposes the United States, the Soviet Union, Britain, France, and China, as permanent members of the council, insisted from the outset that on matters related to peace and security, council decisions would require a majority vote of the council, "including the concurring votes of the permanent members." This passage, which appears in Article 27 of the charter, constitutes the so-called great-power or permanent-member veto.)

For fully nine-tenths of its life the United Nations was paralyzed in its efforts to use its sanctioning authority effectively. The Cold War, dominated by the incompatible global objectives of the United States and the Soviet Union, made the veto a familiar diplomatic instrument, each side thwarting the goals of the other. Matters were further complicated by the change in China's representation from Taiwan to Beijing in 1971, bringing to the forum a third potential military giant, alienated from both Washington and Moscow. Some would argue that the Korean War, often referred to as a United Nations police action (partly because the U.S. Congress never declared war), was the exception to the UN's failure, but this is not technically accurate. In the early days of North Korea's aggression (1950), the Soviet delegate to the council was absent in a protest boycott over the organization's refusal to seat a delegate from Beijing after communist forces had sent the nationalist government into retreat to Taiwan. Upon his return, the United States moved its diplomatic offensive to the General Assembly, where the powerful Western majority shielded it from Soviet interference. Hence despite the early Security Council resolutions adopted in the absence of Soviet influence, the Korean War was not conducted pursuant to the authority of Chapter VII.

These circumstances persuaded many scholars that Chapter VII of the charter ought not to be listed prominently among multilateral sanctioning devices. As late as 1988 one observer dismissed the council's authority as "paper enforcement powers." He concluded that the charter "appears to confer upon the Security Council substantial power to issue commands in matters relating to international peace and security, but the power has seldom been used and in practice has not been very significant."[10] But by the time the crucial test of Iraq's invasion of Kuwait arose in 1990, the New World Order was in its infancy. The Cold War obstacles to effective multilateral sanctions had gone the way of the Soviet empire in Eastern Europe, the Soviet-American nuclear arms race, and many communist governments. The dissolution of the Soviet Union was, in fact, imminent. In a convergence of political wills anticipated by the framers of the charter as part of the grand design, but obstructed by forty-five years of Cold War, the Security Council was able to act with the concurring votes of the five permanent members, first to impose an economic embargo on Iraq and then, with explicit reference to Chapter VII, to authorize member states "to use all necessary means . . . to restore international peace and security" in the war zone, to liberate Kuwait, and to force Iraq to surrender. Without question this time, the war called Operation Desert Storm was a full implementation of the Security Council's powers under Chapter VII, with twenty-seven member states contributing armed forces under a single command to carry out the sanctions adopted by the council.[11]

After Desert Storm, the council exercised its authority in a variety of ways in efforts to restore stability in Cambodia, Rwanda, Somalia, Haiti, and elsewhere. Actions ranged from peacekeeping to peace observation, humanitarian aid distribution, refugee transportation, civil policing, and self-defense. While variously effective, these were all situations in which domestic ethnopolitical violence was the root cause of instability. (In two other large situations, Liberia and Algeria, the council played no significant role.) The big test, however, was Bosnia, one of the former constituent republics of Yugoslavia plunged into civil war after the dissolution of the parent country. Sent originally to provide relief to Bosnian nationals and Muslim settlers subjected to the UN's own arms embargo, the UN role on the ground escalated from aid distribution to self-defense and artillery combat in defense of safe zones. Still, however, the UN role was restricted by Russia's unwillingness publicly to oppose its Serbian friends, and so real enforcement measures were undertaken by NATO in the form of aerial strikes on Serb military installations, over Russia's objections. Nonetheless, despite the limited contribution of the UN to the Bosnian War, reliance on multilateralism, up to and including Chapter VII of the charter, may be supplanting the chaotic world order of nationalistic power politics.

Enforcement measures are not the sole means of UN sanction. Indeed, skeptics of the coercive theory of international law note that forceful sanctions through the United Nations are limited to situations involving threats to the peace, breaches of the peace, and acts of aggression. In all other instances of noncompliance with international law, the charter's own general provisions outlawing the threat or use of force actually prevent forceful sanction. Those same skeptics regard this as an appropriate paradox in a decentralized state system of international politics.

Nonetheless, nonmilitary means of collective sanction through the United Nations are other multilateral alternatives, and they focus principally on economic power. In the economic sphere, the United Nations has followed in the path of the League of Nations, which undertook economic sanctions against Italy in 1935–36 for its attack on Ethiopia. In the UN period, the most celebrated economic sanctions have been those voted against China by the General Assembly in 1951 as a result of its intervention in the Korean War and the Western determination to isolate the new communist government; the 1967 decision of the Security Council to isolate Southern Rhodesia (now Zimbabwe) for its policy of racial separation following its unilateral declaration of independence from Britain;

---

[10] Robert E. Riggs, "The United Nations and the Politics of Law," in Lawrence J. Finkelstein, ed., *Politics in the United Nations System* (Durham, N.C., and London: Duke University Press, 1988), pp. 41–74, especially pp. 53 and 63.

[11] For the full text of the Security Council Resolution, see *The New York Times*, November 30, 1990, p. A10.

A Bosnian Serb in the custody of NATO peacekeeper awaiting trial as a war criminal, 1996. (*Source:* © Jerry Lampen/Bettmann)

and sanctions reaffirmed against Iraq by the Security Council for failure to comply with 1991 terms of settlement, particularly with respect to "no-fly" zones, immunity of the northern Kurds from genocidal attack, and full disclosure and inspection of chemical, biological, and nuclear warfare facilities.

Establishment of sanctions through a political process does not guarantee their universal imposition. In the Rhodesia case, for example, the United States voted with the majority in the council (otherwise it would have vetoed a major British policy goal). Yet by executive order of the president, Washington imposed restraints on imports originating in Rhodesia,

> *Provided,* however, that the prohibition against dealing in commodities or products exported from Southern Rhodesia shall not apply to any such commodities or products which, prior to the date of this Order, had been lawfully imported into the United States.[12]

---

[12] U.S. Department of State Release no. 176, July 29, 1968; in U.S. *Department of State Bulletin,* vol. 59, 1968, p. 199, and as reprinted in *American Journal of International Law,* vol. 63, 1969, pp. 128–130, in the section entitled "Contemporary Practice of the United States Relating to International Law."

The reason for this divergent exception to multilateral policy was Southern Rhodesia's chromium exports to the United States, the continued flow of which was necessary for production of steel alloys needed in, among other things, military hardware. These events illustrate that even when the most powerful governments act multilaterally, resort to decentralization of sanctions cannot be prevented fully. This is a major obstacle to reliability in the implementation of international law. For as long as multilateralism and sovereign equality coexist, states will continue to be the importers and exporters in the international system. They will command industrial economies and the passage of goods across national boundaries. Just as Stalin once remarked that the pope has no military divisions, so too does the United Nations have no troops or funds of its own, no industries to produce the coveted commodities that, if withheld, might alter states' policies. The UN has no chromium deposits to withhold from the United States! Governmental resistance to a financially independent UN arises principally from members' insistence on maintaining control over sanctioning processes in international politics.

Individual Sanctions in International Law

In the absence of a reliable system of collective sanctions, individual and group sanctions remain legitimate provided they are responses to illegal acts and remain within the rules of proportionality. Such sanctions are more often threatened than implemented, however, to the extent that the threat of sanctions is a common diplomatic device used to dissuade a government from undertaking or continuing a noxious practice. In 1995, for example, Washington threatened to impose huge increases in import duties on Japanese luxury automobiles if certain concessions were not made regarding the sale of American goods in Japan previously banned or sharply limited. An eleventh-hour settlement avoided a crisis. In fact, establishment of the World Trade Organization in 1994 as part of the Uruguay Round of worldwide trade negotiations was aimed at settling such disputes in order to reduce the frequency of sanctions.

Threatened sanctions may occasionally involve third parties. Virtually since Fidel Castro's rise to power in the late 1950s, Washington has imposed strict economic sanctions on Cuba. Despite frequent demands in the United States that they be relaxed or removed, they remained in force as the Republican party gained control of both Houses of Congress in 1994. Immediately thereafter, Senator Jesse Helms, chairman of the Senate Committee of Foreign Relations, announced that he would submit legislation forcing U.S. sanctions on all third parties that do not also embargo Cuban trade. Foremost among these would be Canada, largest trading partner of the United States and fellow member of the North American Free Trade Area (NAFTA). The legislation was acted on and signed by President Clinton in 1996 after Cuban jets downed two small American planes known to have been penetrating Cuban air space for political reasons. The president's action evoked immediate protests from Canada and the EU.

There are, of course, many instances in which unilateral sanctions are carried out. The United States, for example, imposed limited restraints on agricultural trade in light of the Soviet Union's refusal to permit Jewish citizens to emigrate during the 1970s without having paid an exorbitant "education tax," and in 1980 terminated treaty-controlled grain trade when Soviet troops invaded Afghanistan. Similarly, only Egypt and Jordan have lifted the decades-long trade embargo against Israel. In a loosely coordinated fashion, the United States, most of the states of the British Commonwealth (with Britain itself the notable exception), and many developing countries maintained sanctions against South Africa in protest of its racial separation policy (apartheid) until the policy was discontinued and former political prisoner Nelson Mandela was elected president. American sanctions

against Vietnam, dating to the end of the Vietnam War in 1974, were relaxed when relations were normalized, but not dropped until formal diplomatic recognitions were exchanged in 1995. Washington still maintains sanctions against Iran for having held dozens of American diplomatic personnel hostage for more than a year after the fall of the Shah and the ascent of the Ayatollah, a detention that violated the international law of diplomatic and consular privileges and immunities.

Some argue that the freedom of individual states to impose forceful and nonforceful sanctions is proof that power politics rules in the place of international law. This is an inaccurate view. It is fully accepted legal doctrine that until a reliable regime of multilateral sanctions is available to the world order, individual and group sanctions, when conducted according to the pertinent rules, are, in fact, international law. But the dilemma remains: For so long as sovereignty and multilateralism coexist, the tension between globally legislated and individual sanctions will prevail. Moreover, it is the goal of powerful governments to preserve that tension, thus always having available the choice to use traditional state-oriented international law when they either cannot or wish not to use system-oriented international law.

The Effectiveness of International Law

To conclude that international law provides effective restraints on states, we must demonstrate not only the existence of legal principles but also the willingness of states to comply with them. Compliance is a function of several factors, among them: (1) the subject matter that law seeks to regulate, (2) changes in the motives and needs of governments, (3) the ability of states to violate the law without serious threat of sanctions, and (4) the importance of the outcome of an issue. Each of these elements is subjected to the political judgment of the state. The decision as to whether one will be

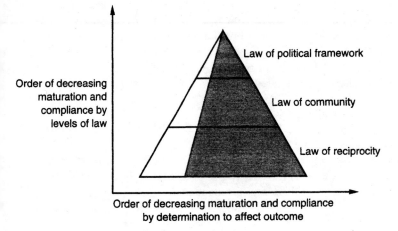

Order of decreasing maturation and compliance by levels of law

Law of political framework

Law of community

Law of reciprocity

Order of decreasing maturation and compliance by determination to affect outcome

FIGURE 14–1 Levels of compliance and political salience.

law-abiding is a decision for the state's political apparatus. A state's compliance with legal obligations is a function of (1) the degree to which issues are politicized and (2) the state's ability to behave in a lawless manner without serious threat of adverse consequences.

International law consists of norms of varying political levels (see Figure 14–1).[13] On subjects that are relatively mechanical and depoliticized, states readily recognize the utility of collective regulation. This level of law, referred to as the law of reciprocity, is a network of treaties and customs through which governments acknowledge reciprocal benefit. Compliance with these norms is predictable and consistent.

But as the subject matter of the law becomes more politicized, states are less willing to accept formal regulation or do so only with loopholes for escape from apparent constraints. In this area, called the law of community, governments are generally less willing to sacrifice their sovereign liberties. In an international system where change is rapid and direction unclear, the integrity of the law

of community is weak, and compliance with its often flaccid norms is correspondingly uncertain.

The law of the political framework resides above these other two levels and consists of the legal norms governing the ultimate power relations of states. This is the most politicized level of international relations; hence, pertinent law is extremely primitive. Those legal norms that do exist suffer from all the political machinations one might expect. States have taken care to see that their behavior is constrained only minimally. The few international legal norms they have created always provide avenues of escape such as the big-power veto in the UN Security Council.

The question of states' compliance with international law, and therefore the effectiveness and credibility of international law, has been crucial throughout interstate system history. Some theorists base effectiveness exclusively on the built-in sanctions of the law, but more modern studies tend to emphasize the behavioral aspects of political decision making related to law, such as domestic political considerations or profit-maximization strategies of foreign policy.[14] A third school finds

---

[13] Although this concept has been expressed by several legal scholars, this analysis follows most closely that of Stanley Hoffmann, "International Systems and International Law," *World Politics*, vol. 14, 1961, pp. 205–237.

[14] Oran Young, *Compliance and Public Authority* (Baltimore: Johns Hopkins University Press, 1979).

problems of compliance rooted particularly in global cultural and ideological diversity, a condition that makes it difficult to frame a cohesive world order without attempting simultaneously to bring about fundamental changes in political relations.[15] A fourth view concerns the diversity of ethical standards.[16] One scholar examined these several literatures and found no fewer than thirteen explanations of compliance and noncompliance with international law. In addition, taking for granted the problems associated with weapons technology, he summarized the political foundations of change in the global environment during the Cold War.

1. The emergence of the quasi-legislative functions (see Chapter 15) of the United Nations and other international institutions that purport to prescribe conduct without any formal legal codification

2. The evolution of informal international rules regarding apparent understandings or unilateral actions and acquiescence

3. The frequency with which social revolutions have overturned traditional order and challenged assumptions on which authority was previously based

4. Cooperation and reciprocal behavior resulting from global interdependence but not yet institutionalized in traditional forms of law

5. The increased permeability of states by technology and economic interdependence, which blurs traditional distinctions between domestic matters and those of international concern

6. Scientific and technological expansions that have led to informal means of setting standards and exercising supervision without formal legal instruments[17]

Placed in the Cold War context, others concluded from this list that the normative basis of international law was deteriorating alongside threat to world order itself.[18] But has the New World Order reversed this trend? Consider the following strategic and economic characteristics of the post–Cold War world:

1. The profound East-West ideological confrontation has abated almost entirely, though China remains a passive player in the New World Order save for its role at the Security Council.

2. Sharp reduction in both Russian and American nuclear weapons has moved the world back from the precipice of mass destruction.

3. Almost everywhere, with exceptions in North Korea, Cuba, and China, emerging market economies are supplanting strict socialism, eliminating the Cold War threats of economic isolation, encirclement, and strangulation.

4. Long-stalled negotiations within the General Agreement on Tariffs and Trade (GATT, a post–World War Two organization) have concluded with new machinery for resolving economic disputes and reducing barriers to international trade.

5. In both the economic and military realms, there is growing evidence of governmental preference for multilateral rather than nationalistic approaches to international crises.

6. Regionalism, intermediate between individualism and global multilateralism, is on the rise in Latin America, the Pacific Rim, Europe, and North America, improving cooperation and generating constitutional or quasi-constitutional bases for the progressive development of international law.

[15] George Schwarzenberger, "The Credibility of International Law," *The Year Book of World Affairs* (London), 1983, pp. 292–301.
[16] George Schwarzenberger and Stanley Hoffmann, *Duties Beyond Borders: On the Limits and Possibilities of Ethical International Politics* (Syracuse, N.Y.: Syracuse University Press, 1981).
[17] Oscar Schachter, "Towards a Theory of International Obligation," in Stephen M. Schwebel, ed., *The Effectiveness of International Decisions* (Dobbs Ferry, N.Y.: Oceana Publications, 1971), pp. 9–31. Schachter identifies the explanations of compliance as consent, customary practice, juridical conscience, natural law or natural reason, social necessity, international consensus, direct intuition, common purposes of governments, effectiveness, fear of sanctions, systemic goals, shared expectations, and rules of recognition.
[18] See, for example, Richard A. Falk, *The Year Book of World Affairs* (London), 1982, pp. 3–16.

Given these circumstances, one may conclude that the law of the political context is in a condition of political moderation, and that the prospect for its normative improvement is far greater than it was during the Cold War. This is certainly true of the strategic content, though one might argue that as economic subjects replace military subjects in defining power, there is a mere content shift in the political context rather than an absolute improvement. In making such an argument one would also have to acknowledge that the parties to the debate over context have changed too, with Japan, NAFTA, the European Union, the Pacific Rim, and the Developing Nations the major contestants while Russia, Central Europe, and China find their way. Conversely, the law of community has vastly expanded as the modified political context enables more subjects to come to the table for normative regulation. And finally, as the temperature declines in the context, as states demand less change in one another's policies and have less compulsion to command outcomes, the normative law of reciprocity has a greater oportunity to expand. Consequently, if the New World Order is itself progressive, then the opportunity arises once again to expand the normative basis of international law.

Areas of Urgency in International Law

While no list is thorough, there are a number of issues of international politics in which effective normative regulation is visibly insufficient. A few are noted here.

Prevention and Control of Aggression

No issues are more vital to the global political context than are prevention of aggression, serious disruption of important international transactions, and massive destruction and death. Once preventive measures have failed, control of territorial scope of conflict is the next most crucial issue, along with restrictions on the number and power rankings of participants and the types of weapons engaged, particularly in instances that may involve the crucial interests of the most powerful and nuclear-armed states.

In the war-peace cycles of the twentieth century, enormous effort has been invested in preventing and controlling armed conflict. The turn-of-the-century Hague Conferences attempted to freeze the European balance of power and to create institutions for arbitrating international disputes. Woodrow Wilson's Fourteen Points, a statement of principles about U.S. entry into the First World War and its post-war diplomatic objectives, set the tone for the League of Nations Covenant, presumably a global constitution for peace and prosperity. The General Pact for the Renunciation of War (also called the Kellogg-Briand Pact) and the Washington Naval Treaties, which attempted to freeze the global balance of naval power through formal ratios of different ship classes, were major preventive instruments of the interwar period. The United Nations Charter, the Washington-Moscow Hotline Agreement, the Strategic Arms Limitations Talks (SALT) agreements (the second of which was never ratified by the U.S. Senate), the Anti-Ballistic Missiles Treaty, the Intermediate-range Nuclear Forces Reduction Treaty, and the intercontinental ballistic missile reductions achieved through the Strategic Arms Reduction Talks (START) were all post-war achievements designed to reduce the threat of nuclear holocaust during the Cold War.

Obviously, however, not all armed conflict is between major powers; nor are all wars international. Indeed, one of the great fears of the Cold War era was that civil or small regional wars would threaten the interests of one or more of the major powers, thus inviting intervention, escalation, and possibly superpower confrontation. A short list of recent civil and small regional wars will serve to remind us of these threats: Cuba, Vietnam, Korea, Nicaragua, Israel and its Arab neighbors, Iran and Iraq, and so forth. Though in each the circumstances differed, they were all fraught with the same threats to international stability, in varying degrees. In some, territorial integrity was at stake, as in the Chinese intervention in the Korean War after the United States went to the aid of South Korea. In others, the threat was more indirect: Western and Japanese economic interests were threatened by the OPEC oil embargo of 1973–74, brought on in retaliation for support of Israel. In other circumstances, the worst prospects did not materialize: While both the Soviet Union and China supported North Vietnam against American force, neither intervened physically; and while the United States took no part in combat in Afghanistan, it did support the rebel forces against Soviet intervention in their civil war. And because of great-power interests in most of these conflicts, the United Nations was able to do little. (Remember, we are examining the Cold War period here.) The principal exception was the invention and subsequent multiple uses of peacekeeping in the Middle East, a topic explored at length in the next chapter.

The articulation of legal norms invariably begins with a definition of the problem, and accordingly, the General Assembly of the United Nations worked for years attempting to define "aggression." In 1974 it adopted a generic definition without voting, a gesture that indicated that its effort was more hortatory than practical. Aggression, it said, is "the use of armed force by a State against the sovereignty, territorial integrity or political independence of another State, or in any other manner inconsistent with the Charter of the United Nations." This ignores many of the critical subtleties of international conflict. When, for example, is armed action actually legal reprisal rather than aggression? When, on the other hand, is a presumed reprisal a calculated ruse for aggression? Take a single important debate as an example. When the United States escalated its offensive in Vietnam (1964) after two small gunboat attacks on ships in the Tonkin Gulf, was it undertaking a legal retaliation? If so, it was not guilty of aggression. Alternately, did it use an insignificant skirmish of Davids and Goliaths to formulate a justification for a major assault aimed at

defeating communist forces and reunifying the two Vietnams under a Western-oriented government? If so, it was involved in aggression.

From a political perspective, these matters may be somewhat clearer in the New World Order. While Saddam Hussein claimed, for instance, that his assault on Kuwait in 1990 was not aggression but a legal attempt to recover a province separated by Britain decades before, the Security Council with the concurrence of the five permanent members deemed it aggression even though Russia had close economic ties to Baghdad. Before casting its ballot at the Security Council, however, Mikhail Gorbachev sought and received from President George Bush assurances that if war were to ensue, the United States would not maintain a permanent military presence in Iraq. Time will tell whether this is an isolated example or a trend in post–Cold War politics to distinguish among military, territorial, and economic interests when opting for multilateral rather than nationalistic solutions.

Normative controls on domestic conflict are technically beyond international law. Unilateral intervention, in contrast, is generally illegal. During the Cold War, UN peacekeeping was used in a number of situations in which it was requested by one or more of the combatants, with moderate success and not without controversy. In the New World Order, its definition has been expanded considerably (see next chapter) and used with renewed enthusiasm as an alternative to individual intervention, in part because of its presumed neutrality (though there was never a doubt that first the U.S. and then the UN presence in Haiti was for the purposes of eliminating an insurgent government, returning an elected president from exile in the United States, and establishing stability on behalf of the elected government). The larger question for international law, however, is the regulation of individual third-party involvement that transforms civil war into international war.

Three issues closely associated with controls on aggression—arms control and disarmament, international arms trade, and nuclear proliferation—are discussed elsewhere in this book.

International Economic Order

Until the past quarter-century, international economic law was restricted largely to trade and currency agreements, international economic aid, and agreements between (or among) imperial states competing in colonized territories. The formation of the European Economic Community and other regional customs unions expanded the scope of interest to investment controls, labor markets, and tariff reduction within protected areas. But the commencement of the New International Economic Order (1973) called for a comprehensive legal order.

Views of what the content of that law should be depend on national perspectives. The industrializing countries call for a legal order that limits the political activities of the transnational corporations, ensures the transfer of technology, protects agricultural and semifinished products from dangerous fluctuations in international prices, protects natural resources from foreign exploitation, removes political strings from intergovernmental aid, places restrictions on foreign direct investment, and limits the growth of debt by improving terms of trade (cost of imports as against value of exports). For their part, the industrialized states call for protections against nationalization of property by host governments, assurances of controlled increases in prices of natural resources, guarantees against repudiation of contracts to purchase industrial produce, and guarantees of a steady export flow of raw materials. The concern of the latter group is directed especially to the oil-exporting countries, which from 1973 to 1983 demonstrated their ability to influence the industrial productivity of the West and Japan by controlling the export volume and price of oil, and which in the meanwhile disrupted the international currency exchange system by amassing nearly $100 billion annually in reserve currencies.

President Clinton undoubtedly was right when he remarked to a reporter in the Philippines in 1995 that in the future, national power will be measured more in economic than military terms. This is, in fact, one of the defining characteristics of the New World Order. Already many changes in the global economy have occurred, among them the creation of the North American Free Trade Area (NAFTA) among the United States, Mexico, and Canada; acceleration of economic integration in Europe through the European Union (formerly the European Economic Community); and completion of the Uruguay Round of GATT negotiations with revised tariff structures and dispute-resolution machinery. Western aid is flowing to Russia, other former parts of the Soviet Union, and Eastern Europe to accelerate transformation to market economies. Japanese and Western manufacturers are competing to open plants in Russia, China, Central Europe, and Vietnam. Many of these events constitute new international law themselves; others call for it lest they degenerate into new varieties of neoimperialism. Furthermore, with Soviet-American ideological competition gone, foreign economic aid has become unpopular with taxpayers and conservative legislators, threatening a sharp reduction in investment capital for development. Only new and expanded multilateral devices can compensate for these prospective losses.

A popular bumper sticker exhorts, "If you love peace, seek justice." Poor people the world over add that a prerequisite of justice is universal prosperity, as the failure of peace and justice stems from interracial hostility, economic disparity, and exploitation of the poor by the wealthy. One of the paramount responsibilities of the New World Order is to articulate a normative regime to address these issues as never before.

The Natural Environment

Earth, water, and air—all the components of our physical environment are under assault. Nuclear and chemical contamination of soil and water, millions of tons of greenhouse gases released into the atmosphere, deforestation pushing back the rain forests, changing weather patterns and reducing the global production of oxygen: These comprise only a sample of the untoward consequences of economic development, industrial production, and technological advancement. One of the great paradoxes of our time is that the more we advance, the more we destroy. The manufacturer will claim that he cannot produce coveted goods if he cannot pollute; and the starving Ethiopian farmer will claim that he cannot survive if he cannot plant, and he cannot plant until he levels and burns yet a few more acres of the rain forest. Such are the tensions between humankind's quest for comfort and the natural environment from which all springs.

From the perspective of international law, the problem is that oceans and atmospheric space know no national boundaries; nor does pollution. Furthermore, it is unreasonable to expect that national governments will be able to impose rigorous environmental controls that will impede development or start a deflationary cycle by closing plants, displacing workers, reducing public revenue, driving down gross domestic product, and diminishing competitiveness in the global market. These are not in the interest of governments and are less so for the powerful economic elites and millions of people whose retirement planning rests on effective investment. In the United States, the Environmental Protection Agency assigns emission quotas to industries, but the major polluters can buy unused emission credits from the minor! The consequences for the United States are not of international concern, but the consequences for the world are significant.

Worse, most countries have very little in the realm of effective environmental legal restraint.

In a New World Order defined in economic rather than military terms, these problems will be accentuated. The replacement of national economies by huge international consortia is likely to add another damaging contribution. Rapid population growth in the world's poorest areas will intensify the demand for development, leading to more environmental exploitation and spoliation. Even nuclear arms reduction will complicate environmental controls, as radioactive isotopes from disarmed nuclear weapons will have to be stored for thousands of years before they lose their potency. The New World Order cannot survive if it fails to address these monumental problems in the form of normative regulation.

Terrorism

Aggression is not the exclusive province of national governments. In recent years, terrorist violence by national and transnational extremist groups has become a common political activity. Although most of it is purely domestic, it often affects foreign nationals, as in the many cases in which foreign businesspeople have been shot by Italian and Latin American terrorists. Other terrorist acts have occurred in the territories of third parties,

A French frigate maneuvers against a Greenpeace protest vessel in an area of the South Pacific where France renewed nuclear weapons testing in 1995. French commandos later boarded the vessel and removed it from the test area.
(*Source:* New York Times)

most notably the massacre of Israeli athletes by Arab terrorists at the 1972 Olympic Games in West Germany. In 1995, a planned assassination attempt on the pope was narrowly foiled in the Philippines, and the Middle Eastern terrorist who is alleged to have planned it was captured in Pakistan. Arab terrorists were convicted of truck-bombing the World Trade Center in New York City, and others of plotting to attack other public structures such as the United Nations building and the tunnels under the Hudson River. On at least three occasions terrorists have blown up commercial aircraft in flight, killing hundreds of people. Many more have died in terrorist skyjackings. And when a cruise ship was hijacked in the Mediterranean, one person was murdered. Seven horses of the Queen's guard were killed by a car bomb in London in 1982. With the 1994 truce agreement between Catholic and Protestant militants in Ireland, terrorism traditionally attributed to the IRA stopped but resumed in 1996, the same year in which several Americans were killed in a terrorist attack on their barracks at a Saudi Arabian base. International terrorism itself goes on, much but by no means all of it a product of a *jihad* (holy war) of Islamic extremists against the supporters of Israel. (It is important to note in this connection that some of the most heinous terrorist attacks are wholly unrelated to international activity. Two cases in point are the truck-bombing of the federal building in Oklahoma City and the poisonous gas attack on a Tokyo subway station, both in 1995, and both known to have been entirely domestic in origin. The assassination of Israeli Premier Yitzhak Rabin in 1995 was a domestic act, but provoked by opposition to his peace policy of ceding territory to the Palestinians.)

State-sponsored terrorism is a special problem. The U.S. government has identified a number of

Terrorism returns to the Middle East with the bombing of a crowded Israeli bus, 1996.
(*Source:* © Heidi Levine/Sipa Press)

terrorist states, that is, states that sponsor terrorism as a matter of policy. These include Iran, Iraq, Tunisia (as the home of the Palestine Liberation Organization during its terrorist days), Libya, Albania, and Syria. A shooting of the pope over a decade ago is known to have been the work of an Albanian agent on assignment. In 1986, having determined that the Libyan government had participated in a terrorist attack in Germany that killed an American soldier, President Ronald Reagan ordered air attacks on the Libyan central government compound. Among the several people killed was a daughter of the Libyan chief of state, Colonel Muammar Qaddafi. This sort of self-help retaliation is invited by the absence of adequate international legal remedies.

In recent years there has been much intergovernmental cooperation in these matters. Colombia has agreed to extradite for trial persons suspected of drug-related crimes in the United States. Many countries, including Cuba, have agreed to return skyjackers who seek refuge. But to date there is no comprehensive international legal code covering prevention, apprenhension and prosecution obligating governments to assist one another in the matter of international terrorism.

International Refugees

Throughout the twentieth century, one of the principal objectives of international law and organization has been to extend legal rights to the millions of people who, displaced from their homelands, swarm across the world as refugees. Handling of the refugee problem was one of the main activities of the League of Nations after the First World War; and at the close of the Second World War, the United Nations, as one of its earliest efforts, organized machinery on behalf of refugees.

Not all homeless people crossing international boundaries are refugees by international legal definition. It is doubtful, for example, that thousands of East Germans who, in 1989, reached the West when Hungary, in defiance of a demand from its East German ally, opened its boundary to Austria

in deliberate assistance to East Germans wishing to leave the Eastern bloc territories permanently, were refugees due protection under international law. Nor are Mexicans seeking better economic conditions in Texas or California, and who cross the border into the United States in violation of American immigration law. They are, instead, illegal aliens subject to involuntary repatriation. In contrast, Cambodians seeking refuge in Thailand from the civil war at home were refugees by international legal standards, as were Ethiopians in Sudan, Nicaraguans in El Salvador, and Rwandans in Burundi. What, then, constitutes a refugee in international law?

The 1951 UN Geneva Convention on Refugees stipulates that refugee status depends on "a well-founded fear of persecution for reasons of race, religion, nationality, membership in a particular social group or political opinion." The narrowest view, accordingly, is that an international migrant is a true refugee only if the cause for migration were political persecution, and only if repatriation carries the threat of its resumption. Generally, faced with demands to expand the definition to include natural disasters and famine, states have appreciated this narrow definition, as it places rather strict limits on their obligation to undertake the costs and logistics of housing, feeding, and caring for refugees.

In 1987, when a number of civil wars in Asia, Africa, and Central America swelled the number of international refugees to more than 10 million, the UN General Assembly recieved a report on International Cooperation to Avert New Flows of Refugees that advocated the broader definition, including as internationally protected refugees people escaping natural disasters as well as political persecution.[19] The definition alone adds to the global refugee popoulation, reset in 1988 at 14.5 million. Since that time, several events have inflated those

---

[19] Luke T. Lee, "United Nations Group of Governmental Experts on International Cooperation to Avert New Flows of Refugees: Part II," *American Journal of International Law,* April 1987, pp. 442–444. For a thorough history of the issue that adopts the narrower definition, see Guy S. Goodwin-Gill, *The Refugee in International Law* (New York: Clarendon, 1984).

numbers yet again: civil war in Rwanda that may have displaced as many as 2 million; civil war in Mozambique that sent 930,000 refugees to Malawi at one time; protracted war in Bosnia; the Russian war to thwart Chechnyan secession; civil wars in Somalia and Liberia; a coup d'état in Haiti; Iraq's invasion of Kuwait; Iraqi genocidal attacks on the northern Kurds; and resumption of political oppression in Nigeria. To underscore the magnitude of the refugee numbers, think of them as approximately equal to the total population of Venezuela, or equal to the combined populations of Sweden and Switzerland. The global refugee population doubled between 1980 and 1990, and it continues to grow.[20]

But the refugee problem is far greater than mere definitions and numbers. All these people are without homes, food, protection from weather, sources of income, medical care, education, clothes, stable social and political organizations, and protection from violence. Most are unable to communicate in the languages of the host countries. And because all the basic necessities of life must be provided by the host countries when international relief efforts fall short, in the main they find themselves inhospitably received as added burdens on the public revenue systems of poor countries already unable to meet the needs of citizens. Moreover, their international legal protection means that they cannot be forced to return to their homelands, thus prolonging indefinitely their absolute dependence on international and host-country assistance. It is, therefore, the role of international law to protect them from the threat of involuntary return to the ravages of war, to political persecution, or to the consequences of natural disaster.

International Illicit Drug Trafficking

As dependence on illegal drugs sweeps many countries, and as the documentation of drug-related violence begins to dominate the front pages of many urban daily newspapers, virtually every legal jurisdiction in the world has attempted to find solutions to the problem of illicit drugs. City, state, and national governments turn to law enforcement, border patrols, searches of suspicious vessels, and surveillance of airports to stop the flow of drugs, while they attempt to find programs of drug treatment and education that will reduce the demand for these substances. Many aspects of the global drug problem belong properly within national and local jurisdiction, but there can be little progress in reducing the international flow of supply without effective international law.

Although several bilateral and multilateral agreements on drug trafficking existed prior to 1984, the huge increase in social problems—addiction, drug-related violence, and drug-related spread of acquired immune deficiency syndrome (AIDS)—prompted the UN General Assembly in 1984 to call for the creation of new global measures for dealing with international drug trafficking. It was reiterated by an International Conference on Drug Abuse and Illegal Trafficking in 1987. At the end of 1988, the United Nations convened a conference at the home of its drug-control agencies in Vienna, Austria, from which emerged a new UN Convention Against Illegal Traffic in Narcotic Drugs and Psychotropic Substances. One indication of the urgency with which governments viewed the situation was that the convention was adopted unanimously by the representatives of 108 participating governments. As national governments formally adopt this treaty by their normal constitutional processes, and as it gains enough national ratifications to go into effect, the participating states will acquire new rights and obligations. Among the rights will be the ability of courts to confiscate drug profits and to extradite drug offenders to the countries in which they conduct their illegal acts. And among the obligations will be passing laws to open banking practices so that drug money laundering will become more difficult, and to forbid the employment of children in any aspect of creating, processing, transporting, or disseminating illicit drugs.

---

[20] *World Social Situation in the 1990s* (New York: United Nations, 1994), pp. 111–121.

Promising as this may sound, at the close of 1988 the United Nations had 155 state members plus the Holy See, so even if all 108 of the conferees were to ratify the treaty, its privileges and obligations would be far from universal. The greater probability is that most of the original 108 participants will ratify as will most states that have joined the UN since 1988, but that most of the remaining 47 will not. The threat of antistate violence will prevent some from joining, as will the domestic Robin Hood image of the principal drug producers in some countries. In others, where drugs have been decriminalized or made legal, in some of which they are sold legally and openly, there will be no incentive to join.[21] The world is thus very far from an effective normative regime on this important subject.

Questions of Jurisdiction

One of the frequently debated topics·among theorists of international law is the relationship of domestic law and jurisdiction to international law and jurisdiction. Although most theories and judicial findings subordinate domestic law to international law, there are several that endorse the superiority of national law and jurisdiction. In drafting the Statute of the Permanent Court of International Justice and later of the International Court of Justice, negotiators debated this relationship in connection with the obligation of states to submit international disputes to the jurisdiction of the court. Still today, international organs and jurisdiction extend into the state only on the rarest of occasions. As we will see, such instances almost always involve regional courts in integrating international communities.

Until states agree on the extent to which national jurisdiction is subordinated to or defined by international law, there will be little opportunity

for international organs to pursue criminals into protective jurisdictions. Furthermore, only under certain regional codes of law (such as those of the European Court of Human Rights) does international jurisdiction address itself to individuals rather than to governments. These twin problems of jurisdiction—the place of the individual in international law and the relationship of international jurisdiction to national jurisdiction—are major obstacles to a more effective international legal order.

The American View of International Law

The United States' view of international law arises from America's European origins and from the fact that the United States is heir to the central political position previously held by Great Britain. United States law is a by-product of West European culture and civilization.

International law evolved in a Eurocentric world, its norms originally serving the reciprocal convenience of European monarchs. But as the trade of the European states became global and as European empires swelled, the European view of international law became imprinted upon much of the inhabited world. Law came to protect and serve capitalist economic interests; the doctrine of noninterference in the policies of other states was used in part to foster imperialism; and maritime law facilitated the commercial and military shipping of the richest and most powerful. Many of these laws were oblivious—and occasionally hostile—to the interests of competing economic systems and to colonized populations. Yet they enjoyed a high degree of integrity, because they had the political protection of the states whose interests they served.

The United States, reared in the cultural, economic, and legal traditions of Britain and Europe, inherited dominance of a Euro-American world prior to the Second World War, in which existing international law was much to its advantage. In the interwar period, the United States had taken a major role in expanding this legal system along the same lines, seeking, for example, to sponsor a vast network of treaties for the peaceful settlement of international disputes. It had also participated in the functional activities of the League of Nations (though it never joined the League) and sought international economic regulation through bilateral and limited multilateral pacts.

The revolutionary international system that followed World War Two was not always receptive to the positivist concept of international law that Washington sought through the United Nations. As new forms of Cold War politics appeared, they averted positivist regulation. Finally the United States was forced by Soviet policies to adopt neorealistic attitudes toward the law. Hence the Truman Doctrine occurred outside the United Nations, the occupation of Japan was replaced by a close Japanese-American security arrangement for the Far East, and West Germany was rearmed. Whenever possible, then, Washington pursued a policy of enhancing the positivist approach to international law; but whenever Soviet foreign policy prevented this, the United States was forced to resort to the broader standards of neorealism.

But it was the Soviet-inspired revolutionary policies of the Developing Nations (then called the Third World because the members were tied to neither the United States nor the Soviet Union) that brought on Washington's greatest impatience with the changing foundations of international law, the dramatic last straw appearing in Nicaragua. Fed up with the continued Soviet supply of the socialist Sandinista forces in Nicaragua and determined to reverse the revolution (a policy that became known as the Reagan Doctrine), the United States intervened by giving military aid to the Western-oriented rebel forces and assisted directly by mining Nicaraguan harbors. When the leftist government of Nicaragua submitted to the International Court of Justice a legal claim against American actions, Washington announced the first modification in its forty-year-old declaration of acceptance of the

court's compulsory jurisdiction, excepting from the declaration all matters pertaining to Central America, and declaring that it would neither participate in the proceedings nor comply with the outcome. Despite subsequent findings in favor of the Nicaraguan government, and in defiance of several attempts to embarrass the United States at the United Nations, Washington held fast to its refusal to be subjected to the court's jurisdiction in the Nicaraguan matter.

Since the end of the Cold War, global political circumstances have encouraged a return to a more positivist approach to the progressive development of international law. NAFTA, the Uruguay Round of trade negotiations, the Berlin Conference to limit emission of greenhouse gases, renewal of the Nuclear Non-Proliferation Treaty, growth in sentiment for a complete and universal ban on nuclear testing, and diplomatic recognition of Vietnam all illustrate this trend. Moreover, in the security realm the United States has consistently opted for multilateral action rather than individual. Desert Storm was conducted under Security Council mandate, as were the American peacekeeping roles in Haiti and Somalia. A major break from these policies occurred in Bosnia, where the United States elected to act within NATO rather than the Security Council. This was prompted by Russia's reluctance to oppose the Serbians publicly and the fear of (or to avoid New World Order embarrassment to everyone?) a Russian veto.

The View of America's Major Partners

Because of the Cold War, rapid industrialization, and the Westernization of Japan after 1945, Washington's principal allies evolved similar attitudes toward positive international law in all three categories: community, reciprocity, and the political context. Indeed, because of the social and economic origins, the United States and Canada derived much of their perceptions of international law from Europe. Japan, earlier a victim of such a legal order, after 1950 came to enjoy its fruits and thus adopted a Western-sympathetic attitude.

But as the Cold War ended and the New World Order began to evolve, with security imperatives giving way to the economic bases of national power, attitudinal changes have been common. Burgeoning resource scarcity in Europe and Japan, Tokyo's dependence on Middle Eastern oil, rancorous diplomacy over access to one another's markets, huge balance-of-trade discrepancies, competition to exploit labor markets in newly opened areas (e.g., Vietnam, China, Russia, eastern Germany, and Central Europe), and fundamental differences over trade in government-subsidized goods (for example, the subsidized European Airbus industry has eroded American dominance and, with it, export volume) have all strained political relations and evoked threats of economic coercion. Completion of the Uruguay Round of GATT negotiations may reduce much of the tension, but the new global conditions demand more than previously the steady development of international economic law.

The Russian View of International Law

Unlike the United States, the Soviet Union gained major-power status in a world fundamentally hostile to its political, ideological, and economic principles. Its view of international law arose from the writings of Karl Marx, who viewed the state as an instrument of class oppression. To Marxist jurists, law is the formal instrument of such oppression. The law of nations, therefore, is a body of rules and principles by which the powerful promote class exploitation in the international system. International law, like all other law, is of class origins.

Yet Soviet leaders found reason to cooperate with prevailing international law. Their principal justification was the Stalinist premise that the withering away of states must await the universal socialist revolution. Meanwhile, Soviet politics was motivated partly by the fear of capitalist encirclement. It was necessary to participate at least minimally in capitalist international law to escape this encirclement. In later years, after Nikita Khrushchev introduced his notion of peaceful coexistence, it became the fashion of Soviet international legal science to promote cooperation with the institutions of interstate law as a means to achieve peaceful coexistence.

Although it was denied officially by Soviet spokespersons, the Cold War practice rested on the notion that three bodies of international law existed concurrently. The first was the body of law that regulated the class interests of the capitalist nations and was called capitalist international law. The second pertained to the relations between the capitalist and socialist worlds, interbloc law. Finally, there existed a totally separate body of law among socialist states, intrabloc law.

Interbloc law was also called the law of peaceful coexistence. It was understood that a body of rules and principles existed to govern diplomatic and economic relations between East and West. While positivist in content, the formalities of textbook law had to be distinguished from political reality. Treaties, and particularly bilateral treaties, were the preferred source of law, but any politically outmoded rules had lost the force of law. Probably because of Moscow's political minority status in international organizations, Soviet jurists and diplomats alike were more sensitive than their American rivals to political controls of international law. And they were the utter foes of multilateralism.

Intrabloc law was a matter on which there was little theorizing and much political legitimacy. It noted that while Americans purport to respect the territorial integrity and political independence of states within their sphere of interest, history is replete with examples of American intervention. From the Soviet juridical viewpoint, America's lip service to these general principles of international law is a hypocrisy, and the Monroe Doctrine little more than a legal justification for U.S. intervention at will rather than a doctrine of hemispheric self-determination.

Cold War Soviet intrabloc law and practice were very different. Starting from the premise (much later articulated as the Brezhnev Doctrine) that states within the Soviet sphere of influence were subordinate to the system itself, all systemic components, particularly economic and military, were centralized in Moscow. Although purely domestic matters were locally determined, any aspect of statehood that had a potential impact on the solidity of the system was directed centrally. Hence independence movements in East Germany and Czechoslovakia were crushed by Soviet force. In 1980 Poland's recognition of labor's independence from government and the Communist party resulted in a Moscow-sponsored change in governments. This was considered consistent with the dictum that member states of the socialist commonwealth were politically independent up to the point at which their actions or policies countervened the basic ideological foundations of intrabloc law.

Despite the prominence of this thinking prior to the Gorbachev era, events in Poland in 1989 revealed the legal implications of *perestroika*. In that year, the growing strength of the Solidarity union forced the government to grant it legal status for the first time in seven years (despite the 1980 recognition). Mikhail Gorbachev, without explicit reference to the Brezhnev Doctrine, hinted that intervention would no longer be part of Soviet intrabloc policy. There followed general elections in which the Solidarity union became the Solidarity party, and in every contest in which it fielded a candidate, it defeated the incumbent communist. In a rapid rush of events that captured global attention, Gorbachev publicly implored the Communist party to cooperate in establishing the first noncommunist government in Eastern Europe since immediately after the Second World War. In place of the tanks of the summer in 1968 in Czechoslovakia and the forced change of Polish governments in 1980, the Kremlin of the *perestroika* era openly encouraged political self-determination. This formed the first indication that in law, politics, and even ideology, *perestroika* would alter vastly not only the

Brezhnev Doctrine, but intrabloc law, the law of peaceful coexistence, and even the notion of proletarian internationalism. The final blow was dealt to the Brezhnev Doctrine when the Kremlin gave its blessing to the reunification of the two Germanys and its consent for the new Germany to be a member of the North Atlantic Treaty Organization, the very alliance that had been the adversary of the Warsaw Treaty Organization throughout the Cold War.

These events occurred as the Cold War was passing into history. At about the same time, evidences began to appear of what the subsequent Russian view of international law would be. Declaration of willingness to pay old UN assessments for peacekeeping operations, reduction in economic support for Cuba, allowing the Contras to prevail over the Soviet-supported Sandinista government in Nicaragua, and the removal of armed forces from Afghanistan undoubtedly are related more closely to the demands of the Soviet economy and to the thaw in Soviet-American relations than to international law. Russian scholars, on the other hand, have adjusted their views of international law as the New World Order has taken hold. One has written, for example, that Russian jurisprudence rejects neorealism because it causes "complete uncertainty in international law." Instead, Russian scholars now prefer a theory based on "the coordination of wills" among governments, a doctrine more nearly correlated to the consensual theory of Western positivism. In this Russian theory, international law is a body of principles and norms that form a subsystem of the larger global system designed to regulate the common interests of the market economies and the socialist economies, shaped by a variety of economic, political, sociological, ideological, and other factors.[22] This residual sound of interbloc law is likely to be modified further as

---

[22] R. A. Mullerson, "Sources of International Law: New Tendencies in Soviet Thinking," *American Journal of International Law*, July 1989, pp. 494–512. At the time of publication, the author was Head of the Department of International Law, Institute of State and Law of the Academy of Sciences of the USSR.

the Russian Federation progresses toward a market economy of its own.

In broader terms, the new Russian theory of international law begins with the declaration of the Soviet Communist Party in 1986 that peaceful coexistence is no longer understood to be a specific form of class struggle. Even in the closing years of the Cold War, then, it was recognized that Soviet interbloc law no longer needed to focus on the threats of war and capitalist encirclement. Nor could it any longer defend the premise that massive war among capitalist states, a central Marxist concept, would result in a worldwide socialist revolution. Peaceful coexistence, in the face of these doctrinal developments, was no longer an instrument of international class struggle, but of urgency to all humankind. The liberalization of intrabloc law, the weakening of Washington's grip on world capitalism, and the reduced threat of East-West war all introduced changes to the Kremlin's ideology, thus enabling the Russian view of international law to shift markedly. The result is an appeal to a more positivist concept of international law; greater reliance on institutions such as the United Nations to foster legal norms, security, and economic development; and a greater distribution of economic produce by increased trade between the market economies and the transforming socialist economies regulated by treaties and other formal arrangements.[23]

The Chinese View of International Law

Although the Chinese share the old Soviet notion of the class origins of international law, they face the additional problem of having been a major

victim of Western treaty law. During the Century of Humiliation, China was subjected to treaty relations based on Western power superiority and the ability of other states to imperialize its territory and its commerce. More recent events, such as exclusion of the People's Republic of China from the Japanese Peace Treaty (1951) and the long delay in seating Beijing's representative at the United Nations, have accentuated the Chinese alienation from prevailing international legal norms. All Chinese governments of the present century have deplored the unequal treaties and have shared the determination to repossess territory granted to other states, yet none has coupled these determinations with other diplomatic grievances more vigorously than has the government that has ruled China since 1950. It looks upon Western-oriented international law as vacuous humanistic platitudes designed to lure China's support and participation on Western terms. The concept of President Woodrow Wilson's Fourteen Points as the gospel of the First World War and the Atlantic Charter of the Second World War, with their stress on fundamental freedoms, seem to the Chinese to have been withdrawn in time of peace and the actual destiny of China to have been given over cynically to other "legal" agreements. Most vexatious among these is the Soviet-American Yalta Protocol (1945), which enlisted Soviet military assistance against Japan at the cost of Chinese political and territorial integrity.

The contemporary Chinese view of international law is shaped by three factors: (1) the historical perception that Western-oriented law has aided Western growth at the expense of China and that Russia benefits increasingly from the same; (2) that international law has class origins that make it a peculiar instrument of transnational class struggle through economic oppression and intervention; and (3) that as an industrializing socialist state, China's sympathies on the restraints and licenses of law lie with the Developing Nations rather than with the economic powers with worldwide interests.

The Chinese view rejects the old Soviet idea that several types of international law operate

[23] G. I. Tunkin, Address to the American Society of International Law, Washington, April 21, 1988. This paragraph is based on John Quigley, "*Perestroika* and International Law," *American Journal of International Law*, July 1988, pp. 787–797. Quigley based his comments on a translation of Tunkin's address prior to its publication in English.

simultaneously. It accepts the notion of a single general international law that represents the will of the ruling classes. With respect to the theoretical basis of international law, however, the Chinese strike a difference between a bourgeois theory derived to preserve the capitalist world order, and a proletarian theory founded on assumptions designed for a socialist world order uniting classes across national boundaries. The first emphasizes the state and the ruling class; the second stresses the liberation of the working class (proletariat). This view concludes that "only the proletarian science of international law established on the base of Marxism-Leninism is genuine science."[24]

China's interest is not so much in expanding its rights as in attempting to restrict the rights, and formalize the obligations, of other major powers that have interests in Asia. Thus China argues for the sanctity of treaties, although it acknowledges membership in few. As its fundamental statement on international law, it has accepted the content of a Sino-Indian declaration of 1954, which encompasses the five Primary Principles of Peaceful Coexistence:

1. Mutual respect for sovereignty and territorial integrity
2. Mutual nonaggression
3. Mutual noninterference in internal affairs
4. Sovereign equality and mutual advantage (or benefit)
5. Peaceful coexistence

(Unlike the Soviet formulation enunciated by Khrushchev in 1961, peaceful coexistence in Chinese terms does not mean peaceful competition. By the same token, there has been no formal restatement subsequent to Gorbachev's reformation of the peaceful coexistence concept in the era of *glasnost*.)

Although most of these principles do not depart substantially from the classical notions of Western international law, the Chinese formulation stresses mutual advantage more than others do. Imbued with a historical sense of inequality in treaty relations, the Chinese argue that unless a treaty exists for mutual benefit, it is not binding, regardless of the apparent formalities of consent. Chinese jurists argue explicitly that treaties need not be renegotiated or terminated formally if their obligations were imposed imperialistically. It is held, rather, that in these cases the victim state may simply renounce its obligations. Despite ideological origins similar to those of the Cold War Soviet Union, the Chinese view of international law is tempered more by history and policy imperatives than by ideology.

The Developing Nations' View of International Law

The Developing Nations share China's perception of having been victimized by the Western international order, and they view much of its legal content as designed to facilitate Euro-American growth at their expense. New states of revolutionary birth sympathize, furthermore, with the Chinese view that the law of nations still is pitted against their interests. But even old Developing Nations, and those that became independent through peaceful means and with formal preparation for self-government under UN surveillance, consider much existing international law inimical to their needs and policies.

The element of succession that distresses these states most is devolution. Upon achieving independence, many states found themselves left with debts and commitments they are expected to honor. Certain obligations have devolved upon new governments, some informally and others through inheritance agreements. Some of these may be bilateral obligations easily renegotiated into modified arrangements called novations. In other cases, however, the partner may be unwilling to

---

[24] For a traditional Chinese statement on the basis of international law, see Ho Wu-shaung and Ma Chun, as reprinted in Jerome Alan Cohen and Hungdah Chiu, *People's Republic of China and International Law: A Documentary Study*, 2 vols. (Princeton, N.J.: Princeton University Press, 1974), vol. 1, pp. 33–36.

change the agreement. Here the new state is likely to adopt the Chinese view that conditions having changed, the obligation no longer holds. Some new states have taken up the clean-slate doctrine, which insists on the nullity of all prearrangements.

Multilateral treaties present a more complex problem, because renegotiation with multiple partners is more difficult. Furthermore, upon entry into international organizations, the new state assumes obligations that it did not create. Certain unwanted restraints may have to be undertaken as the price of membership benefits.

Customary law creates larger problems too. The Developing World countries are expected to partake virtually without consent, and it is here that they find themselves most disadvantaged by the legal rules and principles that preserve the interests of the more powerful states. This is especially true in the economic sphere, where the desperate need for investment capital and favorable terms of trade may be held captive to externally imposed trade principles, liquidity agreements, and tariff regulations. In this regard, the Developing Nations have combined to develop a more advantageous structure of positive international law to help them deal with the collective economic strength of the industrialized states. Their principal mechanism has been the United Nations Conference on Trade and Development (UNCTAD) and its use to press their common needs upon the wealthier countries within the UN system. In 1973 their voting majority at the UN enabled them to pass the Declaration of the Establishment of a New International Economic Order and its companion Programme for Action, as well as the Charter of Economic Rights and Duties of States. The efforts of the underindustrialized world toward establishing an international legal order depend on an effective law for economic self-determination. Accordingly, it welcomes the efforts of both the Organization for Economic Cooperation and Development and the United Nations Task Force on Multinational Corporations to conclude codes of conduct for international business, with the hope

of reducing by law some of the neoimperialistic patterns justified under existing Western-oriented international law. So too does it welcome the effort of the International Criminal Law Commission to define international economic crimes.

To the Developing Nations, and especially to its newly independent members, the main objection to international law combines the notion of sovereignty with the philosophical understanding of self-determination. The achievement of independence illuminates a bold fact of international life—that in the face of disparate power, sovereignty is an abstraction. Although formal self-determination may have been achieved, it does not confer all the latitudes of an economically powerful state. The destiny of the state is in large measure determined from without, both because it is expected to comply with certain established rules and because relations with more powerful states and corporations may limit economic and political alternatives. In place of formal colonialism, the economically less developed states find that international law provides few, if any, defenses against the neoimperialistic trend by which the developed states encroach upon their economies.

It remains to be seen what consequences the New World Order will have for the Developing Nations from a legal perspective. For those, such as Mexico, that find themselves in large post–Cold War trading collaborations, new advantages should follow. But the withdrawal of financial support from both Washington and Moscow may be damaging. Furthermore, important as the Uruguay Round agreements may be for the industrialized countries, they may have no benefits for the Developing Nations. Forthcoming meetings of UNCTAD, against the backdrop of NAFTA and the Uruguay Agreements, undoubtedly will address this matter.

Conclusion

The diverse outlooks toward contemporary international law that prevailed during the Cold War period arose because four fundamental bases of the Western legal order no longer enjoyed universal validity. First, a fundamental distinction between law, on the one hand, and ideology and politics, on the other, was no longer assumed. Second, the very existence of the Cold War revealed the breakdown in any practical distinction between war and peace. Third, the revolutionary international system partially rejected the traditional presumption of the coexistence of independent, territorially discrete states. And finally, that governments were able to undertake mutually binding obligations through consent and voluntary compliance no longer was assumed universally. These premises deteriorated primarily because of the maturation of multicultural forces that eroded the West's control of global politics and international law.[25]

Multicultural forces are even more pronounced in the post–Cold War international system, as is seen in the heightened instances of ethnopolitical violence, the spread of Islamic political power from the Middle East to North Africa and Eurasia, and the nearly global spread of Islamic militance. The dominant imperative of the New World Order, however, is security through economic strength, and it is this that improves the environment for the progressive development of normative international law. One of the characteristics of security through economic strength is material interdependence. This is ensured by economic development and well-regulated trade on equitable terms, each of which requires the guidance of international law. As we have seen, however, there are major tensions in the law-generating environment at least as important as the existing political and social hostilities. On the one hand, the post–Cold War system opens the way to normative rule-making for mutual benefit. But on the other hand, the demise of Soviet-American ideological hostility has removed one of the major incentives for development aid. Previously, the prime goal of this aid was political, and economic goals were secondary. (This was less the case with other aid-extending states.) It would be naive to assume that governments will abandon their political goals in the global system, but reasonable to expect that in the New World Order, the gap between political motive and economic security motive will be reduced. The prospects for effective international law-making are thus restored. This is particularly the case if multilateralism progresses along with multiculturalism.

During the Cold War, the law of community and the law of reciprocity were relatively well developed, but the law of the political context was primitive, hindered as it was by the threat of nuclear destruction. The New World Order, with its focus on security through economic strength, at least opens the opportunity for renewed progress in the development of normative international law.

One observer, concerned that the Security Council not become an oligarchy of great powers acting in concert when policy convergence permits, casts even a brighter light on the future of international law. Referring to the UN Charter he wrote, "The end of the Cold War has once again moved constitutional law to the forefront . . . on a planetary scale. . . ," as many powerful states "have begun to discover that in an increasingly organized, but still asymmetrical, world political system, it is safer to depend on the structural restraint of a constitution than on the good will and shifting interests of the Prince. In short, they have begun to appreciate the need for a better approximation of a modern constitution."[26]

---

[25] Adda B. Bozeman, *The Future of Law in a Multicultural World* Princeton, N.J.: Princeton University Press, 1971), pp. 35–48 and 180—186.

[26] W. Michael Reisman, "The Constitutional Crisis of the United Nations," *American Journal of International Law*, January 1993, pp. 100 and 95, respectively. See also by the same author, "International Law After the Cold War," *American Journal of International Law*, October 1990, pp. 859–866.

CHAPTER 15

International Organization

The preceding discussion of international law emphasized repeatedly that the development of an effective international legal order is impeded by both the sovereign equality of states and the absence of authoritative international institutions competent to govern the global system. Since 1648, and more especially since 1815, creative statespersons have sought to remedy this defect by founding a network of international decison-making agencies. Although these will hardly replace nation-states as principal actors, there is considerable evidence that their presence contributes to the settlement of disputes, prevents their occurrence, and facilitates decision making and conflict resolution on a broad spectrum of problems.

But their contribution necessarily is limited. Only in rare cases are international institutions authorized to impose their decisions on member states. They conduct their business among states and do not exist separately from them. *Suprana-tional* organizations, in contrast, have authority above the state and are capable of dictating to it, within carefully defined limits as set in advance by the members. *International* organizations do not pretend to supplant the nation-state or its authority over internal or external policies. This chapter deals with international organizations, and the following with supranational.

In a world of hostilities and power politics, students of international relations traditionally have focused their attention on public international organizations (also called intergovernmental organizations, or IGOs). Recently, on the heels of

communications and travel revolutions, and recognizing that business and other interests often transcend international boundaries, attention has been directed to private international organizations (also called nongovernmental organizations, or NGOs). These facilitate transactions by means other than governments, and they are the vehicles of transnational participation. Governments become involved in their business only indirectly or secondarily. Their principal subjects are individuals and organized social groups, corporations, and so on. Whereas the IGO is a government-to-government institution, the NGO deals people to people. They are, respectively, intergovernmental and intersocietal.[1] Our concern here is with the intergovernmental organizations. The following chapter deals with transnational participation.

Throughout the last century there has been a steady growth in the numbers of both IGOs and NGOs. At present there are more than 300 IGOs and in excess of 2000 NGOs. Moreover, even

---

[1] Historically, the study of international organizations has concentrated entirely on intergovernmental organizations as defined here. Now, however, it is recognized that not all organized intergovernmental activity occurs in formal institutions such as the United Nations. Many take place, rather, in less formal "regimes," defined as "sets of implicit or explicit principles, norms, rules, and decision-making procedures around which actors' expectations converge in a given area of international relations." See Stephen D. Krasner, ed., *International Regimes* (Ithaca, N.Y.: Cornell University Press, 1983). Although the treatment here makes occasional reference to regimes, its central focus is on the more formally constituted international institutions.

among the IGOs the variety of content and intent is so wide that further subdivision is needed. That the North Atlantic Treaty Organization (NATO) and the International Court of Justice (ICJ) both are IGOs ought not to imply that they have very much in common, except that each has several member governments! The following typology (breakdown of types) suggests some of the important classifications and provides familiar examples:

I. Global Organizations
   a. Multipurpose (United Nations)
   b. Single purpose or functional
      1. Economic (Economic and Social Council)
      2. Security (Security Council)
      3. Anti-imperial (Trusteeship Council)
      4. Nutrition (Food and Agricultural Organization)
      5. Transportation—sea (International Maritime Consultative Organization), air (International Civil Aviation Organization)
      6. Communications—mail (Universal Postal Union), telegraph (International Telegraphic Organization)
      7. Judicial (International Court of Justice)

II. Subglobal Organizations
   a. Intrabloc organizations
      1. Economic (International Monetary Fund)
      2. Security (North Atlantic Treaty Organization)
   b. Regional Organizations
      1. Economic (European Union)
      2. Security (Organization of American States: Rio Pact aspects)
      3. Sociocultural and economic (Organization of American States: Bogotá Pact aspects)
   c. Integrating Organizations
      1. Economic (European Coal and Steel Community)
      2. Judicial (European Court of Human Rights)

International Organization and World Politics

The expression "international organization" has two related but different meanings. First, the expression can be considered synonymous with "international institution." The United Nations, for instance, may be labeled an international organization or an international institution (or group of institutions). In the other context "international organization" refers to a major international political process, one in which member states attempt through institutionalized collective measures and diplomatic experimentation to facilitate their transactions, particularly when the subject matter is deemed to be handled more efficiently collectively than competitively.

Whatever form an IGO may take, states enter into it because of anticipated benefits. But in determining the effectiveness of such institutions from a collective viewpoint, it is not mere service to governments that matters. There are three critical measures of organizational ability to draw states into collective policies and, therefore, to overcome the potentially anarchical characteristics of the nation-state system.

Association or Disassociation?

Does the activity of membership tend to draw states closer together, or does it accentuate their differences and drive them farther from collective decision making? Does parliamentary diplomacy facilitate the discovery of workable common denominators, or does it magnify the differences among states? Does it help to clarify peoples' clouded images of one another, or does it further distort them?[2] From a global perspective, even associating organizations have a paradoxical component: The more associating they are among members, the more disassociating they may be in

---

[2] Bruce Russett, *International Regions and the International System* (Chicago: Rand McNally, 1967).

relation to outside states. NATO is a case in point. Although it intends to be associating among the members, its existence maintains the disassociation of Europe, especially in the New World Order. But it exemplifies also a second phenomenon: As Europe has embarked on other paths of association, NATO has come to have internal disassociating effects, particulary between the European states, on the one hand, and the United States, on the other.

Contributions to Future Improvements

What is an institution's capacity for contributing to change in the international system? Although institutions often are imprisoned by the will and power of their members (which, as sovereign states, safeguard their supreme decision-making capability), they may make independent contributions to world politics, often by helping members clarify obscured possibilities in their relations. But they may also contribute through a more complex mechanism. Dag Hammarskjöld, second Secretary-General of the United Nations, visualized two distinctly different models of UN effectiveness. The organization might be either a "static conference machinery" or a "dynamic instrument of governments" for introducing a new world order. Far from prescribing a supranational role, Hammarskjöld hoped only that a politically immune international civil service, together with quasi-legislative competence of the deliberative body, might help states overcome their immediate and narrow interests.[3] The extent to which an international organization is able to emulate the second model may be taken as one of the criteria of its effectiveness in stabilizing the international system.

Most studies of international organization suggest that regional organizations are, understandably, more effective than global organizations. The usual explanation is that regional neighbors share historical understandings, have had a long history of diplomatic and international relations, and have built an informal sense of understanding among themselves because of the frequency of their transactions. Although the West European experience with international integration partially vindicates this outlook (see Chapter 16), at least one quantitative study suggests that global organizations actually are more effective in improving the relations of members than are regional institutions. Based on comparative data, the study concludes that through international institutions, states may find solutions to problems that they are unable to resolve through bilateral diplomacy; that the degree of cooperation in international institutions is determined more by the expanse of the organization's mandate than by the characteristics of the member states (ideological, economic, and so on); and that, on balance, global institutions are more effective than are their regional counterparts.[4] One plausible interpretation of these findings is that in multipurpose global institutions, competing states are able to isolate their conflicts, so that while they undertake bilateral diplomacy on those issues, they are free in the multinational forum to cooperate on other issues.

Constraints on Member States

It is taken for granted (1) that states enter IGOs in anticipation of benefits to their individual interests and (2) that institutions become the instruments of their members' foreign policies. Under these circumstances, are such institutions ever capable of restraining the states' behavior? True, they serve definite purposes for specific governments; but in the long run, are they able to constrain governmental behavior? The third criterion of institutional effectiveness, therefore, is the ability of

[3] Dag Hammarskjöld, "Two Differing Concepts of the United Nations Assayed," *United Nations Review*, September 1961, pp. 12–17.

[4] James M. McCormick, "Intergovernmental Organizations and Cooperation Among Nations," *International Studies Quarterly*, March 1980, pp. 75–98.

multilateral diplomacy to constrain members' behavior. Boutros Boutros-Ghali, sixth Secretary-General of the United Nations, addressed the classic tension between nationalism and multilateralism in the New World Order context. In 1995, in reviewing the post-Cold War activities of the United Nations and outlining proposals for the organization's future, he wrote:

> The foundation-stone of [the UN's] work is and must remain the State. Respect for its fundamental sovereignty and integrity are crucial to any [collective] international progress. The time of absolute and exclusive sovereignty, however, has passed; its theory was never matched by reality. It is the task of leaders of States today to understand this and to find a balance between the needs of good internal governance and the requirements of an ever more interdependent world.[5]

If the principal objective of international organization is to overcome some of the anarchical characteristics of a decentralized, state-centered global system, then institutional capacity to be associative, to contribute constructively to systemic transactions, and to constrain the behavior of member governments become important measures of effectiveness. Because we are concerned here with the global system, the discussion that follows addresses only global organizational efforts, and because of space limitations, the discussion centers entirely on the components of the UN organizational system.

The United Nations System

The United Nations consists of six permanent organs and a vast array of specialized agencies, conferences, funds, and commissions. Table 15–1 categorizes some of these. Each body has different objectives and capabilities. As a result, each relates

differently to the sovereignty of the state, and each has a different potential impact on the international system and change therein.

The General Assembly

In the division of responsibilities among UN organs, the General Assembly may be said to be the legislative branch to the extent possible in a setting of 185 equally sovereign members. Each member of the organization, irrespective of size, financial contribution, or world status, has a single vote. Because, therefore, the General Assembly embodies global pluralism and multiculturalism as does no other, it is not a forum to which governments are generally willing to subordinate their sovereign controls. These limitations have led to the description of the General Assembly as a *quasi*-legislative body despite its broad competence to consider virtually any subject so long as it does not intrude on the domestic jurisdiction of states.[6] Its authority to make binding decisions is limited to certain matters internal to the organization (budget, membership, temporary members of the Security Council). Beyond these, its work is done through parliamentary diplomacy, a process that combines the techniques of legislation with those of negotiation,[7] and its conclusions are expressed in three forms, none of which is decisive.

Declarations are pronouncements of principle that lack binding capacity, although they may result in subsequent treaties and may have moral impact or may evolve into customary international law. One of the declarations of the General Assembly that has been most celebrated but least observed is the famous Universal Declaration of Human Rights (1948). Its principles have found their way into several constitutions, and it has

---

5 Boutros Boutros-Ghali, *Agenda for Peace, 1995* (New York: United Nations), p. 44.

6 See, for example, Richard A. Falk, "On the Quasi-legislative Competence of the General Assembly," *American Journal of International Law*, 1966, pp. 782–791.

7 Philip C. Jessup, "Parliamentary Diplomacy," *Recueil des Cours*, vol. 89 (The Hague: Academy of International Law, 1956), pp. 181–320.

TABLE 15–1

THE UN SYSTEM

All Permanent Organs	All Specialized Agencies	Some Commissions, Funds, and Institutionalized Programs
General Assembly	World Health Organization	Conference on Trade and Development
Security Council	Food and Agricultural Organization	Children's Fund
Trusteeship Council		Special Fund
Economic and Social Council	Intergovernmental Maritime Consultative Organization	Peacekeeping and Observer Forces
Secretariat	International Civil Aviation Organization	Disarmament Commission
International Court of Justice		High Commission for Refugees
	Universal Postal Union	Institute for Training and Research
	International Telecommunications Union	Development Program
	World Meteorological Organization	Environment Program and Earth Watch
	International Labor Organization	Disaster Relief Office
	Educational, Scientific, and Cultural Organization	Fund for Population Activities
	International Atomic Energy Agency	World Food Programme
	International Monetary Fund	World Food Council
	World Bank Group[1]	Center for Transnational Corporations
	General Agreement on Tariffs and Trade	Drug Control Program
	World Intellectual Property Organization	
	United Nations Industrial Development Organization	

[1] The World Bank Group consists of the International Bank for Reconstruction and Development, the International Development Association, and the International Finance Corporation.

become the substance of two international covenants on human rights. But the declaration itself lacks the force of law, despite adoption without a dissenting vote.

Resolutions are both more common and more controversial results of the General Assembly's work. When a resolution stems from existing international law, it illuminates the law and states' obligations under it. But when it imposes a new standard, is it a source of new international law? Because the General Assembly cannot impose decisions on states, presumably such a resolution

The founding of the United Nations, San Francisco, June 1945. U.S. President Harry S Truman stands on the speaker's right, in front of the assembled delegates. (*Source:* © United Nations)

would not enjoy the force of law until general acquiescence is shown in the behavior of member states. But there is a third possiblity, namely, that a General Assembly resolution will recommend, authorize, or enable member governments to undertake certain policies, giving legitimacy to those policies. Such a resolution may not be legally binding on members, but it frees any member or group of members to act as agents of the General Assembly, thus condoning international policy where it cannot generate international law. The supreme instance of a recommendatory resolution of the General Assembly legitimizing foreign policy activity was the Uniting for Peace Resolution (1950), under which the body extended its jurisdiction into matters of international peace and security, an area

previously the exclusive domain of the Security Council. Frustrated by Soviet vetoes there, the United States moved its Korean War policy into the General Assembly, where it sought, and was granted, legitimacy under the Uniting for Peace Resolution.[8]

Conventions are multilateral treaties adopted by the General Assembly for ratification through

---

[8] For various well-known perspectives on this subject, see Leo Gross, "The United Nations and the Role of Law," *International Organization*, 1965, pp. 537–561; Jorge Castañeda, *Legal Effects of United Nations Resolutions* (New York: Columbia University Press, 1969); and Inis L. Claude Jr., "Collective Legitimization as a Political Function of the United Nations," *International Organization*, 1966, pp. 367–379.

the constitutional processes of the member states.[9] Because they require multiple ratifications to enter into effect, the ultimate decision-making authority is not with the General Assembly, but with the members in their respective domestic settings. The General Assembly's treaty-making capacity is not, therefore, a centralized legislative authority, but one dependent for its culmination on the vagaries of domestic politics in 185 diverse capital cities.

The strictures placed on the General Assembly by the charter ensure the infrequency of its authoritative decisions regarding the vital interests of states. Yet through its legitimizing role, the assembly has occasionally made significant contributions to the theory and practice of international stability. The Uniting for Peace Resolution, for all its political aftershocks, is one such example. Another, much more original in form and reusable in content, was an action of the General Assembly pursuant to an initiative of the secretary-general in 1956. Because of their participation in Middle East (Suez) combat, Britain and France had immobilized the Security Council. When the issue was shifted to the General Assembly, it was suggested that Britain and France remove their forces in favor of a UN presence. The result was an assembly mandate to Secretary-General Hammarskjöld to formulate the principles of a new system that came to be known as "peacekeeping"—a specific way of keeping peace. The idea was not to enforce a political objective of one party against that of another, but to interpose a lightly armed force between the belligerents to gain time for diplomacy. Although the Soviet Union opposed bitterly what it considered another erosion of Security Council authority by the General Assembly, these initial

moves evolved into one of the most profoundly important adaptations of UN authority in maintaining international peace and security and in modifying multilateral relations. In the area of global economics, the assembly's Declaration of the New International Economic Order is another example of its ability to alter the course of international relations despite the severe limits of its legislative authority.

Although national viewpoints on the effectiveness of the General Assembly may differ from one event to the next (with their differing evaluations resulting from the incompatibility of their objectives), scholars have concluded that the General Assembly's effectiveness is greater than public opinion and conventional wisdom will admit. One study, for example, that attempts to correlate effectiveness of action with the willingness of states to comply with assembly resolutions, concludes that in twenty-nine resolutions concerning international political situations between 1946 and 1962, effectiveness of action reached 87 percent among those resolutions complied with by states. Where compliance was not forthcoming, the level of effectiveness was a scant 21 percent. The study also substantiates that in matters dealing with threats to the peace, breaches of the peace, and acts of aggression, the level of compliance and effectiveness was higher than in less dangerous and nonmilitary situations.[10] But these data pertain only to compliance with, and effectiveness of, General Assembly resolutions, which often deal only with parts of disputes. To this extent, and except for specified situations, the General Assembly shares other international agencies' failure to prevent war situations, as detailed in the empirical data of yet another study.[11]

---

[9] There is a second form of "United Nations Treaty" in which the organization enters into an agreement with a government. The Headquarters Agreement with the United States is an example. In an instance in which the United Nations and Egypt entered into an agreement to permit peacekeeping troops to utilize Egyptian territory in the 1956 Suez crisis, over which lightly armed peacekeeping was invented, the political circumstances of the region were changed significantly.

[10] Gabriella Rosner Lande, "An Inquiry into the Success and Failures of the United Nations General Assembly," in Leon Gordenker, ed., The United Nations in International Politics (Princeton, N.J.: Princeton University Press, 1971), pp. 106–129.

[11] J. David Singer and Michael Wallace, "Preservation of Peace, 1816–1964: Some Bivariate Relationships," International Organization, vol. 24, 1970, pp. 520–547.

The Security Council

In comparison with the General Assembly, the Security Council of the United Nations is both more complex and simpler. It is more complex because it is more the forum of intensive great-power politics than is the General Assembly; here, clashes of opinion can incapacitate the UN system more profoundly on crucial issues of war and peace. Throughout the Cold War period, the Security Council's political paralysis in one crisis after another dramatized the shortcomings of intergovernmental organization far more than anything that occurred—or did not occur—in the General Assembly. Yet herein lies the organ's simplicity as well: The veto power of the five permanent members (the United States, Russia, Britain, France, and China out of a total membership of fifteen) often prevents effective decision making in the Security Council, and if it cannot establish policy, the global problem of ensuring compliance and effective implementation is obviated. Until the New World Order, the Security Council was the principal public forum of East-West conflict, a forum long on ideological rhetoric and short on responsible collective management of international crises.

The Security Council grew out of the so-called grand design or grand alliance of the Second World War. Despite the mutual suspicions and antipathies between the West and the Soviet Union, the necessity of alliance against the fascist menace fostered cooperation that many assumed could survive into the post-war period as a collective means of ensuring international peace and security. But underlying differences, together with the historical American fear of being dragged into foreign wars, were expressed in the Security Council's complex voting formula: On matters of substance, decisions are made by a majority of nine votes "including the concurring votes of the permanent members." The final phrase is the veto power of the permanent members. Abstentions and absences do not affect the outcomes of decisions. Earlier, however, a controversy raged over the meaning and political

impact of abstentions, because it was during the Soviet absence in June and July of 1950 that Washington's Korean War policy was legitimized by the Security Council. At that time, many observers (including Soviet) held that in the absence of one of the five permanent members, the votes of the council had no binding effect on the organization.[12] More recently, the issue has ceased to have meaning, and often votes are recorded as "in favor," "opposed," "abstaining," and either "absent" or "not participating."

Great-power dominance has been the chief impediment to effective Security Council action. For the five permanent members, decision making remains absoutely decentralized, because any one of them can tie the council's hands. For the ten governments holding the temporary seats, the council's decision making is relatively centralized, because none alone can prevent a decision if the permanent members are unified. For the remaining bulk of UN members (170 as of December 31, 1995), who face being obligated by policies formulated without their participation, Security Council actions appear highly centralized. But the ability of any single permanent member to prevent action means that ultimately the Security Council is highly decentralized. It is true that if all five permanent members abstain and nine of the others constitute a majority, then a decision can be reached. But in the Security Council as in the General Assembly, the making of formal norms by majority voting can be deceptive; unless states are willing to put their power behind decisions, there will be no effective impact on the international system. And if, as is often the case in the Security Council, the issue at hand involves a threat to peace, a breach of peace, or an act of aggression, even successful collective decision making

---

[12] For starkly contrasting interpretations of this matter, see the works of a positivist and of a neorealist, respectively: Leo Gross, "Voting in the Security Council: Abstention from Voting and Absence from Meetings," *Yale Law Journal*, 1951, pp. 210–257; and Myres S. McDougal and Richard N. Gardner, "The Veto and the Charter: An Interpretation for Survival," *Yale Law Journal*, 1951, pp. 258–92.

The United Nations Secretariat Building in New York celebrates the institution's golden anniversary, 1995. (*Source:* © AFP/Corbis-Bettmann)

may not provide benefit unless it is backed by sufficient will to implement it.[13]

Increasingly, the Security Council's membership fails to reflect the facts of world politics. Twice in the past it has been altered, once by General Assembly policy (granting to Beijing in 1971 the UN membership, and with it the council seat, formerly held by Taiwan), and once by charter amendment

(expanding the membership from eleven to fifteen and the voting majority from seven to nine). But the vast structural changes in world politics in the past decade—end of the Cold War, breakup of the Soviet Union and its Eastern European empire, reunification of Germany, cohesiveness of the Developing Nations, the European Union, Japan's economic position and independence of Washington, Middle East political realignment—have provoked competing demands for more change in the Security Council. The governments of many Developing Nations prefer eliminating the veto but, aware that the permanent members will not sacrifice it, propose a veto seat for one of their own. A permanent seat for Germany? For Japan? If so, with or without veto? On the other side of the debate, does increasing the number of potential vetoes improve or diminish prospects for Security Council effectiveness? Furthermore, the five permenent members achieved their status through victory in World War Two, and the system they created in the Security Council was one of collective security in which they would provide the power to achieve, enforce, and maintain peace. In the New World Order, is it in the world's interest to expand the number of military powers?

The answers to these questions about the Security Council's membership lie not so much in the world's power equation as in the future role of the council itself. The only time the Security Council implemented collective security as envisioned in 1945 was in the case of Iraq's conquest of Kuwait in 1990 and 1991, after the collapse of the Cold War order. Since then, however, the council has been called upon repeatedly to undertake peacekeeping missions, a concept that it has reshaped greatly in the early years of the New World Order. If peacekeeping is to become the major mode of Security Council operation, then expanding the number of permanent members, assuming they are granted veto status, is unlikely under contemporary political circumstances to diminish the council's effectiveness. But if, as the Iraq example demonstrates, collective security survives as a Security Council mission into the next century, then expansion may

---

[13] Leo Gross, "Voting in the Security Council: Abstention in the Post-1965 Amendment Phase and Its Impact upon Article 25 of the Charter," *American Journal of International Law*, 1968, pp. 315–334.

have deleterious consequences. History may yet prove that the consensus on Iraq was such a rare combination of historical timing (end of the Cold War), East-West leadership collaboration (Gorbachev and Bush), unjustified aggression, and threat to great-power interests (Kuwait's moderate oil policy regarding Japan and the West) that it was unique and unreplicable. If this were the case, collective security would become as elusive in the future as it was prior to 1990. Meanwhile, a Security Council Summit Declaration of 1991 expands the definition of threats to international peace to include non-military sources of instability in the economic, social, humanitarian and ecological fields, suggesting that a new interventionary role may evolve for the Security Council that combines the enforcement legitimacy of Chapter VII with the nonmilitary service roles of modern peacekeeping.

The International Court of Justice

The International Court of Justice (ICJ), or World Court, enjoys a dual role in the international system as it is simultaneously the constitutional court of the United Nations and the court of law among states. In its relation to the United Nations, the court has the authority to render advisory opinions on formal request from official UN bodies. As we have seen in the *Certain Expenses* case concerning the funding of UN peacekeeping in the Congo and the Middle East, these opinions may strengthen and expand the operating scope of the organization. At the same time, however, the opinions are unenforceable, so that their effectiveness is determined by the willingness of member states to comply voluntarily with any organizational policy that results from an advisory opinion of the court.

In its role among states, the World Court is authorized to hear contentious cases, or cases involving disputes between or among states, and to render judgments. But unlike domestic courts, the ICJ is limited in this activity by the willingness of states to bring their disputes before it. Domestic courts possess compulsory jurisdiction, which means that they determine their own jurisdiction according to

law and that subjects of the legal system are bound to appear when called. In the United States, for example, individuals can be summoned into court, corporations can be sued against their will, and governmental officials can be enjoined from certain acts. The ICJ has no comparable authority. All members of the United Nations are members of the ICJ, but their obligation to utilize the court is restricted by the court's own statute.

The statute was created by a Committee of Jurists in 1921 for the Permanent Court of International Justice, a court affiliated with (but not a permanent organ of) the League of Nations. The committee recognized both the desirability and the political impracticability of imposing compulsory jurisdiction on states, knowing from the outset that including it in the statute would prevent many states from embracing the court. Accordingly, they adopted what was to be an interim arrangement under which governments voluntarily could accept the the court's limited compulsory jurisdiction on certain matters, with or without reservation, and on condition of reciprocity. These conditions comprised the "optional clause" of the statute.

When the ICJ was established as a permanent organ of the United Nations, the statute was adopted virtually unchanged. The critically important passages regarding member obligations to use the UN's principal judicial organ are found in Article 36.

> Article 36.1. The jurisdiction of the court comprises all cases which the parties refer to it and all matters specially provided for in the Charter of the United Nations or in treaties and conventions in force.

> Article 36.2. The states party to the present Statute may at any time declare that they recognize as compulsory *ipso facto* and without special agreement, in relation to any other state accepting the same obligation, the jurisdiction of the Court on all legal disputes concerning:

> a. the interpretation of a treaty;
> b. any question of international law;
> c. the existence of any fact which, if established, would constitute a breach of an international obligation;

d. the nature or extent of the reparation to be made for the breach of an international obligation.

Article 36.3. The declarations referred to above may be made unconditionally or on condition of reciprocity on the part of several or certain states, or for a certain time.

...

Article 36.6. In the event of a dispute as to whether the Court has jurisdiction, the matter shall be settled by the decision of the Court.

Because the court is a permanent organ of the United Nations, all UN members are automatically its members. Yet, as Article 36.2 indicates, recognition of the court's limited compulsory jurisdiction requires an act separate from joining the organization. Fewer than one-quarter have executed that step, virtually all of them with substantive reservations. Reservations typically excuse the state from use of the court on matters that lie within the domestic jurisdiction of the state or that are classified as matters of vital national security interest.[14] Some national reservations effectively nullify Article 36.6 by declaring that the state alone shall determine whether or not an issue lies within its domestic jurisdiction. Moreover, states are free to terminate their declarations of acceptance (as France and the United States have done), to allow them to lapse after a given period of time (Turkey), or to modify them to fit new and unforeseen circumstances. In a most celebrated instance, before withdrawing its declaration of acceptance the United States notified the secretary-general of a change in order to avoid responding to a Nicaraguan suit in the ICJ regarding American intervention in the Nicaraguan civil war. Washington

indicated that the declaration would no longer pertain to matters in Central America. Given all these protections against the court's compulsory jurisdiction, there now exists a brisk debate among scholars on the value of retaining Article 36 of the statute, at least in its classical form.[15]

Under the conditions of membership, then, there is little obligation to use the court; thus a decision to use the World Court is a political rather than a legal matter. Studies have considered why nations use the court. One compared the decision processes on each side of four suits brought to court: the *Nuclear Test* case, in which Australia and New Zealand sued to prevent France from conducting nuclear tests in the South Pacific; the *Fisheries Jurisdiction* case, in which Britain and Germany brought suit against Iceland to determine the territorial limits of exclusive fishing rights; the *North Sea Continental Shelf* case, in which Germany sued both Denmark and the Netherlands on division of the North Sea continental shelf for purposes of fishing and mining rights; and the *Prisoners of War* case between Pakistan and India. The study determined that six motives lead plaintiffs to invoke the authority of the World Court. First, such a decision may be a tactical move to speed up negotiations. Second, it provides the suing party an opportunity to save face in domestic politics. Third, such a suit may focus worldwide critical attention on the opponent and its international policy. Fourth, although the

---

[14] For example, one of the four reservations included in the recently canceled U.S. acceptance read: "Provided that this declaration shall not apply to . . . [d]isputes with regard to matters which are essentially within the domestic jurisdiction of the United States of America *as determined by the United States of America*" (emphasis added). The emphasized final clause is referred to as the Connally amendment, after the senator who sponsored it.

[15] Withdrawal of the American declaration set off a modern debate about the meaning of Article 36.2. For various viewpoints, see Anthony Clark Arend, ed., *The United States and the Compulsory Jurisdiction of the International Court of Justice* (Charlottesville, Va.: Center for Law and National Security, 1986); Thomas J. Franck, *Judging the World Court* (New York: Priority Press Publications, 1986); Jonathan I. Charney, "Compromissory Clauses and the Jurisdiction of the International Court of Justice," *American Journal of International Law,* October 1987, pp. 855–887; Gary L. Scott and Craig L. Carr, "The International Court of Justice and Compulsory Jurisdiction: The Case for Closing the Clause," *American Journal of International Law,* January 1987, pp. 57–76; and Robert E. Lutz, "The World Court in a Changing World: An Agenda for Expanding the Court's Role from a U.S. Perspective," *Stanford Journal of International Law,* spring 1991, pp. 265–343.

parties may not be equally powerful and influential in world politics, the judicial environment tends to equalize them and to remove disparities. Fifth, the acting state may wish to use the court in order to establish or clarify a rule of international law. And sixth, in cases of suits between states that have generally friendly relations, utilization of the court permits isolation of the dispute from the full body of their relations, thus preventing contamination of other issues between them.[16]

If the decision to bring suit in the World Court is political, then a decision to be sued will be doubly political. When threatened with action in the World Court, states generally react by claiming that they have exempted themselves from the court's jurisdiction. In the cases examined in the same study, the respondent states also felt that politically it is preferable to seek a partial solution by agreement or compromise than to await an absolute solution based on court procedure and a potentially embarrassing decision. In other words, states prefer to avoid suit than to face outcomes that politically they are unwilling to execute. Finally, states attempt to avoid the jurisdiction of the court because of the vagueness, uncertainty, or absence of the law to be applied—all circumstances that make it more difficult for respondents to assess probable outcomes.

In rare cases when disputing parties agree to adjudicate and the court renders a final judgment, the international legal system is faced with its second problem: compliance. It commonly is thought that states ignore or violate the court's decisions. In fact, however, there is a high degree of compliance for two reasons. First, the ICJ is capable of rendering either declaratory or executory judgments. In declaratory judgments, it declares itself on a point of law and may in effect advise states as to their rights or may limit behavior by clarification of existing law. These judgments are not intended to

favor one state over another in specific issues, and neither disputant need make restitution to the other. Executory judgments are quite a different matter. These occur when the court finds for one contestant over the other and orders one to undertake remedial or compensatory action. Much misinformation has circulated about these judgments, leading to the impression that states rarely have carried out judicial awards made against them. In fact, however, such cases of noncompliance are exceptional.

The second reason for a high degree of compliance is closely akin to an argument used in earlier discussion of states' compliance with treaties. Because, in the absence of compulsory jurisdiction, use of the court is almost wholly voluntary, it stands to reason that a government will not make the political decision to seek a judicial settlement without having assessed possible outcomes and accepted in advance the obligation to carry out an award in case of an adverse decision.

What remedies exist when states refuse to comply with judicial awards? As the traditional standards of sanctions suggest, a judicial award gives a state an actionable right. This may be exercised through general IGOs, functional organizations, or regional organizations. Conceivably, even the Security Council might be called upon to enforce compliance, as provided by Article 94 of the UN Charter. Such actions, however, may serve merely to repoliticize a dispute previously depoliticized by having been taken to the court in the first place. The other alternative is to rely on self-help, with all its potential anarchical and escalatory effects.

Remarkably illustrative of many of these principles and their limitations was Washington's behavior regarding the *Case Concerning Military and Paramilitary Activities In and Against Nicaragua*, a suit entered in the ICJ by Nicaragua in 1984. The Nicaraguan government sought court orders terminating alleged American intervention in its country's civil war, in the form of arms supplies to the Contra (antigovernment) forces and mining of the Nicaraguan port. It also sought $370 million in

---

[16] Dana D. Fischer, "Decisions to Use the International Court of Justice: Four Recent Cases," *International Studies Quarterly*, June 1982, pp. 251–277.

reparations for damages attributed to American intervention.

Just three days before the action was filed, the Reagan administration notified the Secretary-General of the United Nations of a change in the long-standing American acceptance of the court's limited compulsory jurisdiction. Effective immediately and for a two-year period, the notification stipulated, American acceptance "shall not apply to disputes with any Central American State or arising out of or related to events in Central America, any of which disputes shall be settled in such manner as the parties to them may agree." The purpose, according to Washington, was "to foster the continuing regional dispute settlement process."[17] The logic, however, was to deny the court's jurisdiction in anticipation of its refusal to evaluate American policy in the full political and ideological context of regional events to which the United States was reacting.

In its response to Nicaragua's application for trial, the United States formally argued that the court was without jurisdiction for several reasons.[18] Principal among them was that Nicaragua's own acceptance of the court's compulsory jurisdiction, a carryover from the Permanent Court of International Justice in 1929, was procedurally incomplete and, therefore, invalid (even though Washington never before had presented this analysis in judicial dealings with Nicaragua). Assuming its invalidity, then, Washington claimed its reciprocal right under the statute not to be subjected to the court's compulsory jurisdiction, despite its historic acceptance and notwithstanding its recent modification. Over these objections, the court ruled unanimously that the case fell properly within its jurisdiction, and it agreed to proceed with an examination of

the facts and merits. At the same time, it decided that the United States should desist from restricting access to Nicaraguan ports and that Nicaragua's sovereignty should not be endangered by any military or paramilitary activities prohibited by international law. Now, having lost its argument regarding the court's jurisdiction, Washington declared that it would not participate further in the deliberations. Nicaragua's case was branded "a misuse of the Court for political purposes." Furthermore, the State Department rationalized, "The haste with which the Court proceeded to a judgment [on the matter of jurisdiction] . . . only adds to the impression that the Court is determined to find in favor of Nicaragua in the case." Under such circumstances, American participation was unjustified.[19] Washington had decided that it could ill afford the political consequences of an adverse judicial decision.

Nicaragua and the court proceeded without the United States, and in 1986, the court ruled in favor of Nicaragua's claims. In a series of sixteen votes on individual matters, the court found the United States in violation of customary international law regarding the use of force, violations of Nicaraguan sovereignty, and intervention in the internal affairs of another state. It rejected only Nicaragua's claim that all damage done should be attributed to the United States. Although the court determined that Nicaragua was due reparations, it declined to establish an amount.[20] Having by these decisions acquired an actionable right, Nicaragua proceeded to the Security Council, where it invoked its right under Article 94 of the UN Charter to seek council enforcement of the court's decisions. Taking full advantage of its permanent-member prerogatives under Article 27.3,

---

[17] *Case Concerning Military and Paramilitary Activities In and Against Nicaragua (Nicaragua v. United States of America)*, 1984 *ICJ Reports*, pp. 169 ff. at pp. 174–175. For a summary, see a case note by Monroe Leigh, *American Journal of International Law*, October 1984, pp. 894–897.

[18] For a transcription of the American argument on jurisdiction, see *U.S. Department of State Bulletin*, January 1985, pp. 24–29.

[19] For the text of the State Department's news statement on the discontinuance of participation, see *U.S. Department of State Bulletin*, March 1985, pp. 64–65. The statement was released on January 18, 1985.

[20] For the summary of the court's findings and the Security Council's debate, see *United Nations Chronicle*, August 1986, p. 110; and *U.S. Department of State Bulletin*, November 1986, p. 57.

Washington vetoed action against itself and nullified Nicaragua's only political recourse to the enforcement of a judicial award.

The case prompted within the Reagan administration a comprehensive review of the American acceptance of the court's compulsory jurisdiction. Even before the court's final award to Nicaragua, the United States had determined that for a number of reasons, acceptance of compulsory jurisdiction no longer benefited its foreign policy. Using classic Cold War logic, it noted the imbalance between its obligations and those of the Soviet Union and the East European nations, none of which had accepted compulsory jurisdiction. Its principal argument was that as a founding member of the United Nations, it never had expected the principal judicial body to become involved in matters of high politics that presumably were reserved for the Security Council. Hence, in accepting jurisdiction in the *Nicaragua* case, the court had enlarged its scope in a manner potentially injurious to American security interests. In explaining the administration's decision to the Senate Foreign Relations Committee, the legal adviser to the State Department argued as follows:

> The fact that the ICJ indicated it would hear and decide claims about the on-going use of force made acceptance of the Court's compulsory jurisdiction an issue of strategic significance. Despite our deep reluctance to do so and the many domestic constraints that apply, we must be able to use force in our self-interest and in the defense of our friends and allies. We are a law-abiding nation, and when we submit ourselves to adjudication of a subject we regard ourselves as obliged to abide by the result. For the United States to recognize that the ICJ has authority to define and adjudicate with respect to our right of self-defense, therefore, is effectively to surrender to that body the power to pass on our efforts to guarantee the safety and security of this nation and of its allies.

Having thus constructed its case, the United States notified the secretary-general in 1985 of the withdrawal, effective six months later, of its acceptance of the ICJ's limited compulsory jurisdiction, under Article 36.2 of the statute.[21]

Social, Economic, and Humanitarian Functions

Although media attention usually focuses on the contribution of the United Nations to global security, the organization engages in a vast array of social, economic, and humanitarian activities that receive far less attention or acclaim. These activities are consistent with the functional theory of international relations, introduced in the early 1930s, which posits that in the long run, peace is preserved by growing international trust and reciprocity constructed around specific common objectives of states. It assumes, not entirely accurately, that as trust builds around relatively nonpolitical interests, it will spill over to the crucial political interests of governments. Its first practical verification occurred in 1936 when, even while the African and Asian conflicts of the Second World War were already in progress, with little lingering hope of effective action on the part of the League of Nations, a major evaluation of the nonsecurity activities of the League found them to be still healthy and productive.

The post-war endorsement of functionalism was signaled by inclusion of the Economic and Social Council and of the Trusteeship Council among the permanent organs of the United Nations. Thereafter, specialized agencies were created on the basis of perceived international needs with respect to health; refugees; economic development; children; educational, social, and cultural activities; labor; trade; and so forth. Two venerable functional organizations, the Universal Postal Union and the International Telecommunications Union, were incorporated into the UN system. Special programs, commissions, and funds continue to be added as

---

[21] For the full statement and the text of the letter to the secretary-general, see *U.S. Department of State Bulletin*, January 1986, pp. 67–71.

world attention is focused on new humanitarian needs: the environment program, the development program, the population program, and so forth. Today, a survey of the activities of the United Nations in areas not directly related to international peace and security is a virtual tour of world political, social, economic, and humanitarian concerns. Although the world has stumbled into nearly 100 wars since the World War Two armistice, functionalism through the United Nations (and elsewhere) has flourished and has been a major force of change.

Many of these functional activities are discussed elsewhere in this book, particularly those related to international economic development. One that merits specific mention here, however, is the progress made through the United Nations toward self-government of formerly colonized peoples. The United Nations shares with the League of Nations, however delicately, formal commitment to the self-determination of national peoples, largely on the ground that competitive imperialism is a cause of war. To deal with this problem, the League created a system of mandates by which established states undertook formally to prepare colonized peoples for self-government in the League's behalf. The United Nations has provided a dual system, consisting of a Trusteeship System and a Declaration Regarding Non-Self-Governing Territories.

The Trusteeship System was arranged (Chapters 12 and 13 of the UN Charter) for international surveillance of progress toward self-government. To colonized peoples, the trusteeship was a progressive mechanism, for it included formal terminal dates and the promise of international pressure to enforce major-power compliance with the terms of the agreement. But to the major states, trusteeship agreements involve too much obligation and exposure. As a result, trusteeship has not been the main route to independence.

But out of this gap between plan and performance emerged one of the great success stories of UN history. In Chapter 11 of the UN Charter, the framers had arranged a Declaration Regarding Non-Self-Governing Territories. Although it was initially assumed merely to inscribe principles rather than legal obligations, this declaration became the United Nations' prime peaceful mechanism through which sovereign status has been achieved by formerly colonized peoples in the postwar era.[22] The focal point of this development has been the evolution of Article 73(e). Here UN members who controlled non-self-governing territories accepted as a "sacred trust" the responsibility to achieve well-being for the inhabitants, and in pursuit of this goal they consented

> to transmit regularly to the Secretary-General for information purposes, subject to such limitation as security and constitutional considerations may require, statistical and other information of a technical nature relating to economic, social and educational conditions in the territories for which they are respectively responsible.

By evolution, this hope was transformed into an obligation. Article 73(e) became a source of international scrutiny. (It would be excessive to say surveillance.) It shares significant responsibility for the huge increase in the total number of states and in the membership of the United Nations. More than half of the UN member nations have become independent in the last thirty-five years. Even more remarkable as the result of this emancipation, between 1945 and 1985 the number of people living in dependent territories declined from 750 million to 2.8 million.[23] This reduction occurred while the

---

[22] Much of the expansion in UN membership has occurred from achievement of sovereign independence. The first boom was after 1956, when the old European empires in the Developing World began to crumble and former colonies by the dozens became independent. The second followed the breakup of the Soviet Union and the subsequent disintegration of Yugoslavia and division of Czechoslovakia.

[23] *United Nations Chronicle*, January 1986, pp. 76–80 at p. 79. The decline is the more dramatic in light of the continuing and alarming increase in population in the Developing World. In 1982, for example, the number was estimated as 4 million, out of a Developing World population several hundred million fewer than in 1985. See United Nations, *Report on the World Social Situation, 1982.*

world's total population increased by 50 percent, with a disproportionate amount of that increase in the newly independent, underindustrialized areas of the world. By 1991 less than one-twentieth of 1 percent of the global population lived in dependent or colonized territories, half of them in British Hong Kong and Portuguese Macao, both of which will rejoin China in 1997. This remarkable reduction in the number of dependent peoples occurred over a span of barely forty years, during which the last of nineteenth- and twentieth-century empires dissolved. Belgian and Portuguese power yielded to black self-government in Africa; the French abandoned virtually all their colonial holdings from Southeast Asia to Africa; and the once nearly global British Empire dwindled to a few remnants—Gibraltar, eight Caribbean sites, and Hong Kong. To underscore the rapidity of these events, one historian wrote the following comment more than a decade ago about the sun's setting on the British Empire:

> Until 1947—within the lifetime of half the world's population—the Government in London ruled more land and people than any other government in history. In the thirty-three years between India's independence in 1947 and Southern Rhodesia's in 1980, the British Empire ended. Territories that gained independence from Britain before then—for example the American colonies and Ireland—were part of the imperial ebb and flow. After 1980 the dozen territories that remained—were no longer an empire, merely the leftovers. Relative to its size, no great ship ever sank so quickly.[24]

Encouraged by the great progress made toward the elimination of colonialism in sub-Saharan Africa, the states of the Non-Aligned Movement within the United Nations persuaded the General Assembly to adopt in late 1988 a resolution declaring the 1990s as the International Decade for the Eradication of Colonialism. The reader is cautioned,

however, that political independence is not necessarily independence in its entirety. As Chapter 6 has indicated, political independence in the underindustrialized world has often been followed by economic subservience and neoimperialism.

The United Nations and International Peace

By the time of its fiftieth anniversary in October 1995, the United Nations had accumulated a spotty record on its foremost objective: the preservation of international peace. Its critics, especially those who prefer nationalistic realism to multilateralism, argued that the historical foundations on which collective security was built were faulty and fatuous; that irreconcilable intergovernmental differences make the Security Council's mission unattainable (Desert Storm having been a historic exception); that peacekeeping is too expensive, inconsistent with normal military purposes, and insufficiently designed tactically; and that aggression can only be turned back when the vital interests of powerful states or coalitions move those governments to responsive action under their respective constitutional authorities. Its supporters, on the other hand, among them multinationalists committed to ending the anarchy of individually-determined counterforce, respond that UN programs other than in the Security Council have reduced the impetus to war; that it was the Cold War and not the UN Charter that paralyzed the council; and that while peacekeeping is imperfect, no alternative to counteraggression has ever contributed as much to the pacification of hostile situations. The only agreement in this debate is one historical fact, namely, that for whatever reason, collective security has not served the world effectively. Despite the end of the Cold War and the unusual circumstances that merged into the Security Council–sponsored coalition that drove Iraq out of Kuwait in 1991, there is little reason to expect that it will do much more than deter aggression in the future.

---

[24] Brian Lapping, *End of Empire* (New York: St. Martin's Press, 1985), p. xiv.

Peacekeeping has emerged as the principal method of UN response to breaches of the peace and acts of aggression, provided that major military powers are not initial combatants. Although its origin is often set at 1956, when the UN's first lightly armed interventionary force was dispatched to the Middle East to quiet the Suez crisis, the history of peacekeeping actually dates to the UN's infancy. In 1947, a fact-finding mission was sent to the Balkans to determine whether or not the forces of Soviet-allied governments were conducting incursions into Greece. Thus began a lengthy evolution that, in the view of one author, has gone through five distinctive stages.[25]

Stage I, 1946–1955. In these years, four unarmed missions were sent to inquire into possible breaches of peace or to supervise cease-fires. During this phase, the initial rules of peacekeeping were articulated: host-state consent, political neutrality in contrast to enforcement, and non-use of force. Except in the first instance, which was limited to Security Council members, the concept was also developed that peacekeeping missions should exclude the major powers.

Stage II, 1956–1965. A total of eight undertakings included the first two armed peacekeeping missions, UNEF I (United Nations Emergency Force in the Middle East) and ONUC (United Nations Operation in the Congo, using initials as per the French language). Both were severe tests of this new adaptation. UNEF was created by the General Assembly so as to avoid French and British vetoes in the Security Council; and while ONUC was a Security Council creation, the Soviet Union objected to what it considered the Western-sympathetic manner in which it was directed by the secretary-general.

Stage III, 1966–1985. Although there were but three peacekeeping missions in this phase, all to the Middle East, the period is important because it was in these years that the primacy of the Security Council in matters of peacekeeping was accepted, placing the doctrine in a more stable political environment than it had enjoyed previously. From theoretical and diplomatic perspectives, this was the most important phase.

Stage IV, 1986–1989. Though it occupied the briefest period, this phase is of lasting importance because it foreshadowed the end of the Cold War. Among the four actions, one was to oversee withdrawal of Cuban troops from Angola, one to oversee Namibia's final liberation from South African control, and one to oversee and verify the discontinuance of foreign intervention in Central America's civil wars. The last of these is important because the Bush administration had made the withdrawal of Soviet troops from Nicaragua and El Salvador virtually the final test of Mikhail Gorbachev's commitment to a post–Cold War order.

Stage V, 1990–present. This is the post–Cold War phase of peacekeeping's history, and the vast political changes of the New World Order have also made it the most prolific. By the end of 1995, a total of fifteen missions has been created and dispatched. Remarkably, one of these was to Georgia, a former constituent republic of the Soviet Union, where civil strife threatened to break into war. But because Russia was a party to the civil war in Chechnya, the certainty of its veto in the Security Council prevented collective action there.

---

[25] David R. Segal, "Five Phases of United Nations Peacekeeping: An Evolutionary Typology," *Journal of Military and Political Sociology*, summer 1995, pp. 65–79 with adaptations.

These preceding stages address historical evolution. Another scholar has made a similar effort to organize the functions of peacekeeping.[26]

Type I. Preventive deployment of troops. Here troops are dispatched to areas where conflict is threatened but has not yet erupted.

Type II. Traditional peacekeeping. Troops may be either unarmed or armed, and they are charged with separating combatants in order to accelerate diplomatic exploration of alternative settlements. They do so by monitoring troop movements, protecting buffer zones, policing cease-fire agreements, disarming troops, confiscating weapons, and so forth.

Type III. Implementation of comprehensive settlements. Particularly in the last decade, the functions of peacekeeping forces have expanded considerably. In the past they served almost exclusively in military roles or the supervision of military operations. Based on experience in such places as Cambodia and Namibia, however, "[i]ncreasingly, peace-keeping requires that civilian political officers, human rights monitors, electoral officials, refugee and humanitarian aid specialists and police play as central a role as the military."[27]

Type IV. Conduct or protect humanitarian relief supply. In both Somalia and Bosnia, this was the UN's principal role. In Bosnia, however, because peacekeeping troops were armed and authorized to use force to fulfill their mission, they frequently found themselves in a quasi-combat role, particularly in protecting the supposed "safe" (demilitarized) civilian areas.

Type V. Deployment to states in anarchy. Used successfully in the Congo in the 1960s and unsuccessfully in Somalia in the 1990s, this is a UN response to a nation in which the organs of government have ceased to function because of civil chaos. Its substance may include all the attributes of Types III and IV, and it may require enforcement.

Type VI. Peace enforcement. Technically, this is new to the United Nations, though it is an adaptation of some aspects of cease-fire enforcement that requires greater firepower. In early 1995 it was thought that the UN might undertake this role in Bosnia, but the function was taken up by NATO instead.

As these two typologies indicate, peacekeeping underwent a rapid evolution in the early days of the New World Order. It did so because of the rapid and profound changes in the global power distribution, removal of Cold War politics from the Security Council, disintegration of the Soviet Union, and Russia's abandonment of its Cold War client states. But the evolution is of even greater significance because UN actions have occurred in "disputes which formerly would have been vigorously excluded from the United Nations agenda by virtue of the fact that they take place in the back yard of one or other superpower."[28] One needs only to consider Haiti, Nicaragua, the former Yugoslavia, and Georgia to verify this claim. But popularity does not ensure success. In fact, the serious setbacks suffered by UN peacekeepers in Bosnia (where several deaths and hostage takings together with inability to protect the safe towns resulted in combat and resort to NATO aerial bombings) caused a reconsideration of the enthusiasm with which the Security

---

[26] Marrack Goulding, "The Evolution of Peacekeeping," *International Affairs* (London), March 1993, pp. 451–464, especially pp. 456-460.

[27] Boutros Boutros-Ghali, *An Agenda for Peace, 1995*, pp. 59–60.

[28] Alan James, "Peacekeeping in the Post–Cold War Era," *International Journal*, spring 1995, pp. 241–265 at p. 258.

Council embraced peacekeeping in the first half of the 1990s. The murder and public display of the remains of an American soldier in Somalia added to the decline of peacekeeping's popularity in the United States. The sudden change in public opinion prompted one observer to write that it is "a mirror of the commotion and ill-considered enthusiasm which have accompanied the end of the Cold War, rather than indicative of a basic flaw in the concept of peacekeeping."[29]

Despite its imperfections, however, peacekeeping is the most important UN contribution to international security and one of its most important innovations. A comment written nearly three decades ago still applies:

> Perhaps the most significant development in the thinking of scholars and statesmen about international organization in the [post–World War Two] period has been their gradual emnancipation from the collective security fixation, their breaking out of the intellectual rut in which it was taken for granted that the suppression of aggression was so crucial a function of general international organizations that if this function could not be exercised, the only issue worth thinking about was how to make its exercise possible. Dag Hammarskjöld gave dramatic and forceful expression to the new and less constricted approach to international organization when he put the question of how the United Nations could contribute directly to keeping the peace when it could not enforce the peace and answered the question by formulating the theory of preventive diplomacy, now generally known as peacekeeping.[30]

Because peacekeeping is preferable to war and more pratical politically than collective security, its adaptations are likely to progress in the New World Order. In his *Agenda for Peace*, Secretary-General Boutros-Ghali recommended several specific changes.[31]

1. Improvement of preventive deployment by dispatching troops to international borders with the consent of one or both parties, if either senses that conflict is imminent.

2. Maintenance by member governments of troops earmarked to UN service, on a permanent basis rather than an emergency, ad hoc basis. This would deter aggression as well as respond to it, thus removing the initial advantages of quick military strikes. Such a step would globalize the concept of "standby agreements," by which several small powers such as Canada, India, and Ireland frequently have contributed troops to UN peacekeeping.

3. Donation to the United Nations by members of prepositioned logistical equipment such as communications equipment, vehicles, and generators, so that they will be available readily. As an alternative, states should hold these in preparation for assignment to the United Nations in emergency situations.

4. Utilization of peace enforcement units consisting of more heavily armed forces than used in traditional peacekeeping. (This is a controversial proposal, because peace enforcement may involve combat. But successful limited enforcement has been undertaken in Iraq, where UN-authorized warplanes maintain "no-fly" zones to prevent Iraqi air strikes on Kurdish populations. In addition, a UN commission is responsible for monitoring Iraq's defense developments, especially its chemical and nuclear components, by having UN-mandated access to all research and storage facilities, as part of the agreement that terminated the Desert Storm War.)

[29] Alan James, "Peacekeeping in the Post–Cold War Era," p. 265.
[30] Inis L. Claude Jr., "The United Nations, the United States, and the Maintenance of Peace," *International Organization*, 1969, pp. 621–636. While this statement gives full credit to Hammarskjöld, Lester Pearson, Canadian ambassador and later prime minister, generally is credited with having formulated much of the original peacekeeping concept.

[31] Boutros Boutros-Ghali, *Agenda for Peace, 1995*, pp. 49–58. Many of the secretary-general's thoughts also appear in "Empowering the United Nations," *Foreign Affairs*, winter 1992–93, pp. 89–102.

5. Funding of UN peacekeeping operations from the defense budgets of member states rather then their foreign affairs budgets, because the former are much the greater, and because the cost of peacekeeping is trivial compared with the cost of war. This argument undoubtedly is designed to resolve the UN's debt crisis, discussed below and outlined in Table 15–2.

It is not immediately clear how these proposals apply to imminent or actual civil wars, which have become the main conflicts of the post–Cold War era. Nonetheless, they underscore once again the limitations of the United Nations as an international organization, even in relation to its central mission: It is not a sovereign entity; it has no standing military forces; it lacks a defense budget; and it is totally dependent on its members both politically and budgetarily for the effective fulfillment of its responsibilities. In the words of the Swedish prime minister: "The United Nations is not a third party, somehow separate from member governments. It is not the property of the officials appointed to head its secretariat or agencies. The United Nations belongs to its members—with all the benefits, problems, and, above all, responsibilities of ownership."[32]

Evaluation of United Nations Performance

Secretary-General Dag Hammarskjöld, who was killed in an airplane crash in 1964 while viewing UN peacekeeping operations in the Congo, would have taken issue with the preceding characterization of the United Nations, not because it is inaccurate, but because it is incomplete. He propounded strongly the view that despite its dependence on its members, the United Nations can, by the good example of what it can do through multilateral cooperation, become a significant force in world politics, not separate from its members, but in concert with them. He viewed the UN as having a catalytic or coalescing capacity to bring governments together around specific issues in a way they cannot bilaterally. One can reasonably speculate that had he been secretary-general at the birth of the New World Order, his conviction would have been argued all the more forcefully.

But even under New World Order conditions, skepticism about the value of the United Nations abounds. During its many successes in the peaceful wake of the Cold War, it enjoyed unusual popularity, only to be discredited again five years later in public opinion. Untoward images of operations in Rwanda, Somalia, and the former Yugoslavia seemed to underscore the organization's inherent weaknesses, though its supporters argued that the real weaknesses were in the faltering resolve of the UN's most powerful members. While one school of thought celebrated the "recovery of internationalism," partly through the UN, another charged the UN with being incapable of achieving regional peace and challenged it to leave peacemaking to interested states.[33]

Arguments about the inconsistency of UN performance range from theoretical comment on the nature of international organizations to comment steeped in a preference for unilateral nationalism or ideological regionalism over multinationalism. A few representative arguments follow.

1. The United Nations cannot function unless its members permit it to by wanting it to. This requires policy convergence outside of the UN's organs, as it is a policy decision of individual national capitals. This is commonly the argument of political realists, who hold firmly to state-sovereignty and national-interest theories of world politics.
2. Bureaucratic wastefulness at the UN erodes its budget and its credibility in the realm of bud-

---

[32] Ingvar Carlsson, "The U.N. at Fifty: A Time to Reform," *Foreign Policy*, fall 1995, pp. 3–18 at p. 3.

[33] Contrast as examples David C. Hendrickson, "The Recovery of Internationalism," and Saadia Touval, "Why the U.N. Fails," both in *Foreign Affairs*, September–October 1994, at pp. 26–43 and pp. 44–57, respectively.

getary management, thus discouraging governments from making special contributions for emergencies except those in which they have particular interests or stakes. Otherwise, the UN should be prevented from acting by denial of funds. This argument is common among those who would restrict the UN to occasional, special multilateral functions where effective state coalitions fail to form. Table 15–2 summarizes the main outstanding debts to the UN at the end of 1995, revealing a debt crisis of about 2.4 billion dollars. Note that the United States accounts for virtually all the debt in the general operating budget, and half the debt in the peacekeeping budget, most of which is owed by the UN to member states that have taken part in peacekeeping. To complete the record, recall that the United States is also the largest contributor to the United Nations despite its arrears. (Embarrassed by the American situation in this respect and committed to a course of multilateralism, President Clinton asked lamentingly in a 1995 address: "Why is the United States the biggest piker at the UN?"[34])

3. Despite the vast changes in its membership since 1945, and transformations in both the political stage and the global agenda, the permanent members of the Security Council and their principal partners still conduct their foreign policies, in the council and out, by Cold War principles. An appropriate New World Order agenda becomes lost in this context. This argument comes especially from the Developing Nations, who hold that in the New World Order conditions, attention to economic development has declined in all but rhetorical terms.

4. The end of the Cold War and the Soviet-American nuclear confrontation, together

---

[34] *The New York Times*, October 7, 1995, pp. A1 and A5 at p. 5. The answer to his question is the 1985 Kassebaum-Solomon Congressional Resolution, described subsequently.

TABLE 15–2

ARREARS IN PAYMENTS TO THE GENERAL BUDGET OF THE UN AND PEACEKEEPING OPERATIONS AS OF OCTOBER 1995

	Regular Budget	Peacekeeping Operations	Total
United States	$432 million	$823 million	$1.255 billion
Russia	0	497	497 million
Ukraine	52	185	237
Japan	0	197	197
France	0	101	101
Italy	0	72	72
Spain	0	30	30
Totals	$482 million	$1.905 billion	$2.387 billion

Source: United Nations, as reported in *The New York Times*, October 21, 1995, p. A4.

---

with the collapse of Soviet power on a global scale, enables the United States alone to pursue hegemonic policies of world domination, thus diverting the UN from an agenda appropriate to the New World Order. This argument comes from the remaining radical states such as China, Cuba, North Korea, Libya, Iraq, and Iran.

5. Historically, the greatest value of the UN to the West was its use as a forum for organizing world opinion against communism and against Soviet foreign and domestic policies. Extravagant contributions to the UN were justified by the worldwide character of the Soviet threat. With the Cold War's end, this rationale is gone. This argument, most common in the United States, is repeated by those who understand the UN only to be a convenient extension of national foreign policy for selective purposes.

6. A comparison of the major powers' response to Iraq's invasion of Kuwait (1990) with their responses to civil war, starvation, genocide, and

so forth in the Developing World demonstrates that their focus is on aggrandizing their own power and wealth without fulfilling the UN Charter's promise of removing the scourge of war through social, economic, and humanitarian development. Because of its nature, the UN is capable of advancing the policy goals of the rich, but not those of the poor. This is heard from representatives of the world's poorest peoples.

7. The explosion of new states and the membership of the UN effectively has reversed the organization's priorities in a way that favors the vast number of poor and predominately small states ("the mini-state problem") that would exploit the advances of the more powerful and wealthier states without attention to their needs. These problems have overwhelmed the UN. Hence there is a declining incentive to support the UN. This comes from elements in the wealthier nations that hold the poor people of the world responsible for their own plight and future development. Table 15–3 shows the evolution of the UN membership.

8. We have so many unmet needs of our own, in areas such as homelessness, child and maternal health, poverty, unemployment, deteriorating schools, and so forth, that foreign aid has become senseless, particularly when the UN and not the national government determines where and for what it will be spent. This is a common nationalistic taxpayer revolt in the West among conservative political elements that find little of intrinsic value in internationalism.

9. The UN is a function of states and should be permitted to operate only where it is in the interest of states; and if it takes withholding funds or exercising the veto to ensure such limits, then such tactics should be used. This argument is heard from conservative political elements in the more powerful states, which are committed ideologically to sovereign unilateralism in foreign policy.

Despite these and other critiques of the United Nations, and despite its budgetary crisis and fickle popularity in the United States and elsewhere, its various roles continue to evolve in the New World Order. The International Monetary Fund and the International Bank for Reconstruction and Development (or World Bank) are accepted almost universally as vital partners in the global economy. United Nations programs on children, women, development, the natural environment, public health and disease control, refugees, human rights, population, and other subjects vital to global stability proceed daily, almost unseen by national publics that understand the UN narrowly as a forum for cantankerous diplomacy. The UN achieved in Namibia, Cambodia, the Middle East, the former Congo, Rwanda, and elsewhere what governments could not, often for decades—in the case of Namibia, more than seventy years.

Nonetheless, because of inconsistent satisfaction with the United Nations, there are repeated calls for reform of its charter. Some come from devoted multilateralists whose purpose is to strengthen both the roles and authority of the UN organs; equally often, however, they come from disgruntled members or commentators who long either to weaken the UN or to reshape it to meet evolving needs. As we have seen, for example, Developing Nations would like to modify the composition of the Security Council and break the hold of the five permanent members. For the most part, however, UN adaptation to evolving world circumstances has come through policy and practice rather than constitutional redefinition. Many argue that the advent of the New World Order offers an opportunity to abandon this history and reshape the UN to the post–Cold War period much as its founders did to revise the League of Nations principles at the end of World War Two. It is unlikely, however, that the permanent members of the Security Council will permit dramatic change in the foreseeable future because, despite the end of the Cold War, the enduring frequency of international violence preserves classical notions about a global

TABLE 15-3

GROWTH OF UN MEMBERSHIP, 1945–1995

Year	Number	Original Member States
1945	51	Argentina, Australia, Belgium, Bolivia, Brazil, Byelorussian SSR (now Belarus), Canada, Chile, China, Colombia, Costa Rica, Cuba, Czechoslovakia, (divided in 1993), Denmark, Dominican Republic, Ecuador, Egypt, El Salvador, Ethiopia, France, Greece, Guatemala, Haiti, Honduras, India, Iran, Iraq, Lebanon, Liberia, Luxembourg, Mexico, Netherlands, New Zealand, Nicaragua, Norway, Panama, Paraguay, Peru, Philippines, Poland, Saudi Arabia, South Africa, Syria, Turkey, Ukrainian SSR (now Ukraine), United Kingdom, USSR (now Russia), United States, Uruguay, Venezuela, Yugoslavia

Year	Number	New Member States
1946	55	Afghanistan, Iceland, Sweden, Thailand
1947	57	Pakistan, Yemen
1948	58	Burma
1949	59	Israel
1950	60	Indonesia
1955	76	Albania, Austria, Bulgaria, Democratic Kampuchea, Finland, Hungary, Ireland, Italy, Jordan, Lao People's Democratic Republic, Libyan Arab Jamahiriya, Nepal, Portugal, Romania, Spain, Sri Lanka
1956	80	Japan, Morocco, Sudan, Tunisia
1957	82	Ghana, Malaysia
1958	83	Guinea
1960	100	Benin, Burkina Faso, Central African Republic, Chad, Congo, Côte de'Ivore, Cyprus, Gabon, Madagascar, Mali, Niger, Nigeria, Senegal, Somalia, Togo, United Republic of Cameroon, Zaïre
1961	104	Mauritania, Mongolia, Sierra Leone, United Republic of Tanzania

Year	Number	New Member States
1962	110	Algeria, Burundi, Jamaica, Rwanda, Trinidad and Tobago, Uganda
1963	112	Kenya, Kuwait
1964	115	Malawi, Malta, Zambia
1965	118	Gambia, Maldives, Singapore
1966	122	Barbados, Botswana, Guyana, Lesotho
1968	125	Equatorial Guinea, Mauritius, Swaziland
1970	126	Fiji
1971	131	Bahrain, Bhutan, Oman, Qatar, United Arab Emirates
1973	133	Bahamas, Federal Republic of Germany, German Democratic Republic
1974	136	Bangladesh, Grenada, Guinea–Bissau
1975	142	Cape Verde, Comoros, Mozambique, Papua New Guinea, São Tomé and Principe, Suriname
1976	145	Angola, Samoa, Seychelles
1977	147	Djibouti, Vietnam
1978	149	Dominica, Solomon Islands
1979	150	Saint Lucia
1980	152	Saint Vincent and the Grenadines, Zimbabwe
1981	155	Antigua and Barbuda, Belize, Vanuatu
1983	156	Saint Kitts and Nevis
1984	157	Brunei Darussalam
1990	159	Liechtenstein, Namibia
1991	168	North Korea, South Korea, Estonia, Latvia, Lithuania, Marshall Islands, Micronesia
1992	179	Armenia, Azerbaijan, Bosnia, and Herzegovina, Croatia, Georgia, Kazakhstan, Krygyzstan, Moldova, San Marino, Slovenia, Tajikistan, Turkmenistan, Uzbekistan
1993	184	Andorra, Czech Republic, Eritrea, Monaco, Slovakia, Macedonia (formerly Yugoslavian)
1994	185	Palau

Note: All names appear as they were at the time of admittance to the UN. After the break-up of the USSR, Russia succeeded to the Soviet seat and the newly-independent republics were admitted individually. The Ukrainian SSR changed its name to Ukraine and Byelorussian SSR to Belarus. Upon the disintegration of Yugoslavia, Serbia assumed the original seat and the new republics were admitted separately. Czechoslovakia divided into the Czech Republic and Slovakia for a net increase of one member. Burma is now called Myanmar.

Source: United Nations Chronicle, June 1995, inside back cover.

power distribution, though greatly changed by the collapse of the global Soviet reach. It is far more probable that in the New World Order, dramatic change will occur elsewhere in the UN system, as it has already in the evolution of the General Agreement on Tariffs and Trade (GATT) into the International Trade Organization (ITO) with new dispute-resolution authority. As the focus of world politics shifts in the New World Order from military confrontation to global economic competition, it is altogether fitting that the substantive organizational changes should occur in the realm of the global political economy.

The United States and the United Nations: A Special Case

Historically, the United States has had a special meaning to the United Nations for at least three reasons. First, the United States is the largest contributor to the UN, providing 25 percent of the general operating budget and a large voluntary share of funds for special projects. Second, the United States is the most powerful of the UN's members, a fact that endows the organization with great strength, but can also cause agonizing division when Washington chooses to pursue its policies unilaterally or through non-UN multilateral organizations such as NATO. Third, the United States is the host state of the UN (though some of its agencies are headquartered elsewhere), presenting unique diplomatic problems. Most of these involve the diplomatic privileges and immunities of the national delegations to the UN, placing them largely outside of American jurisdiciton when their behavior is unlawful. In addition, the host-state status provides special security problems, because UN affiliation may ensure entry into the United States of people who would otherwise be excluded for security reasons.

In the post–Cold War context, the uniqueness of this relationship is accentuated by a number of new factors. First, the United States is now without peer as a world power, freer than ever to select unilaterally the means by which it will pursue its foreign policy. Second, with the Soviet-American confrontation removed from both the world stage and the Security Council, American public sentiment for the United Nations is in jeopardy, as is American support for continued assistance to the majority Developing Nations in the UN membership. Third, the conservative tide that swept the United States in the Congressional elections of 1994 produced an unprecedented standoff between President Clinton's preference for multilateralism and internationalism, and the conservative demand for unilateralism and the primacy of domestic issues over internationalism. A 1996 conservative sweep would resolve this confrontation in a manner unfavorable to the UN's global role. Given the unwillingness of Congress to make good on the debt in its contribution to the United Nations, all these issues fuel the UN's anxiety about its most powerful member.

All this is consistent with the political history of the United States with respect to global organizations. Although the League of Nations was the brainchild of President Woodrow Wilson and the foundation on which post–World War One peace was built, the U.S. Senate never ratified a membership agreement out of fear of being dragged again into a European war. Furthermore, although the Permanent Court of International Justice (precursor of the UN's International Court of Justice) made a special provision to attract U.S. membership as a nonmember of the League, such a membership never was approved. Throughout the interwar period, Washington did participate in the League's functional activities, but it always dealt with the organization from a political arm's length.

By 1943, however, the public and official moods shifted in favor of post-war internationalism, with both the House of Representatives and the Senate adopting resolutions calling on the country to help create and to join a new global organization with the capacity to maintain international

French UN soldiers unloading relief supplies from American aircraft for distribution in Bosnia, 1994. (*Source:* AP/Wide World)

peace and security.[35] The work of preparing the United Nations Charter was done largely by a committee in the State Department headed by one Leo Pasvolsky, and the United States hosted the Dumbarton Oaks Conference at which the draft charter was presented to the World War Two allies. After final arrangements were discussed with Winston Churchill and Josef Stalin at the 1945 Yalta Conference, Washington hosted the San Francisco Conference at which the charter was adopted and the United Nations system born.[36] To avoid the

dilemma of separate memberships in the organization and in the World Court, the charter included the new International Court of Justice as one of the UN's permanent organs.

As the post-war peace evolved into Cold War and the Soviet Union transformed the American atomic bomb monopoly into a global standoff, American sentiment toward the United Nations ran high. When first the Security Council (in the Soviet delegate's voluntary absence) and then the General Assembly approved Washington's military response to North Korea's invasion of the South, Americans by the scores of millions adopted the UN as the nation's partner in stemming the bloody advance of the hated communist ideology. But as world conditions changed, so did the American attitude about the UN. The explosion of impoverished, newly independent states in and around 1960 required huge contributions of the United States that could be justified only in Cold War terms, not humanitarian. Later, although the United States officially supported the declaration of the New International Economic Order (NIEO), it was never popular.

In addition, in contrast to the Korean War experience, the United Nations declined to endorse

---

[35] House Concurrent Resolution no. 25, 78th Congress, 1st sess., sponsored by Congressman J. William Fulbright of Arkansas, adopted on September 21, 1943. *Congressional Record,* vol. 89, p. 7729, and reprinted in Ruhl J. Bartlett, ed., *The Record of American Diplomacy,* 4th ed. (New York: Alfred Knopf, 1964), p. 675. Senate Resolution no. 192, as amended, 78th Congress, 1st sess. vol. 89, p. 9222, sponsored by Senator Tom Connally of Texas and adopted on November 5, 1943. The Senate action is commonly referred to as the Connally Resolution.

[36] For a comprehensive history of the American effort to establish the United Nations with emphasis on the new commitment to internationalism, see Robert A. Divine, *Second Chance: The Triumph of Internationalism in the United States During World War II* (New York: Atheneum, 1967). See also Ruth B. Russell (with the assistance of Jeannette E. Muther), *A History of the United Nations Charter* (Washington, D.C.: Brookings Institution, 1958). Russell was a staff member of the Pasvolsky Committee.

American policy in Vietnam, and it became a hotbed of criticism. Furthermore, the General Assembly expelled the Taiwan delegation and awarded the single China seat to Beijing, poking a huge hole in Washington's Cold War policy at the time. The assembly matched this by declaring Zionism to be racist, and by identifying Israel, a close American partner, as an aggressor. Later, fearful of an embarrassing loss at the International Court of Justice over military support of the Contra forces against the Soviet-oriented and Soviet-aided Nicaraguan government, the United States withdrew its acceptance of the court's limited compulsory jurisdiction. Subsequently Washington withdrew from the UN's Economic, Social and Cultural Organization (UNESCO) over a long dispute regarding what it considered anti-Western practices by the organization's secretary-general.[37] By now fully frustrated with the UN, Congress adopted the Kassebaum-Solomon Amendment of 1985. This mandated a 20 percent annual reduction in the American contribution to the UN's general operating budget and reduction in voluntary contributions to special operations such as peacekeeping. These cuts went into practice in 1987 and are required to continue until the UN adopts a voting formula that gives greater decision-making power to those members that make the greatest contributions.[38] Because this has not occurred (and probably will not), the deficit in American contributions continues to mount, and with it the deepening financial crisis of the United Nations.

American frustrations regarding the United Nations were expressed forcefully in 1983 by Charles Lichenstein, a member of the U.S. delegation. After having heard his government accused of violating the Headquarters Agreement in events

following the Soviet destruction of a Korean civilian airliner in flight, Lichenstein declared:

> If in the judicious determination of the members of the United Nations, they feel that they are not welcome and that they are not being treated with the hostly consideration that is their due, then the United States strongly encourages such member states seriously to consider removing themselves and this organization from the soil of the United States. We will put no impediment in your way. The members of the US mission to the United Nations will be down at dockside waving you a fond farewell as you sail into the sunset.[39]

It was only the Security Council's response to Washington's goals against the Iraqi invasion of Kuwait in 1990 that restored American public support of the United Nations. But that response would not have been possible had Mikhail Gorbachev not agreed in advance to discontinue Soviet intervention in Central America and, in general, to thaw the Cold War. The tide of sentiment carried through an American peacekeeping action in Haiti and into Somalia, but there it suffered a setback consistent with the predictable failings of the operation. Humiliating peacekeeping losses in Bosnia, not involving American personnel, deepened once again the skepticism of Americans about the United Nations and its special operations, despite the end of the Cold War and general Russian-American agreement on matters under consideration by the Security Council. Two resolutions offered by Senate Democrats calling for

---

[37] For the full text of the notification from the State Department to the secretary-general, see American Journal of International Law, April 1984, pp. 428–429.

[38] For a comprehensive review of the political and legal aspects of this event, see Elizabeth Zeller, "The 'Corporate Will' of the United States and the Rights of the Minority," American Journal of International Law, July 1987, pp. 610–634.

[39] The New York Times, September 20, 1983, p. A1. The statement was made in reference to charges made by the Soviet Union that the United States had violated its responsibilities as the host state of the United Nations by refusing permission to Soviet Foreign Minister Andrei Gromyko to land at a civilian airport in the United States on his way to the fall session of the General Assembly. Both New York and New Jersey had announced that in retaliation for the Soviet downing of a Korean civilian aircraft, the Soviet jetliner would not be permitted to land at any of its accustomed destinations. The federal government had offered use of a U.S. Air Force base as a substitute, but the Soviets declined the offer and announced that Gromyko would not attend the session.

the Defense Department to train and equip American peacekeeping forces went nowhere, and these were countered by a Republican resolution designed to prevent the president from placing American troops under UN command. In the midst of this, President Clinton released Presidential Decision Directive 25 (PDD-25) in 1994, in which he outlined the conditions required for U.S. support of UN peacekeeping, and the conditions under which he would commit American troops. American support will be given only if (1) the operation serves American foreign-policy interests; (2) the operation is backed by adequate means to achieve the stated goals; and (3) it is accompanied by realistic criteria for termination. American troops will be committed to peacekeeping operations only if (1) the risk is deemed acceptable; (2) personnel, funds, and other resources are available; (3) American participation is necessary for success; (4) both Congress and the public support American commitment; (5) the mission has clear objectives; and (6) command-and-control arrangements are acceptable to Washington. London's Institute for International Strategic Studies characterized PDD-25 as a "retreat from multilateralism."[40]

But American dissatisfaction with the United Nations does not focus exclusively on activities related to international security. Even more, it concerns the world economy and the expectations of the poor nations. One thoroughly dated scholarly effort to explain dissatisfaction with international regimes correlated it directly to American dissatisfaction with the international system as represented by the increased frequency of American dissent from majority votes in the UN's political organs.[41] In the New World Order, the political agenda of those bodies leans heavily toward the expensive needs of the Developing World and away from the competitive needs of the United States. Hence, while Americans are less concerned with the geomilitary aspects of the global system than during the Cold War, they remain dissatisfied with those aspects of the international political economy that crowd the agendas of UN organs and agencies. Hence a conclusion drawn from data now nearly two decades old still applies. Moreover, from the American perspective, more even than when the phrase was coined (1984), the UN is dominated by a "Developing World ethos" that is inimical to American policy interests.[42]

The essence of this summary history is that the United Nations cannot contribute consistently to the peace and stability of the international system without the power, cooperation, and economic and political support of its most powerful member and host state. Once again, a great irony of the New World Order is that removal of the Soviet-American confrontation from the Security Council has produced not a stronger United Nations, but one more reliant than ever on an American commitment to multilateralism, just as world conditions encourage the abandonment of multilateralism in America's domestic politics.

[40] Institute for International Strategic Studies (London), *Strategic Survey 1994/95* (London: Bassey, 1995), p. 57.

[41] Ernst B. Haas, "Regime Decay: Conflict Management and International Organizations, 1945–1981," *International Organization*, spring 1983, pp. 189–256.
[42] Richard Bernstein, "The United States Versus The United Nations," *The New York Times Magazine*, January 27, 1984, pp. 18–24, 26, and 68. The present text modernizes Bernstein's original reference to a "Third World ethos," but the meaning and significance are unchanged.

CHAPTER 16

International Integration and Transnational Participation

Centuries of experience with the nation-state system cast doubt on the ability of governments to preserve international peace and stability. International law and organization have contributed modestly, but neither can ensure lasting international harmony. What, then, are the alternatives to the nation-state system? What other political contexts might there be that would both conduct familiar global functions and, at the same time, safeguard peace more effectively? Will political history reach beyond the nation-state? This chapter considers two modern trends that address these questions in different ways: international integration and transnational participation.

International Integration

International integration is the process by which a supranational condition is achieved, in which larger political units conduct the business now carried out by national governments. Defined succinctly, it is

> the process whereby political actors in several distinct national settings are persuaded to shift their loyalties, expectations, and political activities toward a new and larger center, whose institutions possess or demand jurisdiction over the pre-existing national states.[1]

Unlike international organization, which establishes institutional machinery *among* states, international integration provides decision-making machinery *above* them. It constructs procedures and institutions capable of making obligatory decisions on behalf of national governments. It consists of the merger of separate authorities and jurisdictions, usually in a well-defined geographic region, into a larger unit, a higher unity, and a single polity. This slow and gradual process, which may occur unevenly in different sectors of interaction, leaves different states intact; but it blurs progressively the distinctions of international policy among them.

Overwhelmingly, the goal of integrating movements is economic prosperity particularly through trade, so that virtually all such movements begin as preferential trading arrangements such as customs unions or free trade areas. Often the goal is no more than this; there is no plan to integrate nontrade economic issues such as fiscal or monetary policies, let alone a plan to integrate governments, judicial systems, or foreign policies. The limited purpose usually is made clear by such names as the European Free Trade Area (EFTA), the Latin American Free Trade Area (LAFTA), the Central American Common Market (CACM), and the North American Free Trade Area (NAFTA). Often the purpose is not recorded in the name, but explicit nonetheless. Examples include the Andean Group, the Association of Southeast Asian Nations (ASEAN), and the Special Economic Arrangement of Australia and New Zealand. On rare occasions, however, the goal is broader than

---

[1] Ernst B. Haas, *The Uniting of Europe: Political, Social and Economic Forces 1950–57* (Stanford, Calif.: Stanford University Press, 1958), p. 16.

advantageous trade regulation. Yet it still may not reach into activities of the state beyond economics. And even more rarely, the goal may be complete economic integration along with political and security integration, the creation of a virtual superstate. This is why the European Economic Community (EEC) gave way to the European Community (EC) and then to the European Union (EU).[2] Because the Western European experience most nearly exemplifies comprehensive international integration, the pages that follow concentrate exclusively on it.

Integration and the Functional Model

Integration by any means is a long and arduous process. Although some observers have predicted integration through federation, most hold that integration is a testing process tied to compiled successes. This functional model of integration rejects rapid constitutional consolidation and looks instead to progress in specific sectors. The functionalist view holds that even compatible societies cannot integrate all public functions simultaneously. Collectivization may be based on economics, on politics, or on security. Gradual and parallel progress in several sectors may converge into general, cross-sectoral integration. Without this convergence, integration is encapsulated or isolated, having no carryover effects in other sectors.[3]

---

[2] The first three institutions of Western Europe's integration process were the European Coal and Steel Community (ECSC), the European Atomic Agency Commission (EURATOM), and the European Economic Community (EEC), also called the Common Market. The Single European Act of 1987 formalized the practice of calling them collectively the European Community (EC). With completion of the common market in 1992, the Maastricht Treaty (1991) dropped EC and formalized the collective name European Union (EU). In this presentation, pre-1992 references are generally made as "the community," and after 1992 the European Union or EU.

[3] For a study of the distinction between the federationist and the functionalist approaches, see particularly David Mitrany, "The Prospect of Integration: Federal or Functional?" *Journal of Common Market Studies*, vol. 4, December 1965. A useful study of the multivariate nature of integration is found in Leon N. Lindberg, "Political Integration as a Multidimensional Phenomenon Requiring Multivariate Measurement," *International Organization*,

1. The Sectors of Integration

What functions have been given over to the integrative process? What purposes, normally served by national governments, have been entrusted to higher political levels? The answers to these questions lie in the different sectors of integration.

Economics   Historically, the sector most frequently integrated has been the economic. The most familiar integrative organizations are free trade areas and common markets.[4] In the former, the members eliminate barriers to trade among themselves and establish common barriers with respect to outside competitors. The common market goes the extra step of allowing free trade of the means of production among members as well as goods. This means the free flow of labor and capital. This was achieved by the European Community in 1992. The next phase, monetary union including a common currency, now is scheduled for 2002.

Because economic interaction is highly complex, it is instructive to consider economic subsectors. In the European experience, for example, progress toward a full free trade area has developed at different rates and with vastly different amounts of enthusiasm in the industrial and agricultural subsectors. Although it has not been easy, principles for industrial free trade areas were achieved more readily than were those for agriculture. In addition, Britain's entry into the Common Market was delayed not only by French politics (on Britain's first serious attempt to gain entry in 1963, French President Charles de Gaulle vetoed its membership), but also by British fears of the impact on its agricultural subsector. Upon entry in 1973, Britain suffered inflation in food prices but anticipated that

---

vol. 24, 1970, pp. 649–731. The neofunctionalists hold that federation ultimately can occur on a well-established and solid functionalist base. See, for example, Joseph S. Nye Jr., "Comparing Common Markets: A Revised Neo-functionalist Model," *International Organization*, vol. 24, 1970, pp. 796–835.

[4] For detailed definitions of the various types of integrating organizations in the economic sector, see Miroslav N. Javanovic, *International Economic Integration* (London and New York: Routledge, 1992), pp. 8–10.

gains in industrial trade would favorably affect its balance of payments (increase exports over imports) and would stabilize the British economy. French farmers have repeatedly protested the community's agricultural policies. And a dispute on red wine trade between France and Italy required a community-wide agreement on trade in alcohol before the common market could be completed in 1992.

Another distinction is between production and labor. There are important labor aspects to a free trade area—standardization of wages in industries, community agreement on fair labor practices, free flow of labor across national boundaries, subsidy programs, and agreement on pension and unemployment benefits.

Still another aspect of economic integration is the availability of capital, without which efficient, coordinated growth cannot occur. If this means borrowing from abroad, then one state (even perhaps an outside state) may dominate growth by controlling both capital and decisions about capital utilization. Creation of a common medium of exchange among participating central banks facilitates payments. West European integration achieved this milestone in 1971 with the establishment of the Euronote or European Currency Unit (abbreviated as E-Note or ECU, and commonly symbolized as $).

Full monetary integration is the next step. The Maastricht Treaty on European Unity (1992) charges the European Monetary Institute (EMI), which will evolve into the European Central Bank, to achieve this in three steps by 1999 (now postponed to 2002). This will include transforming the ECU into a common currency. Not surprisingly, this has been the most controversial issue in European integration to date. The Maastricht Treaty led Norwegians to reject membership in the EU after having been invited to join, and Danish voters first rejected membership and then, on a second vote, accepted it. A "Eurobarometer" poll taken in early 1994 indicated that more than half of Belgians had lost interest in integration, and half of Britons and Portuguese. Among the twelve members at the time (there are now fifteen), the average who

considered themselves disaffected was 40 percent.[5] (In fairness, not all of the unhappiness was over monetary union. In completing the common market component, Maastricht declared the free flow of labor within the community, but also pronounced it the right of any community citizen to vote wherever he or she settles. The French especially were astounded to learn that non-French had gained the right to participate in French national elections.)

Social Considerations The second major sector is the social. Although it may be feasible technically to integrate economies, ultimate integration requires mutual toleration and common social and political values. Social integration means transforming national preferences into loyalty to the larger political community. *Supra*national attitudes must evolve.

From 1970 through 1992 there was a steady growth of survey evidence that a sense of social community, or "Europeanness," was evolving in Western Europe, and that the supranational consciousness included confidence that a united Europe would have a stabilizing effect on international relations. This trend took a sharp dip after Maastricht, though for how long is yet to be determined.[6] Although it was evidenced most vividly by the Norwegian and Danish actions and by public opinion polls, the underlying reasons are less clear. Among them, however, are the following:

1. A swing to pro-nationalist, conservative politics in Britain and France.
2. A growing discomfort over Germany's aggressive leadership on integration in general and monetary unity in particular, in view of Berlin's commanding position in the EU economy and in international trade.
3. A mounting public attitude that planning for the next phases of integration is a closed rather

[5] Reproduced in *World Press Review*, February 1994, p. 34.
[6] Mark Franklin, Michael Marsh, and Lauren McLaren, "Uncorking the Bottle: Popular Opposition to European Unification in the Wake of Maastricht," *Journal of Common Market Studies*, December 1994, pp. 455–472.

French farmers having their own
"Boston Tea Party" in protest over
the Maastricht Treaty on
European union.
(*Source:* © AP/Wide World)

than an open process, that it is not democratic, and that it lacks appropriate accountability, because at present the Council of Ministers is accountable only to sitting governments, not to the electorates of the fifteen member states.

4. Increasing fear that the dual processes of "widening and deepening" (i.e., increasing membership and extending the integrative process into more subject matters) are gathering momentum not subject to the public's control, and that expansion of the social and ideological pluralism (such as by considering membership applications from Cyprus, Malta, and the former communist Central European countries) creates unintended liabilities for the EU.

5. The ambiguity of both the Maastricht Treaty and the Council of Ministers on the issue of "subsidiarity," meaning definition of the division of responsibilities among the institutions of the EU, the member governments, and the subnational political institutions of the member states.[7]

Politics A third sector of concern to integration theory is the political, though it is not distinguished neatly from other sectors. Societies are replete with bonds of patriotism, loyalty, historical mythology, and a sense of national difference. Political integration refers, therefore, to the relatively narrow concept of integration of basic political institutions—with transfer of sovereignty over external policy to common international institutions. It aims not to eliminate national governments but to alter their control over specific functions. These changes may affect internal matters of the state, such as fiscal policy or production policy. In integration short of full federation, there is no pretense to transfer of full sovereignty over internal matters.

Despite this limited expectation, political integration is more difficult to achieve than is economic integration, chiefly because the latter is expected to strengthen the national economy, thus encouraging dual loyalty to nation and larger community. Political integration, in contrast, directly affects the state's sovereignty over decision making with respect to its nationals. Its institutional effects are more visible, and the assault on nationalism is more nearly frontal. The state is reduced in stature. Only where this is regarded as a desirable objective has the concept of political integration caught on.

A variety of interpretations exists about the relationships among political integration, social integration, and general governmental cooperation. Some hold that social predisposition is the critical measure of integration potential. Others insist that the creation of institutions among generally sympathetic states will create the social conditions necessary for political integration. Empirical studies indicate, however, that improvements in intergovernmental relations must precede both institution-building and changes in societal attitudes.[8] West European integration illustrates this point.

Systematic consideration of political union was launched after the passing of Charles de Gaulle, who had intended no more integration than would benefit the French economy, and the entry of Britain in 1973. Immediately there was signed an agreement on a phased schedule of political unity by 1980. The crowning achievement was to be the public election of the European Parliament, the legislative body of the community, the members of which had previously been appointed by the participating governments. The spirit of political supranationalism grew rapidly, with publication of the Tindemans Report on progressive integration, a common stance on matters at the United Nations on the New International Economic Order, and the quiet dispatch of more than fifty community ambassadorial representatives to such places as Washington, Tokyo, Beijing, and Ottawa. New political alliances formed within the community, with cross-national parties and interest groups policy, as well as doing so within their respective national caucuses.[9]

Though the 1980 deadline for political unification passed with little notice, the activity continued. A draft treaty on a European Union was formulated alongside a Solemn Declaration on European Union, each calling for institutional improvements to deal with financial, social, and trade issues and international policy beyond the community's borders. At the end of 1985, the European Council of Ministers met to consider a report of its Institutional Affairs Committee, and adopted the Single European Act, often simply called the

---

[7] Kers Van Kersbergen and Bartjan Verbeek, "The Politics of Subsidiarity in the European Union," *Journal of Common Market Studies*, June 1994, pp. 215–236.

[8] See Barry B. Hughes and John E. Schwarz, "Dimensions of Political Integration and the Experience of the European Community," *International Studies Quarterly*, vol. 16, 1972, pp. 263–294.
[9] The New York Times, February 9, 1976, pp. A1, and A18.

Single Act, for ratification by member governments by 1987. This accelerated integrative progress by calling for completion of the common market (with free flow of labor and capital, interchangeability of academic degrees, and so on) by the end of 1992. Two British writers assessed its importance in 1989 as follows:

> The Single Act has unexpectedly become the [European] Commission's vehicle for . . . ambitious aims. The Act is no longer a modest intergovernmental compromise, or even a framework treaty . . . , but is instead to be regarded as binding law. . . .

They characterized the goal of the commission as one in which a single economic market will create a single economy, and with it a single currency managed by a treaty-based institution with power to control credit within the EC. They cited the president of the commission as predicting that by 1995, some form of European government would be needed, perhaps a higher form of American-style federalism in which the member states and the community-wide organs of government would share social and economic power on a prescribed basis.[10] These predictions were based on the expectation that by the turn of the century, as much as 80 percent of all economic matters, and perhaps fiscal and social matters as well, will be regulated by community legislation rather than by the laws of the individual member states.

These remarks were prophetic. As the 1992 deadline neared, 70 percent of the public favored further progress to unity,[11] and the Council of Ministers began to consider in earnest the next phases of integration. They finalized them in the Maastricht Treaty on European Union (1991). Though broadbased institutional reform did not occur, the European Monetary Institution was given greater

powers in the area of monetary integration, and full fiscal and monetary integration were specifically articulated aims. But the public reaction was the first serious setback to a united Europe since de Gaulle's rejection of British membership in 1963. The EMI's recommendation of 1995 on postponing monetary unity until early in the next century was designed explicitly to allay "citizen shock" and neutralize some of the adverse public opinion.[12]

Security   The fourth major area in integration is security. Integration may follow from existing alliances, but it implies considerably more than mere alliance. Generally, an alliance is a political instrument through which the dominant member gains political access to the decision-making processes of the lesser members, in return for which the weaker states are guaranteed strategic assistance. Integration calls upon all members, whatever their relative power potentials, to contribute to decision making at all levels of planning, deployment, and command.

Integrated alliances are rare because governments generally have resisted giving total strategic control to common institutions. The Warsaw Pact—the military alliance of the Soviet Union and its East European allies—was about as integrated as any has been. The Soviet Union, through its political control and economic supremacy, regulated the power and the respective roles of the other allies, thus virtually dictating policy. The North Atlantic Treaty Organization (NATO) has more collective decision making, although in nuclear affairs Washington consistently has dominated despite the presence of British and French nuclear forces. Much of the late–Cold War history of NATO diplomacy revolved around attempts by the West European members to break down this American position. Although troops and conventional war materials have been integrated to a considerable extent, fully integrated decision making does not yet exist.

---

[10] Christopher Brewin and Richard McAllister, "Annual Review of the Activities of the European Communities in 1988," *Journal of Common Market Studies,* June 1989, pp. 323–357 at pp. 323–324. The remainder of this paragraph relies on the same source.

[11] "Eurobarometer: Public Opinion in the European Communities," *European Affairs,* autumn 1989, pp. 26–32.

[12] *The New York Times,* November 15, 1995, p. D7.

With the advent of the New World Order, the Single European Act, and the Maastricht Treaty on European Union, the question of Western Europe's security arose in a new context. There always had been differences between the Europeanists and the Atlanticists (i.e., those who wanted more security autonomy and those who favored a strong American presence), but these always were resolved by the practical necessity of having America's military strength. In the new context, however, with the threat of pan-European war gone, the debate took on new facets. Many people denied forcefully the need for a continued American role. Others opted for a continued American presence, but through something other than NATO so as to (1) diminish American domination and (2) make room for Russia as a continental power. A third camp called for an integrated European armed force under a single command. Any who wished to exclude American forces had to recognize that a single-command regional defense system was unavoidable, because none of the EU member governments was prepared to undertake the expense necessary to substitute for Washington's historical commitment through NATO.[13]

In anticipation of changes in the security structure, the community members established (1992) the Western European Union (WEU) as the military arm of the EU and "the embryo of future European armed forces."[14] (The titles seem redundant, but WEU explicitly connotes security affairs, whereas EU addresses economic, social, and political matters.) At the outset, 40,000 troops were committed to this effort, most of them from France and Germany. Greece, Ireland, and Denmark declined to particpate. The subsequent admission of Finland, Sweden, and Austria added to the EU three non-NATO governments with generally neutral international policies and not likely participants in

WEU. In essence, however, it is apparent that the EU is laying the foundation for an integrated security system at some indefinite point in its political integration.

2. The Momentum of Integration

What causes integrating energy to continue to gain? If the impetus exists for sector integration at all, what forces permit it to surpass mere organization and to enter into supranationalism? And what are the prospects that success in one sector will catch on in others?

Sector integration, once begun, gains steam by *feedback*. This is analogous to gravity: A falling object gains velocity. Similarly, a snowball rolling down a steep grade gains mass. Put simply, integration theory posits that if a formal process of sectoral interaction is allowed free forward propulsion, it will gain in intensity.

The analogy is oversimplified, of course. Social phenomena are obstructed from free forward propulsion, in the same way that wind alters the free downward fall of an object or friction reduces the energy of a rolling snowball. Social scientists have as their laboratory only political systems, and invariably the data show the feedback process to be halting and sporadic. The ideal condition is continuous, growing, and mutually perceived success and equal sharing by all the participants in the continuing benefits. Generally, these inside conditions must be accompanied by external inducements. The impetus to advancement must, on the whole, exceed occasional setbacks.

What of the second question: What forces carry the energy of integration from one sector to another? The answer is found in the *spillover* phenomenon, in which integrative successes in one sector awaken integrating objectives in another and the integrative energy from one sector spills over to and energizes another. But once spillover has occurred, there is no assurance that feedbacks within the new sector will keep pace with the first, or that one spillover will energize the next.

---

[13] Stockholm International Peace Research Institute, *SIPRI Yearbook, 1992, World Armaments and Disarmament* (London: Oxford University Press, 1992), pp. 234–236.
[14] The expression is from the weekly *Expresso* of Lisbon, Portugal, in an article reprinted in *World Press Review*, August 1992, p. 13.

The relatively rapid pace of economic integration in Western Europe, as contrasted with political and security integration, illustrates both the necessity for spillover in the aggregate integrative process and the practical limitations of its progress. One writer finds four basic causes for the slower speed of spillover than originally was predicted by the neofunctionalist theory: (1) the mixed quality of performance by the community from national perspectives; (2) the failure of the community to select and administer policies that would become self-evidently critical to the national publics; (3) the difficulty of securing either public or governmental identification with processes with constantly shifting definitions and emphases; and (4) the tendency of national governments to prefer intergovernmental cooperation through the community organs to a direct shift of authority to the the community.[15]

Thus far we have considered four basic issues of the integrative process: (1) the distinction between organization and integration (or internationalism and supranationalism), (2) the notion of sector differentiation, (3) the concept of feedback, and (4) the concept of spillover. Behind these is an array of social and political conditions that determine the start of the process, as well as its pace, progress, and end products.

3. Goals of Integration

Integration is a conscious process, and so nations and governments must have explicit motives for seeking it. This especially is true because self-preservation is one of the major aims of statehood. What expectations are sufficiently intense to motivate governments toward integration?

Economic Potential   Historically, the largest single motive has been the desire to maximize economic potential. In the presence of a few giant

economies, smaller states have been unable to keep pace with competition. Whether they are less developed states or old industrial states, the hope of fully competing may be a call to integration.

After the Second World War, the West European states rebuilt their industries only to discover that once-great national economies were lost in the American shadow. The economy of the Western world had become asymmetrical, with the United States commanding the greatest produce for export, the largest and most technically developed labor force, and the most innovative entrepreneurial skill. For reconstructed Western Europe to compete, it was necessary to merge national economies. Despite the predictable hardships for nonindustrial portions of their economies, six governments committed themselves to this goal in 1957. Later their membership grew to nine, then to twelve and fifteen. In Chapter 4 we studied the consequences of this growth in Europe's competitiveness with the United States and Japan. The subsequent rise of Japan's power in the global economy was another stimulus to integration, and perhaps to territorial expansion as well. While a grand superstate may have been in the backs of a few leaders' minds, steady progress in economic competitiveness is what persuaded the publics to lay aside questions of national grandeur and identity and permit the forward march of integration's forces.

Political Potential   A second major motive for integration is the desire to maximize political potential. With rare exception, small and politically powerless states have had little impact on the international system, especially during the bipolar era that followed the Second World War. Small states felt either left out of, or victimized by, a world of two massive power centers. Some viewed integration as the route to a multipolar world in which their diplomatic goals might be recieved better.

The European experience demonstrates the dual-edged nature of political union as a motive for integration. Although some Europeans view political integration as a route to a stronger role in a politically multipolar world, others think it too great a price with respect to national sovereignty. The

---

[15] William Wallace, "Less than a Federation, More than a Regime: The Community as a Political System," in H. Wallace, W. Wallace, and C. Webb, *Policy-making in the European Community*, 2nd ed. (London: Wiley, 1983), pp. 1–41.

latter generally would prefer to settle for economic integration. The unpopularity of the Maastrict Treaty suggests that something even less than full economic integration would be satisfactory to large numbers.

Conflict Resolution
A third impetus to integration is the desire to resolve potential conflict among territorial neighbors. If there be nascent conflict among states forced by geography to be interdependent, integration of vital sectors of their interaction may outweigh the existing sources of strife.

The most notable instance of such motivation was the founding in 1951 of the European Coal and Steel Community by the same six states that founded the European Economic Community a few years later. Although the ECSC was the first implementation of a long-range plan for European economic integration, it had a more specific immediate mission: to resolve the age-old Franco-German rivalry over coal and steel resources. At a press conference in 1950, French Foreign Minister Robert Schuman declared:

> The gathering of the nations of Europe requires the elimination of the age-old opposition of France and Germany. The first concern in any action undertaken must be these two countries.
>
> With this aim in view, the French Government proposes to take action immediately on one limited but decisive point. The French Government proposes to place Franco-German production of coal and steel under a common "high authority," within the framework of an organization open to the participation of the other countries of Europe.

The Schuman Declaration, previously approved by the French Council of Ministers, resulted in the ECSC. Most important, however, is the specific intent that Schuman emphasized—the interdependence of European economic integration with elimination of this historic cause of war.

How effectively does progress toward supranationalism actually diminish conflict among the participants? Although integration does not eliminate strife, it does reduce its frequency. Denying that this proves a casual link, one scholar, examining a non-European context, contends that "when combined with awareness and concern on the part of Central American elites about the relationship between economic integration and violent conflict, it does provide some useful evidence for the existence of the probable relationship."[16]

But not all students of integration are persuaded that organizations reduce the likelihood of war among members. Using five measurements of integration (common institutional membership, proximity, economic interdependence, sociocultural similarity, and UN voting behavior), for example, another scholar reviewed the history of conflict among forty-one pairs of states. He found that "all five of these conditions may be necessary to prevent war between states . . . , but not even all five together are sufficient to do so." The greater the interdependence among nations, the more sensitive their interests will become, and the greater will be their prospects of conflict.[17] Unfortunately, the closest neighbors may have the largest number of chances to fight—and may do so despite their interdependence. Thus, the desire to resolve conflict is not invariably an adequate cause for integration. Even in such circumstances the duties and expectations placed on integrative processes may exceed the stabilizing capabilities of organization.

Even where there is steady integrative progress in one sector, conflict is common. Writing more than thirty years ago about the European Economic Community, one scholar reminded us that the members

> do not confront each other only or chiefly as diplomatic gladiators; they encounter each other at almost every level of organized society through constant interaction in the joint policymaking contexts of officials, parliamentarians, interest group leaders, businessmen, farmers, and trade unionists. Conflicts of interest and purpose are inevitable. *There is no*

---

[16] Joseph S. Nye Jr., *Peace in Parts: Integration and Conflict in Regional Organization* (Boston: Little, Brown, 1971), p. 120.

[17] Bruce M. Russett, *International Regions and the International System* (Chicago: Rand McNally, 1967), chapter 12, "Conflicts and Integration," especially pp. 198–201.

paradox between the progress of economic integration . . . and sharpening political disagreement; indeed, the success of economic integration can be the cause of political disagreement. The member states are engaged in the enterprise for widely different reasons, and their actions have been supported or instigated by elites seeking their own particular goals. Therefore, conflicts would seem endemic as the results of joint activity come to be felt and as the prointegration consensus shifts.[18]

Progress aside, integration is a dynamic process. Goals change, roles shift, and new leaders and elites emerge; old influences wane, and new ones burst onto the scene. Integration thus may proceed in a regional system of constant conflict. Indeed, because progress toward supranationalism creates stresses of its own, the process may have negative effects on the overall relations of members. Reason dictates that although the resolution of regional conflicts may be one of the expectations of integrating members, the very process itself may be the cause of strife. But shared commitment reduces the likelihood that strife will degenerate into war.

4. Background Conditions for Integration

Alone, common expectations about the regional future are not sufficient to promote integration. Certain preconditions must be satisfied, although subconsciously for the most part.

Social Assimilation   To some observers, the foremost precondition of regional integration is social causation, resulting in a so-called sociocausal paradigm of integration.[19] Focusing on transnational attitudes, this posits that social assimilation is a precondition of integration. Critics of this concept reject the assumed necessity of social assimilation. Nevertheless, most observers agree that minimal social prerequisites do exist and that among them are mutual tolerance of cultures, common identity of foreign-policy goals, and generally cordial contacts of governments and respective nationals.

Value Sharing   A second precondition is value sharing, especially among national policymaking elites. In the economic sector, for example, unless the elites of participating states share common values, such as capitalism or socialism, or free markets as contrasted with central controls and subsidies, they will expend little energy on integration, and little pressure will be exerted on governments. Again, this is a sociopolitical condition.

Mutual Benefit   Expectation of mutual benefit is the third precondition. Because states will enter into a process that fundamentally alters national prerogatives only with sufficient incentives, states must be able to predict that benefits will accrue from the process. Some states may expect to profit in one sector, whereas others seek advancement in another. Remember, however, that the integrative process involves not only international politics but intense domestic bargaining as well. A government may be willing to sacrifice major industrial gains to achieve agricultural integration, but the industrial elites may resist. Thus, their expectation of benefit is just as important as are aggregate national expectations.

Congenial Past Relations   A fourth precondition is experiential: a history of frequent pacific transactions. This acknowledges the functionalist

---

[18] Leon N. Lindberg, "Decision Making and Integration in the European Community," *International Organization*, vol. 19, 1965, p. 80. The emphasis has been added.
[19] See particularly the classic study by Karl Deutsch et al., *Political Community and the North Atlantic Area* (Princeton, N.J.: Princeton University Press, 1957). See also Deutsch's several contributions to Philip E. Jacob and James V. Tascano, eds., *The Integration of Political Communities* (Philadelphia: Lippincott,

1964), including "Communication Theory and Political Integration," "Transaction Flows as Indicators of Political Cohesion," and "Integration and the Social System: Implications of Functional Analysis." For an evaluation and critique of the sociocausal paradigm, see William E. Fisher, "An Analysis of the Deutsch Sociocausal Paradigm of Political Integration," *International Organization*, vol. 23, 1969, pp. 254–290.

precept that nothing succeeds like success itself; and it posits that elites, nations, and governments are unlikely to integrate without already operating cordiality. This clearly was not the case with French and German coal and steel. In that instance, the shared desire to avoid future conflicts was more important than the fact that conflict had existed historically.

The Importance of Integration Itself Closely related to congenial past relations is the fifth criterion—the salience of transactions. If interests are related only remotely, integration is unlikely; but if participants recognize the importance of activities in other countries, impetus for integration may awaken. The prospects for integration in these cases are governed by "the law of inverse salience," which holds that the growth of integration is related inversely to the political importance of the subject matter. Another functionalist proposition, this argues that because integration proceeds only with prior progress, it is seen usually first in matters that are politically expendable. Only through feedbacks and spillovers does the process begin to invade politically sensitive areas.[20] Again, the ECSC does not fit the rule, suggesting that a shared desire to avoid future conflict on the basis of history is a more powerful motive for integration.

Low Relative Costs Because there are bound to be costs as well as benefits, another precondition must be the anticipation of low costs relative to benefits, measured economically, socially, or nationalistically.[21] Likewise, such costs will probably be assessed principally in domestic policy, yet a prospective participant may wish to predict the effects on other foreign policies or other regions. Britain's delayed entry into European Continentalism resulted partly from the potential effect on the

British agricultural sector, on its relations with members of the British Commonwealth, and on its special relationship with the United States.

External Influences The last issue raises what generally has been an underestimated precondition of integration: external influences. Virtually every integration movement can be attributed in part to external stimuli. In Western Europe, for example, the threat of American domination of European economies after the Marshall Plan unquestionably increased the demand for economic consolidation. Also, the desire to coordinate trade policy with respect to the United States contributed to the establishment of the Central American Common Market and the Latin American Free Trade Area. External conditions even may have spillover effects. For example, although French military policies during the 1950s in Algeria and Indochina may have contributed to the French defeat of the European Defense Community (EDC), they also helped change the older notion of forceful maintenance of an overseas empire and inspired new demands that the de Gaulle government turn French national resources and energies inward to Europe.

5. Maintaining the Momentum of Integration

Starting along the integrative path and maintaining progress toward the goal of supranationalism are quite separate issues. In addition to certain preconditions that permit the process to begin, certain combinations of "process factors" must be present to govern steady progress.

Functional Satisfaction First among these process factors is functional satisfaction, or recognition by pertinent elites and officials of the degree to which integrated policy is serving their interests. This recognition promotes feedback, thus fueling greater sectoral integration and encouraging spillover.

Public opinion polls taken during the West European integrating experience reveal an almost steady faith in the process. Even during the years

---

[20] Joseph S. Nye Jr., *Peace in Parts*, pp. 23–24.
[21] For a systematic study of costs and benefits in supranationalism, whether or not in regional settings, see Todd Sandler and Jon Cauley, "The Design of Supranational Structures: An Economic Perspective," in *International Studies Quarterly*, June 1977, pp. 251–276.

following the first OPEC petroleum boycott, when the Western industrial states suffered declining productivity and high inflation and unemployment, functional satisfaction continued to be high in the participating countries. Satisfaction with functional performance was correlated directly with national economic condition and with the duration of membership in the EC. Satisfaction was lower in Britain, Ireland, and Denmark, which joined in 1973, but these were also the member states that suffered the worst inflation during this troubled period. Later, when Greece, Spain, and Portugal were admitted, satisfaction reached new heights, particularly because of satisfactory settlement of common agricultural policies in 1988 and 1989. During the post-Maastricht doldrums, satisfaction remained highest in the four countries with the lowest GDP/capita: Greece, Portugal, Ireland, and Spain. Among the more industrialized members, only Italians continued to report high satisfaction.[22]

In calling for the free flow of capital within the community as part of completing the common market, the Single European Act had bitten off a large piece. To governments, control of capital is the economic equivalent of sovereignty in the political realm. Why, then, would the member governments risk going beyond a unified trade market toward a unified monetary system? Two British authors explained this on the basis of functional satisfaction. They demonstrated that in the first ten years of the EMS (European Monetary System), there had been three major successes: (1) inflation had been reduced and maintained at tolerable levels; (2) there had been a sharp reduction in exchange rate volatility among the member currencies; and (3) money-supply growth rates had been held down and their unpredictability reduced. All these had contributed to low inflation and general economic stability. The authors concluded that it was as a result of this successful EMS performance that the community members were willing by 1988 to risk its growth as a

regulatory influence in the final phases of integrating the West European economies.[23]

Increased Pacific Transactions A second process factor is an increased frequency of pacific transactions. The rate and number of transactions are measures of mutual reliance, revealing governmental willingness to compromise sovereignty in specific sectors. Because increasing interdependence is indispensable, the rate of transactions is a critical measure of progress. One study, however, has cautioned against overvaluing transactions as a causal factor in the growth of integration; increased transactions are more a reflection of integration than a cause.[24] Yet it is probable that satisfaction in these contacts, originally an effect of integration, now encourages additional contacts and is thus a major determinant of sectoral feedback.

Institution-building and Regulation Gradually, the transactions of integrating sectors must become institutionalized. Informal regulation cannot serve continuously the objective of formal integration. Hence a third major process condition is the proliferation of institutions with sufficient authority to regulate. Ultimately, these institutions must assume the national governments' normal legislative and executive prerogatives. Complete transfer of such authority from national governments to common institutions is the final stage of the integrating process, and with its completion a supranational community may be said to exist. At present, the maximum progress toward complete integration of a subsector is represented in the High Authority of the ECSC, which has been authorized by its members to exercise sovereign authority over the allocation of the pertinent resources. While the Council of Ministers has substantial powers on matters of

---

[22] Eurobarometer survey reprinted in *World Press Review*, August 1992, p. 10.

[23] Frank McDonald and George Zis, "The European Monetary System: Toward 1992 and Beyond," *Journal of Common Market Studies*, March 1989, pp. 183–202 at p. 184. This entire issue of the *Journal of Common Market Studies* is devoted to the European Monetary System.

[24] Donald J. Puchala, "International Transactions and Regional Integration," *International Organization*, vol. 24, 1970, pp. 732–763.

trade and other economic subjects, it cannot be expected to act wholly without regard to its members' national views. As a denationalized body, the High Authority of the ECSC has, therefore, more nearly supranational authority.

Bureaucracy   Institutionalizing a political process requires the creation of a bureaucracy, specially trained to manage sectoral activities. Because a high degree of technical competence is needed in addition to administrative and political skills, these bureaucracies customarily are referred to as "technocracies." Technocrats not only manage the day-to-day affairs; they must also coordinate the expectations of elites, soothe the sensitivities of governments, and make the unremitting case for further development. They are at once technical experts, intergovernmental managers, and the guardians of the integrative process.

Bureaucratic development in a multinational and multilingual community is far from automatic. From the start, the integrating European states established national formulae and quotas for employment in several of the important organs of community. These were designed for equity and balance, but they have had some divisive consequences. The tensions of multinational staffing have accentuated the contrast of national loyalties with community loyalty. In addition, it has been shown that nation-based informal organizations of staff members develop spontaneously, and the tensions among these groups have significant impacts on community work.[25] Moreover, such organizations may serve as vehicles for special-interest groups in the decision making of the community.[26]

Community Jurisprudence   Another, though less visible, process condition is the development of a community jurisprudence, a commonly recognized body of law that governs the legal relations of the respective states and has independent authority over constitutional evolution. Where the goal is supranationalism, national courts and bodies of law can have but a diminishing salience. The European Court of Justice serves this need and already has developed a large body of case law governing the integrative process.

In the area of jurisprudence the potential for strife between state and community is particularly acute, especially when basic constitutional premises are at stake. Although the primacy of community jurisprudence was established firmly as early as 1963, a decision of the Court of Justice in 1978 provoked a sharp constitutional debate in Britain, at the time a member for only five years. In the *Simmentha* case, the court declared that "every national court must, in a case within its jurisdiction, apply Community law in its entirety and protect rights which the latter confers on individuals and must accordingly set aside any provision of national law which may conflict with it, whether prior or subsequent to the Community rule." Such a prescription boldly subordinates all pertinent acts of Parliament, those that occurred before entry into the community as well as those that succeeded entry, to the law of the EU.[27] Subsequently, in the case of *Factortame, Ltd. v. Secretary of State for Transport*, the British House of Lords, acting on a request of a lower court to determine the relationshilp between British law and pertinent EU law, not only acknowledged the supremacy of community law, but deferred to the Court of Justice on the subject of appropriate British interim remedies.[28]

Referring to the evolution of community jurisprudence within the EU system, two American authors have concluded that "no other international organization enjoys such reliably effective

[25] Hans J. Michelmann, "Multinational Staffing and Organizational Functioning in the Commission of the European Communities," *International Organization*, spring 1978, pp. 477–496.
[26] Juliet Lodge and Valentine Herman, "The Economic and Social Committee in EEC Decision Making," *International Organization*, spring 1980, pp. 265–284, deals generally with the role of interest groups in functional integration.

[27] J. D. B. Mitchell, "The Sovereignty of Parliament and Community Law: The Stumbling Block that Isn't There," *International Affairs* (London), January 1979.
[28] Claire Francis, "Casenote on *Factortame, Ltd. v. Secretary of State for Transport*, 1989, House of Lords," *American Journal of International Law*, January 1990, pp. 269–274.

supremacy of its law over the laws of the member governments." And of the European Court of Justice they have concluded that "of all the [EU's] institutions, the Court has gone farthest in limiting national autonomy, by asserting the principles of superiority of Community law and of the obligation of member states to implement [it]."[29] Another study concludes that the European Court of Justice has evolved into one of "the world's great constitution makers." Noting that few courts enjoy the power of judicial review (that is, the power to declare a legislative act unconstitutional), a reviewer of this study concludes that "[o]nly the European Court of Justice . . . has taken what proclaims itself as something else, namely, a treaty, and turned it into a constitution so that it itself could engage in constitutional judicial review. And no other court . . . has ever played so prominent a role in the creation of the basic governmental and political process of which it is a part."[30]

Increased Decisions   Increased transactions, formation of institutions and technocracies, and the establishment of a common core of jurisprudence all point to the next process condition: increased decisional output. It cannot be said that integration is under way merely because of institutional appearances; rather, measurable and reliable decisions, on which governments and pertinent elites depend willingly and with which they comply consistently, are indispensable. Institutions can have no productive effect on national elites unless they are able to command the external transactions of those elites. Only through actual decisions does the institution become the authoritative vehicle of an international process.

Mass Attitudes   All the foregoing process factors imply increased relations and communications among elites and officials. But the process of integration requires that mass political and social attitudes also be nurtured. Thus, a seventh important process factor is the development of mutual mass attitudes. Although progress toward integration may build on elite pressures, governments are not likely to sacrifice national prerogatives or to respond to narrow demands for supranationality until appropriate attitudes have been established among their electorates. This development must take place in most of or all the participating nations. In this way, mutual expectations are communicated regularly across national boundaries; the benefits of continued progress become more familiar to individuals; and nationalistic attitudes begin to recede.

The issue of mass attitudes is one of human nature. Attitude formation and manipulation are at the foundation of all modern political movements, as we saw in Chapter 1. As a result, they are not linear. It is not true that because 55 percent of people polled hold a specific political view one day that 60 percent will hold it the following day. Attitudes are subject to all kinds of political and economic changes from succession in leadership to unemployment, inflation, sudden changes in international trade, and hundreds more. Weather conditions severely affecting crop yields may cause people to alter their attitudes about agricultural policy or trading partners. For these reasons, the evolution of mass attitudes about something as profound as international integration can be evaluated only over a long trend line. A progressive trend line demonstrates, among other things, the durability of the supranational goal in face of occasional setbacks. It is for this reason that the sudden decline in support for integration in the post-Maastricht years cannot be evaluated yet. It is not the first setback, and presumably it will not be the last.

External Factors   External factors of two types may influence the integrative process. First, they may be external events that absorb the energy of one of the community members. These events may

[29] Robert O. Keohane and Stanley Hoffmann, "Institutional Change in Europe in the 1980s," in Robert O. Keohane and Stanley Hoffmann, eds., *The New European Community: Decisionmaking and Institutional Change* (Boulder, Colo.: Westview, 1991), pp. 11–12.

[30] Quoted from Martin Shapiro's review in *American Journal of International Law*, October 1987, pp. 1007–1011 at pp. 1008–1009, of Hjalte Rasmussen, *Law and Policy in the European Court of Justice: A Comparative Study in Judicial Policymaking* (Dordrecht, Boston, and Lancaster: Martinus Nijhoff Publishers, 1986).

prevent full and earnest participation or, in some cases, accentuate regional preferences. French foreign policy provides examples of both phenomena. Before the Gaullist era, French participation in European integration was impeded by preoccupation with problems in North Africa and Indochina. But for a decade commencing in the mid-1950s, President de Gaulle turned those problems around and directed energy inward. Those years witnessed the most vigorous steps toward European supranationalism. Hence, integration may depend on external events in which one of the community members is vitally engaged. These are *member-centered external events*.

Other external events focus on nonmembers, but may nevertheless have major impacts on the integrative process. The foreign policies (potentially even the domestic policies) of other nations may touch on one or more of the members of a growing community with either integrative or disintegrative effects. The unpopularity among Europeans of American policy in Southeast Asia during the 1960s heightened their sense of Europeanness and correspondingly diminished their psychological bonds with Washington. Except in the security sector (NATO), then, the Vietnam War (as a *nonmember-centered external event*) had integrative effects on Europe. Warsaw Pact occupation of Czechoslovakia in 1968, a resort to long-invisible Soviet politics, was an event of similar meaning to Western Europe. Conversely, the Soviet-inspired imposition of martial law on Poland in response to the liberal demands of the Solidarity labor union had little integrating impact on Western Europe. Indeed, these events unfolded even while a new peace movement resisted the deployment in Western Europe of new American nuclear-tipped missiles.

A most instructive nonmember-centered external event occurred in 1962, with telling effect on European economic integration. Already concerned about future competition from Europe, American merchants sought long-term relief from tariff barriers. As a result, the Kennedy administration sought and secured from Congress discretionary authority to negotiate substantial reciprocal tariff reductions. The Trade Expansion Act of 1962 authorized executive discretion for a period of five years, during which major changes in American trade policy might be negotiated. The Europeans entered into the subsequent GATT negotiations, called the Kennedy Round, with full awareness of the American intent to safeguard industrial exports against future competition. This awareness sparked renewed activity in Europe toward eliminating internal restraints to trade and resulted particularly in the resolution of many of the thorny agricultural problems that previously had retarded progress toward a full free trade arrangement. Thus the initiative of an external power clearly accelerated the completion of the free-trade-area aspects of West European integration.

The events that led to the New World Order once again accelerated the supranationalist quest. The liberation of even Russia from communism meant that in the place of threat, there were new markets and new opportunities. The removal of the pan-European war threat renewed and expanded the desire for security independence from Washington. And the primacy of economic prosperity and peaceful competition that define the New World Order called for renewed energy. It came in the form of completing the customs-union phase of integrating and the Maastricht Treaty on European Union, which called for deepening integration through monetary union.

Transfer of Loyalty The final process condition is really the measure of all the others: the transfer of loyalty gradually from national to community values, objectives, and institutions. It means the adoption by national majorities of far-reaching supranationalist attitudes. As this itself is a functional requisite, such a development does not occur except through individual recognition of the profitability of integration. Nor will it occur in several nations unless there is sufficient communication by which societies can measure attitudinal progress in neighboring lands. Social communication is thus vital to the transfer of loyalties.

The loyalty-transfer process is one of continuing socialization in which positive value communication substantiates the need for community-oriented attitudes. Public opinion surveys from the late 1960s forward have shown this to be developing, with occasional setbacks following disruptive events such as the original French veto of British membership and the controversial Maastricht Treaty. Generally the socialization data have underscored the public preference for, and acceptance of, regional integration in the economic, political, and security realms.

As important as these indicators may be, however, they deal with the business of state rather than the nature of the state. Loyalty transfer at the economic level—even at the extreme level of the proposed full economic and monetary union in the 1992–2002 phase—falls short of the most elemental issue in loyalty transfer: recognition of a political authority higher than the state, and its assumption of duties previously exercised by the state and, indeed, demonstrating its sovereignty. The direct election of the European Parliament over a decade ago was the first substantial step taken by the community toward transformation of sovereignty. The growth in the influence of the European Commission is another, particularly in view of the political advantage it has taken of the Single European Act. By late 1989, opinion surveys were beginning to reveal the attitude of the public toward this change in the balance of political forces between the community, on the one hand, and its member states, on the other. Fully 82 percent of those questioned recognized the importance of community affairs even though only 45 percent of respondents considered themselves interested in political affairs and only 42 percent expressed interest in specific community policies.[31]

The post-Maastricht uneasiness of the European electorates has special significance in this regard. The treaty's unanticipated scope, broadly considered not a measured extension of the Single European Act but a radical leap, sharpened the perception that planning the latter steps of integration is undemocratic, and that parties in power are striking political deals untested in national politics. Ironically, the fear expressed is directed less at the institutions of the EU than at the national governments, which are seen to be tampering with statehood in order to aggrandize their own power within the EU. Consequently, the subsidiarity issue—division of governing authority among EU, national, and subnational institutions—has blossomed. At the subnational levels (lander, states, provinces, counties, precincts, etc.), there is a growing sense that local interests are being dealt away without adequate airing. This has generated a new level of politics. In Germany, for example, as an inducement for public endorsement of the Maastricht Treaty, Chancellor Kohl pledged access of the lander (states) to the European Council of Ministers, and then he sponsored a successful resolution among the Ministers to meet with representatives of regional governments provided they were authorized to speak on behalf of their national governments. This has led to the new concept of "a Europe of regions," in which subnational governments might play a role parallel to national governments within the EU machinery. In Britain, which has a much more centralized political system, the national government has no interest in autonomous regional voices within the EU. Some speculate that should the Europe-of-regions concept take root, London's refusal to permit its regional governments to participate might precipitate a constitutional crisis in the United Kingdom.[32] The important point here is that after decades of recognizing the value of integration, as the final steps near, those that strike closest to national sovereignty and popular government, the older tension between integrating institutions and

---

[31] "Eurobarometer: Public Opinion in the European Communities," *European Affairs*, autumn 1989, pp. 26–32.

[32] Andrew Scott, John Peterson, and David Millar, "Subsidiarity: A 'Europe of Regions' v. the British Constitution?" *Journal of Common Market Studies*, March 1994, pp. 47–68.

national governments is being replaced by one between national and subnational governments. In the current EU context, this is called "the problem of subsidiarity."

This concludes our discussion of the sectors, objectives, preconditions and process conditions of integration. For easy reference and review, they are summarized in Table 16–1.

An Evaluation of Integration

This examination of integration assumes that supranationalism is healthy and that it is to be encouraged and lauded. But if integration occurs, its impact on people and international order is worth exploring.

First consider the effects of integration on the population of an integrated community. Although it is assumed conventionally that it will, for the most part, profit from integration, some observers raise negative aspects. Integration very well may raise standards of living, indices of production, and so on, but what will life be like? Does supranationalism necessarily make the individual's life more pleasant?

Although these questions remain unanswerable, perhaps skepticism is appropriate. The consolidation of economies and politics does, to be sure, have the effect of eliminating competition and some differences among participants, but it creates a new form of political community. Is this new form merely an enlarged nation-state? Is there anything fundamentally different between an integrated

TABLE 16–1

SUMMARY OF INTEGRATION FACTORS

Integration Sectors	Momentum	Objectives	Preconditions	Process Conditions
Economic	Feedback (intrasector)	Maximize economic potential	Social assimilation	Functional satisfaction
Social	Spillover (intersector)	Maximize political potential	Elite value sharing	Increased frequency of transactions
Political		Resolve regional conflict	Expectation of mutual benefits	Institution-building
Security			History of pacific transactions	Technocracy-building
			Favorable ratio of costs to benefits	Community jurisprudence
			External influences	Growing decisional output
			a. Member-centered	Mass attitude assimilation
			b. Nonmember-centered	External factors
				a. Member-centered
				b. Nonmember-centered
				Transfer of loyalty

community and a large nation-state that is multilingual and culturally and socially heterogeneous?

These are not merely abstract questions. In their concerns with mass anxiety, crises of identity, breakup of the nuclear family, lack of pride in work, and the generation gap, social observers today have begun to explore the social and psychological consequences of mass industrialization. They have turned their attention to whether there are ill effects from the philosophy of the modern industrial state: "There's more of it where that came from!" Does integration for purposes of successful international economic competition rush a society blindly toward these effects? Does it hasten the alienation of men and women from the politics, institutions, and stated ideals of mass society?

Another concern is with the antidemocratic effects of centralization and bureaucratization. As policy becomes less the result of public participation and more a consequence of administrative pragmatism, does a society relinquish to functional technocracies its grip on its own destiny? What is the likelihood that increased reliance on technocracy will degenerate into new forms of oligarchy? Are there major divergences between the values, needs, and expectations of technocrats, on the one hand, and those of society, on the other? What is the future of the political role of nonelite social sectors? At the most practical level, the post-Maastricht debate about subsidiarity illustrates the importance of these questions.

These and other quality-of-life questions have led to a call for a normative critique of integration theory and for research into the social consequences of regional supranationalism. To be socially tolerable in the long run, life in supranational communities must be preferable or superior to life in contemporary nation-states. Otherwise, the achievement of higher political community may be merely a new organizational stage in the destruction of societies.

The view from outside raises equally troubling questions. Even if one accepts the intragroup benefits of integration, what are the effects on intergroup relations? Do the consolidated policies of like-minded states contribute positively to international order, or do they merely accentuate the effects of the nation-state with greatly enhanced power resources? The possibility exists that even if regional integration tends to have associating characteristics among its members, it may have disassociating consequences in overall international stability. We know from history, for example, that early EU development benefited from certain nonmember-centered external events including protectionism and the American Trade Expansion Act of 1962. Will the EU's success provoke more such events, and if so, what will be their consequences for world order? It is clear that the future of the EU's trading relations, especially with North America, cannot be stable without the parallel maturation of the plurilateral trade regime of the Uruguay Round and the WTO. The EU's success and North America's most recent response, NAFTA, make it the more necessary that the contemporary world trade regime evolve into a comprehensive *lex specialis* in international law.[33]

The potential for global disassociation is apparent especially in security communities. Because conflict usually precedes security arrangements, disassociation is a product of earlier political relations. Yet, like all other institutions in society, security institutions tend to become self-sustaining. Their managing elites continue to have interests, and their operations may depend on perpetuating the initial causes. In security communities, the original cause is a threat; and the perpetuation of security institutions thus may depend on the ability to convince public and appropriating agencies of the persistence of potential crisis. Should this occur—if persons propagandize and even romanticize crisis potential for institutional or personal aggrandizement

---

[33] Alberto Tita, "A Challenge for the World Trade Organization—Toward a True Transnational Law," *Journal of World Trade*, June 1995, pp. 83–90. Tita's paper is based on the WTO's creation of a Preparatory Committee charged to make recommendations on its agenda for the future, which he sees as an invitation to expand the jurisdiction of the organization.

—then institutions may prolong crises, contributing to the disassociating effects of the original antipathy. Institutionalized alliances always carry this danger; and because integrated institutions magnify the political potential of elites, supranational security communities may impede global stability.

Uniquely, this logic does not seem to apply to the EU and the WEU. In this case, the vestigial security arrangement is NATO, and it is principally Washington that is trying to sustain it. The recent establishment of the WEU as the forerunner of a European armed force is a deliberate break from the pre–New World Order security assumptions and an effort at spillover into the security sector without having a preidentified enemy.

Despite the dangers implicit in integration from both domestic and international perspectives, at present the prevailing attitude is that regional integrative trends are healthy, productive, and promising of a brighter future for national peoples and for global stability. Indeed, one French student of EC affairs went so far as to write that "Europe as a whole could well become the first example in history of a major centre of the balance of power becoming in the era of its decline not a colonised victim but the exemplar of a new stage in political civilisation."[34] But two others have entered an incisive condition: "[T]he Community's capacity to act constructively in the world depends in the last resort on its success in establishing within its boundaries a more united and more just society."[35] It is safe to conclude that integration over any geographical region will encounter a similar variety of pressures. And while these statements are a quarter-century old, there is no reason to think that they have lost their value.

[34] François Duchêne, "The European Community and the Uncertainties of Interdependence," in Max Kohnstamm and Wolfgang Hager, eds., *A Nation Writ Large? Foreign Policy Problems Before the European Community* (New York: Wiley, 1973), pp. 1–21.
[35] Max Kohnstamm and Wolfgang Hager, "Conclusion" to *A Nation Writ Large?* pp. 256–264.

Is the European Experience Reproducible?

It was noted earlier that integration is not uniquely European, but that the progress made in the EU is so far advanced of other experiments that it has generated the most interest and the richest literature. In addition, in the discussion of economic development in Chapter 6, we inquired into theoretical models for the Developing Nations. We now combine these into the question of whether or not the European experience is reproducible in the Developing World.

In general, the answer is no. Unlike Western Europe, the Developing Nations lack independent industrial bases for accumulating capital. (Overdependence on natural resources and other primary products suggests that temporary cartels, such as OPEC, are practical, but unless the product has the political weight of oil, they are not a useful route.) Their economies are dependent rather than independent, as were those of Western Europe in the 1950s. In many places tribal and other ethnic animosities prevent domestic social assimilation, so that prospects for cross-border social accretion are not good. Usually when we think of development we really mean economic development. But effective integration presupposes a certain level of political development as well, and in many of the poor nations the requisite level has not been achieved. This has the dual liability of uncontrollable domestic factionalism and the absence of transnational party coalitions that were so helpful in promoting common interests in Europe.

This does not rule out some forms of integration, however. The relative simplicity of economic activity in much of the Developing World is a fertile basis for functionalism. In fact, regional trading arrangements are fairly common among the Developing Nations, especially in Central and South America, the Caribbean, and Southeast Asia. Free trade areas and limited customs unions will continue to be popular. So will special trading relations such as the Lomé and Yaoundé Conventions that tie more then 100 Developing Nations to the EU through France, within the GATT and WTO preferential provisions for Developing Nations. Just as some of the post-Soviet transitional economies of Central Europe covet EU membership, so too do some Latin American lands expect a NAFTA expansion (Peru already has expressed an interest), some of them hoping openly for a Western Hemisphere Free Trade Association in the future. ASEAN may expand to embrace other developing Asian economies. As the transitional economies approach the goal of becoming market driven, the CIS, including Russia, will undoubtedly evolve into a free trade area. The same is potentially ahead for Syria, Lebanon, Jordan, and Palestine once Middle East peace is consolidated and Palestine evolves to sovereignty from self-rule. The prospects are dimmest, alas, for sub-Saharan Africa, home of most of the states with the lowest GDP/capita.

Beyond free trade areas and limited customs unions, integration is not likely in the Developing World's foreseeable future. The political and social bases for institution-building are absent, as are the preconditions for supranational jurisprudence.

Transnational Participation

Every structure of world order that we have considered thus far presumes as its central feature the nation-state, intergovernmental organization, or the integration of states into higher political units. Sovereignty, power, and official diplomacy lie at the heart of each of these systems. All of them are considered to be state-centric models of world order, though the EU may eventually introduce the concept of the superstate as a central actor. Yet every traveler, every student of other cultures, every devotee of the creative arts, and every businessperson is aware that many transactions of the international system do not involve governments alone, and that much of what happens across international boundaries is removed from sovereignty and intergovernmental negotiations. Despite the

omnipresence of governments and official regulations, many international transactions occur on a people-to-people basis or between one government and the corporations of another state. This process, referred to as transnational participation, has become the focus of new forms of research and analysis in international relations.

Transnational interaction is defined as "the movement of tangible or intangible items across state boundaries when at least one actor is not an agent of a government or an intergovernmental organization."[36] It may involve contact between two or more nongovernmental actors or between one official actor and one or more private actors. The nongovernmental participants may be corporations, social organizations, interest groups, political parties, elite structures, or formally instituted organizations designed to facilitate private relations. An agreement between an oil company and a foreign government falls into this category, as does contact between the International Red Cross and the government of Cuba. An International Youth Conference, involving no governments, is also transnational.[37]

Goals of Transnational Participation

Although these forms of international contact always have taken place, their impact traditionally has been minimized because of state domination of the global system. Now it is acknowledged, however, that such contacts contribute to the quality of

---

[36] Robert O. Keohane and Joseph S. Nye Jr., "Transnational Relations and World Politics: An Introduction," *International Organization*, vol. 25, 1971, pp. 329–349. This section borrows extensively from this article.

[37] The summer 1971 edition of *International Organization* is devoted to the subject "Transnational Relations and World Politics," Robert O. Keohane and Joseph S. Nye Jr., eds. Among its many papers it considers the Ford Foundation, the Roman Catholic church, airlines flying international routes, labor unions, and scientific societies as transnational actors. Although these papers are not specifically cited here, the reader is alerted to this edition of the journal as the best single source of papers on the theory and illustrative studies of the transnational phenomenon.

coexistence, either directly (by improving perceptions and tolerances) or indirectly (by affecting intergovernmental relations). With increasing private contact, ubiquitous international trade and social communication, transnational participation can no longer be overlooked as a major aspect of international stability or integration.

These interactions have six kinds of prospective impact. First, transnational contact is assumed *to promote changes in attitude* among the actors. Contact may break down perceptions, erase social and cultural barriers, enlighten outlooks, and dissipate animosities. In general, such attitudinal changes may help transform the international system by raising levels of tolerance among peoples, especially elites.

The second identifiable impact is *the promotion of international pluralism*. More and more linkages will be developed between domestic political processes and the international system. More interests will come to be involved in decision making; more national elites will gain contact with their counterparts abroad; and more services will be provided for more people.

The creation of new avenues of dependence and interdependence is the third expectation. Transnational contact illuminates mutual needs, and in the long run it may obviate some causes of intersocietal conflict. In addition, reliance will be built on other societies, on their productivity, and on their unique forms of creativity. In this manner, transnational contact may assist in "denationalizing" the energies of national peoples, thus taking governments out of the center of international transactions.[38]

Fourth, increases in transnationalism may *create beneficial side effects* for those aspects of the international system that remain state centered. Specifically, stabilization of relations among peoples, with increasing intersocietal dependence, may enlarge the peaceful contacts of governments and actually create for them new avenues of influence. A dramatic and unusual example of this impact was President Richard M. Nixon's historic trip to the People's Republic of China in 1972, a trip that, in American public opinion, was made possible by the prior amicable visit of a table-tennis team. Following the president's sojourn, informal contact was utilized further to break down long-standing barriers by exchanges of scientists, physicians, and surgeons. This feature of transnationalism led one observer to describe the process as "transactions which bypass the institutions of government but strongly affect their margin of maneuver."[39]

Fifth, transnational participation, when institutionalized, may *create new influential autonomous and quasi-autonomous actors* in the international system. Among these are hundreds of nongovernmental organizations (NGOs) and informal institutional arrangements through which transnational interactions are regulated. The International Red Cross is the best known of these, one that not only conducts its own relief operations but also to which governments frequently turn to arrange official contacts. Another important NGO is the International Chamber of Commerce, which already has contributed to international stability and amicable exchange by formulating norms of international business relations.[40]

The sixth possible effect of transnationalism is the *gradual institutionalization of intersocietal transactions* that may become the private counterpart of functional international organizations. Although public single-purpose organizations go about formulating international norms in their respective fields, transnational groups may proceed to develop the norms of their own relations. Furthermore, the national elites that direct functional organizations will be identical in some instances to those that

---

[38] These first three features of transnationalism are illustrated especially well in the study of Robert C. Angell, *Peace on the March: Transnational Participation* (New York: Van Nostrand Reinhold, 1969).

[39] Karl Kaiser, "Transnational Politics: Toward a Theory of Multinational Politics," *International Organization*, vol. 24, 1971, pp. 790–817.

[40] Percy E. Corbett, *From International to World Law* (Bethlehem, Pa.: Lehigh University Department of International Relations, research monograph no. 1, 1969).

regulate transnational contact. Such a process would maximize the linkages between national and international decision-making processes.

Types of Transnational Participation

Having noted the functional characteristics of transnational research, we may now classify and exemplify types of transnational participation. Most informal among them are the sociocultural activities, of which there are thousands annually. Most common is individual travel, which has some cumulative effect on international attitudes. Other sociocultural activities of significance are international visits of symphony orchestras, touring exhibits, lecture series, touring dance companies, and so on. International athletic events, particularly the Olympics, the Pan-American Games, and the old Soviet-American games, also are in this category.

Political transnational activity is another. The earliest events were the International Peace Congresses of the nineteenth century, which met to formulate treaties for world peace. These were returned to national societies and national governments, with the Congress members serving as interest groups. At present, the World Peace Through Law movement does much the same thing. Other political transnationalism involves the international communications and meetings of some political parties, such as the socialist parties of Western Europe, national communist parties, and the several National Liberation Fronts. The International Youth Conferences sponsored periodically by the United Nations and other organizations are also examples of political transnationalism, because they present and discuss the political attitudes of young people from different lands.

By far the most numerous transnational activities are in the economic realm. Although many aspects of the international political economy are conducted by governments and although most are regulated by official norms, much of the modern international economy is regulated privately. At present, the transnational actor with the greatest power to affect national economies and the flow of international transactions is the transnational corporation (TNC), also called the multinational corporation (MNC) and, in the European literature, the transnational enterprise (TNE). Its center of operations is in one country, but it has subsidiaries in several others that have major effects on international economics and the host economies. In 1993 the United States alone has more than 18,000 such operations. Japan ranks second, followed by Britain, Germany, and France. In both 1992 and 1993, 45 percent of the productivity of all American MNCs was created at the foreign sites. Table 16–2 summarizes some of the other attributes of these corporations. So large and powerful are these corporations that in 1972, when the domestic and overseas operations of ITT came under fire, the solicitor-general of the United States remarked that the company was beyond the laws even of the United States!

Looked at from the viewpoint of a host government, the power of these corporations is equally great. An anecdote may suffice to illustrate. The British Ford subsidiary manufactures approximately 650,000 automobiles per year, slightly fewer than the Belgian and German subsidiaries. In 1971, when corporation president Henry Ford II arrived in Britain during a strike, he warned that unless the

TABLE 16–2

UNITED STATES MULTINATIONAL CORPORATIONS WORLDWIDE

	1982	1987	1993
Assets	$3.5 trillion	$5.3 trillion	$8.1 trillion
Sales	3.3	3.7	5.1
Net Income	NA	NA	105.1 billion
Employees	25.3 million	24.3 million	24.4 million

Source: U.S. Department of Commerce, Survey of Current Business, June 1995, p. 32.

British economy presented less threat to productivity, Ford would consider closing the British operations and expanding productivity on the continent. Although labor reacted with a "we're-not-afraid" attitude, Ford was generally "treated more like a visiting head of state than an ordinary industrialist." The story illustrates the immense power held by these corporations.[41]

Multinational corporations are growing at an average rate greater than the world's most vigorous national economies. It is estimated that by the year 2000, they will produce upwards of one-half of the gross world product. And the more they grow, the more they dominate world trade. Many of them, if not most, do not produce a commodity from start to finish at a single site. Instead, they build some parts in some areas and export them to second subsidiaries, where they are joined to other parts of the whole and then exported to yet a third place. It is not at all unusual for an automobile made by an American-owned corporation to consist of a transmission made in one country, a motor made in a second, a body made in a third, and tires and fixtures made in a fourth. Twenty-five percent of all American exports are to the overseas subsidiaries of American-based TNCs.

More than merely uncloaking the enormity of these corporations, these characteristics reveal the extent to which they—largely unregulated by governments or by international agreement—are able to control the world economy and the economies of the host states. Often their operations lead to political controversy, as in de Gaulle's insistence on "de-Americanizing" Europe, ITT's CIA-assisted coup d'état in Chile, and rampant scandals resulting from corrupt business practices abroad. In both developed and less developed economies, TNCs can penetrate fiscal policy and labor relations; they are able to profit

by dispersing earnings and losses among subsidiaries without regard for the host economy; and they can remove their economic activity to the detriment of the host. Although they are able to contribute to economic development, they are also able to globalize such injurious phenomena as inflation and to use their economic might for political intervention. As a result, many governments have experimented with restrictions on foreign ownership of production, and the governments of the Developing World have heightened their demand for international regulation of multinational corporate activity. Both the United Nations and the Organization for Economic Co-operation and Development (OECD) have labored long over this issue, and in 1976 the OECD adopted a series of declarations comprising guidelines for the behavior of multinational enterprises.[42] Despite this progress and despite the annual review of performance under the guidelines by the OECD, the Developing Nations continue to consider this a major area of need.

The capital-lending institutions also affect the world economy and the domestic economies of the host states. Although no one disputes the need for operating capital in industrial modernization, some would argue that the rapid growth of branch banks overseas is an instrument of neoimperialism. If American capital is the only available source of funds, then American banks and American fiscal policy actually regulate interest rates and growth rates overseas. Furthermore, both in the banking business and in commodity industries, profits are

---

[41] As related in Christopher Tugendhat, "Transnational Enterprise: Tying Down Gulliver," *Atlantic Community Quarterly,* vol. 9, 1971–72, pp. 499–508.

[42] The OECD guidelines and review documents for 1979 can be found in "Review of the 1976 Declaration and Decisions on Guidelines for Multinational Enterprises, National Treatment, International Investment Incentives and Disincentives, and Consultation Procedures," OECD, 1979. For background information, see particularly Robert O. Keohane and Van Doorn Ooms, "The Multinational Firm and International Regulation," *International Organization,* vol. 29, 1975, pp. 169–212; and Paul A. Tharp Jr., "Transnational Enterprises and International Regulation: A Survey of Various Approaches in International Organization," *International Organization,* vol. 30, 1976, pp. 47–74.

siphoned off and returned with minimal reinvestment, with the result that the principal gains from the multinational enterprise accrue solely to the country of origin.

Apart from their own economic goals, the MNCs hold special significance in the study of transnationalism because they are considered widely to be the principal instruments of technology transfer. When an innovative corporation takes its operations to a Developing Nation, the labor force, banks, government, and entrepreneurs of that country gain firsthand technological experience that is presumed to be transferable to domestic industry and investment. Furthermore, because it is the MNCs that conduct most of the world's direct foreign investing, they are capital disseminators as well. In this role they are considered to be major "engines of growth."[43]

There is a division of opinion as to whether or not these effects actually occur. On the one hand, as Table 16–2 indicates, there are tremendously beneficial employment consequences from the MNCs' global activities. Jobs mean income; income means public tax revenue and capital accumulation. On the other hand, Table 16–3 indicates that at least in the American MNC pattern, the Developing World gets tertiary benefit at best through geographic distribution. This means that only a small fraction of the investment capital goes to the Developing World together with a small fraction of the employment and of the benefits therefrom. Furthermore, unless profits are reinvested where they are earned, capital investment drops off sharply after the initial phase in favor of repatriation. In addition, while practice with the technology elevates the skills of some, it does not include an intense involvement of engineers, scientists, entrepreneurs, and so forth, and thus it really does not become domesticated. In the area of high technology, there is a fear that attempts to direct economic development away from more

---

[43] See, as an example, United Nations, *World Investment Report, 1992: Transnational Corporations as Engines of Growth*.

TABLE 16–3

GEOGRAPHIC DISTRIBUTION OF U.S. MULTINATIONAL CORPORATIONS, 1993

Western Hemisphere	
Canada	1,941
Mexico/Brazil	1,075
Other	1,849
Europe	9,202
Asia/Pacific	
Japan/Singapore/Australia	1,976
Other	1,705
Africa	493
Middle East	313
Other	153

Source: U.S. Department of Commerce, *Survey of Current Business*, June 1995, p. 35.

traditional industries actually may be injurious to the developing economies.

Considered from political and economic perspectives, the multinational corporation is a mixed blessing. But what is it when viewed from the perspective of transnationalism? What is its value as a nongovernmental actor capable of creating new intersocietal communications?

At present, the transnational corporation may contribute to integration through its ability to forge shared values among participating elites. There is a growing consensus that the managers of overseas subsidiaries must subordinate nationalistic attitudes to corporate profit, regardless of the country of central operations. Because the principal decisions are economic rather than political, and because the function of capitalist business is to achieve profit in competitive markets, the tendency in these corporations is to minimize national feelings. Yet it is also probable that this attitude does not filter down very far within the company. Below uppermost management, few employees are aware of the full meaning of their participation in a multinational enterprise. Their objective in most cases is to progress in the plant rather than in the corporation, or in the industry rather than in the conglomerate.

The multinational business enterprise has not had a deep overall impact on national economic attitudes. There are many who feel that such organization is vital to efficiency in a technological world, and there are those who insist that regional supranationalism is dependent on multinational business. But there is little evidence to suggest its positive effect on international stability through attitudinal change at the mass level. The opposite may be quite the case, in fact, because these huge operations tend to be exploitative and ready to use their considerable political weight. Often, they make themselves unwelcome guests by aggravating existing tensions. Although there is considerable evidence that the TNCs are effective agents for the transfer of technology from the developed to the developing economies, the overall effects on national and international political economies remain controversial, as does the broader role of the TNCs in social change and in the emerging world order.

To whatever extent transnational participation contributes to world stability, then, its virtue must be found in less visible places. Most such progress at present is found in the sociocultural sector. At its roots, the transnational process is one of awareness; and the indications are that at the individual level, maximum attitudinal change through awareness occurs through sociocultural contact only.

Governments cautiously safeguard their prerogatives and prevent escape of political functions to external agencies. But the intersocietal linkages created by the movement of persons, information, goods, and capital across national boundaries challenge the purely state-centered model of international stability. They ultimately may alter the supremacy of the state as an actor in the international system, although to date such transformation is minimal. All in all, however, the several alternatives to absolute sovereignty that we have studied in this chapter and the preceding two (international law, international organization, supranationalism, and transnational participation) all press in upon the nation-state and challenge its ability to remain the paramount actor in international relations. Under these circumstances, it has become fashionable to argue that in the New World Order, in which dependence on the state for security is diminished greatly, national sovereignty already is being eroded by the simultaneous but opposite forces of supranationalism, on the one hand, and subnational power, on the other hand. And the forces of the latter range from ethnic separation to the unprecedented global power of the transnational corporations.

CHAPTER 17

The Future World Order

During the era of the Apollo moon probes, an American astronaut told mission control that the most remarkable thing about space travel is seeing earth as a planet without boundaries. From his vantage point deep in space, temporarily removed from armed conflict and the rhetoric of enmity, he voiced the long-standing view of many people—if enduring peace is to dawn, the international system first must be substantially altered. If war is a product of the nation-state system, then the role of the state must be diminished and that of other governing and social processes increased. Disillusioned with the balance of power, the balance of terror, and all known power distributions, observers ranging from nineteenth-century utopians to contemporary futurist scholars have sought alternative worlds, all focusing on one problem: how to supplant the nation-state's capacity for disruption.

Until recently, many observers held naively that the end of the Cold War would eliminate the need to imagine new futures, but its passing only showed that war-peace issues alone do not monopolize inquiries into the future. On an overcrowded planet nearing depletion of resources and extinction of species, the dynamics of the international system have come upon new emergencies. Stability relies not only on the willingness of governments to put aside their arms but also on their ability to correct anarchical ways. Consider briefly a few areas in which the nation-state record is dismal and which cry for international regulation.

1. Ecology

First among them is ecological anarchy. States have exploited the earth's natural riches without regard for the problem of exhaustibility and with little consideration of future generations or the needs of others. Growing energy demands deplete fossil fuels; deposits of hard metals have been used up; and supplies of fresh water are dangerously low. Meanwhile, we have poisoned the air, despoiled most of the major rivers of the world, toxified vast areas of the seas, made urban living a painful clatter, and outgrown designated dumping areas. These problems have become so nearly universal that national regulation is too little and too late. Without new levels of cooperation and international regulation, we are bent upon ecological suicide.

Sadly, international cooperation on this issue scarcely has commenced, despite the best efforts of the United Nations. Under its auspices, after fully four years of preparation, the Global Conference on the Human Environment was convened at Stockholm in 1972. Fraught with politics and beset by Developing World insistence that environmental preservation is a luxury for the industrialized, the conference achieved but modest ends. It established the seeds of a global environmental monitoring system, promulgated an action program, and established UN oversight machinery. But beyond dramatic recognition of the need for international cooperation and the establishment of functional machinery, the Stockholm meeting itself was a less compelling impetus to cooperation than were subsequent events.

The years that followed Stockholm saw a number of dramatic environmental calamities. They ranged from nuclear accidents in the Soviet Union and the United States, to catastrophic chemical explosions in India and Mexico; from the Russian acknowledgment of years of dumping nuclear waste in the sea, to vacating entire American towns because of chemical contamination; from the deliberate Iraqi torching of scores of Kuwaiti oil wells with resulting widespread smoke pollution, to acid rain that killed all indentifiable life in some streams and lakes in the Rocky Mountains; from marine shipping accidents, some from human error and some related to weather, that killed untold millions of aquatic animals, to chemical pesticide runoff that virtually wiped out much of the seafood industry in the Chesapeake Bay. Even interplanetary space has not been immune, as there is now so much "space junk" in orbit (e.g., breakaway pieces of spaceships and satellites, errant and inoperative satellites, some of which reportedly contain nuclear reactors that fueled now-spent Soviet satellites) that both the United States and Russian governments fear for the safety of astronauts. Closer to home, the environmental disasters have poisoned and irradiated the food chain, killed thousands of humans, burned and maimed thousands more, wiped out industries dependent on wildlife, soil, or clean water, and cluttered both the floors and surfaces of the oceans with unclean and potentially lethal debris. And in some places, the air nearly is unbreathable.

Less dramatic but equally alarming are the quieter cumulative effects of environmental spoliation. In the industrialized state, the last years have seen considerable measures against industrial smoke discharge; in control of health hazards in mines; in diminished strip mining or, alternatively, strip mining followed by reconstitution of the landscape; and in reduction of waste release into rivers and bays. Recycling of reusable metal, plastic, and paper products is spreading as a legal requirement, both to preserve resources and to minimize dumping. Laws regulating the transport of dangerous materials are more prevalent, as are those pertaining to fossil fuel emissions.

But in recent years scientists throughout the world have sounded alarms about four new, long-term environmental threats, all of which exceed national and continental boundaries and cannot be reversed without global cooperation.

1. **Depletion of the ozone layer**—that portion of the earth's atmosphere that screens out the most harmful of the sun's rays. After a few years of controversy over the scientific certainty of this crisis, both satellite data and information collected by international teams of scientists working at the South Pole have confirmed that a hole has, indeed, developed in the layer. Chemists theorize that this is caused principally by the release of chlorofluorocarbons into the atmosphere, particularly from refrigeration systems, pressurized spray cans, and dry cleaning fluids. The confirmed appearance of the hole (some years it grows, and some it shrinks) is blamed for the sharp increase in skin cancer rates in the United States and elsewhere, the main reason for stern warnings about exposure to the summer sun.

2. **Deforestation**—particularly destruction of the tropical rain forests of Central and South America, Africa, and Southeast Asia, most often to increase agricultural acreage. In Africa, starvation and drought result in large measure from interruption in natural rain cycles by forest destruction. Man made deserts produce little or no nutrition, and at the cost of removing the natural circumstances that create atmospheric moisture. In the equatorial forests of the Amazon basin in South America, there is a major battle between environmentalists, determined to prevent recurrence of the African experience, and land-starved farmers, who see deforestation as their economic salvation. Southeast Asia, lush in forestation in the 1960s, has seen depletion in the range of 50 to 80 percent by nation by the mid-1990s.[1] But not only does

---

[1] Gareth Porter, "The Environmental Hazards of Asian Pacific Development: The Southeast Asian Rainforests," *Current History*, December 1994, pp. 430–434.

Environmental crisis: a (former East) German river boiling with toxic industrial pollution, 1989. (*Source:* © Anthony Suau/Black Star)

deforestation fail as an agricultural policy, it also is dangerous environmentally. First, most of the tree waste is burned, sending aloft tons of toxic smoke that may fall out virtually anywhere in the world. Some remains aloft permanently. Second, because oxygen is a by-product of photosynthesis in plants and trees, massive deforestation diminishes the world's oxygen supply.

3. **Global warming**—the phenomenon by which the discharge of millions of tons of methane and carbon dioxide, the so-called "greenhouse gases," into the atmosphere alters the earth's temperature-regulating mechanisms, principally by blocking radiational cooling. Gradually the temperature rises; and while this may be appealing to those who bemoan cold winter days, its consequences potentially are devastating. Worst among them is gradual polar and glacial melting, leading potentially to massive growth in the oceans' volume,

endangering coastal cities, obliterating farmlands, driving major rivers over continents, and salinating precious sources of fresh drinking water. In 1995, scientists advising the United Nations on a Convention on Climate Change reported that fifteen nations alone discharged over ten million tons of carbon dioxide into the environment in 1990, and they estimated that a doubling of that amount could result in an increase of the earth's temperature by between three and eight degrees.[2] No estimate was published from the burning of felled forests. One study, designed to estimate the costs and benefits of a rigorous global program of greenhouse-gas abatement, estimates that the cost would

---

[2] *The New York Times*, February 21, 1995, p. B8. Subsequently it was reported that the estimated rise in sea level between now and the year 2100 will be between 10 and 31 inches. See *The New York Times*, September 18, 1995, p. A1.

be about 4 percent of the gross world product. In contrast, if the damage from global warming is high, it could reduce the gross world product by 16 percent by the year 2275, and if damage is low, it would remain within 5 percent of the gross world product. Given the current rate of accumulation of the gases, the study estimates that unless an effort costing 4 percent of gross world product is undertaken soon, there will be no way to avoid paying the cost of high damage in only about 75 years.[3] For a summary of these findings, see Figure 17–1.

4. **Disposal of nuclear waste**—the problem of finding safe ways to store thousands of tons of radioactive materials that have half-lives (the time that it takes for half of the radiation to neutralize) measured in thousands of years. Since 1940, approximately 12,000 metric tons (there are approximately 2200 pounds per metric ton) of plutonium have been manufactured from uranium, about half of it for nuclear weapons and the remainder for generating electricity. (See Figure 17–2 for historical production of plutonium.) As nuclear weapons are dismantled in the New World Order, much of this needs to be disposed of in a manner that is environmentally safe, protective against explosion, and inaccessible to political groups that might adopt techniques of nuclear blackmail. At the same time, about 450 nuclear power stations around the world periodically are replacing old material with fresh new plutonium. The old material needs to be stored for thousands of years.[4] In the United States, a decision was made in 1977 to store nuclear waste in specially designed bunkers deep beneath Yucca Mountain in the Nevada desert. Recently, however, scientists have raised the possibility that this might cause a massive nuclear explosion sometime in the distant future, and so the debate rages once again about how to deal safely with this potentially catastrophic problem.[5]

These threats, together with the unknown genetic and disease-causing consequences of ecological anarchy, imperil all the world's peoples as we near the end of this most industrially, technologically, and agriculturally productive century in human history. Our successes, while not distributed evenly around the globe, have been at a high price from this perspective, and the fight—primarily economic and developmental—between environmental preservationists and advocates of rapid development undoubtedly will not end with the century. Moreover, since Stockholm, rapid industrialization and increased dependence on synthetic fertilizers for agricultural advancement have brought about new concern for ecology in the Developing World. The environmental consequences of unplanned urban growth, involving such things as industrial discharge, waste disposal, poor fresh water supplies, and the natural consequences of deforestation, have stimulated this concern. Table 17–1. compares the specific concerns of the Developing Nations with those of the industrialized states. Those in capital letters indicate specific priorities.

In 1992, the United Nations convened the 150-nation Conference on Environment and Development in an effort to establish global standards and policy for promoting economic preservation and economic development simultaneously. The modesty of its outcome was an accurate reflection of the differences between the Developing World and the industrial states, particularly the United States. The developing countries, holding to the notion that most environmental problems result from overconsumption in the West, sought international protection of biodiversity (preservation of animal and plant species), but with few restrictions on their industrial modernization. The United States, in contrast, unwilling to enter agreements that would have added billions of dollars to industrial costs by raising emission standards, sought primarily protections for international climate control, a restatement of preservation of rain forests.[6]

---

[3] *The New York Times*, October 10, 1995, p. C4.
[4] *The New York Times*, March 14, 1995, p. C1.
[5] *The New York Times*, March 5, 1995, p. A1.

[6] "Saving the Earth," *World Press Review*, June 1992, pp. 9–14; Ronald A. Taylor, "The Road to Rio," *Europe*, June 1992, pp. 12–13; and Bruce Babbitt, "The World After Rio," *World Monitor*, June 1992, pp. 28–33.

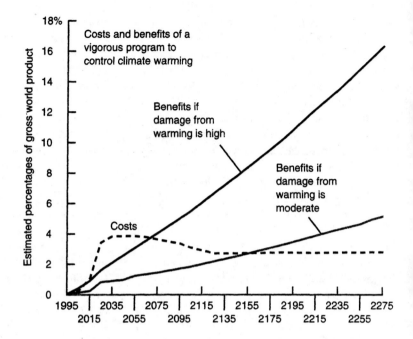

FIGURE 17-1   Abatement of greenhouse warming.

Source: The New York Times, October 10, 1995, p. C4. Reprinted with permission.

The important conclusion is that whether developed or less developed, socialist or market economy, all states now have urgent concern for ecological preservation. Yet because environmental pollution knows nothing of national boundaries, this rising awareness can do nothing more than underscore the inadequacy of national solutions to environmental problems.

2. Population

It took until the year 1800 for the world population to reach 1 billion. From there the extraordinary growth began: The second billion was reached in 1925, the third in 1960, the fourth in 1976, and the fifth in 1987. It is estimated that by the turn of the century, the world's population will have reached nearly 7 billion. Currently at an annual growth rate of 1.7 percent (presently that means an additional 83 million people per year), the total is expected to top off at approximately 10 billion shortly before 2100. Most alarming, the population density is the most stable in the industrialized areas, where many

nations actually have achieved below-replacement reproduction (negative population growth), and is the least stable in the less developed areas. In sub-Saharan Africa, for example, the population is expected to grow by a billion people in the next four decades. Current projections suggest that by 2000, the population density of North America will have increased by only 4 persons per square kilometer, whereas in South Asia it will have increased by 140.[7]

The world order consequences of these projections are many, some of them clearly understood. First, under circumstances such as those of the Developing World, mortality rates decline before birth rates, so that population grows simultaneously at both the upper and the lower ends of the age

---

[7] Scientific projections, though different, convey the same message. See, as examples, Mihajlo Mesarovic and Eduard Pestel, *Mankind at the Turning Point: The Second Report to the Club of Rome* (New York: New American Library, 1974), chapter 6; Wassily Leontief et al., *The Future of the World Economy: A United Nations Study* (New York: Oxford University Press, 1977), summary conclusions on p. 4; and Thomas W. Merrick and the staff of the Population Reference Bureau, "World Population in Transition," *Population Bulletin,* April 1986.

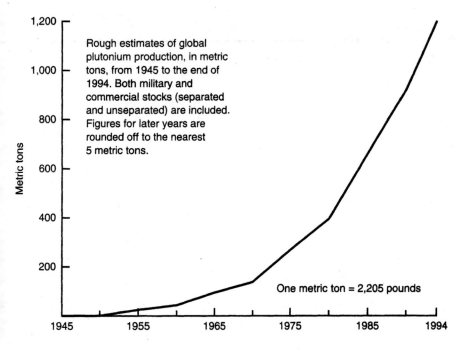

1,200

Rough estimates of global plutonium production, in metric tons, from 1945 to the end of 1994. Both military and commercial stocks (separated and unseparated) are included. Figures for later years are rounded off to the nearest 5 metric tons.

Metric tons

1,000

800

600

400

200

One metric ton = 2,205 pounds

1945   1955   1965   1975   1985   1994

FIGURE 17–2
The worldwide plutonium pileup.

Source: The New York Times, March 14, 1995, p. C11. Attributed to the Institute for Energy and Environmental Research. Reprinted with permission.

scale. At each end are individuals who are resource consumers but not economic contributors. Second, in many of the non-oil-producing Developing World countries, population rates far outrun the rates of economic growth, and so quality of living per capita actually declines, even with actual economic growth. Third, the correlation between deprivation resulting from a declining quality of life and conflict is also well established. And fourth, the current circumstances, when accompanied by domestic violence, result in large population migrations that become international problems.

The global population problem has been the subject of international concern for nearly seventy years, but never more than in the last twenty years as population, human development, economic growth, and environment preservation have come to be considered inseparable. The first UN attempt to address the problem occurred in 1974 at the World Population Conference in Bucharest, a meeting that made little progress because of the Developing World's overriding concern with economic growth and the New International Economic Order. But ten years later, when the United

Nations held the Second International Population Conference at Mexico City, the mood had changed considerably. The final report of the conference called upon all governments to make available birth control information and devices as an urgent international matter. Together with the United Nations Economic Program, the conference's documents were drafted to emphasize the relationship between economic development and population control.[8]

By the mid-1980s, it was apparent that economic growth cannot be considered apart from other important social phenomena. Until then, only a few Developing World countries had undertaken massive programs of population control. In India, for instance, a program of economic penalties was instituted for the failure of at least one spouse to be sterilized after the birth of a third

---

[8] For the final report of the conference, see "Report of the International Conference on Population, 1984, Mexico City, August 6–14, 1984," UN Document E/Conf. 76/19, 1984. For current country-by-country populations statistics, see United Nations Statistical Papers, Series A, vol. XLIV, no. 4, *Population and Vital Statistics Report: Data Available as of 1 October 1992.*

TABLE 17–1

ENVIRONMENTAL CONCERNS OF DEVELOPING
AND INDUSTRIALIZED COUNTRIES

Environmental Concerns	Developing Countries	Industrialized Countries
I. Natural Environment		
A. Air	Air pollution in major cities	AIR POLLUTION
B. Land, soil, mineral resources (including energy)	SOIL EROSION AND DEGRADATION, DESERTIFICATION	Soil loss and deterioration; dumping of waste; risk of radioactive contamination from nuclear-power production
C. Water	FRESHWATER SHORTAGE; freshwater pollution (sewage, pesticides); pollution of coastal waters	Freshwater shortage; INLAND AND MARINE WATER POLLUTION
D. Fauna and flora	DEFORESTATION (especially of tropical forests); loss of genetic resources; endangered species	Loss of genetic resources; endangered species
E. Ecosystems	Pollution of coastal ecosystems (decreasing fish catch)	Disruption of mountain, wetland, freshwater (especially from acid rains and eutrophication) and coastal ecosystems
F. Natural Disasters	FLOODS; DROUGHTS; STORMS; earthquakes, volcanic eruptions	Floods; earthquakes
II. Man-made environment and living conditions		
A. Bioproductive systems	LOSS AND DEGRADATION OF ARABLE LAND; pests and pest resistance, water shortage, pressures on fish population (over-fishing, pollution); IMPACTS OF FUELWOOD CONSUMPTION, food contamination, post-harvest losses	Loss of croplands to urban sprawl; pests and pest resistance; contamination of crops and fish; overexploitation of fishing grounds
B. Human settlements	MARGINAL SETTLEMENTS (RURAL-URBAN MIGRATION, URBAN GROWTH)	URBAN SPRAWL; NOISE
C. Health	MAL- AND UNDERNUTRITION; INFECTIOUS AND PARASITIC DISEASES	CANCER; cardiovascular diseases; genetic and long-term effects of POTENTIALLY TOXIC CHEMICALS

Source: Peter Bartlemus, *Environment and Development* (Boston: Allen and Unwin, 1986), p. 19. Reprinted with permission.

child. And in China, which had run a historically constant birth ratio of six children per woman, the rate dropped to two in the 1970s, the most dramatic birth-rate reduction ever recorded,[9] a remarkable feat particularly in view of the Confucian tradition of "pronatalism" or "reproduction worship."[10] Still concerned with the relationship between population and standard of living, in 1980 China introduced a campaign of "one family, one child," which would achieve negative population growth. By 1995, it remained at the level of two children per family, or actual-replacement rate (stable population). At the 1995 United Nations Conference on the Status of Women, held in Beijing, however, much was made of the fact that China maintained this birth rate by obligatory sterilization and abortion, and even by infanticide of female newborns.

This success was indicative of progress being made throughout the Developing World, where on the whole the population growth rate has declined by 25 percent since the 1960s. Still concerned, the United Nations convened its Conference on Population and Development, its third effort, at Cairo in 1994. Again the political environment was tense because of widespread dissemination of information about China's policies. Moreover, explicit references to abortion in the preparatory documents, though tempered by matching references to sovereign choice, resulted in official Vatican opposition to the conference, followed in its dissent by many developing countries, particularly in Latin America. The move toward conservatism in reproductive politics in the United States prevented the government from taking a strong stand, leading once again to final declarations and action programs that were compromises of little substance.

9 John Bongaarts and Susan Greenhalgh, "An Alternative to the One-Child Policy in China," *Population and Development Review*, December 1985, pp. 585–618.
10 Zongli Tang, "Confucianism, Chinese Culture and Reproductive Behavior," *Population and Environment*, January 1995, pp. 269–284.

3. Natural Resources

As recently as thirty years ago, economic growth throughout the world was predicated on faith that "there will always be more where it came from." World leaders scarcely had begun to predict the exhaustion of the earth's natural riches and, in typical power fashion, were concerned more with the geopolitical location of natural resources than with their potential depletion. But the oil embargo of 1973–74 and the global politics of oil that followed changed that thinking forever.

Mineral resources are being expended at record rates, even at times of reduced industrial activity in the West. That this is most popularly evidenced by the diminishing world supply of petroleum is because individuals depend so directly on petroleum to fuel their cars, heat their homes, and drive the industries that employ them. But the shortages are becoming critical in other areas as well, such as among the nonferrous metals. Although in the long run the depletion of fossil fuels will be compensated by a combination of energy from nuclear fuel, solar power, synthetic fuels, fusion, and ocean thermal energy, many of the basic elements may not be replaceable in manufacturing and other socially important processes.

The deterioration of world mineral supplies may have potential consequences beyond national and international economics. These minerals are not found equally distributed about the globe any more than petroleum is. Although the United States, China, and the Soviet Union have been rich in both coal and petroleum (only China among them now appears to have significant untapped supplies of oil), Britain and the European continental powers were rich only in coal until discovery of oil in the North Sea in the 1970s. Japan, in contrast, until the advent of nuclear power has been dependent wholly on foreign sources of fuel. Metals also are distributed unevenly about the planet, and many of the unutilized supplies now are available only in the developing countries. And while rapid increases in the export of these materials have funded economic development, dependence on them has led to unbalanced exports and raises the prospect of export paralysis upon their depletion.

Beyond these potential consequences, it is important that the external quest for raw materials has been one of the major causes of war in the industrial age and is generally understood to have been one of the principal causes of imperialism. We have seen that the modern efforts to integrate the economies of Western Europe were inspired in the first instance by the desire to eliminate the repeated Franco-German competition for coal and steel. Similarly, it long has been understood that Japan's imperialistic behavior from 1931 to its attack on Pearl Harbor in 1941 was provoked in large measure by the paucity of mineral resources within Japanese territory.[11] More recently, it has been argued that the Americanization of the Vietnam War in 1964 and the general interventionist trend of American foreign policy in that era were driven mainly by the need to control political events in those areas that may still have abundant natural resources.[12]

To the extent that these observations are accurate, deterioration of the globe's mineral supply may portend more than fundamental changes in world economic productivity. Surely, the uneven distribution of oil already has brought a major transition to the world, measured both politically and economically, particularly with the rise of the oil-exporting countries as political and economic powers despite their social and industrial underdevelopment. But such changes may be little more than the first phases of major new alignments in world politics heralded. Japan and all of the West covet China's oil reserves, and they compete for access to them to the point of overlooking China's inhumane politics except in events such as the

massacre in Tiananmen Square in 1989. Without rational control of the politics of declining resources, new forms of imperialism and conquest could emerge. Except for restraint in the UN Security Council ensured by the interests of the veto-holding Russian and Chinese delegations, the first such event might have occurred in Iraq as a result of the Gulf War.

4. Food

Preoccupation with the world's mineral distribution serves only to obscure the global nutrition crisis. In November 1974, just one year after the first major petroleum crisis, the United Nations convened the World Food Conference at Rome to deal with the long-term threat of dwindling food production relative to need. It had projected that by 1985, an increase of production per year of 2.5 percent globally would barely offset the increased demand of the industrialized states, thus leaving none to contribute to the 3.6 percent increase in need from the industrializing states.[13] More recent UN estimates take into account the results of the Green Revolution and increased land yields resulting from modern agricultural techniques. Experts now seem confident that the available agricultural land can be increased by 30 percent during the remainder of the century and that yields can be improved by as much as 60 percent. With massive investment, major crop staples might be increased by as much as two or three times the current annual global yields.[14] Indeed, by 1977, Bangladesh, once considered beyond hope of staple-crop sufficiency, predicted that it would be self-sufficient in rice production within five years. In 1979, American agricultural scientists announced soybean hybrids capable of 15 percent increases in yield.

---

[11] Herbert Feis, *The Road to Pearl Harbor* (Princeton, N.J.: Princeton University Press, 1950).

[12] Gabriel Kolko, *The Roots of American Foreign Policy* (Boston: Beacon Press, 1969).

[13] *Assessment of the World Food Situation: Present and Future*, Item 8 of the Provisional Agenda for the World Food Conference, p. 225.

[14] Wassily Leontief et al., *The Future of the World Economy*, pp. 4–5.

What the Green Revolution was to world food supplies from 1960 through 1990, new agricultural applications of genetic science are today, as these techniques may improve food yields greatly. In one effort, for example, scientists are trying to move a particular nitrogen fixation gene from a soybean into corn. Because nitrogen fixation is an essential step in plants' energy and photosynthetic cycles, successful transplantation of the gene, and the subsequent successful expression of its normal function in a new host, would have profound consequences for corn production worldwide. Similar techniques have been used to increase the size of tomatoes and to improve agriculture by genetically altering insects to prevent reproduction as a means of replacing pesticides. Meanwhile, more controversial genetic techniques have been used to reduce fat in food animals, and hormones to increase milk yield and muscle bulk. Still other scientific methods have been used to increase the shelf life of perishable products so that they can be transported longer distances and stored for longer times without threat of spoiling.

Although closely tied to the problem of population growth, global food shortages also present problems of their own. Aside from the obvious consequences—such as starvation, squalor, and retarded economic growth—maldistribution of food resources introduces other potential difficulties. At present is the fear that those states enjoying plentiful food supplies will use them coercively to ensure steady flows of mineral resources from the mineral-rich Developing World. The introduction of food into the global formula of competitive embargoes would represent a major change in the power resources of international politics, but with individually measurable human costs. In 1979, the prospect of using food as a weapon became a reality. As part of the American reaction to the Soviet invasion of Afghanistan, the Carter administration revoked a trade agreement with the Kremlin and discontinued bulk grain sales to the Soviet Union. At almost the same time, Americans impatient with Iran for holding American diplomatic personnel hostage demanded the discontinuation of food shipments to Iran. As this grew in popularity, some Americans advocated food embargoes as a general policy in dealing with the OPEC countries in response to petroleum embargoes or uncontrolled raw petroleum price increases. Except in the case with the Soviet Union over Afghanistan, however, no such policy was applied.[15]

Despite the efforts of the World Food Conference to establish an international food production program, the large producers jealously safeguard food production as a matter of national policy. Indeed, because food comprises a large portion of international trade, national agricultural policies are linked directly to the international problem. In 1986, for example, the United States recognized publicly the extent to which its international trade balance was deteriorating because of the European Economic Community's successful agricultural policies, and so Washington asked Western Europe to reduce production of such staples as grains and butter. Such nationalistic policies postpone to the future effective international planning of food production and distribution. And in one of the great ironies of modern life, export competition and the preservation of farm subsidy programs in the developed states (many of which actually compensate farmers for not producing!), many argue that agricultural goods are overproduced, even while Developing World populations go malnourished and even starve. In large measure it is the compelling need to redress this problem by domestic food production that has led to deforestation and desertification.

By now it should be clear that while it is handy to consider population, resources, environment, and development as separate issues, they are more realistically parts of a single problem. Together they restrain the living standards of the Developing

---

[15] On the general subject of food export policy as an instrument of international diplomacy, see Raymond F. Hopkins and Donald J. Puchala, *Global Food Interdependence: Challenge to American Foreign Policy* (New York: Columbia University Press, 1979).

World and leave unresolved a myriad of problems that may at any day erupt in ethnopolitical violence, war, swarms of starving refugees, and so forth. In light of this realization, the UN economic development programs have been redrawn partially to integrate consideration of population, resources, environment, and development—PRED.[16] The Second International Conference on Population at Mexico City in 1984 marked the first practical effort to recognize the inseparability of these issues in a comprehensive consideration of the world's economic future. Although only a beginning, it at least represents a broad recognition of the problem's complexity and the willingness of the Developing World to reconsider the social foundations of economic development. But even if these efforts succeed, the stratification of national standards of living will continue unless the competitive urge for nationalistic advantage is replaced at least partially by an effective spirit and program of economic interdependence. A successful initiative of a PRED-oriented world development cannot overcome the problems and miseries of the Developing World except by reversing with it the twilight of internationalism that is sweeping the industrialized peoples.[17]

5. Science and Technology

The dramatic improvements in twentieth-century standards of living are attributable in large measure to advances in science and technology. Particularly since World War Two, scientific discovery

---

[16] Branislav Gosovic, "Population-Resources-Environment-Development Relationships in the United Nations: In Search of an Approach," *CEPAL Review*, no. 23, August 1984, pp. 135–154. This is a publication of the United Nations Economic Commission for Latin America and the Caribbean.

[17] Thomas L. Hughes, "The Twilight of Internationalism" *Foreign Policy*, winter 1985–86, pp. 25–48. This is an American self-criticism based on the supposition that the "traditional internationalist themes are no longer significant outlets for political idealism in the United States." The concept has been expanded for its global application here.

and application have reached into every facet of life in new ways. Biomedical science and engineering have produced chemical compounds that prolong life and machinery that sustains the ill. Recombinant DNA techniques produce enzymes, hormones, and other chemical compounds that afflicted organs fail to produce. Supersonic aircraft have reduced the duration of intercontinental travel to a few hours. Communication has been revolutionized to a point that home computer terminals are replacing daily newspapers and achieving worldwide access to information. New synthetic fertilizers and genetically manipulated seed stocks—notwithstanding their costly ecological effects—enable farmers to increase crop yields. And genetic engineering in animals has resulted in the production of greatly enlarged meat animals and milk cows of greatly increased capacity.

But these miracles are not without liabilities. In the industrialized countries in particular, disposal of chemical waste poses dangers to plant and animal life. Because dumped chemicals eventually find their way back into the human food chain through soil and water and ingestion by lower species, the long-range consequences of carelessly planned dumping may be catastrophic. In 1980, the surgeon general of the United States declared for the first time that the uncontrolled consequences of scientific and technological development are multiplying the disease burden of the American people and the annual national cost of health care. But it is the long-term results of toxification that are most alarming. With the United States alone producing over 300 billion pounds of synthetic chemicals annually, and other nations producing amounts in proportion to their economies, it is certain that national solutions to these problems will be inadequate.

Not all the consequences of scientific and technological modernization are physical or physiological. In recent years, social scientists have begun to focus on their social and political consequences. For some time, futurists have attempted to postulate the characteristics of the post-industrial or technological societies. As some of the liabilities of the age so alarmingly have become apparent, futurists have begun to focus on mechanisms of social control and forms of decision making that will preserve philosophies of government rather than simply respond to technological change. Increasingly they argue that socially responsible decision making is falling prey to decisional reactions necessitated by the lure of scientific discovery.[18] The use of nuclear fuel, for example, was scarcely a topic of public debate until after its dangers became apparent. But by that time so many billions of dollars had been invested in it that rational decision making had no practical application. By the same token, international exchanges of nuclear fuel were licensed by governments largely as a form of commerical competition until controls were demanded after India used fuel provided by the United States for peaceful purposes to construct and explode a nuclear weapon. The prospect of nuclear fuel falling into the hands of terrorists has further prompted demands for controls, yet these have been demanded only after nuclear fuel exchanges have become common and only after reprocessing plants and breeder reactors (which permit certain types of nuclear fuel to be rejuvenated) have been completed and put into use.

The dilemma becomes apparent: Science and technology largely are responsible for the rapid improvement in national standards of living in the current century, and they are major hopes for improved economic competitiveness in the Developing World; yet the cost of such progress is measured not just in economic terms, but in human and social terms as well. We have grown deeply dependent on these advances; but unless we control their long-term physical and political consequences, their forces may be as destructive as they are progressive.

---

[18] See particularly Langdon Winner, *Autonomous Technology: Technics-Out-of-Control as a Theme in Political Thought* (Cambridge, Mass.: MIT Press, 1977); and Roger Benjamin, *The Limits of Politics* (Chicago: University of Chicago Press, 1980).

6. Autocratic Government and Human Rights

From a humanistic viewpoint, another problem looms just as large. Traditionally, each political system has determined its governing philosophy and established the quality of relations between the government and the governed. Many political systems—if not most—have justified stern restrictions on human freedoms and rights. Autocratic politics has been history's rule rather than its exception. In an era of growing literacy, improved mass communications, national liberation, and domestic protest, can the peace of national peoples be preserved against the brutality of governments? Until recently, Taiwan and South Korea enjoyed economic growth rates of 10 percent, twice that of Japan and two and one-half times that of the United States, yet these were two of the world's most repressive regimes. At what price progress? Furthermore, can the world's peace be preserved in the face of government brutality, the ever-present danger of insurgency, or revolution followed by foreign intervention? What role is there for international politics in building a global regime of human rights and dignity in face of absolute state control over national subjects?

In the last decade, much of the world's political consciousness has been riveted on the question of human rights. This has resulted in part from the communications revolution, which has made public spectacles of brutality and political repression. Apartheid (the policy of racial separation practiced by South Africa), the Nobel Prize–winning revelations of Amnesty International regarding the practices of some governments in imprisoning political enemies, worldwide sympathy for Soviet Jews who were prevented by their government from emigrating to Israel, the Tiananmen Square massacre of young Chinese protesting for freedom of the press in 1989, ethnic cleansing (genocide) in the warring factions of the former Yugoslavia, and interethnic slaughter in Rwanda—these have all been issues of

(*Source*: © Gable/Canada/Cartoonists & Writers Syndicate)

popular attention, fanned by global exposure through improved communication.

There have been official stimulants to the world conscience also. The Vladivostok accords called on the United States and the Soviet Union to treat their nationals according to agreed international standards. A quarter-century after the passage by the UN General Assembly of the Universal Declaration of Human Rights, two international covenants (the International Covenant on Political and Economic Rights and the International Covenant on Social and Cultural Rights) finally secured enough signatories to come into effect. The 1978 Belgrade Conference on Human Rights, resulting from the Vladivostok Conference in 1978, was conducted amid much popular acclaim but produced little of significance.

But with what practical result? Despite the expansion of international standards for the protection of human rights, political imprisonment, denial of due process, unethical (and perhaps illegal) economic exploitation of minorities, and other violations of basic human rights abound. This is due in part to the variety of ideological interpretations given to international standards and in part to the impulse of powerful factions to defend their position against rising expectations of political freedom. Without international sanctioning authority competent to monitor the proliferation of declaratory international standards, the protection of human rights will continue to suffer from inconsistencies of national policy and the maldistribution of political power in national political systems.

7. World Economics

Yet another form of contemporary anarchy is the international economic system. Despite foreign aid and international development programs, a powerful few dominate the world economy. Self-serving autocracy of the economically powerful states and of their political elites, together with central planning and allocation, is the guidepost of world economics. Imperialism, neoimperialism, exploitation, discrimination, and manipulation—these are the instruments used by the powerful to subordinate the weak. Stability in economic relations cries out for international supervision and new modes of decision making.

Already new patterns are emerging. The dependence of the Western industrialized nations on the wealthy but socially and economically less developed petroleum exporters of the Developing World changed the face of global economic relations between 1973 and 1983. But this reverse dependency is marked by forms of anarchy of its own: manipulation, retaliation for a century of subordination, and decisions of global impact made as much out of competition within OPEC as out of cooperation. Only in 1979 and 1980 did there begin to emerge a rational pattern of decision making with respect to the quantity of oil production and its price, based at first on the general principle of trying to force the industrial states to control inflation and subjected later to efforts to establish complex formulae giving attention to inflation, declining values of currencies, anticipation of resource depletion, and correlation of the export trade with the rate of internal economic development. But this progress declined in 1982 and 1983 when internal disagreement among the OPEC members flared up, sparked by the radicals who wished to maximize profits and the moderates who wanted to stabilize the world petroleum market. As a result, prices dropped, and incentives for exploration of new sources of oil were removed. In 1985, OPEC's power virtually collapsed. Moreover, it was

weakened greatly when Iraq invaded Kuwait only to be forced out (not before igniting dozens of oil wells) by an American-led UN force. The permanent presence of American armed forces in Kuwait, Saudi Arabia, and the Persian Gulf testifies to the reliance of the politically moderate Gulf oil producers on external powers, thus diminishing their independence within the politics of the oil cartel.

A second new pattern centers on the activities of the multinational corporations. Although they are chartered by states of origin and licensed to operate in host economies, the magnitude and complexity of their operations place them virtually outside the legal control of any government(s) and subject them only to regional controls to the extent of their operations within those regions that have attempted to apply controls.

A third pattern, although perhaps less new, pertains to the imperatives of the welfare state. As the welfare-state concept has spread throughout the industrial world, individual nation-states have strengthened the arsenal of public policies by which they control and maintain the loyalty of their nationals.[19] The political imperatives that follow from this observation ensure that the state's commitment to a more rational international economic order may be secondary. The U.S. Congressional elections in 1994, in which the Republican party seized control of both Houses of Congress for the first time in more than forty years, while unquestionably a backlash to the costs of the welfare state, portend no improvement in support from Washington for economic policies more sympathetic to the poor countries.

---

[19] Melvyn B. Krauss, *The New Protectionism: The Welfare State and International Trade* (New York: New York University Press, 1978); and George R. Neumann, "Adjustment Assistance for Trade-displaced Workers," in David B. H. Denoon, ed., *The New International Economic Order: A U.S. Response* (New York: New York University Press, 1979), pp. 109–140. A different analysis found governments reacting to the breakdown of this kind of order. See James Rosenau, "A Pre-theory Revisited: World Politics in an Era of Cascading Interdependence," *International Studies Quarterly*, September 1984, pp. 245–305.

A closely related phenomenon is the "new protectionism." Although the interdependence of economies and the activities of multinational corporations generally have stimulated technology transfer and industrial productivity, they have had detrimental consequences for some developed economies. At a time when American industrial sales at home and abroad have been challenged by imports from Japan and the European Union, rising imports and troubling balance-of-trade deficits with respect to the Developing World (particularly the OPEC Developing World) have led to new demands for protection of the American economy. And this pattern has been repeated elsewhere.

Superimposed on all these difficulties is the growing scarcity in the world of natural resources, investment capital, and economic leadership. The 1973–74 oil embargo gave rise to the notion of an age of scarcity; and the dwindling wealth of the United States relative to that of the world has, since about 1971, produced the notion that the American Century was really more like twenty-five years in duration. These two phenomena—scarcity and leadership decline—have encouraged new thinking about the future of the world economy. One person in particular has called for a system of global economic management (GEM), under the aegis of international organizations, to establish and monitor global and regional growth rates that do not produce major resource constraints or inflation. The constituent organizations would have the authority to forecast and establish growth rates, to control supplies of funds to nations, and to negotiate bilaterally and multilaterally any structural economic changes necessary to achieve the agreed rates.[20]

It is doubtful that governments will go so far as to institute such a global process. It is clear, however, that in an age of scarcity and decline, states will turn inward, with the result that the normal antagonism between internationalism and nationalism will intensify.[21] The outcome of the struggle on a global basis will determine whether the next quarter-century will see the creation or the decay of a new economic regime. The argument of this book, however, is that the erosion of the international economic regime is an obstacle to effective interdependence and that only reform of basic attitudes, structures, and patterns of interaction can transform the global economy for the next century. Contemporary system dynamics are self-destructive, and any further retreat to narrow national goals at the expense of interdependent solutions to economic problems cannot promote stability.

8. International Public Goods and Property

When we speak of the international economy, we refer to trade, capital, labor, and specific commodities. But there are other aspects of global economic life that do not fall into these categories. These we distinguish as international public goods and international public property and save them for special treatment.

International public goods are not tangible commodities, yet they are the products of domestic manufacture in the sense that they are the products of policy. They are social goods that are not traded in the market, but without which effective global economic activity cannot occur. And although there is no generally accepted list of these goods, there are some that stand out.

From the standpoint of all the social sciences, the most important of these is peace. As contrasted with rights that are elucidated in law, any moral philosophy or political theory posits peace as a public good. In 1984, the General Assembly of the United Nations promulgated its Declaration on the

[20] D. B. Steele, "The Case for Global Economic Management and U.N. System Reform," *International Organization*, summer 1985, pp. 561–578.

[21] Ted R. Gurr, "On the Political Consequences of Scarcity and Economic Decline," *International Studies Quarterly*, March 1985, pp. 51–75.

Rights of Peoples to Peace, but it did so with little support from the Western governments that objected to the political subjectivity of the language.

From an economic standpoint, there are several other international public goods, most of them related to an open system of exchange. These include freedom of the seas, well-defined rights of property in host territories, standards of weights and measures for fair exchange, internationally accepted currencies and exchange rates, politically accepted trading systems, capital flow mechanisms, consistent macroeconomic systems during times of stability, and accepted leaders of crisis management and emergency lending in times of need.[22]

For much of the time since the Second World War, the United States played a leadership role in the global economic system, partly by its direct action (for example, making the dollar available as an international currency, providing a steady flow of capital to the Developing World) or by its leadership in establishing an international regime of institutions to govern the international economy (for example, the International Monetary Fund and the International Bank for Reconstruction and Development). Now, however, because of scarcity and America's own economic decline, attention has been turned inward, and the United States no longer practices this leadership. Without it and without an acknowledged substitute, the intangible international public goods necessary for an effective global economy are in jeopardy.

International public property differs in that it consists of specific commodities, but they occur in nature, they are not fixed to national territories, and they are not for the most part traded in the market. Principal among them are the air and fresh waters shared by two or more nation-states. Seas and oceans also fall into this category, although it has long been established (and reaffirmed by the

Law of the Sea Treaty) that exploitation of the sea and the seabed results in tradable national goods.

Unlike international public goods that support and sustain the economic system, international public properties sustain life. As a result, nations have a shared obligation to protect them against spoilage and pollution, irradiation, and sequestration. In our earlier treatment of ecological issues, we saw the extent to which governments have failed to protect against the former two. Now let us look briefly at the last. Does a government have a right to divert a river that flows to or through more than one nation for its exclusive use? If a downstream riparian state depends on the river's flow for commerce or drinking water or any other legitimate purpose, does its upstream neighbor have a right to divert the flow to its own exclusive irrigation purposes? The concept of international public property says that it does not.

The habit of nationalistic exploitation of international public properties, together with the failure of governments to recognize their joint responsibilities in this domain, has put those properties at considerable risk. Redoubled international efforts for regulation in this vital area of interdependent concern is thus one of the major issues for the future of world order.

Despite intergovernmental efforts to overcome these vexing problems through organization, law, and integration, the magnitude of the problems and the antiquity of national solutions further highlight the dilemma of traditional international remedies. So long as the unique sovereign attributes of the nation-state are preserved, the pace of deterioration will continue to outrun proposed solutions, rendering them always ideas after their times. Accordingly, research has centered on wholly new approaches, although they vary considerably in scope. Some, labeled maximalist proposals, seek a fully structured world government; the minimalist proposals advocate upgrading existing international machinery; and the reformist proposals generally would retain the current systemic

---

[22] This entire section on international public goods is fashioned after Charles P. Kindleberger, "International Public Goods Without International Government," *American Economic Review*, March 1986, pp. 1–13.

features, but they would subject the nation-state to global law.

The Idea of World Order

Although two world wars and the nuclear arms race have prompted new interest in the world order movement, the idea is an ancient one. It has arisen repeatedly in history from peace groups, governments, philosophers, religious thinkers, imperialists, and nationalistic zealots. Often the world order movement has been synonymous with the quest for world government. One of the earliest known forms was that of ancient Rome, whose imperial quest sought to bring all the known world under Roman political control. Other imperial impulses to world domination have been grossly maniacal, such as that of Adolf Hitler, whose aim was to rule Europe and then the world on behalf of the Aryan race.

Several other universalist ideas have arisen. Saint Thomas Aquinas propounded the concept of a universal Christian spirit forging a human community and supplying the ideals and benevolence of Christian rulers roughout the world. He distinguished the power of the state (*imperium*) from that of the church (*sacerdotium*), leaving room for separate governments in different lands, even though he viewed papal power as superior to secular power. Even in a Christian Europe, however, and writing a half-century later than Thomas (about A.D. 1310), Dante saw the only hope for world peace (meaning essentially European peace) in the consolidation of all power in the Roman emperor. "Neither by birth nor breeding was Dante a partisan of the imperial cause. His imperialism was purely an idealization of universal peace."[23]

Thinkers in more modern times frequently have revived these ideas. The Spanish theologian Francisco Suarez, writing in the absolutist era bridging the sixteenth and seventeenth centuries and

imbued with Jean Bodin's notions of sovereignty, moved from the concept of moral law to the hope of world government. Later in the seventeenth century, the English philosopher Thomas Hobbes wrote in *Leviathan* that the political nature of society is that of war of every man against every man and that through social contract, men form governments to which they entrust their security. Applied to international relations, Hobbes's social contract extrapolates to a theory of world order.

The German thinker Georg Hegel, whose dialectical method formed the basis of Marx's arguments about class conflict, introduced the concept of a world spirit of the governing class, with a universal morality in political leadership, freedom, and even the arts. Despite his nationalistic fervor, he saw every state falling to the universal logic of the world spirit. Marx not only adopted Hegel's system of argument, he also made similar historical predictions. Rather than concentrate on a governing class and a mystical world spirit, Marx looked to the working class and the eventual elimination of class conflict. When power resides in the hands of the proletariat, states will wither away, and all people will be ruled in classless harmony. In this utopian prediction, government becomes not state centered but spirit centered.

Not all visions of universal political morality and utopian harmony arise from philosophical abstraction. Indeed, the popularity of world order schemes has paralleled certain events: the frequency of war, the destructiveness of modern industrialized warfare, imperial competition, and the irrationality of ideological fears, to name only a few. There is at least impressionistic evidence of a correlation between world order enthusiasm and warfare. The popularity of such proposals seems highest toward the end of, and upon conclusion of, major wars; the longer and more tranquil post-war periods are, the more rapid will be the decline in popularity of world order ideals. This correlation seems guided by a simple "rule" of world politics: When states serve their functions satisfactorily and with minimal external disruption, only a handful of activists advocate centralized world

---

[23] George H. Sabine, *A History of Political Theory*, 3rd ed. (New York: Holt, Rinehart and Winston, 1961), pp. 257–258.

order; but when the nation-state system breaks down, more people share the organized world order sentiment.

Thus the present century has been one of consistently high interest in world order. The destruction caused by the First World War was unprecedented, and the vision of the further industrialization of war potential forged a solid core of sentiment for some form of centralized world order. In America, the League to Enforce Peace considered several alternative forms of international organization, with some of its adherents arguing for virtual international government. Intent on retaining their sovereign prerogatives, however, national governments were willing to do no more than subscribe to President Woodrow Wilson's League of Nations. Predecessor to the United Nations, the League of Nations (1) prescribed mechanisms for the peaceful settlement of international disputes, (2) called upon its members to guarantee the territorial integrity and political independence of all members, (3) looked forward to general arms limitation, (4) authorized its Council to undertake enforcement action against aggressors, and (5) mandated member states to impose sanctions against violators of the peace.

As an instrument of world order, the League of Nations was generally a disappointment to the advocates of world government. They viewed it as little more than a smokescreen for power politics. Its voting provisions, especially on matters of greatest interest to members of the Council, restricted progress toward effective international decision making and encouraged great-power domination of policy. Although many saw in the Assembly, where all member states were represented, an opportunity to sow and to germinate the seeds of international society, there was general discouragement over the decentralization of sanction procedures and over the great-power control of peace-war issues. But of major long-range interest was the network of functional organizations (single-purpose agencies with specific technical tasks), which seemed to promise greater person-to-person contact around the world and to offer an opportunity for the development of

loyalty to a political entity outside nation-states. Ultimately, the problem of the nation-state system is not simply the existence of multiple sovereignties, but the ability of governments to monopolize the secular loyalties of individuals and to mobilize them for nationalistic rather than universalistic purposes. Any institutional structure that might erode this pattern is acceptable to the advocates of world government and to the proponents of most other doctrines of world order as well.

Some universalists viewed the League of Nations with even deeper suspicion, principally because of its collective security provisions. Collective security could not govern, they argued; it could maintain peace only by the threat of force. Thus, it was a negative approach to international stability, still built on nationalistic preferences. It did not address the causes of conflict; it was powerless to legislate preventative social, political, and economic changes; and it was impotent when international norms were violated, except by the unanimous consent of the Council members. Hence some saw the League not as a steppingstone from the nation-state system to world government, but as a threat to world order.

Although the League of Nations failed to prevent war, its history partly was successful from a world order perspective. It made modest but positive contributions to self-determinism, previously little more than a platitude. Its social, scientific, and economic projects made inroads into problems of squalor and disease. Post-war relief programs, assistance to refugees, and the League's management of intellectual exchanges all earned for the organization a reputation as a helpful intermediary among governments in matters not directly related to national security. One of the celebrated events of the League was its acceptance in 1939 of the Bruce Committee Report, which advocated a broad reorganization of authority for social and economic development. Although the Second World War prevented its implementation, the report formed the rationale for establishing the Economic and Social Council as a permanent organ of the United Nations.

Despite these League successes, the concept of intergovernmental organization generally was not popular with advocates of world government during the interwar period. Like other critics of the League, they found its failings more notable than its successes. But more than that, the Second World War was testimony to the intrinsic weaknesses of collective security in particular, and of intergovernmental organization in general.

The war and its aftermath further heightened the vigor of the world order movement. While the State Department was planning, at first secretly, to revitalize collective security in an organization to be known as the United Nations, the United World Federalists were organizing in support of world government. That the war had been global rather than continental demonstrated the need for universal regulation. The unprecedented devastation, including the use of atomic weapons, accentuated the need for world government before technical advances led to world domination and centralized imperialism. The polarization of world politics and the Soviet-American standoff, along with the growing reality of a nuclear balance of terror, convinced many people that this might be humanity's last half-century to achieve effective world order.

Vigorous advocacy was untimely. At the end of the Second World War, hopes were high for the United Nations, dedicated in part to the principle—the grand design—that the major powers, despite their differences, could cooperate in peacetime to preserve stability as they had cooperated during wartime to establish it. Remembering the problems of 1918, advocates of world government had to contest this sentiment. Meeting together in 1945, "world federalists" and advocates of the "world law movement" debunked the adequacy of the United Nations, called for a world federal government of limited powers, and urged that either the United Nations Charter be amended into federalist form or that a world constitutional convention be called. In 1946, a second conference reaffirmed the need for world federal government, but found the UN Charter the most practicable route.[24]

For the moment, the world government movement remained almost exclusively the province of a few committed activists. In the United States, especially, popular sentiment seemed to lean more toward intergovernmental organization, with the specific hope that this time, with the backing of American power, the UN experiment might prevent cataclysmic war. But the promise collapsed with the onset of the Cold War and the desire of like-minded nations to cluster into defensive alliances outside the United Nations. A new threat to the concept of world order emerged: the willingness of states to entrust the preservation of their sovereignty to their most powerful allies.

One result was the movement for a union of the Western democracies, which frightened the proponents of world government by the threat of a regional central government that could harden the polarity of the world and further delay the universalist dream. There was fear that the North Atlantic Treaty Organization (NATO) might form the base of such a movement.

Faced with two competing movements—intergovernmental organization (UN) and the possibility of counterproductive regional military supranationalism (NATO)—the universalists took to the offensive. In testimony before the House Foreign Relations Committee in 1948, the president of the United World Federalists called upon Congress to champion greater strength for the United Nations through charter amendment, not to strengthen its intergovernmental character, but to advance it toward world government. A year later Grenville Clark, a distinguished lawyer and later director of the World Peace Through Law Movement, sat before the same committee to testify on two bills: for the World Federation Resolution and against the Atlantic Union Resolution. The former called for an American initiative for

---

[24] For a review of early events, see Edward McN. Burns, "The Movement for World Government," *Science*, vol. 25, 1948, pp. 5–13.

the evolution of world government, and the latter for a union of Western democracies. In an eloquent plea, Clark argued that "the distinction is of basic importance. It marks, I believe, the difference between peaceful evolution and a probable or possible third world war."[25]

It is one thing to propound the establishment of government but quite another to equip it to achieve the desired ends in a heterogeneous world. How much power should there be? How should it be divided among governmental organs? To what extent should authority be left to the "local" governments of the former nation-states? What limitations on power ought to be prescribed? How can these limitations be preserved? What sorts of incentives to compliance should be arranged, and what kinds of punishment for violations? Even more fundamental, what aims and values is world government to pursue?

Still, however, not all world order concepts embrace the idea of world government, although such a tendency is typical of maximalist proposals.

World Order: A Maximalist Proposal

Because the maximalist position was held principally by Americans, it is not surprising that the federalist model of government prevailed. Harkening back to U.S. constitutional history, this is a system of government in which state sovereignty is divided so that the central government is sovereign in some matters, smaller units sovereign in others, and the two jointly sovereign in still others. The purpose is to prevent absolutism or a drift toward full centralization, something that the Federalists also had to avoid. They did so by acknowledging the need for nations and nationalism, and claiming that "we need only modify the present absolute nature of

national sovereignty."[26] Hence the movement for world federalism draws a distinct line between world government and the formation of a world state. Nation-states may exist and nationalism may be a permanent feature of world politics, but these cannot prevent the evolution of a world society disassociated from nationalism.

But the idea of world federalism requires not only the erosion of state sovereignty, but of nationalism as well. It requires changing national percpetions, enlightening national views of the ideals and expectations of other peoples, and so on. The goal is to create a global society despite the presence of nation-states and nationalism.

Separation of Powers

A second fundamental concept is also borrowed from the American constitutional model: the separation of powers. A concept traditionally ascribed to the French philosopher Montesquieu, the separation of powers divides the power of the federal government into three branches—legislative, executive and judicial—in order to avert tyranny by a single political authority. As James Madison argued in Federalist Paper No. 47, a pamphlet written to argue for ratification of the American Constitution, "The accumulation of all powers, legislative, executive, and judiciary, in the same hands, whether of one, a few, or many, and whether hereditary, self-appointed, or elective, may justly be pronounced the very definition of tyranny." Imbued with this spirit, major proposals for world federalism usually include separation of powers.

In 1947 and 1948, the Committee to Frame a World Constitution released the first draft of a constitution for the Federal Republic of the World. In good separation-of-powers fashion, it specified areas of substantive powers as well as organs of government. And consistent with the reserved-powers-of-the-states notion in the U.S. Constitution, it provided that "the powers not delegated to the

---

[25] Cord Meyer Jr.'s testimony is reprinted in Julia E. Johnson, ed., *Federal World Government* (New York: H. W. Wilson, 1948), pp. 86–94. Clark's can be found in appendix B of his *Plan for Peace* (New York: Harper and Brothers, 1950), pp. 78–83.

[26] Vernon Nash, *The World Must Be Governed*, 2nd ed. (New York: Harper and Brothers, 1949), p. 4.

World Government in this Constitution, and not prohibited by it to the several members of the Federal World Republic, shall be reserved to the several states or nations or unions thereof." This provision was intended to guarantee within the federal scheme the integrity of traditional governmental units and political communities. Differently stated, "Federalism symbolizes functionally-limited centralization, but centralization nonetheless."[27]

Highly institutionalized maximalist schemes have been rather common in the history of the world order movement. Yet, in their ambition to restructure the international system, they have run afoul of the same criticisms time and again: (1) their social and political practicability, (2) the slender probability of successful implementation, and (3) the philosophical desirablity of world government.

The Practicability of World Government

The theologian and social observer Reinhold Niebuhr once wrote: "Virtually all arguments for world government rest upon the simple presupposition that the desirability of world order proves the attainability of world government."[28] What is the logical link between desirability and attainability?

The critical issue in addressing this question is the relation between society and government. World federalists argue that if people will look beyond their governments, they will be able to shape a supranational government capable of maximizing social integration, effective compliance with law, and perpetual peace. Critics hold, on the contrary, that governments have little ability to integrate communities; rather, the merger of diverse value patterns and heritages is a sociopsychological process to which governments may give direction

but which cannot be legislated into effectiveness, regardless of the type of government. Integration is a matter of will rather than of power.

Studies have been conducted in a number of countries on the images national peoples have of one another. In one, when Americans were asked to rate themselves according to specific descriptive words, only 2 percent chose the word "cruel" and only 2 percent the word "backward." But when the same people were asked to rate the Russian people, no fewer than 50 percent selected "cruel" and 40 percent "backward." By the same token, 39 percent of British questioned thought the Russians cruel, and 36 percent thought them backward. Only 12 percent of both British and Americans thought the Russian people intelligent. In the polling among people of eight different Western countries (Australia, Britain, The Former West Germany, France, Italy, the Netherlands, Norway, and the United States), positive adjectives were applied most frequently to the subject's own people. Consistently, the Soviet people and the Chinese people were assigned positive adjectives least frequently and negative adjectives most frequently.

But even among Western neighbors and allies there appeared to be social barriers to complete trust and mutual respect. Not surprisingly, given historical relations, the German people held the French in low regard, only a fraction above the Russians and the Chinese, though Germans thought the French more intelligent, less cruel, and less backward than the Russians. Yet Germans thought the French less brave, less self-controlled, and less peace loving than Russians, even though the polling was done during the Korean War.[29]

A similar questioning technique presents subjects with pairs of adjectives that have opposite meanings, such as cowardly and brave, stupid and intelligent, lazy and industrious. In a study in which people were asked to select preferable adjectives

---

[27] Inis L. Claude Jr., *Power and International Relations* (New York: Random House, 1962), p. 207.
[28] Reinhold Niebuhr, *Christian Realism and Political Problems* (New York: Scribner's, 1949), as reprinted in Arend Lijphart, *World Politics*, 2nd ed. (Boston: Allyn and Bacon, 1971), pp. 71–80, "The Illusion of World Government."

[29] For a full tabular report of results, see William Buchanan and Hadley Cantrell, *How Nations See Each Other* (Urbana: University of Illinois Press, 1953), pp. 46–47. While these findings are very old and almost certainly no longer accurate, the analytical points are still valuable.

first to describe foreign peoples and then to depict their governments, both ethnic images (people) and national images (governments) were determined. Among Americans polled, the results were tabulated in decreasing order of preference (see Table 17–2).

Note that in the ethnic ratings all noncommunist peoples are ranked higher than all communist peoples with the exception of Nationalist Chinese, who rank behind the European communists but ahead of the mainland Chinese. By contrast, in the national ratings there is no exception. All noncommunist governments rate higher than do all communist governments. The Soviet people and the Soviet government both rate consistently above the peoples and governments of the other communist states about which questions were asked.[30]

Results concerning images and trust among allies were substantiated in a NATO study. Europeans have the highest trust for the Swiss, with the United States ranking second. Although the polling was conducted prior to British entry into the European Economic Community, trust for Britain ranked third among people questioned in Belgium, France, West Germany, Italy, and the Netherlands. Although engaged in the process of economic integration, none of the Common Market members on the list received a majority expression of trust in all four other countries.[31]

These data, old as they may be, underscore the fact that governments are not alone in their resistance to world government. Among allies as well as among enemies, there are still barriers to mass perceptions that are sufficient to rebut the assumption that if national governments were subordinated to a world government, antipathies among the peoples would fade and an integrated world society would result. We thus must be cautious in presuming the practicability of world government.

---

[30] For a full report of findings, see Richard H. Willis, "Ethnic and National Images: People vs. Nations," *Public Opinion Quarterly*, vol. 32, 1968, pp. 186–201.

[31] "Swiss, Then Americans Most Trusted by Europeans," *Atlantic Community News*, March–April. 1973, p. 2.

TABLE 17–2

AMERICANS' RANKING OF ETHNIC AND NATIONAL IMAGES, IN DECREASING ORDER OF PREFERENCE

Ethnic (peoples)	National (governments)
Finnish	United States
West German	Finland
American	West Germany
Russian	Nationalist China
East German	Soviet Union
Nationalist Chinese (Taiwan)	East Germany
Chinese	China

Source: Adapted by permission from Richard H. Willis, "Ethnic and National Images: People vs. Nations," *Public Opinion Quarterly*, vol. 32, 1968, p. 190. © 1968 by the University of Chicago.

Probable Success upon Implementation

What if the social and political barriers to the implementation of a world government were superable? Would the maturation of a world society be sure to deter further warfare? Most critics of the world government ideal argue that on the national level, central government has not invariably deterred civil war. Even in a world state, to say nothing of a global federation, occasional warfare will erupt.

Advocates respond in a utopian way. On the assumption that an effective federation would achieve universal justice (but by what value standards?) and adequate distribution of authority and goods, they insist that the contemporary causes of war would be eradicated. They assume that centralization of military force would provide adequate deterrence to the use of force by members. But this blanket assumption overlooks that hostilities often involve the use of power at other levels—that the ability of force to deter force is not absolute but relative to conditions, situations, and perceptions. Furthermore, these assumptions trip on the same snares as does collective security: Those who threaten the peace are not always identifiable; self-defense may justify the use of force, just as it may be used as camouflage for aggressive intentions; and states sympathize with one another's interests and perceptions, thus minimizing the efficiency of global decision making. The expectation that world government might invariably avert war is untenable in light of these observations. "The hard fact is that the record does not support the generalization that the establishment of government, within a social unit of whatever dimensions, infallibly brings about a highly dependable state of peace and order."[32] The skeptics agree that world government and monopoly of force would not ensure perpetual peace.

Philosophical Desirability

Skeptics also differ with the universalist assumption that world government is necessarily good government, either in efficiency or in quality. In the American federal system, the delicate balance between executive and legislative prerogatives has undergone fundamental change; why might not the same occur in a world federal system? If political conflict is capable of turning even ideal democracy into tyranny or constitutional authoritarianism, is there any prospect that global problems might produce a world government of universal tyranny? How would coalitions of like-minded states utilize their share of political power in a world system? Does world government necessarily eradicate the threat of worldwide absolutism?

These and scores of other related questions plague the theoretical integrity of the world government philosophy, just as does the claim that there is virtue in peaceful diversity. The critics of the world government ideal charge that it carries Hobbes's social contract to logical absurdity.

> Hobbes was right; when a community is so poorly developed that its pre-governmental condition is one of intolerable warfare, and its urge to establish government rests on no other foundation than a desperate desire to escape the perils of anarchy, the only theoretically adequate government is Leviathan, an omnipotent dictatorship. Locke, too, was right; when a community is held together by strong bonds of agreement concerning what is right and just, and common life is reasonably satisfactory, a limited and mild kind of government, based mainly upon consent, may suffice to supply its needs. World governmentalists describe the world's situation in Hobbesian terms, with a view of emphasizing the urgent need for a global social contract, but they depict the resultant government in Lockean terms, with a view of making the social contract palatable. It would be better to recognize that in so far as this is a Hobbesian world, it is likely to require a Hobbesian government.[33]

Yet there are many who hold that supranational world order short of total world government is both desirable and feasible. One such movement is that of World Peace Through World Law, and the other is the growing sentiment of globalism. We turn now to those alternatives of the future world order.

World Order: A Minimalist Proposal

The ultimate objective of the world order movement is to centralize political authority in order to avoid war. However, because of the practical barriers to federation, other movements have proposed partial centralization of authority addressed to the specific problems of arms in international politics. The best known among these is the World Peace Through World Law movement. "World law" is not synonymous with "international law." International law purports to interpose norms of behavior between states. The world law movement, in contrast, is concerned explicitly with the removal of arms from international politics, and the establishment of collective security.

---

[32] Inis L. Claude Jr. *Power and International Relations*, p. 220.

[33] Inis L. Claude Jr., *Swords into Plowshares*, 4th ed. (New York: Random House, 1971), p. 429.

World law ... ties together two very important notions; disarmament and a collective security system. It argues that the present system of international relations ... [is] based on unilateral decision-making sanctioned by armaments, and maintains that this situation results in a spiralling arms race that may very well set off a cataclysmic war. The world law model therefore posits the need for complete and general disarmament of all the states in the world down to the level of police forces, and proposes the establishment of a transnational police force that can maintain the territorial integrity and political independence of each state.[34]

The emphasis is on the elimination of national arms, rather than their mere limitation.

The plan involves two steps. First, it calls for revision of the UN Charter to grant the General Assembly full authority for overseeing total disarmament, and with full power of enforcement through weighted voting. Thereafter, the General Assembly would establish an inspection commission that would begin by taking a world census on quality, quantity, and deployment patterns of national arms. The inspection would be accompanied by a truce on further arms production. In the following decade, each state would reduce its national arms stockpile by 10 percent annually, all reductions being distributed evenly among the several military services so that all are reduced at the same rate. Verification of compliance would be conducted by the United Nations Inspection Service, operating in national territories without governmental barriers.

The plans run into several insuperable barriers. Can there be security without arms? Is international inspection trustworthy in a technological age? What are the possible political consequences of secret unilateral violations that might result in clear military superiority, even monopoly? And there are still other problems. National armaments are the special preserve of arms manufacturers and

certain elites in society, such as rival armed services. What are the prospects of weakening these groups to levels sufficient to make world disarmament proposals attractive to national governments? Do domestic political relationships bode well for the future of total disarmament? The skeptics—and they are legion—see little hope in current national perceptions. Thus these proposals, although humane, remain futuristic, leaving governments to concentrate their efforts on international law rather than world law, and on arms limitation rather than arms abolition. The piecemeal attack on sovereignty remains the method of practical choice, despite the increasingly urgent need for major transformation of the international system.

World Order: A Reformist Proposal

In addition to the maximalist and minimalist proposals for world order, there have arisen other reformist ideas, each of which concentrates on adaptation of existing national and international machinery. The prevailing idea is globalism, a movement tied to the United Nations by virtue of its growing role as a center of international planning. Although the United Nations has limited authority and has had little effect on national arms stockpiles, its record as an innovator and clearinghouse for planning and activity on other issues has been modestly good. The United Nations has been most successful in economic development. Other areas to which globalism might spread are the allocation and preservation of national resources and the distribution of the world's produce.

But there is another dimension to globalism. As societies develop, they both overcome problems and create new ones. Industry, the prime aim of less developed states, is a case in point. Although industrialization may reduce poverty, it also causes environmental degradation, marked domestic economic disparities, problems of urbanization, depletion of natural resources, and scores of other potentially critical problems. The philosophy of

[34] Saul H. Mendlovitz, "Models of World Order," in Richard B. Gray, ed., *International Security Systems* (Itasca, Ill.: Peacock, 1961), p. 191.

globalism attempts to elevate these issues from the national level to the global.[35]

One globalist holds that the need for global planning is evident in a five-item "inventory of mankind's problems": environmental crisis, the widening gap between rich and poor, unemployment, urbanization, and malnutrition.[36] The principal concern is for the development of global planning that is acceptable to governments because it does not alter their status as the principal actors in world politics. Hence future world order will owe its origin not to governments, but to universal satisfaction. In the end, this is a functionalist view of world order.

A British author has enumerated some of the social requisites to this globalist world order.[37] In fields of human rights, labor standards, and monetary controls, in particular, UN coordination is crucially important. If the philosophy of globalism is to rise above futuristic platitudes regarding the human instinct for survival, then institutionalization is essential.

All the proposals thus far studied have one thing in common: They all are political-structural concepts of world order; that is, each deals with international anarchy by adjusting the system's structural characteristics and by prescribing mechanisms for addressing existing evils. Other approaches focus on the universal cultural aspects of international relations, recognizing that international events often are nongovernmentally motivated. They assume that there are universal cultural similarities and that cultural imperatives underlie many international events. Then they argue that "a oneness lies buried beneath the manifold diversities and dissensions of the present fractionated world, and that this latent oneness alone can give life and fire to a new political program of transformation."[38]

This particular look into the future of the international system rests on the concept of universal culture as a basis for effective political cooperation.

The World Order Models Project (WOMP) typified this concern. To restore a humanistic view of the international system, WOMP focused not only on peace and disarmament but also on social justice and welfare. One participant argued that "[i]n a sense, social justice is prior to economic welfare and minimization of violence. Welfare will not be equitably distributed nor violence averted unless justice is done or is in prospect."[39]

Untested Questions in World Order Transformation

Even if one accepts the need for conscious international transformation to achieve peace, justice, welfare, and ecological restoration, many troubling questions remain about transactions in a world without sovereign states. Historically, values have been allocated by power, conflict, and war. Will merely eliminating absolute sovereignty necessarily be more effective for allocating global values? How will crucial value decisions be made? Will such a world be better than the one we have now?

The Problem of Sovereign Transfer

Whether by structural change or universal culture, the creation of world order requires the fundamental alteration of individual states, especially the more powerful. The state, after all, serves many functions, both internally and externally. And whereas the international law of a nation-state system tries to regulate the external functions of statehood, effective world order may have to deprive

---

[35] For an eloquent plea for development of a globalist philosophy, see Philippe de Seynes, "Prospects for a Future Whole World," *International Organization*, vol. 26, 1972, pp. 1–17.
[36] Lester R. Brown, *World Without Borders* (New York: Random House, 1972), pp. 11–12.
[37] C. Wilfred Jenks, *The World Beyond the Charter* (London: Allen and Unwin, 1969), especially chapter 4.
[38] Richard A. Falk, *This Endangered Planet* (New York: Random House, 1971), p. 296.

[39] Ali A. Mazrui, "World Order Through World Culture," *Proceedings*, American Society of International Law (1972), pp. 252–253. A comprehensive study of the traditions and ideas of futuristic research, especially with the universal cultural orientation, appears in Louis René Beres and Harry R. Targ, *Reordering the Planet: Constructing Alternative World Futures* (Boston: Allyn and Bacon, 1974).

the state of control over them. If contemporary international law is only modestly successful, the drive for comprehensive world order will face the same problems in greater magnitude. Whereas consensual international law seeks to limit certain state activities, comprehensive world order attempts to abridge the very sovereignty of states. Thus the requisite new international machinery must have a supranational character and relies on the transfer of loyalty from states.

But the picture is not altogether bleak. Because reformist world order ideas reject world government, the transfer of loyalties, and the readjustment of states' sovereignty, can be both gradual and unified. In this sense, the world order idea is consistent with the philosophy of functionalism, except that the reassignment of public tasks and the redirecting of individual loyalties are determined not by the political intensity of issues, but by (1) the importance of the subject matter as a potential cause or preventer of war, and (2) public and governmental support attainable for transfer away from the nation-state.[40] Even so, unanimity on such issues is unlikely. If issues of transfer are decided by international conventions, it will make little difference whether delegates are appointed by governments or elected by publics. Sentiment to alter fundamental attributes of statehood is not rampant, not even in the European Union, where political disagreements have proved far more intractable than economic.

Mechanisms of Sanction

Under institutionalized world order, what will ensure cooperation among nations? It is assumed that punishment of violators is the responsibility of all members of the community through both centralized and decentralized means. Besides the use of force by legitimized military control, however, the

world order advocates prescribe various lesser sanctions. Foremost among these are the age-old techniques of ostracism—economic boycott, censure, cultural isolation, and so on.

Power and Justice

There is probably universal agreement that power and war, the mechanisms by which international decisions traditionally have been made, have resulted in many unjust decisions. But what guarantee have we that some new mechanism will not occasionally be unjust? Presumably, the core values of different national peoples will continue to collide. In the absence of war and traditional power struggles, what standards of justice will apply? Whose concept of justice ought to prevail in a political process without coercion? International decision making may require a functional equivalent to war and power, which traditionally have resolved fundamental matters of values distribution. Otherwise, states may be tempted to desert cooperative world order in favor of their individual abilities to coerce by means other than armed force.

Furthermore, if states sacrifice warmaking ability by vesting central coercing authority in supranational agencies, they will encounter the problem of those agencies' capacity for justice. Might not such an authority be dictatorial and thus prone to injustice? Alternatively, could it fall under the command of an influential minority of states? Or the converse, could it succumb to the avarice of a tyrannical majority of states that disdain the values and interests of others? These problems especially plague maximalist proposals for world order, but they are only relatively less critical to minimalist and reformist views.

Value Standards and Value Objectives

Underlying all other problems and questions is the matter of what standards are to be used and what objectives pursued in a comprehensive world order. Order requires more than simple institutional mechanics; it reflects the value patterns that create it,

---

[40] Norman L. Hill, "The National State and Federation," in Howard O. Eaton, ed., *Federation: The Coming Structure of World Government* (Norman: University of Oklahoma Press, 1944), p. 131. This world order standard is part of the world federalist intellectual tradition.

and it is expected to perform in accordance with some values. The feasibility of world order depends largely on the pertinence of the larger values to their particular political and social cultures, their economic systems and expectations, and their philosophies regarding rights, freedoms, and other elements of public life. Proposals of world order cannot ignore the sociological imperatives of the international community.

Despite lingering sentiment for a world republic, most formal proposals were products of the early Cold War—an age of extreme ideological sensitivity. As a result, most of them lean heavily on the philosophy of government that broadly is characterized as the Western liberal tradition, with emphasis on civil liberties and economic individualism. At the same time, however, they attempted to lure socialist attention by including collective responsibility for economic development, allocation of natural resources, and distribution of wealth. Nevertheless, there is a distinct Western tone to them, with patent leanings toward an idyllic Western model. Proposals that call for upgrading the United Nations as an instrument of world order, on the other hand, are more realistic in accepting diverse domestic ideologies and political heritages. This realism was imposed on Western thinkers largely by the growing solidarity of the left-leaning Developing World on economic issues at the United Nations.

The Problem of Internal War

Traditionally, students of international relations have distinguished sharply between international war and internal war. In the revolutionary international system of the past half-century, the distinction has faded because of the tendency for internal wars to become international wars through intervention and third-party belligerency. It is by now evident that internal wars are a major threat to international peace and security. Can effective world order instruments avert this threat by resolving internal problems? How much authority should be vested in the international community to intervene for such a purpose? Would the authority of

centralized enforcement be tantamount to a dictatorial world state or a menace of the majority?

A related problem—from the viewpoints of justice and welfare, perhaps a larger one—is the relation of world order to insurgent groups in strife-torn countries. If insurgency threatens world or regional peace, and if international agents have authority to intervene, are they bound to intervene on behalf of incumbents? Or ought they to act on their judgment as to the relative merits of conflicting claims for social justice? What ideological and philosophical standards ought to be invoked? Who ought to create them? Furthermore, in internal situations, what will be the mechanisms for determining and executing value standards in the absence of unchallenged national authority?

Conclusion

In this section of the book, we considered several approaches to world order, and we concluded by exploring some existing proposals for alternative world futures. Despite the contributions made to international peace and stability by intergovernmental organization, international law, transnational participation, and regional integration, the international system generally has pointed toward self-destruction. This is not due entirely to the potential for war. It is also attributable partly to the widening gap between the wealthy countries and the poor, with resulting social and political conflict. Moreover, the presence of egalitarian ideals among virtually all peoples has heightened the demand for international protection of human rights. While all this political demand burgeons, the delicate balance of the human environment is deteriorating at an alarming rate. It is abundantly clear that the international system is in jeopardy unless nations and their leaders accept the critical need to rise above the narrow psychology of nation-states, nationalism, and the kind of contemporary regionalism that is little more than nationalism writ large.

In deciding among alternative world futures, we are faced with several choices. We may proceed in the traditional political-structural manner, through maximalist, minimalist, or reformist means. But the social imperatives, the problems of loyalty transfer, and fears about life in the future retard progress on these choices even while the need becomes clearer. Our choice, it now appears, is not between perpetuation of the present structure and vague alternatives, but between world order based on piecemeal erosions of states' sovereignty, and highly institutionalized and expansionist world government. The longer the choice is delayed, the more the alternatives will narrow to two: expansionist world government or systemic destruction. As neither is desirable, the wise use of precious time is essential.

Contrary to hope and expectation, the passing of the Cold War did not usher in the kind of stability that would erase the need for studious consideration of alternative futures; for though nuclear bipolarity is gone and economic competition has replaced the global arms contest, such universal enemies as waste, deforestation, exhaustion of natural resources, poverty, hunger, refugees, contamination of all the earth's environments, ethnopolitical violence, political repression, and many more await governmental consideration as urgently as did the nuclear arms race a decade ago. And most of these problems can be resolved only through global multilateralism rather than national effort. Multilateralism must evolve with the New World Order, therefore, or the order itself will survive only as a brief transition to a new phase of economic warfare and geopolitical domination by a single superpower.

Index

Note: italicized *f*'s and *t*'s following page numbers refer to figures and tables, respectively.